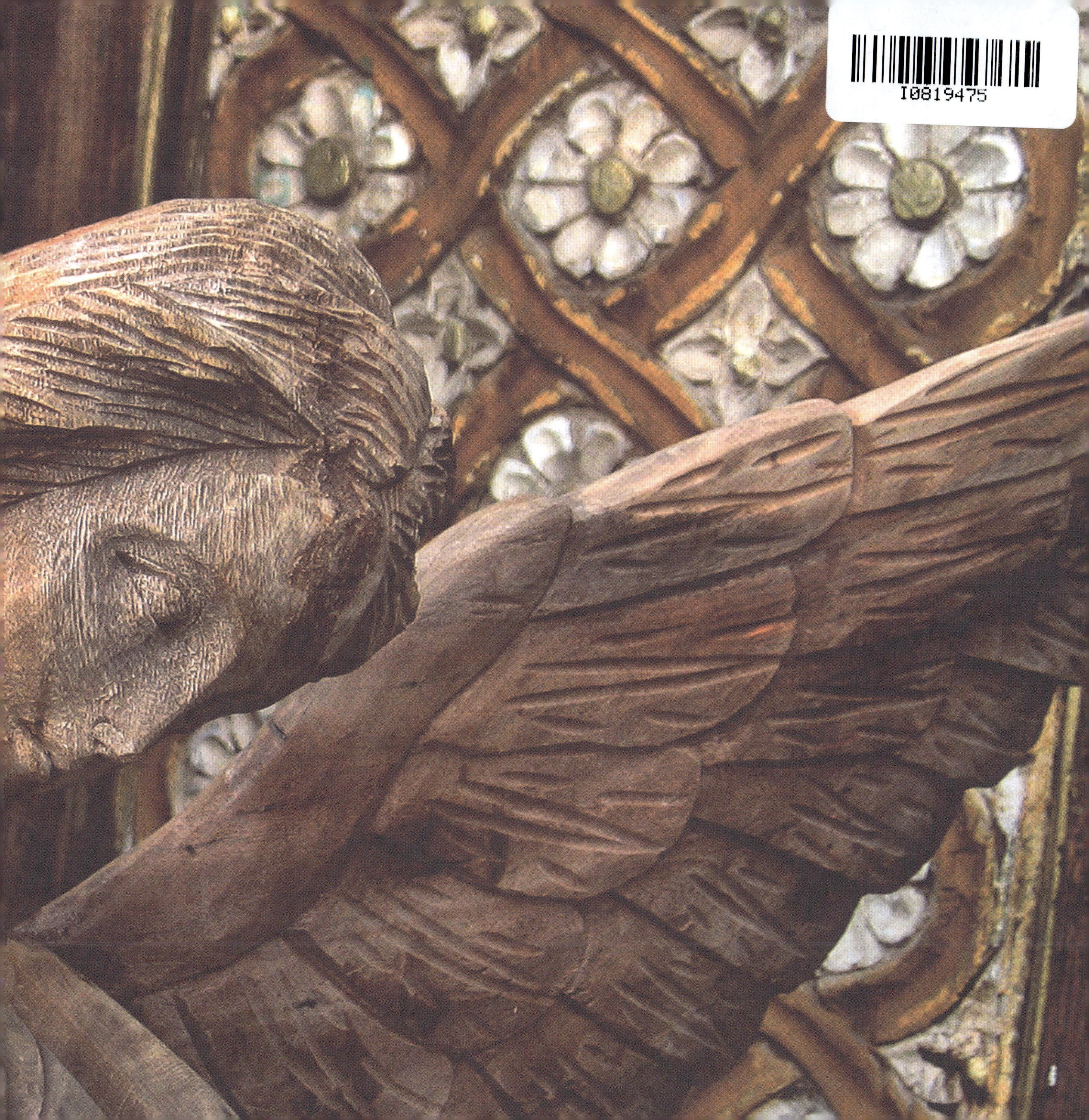
I0819475

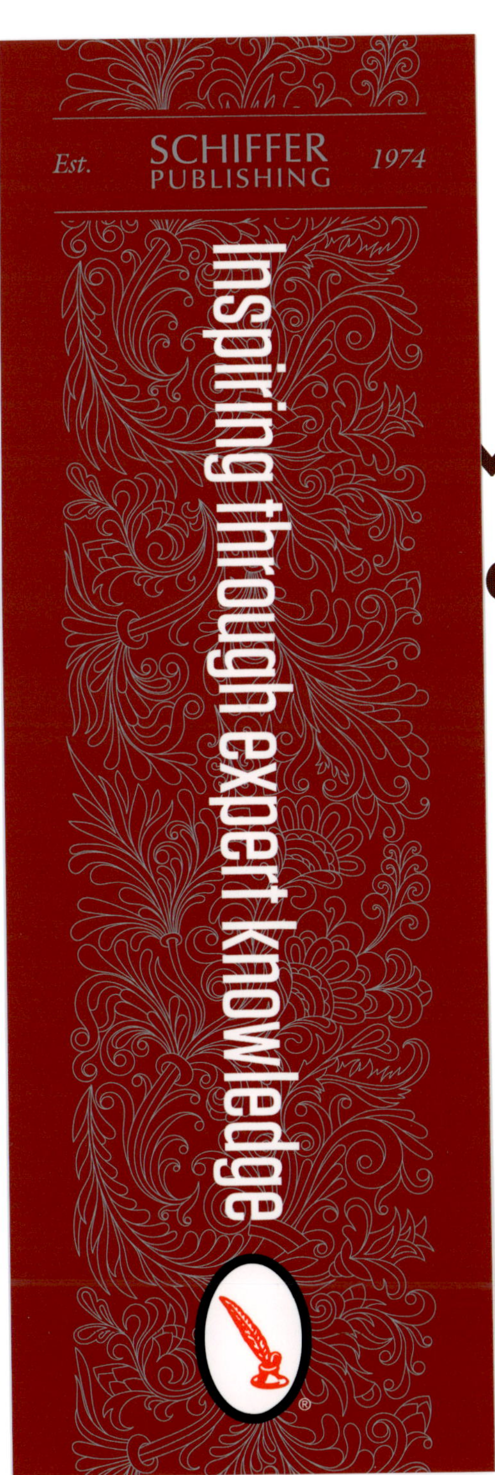

Miguel de Allende

e soul of mexico

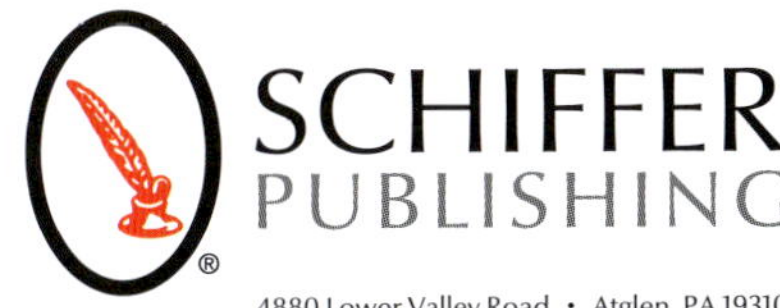

4880 Lower Valley Road • Atglen, PA 19310

For the extraordinary gift of so many years traveling and working in Mexico, we would like to dedicate this book to the people of Mexico and particularly those of San Miguel de Allende, who welcomed us with open hearts and who have shared their lives and their families with us. Through them we have come to know the richness of the different cultures that meld to make Mexico one of the most amazing countries on earth. Their kindness and generosity, the artistry of their craftsmen, and the beauty of their cities and towns have given us a new perspective on life and the wonders to be found in each day.

San Miguel de Allende
the soul of mexico

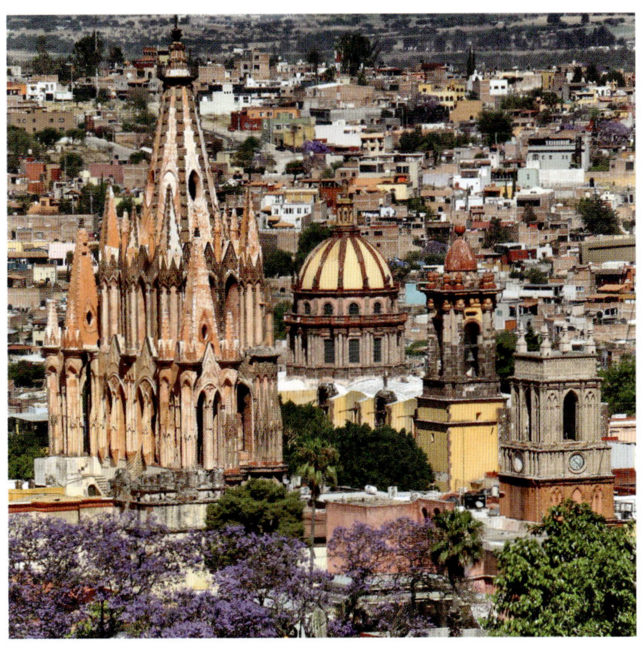

Cathi & Steven House

Foreword by Tony Cohan

Other Schiffer Books by the Author:
Villages of West Africa: An Intimate Journey across Time, Cathi and Steven House, ISBN: 978-0-7643-5481-6

Other Schiffer Books on Related Subjects:
Mexico City: Out and About, Karen and Kenneth Basile, ISBN: 978-0-7643-3672-0

Textile Fiestas of Mexico: A Traveler's Guide to Celebrations, Markets, and Smart Shopping, Sheri Brautigam, ISBN: 978-0-9964-4758-4

Library of Congress Control Number: 2023931160

Type set in Myanmar MN/Gill Sans Nova

ISBN 978-0-7643-6682-6
Printed in China

Published by Schiffer Publishing, Ltd.
4880 Lower Valley Road
Atglen, PA 19310
Phone: (610) 593-1777; Fax: (610) 593-2002
Email: info@schifferbooks.com
Web: www.schifferbooks.com

For our complete selection of fine books on this and related subjects, please visit our website at www.schifferbooks.com. You may also write for a free catalog.

Schiffer Publishing's titles are available at special discounts for bulk purchases for sales promotions or premiums. Special editions, including personalized covers, corporate imprints, and excerpts, can be created in large quantities for special needs. For more information, contact the publisher.

Contents

Foreword

A Community of Souls

by Tony Cohan

Long before travel magazines began declaring the Mexican hillside town of San Miguel de Allende the world's number one tourist destination, it was inhabited by people known colloquially as Chichimecas. In the middle of the sixteenth century, Spanish monks and soldiers arrived and set about establishing a small community here. A forty-year struggle of resistance in the region, known as the Chichimeca War, followed. The Spaniards lost that war but prevailed in the end, and Fray Juan de San Miguel, whose tonsured statue adorns a corner of the main plaza, is now celebrated with a noisy, colorful fiesta every September 29th.

The silver-mining boom in nearby Guanajuato, which produced an estimated 28% of the world's silver for over two centuries, spread wealth throughout the region. In San Miguel, tanneries, textile factories, and artisan work flourished, and by the 1700s the population had reached 30,000. Many of San Miguel's churches and chapels and cloisters, its grand homes and gardens, its abundant crafts and markets, and its extravagant customs and ceremonies, all of which can be seen and savored in this extraordinary book by Cathi and Steven House, date to that era.

After that, San Miguel's fortunes waxed and waned. During Mexico's revolt against Spain, the town played a role, personified in the figure of native son and conspirator Ignacio Allende. But by the beginning of the twentieth century, an influenza pandemic had reduced San Miguel to little more than a ghost town. When a few foreigners began to find their way here in the 1930s, only 9,000 people remained in what was essentially a depopulated ruin. Today, San Miguel de Allende is a UNESCO World Heritage Site, a tourist mecca for both Mexicans and foreigners, and the population stands at about 175,000, of which an estimated 10% are non-Mexicans.

The town seemed to have had a dual nature from the beginning, fervently religious on the one hand and lavishly festive on the other, qualities that still characterize it (and are on full display in the pages of this book). The town center is laid out according to the fourteen stations of the cross, and during Easter Week it becomes an outdoor church as crowds of believers visit each one in turn, while at the nearby shrine of Atotonilco, penitents flog themselves in rituals of purification. Yet, the town adopts an equally fierce, pagan abandon for Day of the Locos. According to some written accounts, San Miguel was censured by the Spanish Crown for having "an excess of fiestas." So faith and fiestas coexist, and sometimes in combination, as on Day of the Dead, when visits to the cemetery are often as celebratory as they are somber.

Currently the town wrestles with its new popularity and consequent gentrification (there are now several hundred restaurants). Little shops close their doors or move away from the center while new shopping plazas erupt on the outskirts. Longtime residents adjust their daily schedules to deal with the complicating presence of so many visitors during weekends and holidays. Yet, in towns like San Miguel, history, religion, architecture, and ceremony soften the effects of change. The balloon sellers still roam the plaza, ice cream is still sold out of tubs on a cart borne by a dray horse, fireworks still erupt at improbable hours. Here there are few ordinary days, each belonging to a saint at least, and life remains in many respects as before: intimate, voluptuous, sense driven. The Virgin appears continually in myriad guises: in a tree, by a river. Marriages are consecrated, children are born, the devout attend daily Mass. San Miguel remains, to those who live here, a community of souls.

The multifaceted Cathi and Steven House, award-winning architects, photographers, authors, and educators, bring a unique perspective to this book on San Miguel de Allende. They have traveled the world documenting vernacular architecture and the people who live and create in these remarkable spaces that have so much to teach us about imagination, survival, and sustainability. Additionally, both draw beautifully and both are exceptional photographers. Products of a unique intensive education at Virginia Tech's College of Architecture, modeled after the Bauhaus, emphasizing design at all scales and the interrelatedness of all forms of art and architecture, they began their firm, House + House Architects, with the full array of practical and theoretical tools at their command.

Anyone familiar with *Mediterranean Villages: an architectural journey*, their book exploring traditional building in the hill towns of Italy, the Greek islands, the Dalmatian coast, and Spanish Andalusia, knows their passionate relationship to these places, their structures, and their people.

More recently, their book *Villages of West Africa: an intimate journey across time* celebrates the beauty of land, architecture, crafts, and people in seven countries of West Africa, binding the memorable settings to the lives lived there.

Here, they turn their gaze upon a community where they have lived, worked, and taught for over thirty years. Their connection to San Miguel de Allende runs deep. They have built homes here (beginning with their own), run an annual school for international architecture students, and have photographed its buildings, its fiestas, and its people across decades. Just as importantly, they have shopped in its markets and stalls and stores, walked daily past its churches and through its plazas, witnessed and participated in its celebrations and ceremonies, and shared their lives with its inhabitants as friends and neighbors. This rich familiarity pervades the book, and this is what makes *San Miguel de Allende: the soul of mexico* sing.

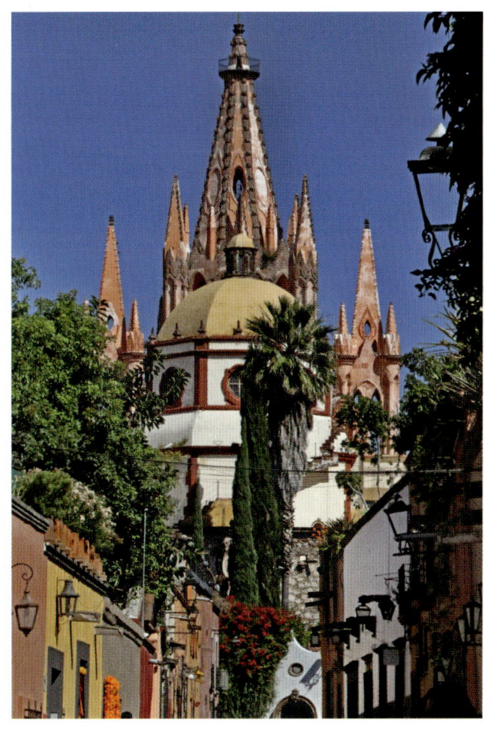

Tony Cohan is the author of the bestselling travel memoirs *On Mexican Time* and *Mexican Days*, as well as *Native State: A Memoir*, novels *Canary* and *Opium*, and numerous short stories. His writing has appeared in the *New York Times*, *Condé Nast Traveler*, and numerous other publications. In addition to his writing, Tony has been a jazz drummer, working with such notable musicians as Dexter Gordon, Bud Powell, Tete Montoliu, and Memphis Slim. Tony has lived for many years in Mexico, both in San Miguel de Allende and in Guanajuato, and divides his time among Mexico, Denmark, and the US.

Reflections on a Life of Discovery

by Cathi House

The first time we came to San Miguel was by chance. In 1988 our firm, House + House Architects, was retained to design a resort on the Caribbean Island of Roatan, in Honduras. Determined to have this resort built by local workers, with skills and products from that part of the world, I spent weeks searching every corner of the country for appropriate craftsmen and materials. Not finding what we needed in Honduras, I continued to search through Mexico and Guatemala. At that time, we were not familiar with these countries or the materials to be found there. We did, however, know about cantera, a lovely volcanic stone that comes in an amazing array of colors. Having used cantera stone in California, we loved this material, and knew that it came from Mexico.

The next step was challenging. In my search for a source of cantera stone, I discovered that every importer of cantera to the US was determined to protect their source. After an exhaustive quest, finally, one man in Texas recommended a stone quarry in Tequisquiapan because it was near San Miguel de Allende, one of his favorite towns in the world. He helped set up the contacts I needed, and even recommended his favorite hotel. Looking back on it now, we feel that this difficult search was part of the universe's plan for us, because it brought us to San Miguel and completely changed the direction of our lives.

I arrived in San Miguel on that first trip in the summer of 1988, late in the day, when the sun was perfectly positioned to illuminate the Parroquia and give that magic glow of dusk to the richly colored walls of the town. San Miguel was overwhelmingly beautiful, especially at that time of day, and what I felt was a confusing sensation. Even though we had traveled extensively around the world, we had no idea that a place of such breathtaking architectural, historical, and cultural combination existed in Mexico.

A few months after that first trip, Steven and I returned to Mexico for a deeper exploration of the country, discovering many stunning cities, towns, and villages. We returned again to San Miguel in 1992, and in a twist of fate, as often happens with so many who fall under the spell of this magical place, we bought a small ruin in the historic center. I designed a home for us, a retreat meant to be a comfortable, inspirational, beautiful place to reassess life away from our normal environment, to give us fresh perspective and to complement our lives in San Francisco.

In San Miguel we have so much more than our home in the historic center of one of the most extraordinary towns we have ever known; what we also have is a community of precious people who have become integral to our lives. Mexico is fascinating, historical, and architecturally spectacular. But it is the people that we count as friends, neighbors, and coworkers who make life so much more than we bargained for. Experiencing the fervor and passion they have for life and faith and love and family, celebrating birthdays, weddings, quinceañeras (a girl's fifteenth birthday), and funerals with them, seeing life and the world through their eyes has transformed us in more ways than we can count. Even simple walks are filled with wonder, and the pleasures of seeing in new light, new details. Days feel longer, filled with the joys of life. Church bells and processions, the calls of the trash truck, the scissor sharpener, the elote (corn) seller, simple things that disappear without notice in the US become joyous in a life that feels more significant, more gracious, more enjoyable, definitely more wondrous.

In San Miguel, a place that Steven and I have come to love so very deeply, I have had the extra pleasure of working here. All that I have learned elsewhere, along with all that I am constantly learning in Mexico, I have been able to incorporate into my architectural work in San Miguel. Working in Mexico has been one of the great joys of my life. During my thirty-four-year love affair with this country, I have designed more than forty homes in San Miguel and two in Baja, working intimately with builders and the artisans and materials that brought us to Mexico in the first place. These men have given me the opportunity to do work not affordable in the US. We are able to make roofs that undulate and create waterfall art in the rain, use hand-cut stone walls and moldings and complex intertwining steel railings, and restore and reuse ancient roof tiles . . . And the men who build my work leave in it their hearts and spirits, adding a quality to my projects that makes my soul sing for joy.

We were fortunate to learn early in our professional lives the transformation that happens when you touch other cultures. When you slowly feel a place, breathe its aromas, taste its delicacies, listen to the stories of those who live there, and stand in awe before its beauty, you allow them into your senses. We learned that to truly experience another culture, we must let it penetrate into our very souls. Travel is our source of inspiration and personal growth, allowing us to see the world with clear eyes and search beyond the limits of our own imagination. As architects, artists, photographers, and educators, Steven and I find inspiration in ancient lands, vibrant colors, and extraordinary people. In some of the most impoverished countries in the world, we have met communities that are joyous and respectful and have created environments that are beautiful and sustainable.

We learned that soulfulness is one of the most important qualities to nourish, not only in ourselves but also in our clients and in the coming generations of architects. In San Miguel we have found a world that combines all that we have learned in our travels with the prospect of actual applications in our work. As residents and as practicing architects in San Miguel, lessons accumulated over our lifetime have become so integral to who we are that there is no distinction between who we are and what we do.

In gratitude for all we have learned in our travels and how it has given our professional and personal lives so much depth, fifteen years ago we established CASA, the Center for Architecture Sustainability + Art, a summer study abroad program based in San Miguel for young international architecture students. Our goal is to help the next generation of

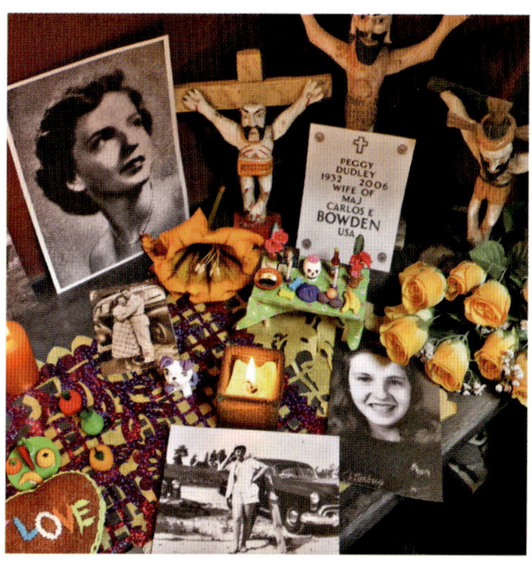

architects step away from their technology and learn how to see, feel, and understand in the deepest recesses of their being that their soul is where their work should be born. San Miguel could not be a more perfect setting to help young architects understand the profound beauty all around for them to draw from.

Life is a journey through places and relationships, with ourselves and with each other. Opening our souls to other cultures with respect and understanding of our different histories, experiences, and hopes has been our greatest joy, for which we are eternally grateful.

Churches

San Miguel de Allende is an exquisitely beautiful, very well-preserved Spanish colonial town. Churches grace every neighborhood, their towers reaching for heaven. The intricately sculpted pink stone spires of La Parroquia de San Miguel Archangel feel as though they actually touch heaven. Visible from all parts of town, the pink stone facade was designed in the late 1800s by Indigenous stonemason Zeferino Gutierrez, inspired, they say, by postcard images of Belgian and German Gothic churches, sketching the design in the sand for his construction crew.

The rhythms of day and night are modulated by the deeply resonant sounds of church bells as they ring out the quarter hours, sometimes softly, other times insistently, waking residents, sharing news, calling for prayer, announcing a celebration, or inviting peaceful meditation. Their rhythmic sounds connect everyone into the web of humanity that occupies this beautiful town. The tones vary with the meaning of the message, the intensity with the nature of the call. Sometimes just one church will ring its bells; sometimes all of the churches' and chapels' bells work in harmonic sequence to alert residents to a particular message. With every hour they ring out life. They are the music and centerpieces that hold the townspeople together. A cacophony of barking dogs, roosters, and twittering birds, sometimes the explosion of fireworks, accompany the bells as this music of life penetrates every corner.

On September 16, 1810, conspiring with Ignacio Allende, Father Hidalgo rang the bells in the call for independence, beginning the Mexican War of Independence. This bell now hangs in Mexico City, rung by the president each Independence Day as he gives "el Grito," the cry for freedom, and reads the names of the heroes of independence. In 2008, when San Miguel was given UNESCO World Heritage status, the church bells rang without pause for days.

Celebrations in the churches are accompanied by the music of mariachis, a uniquely Mexican sound that perfectly harmonizes with the sounds of the bells, the laughter of children playing, and the splashing of fountains. Whether it is a funeral, a quinceañera, a wedding, or a baptism, and especially when they are quietly inhabited by a few souls in deep prayer, the beautiful churches and chapels of San Miguel offer quiet reflection, joyous celebration, and a soulful lesson on faith, community, love, respect, architecture, and history.

By any measure, these churches celebrate the history of Mexico, showing the evolution of Spanish colonial architecture as it mixed with Indigenous traditions and skills. From the lofty pink spires of La Parroquia, to the simple rustic church of La Salud, to the deeply revered and colorful Templo Oratorio de San Felipe Neri, to the original San Miguel Viejo, the churches and chapels of San Miguel offer order, inspiration, reverence, and a place for quiet escape. And each reflects the deep faith the residents feel, not only for their God but for their families, their communities, and their shared history.

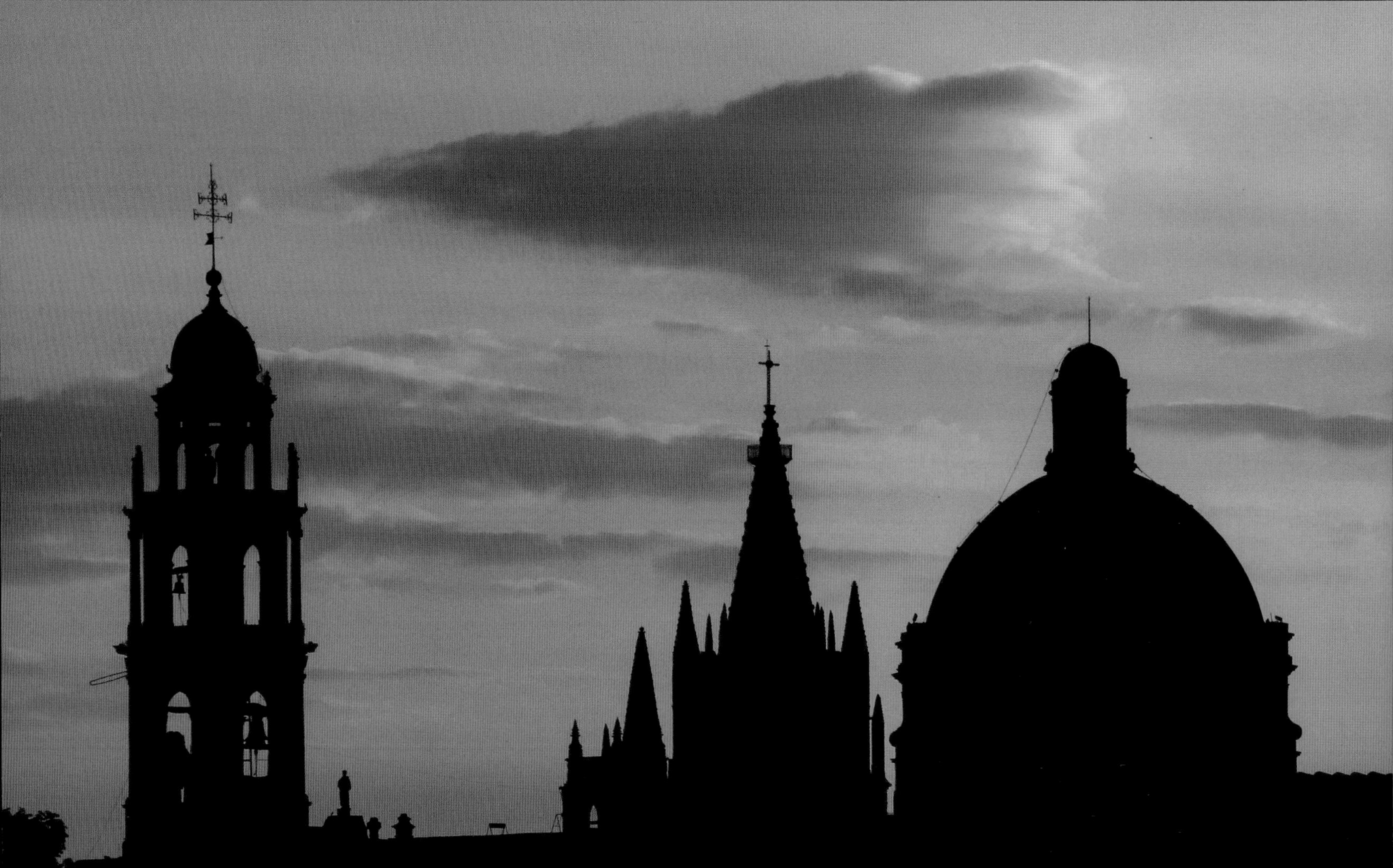

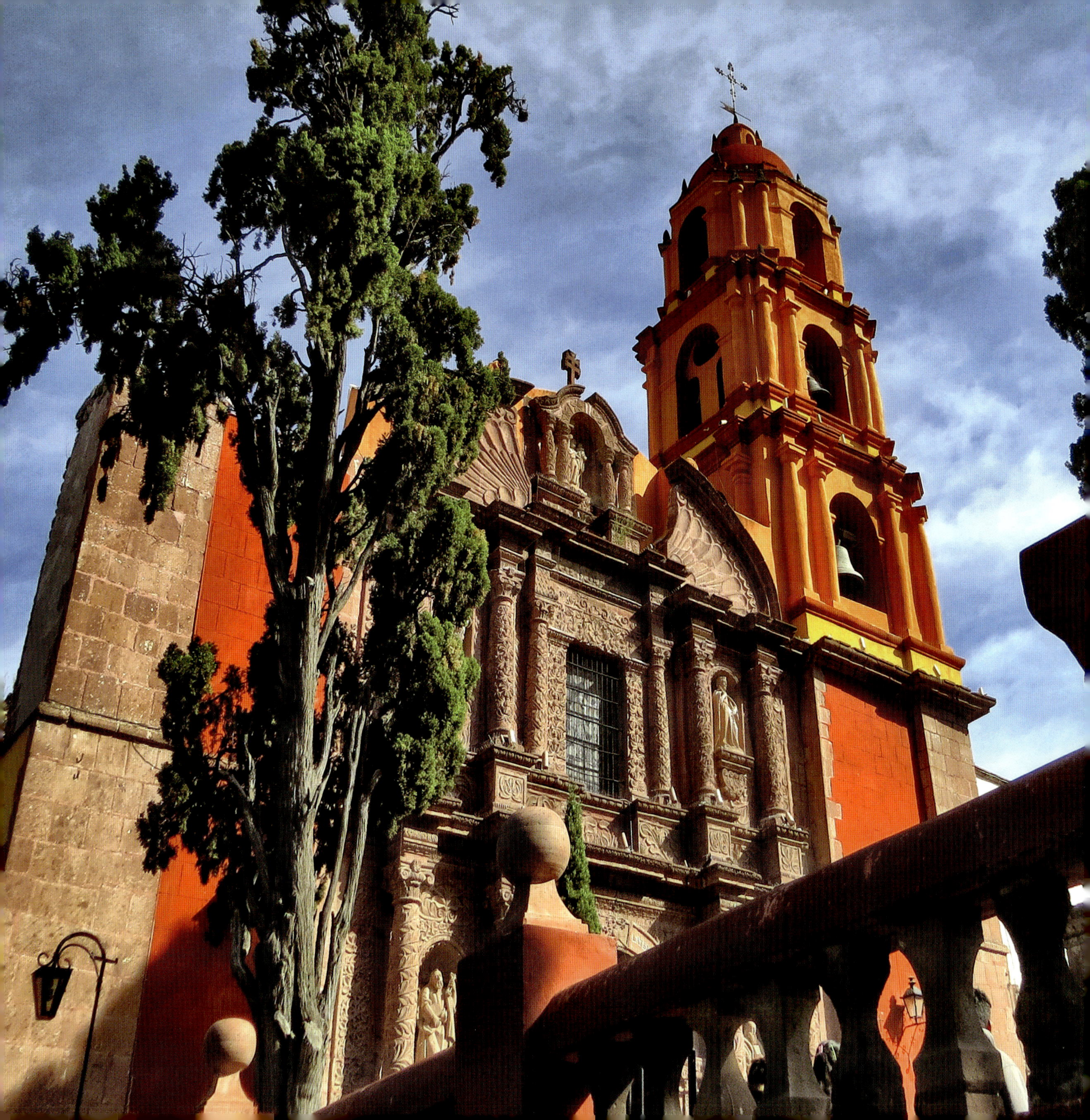

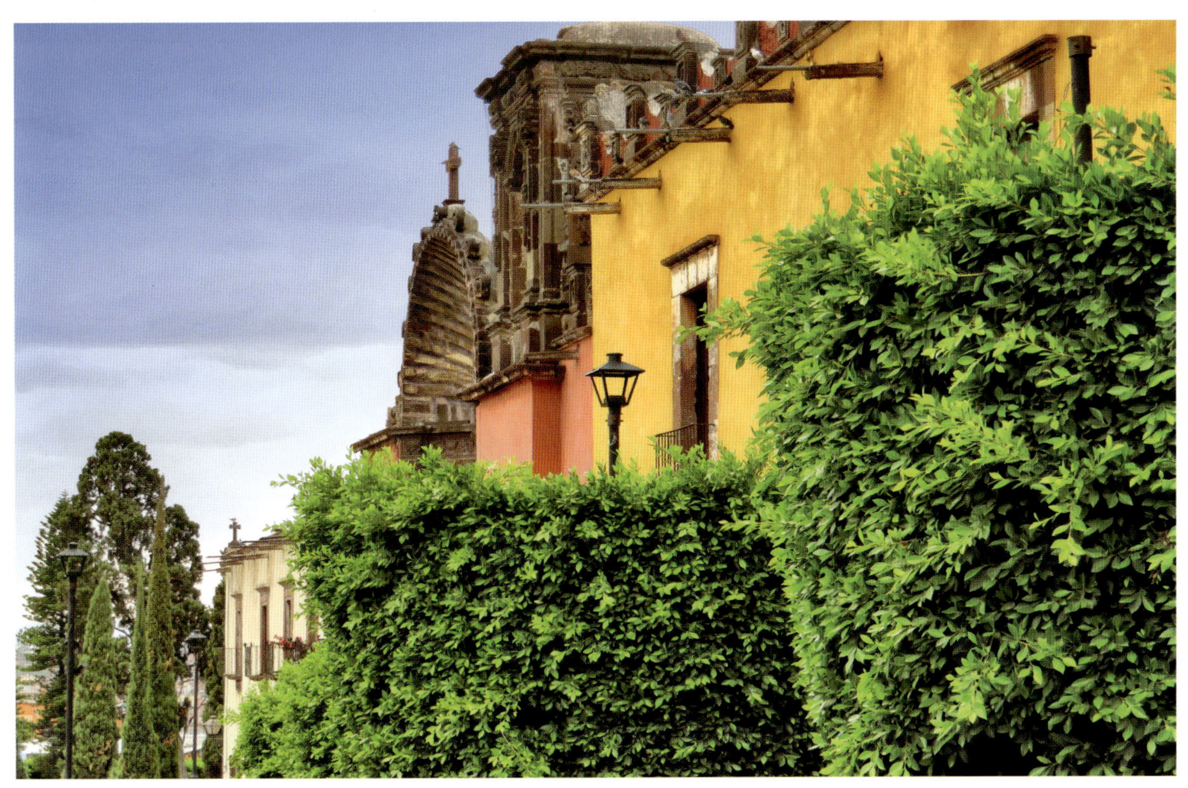

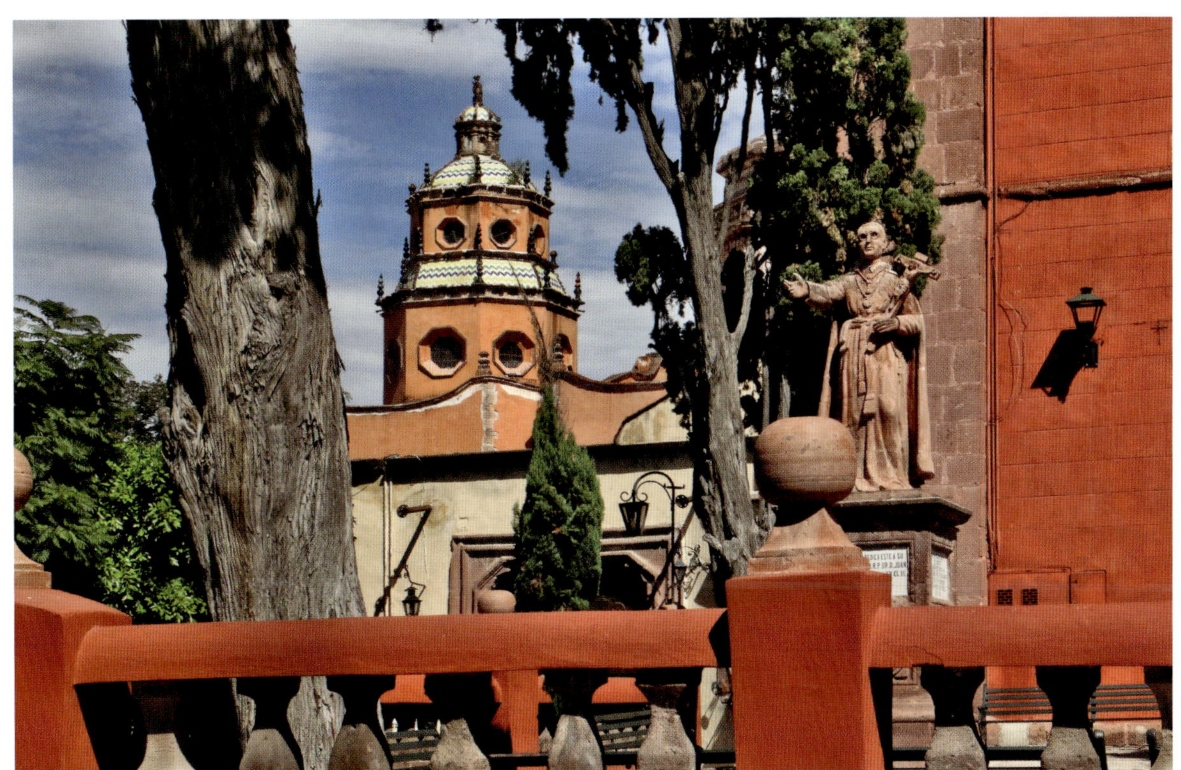

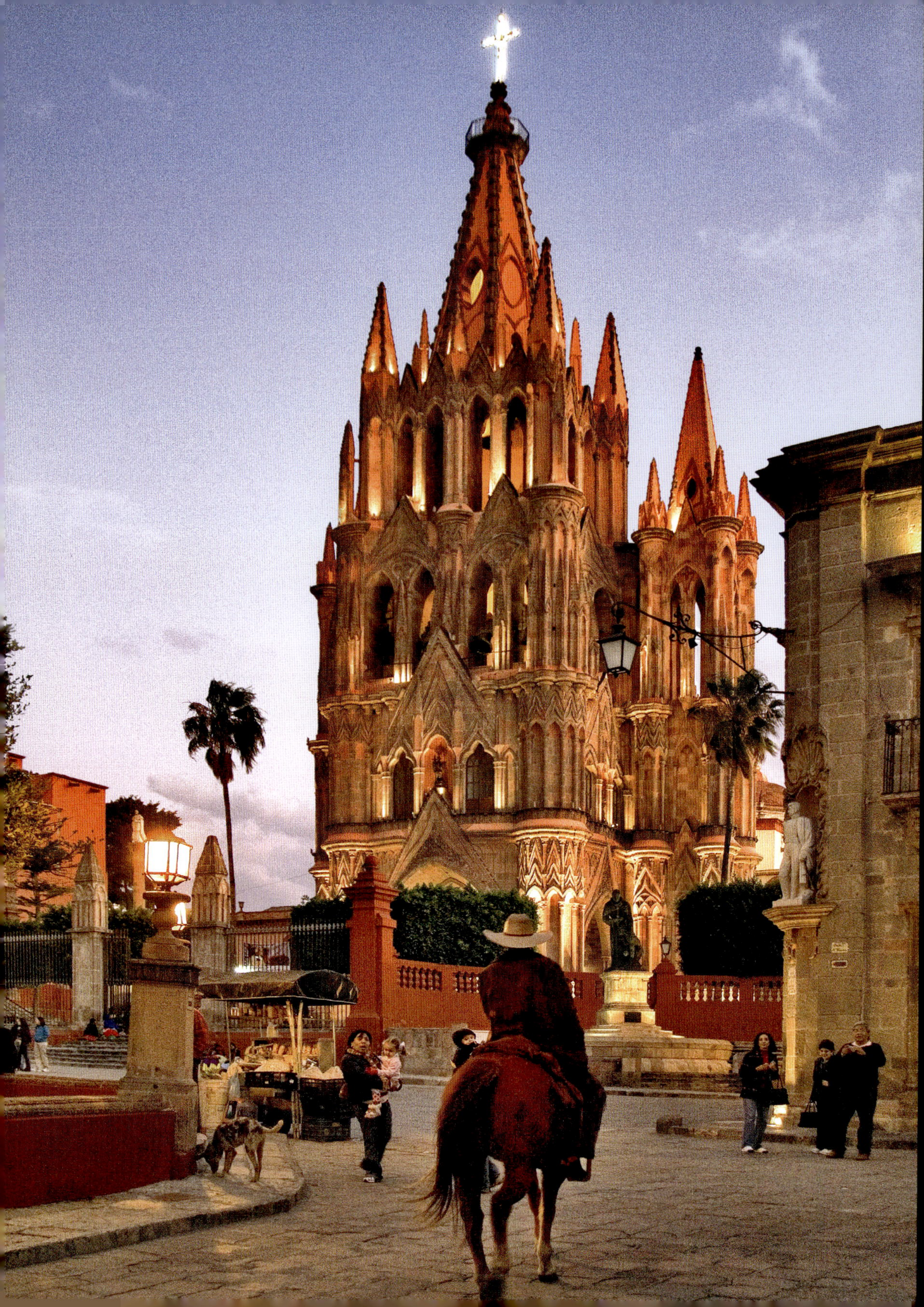

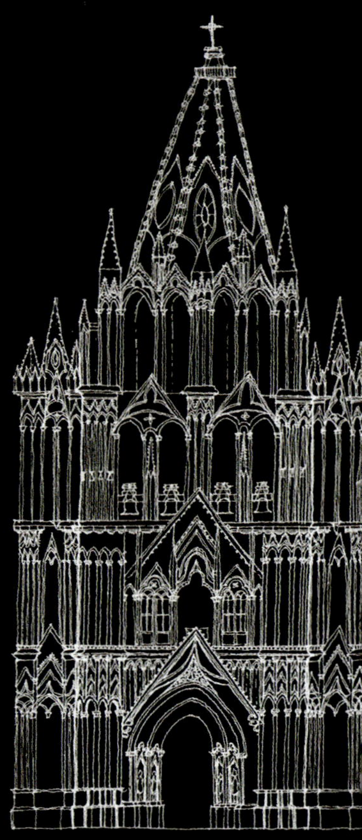

Exquisitely sculpted pink stone spires watch over the residents o San Miguel, calling them to pause in their daily occupations to fee gratitude for the beautiful life here These spires hold court over the Jardín, the beating heart and sou of San Miguel, where families gathe each evening to visit, lovers kiss i the shadows, and grandmother keep an eye on gleeful children. I a courtship dance that has con tinued for centuries, adolescen boys swirl in one direction aroun the Jardín, girls in the other, findin their life partners under the watch ful gazes of their families.

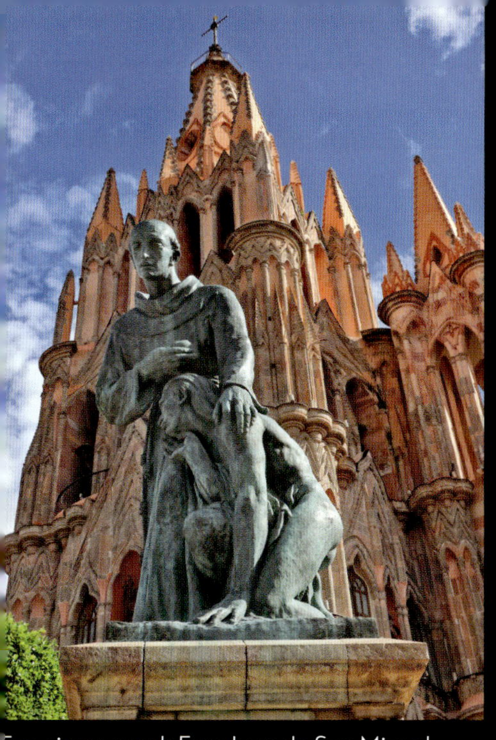

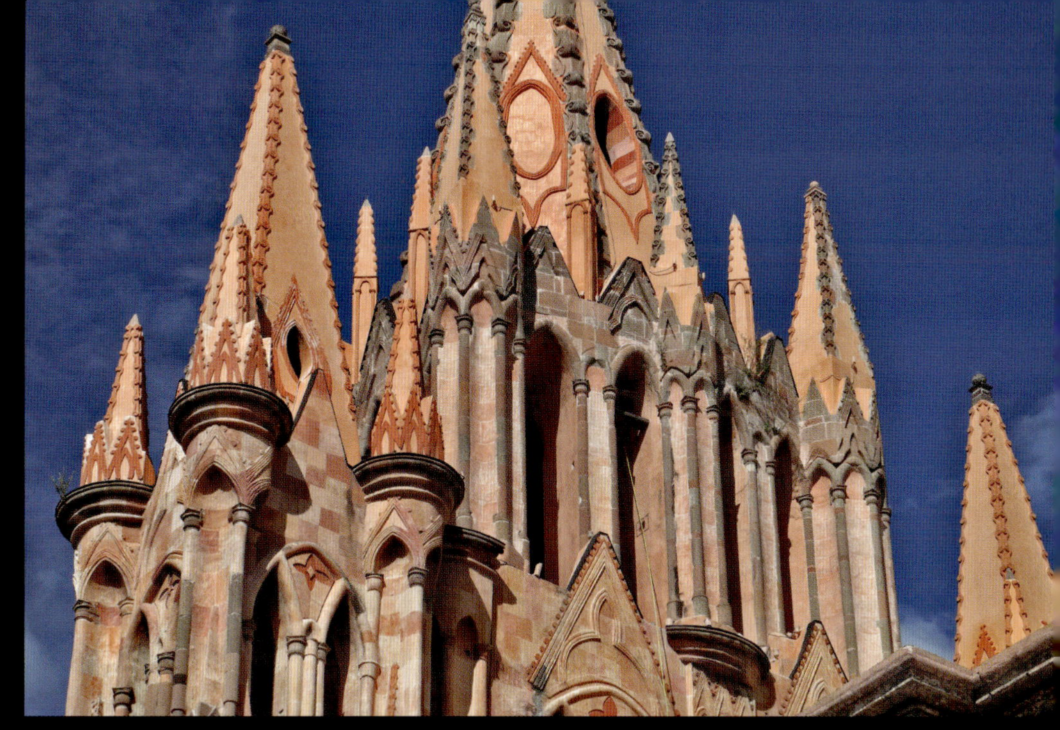

Franciscan monk Fray Juan de San Miguel

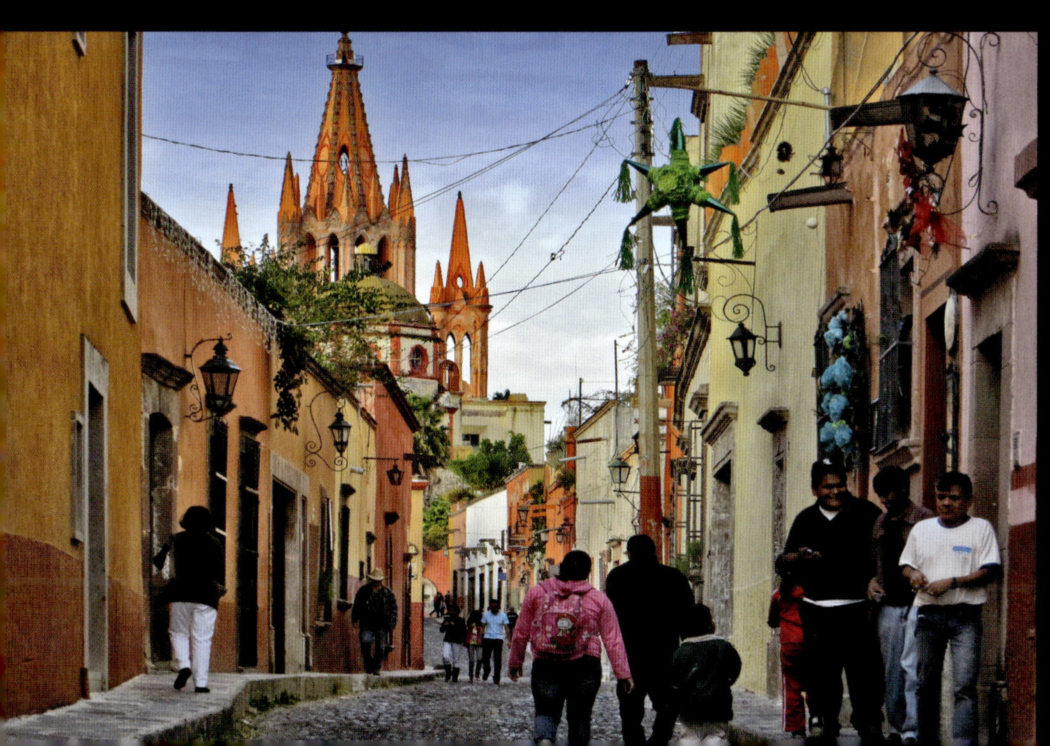

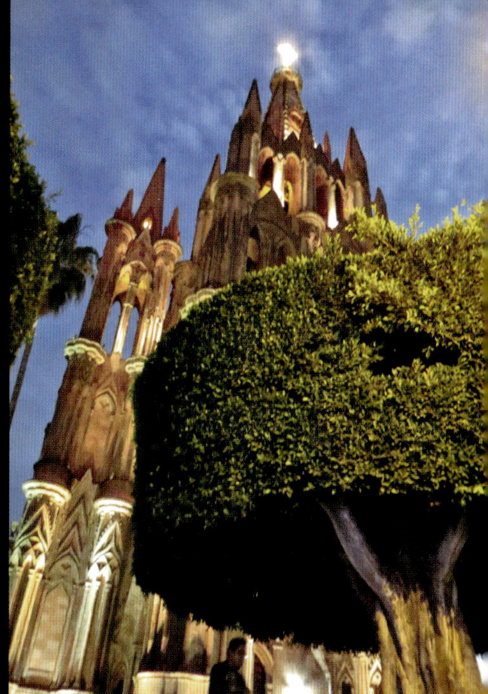

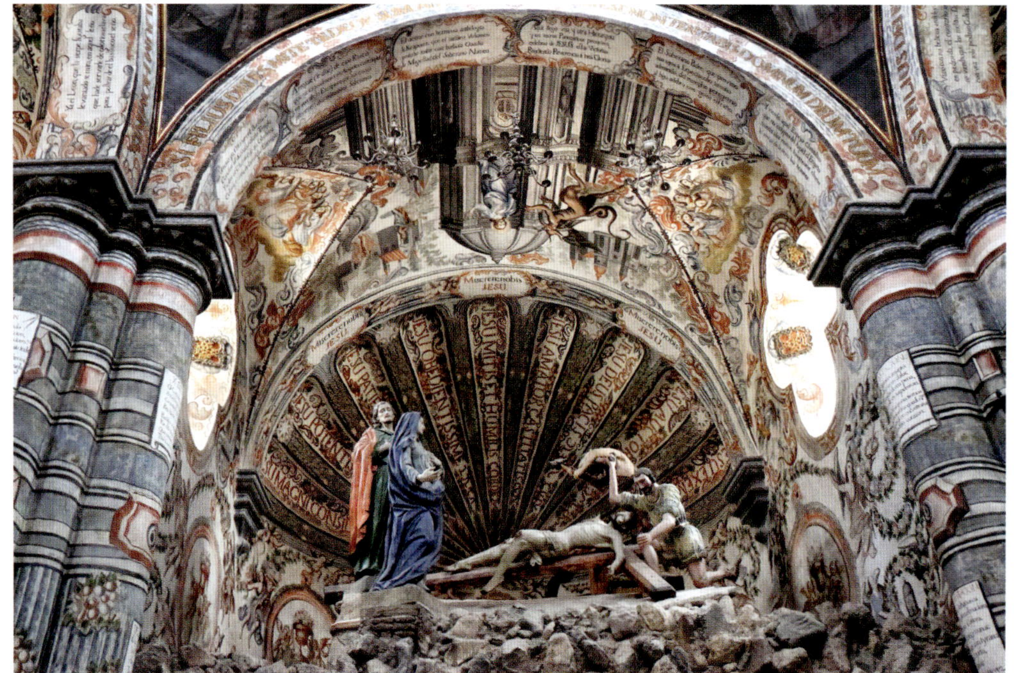

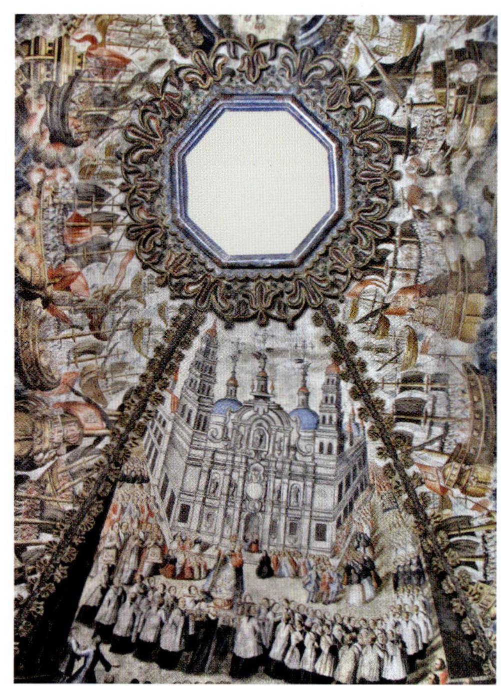

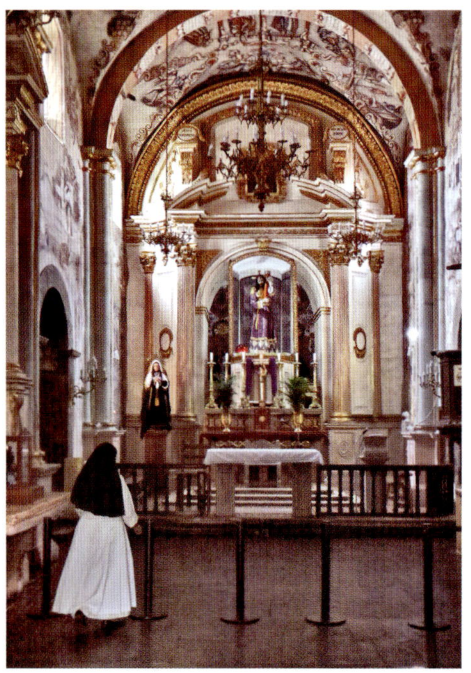

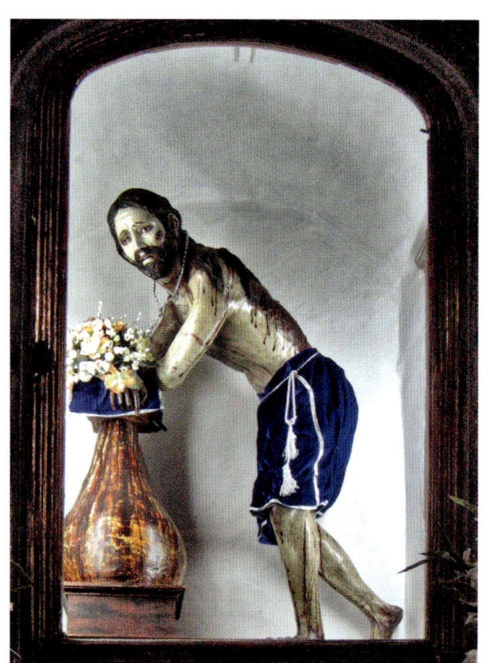

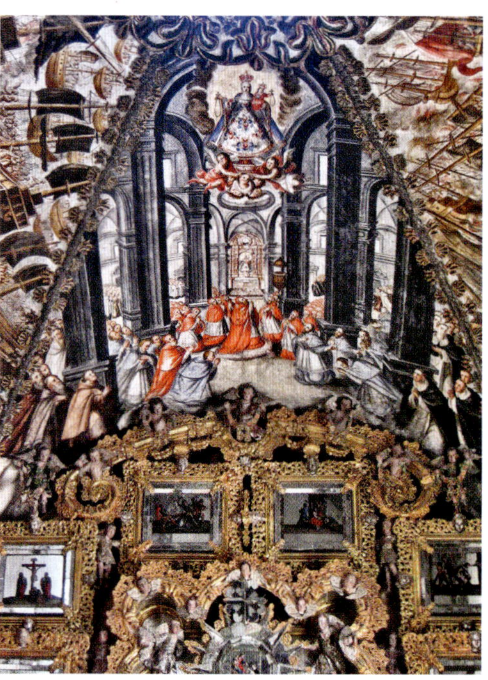

In 1740, Father Luis Felipe Neri laid the first stone in the Santuario de Jesús Nazareno de Atotonilco, located in a rural community 14 kilometers north of San Miguel. The exterior is spare, fortresslike, while the interior walls and ceilings are almost entirely covered by murals depicting stories from the Bible in a rich Mexican baroque style. The deeply revered statue of El Señor de la Columna, Jesus beaten and exhausted, is carried in a massive procession during Holy Week to San Miguel, traveling across a blocks-long carpet of images lovingly made of colored wood shavings. The richness and breadth of the interior murals have led the Santuario to be called the "Sistine Chapel" of Mexico.

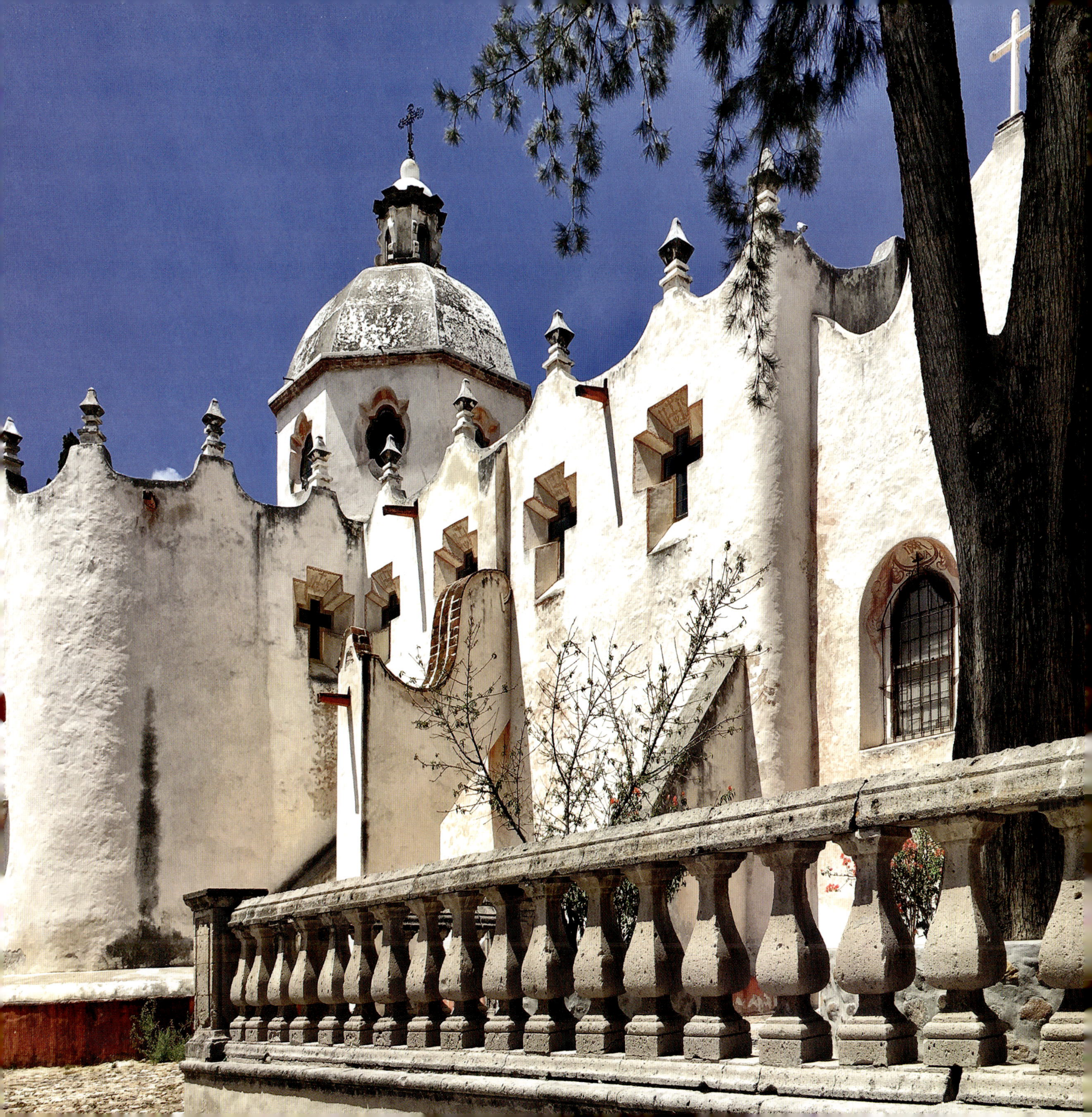

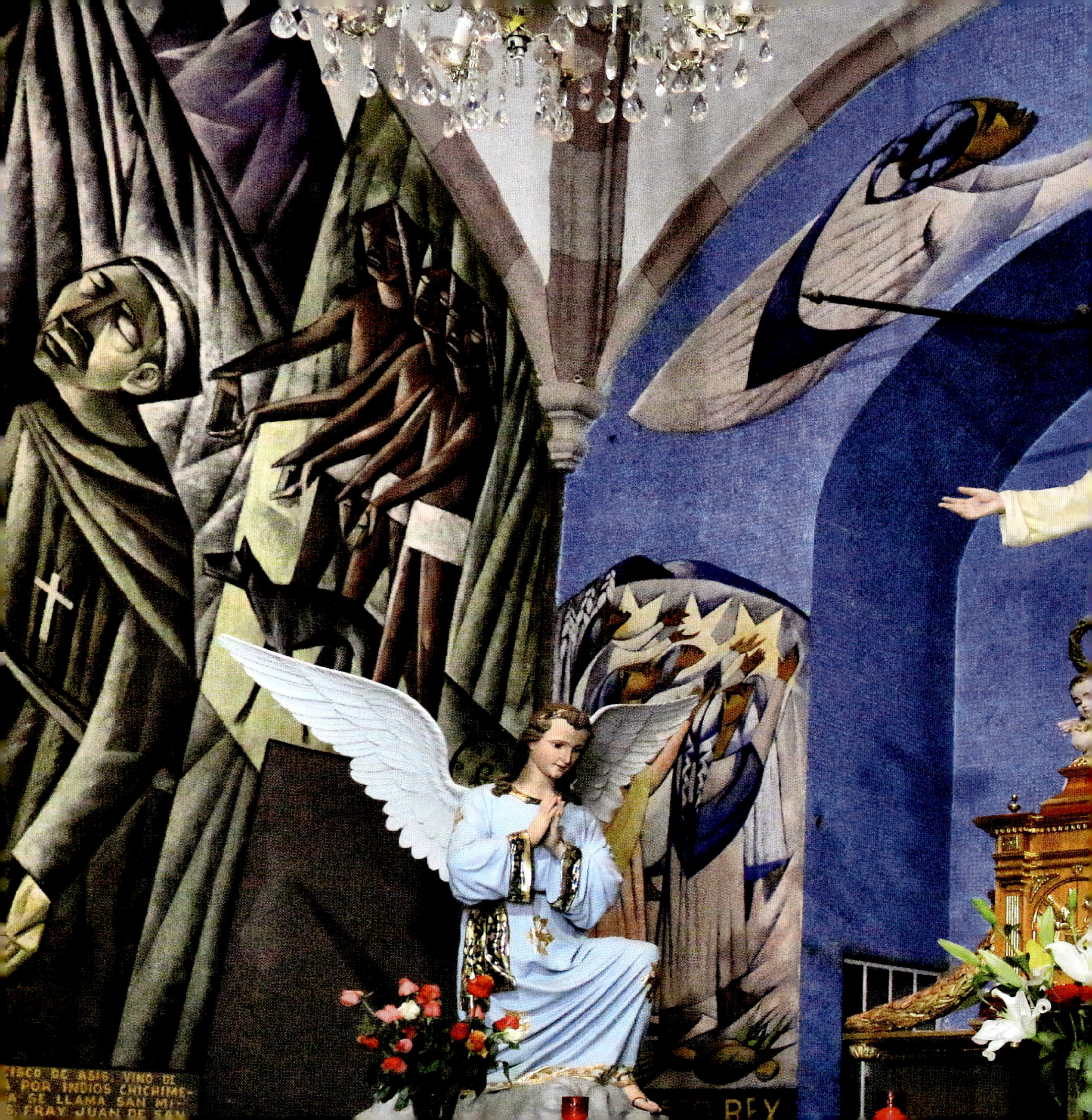
ISCO DE ASIS, VINO DE
POR INDIOS CHICHIME-
A SE LLAMA SAN MI-
FRAY JUAN DE
REY

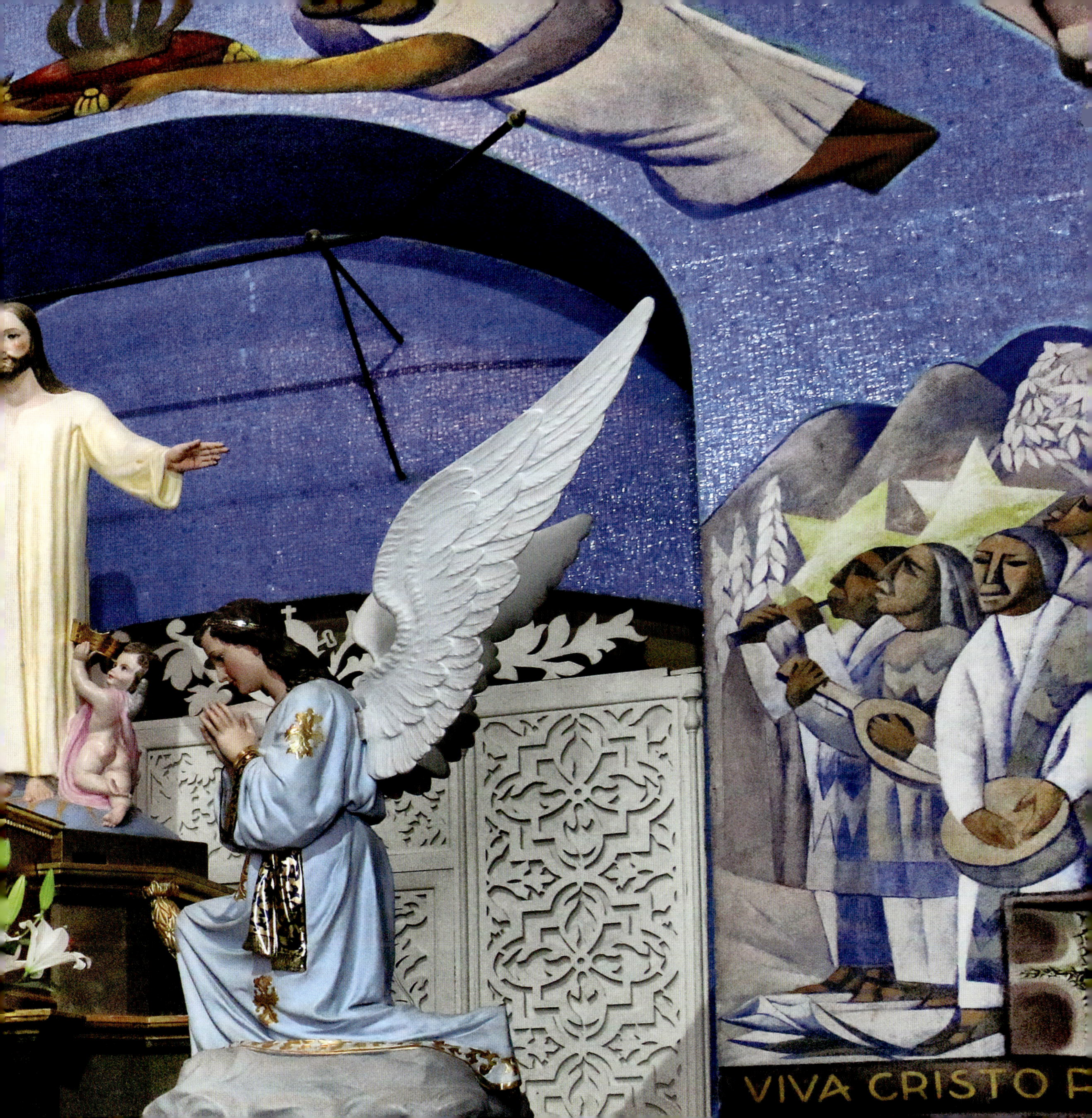
VIVA CRISTO

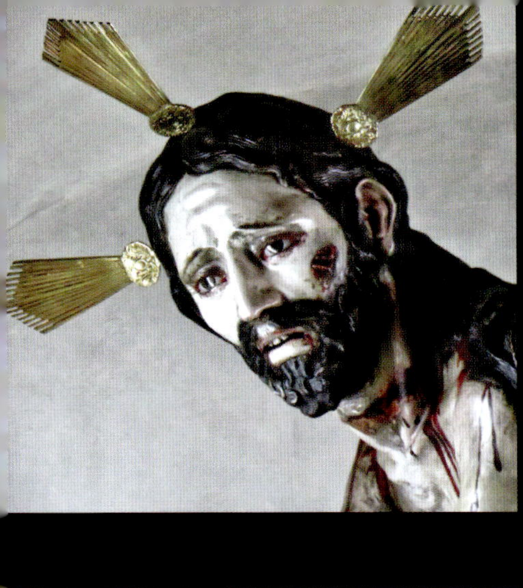
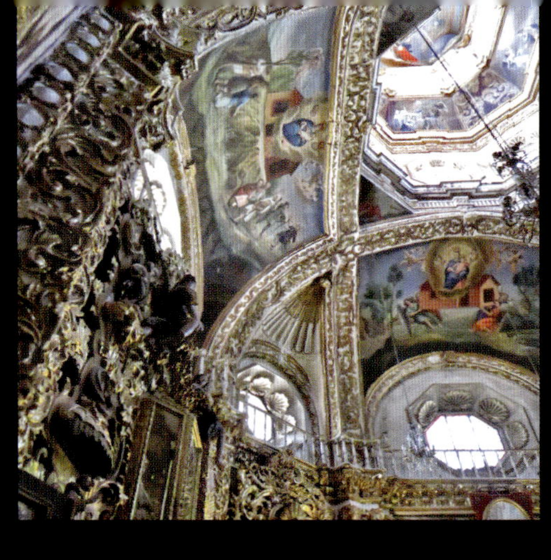
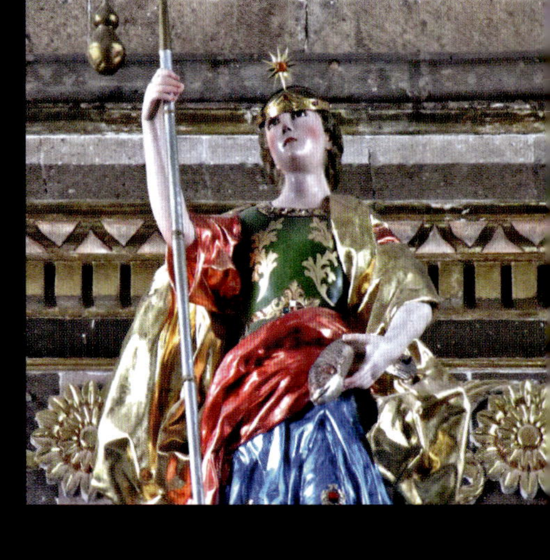
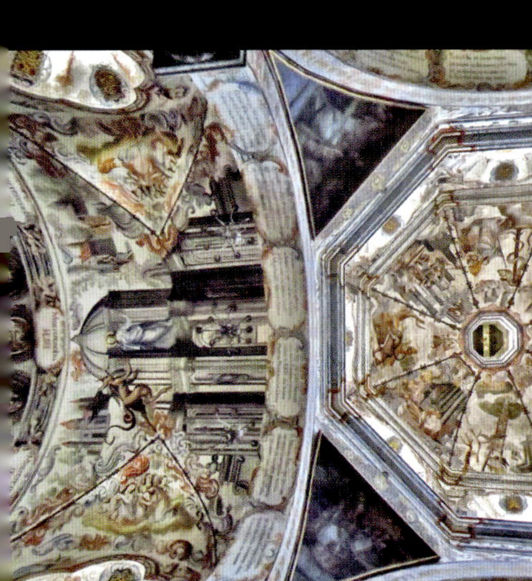
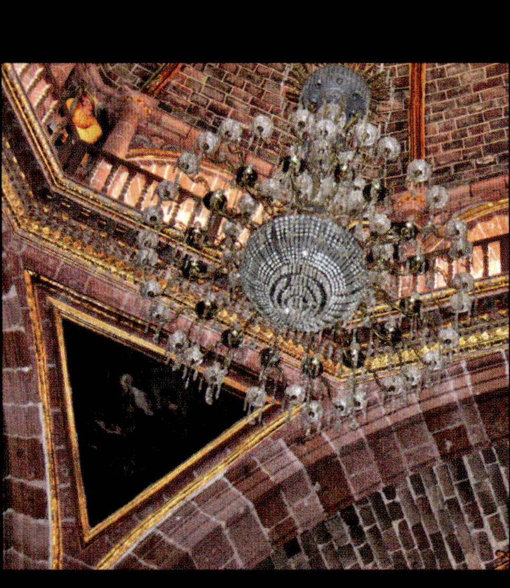
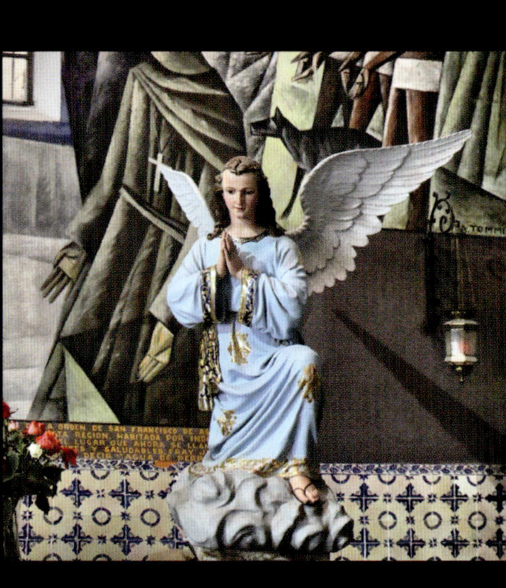
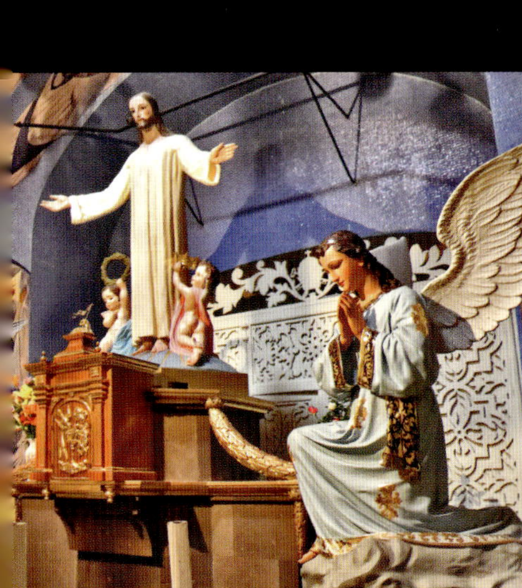
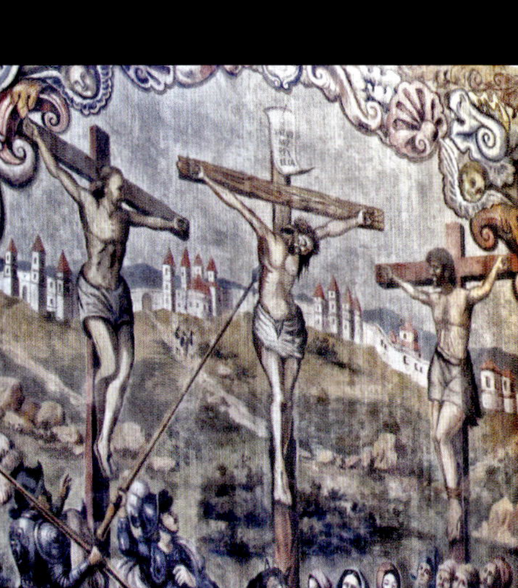
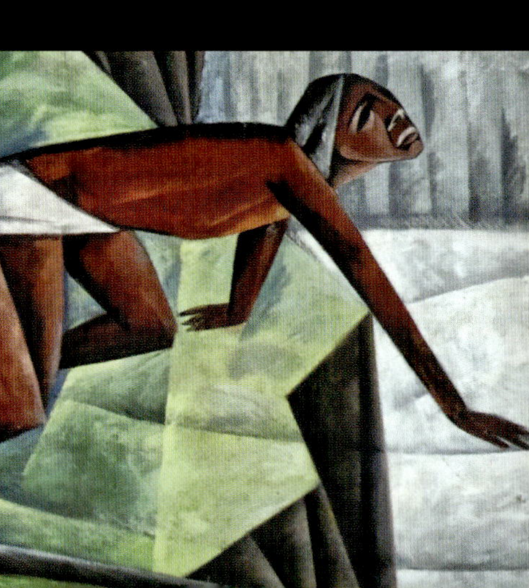

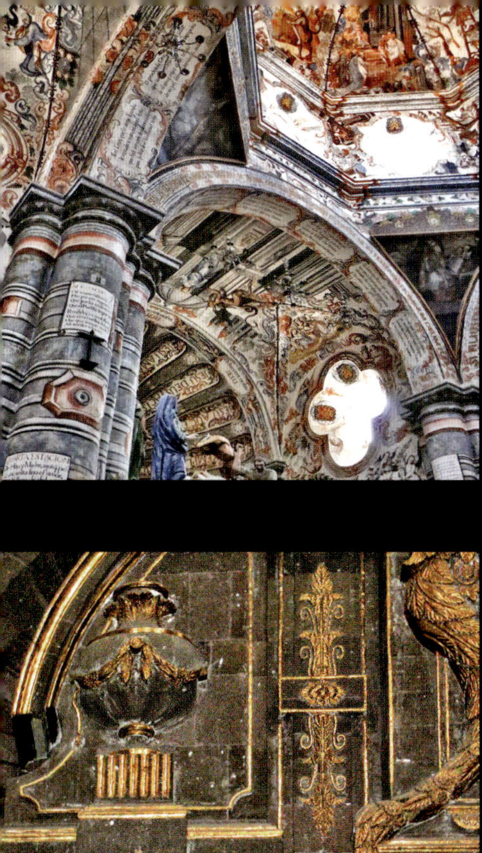
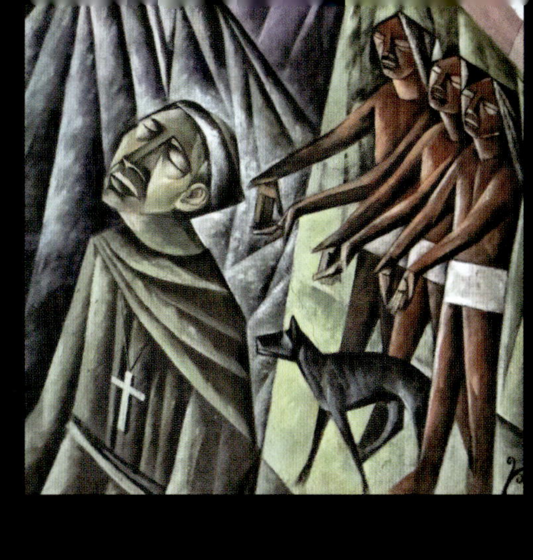
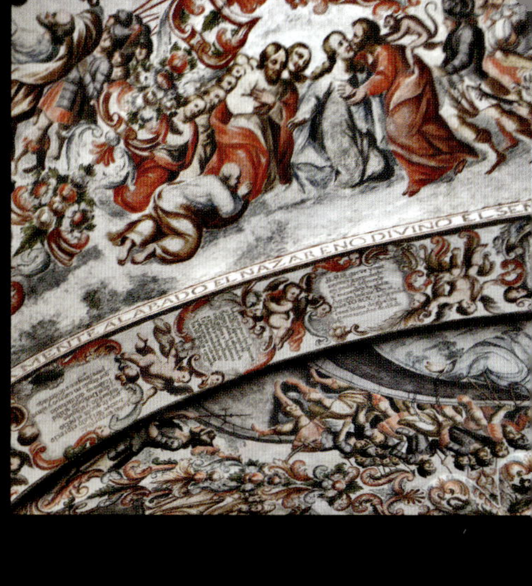
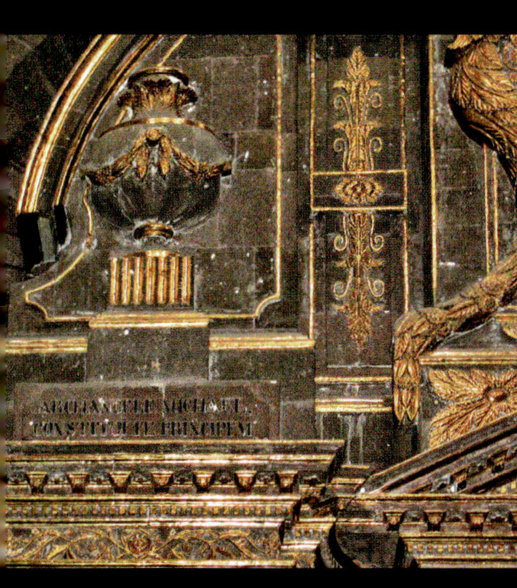
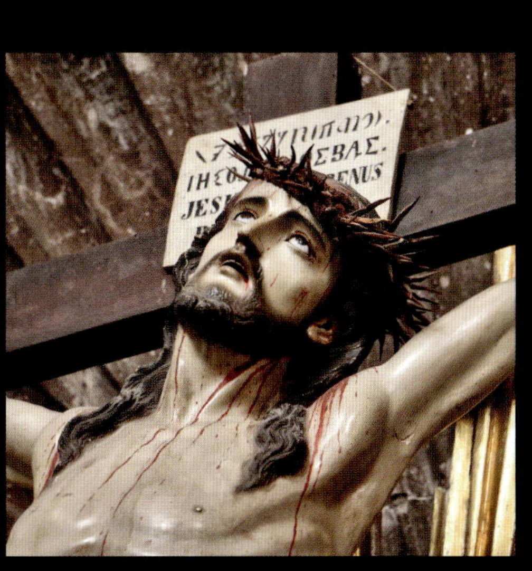
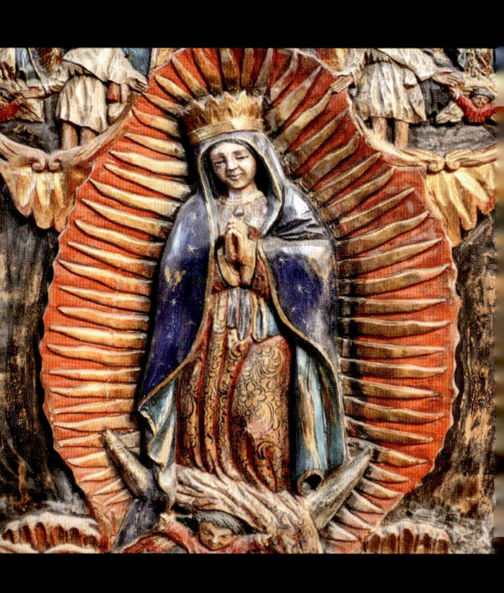
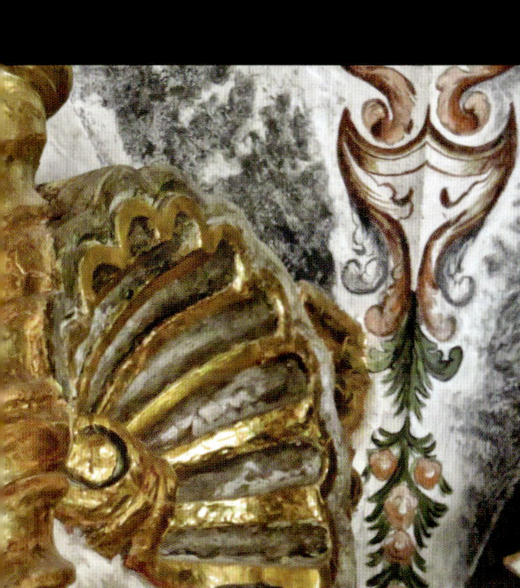
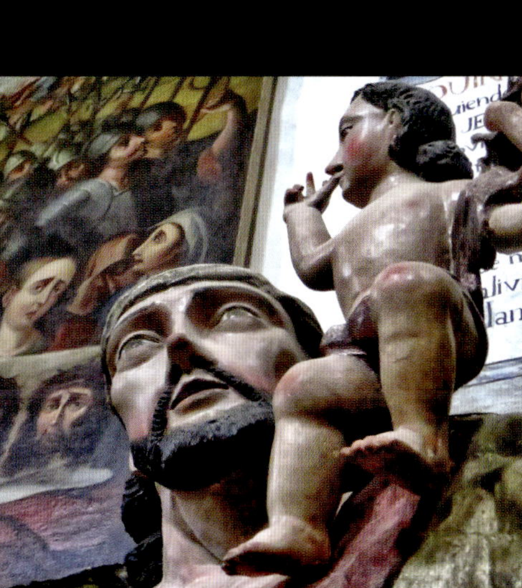
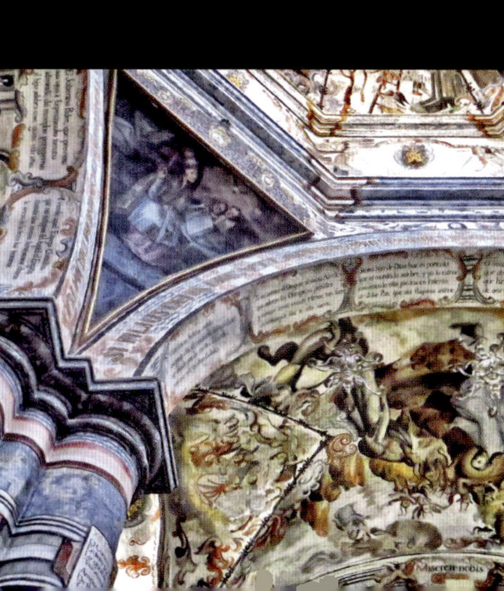

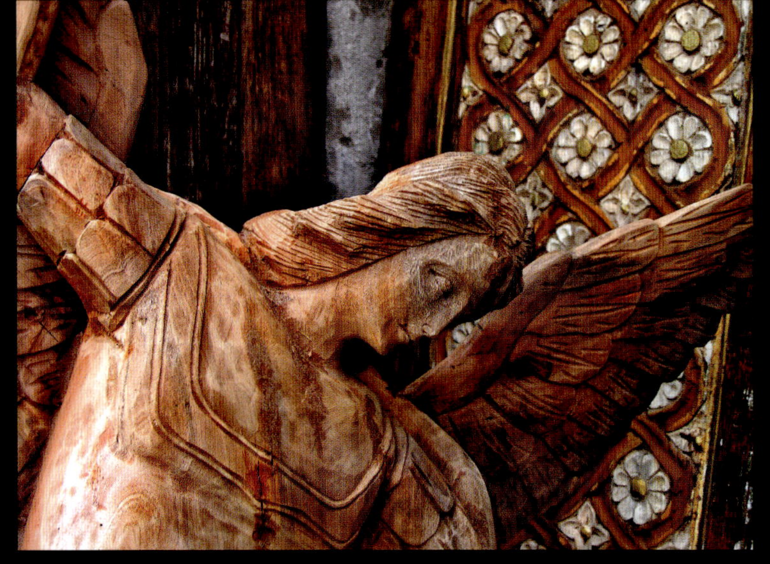

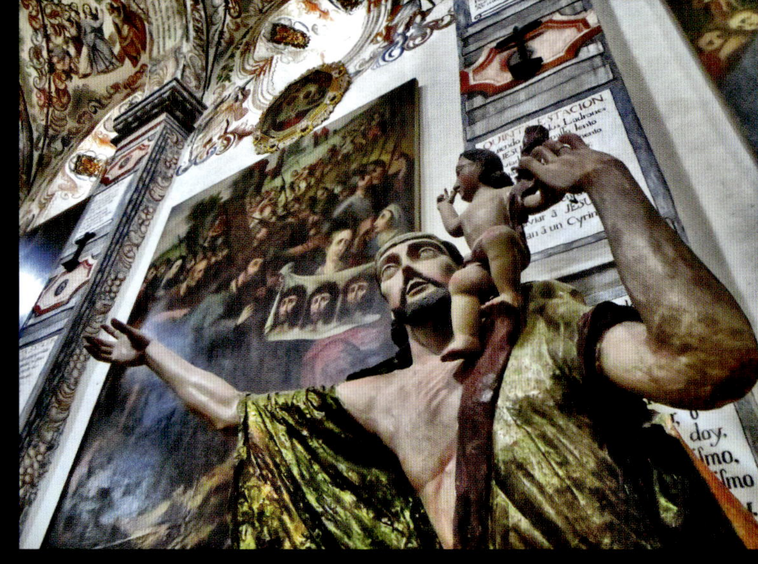

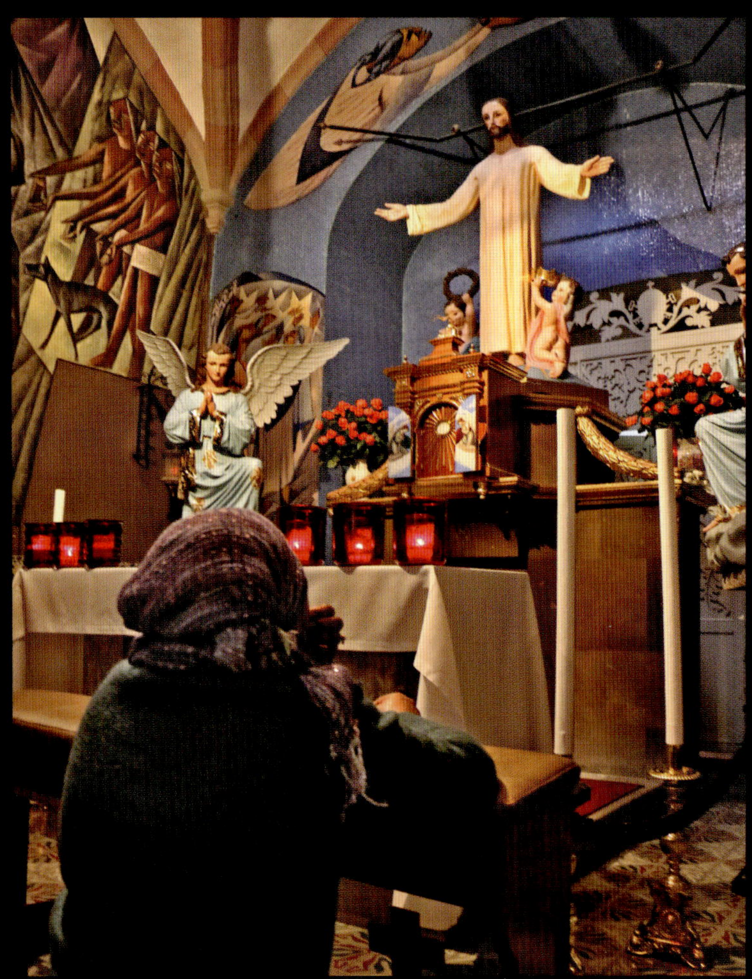

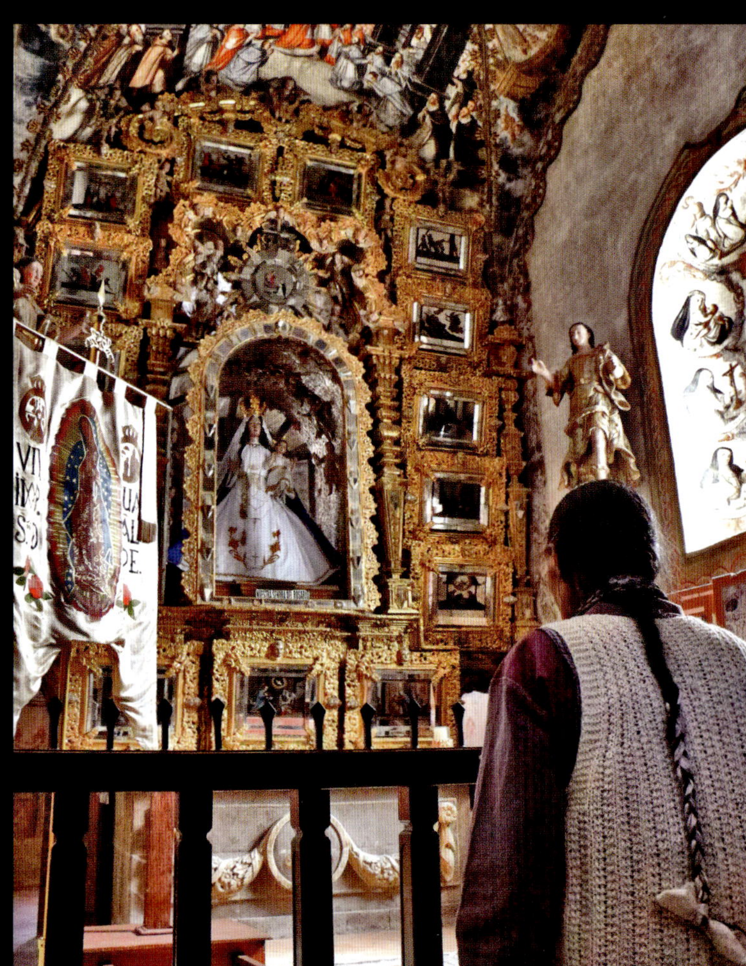

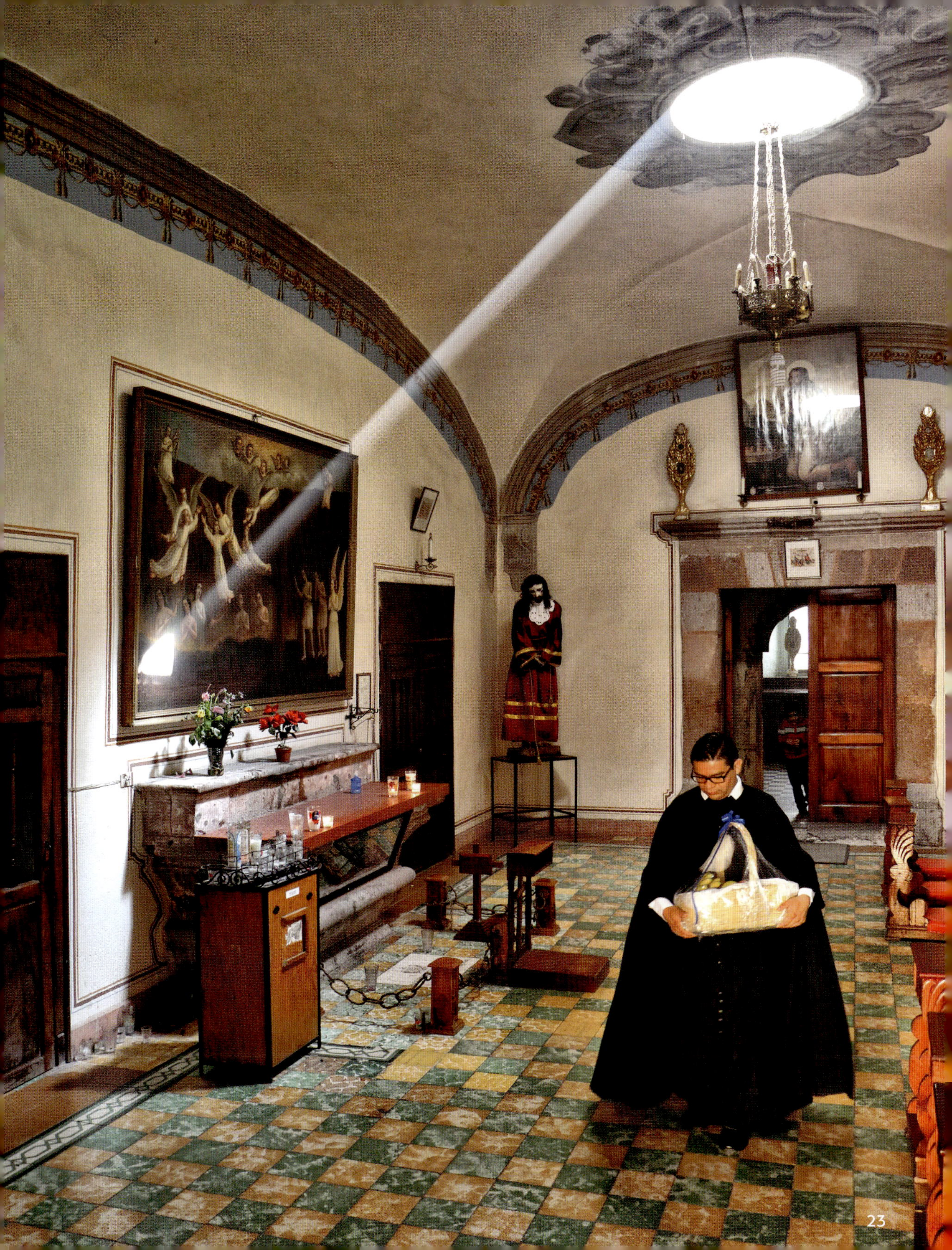

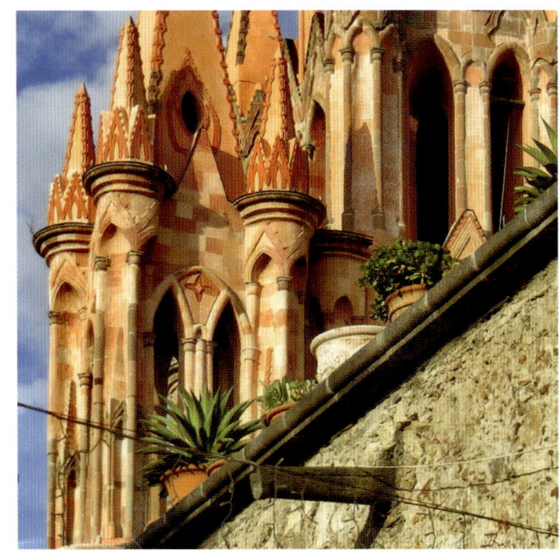
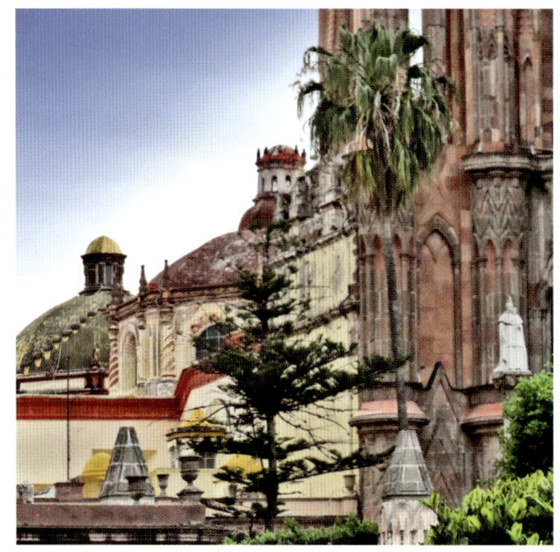
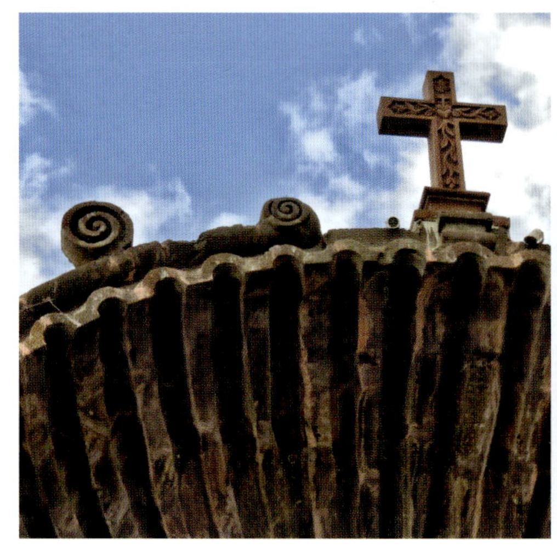
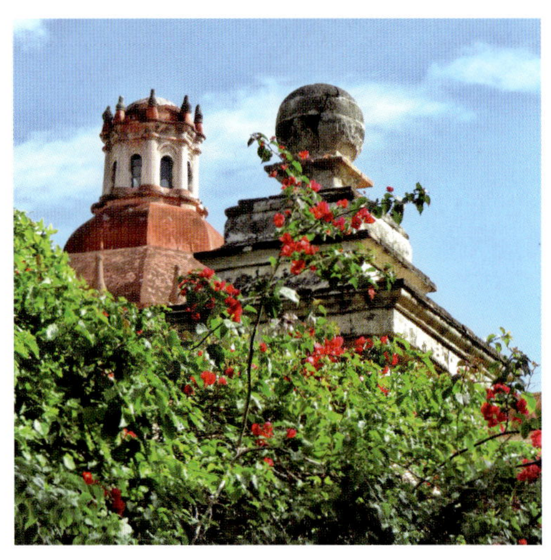
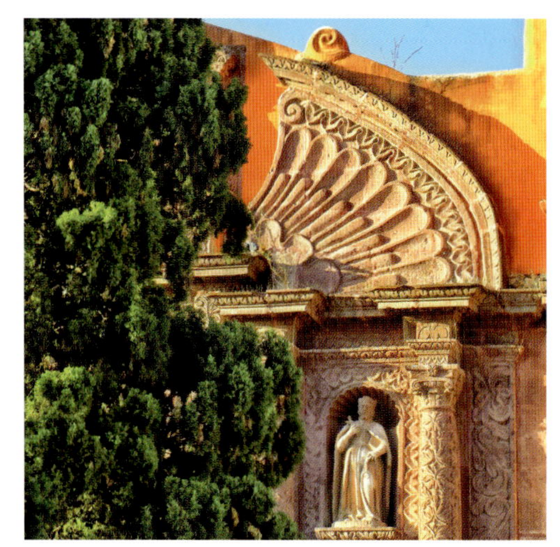
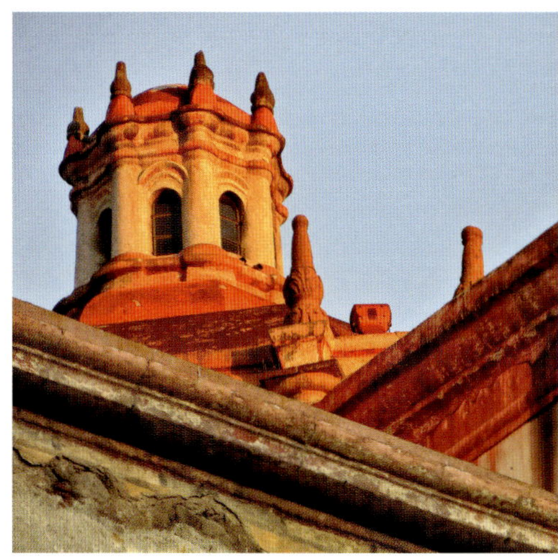
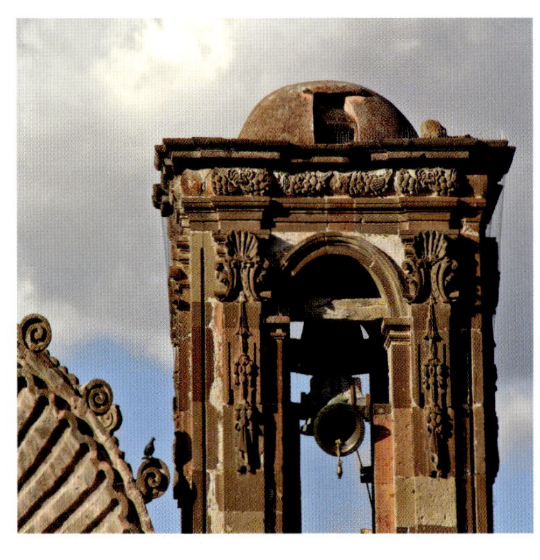
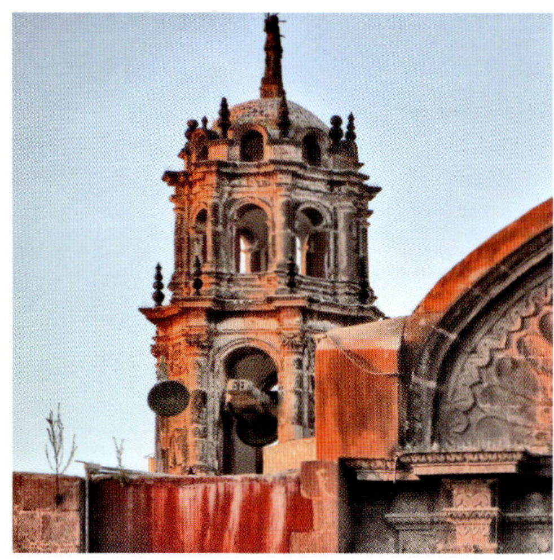
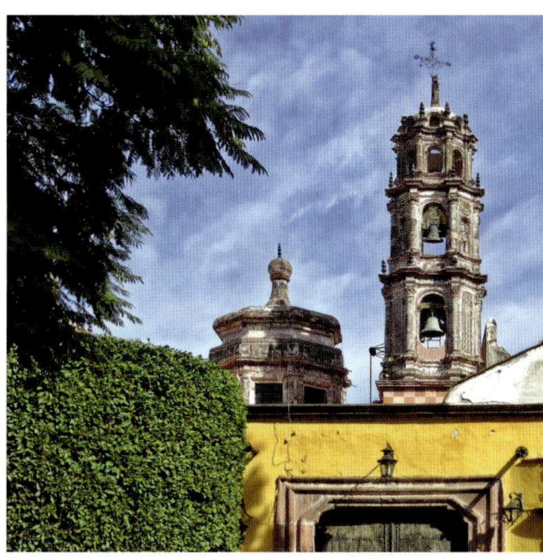

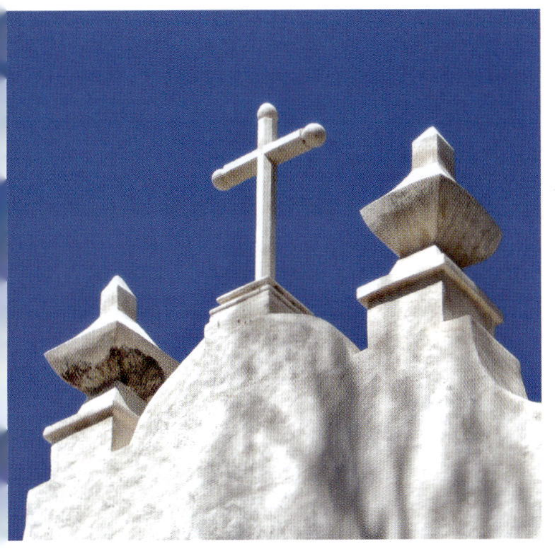
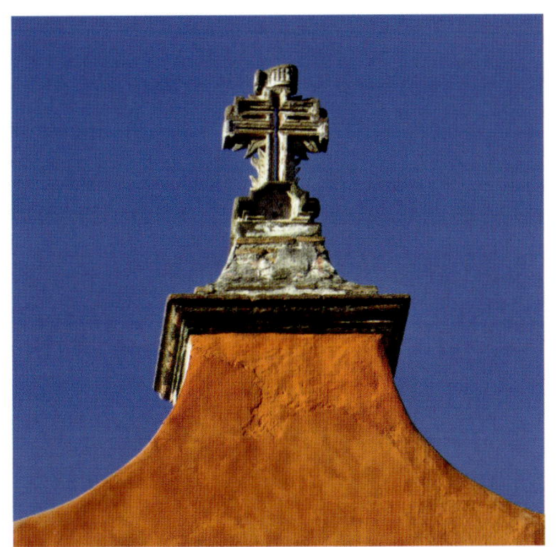
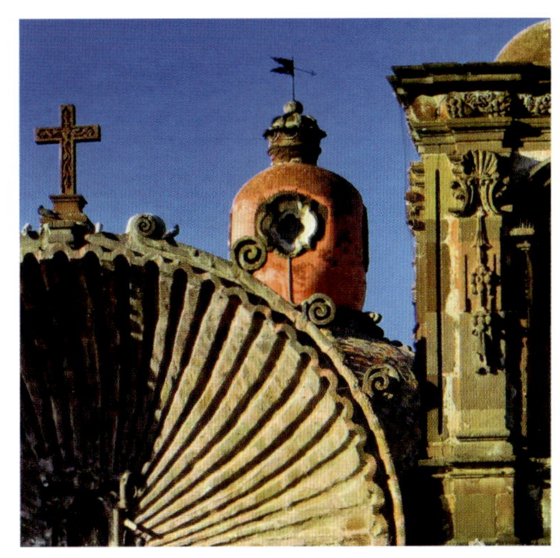
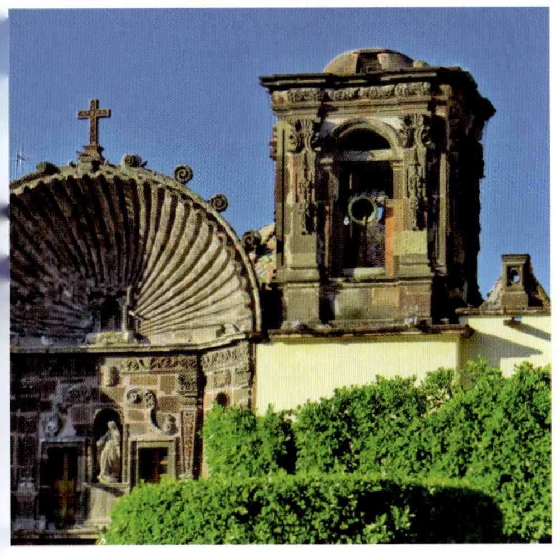
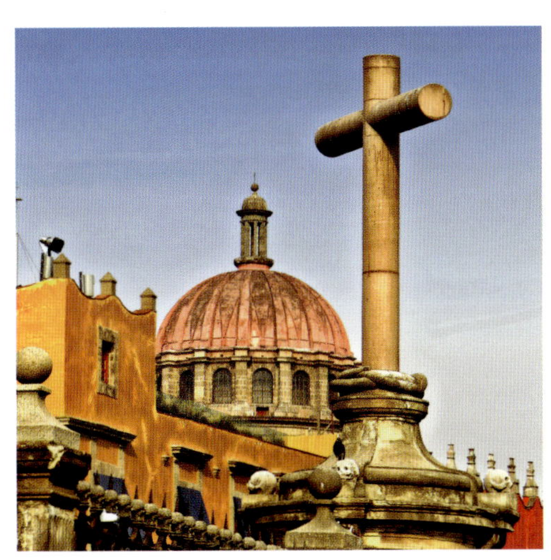
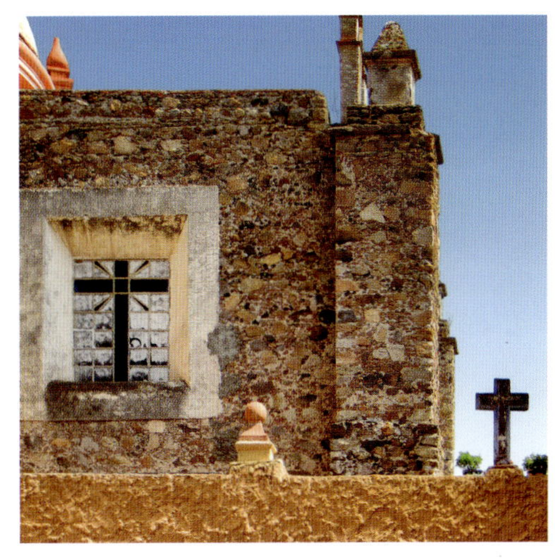
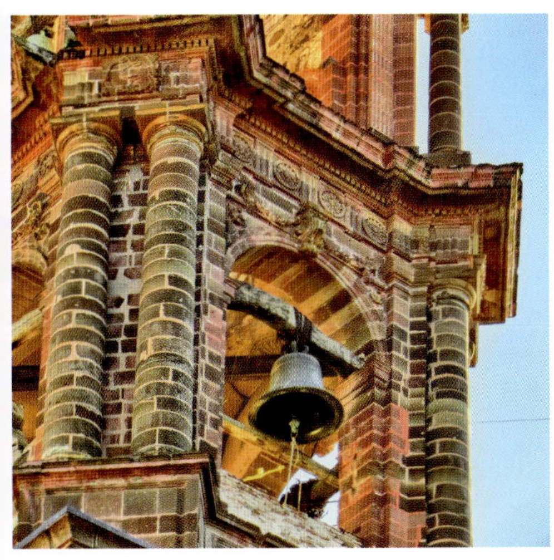
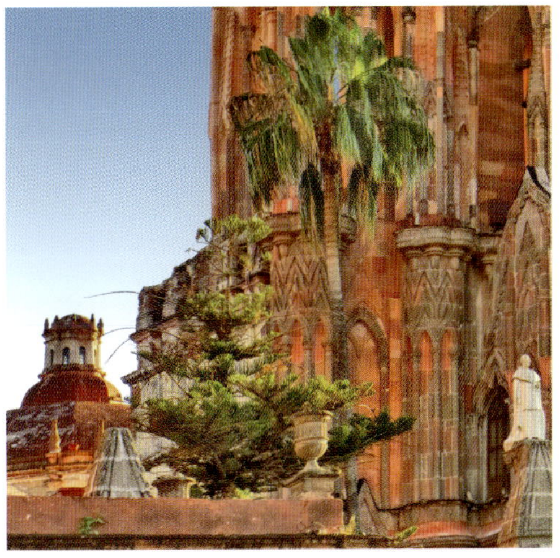
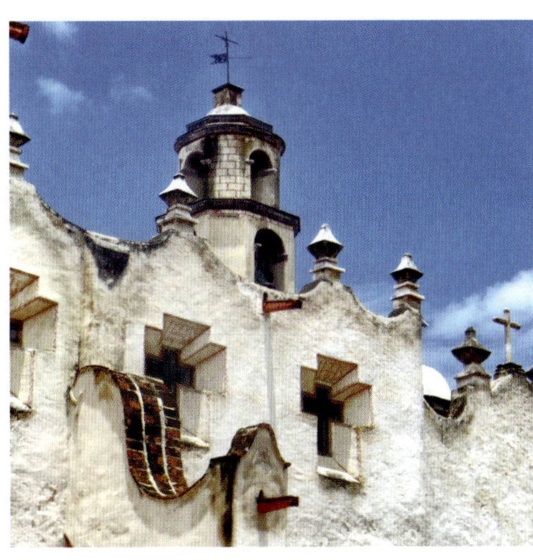

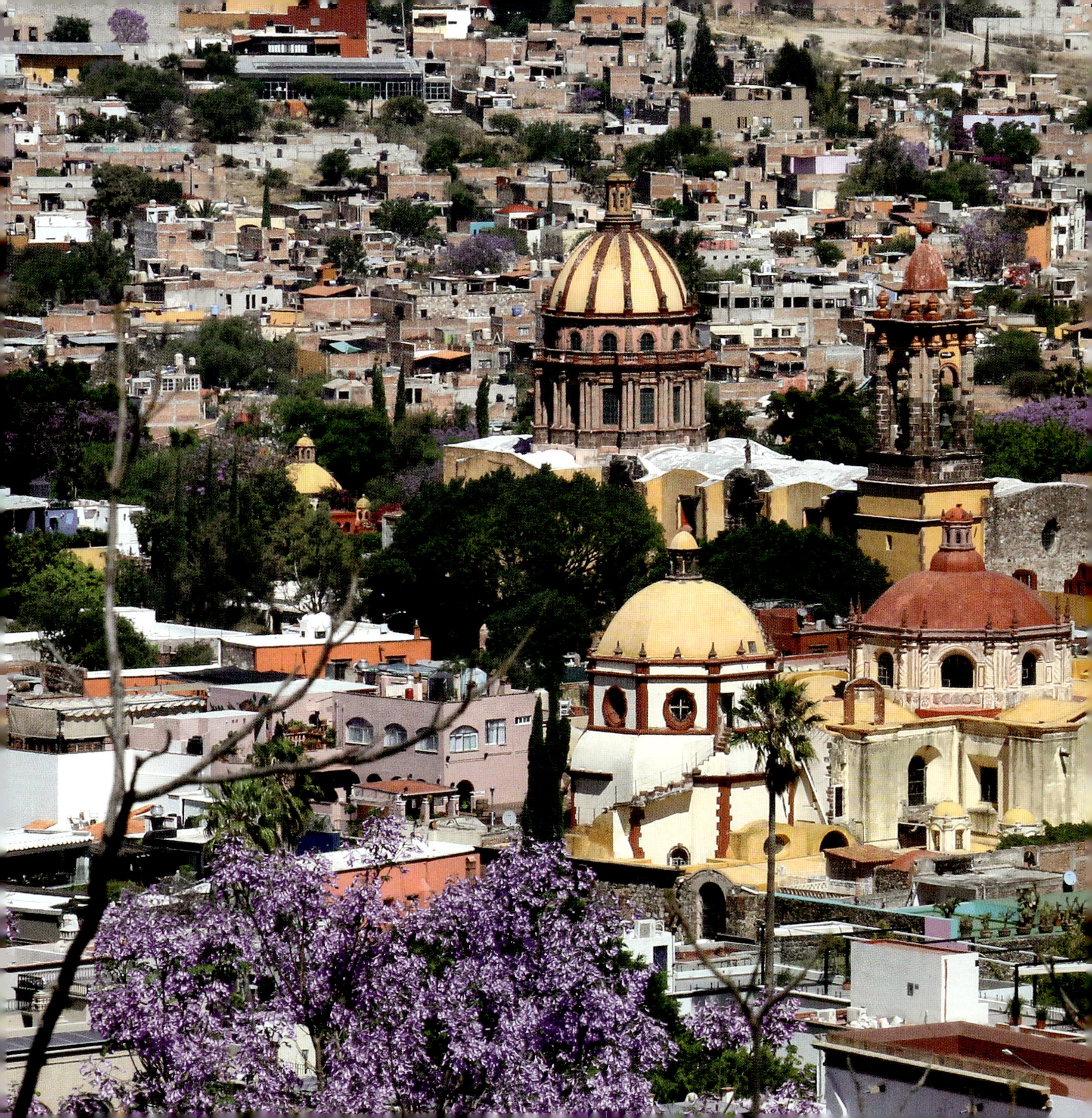

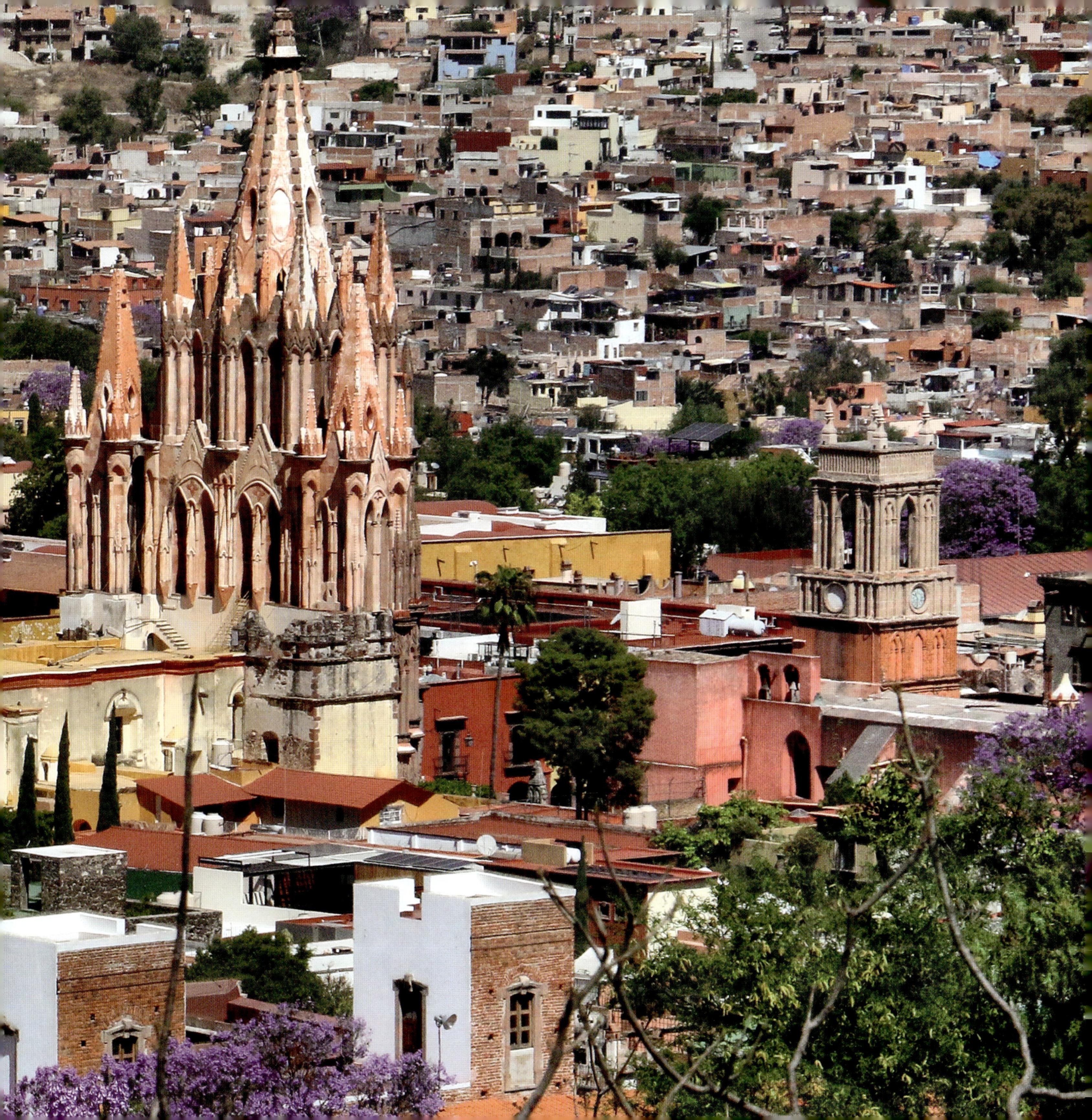

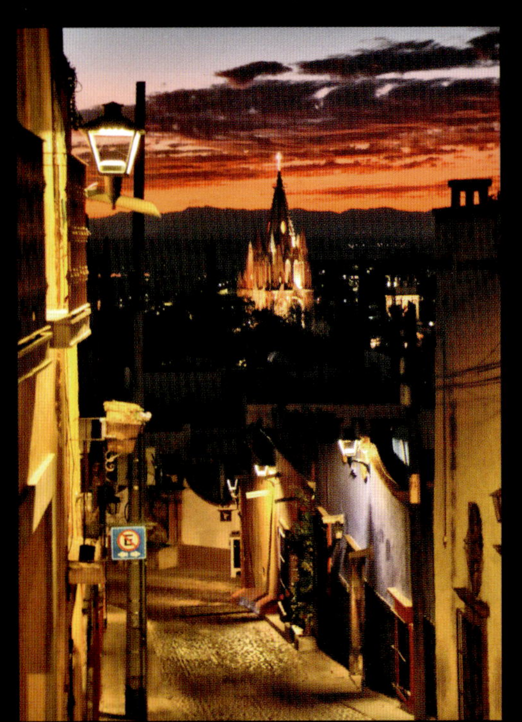

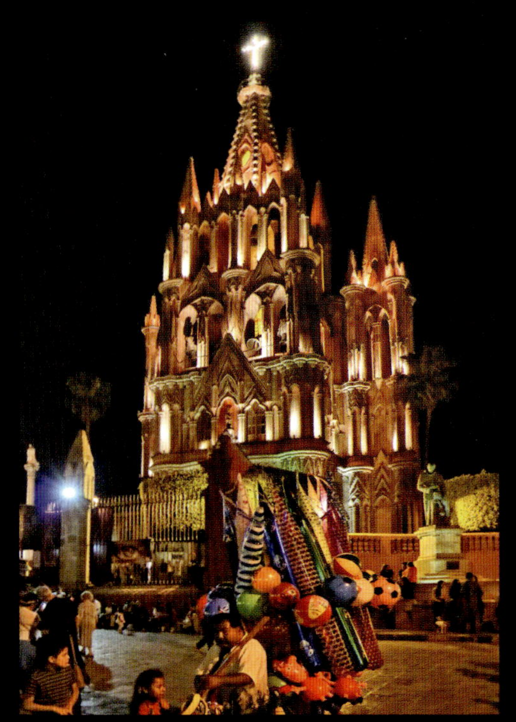

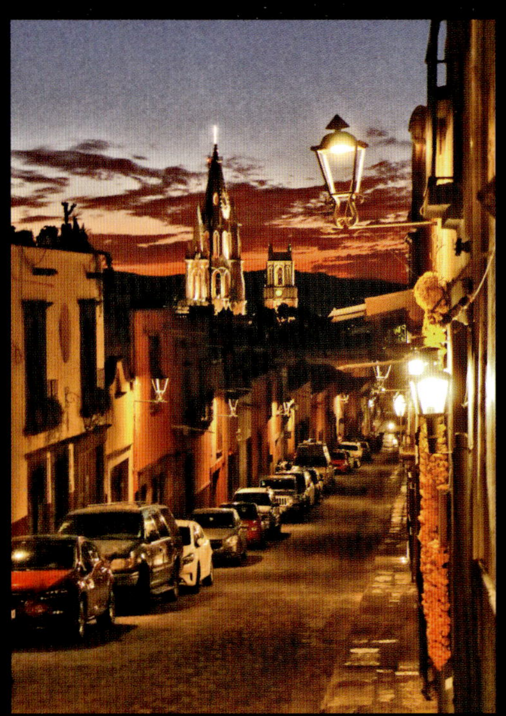

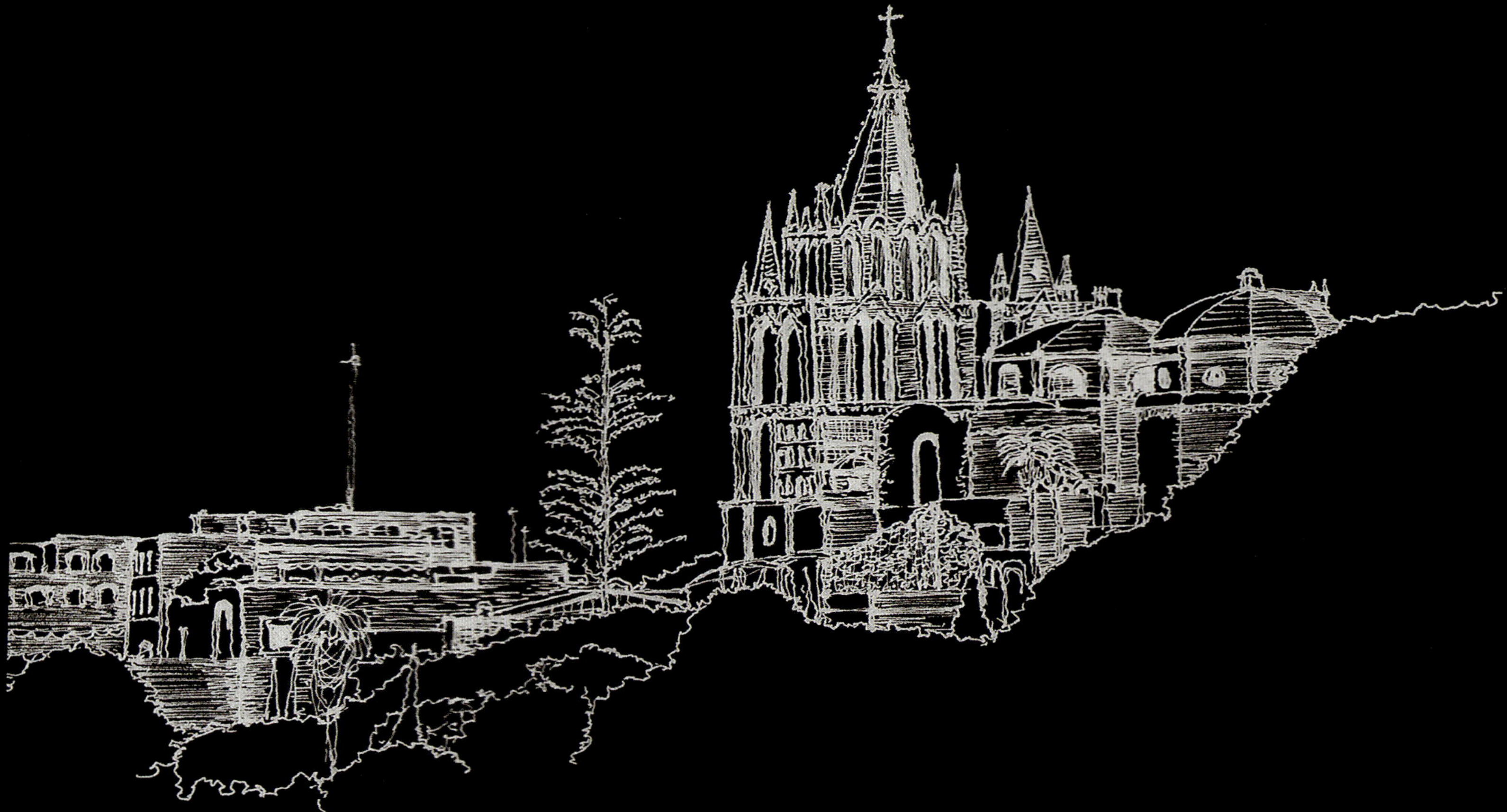

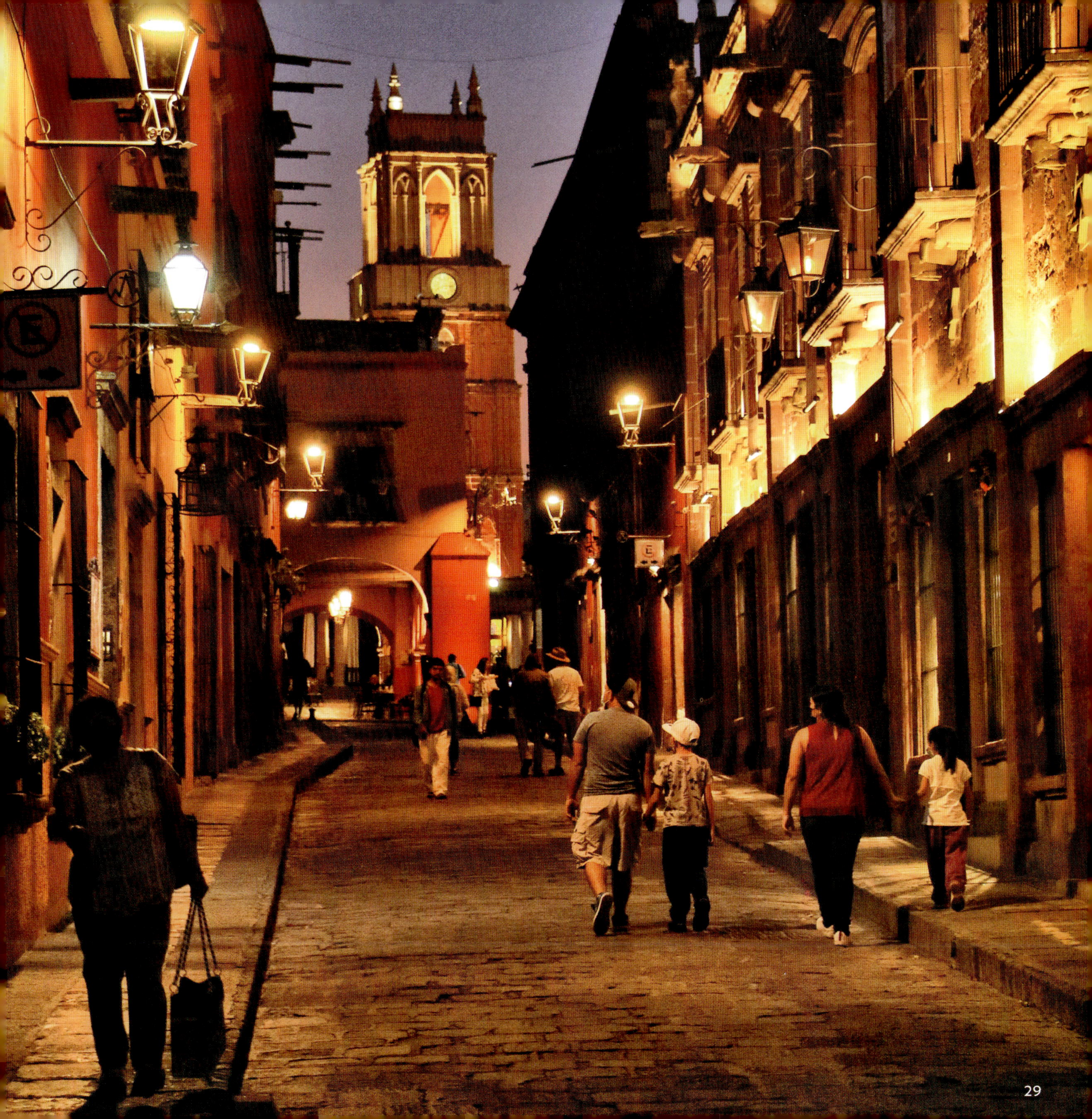

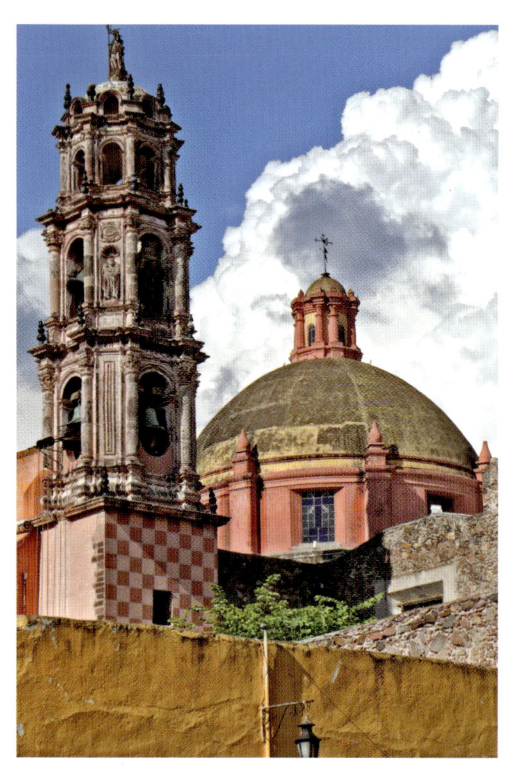

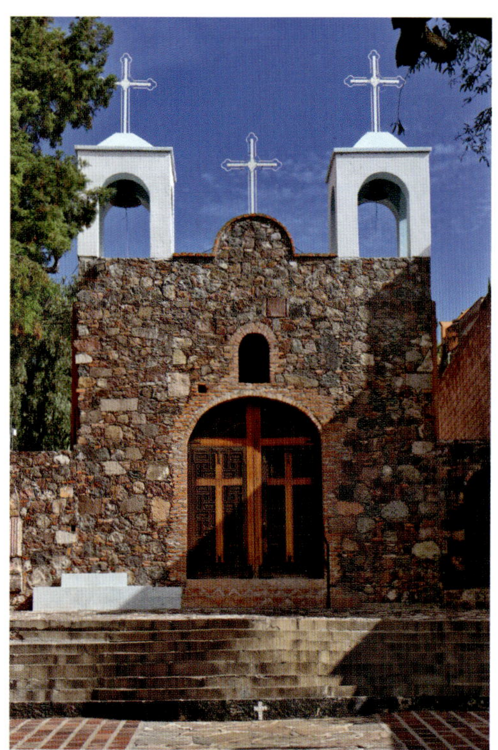

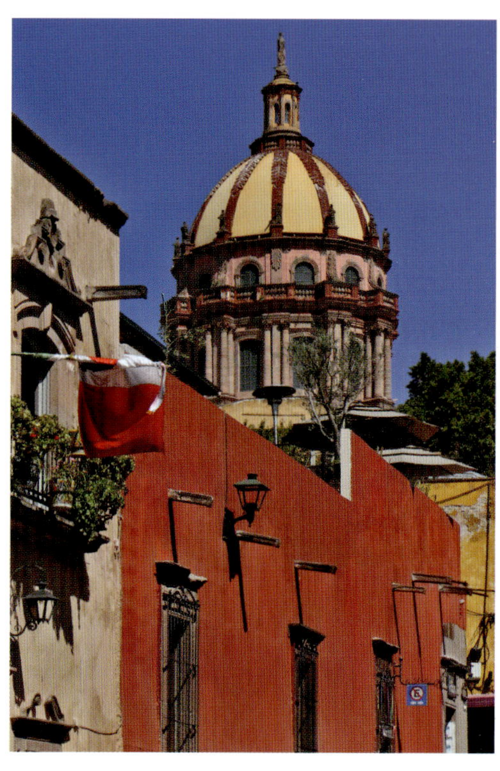

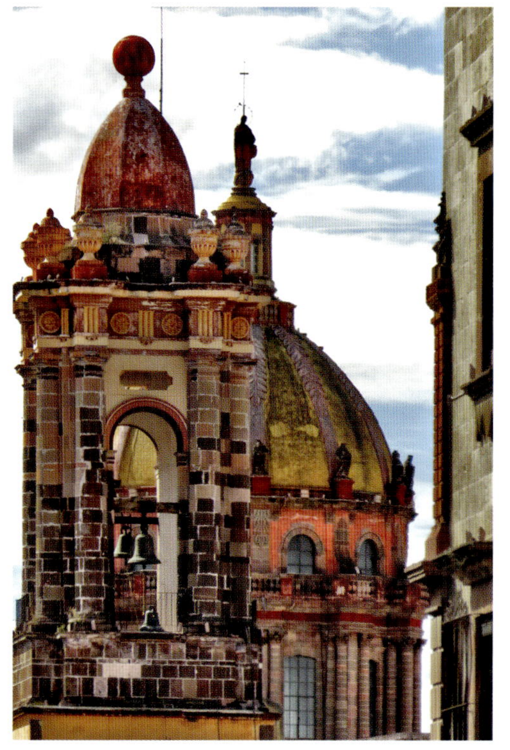

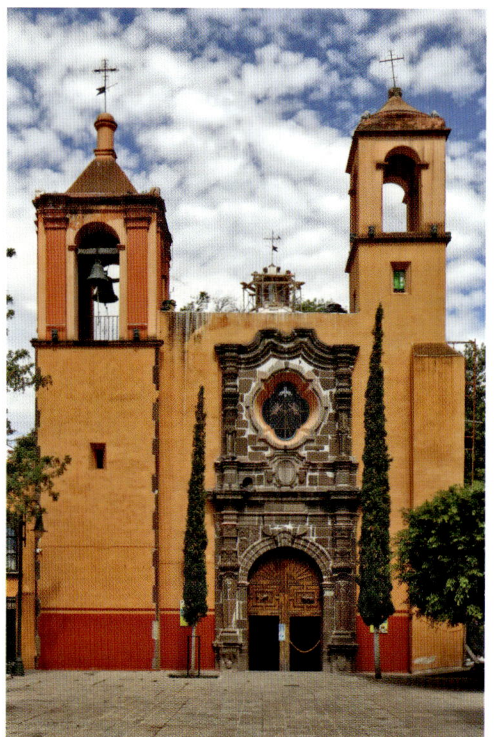

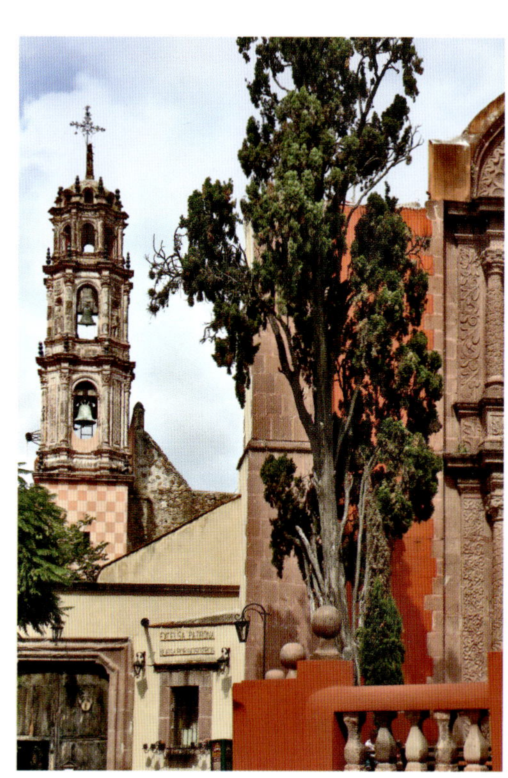

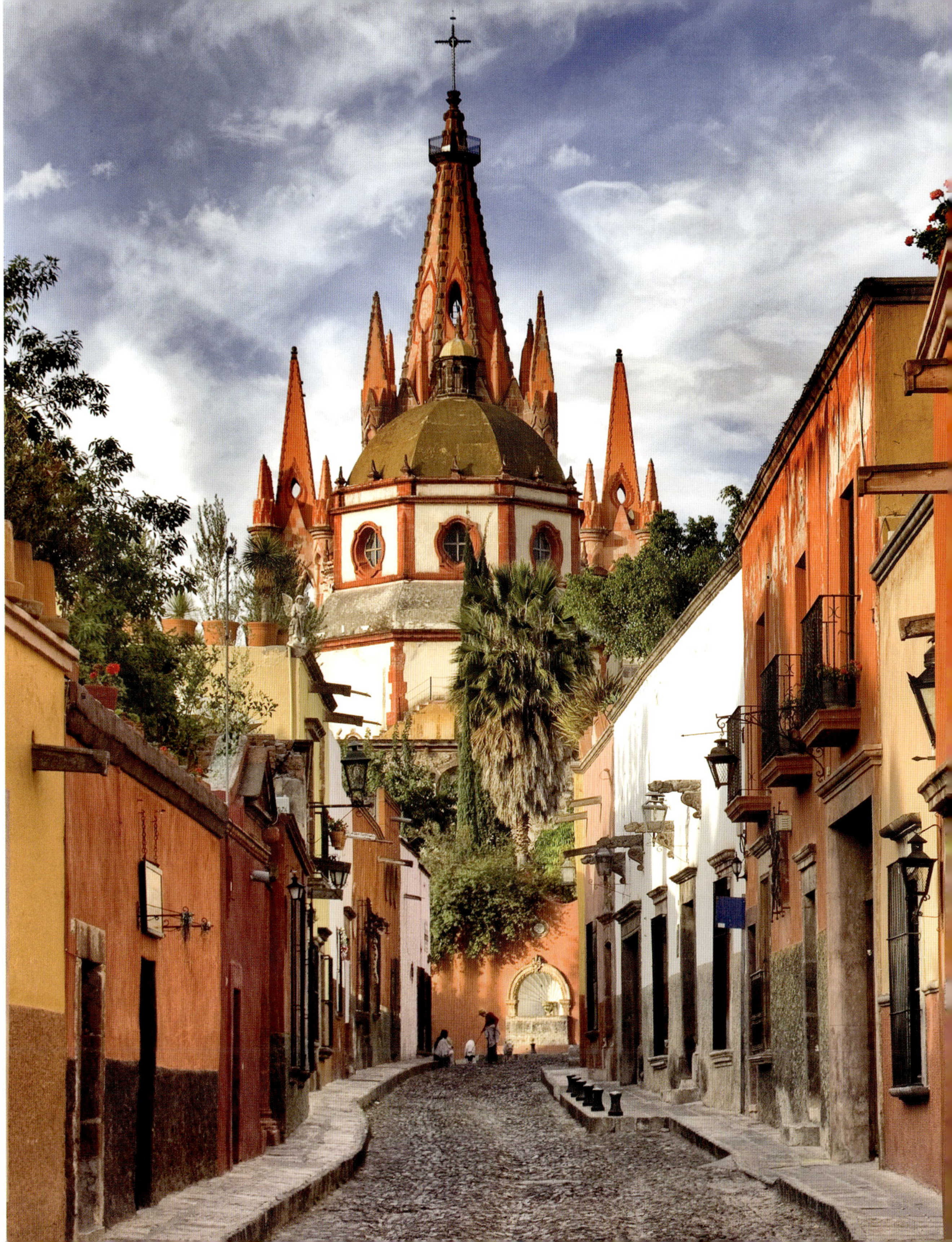

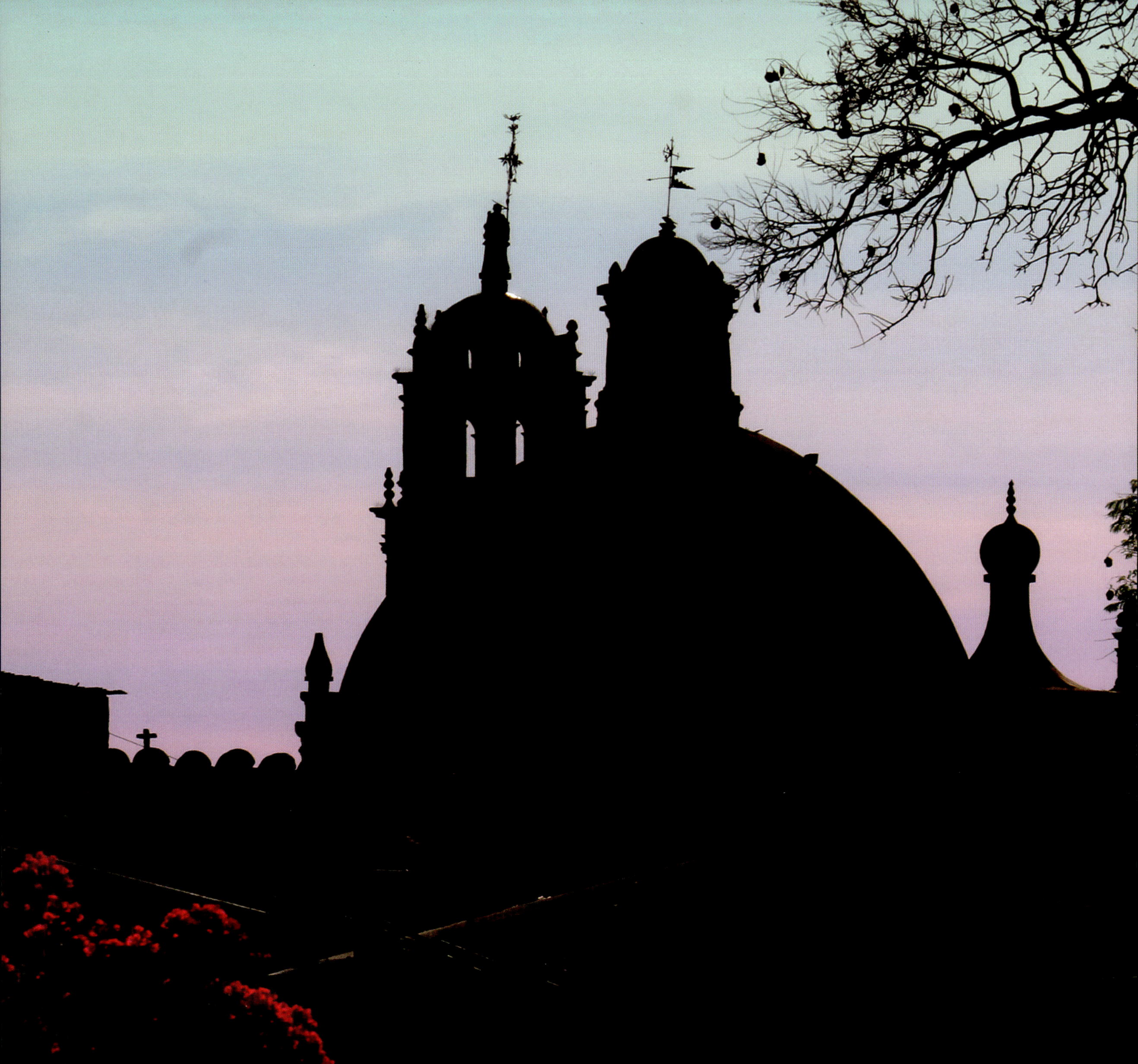

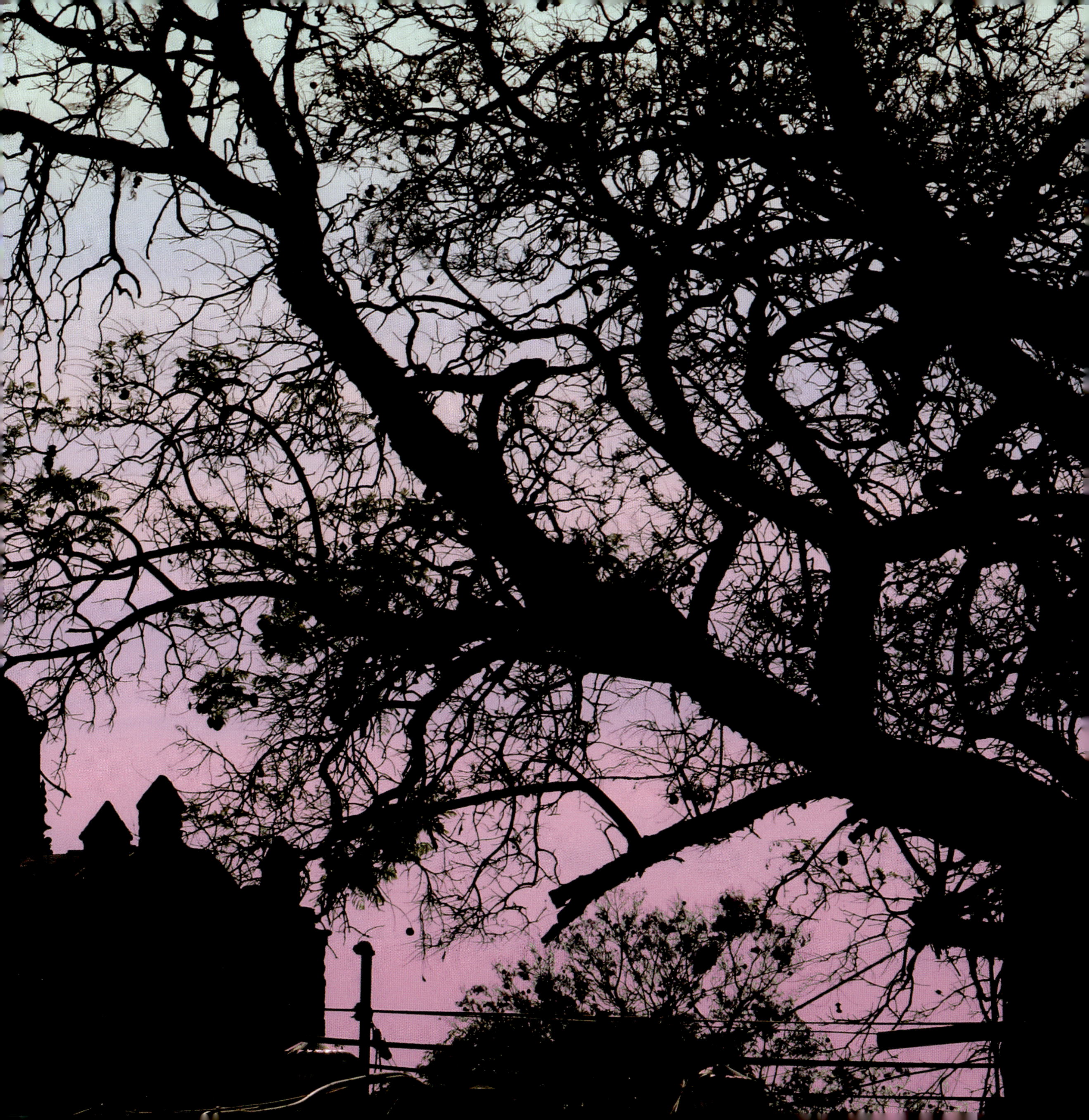

Markets

A riot of bold colors in constantly changing compositions, the sound of birds and vendor calls, the chatter of bargaining and lively conversation, blaring music, the aromas of roasting meats and vegetables, oven-baked pizzas, grilled corn, tacos, fresh tortillas, fruits, vegetables, and flowers all swirl together in San Miguel's markets in that eternal dance of life and commerce that fills your needs and floods your senses with pleasure.

The vast Tuesday market, or Tianguis, takes its name from the Aztec language for open-air market. It is a world of color, texture, sound, and smell, every sense heightened and satisfied. Mounds of colorful produce; piles of clothes being sorted through; tables of school supplies, makeup, and hair décor; stacked cages of exotic birds singing; every vendor calling out his products and prices; people dining on beautifully crafted plates of aromatic traditional foods; live and broadcast music playing loudly; jewelry, bags, antiques, old tools, sunglasses, you name it, you will find it.

A Mexican market is alive and fluid, pulling your attention in every direction. It is possible to find anything you may need, from a sweet songbird to a rooster to an iPad to a chisel or shovel, an ancient wooden statue, or freshly prepared cakes to complement your dinner plans. Young jewelers get their foothold on how to sell their creations; children play among their mothers' skirts; fresh churros are scooped from sizzling vats, sprinkled with sugar and handed over in a bouquet of sweetness; vegetables are shredded into colorful vertical salads in large plastic cups; fruit juices become aqua frescas, ladled from enormous glass jugs to quench the thirst of serious shoppers.

Markets may be vast, like the Tianguis, spread over a large area at the outskirts of town; they may flow down a stairway in town, like the many artisan markets; they may pop up in someone's entryway or on a certain street that celebrates holidays unique to that street. There are moving markets in the form of the women who stroll the town center, their arms filled with hand-strung necklaces, or the men with vertical stacks of hats on their heads, often as tall as the man himself. There are tiny markets of old women who may be selling only a rosebush or freshly prepared gorditas. On certain days, markets unfold in front of churches where women sell home-made tamales and the luscious Mexican drink atole, or nuns sell fresh eggnog or the special ponche at Christmas. And markets accompany any celebration.

Markets in their more traditional form, as shops, overflow with beautifully crafted goods. Hand-blown glass, flowing clothes, hand-painted and sequined jackets, bags, shoes: whatever your heart desires can be found in the many shops and markets of San Miguel.

Life in Mexico is a dance, never more beautiful than the stroll through a market with all its richness of color, texture, and aroma, and with the promise of finding something special.

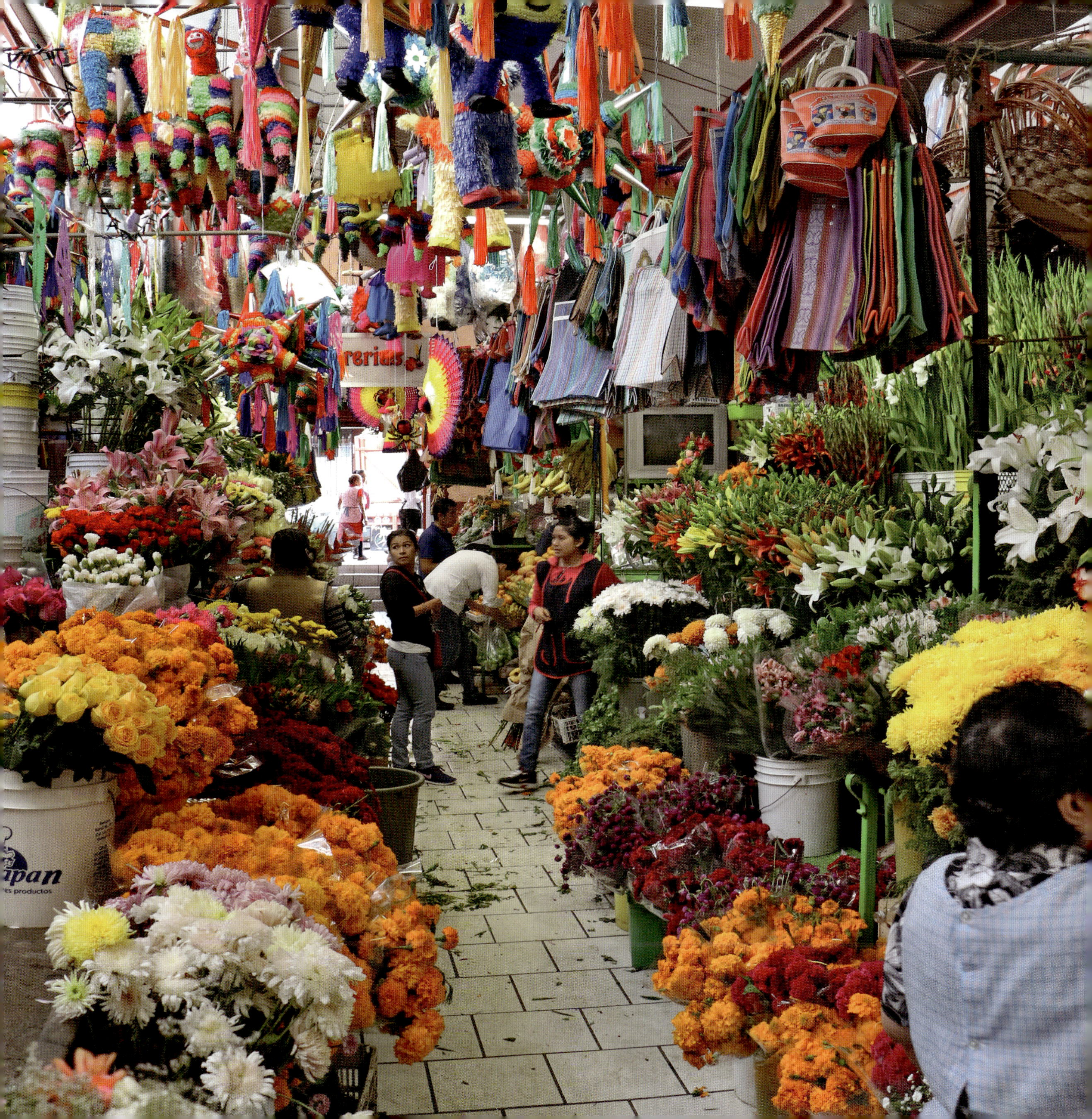

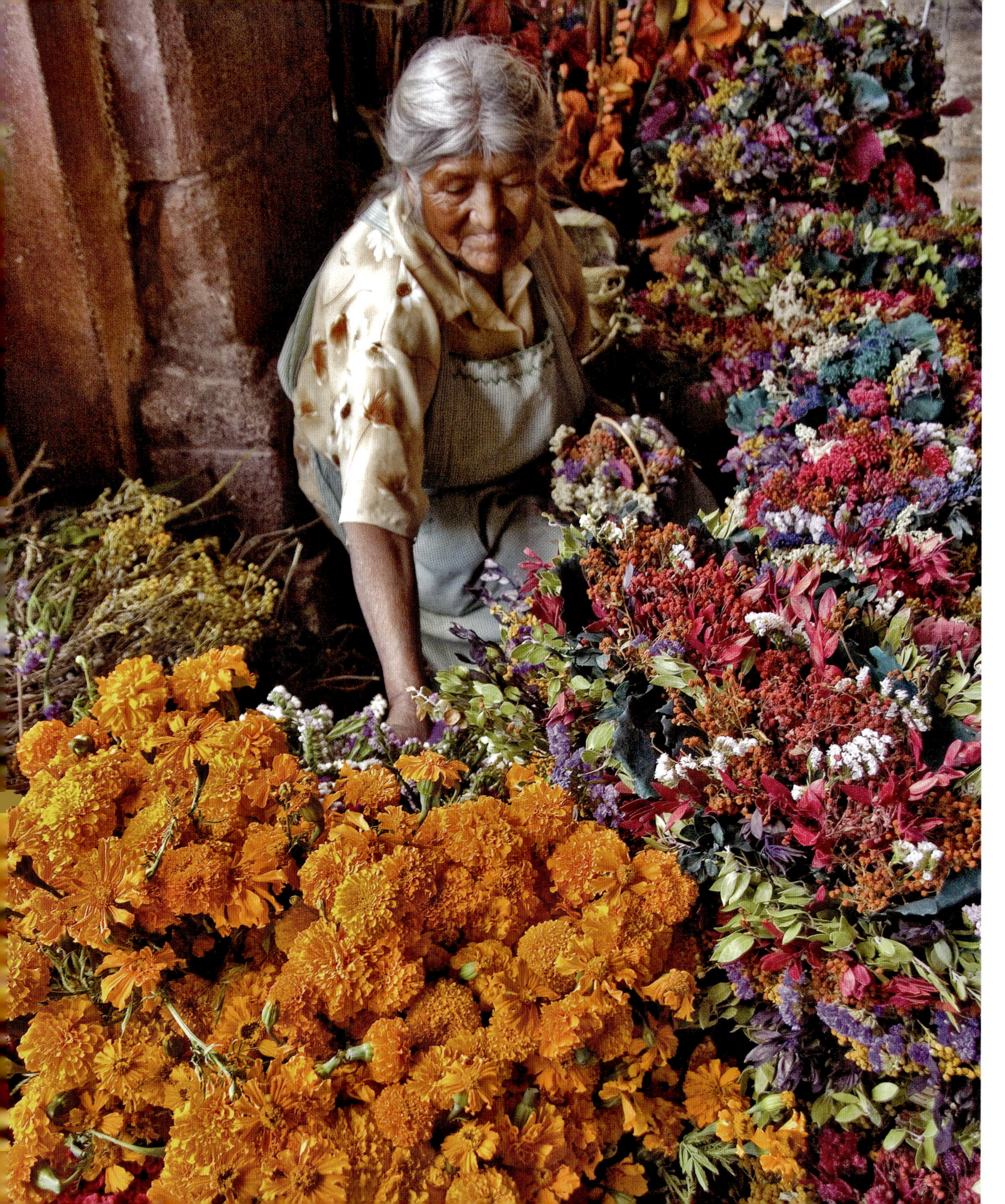

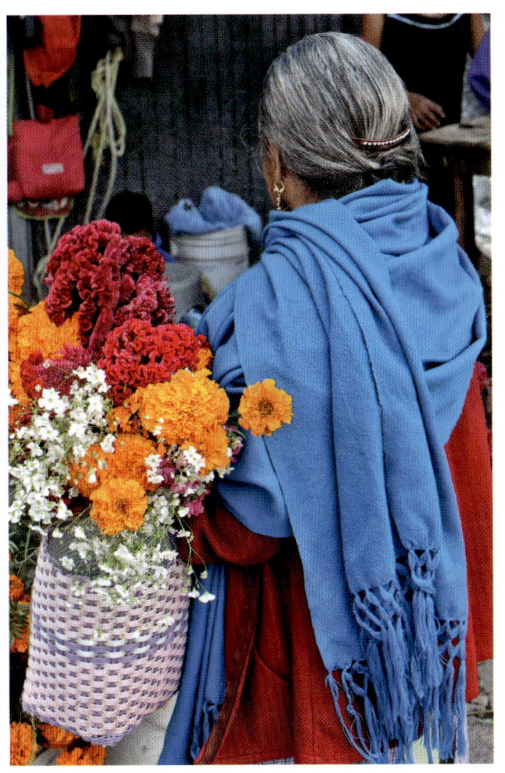

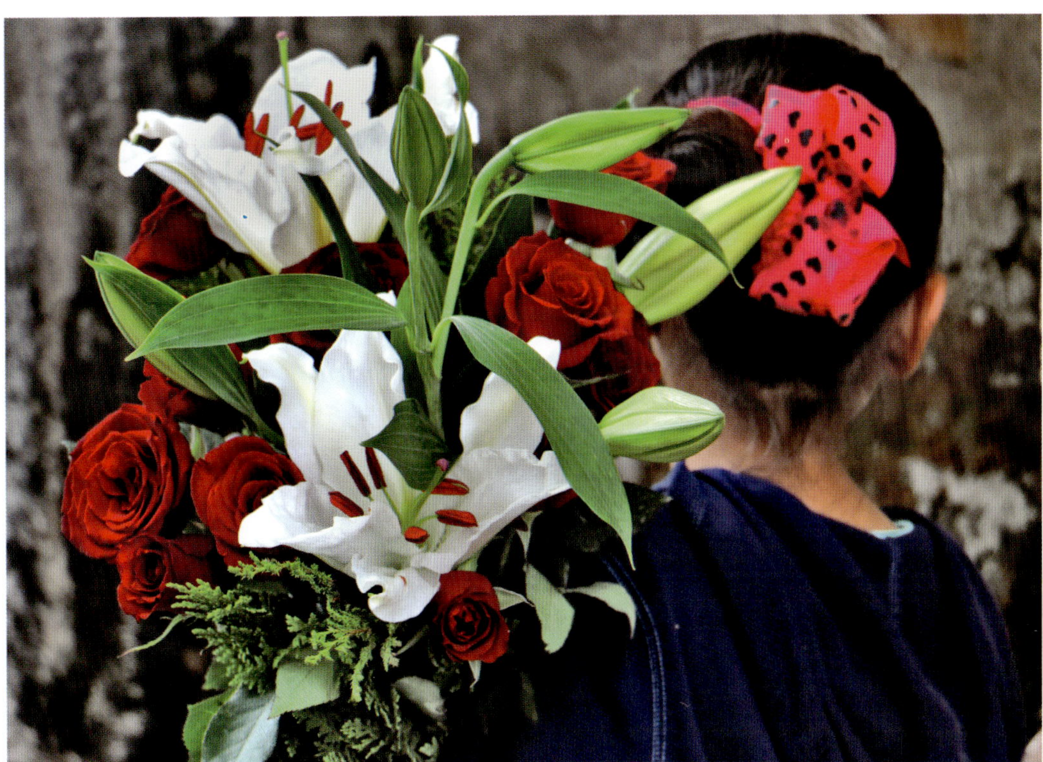

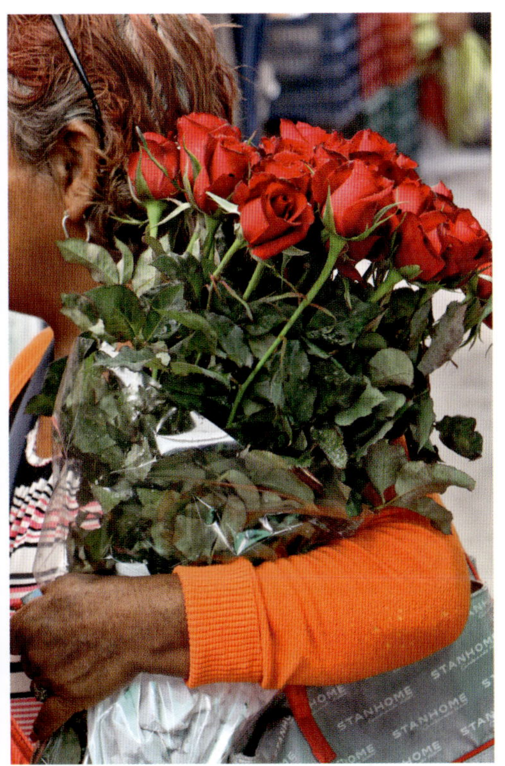
STANHOME

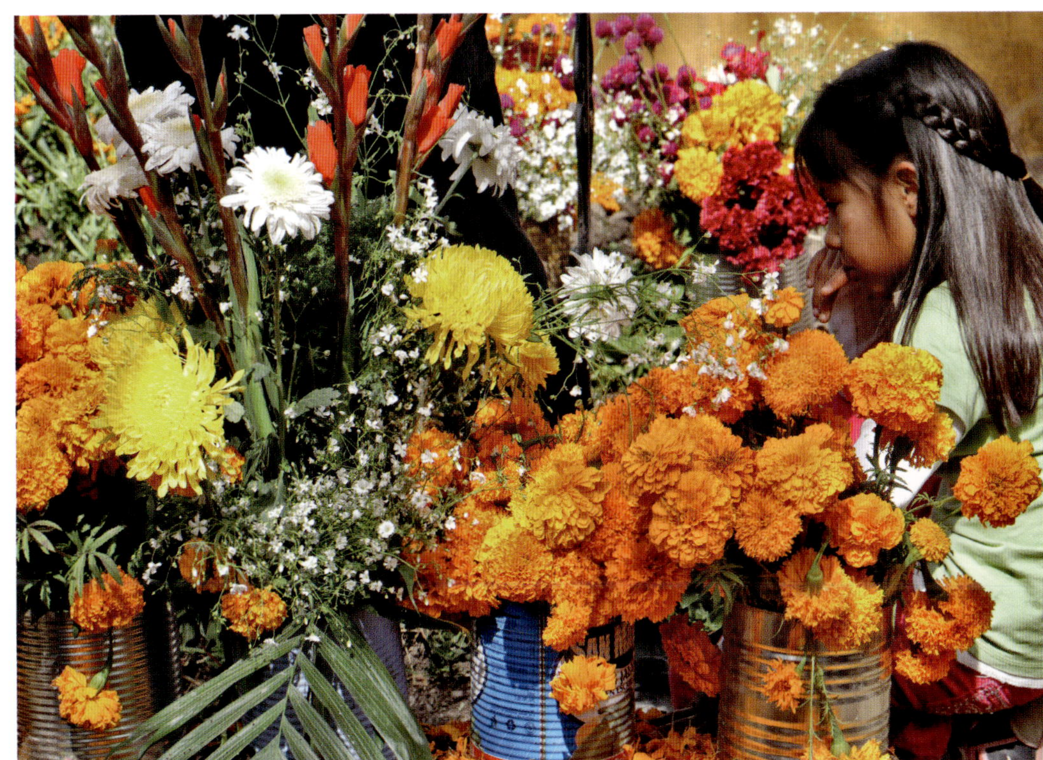

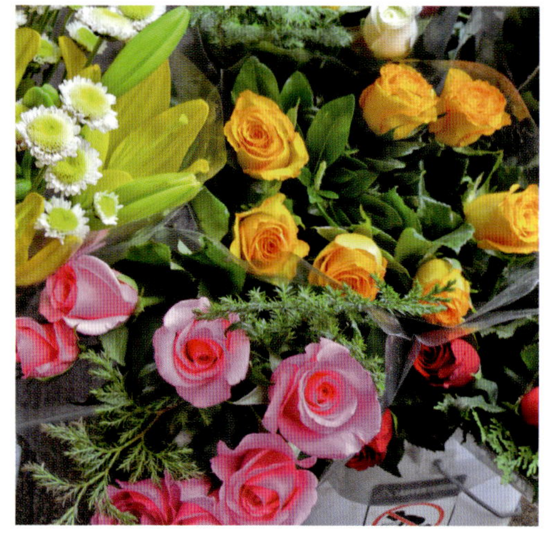
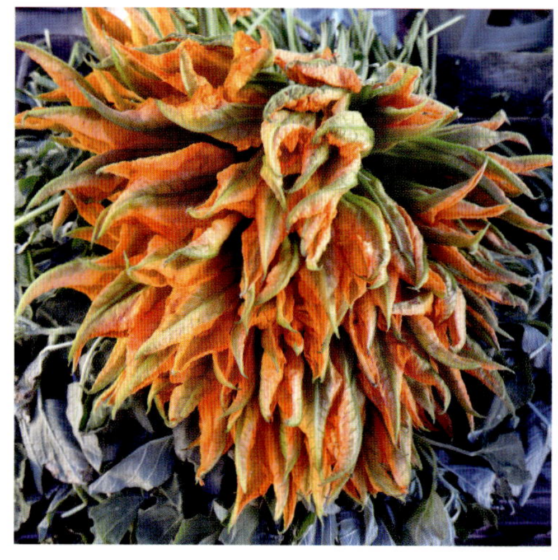
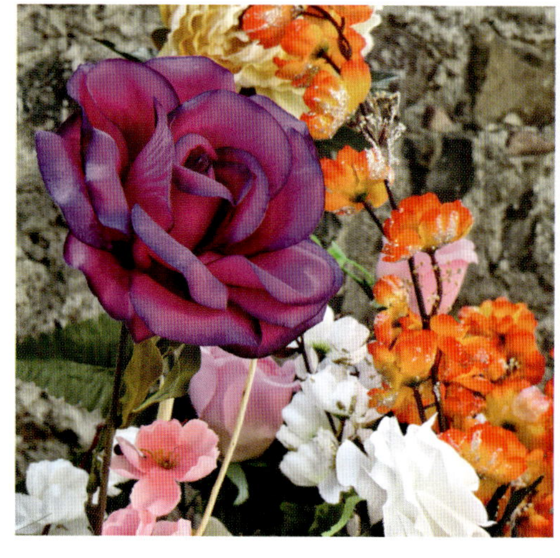
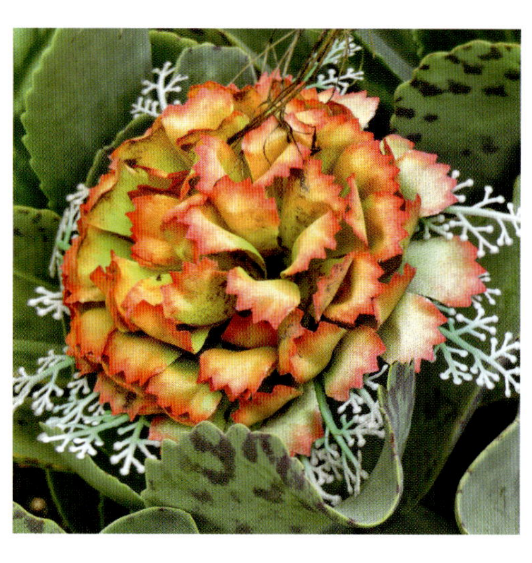
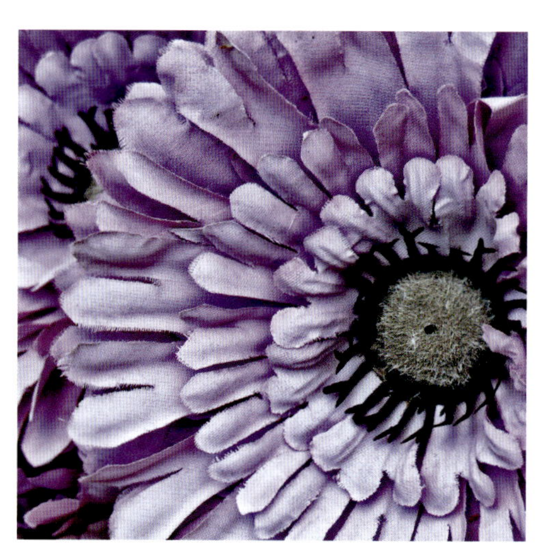
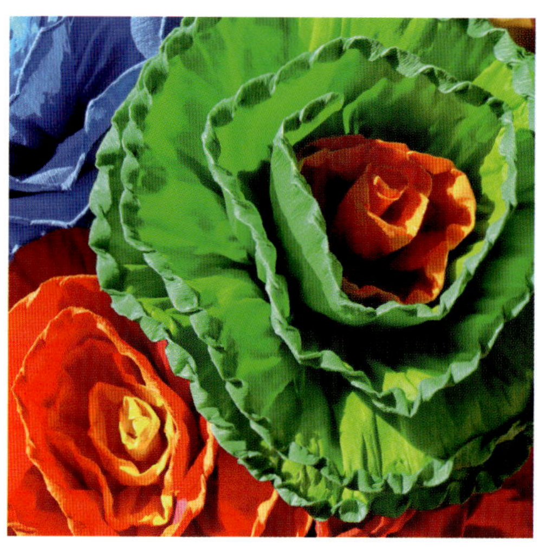
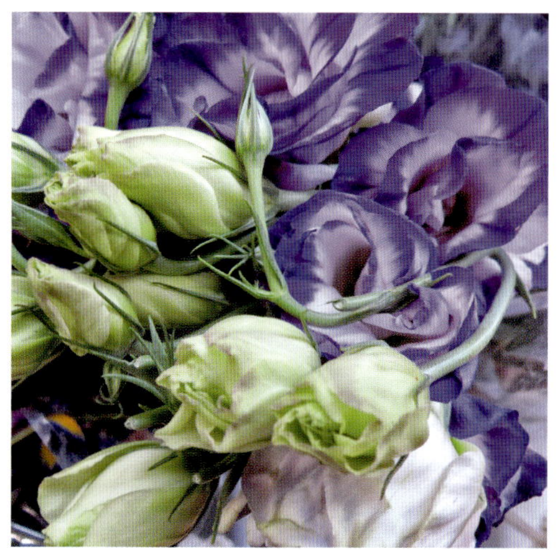
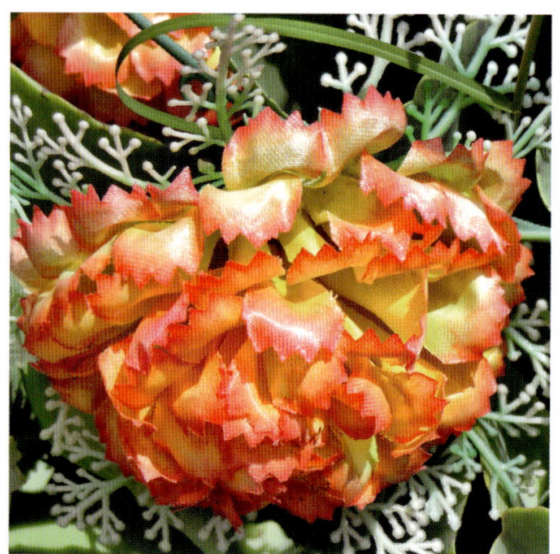
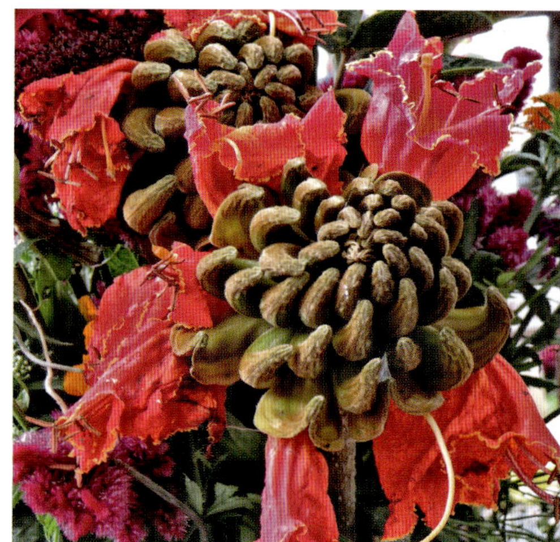

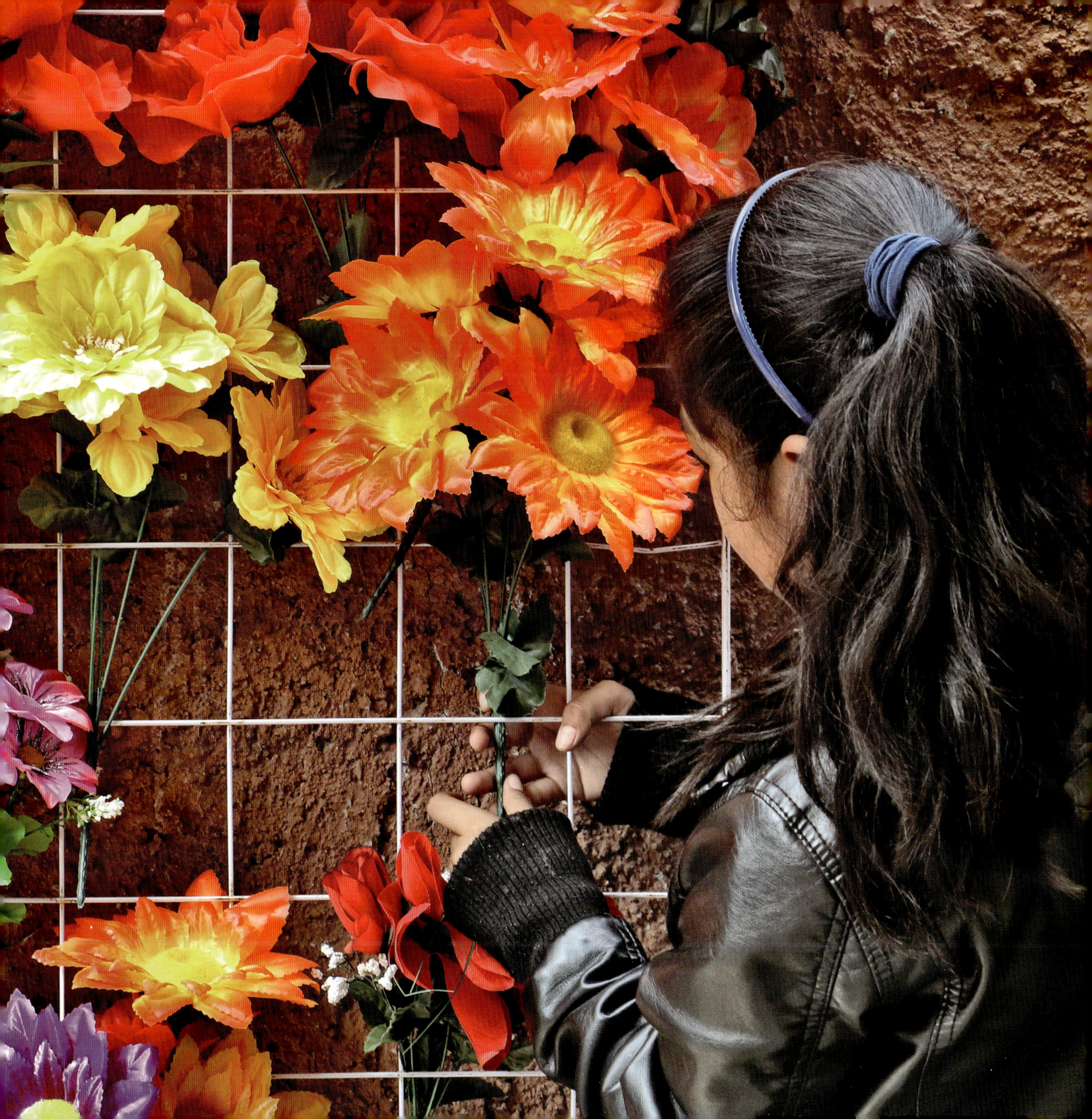

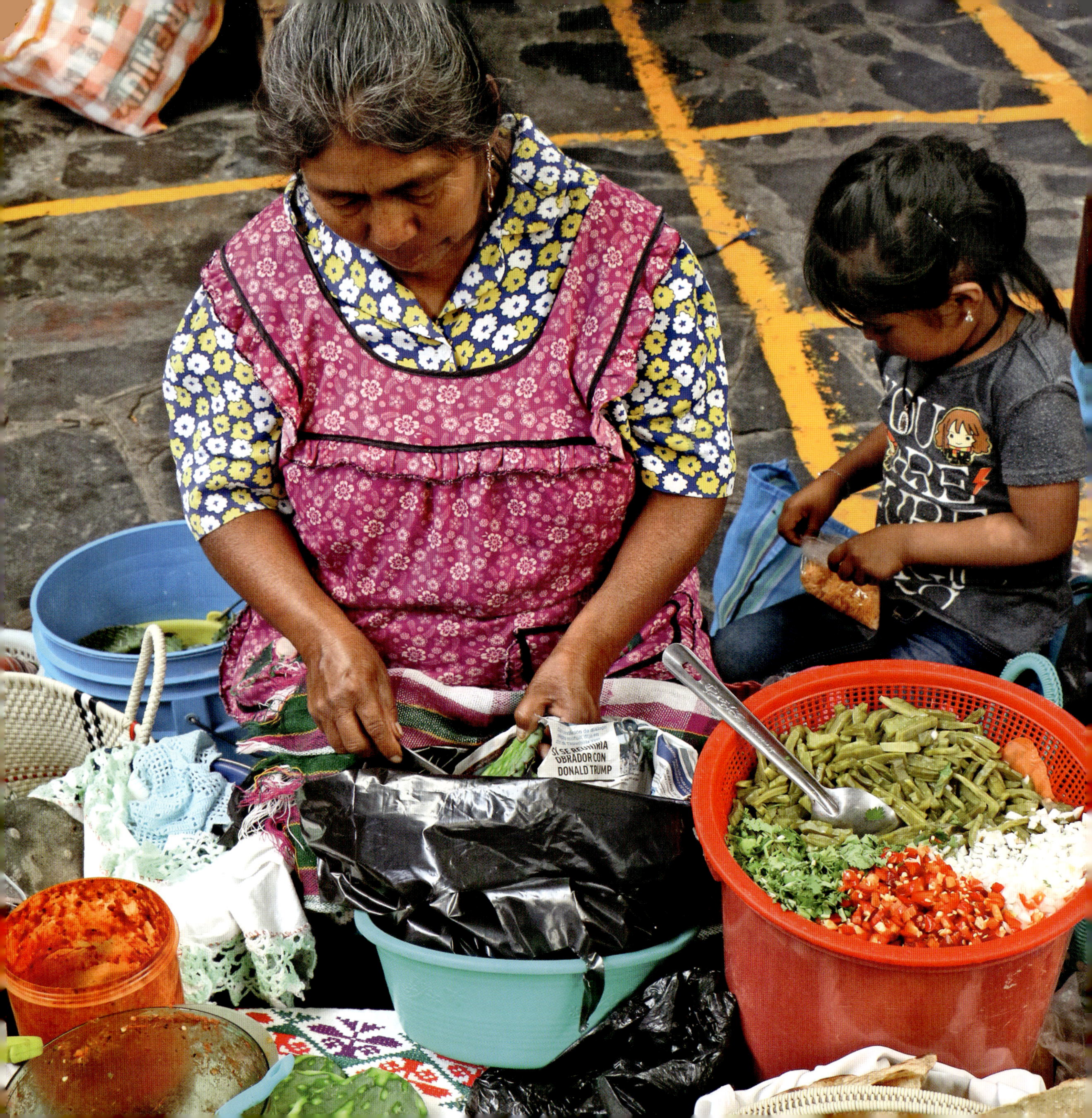
OBRADOR CON
DONALD TRUMP

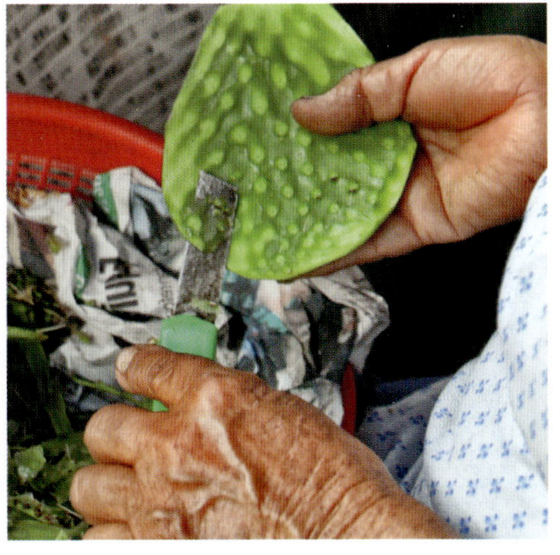

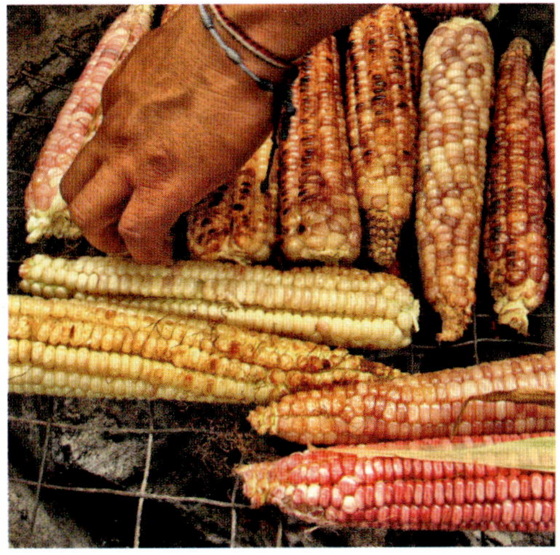

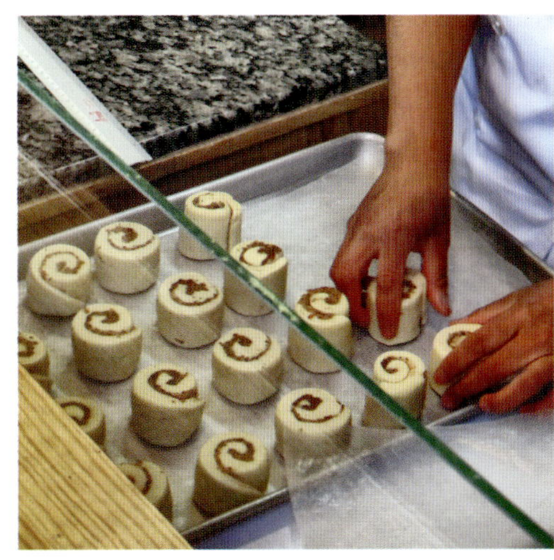

Aromas of roasting meats and corn, fresh strawberries in cream, tacos, gorditas, cakes, fresh fruit juices, luscious pastries, pizzas, churros, and potato chips hot from their vats . . . all swirl around women diligently preparing nopales by removing their spines for ease of use once home, work that has continued since the first peoples occupied this part of the world. San Miguel's markets are a lively alternative to pristine air-conditioned supermarkets with their access to produce from farther afield. This colorful, noisy environment turns buying necessities into one of life's joys.

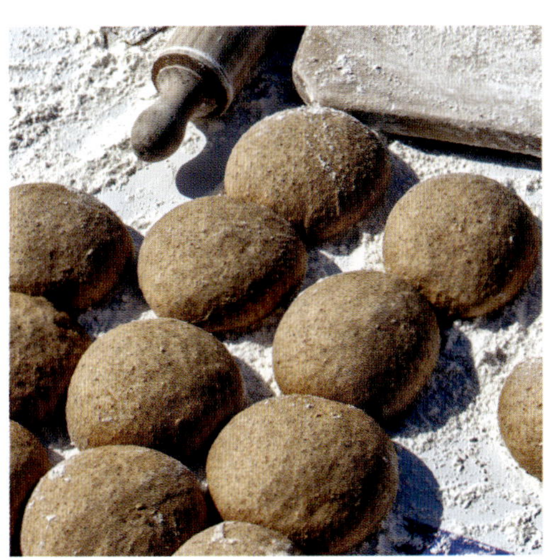

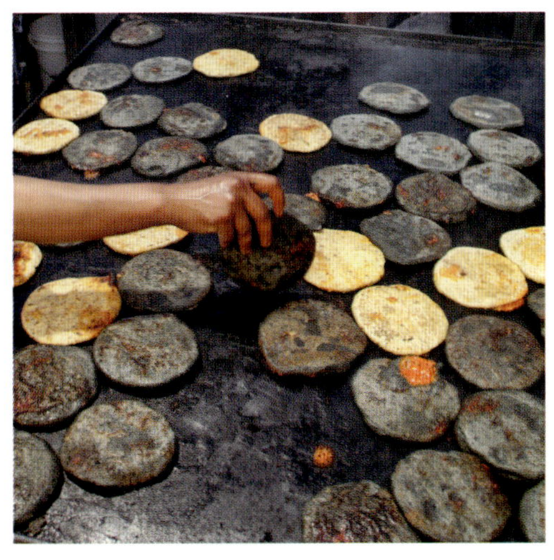

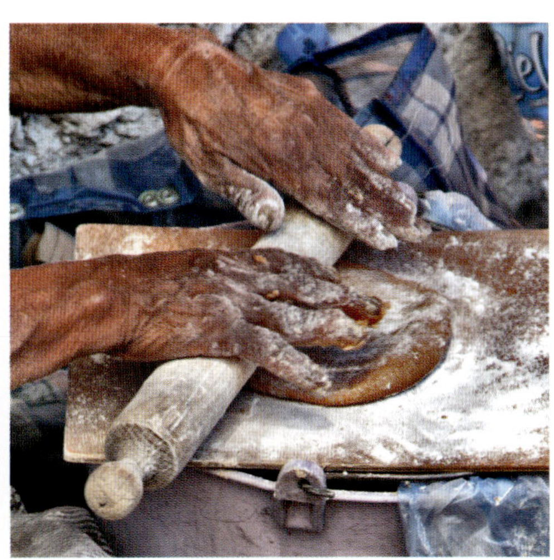

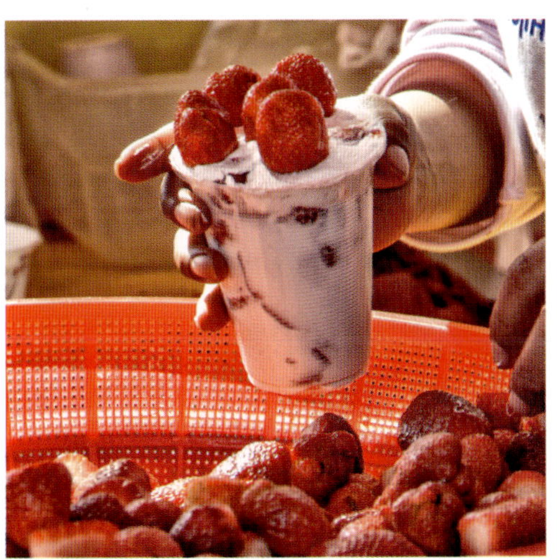

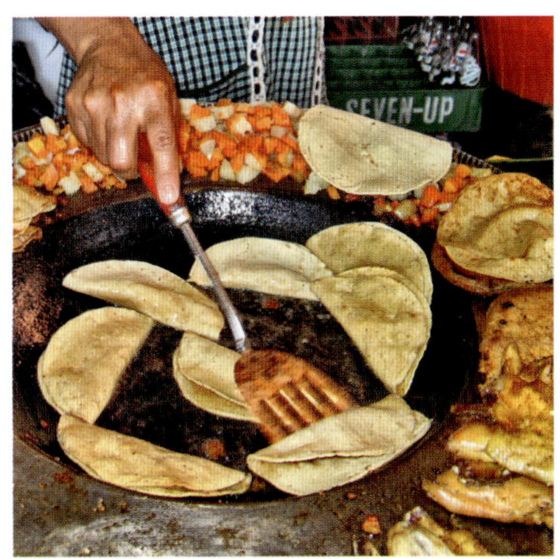

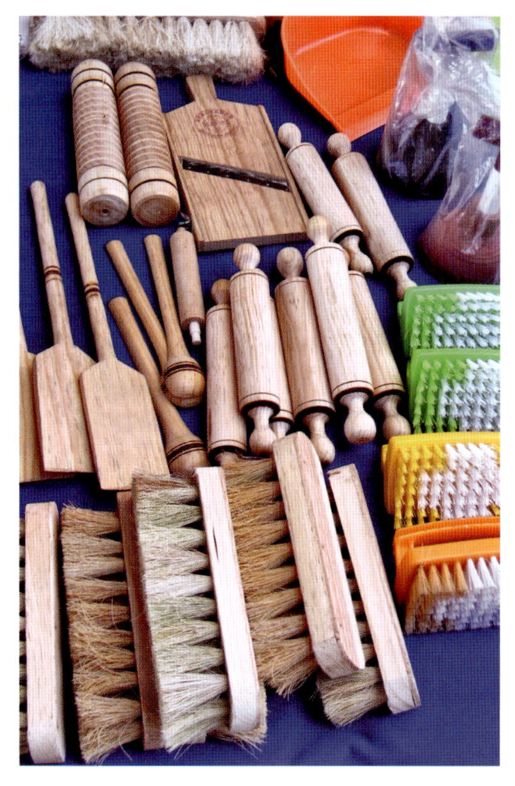

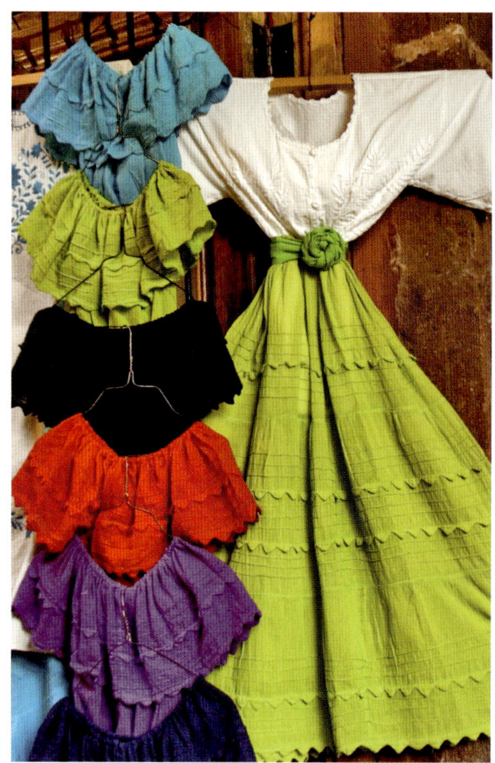

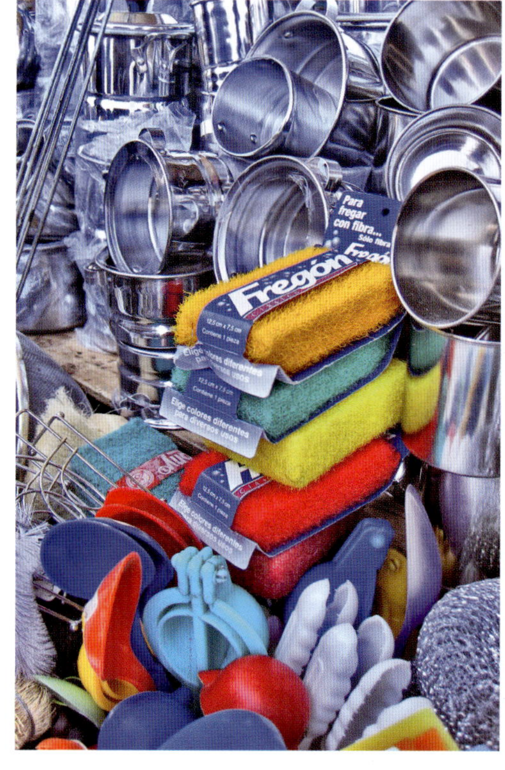
Para fregar con fibra...
Sólo fibra
Fregón
12.5 cm x 7.5 cm
Contiene 1 pieza
Elige colores diferentes para diversos usos

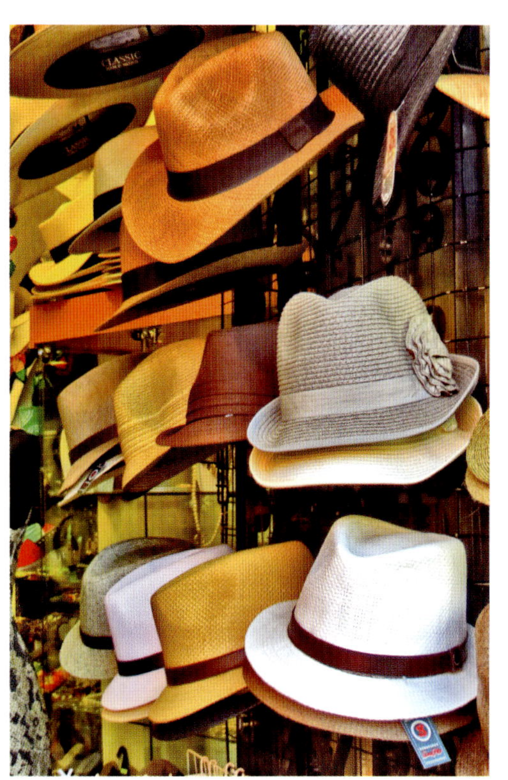

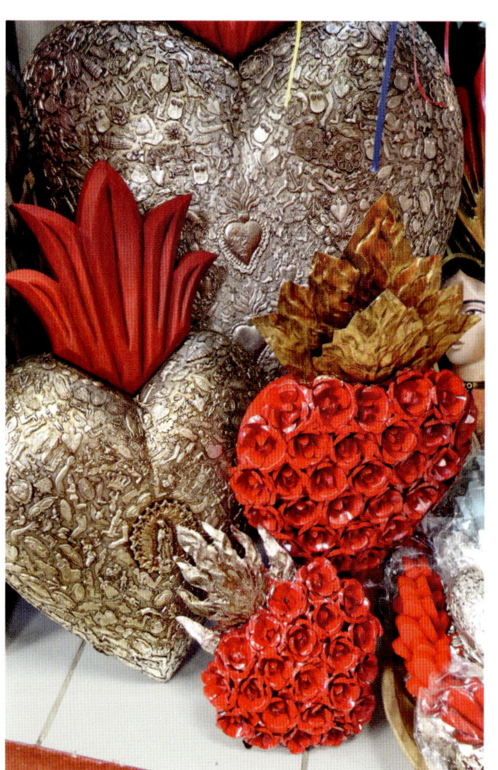

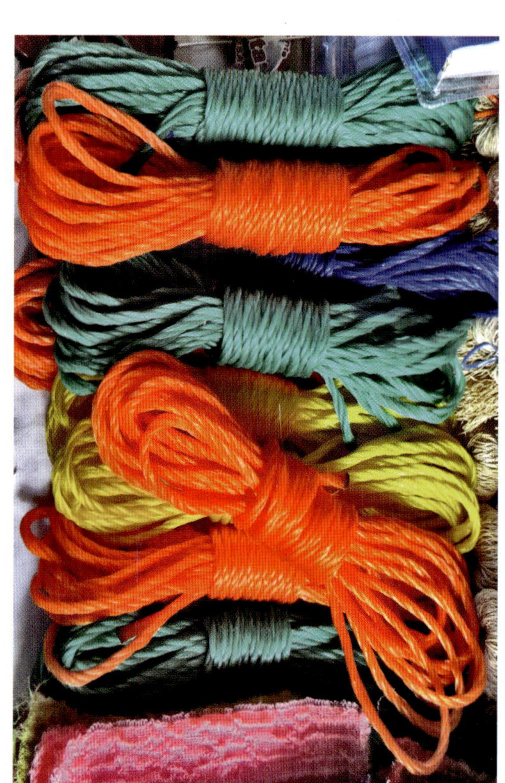

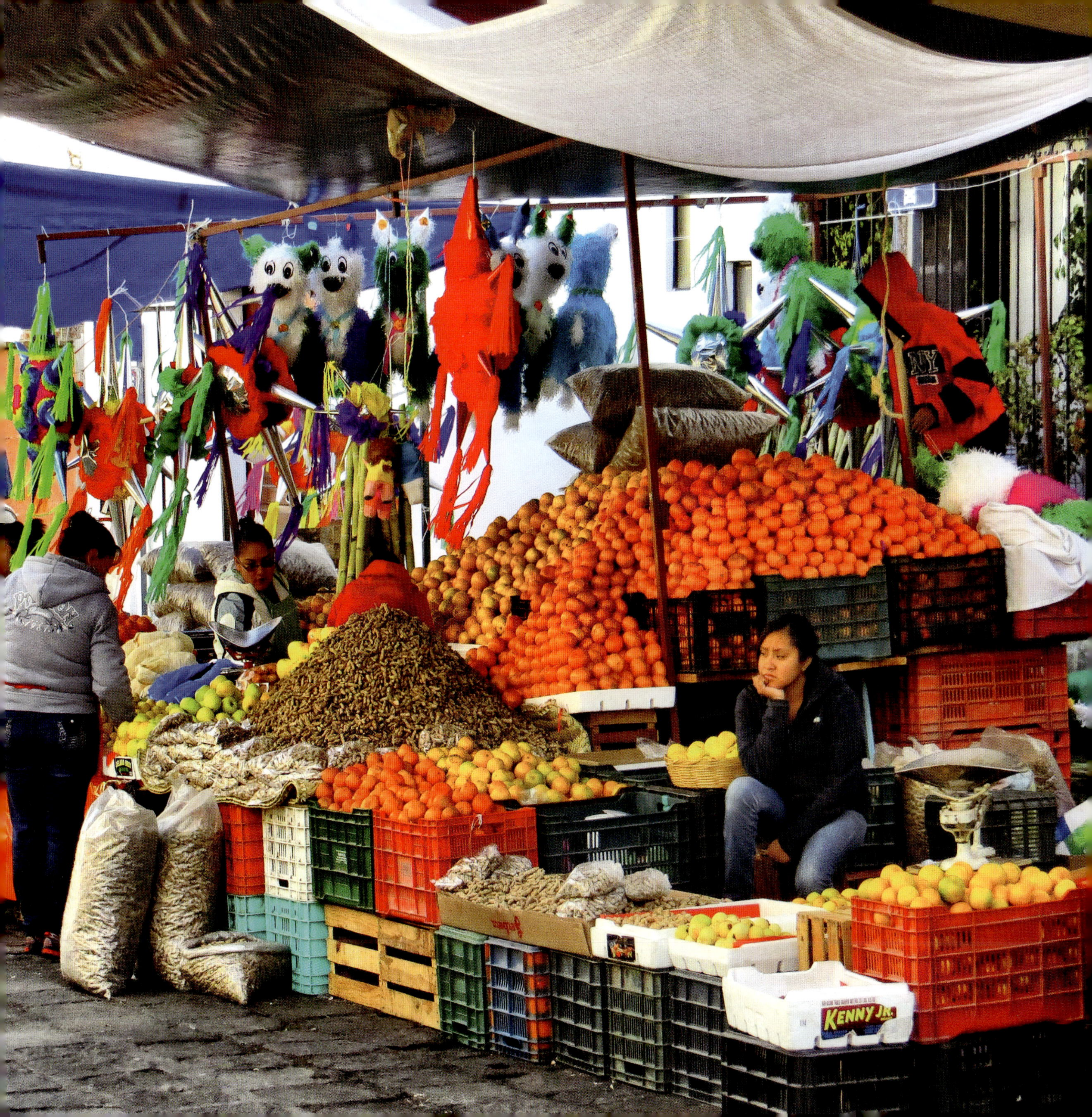
NY
KENNY JR.

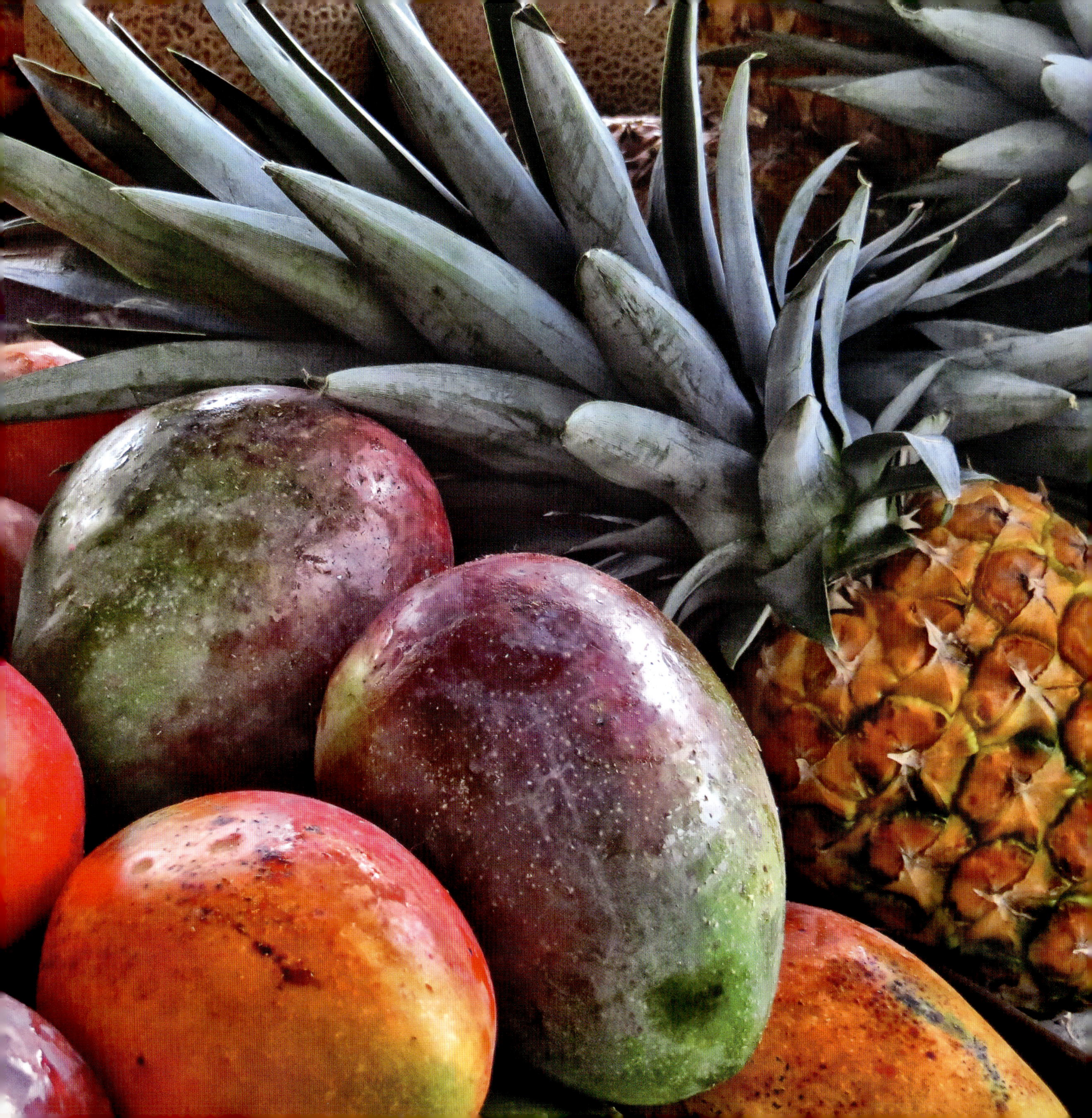

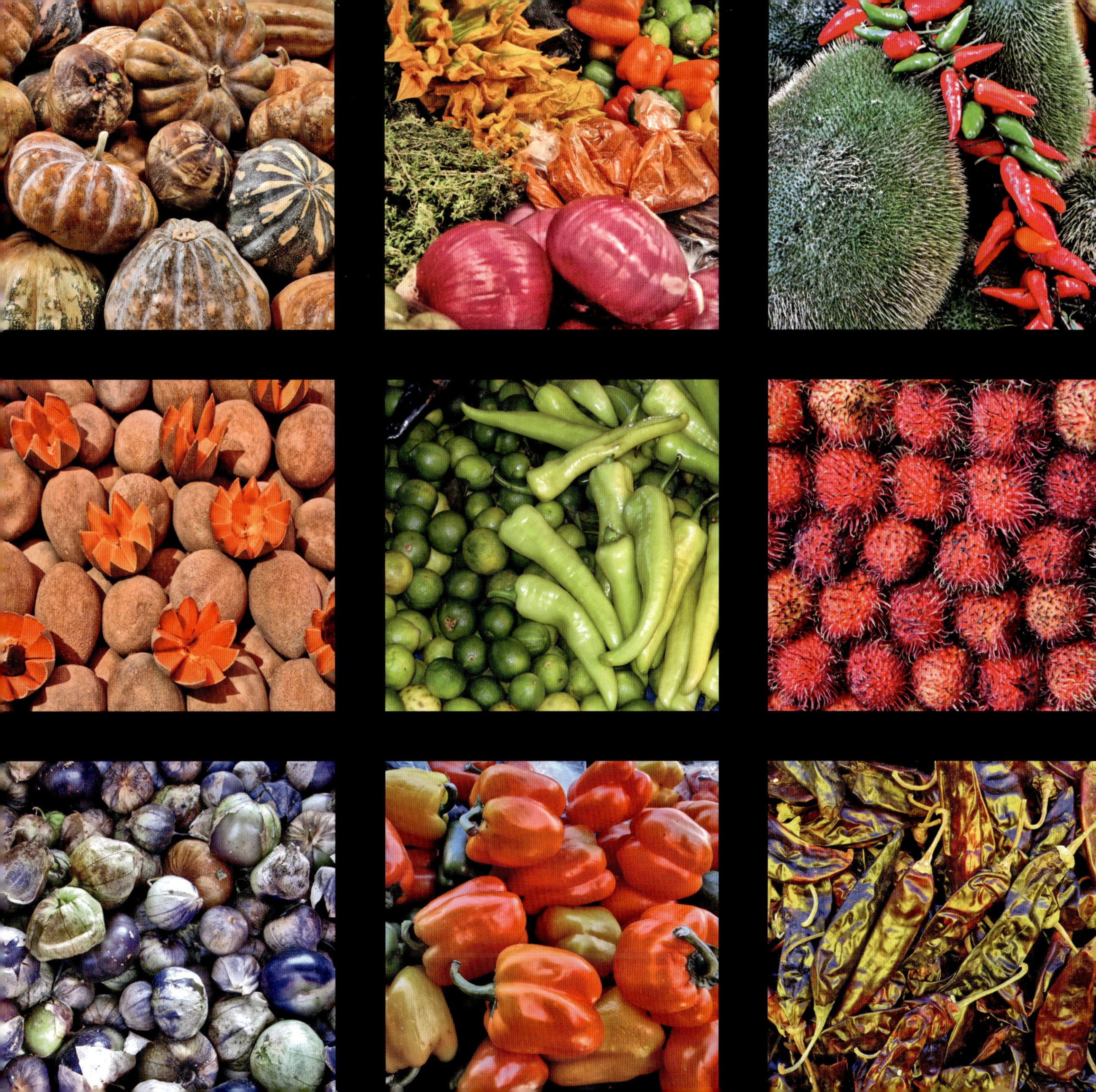

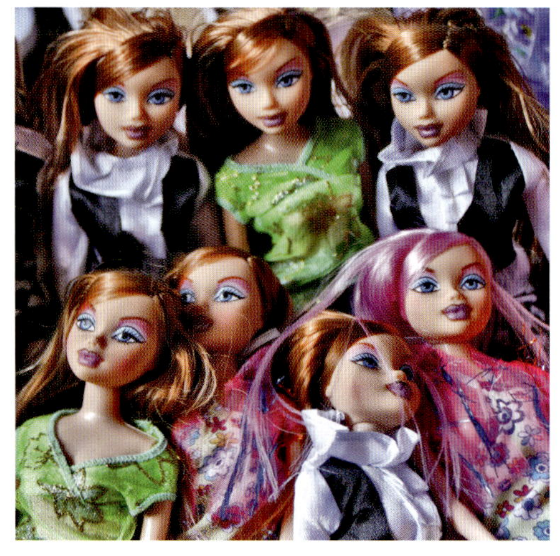

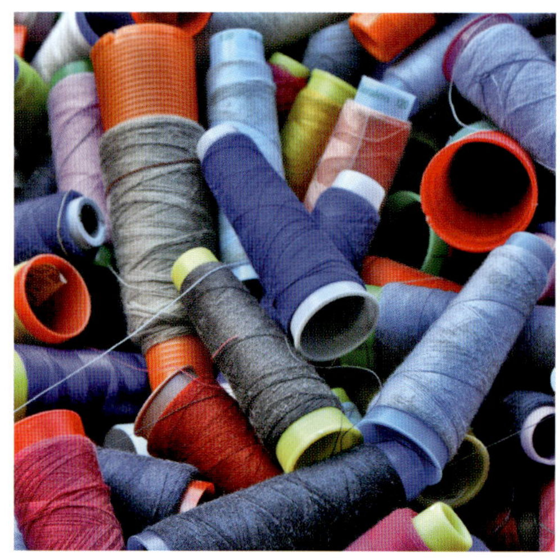

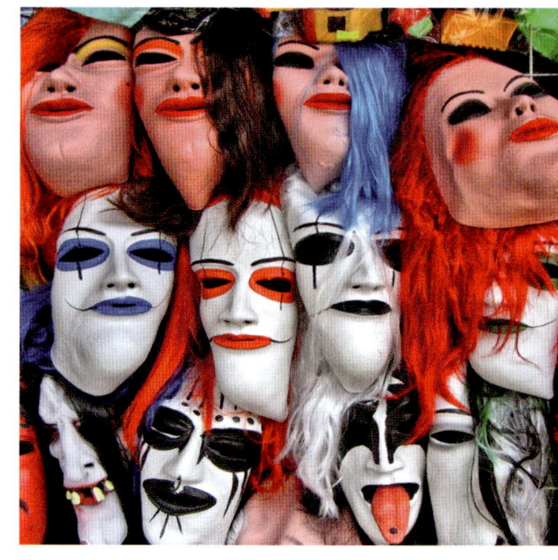

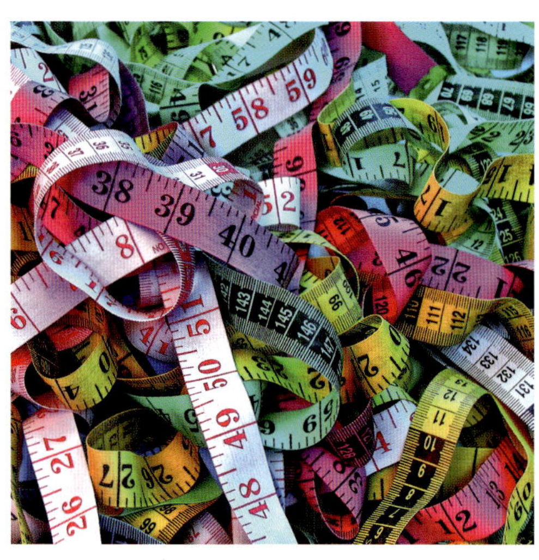

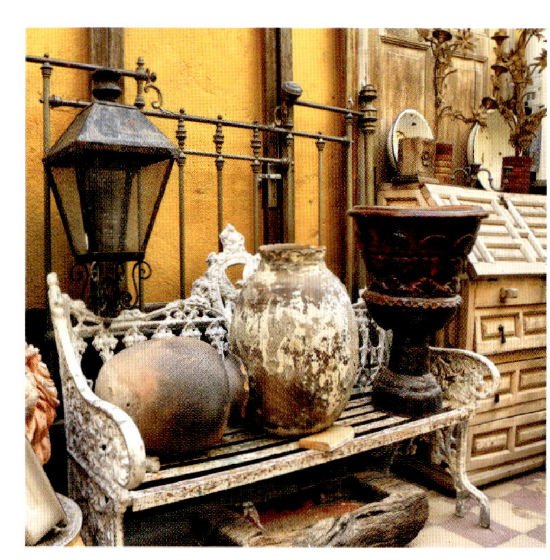

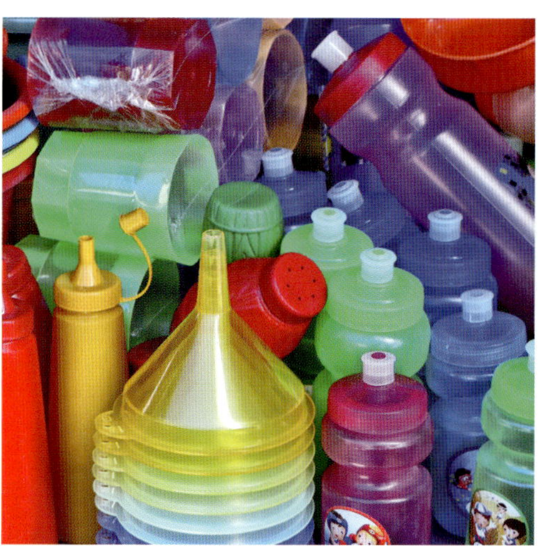

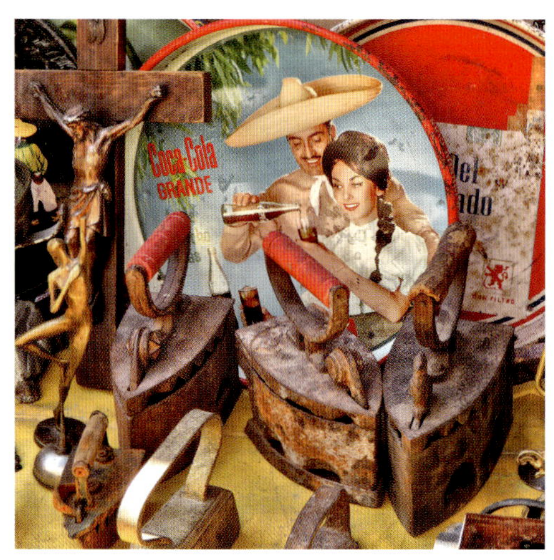
Coca-Cola
GRANDE

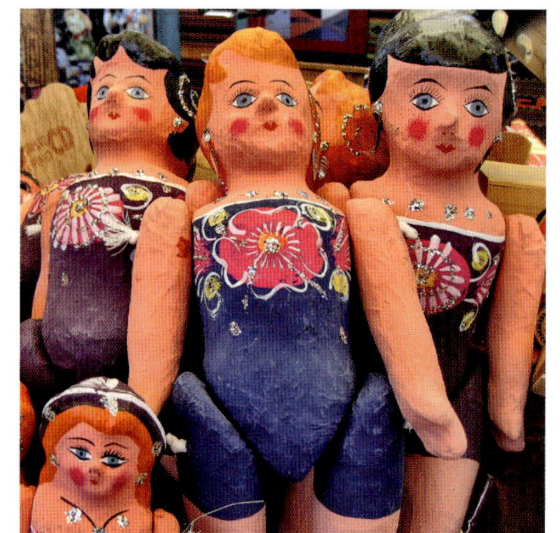

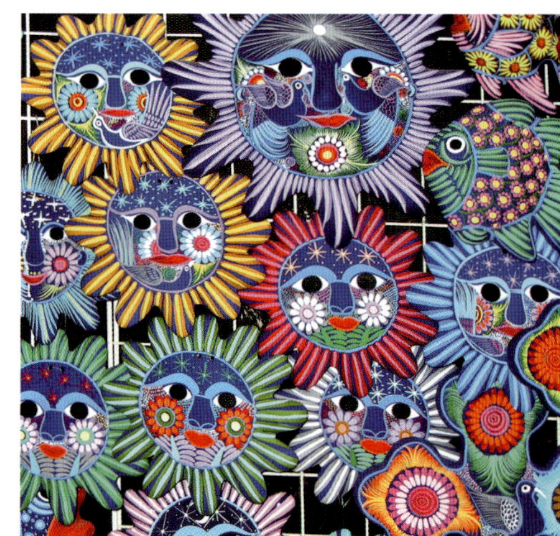

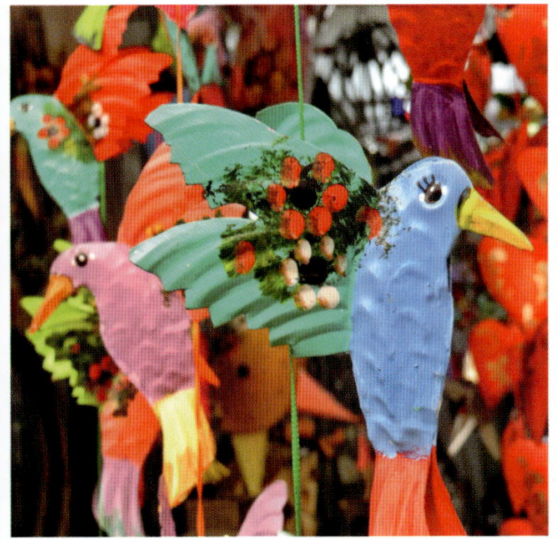
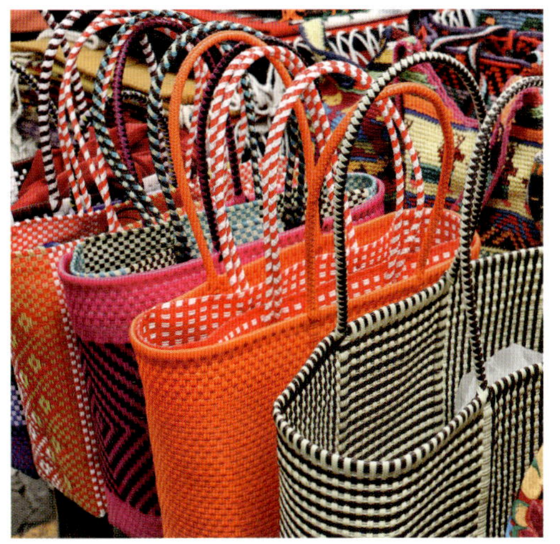
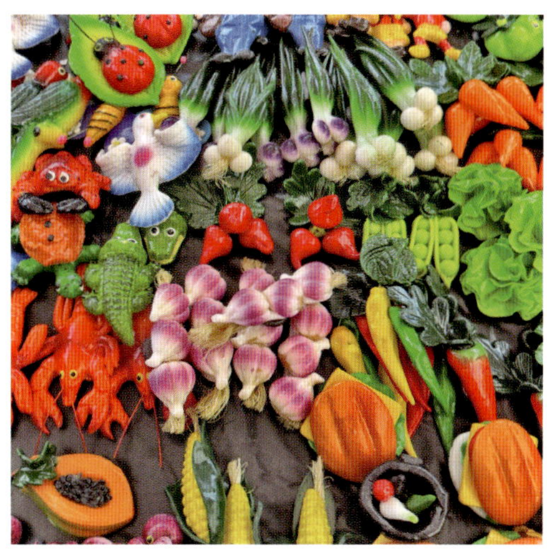
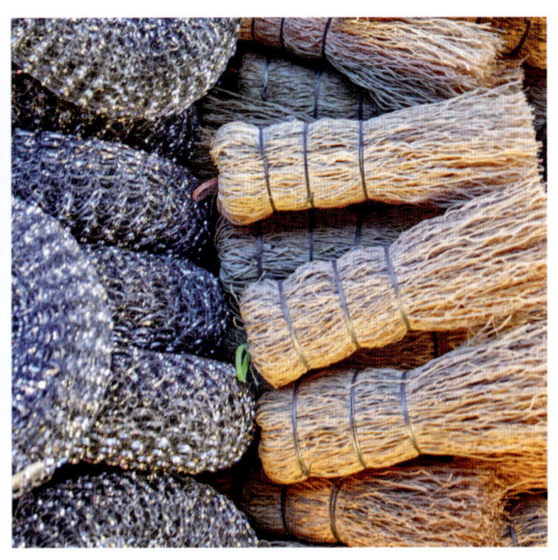
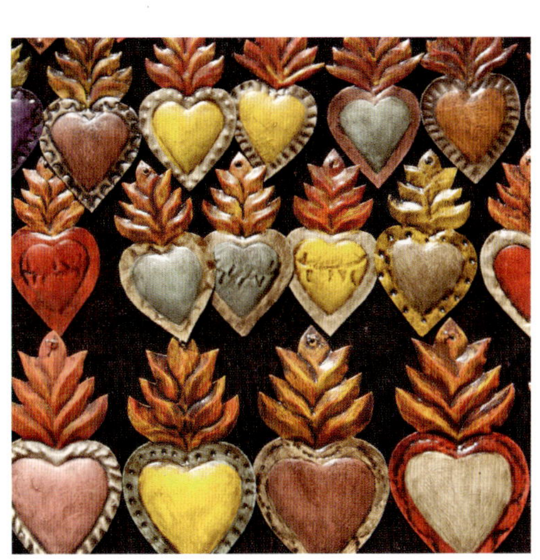
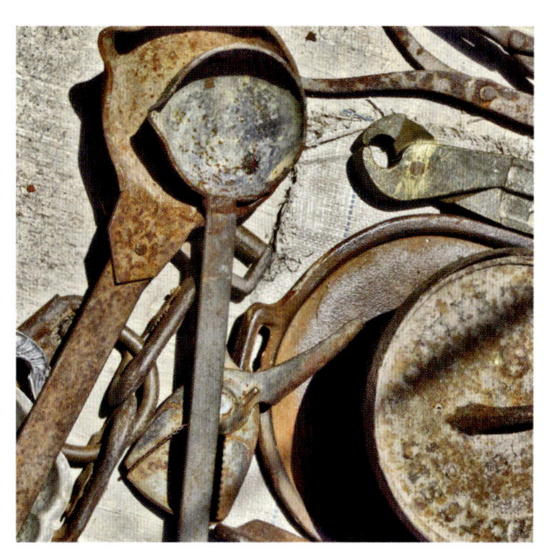
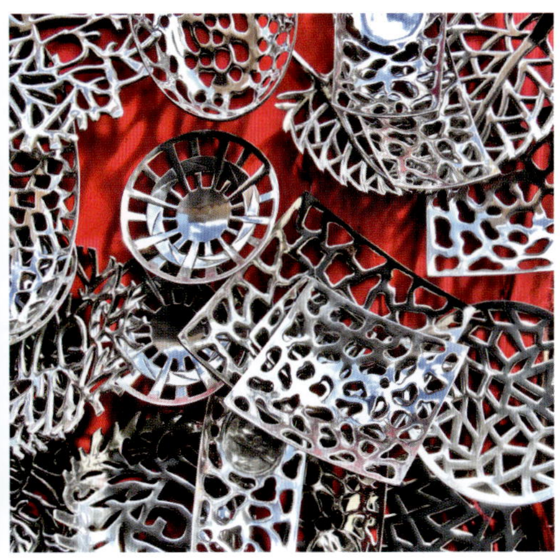
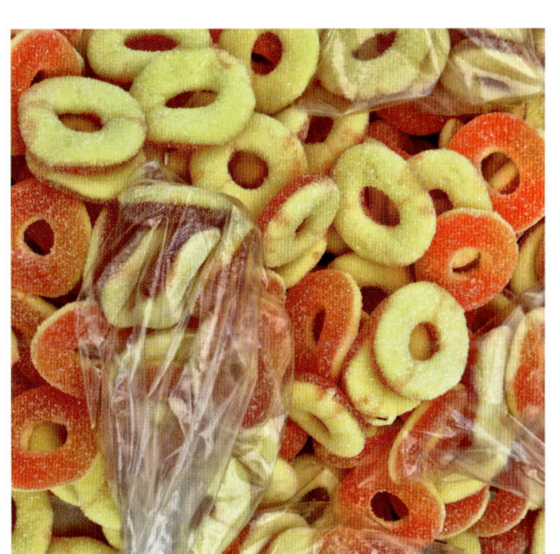
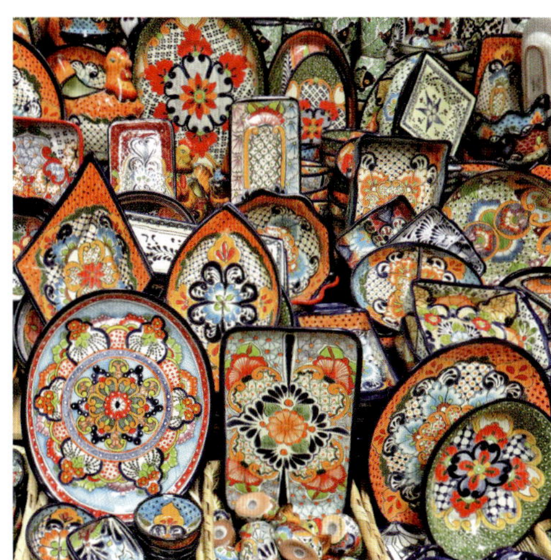

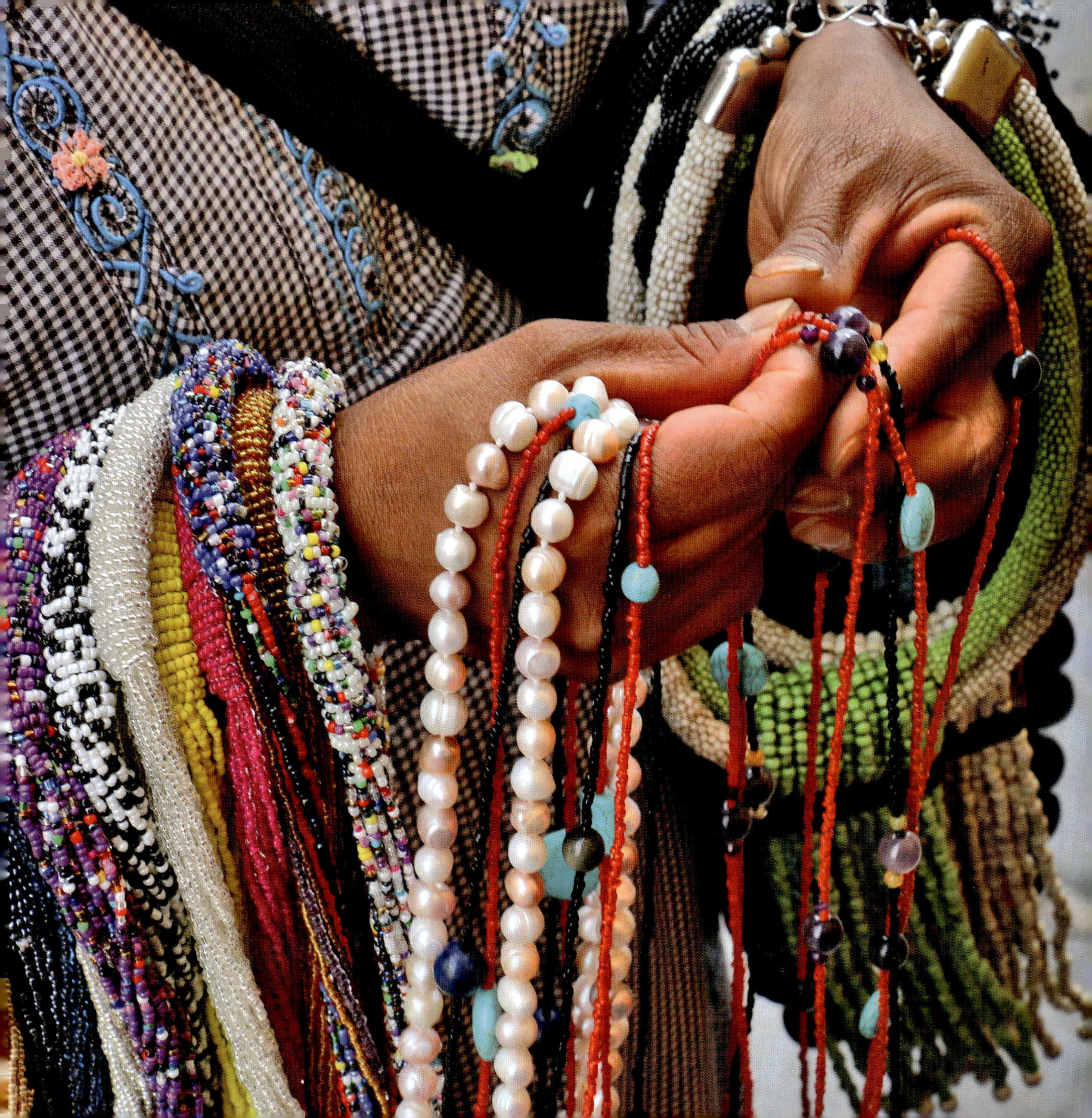

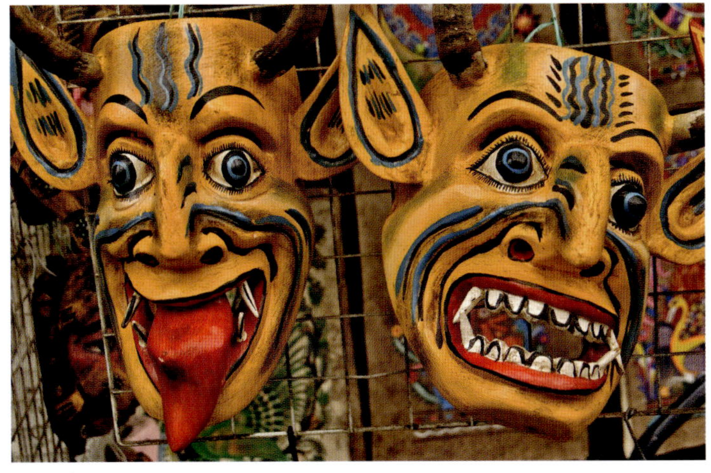

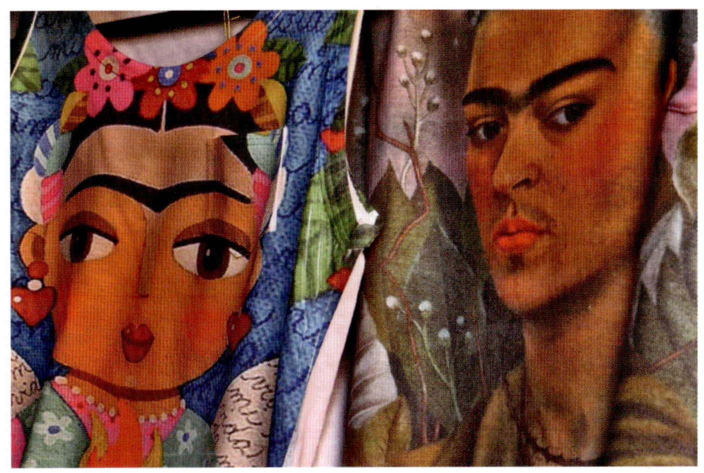

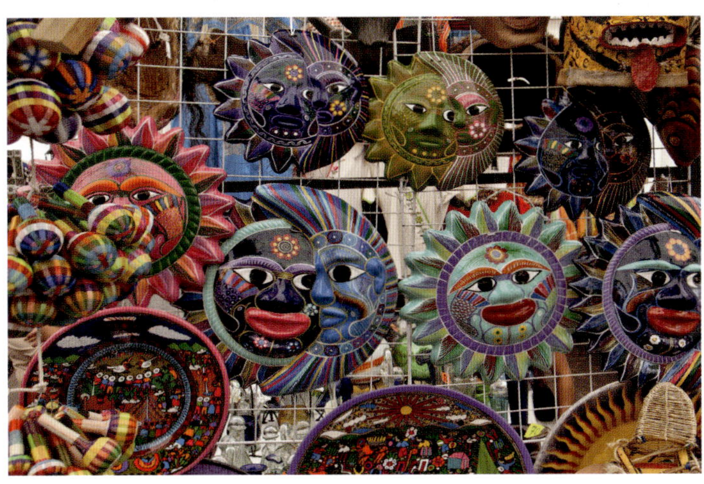

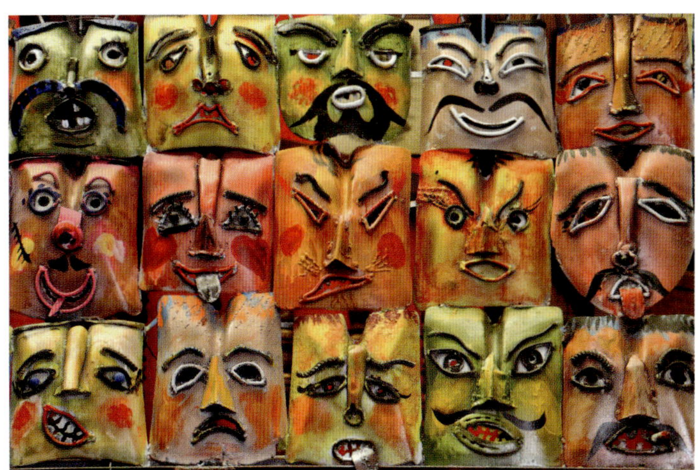

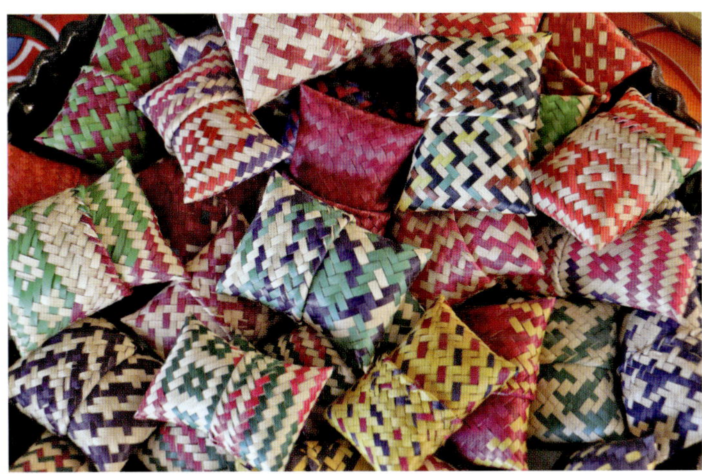

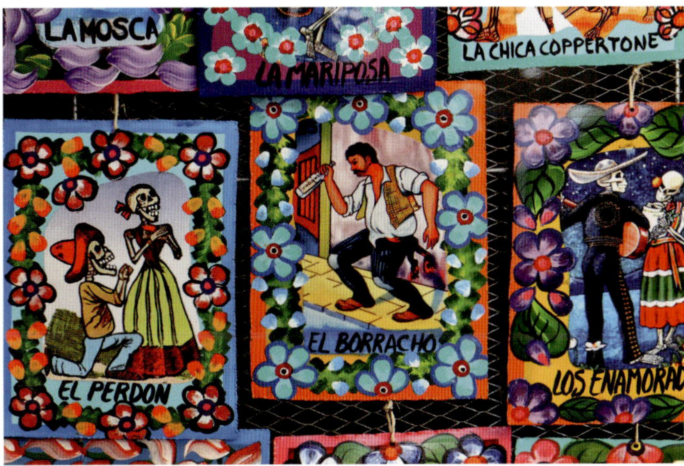

Beauty was the aura surrounding the object, the consequence of the secret relation between its making and its meaning. —Octavio Paz

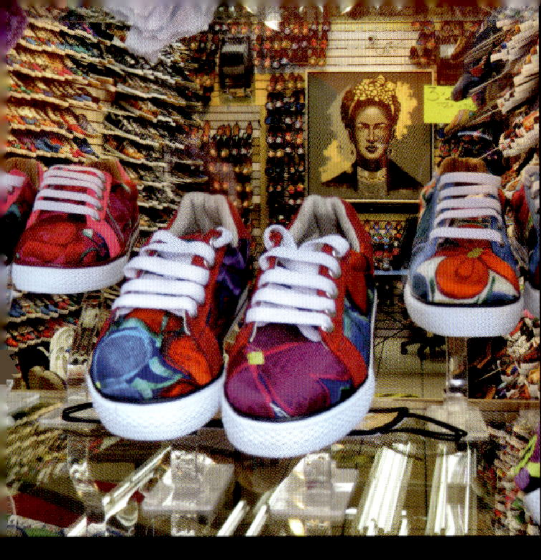

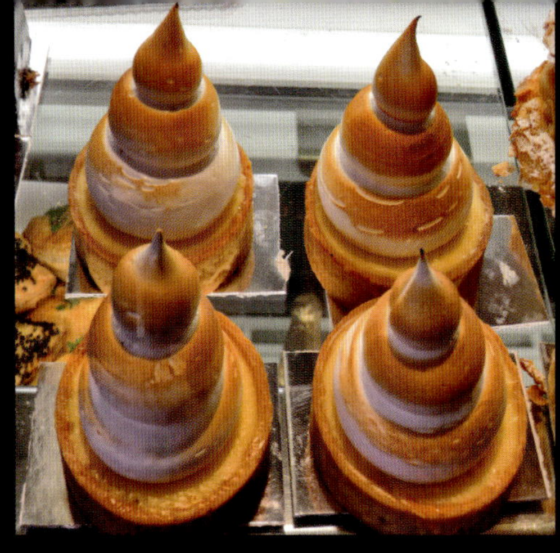

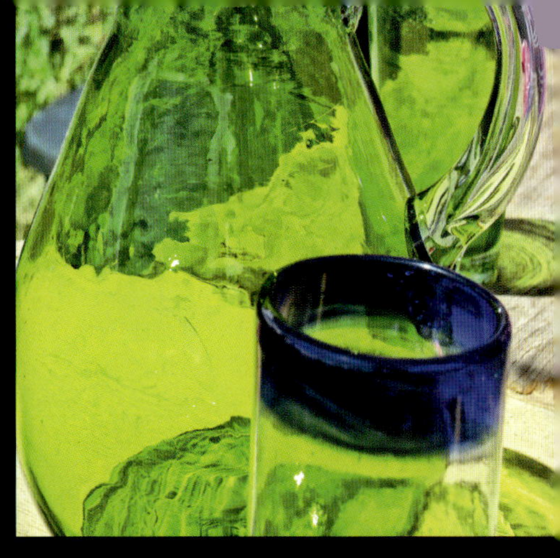

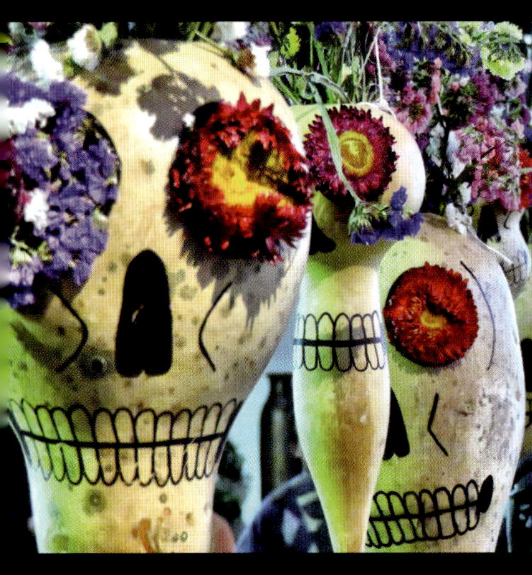

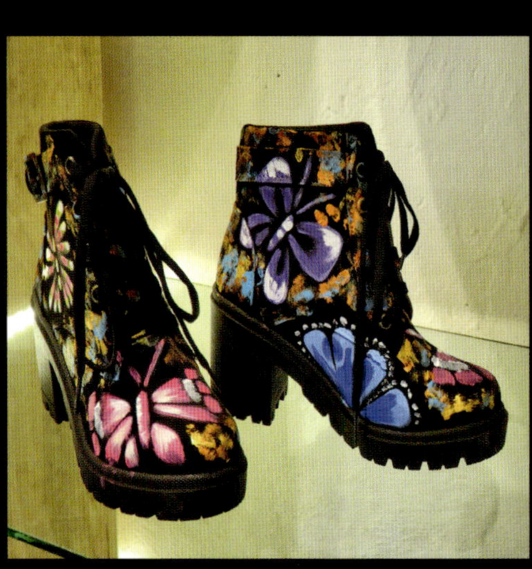

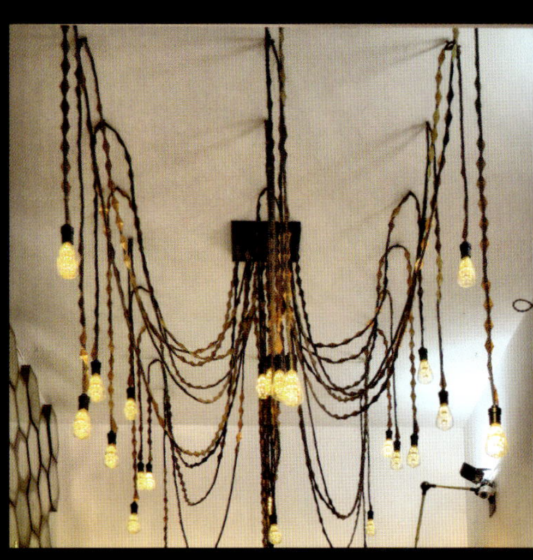

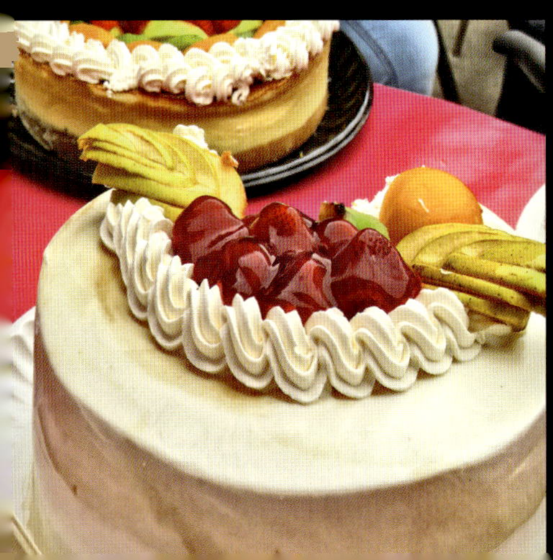

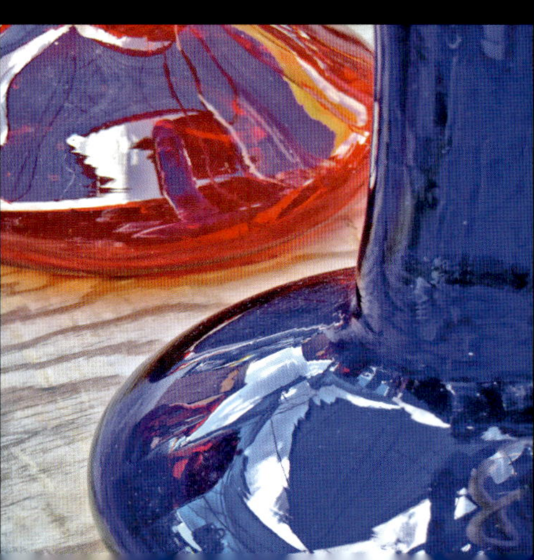

Although San Miguel's historical patterns are protected in the crafts and traditional architecture, there are stunning modern goods available, from hand-blown glass to clothing, shoes, bags, pastries, lighting, furniture, carved stone sinks, and an infinite array of beautiful products designed and made by local contemporary craftsmen, items that rival anything you might see in any of the great cities of the world. These goods and their makers create the balance that makes San Miguel so rich and lush: whatever you need or want, more than you can even imagine . . . there it is, ready to go home with you.

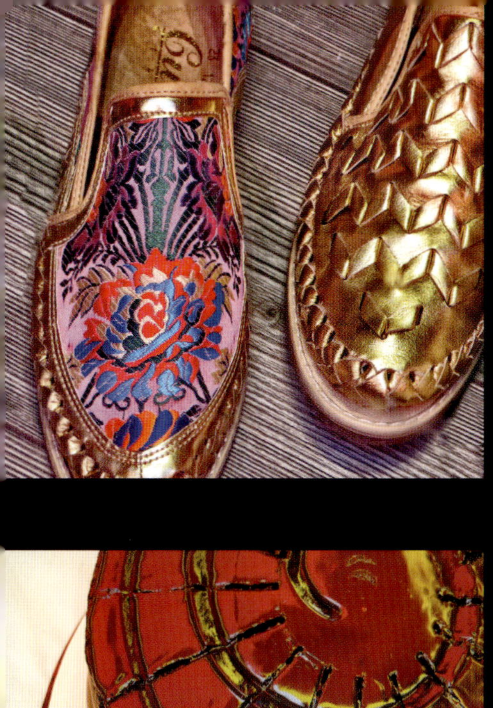
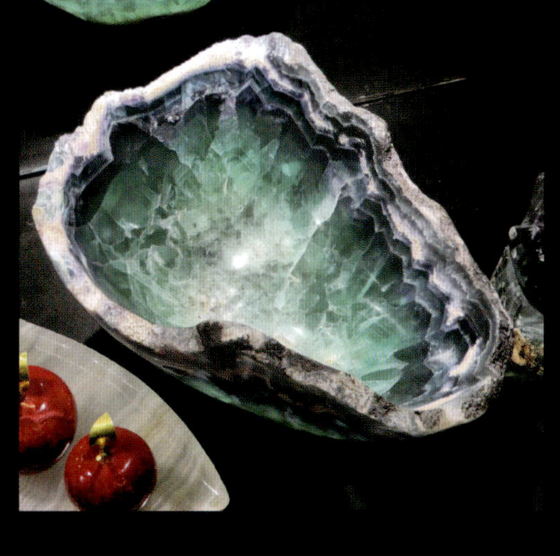
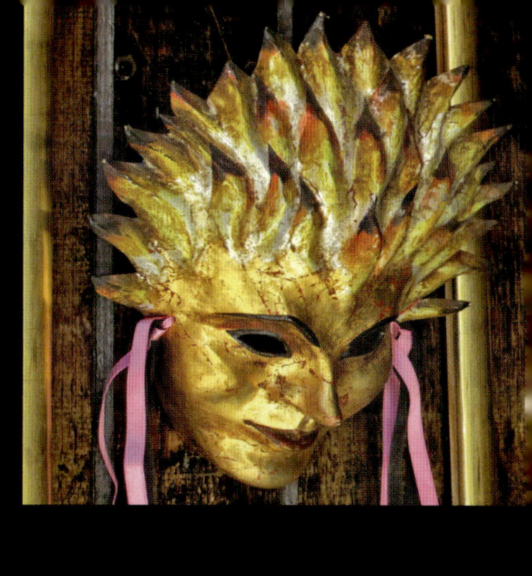
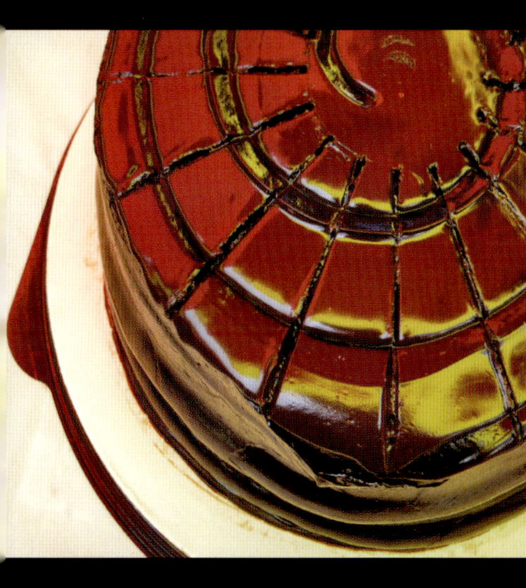
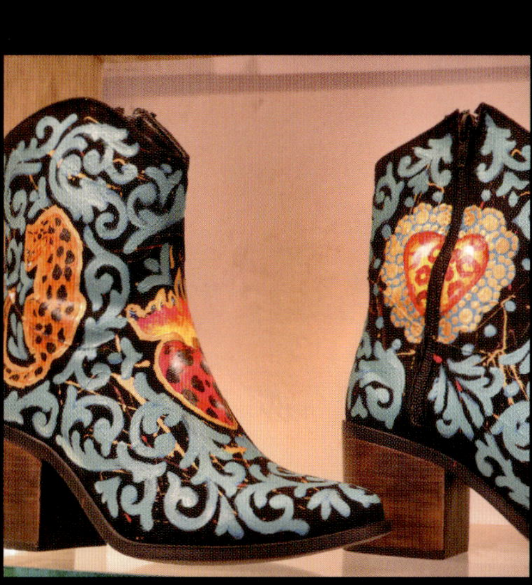
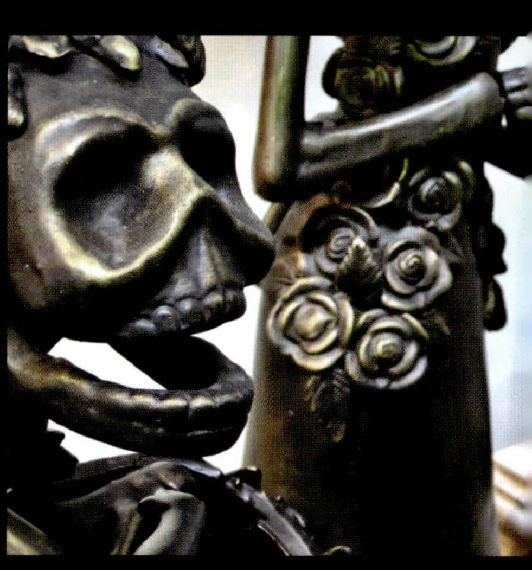
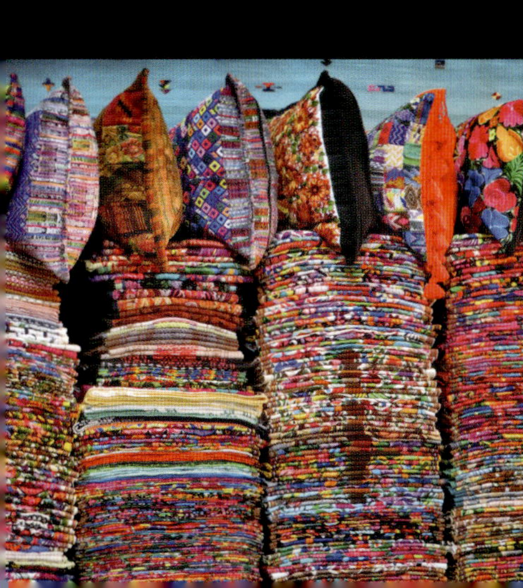
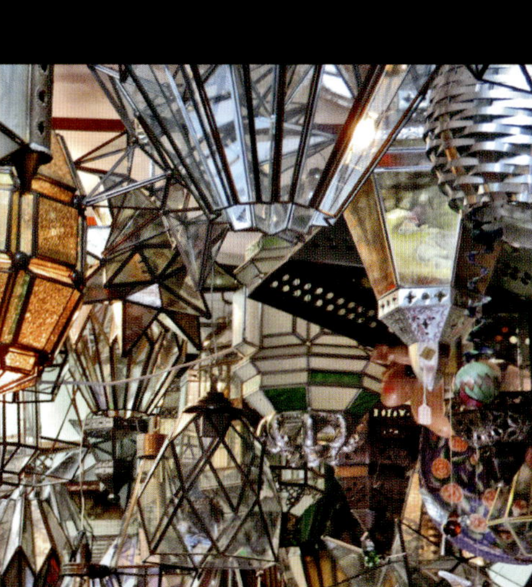
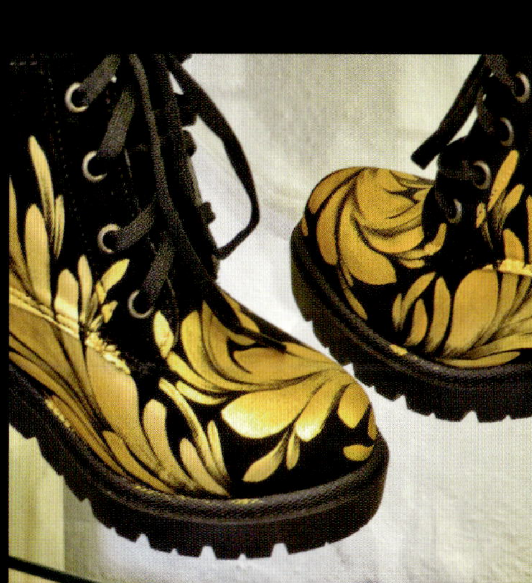

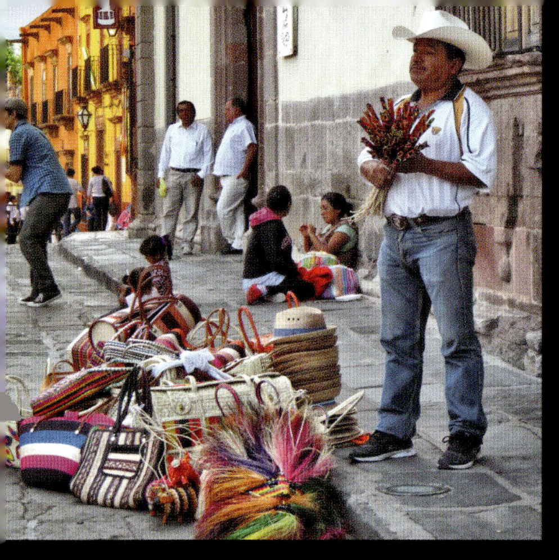

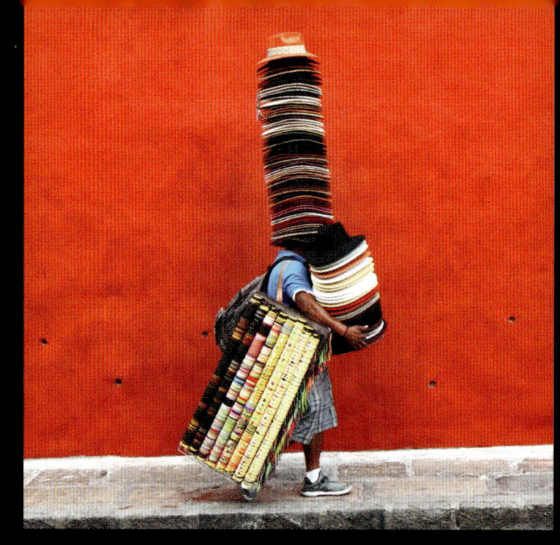

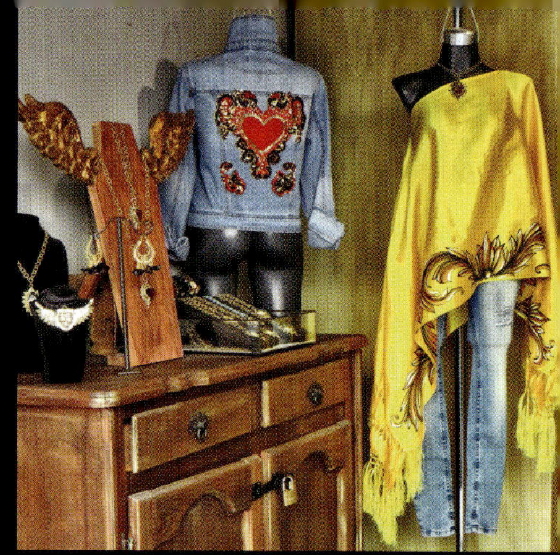

Markets pop up at every turn in San Miguel, from the single man with a stack of hats towering above his head; to the iconic balloon sellers in the Jardín; to the flower vendors that appear for every celebration; to chic shops offering stylish wraps, bags, and shoes; to the basket sellers, the freshly harvested honey, and the old women with their handmade dolls.

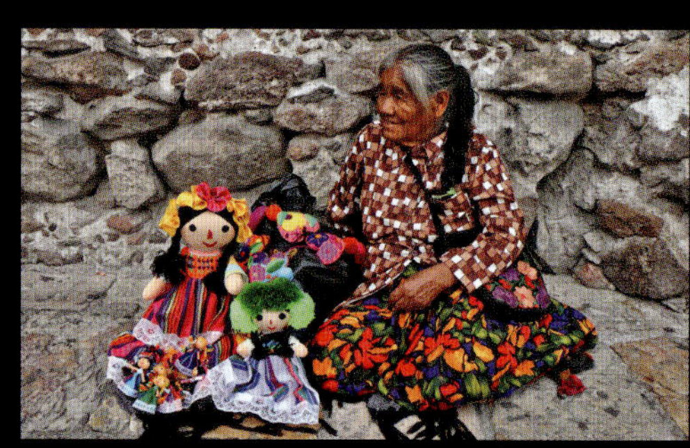

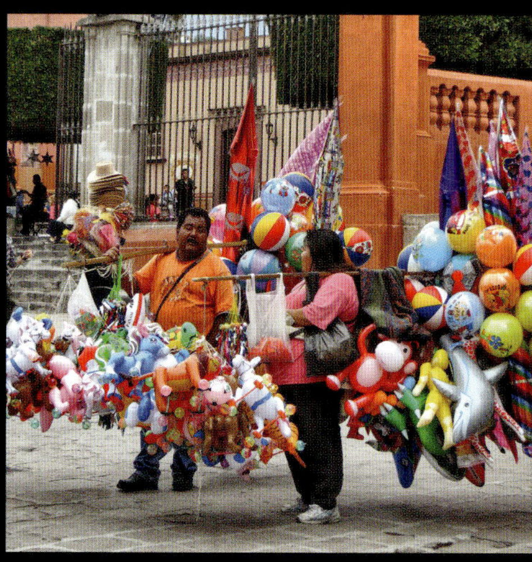

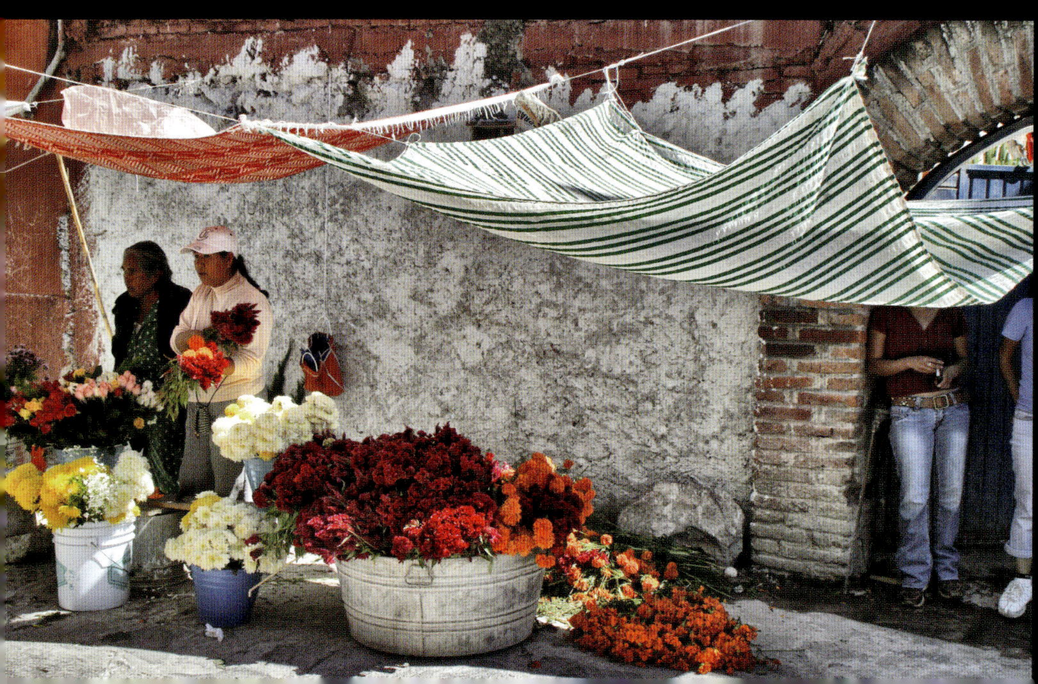

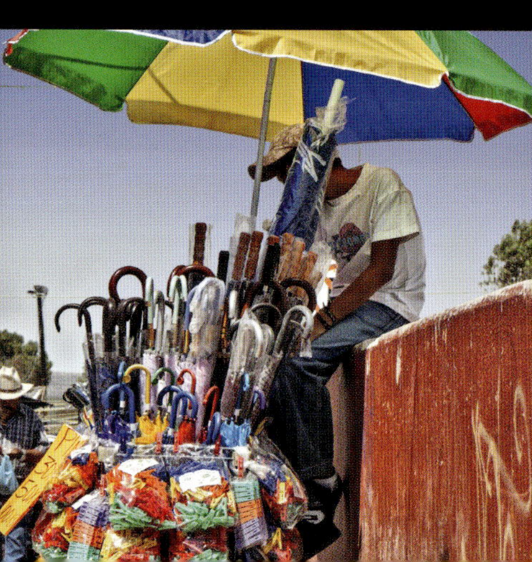

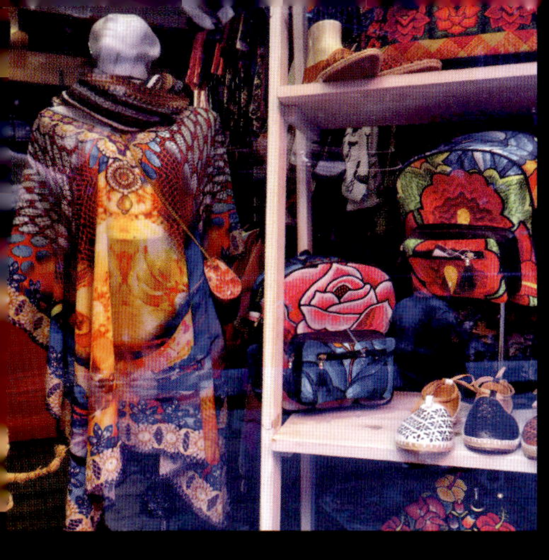
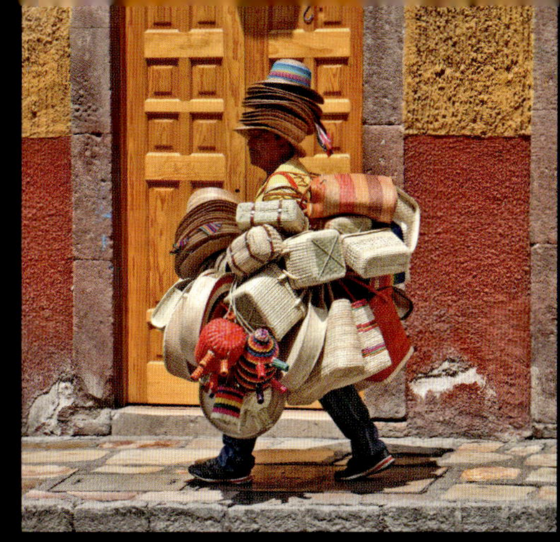
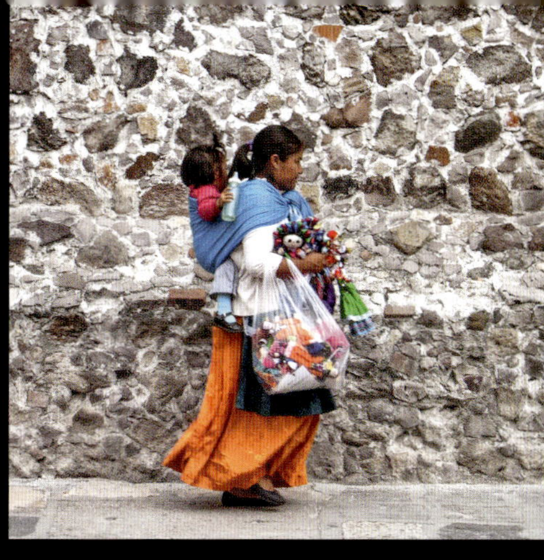
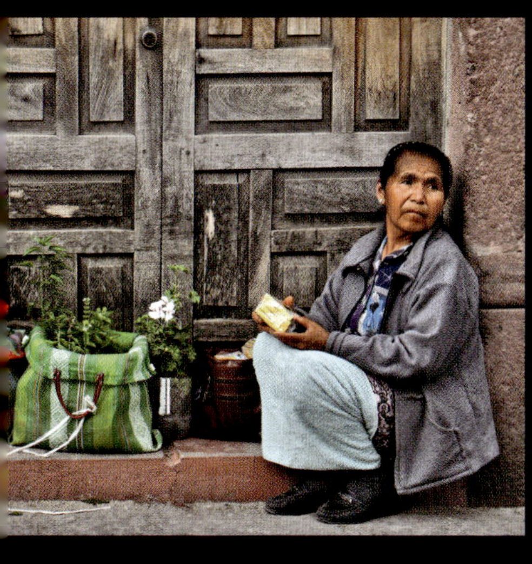
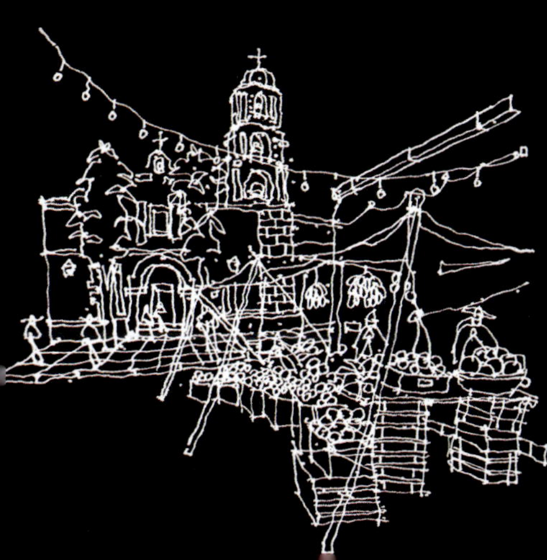

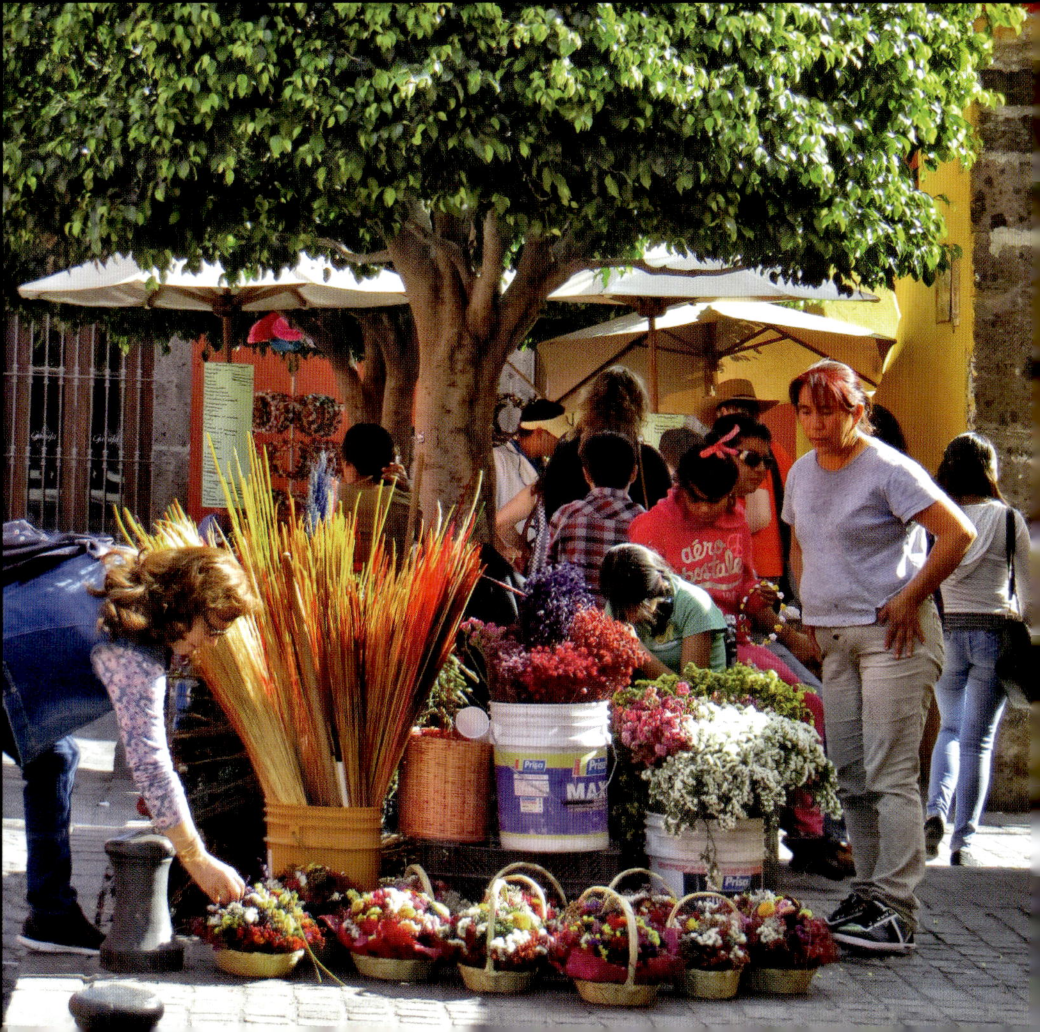

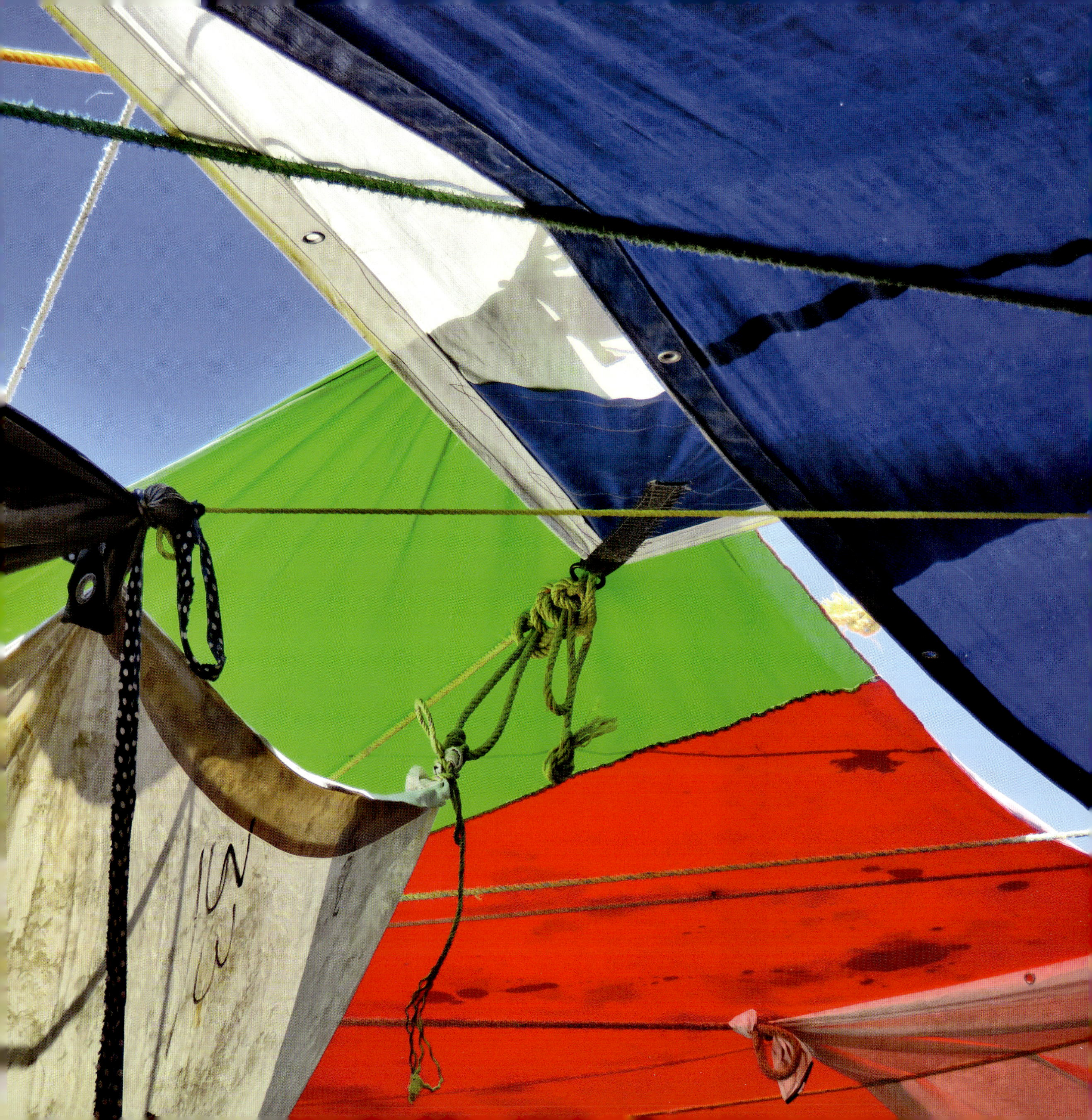

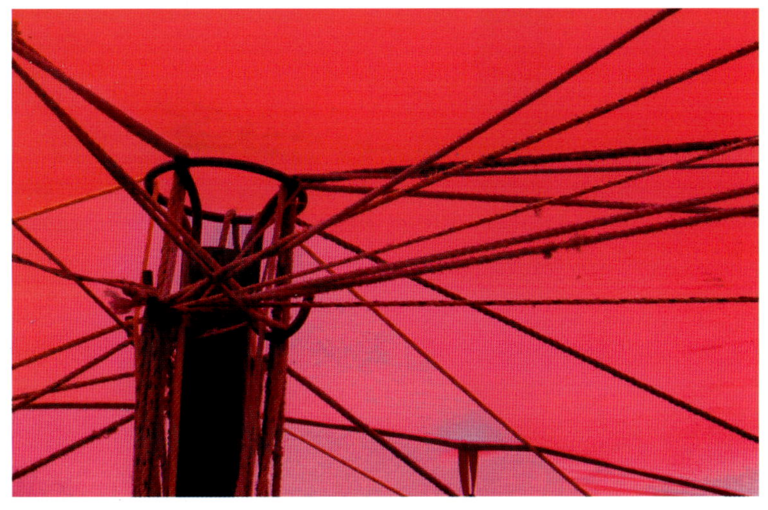

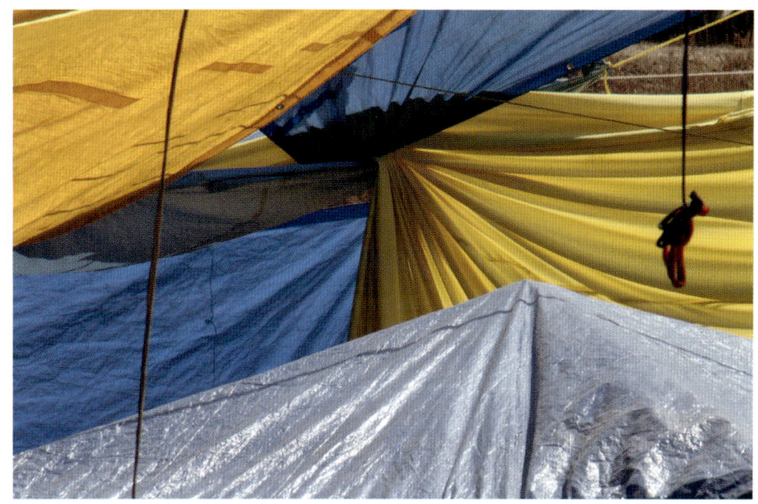

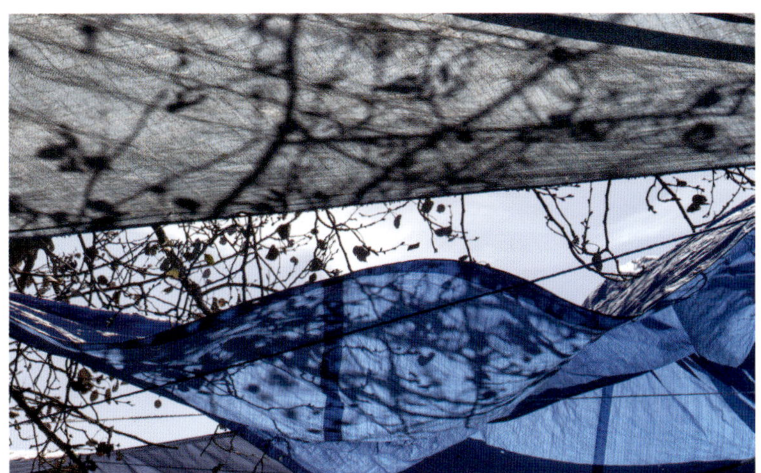

Tarps billow in the breeze, brilliant colors overlapping in abstract patterns against the sky above markets large and small. Their undulating movement is a slow-motion dance above the chaos of people and products in that eternal cycle of commerce, the make-grow-sell that is the most basic exchange between people on earth. Markets are the pulsating center of life, and in San Miguel they sustain and nourish both body and soul.

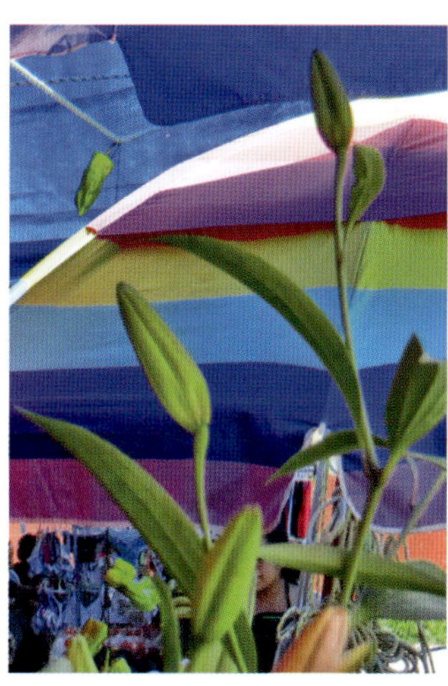

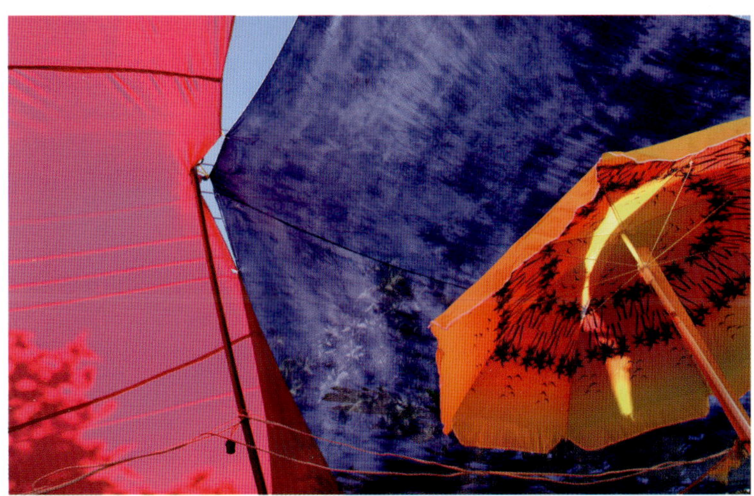

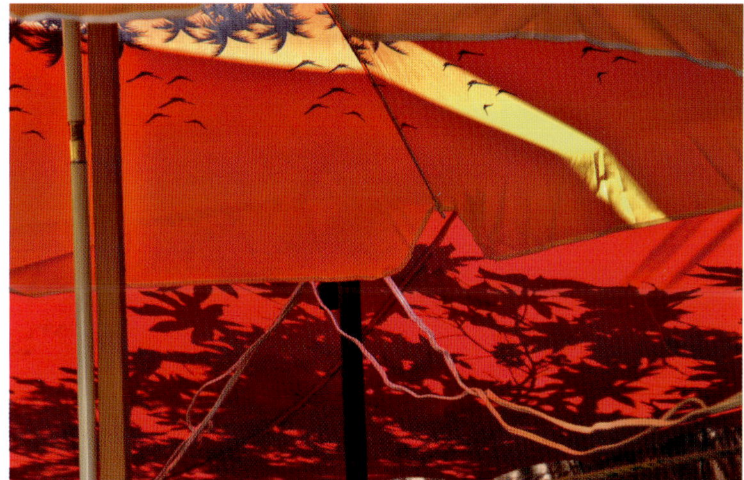

People

Mexican people by nature are kind, loving, helpful, and considerate. And these qualities can be seen and felt in every corner of this beautiful country. In San Miguel de Allende, the mix of cultures has created a multilayered population, a dynamic society that blends the old with the new, traditional with modern ideas, and Mexican culture with a broad spectrum of the cultures of the world.

It was about 9:30 p.m. and the Jardín was full of people; the lights on the church and surrounding buildings were luminous, dreamlike. Children were playing, lovers were kissing, the little old man all bent in half who walks with two canes, inching along, was out, dressed in his best suit. The balloon sellers, children dressed like dolls, and musicians playing at every corner all surrounded us as we sat on a bench among the flowers with Margarita, whose family has sold popcorn in the Jardín for generations, and with her husband, Zarco, a very dear, old friend. We talked of life and poetry and history and philosophy and Zarco's love of the music of Edith Piaff. We walked home through streets that were dark and quiet except for music and laughter spilling from the cantina on the corner. And when we came into our precious little home and looked up, we realized that we could see more than just the Milky Way . . . we could see heaven. We were home.

The great hall was overflowing for the wedding party with stunningly clad, very attractive people . . . and they are beautiful people. Their richly colored skin glows with life, their dark hair shines, their eyes sparkle. Women in San Miguel know how to use makeup to its best effect: eyes that are exotic and mysterious; cheeks with just the right amount of glow; a light dusting of glistening powder on bare, shapely shoulders; full lips in bold, shimmery shades. And their hair . . . they part it in strips and zigzags, lines and grids, and they swirl and curl it into countless manners of gathering; it is mesmerizing and beautiful. And their dresses are so sensual, flowing, artistic, their shoes beyond imagining being able to walk in, yet they move exquisitely, even on the old cobblestone streets. The men are handsome in the real meaning of that word. They are strong and charming, with a twinkle in their eyes that enchants instantly.

Children play fútbol in whatever space is available, laughter filling the streets. Teenagers sit on the sidelines cheering the younger children on; mothers sit just inside their open doors, visiting with each other and keeping an ear on what's going on. Every one of them, from the babies to the grandmothers, wishing good evening to every passerby.

The sounds of San Miguel are unique and varied, carrying in their tones meanings that give texture to each day. The milk truck, the trash truck, the knife sharpener, the fresh corn seller, and donkeys with bags of rich dirt . . . the sounds of each one makes us pause for a moment and appreciate life.

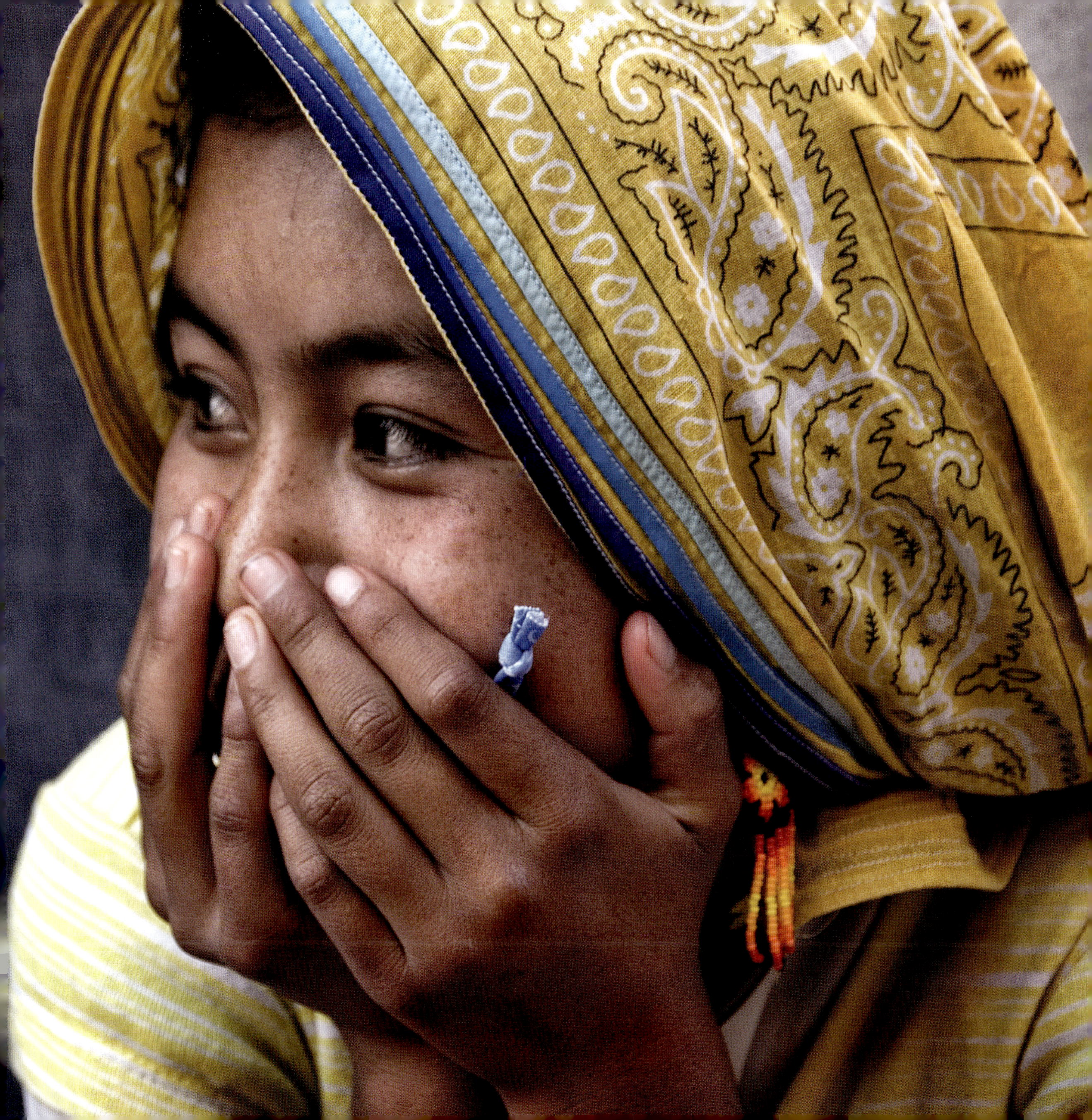

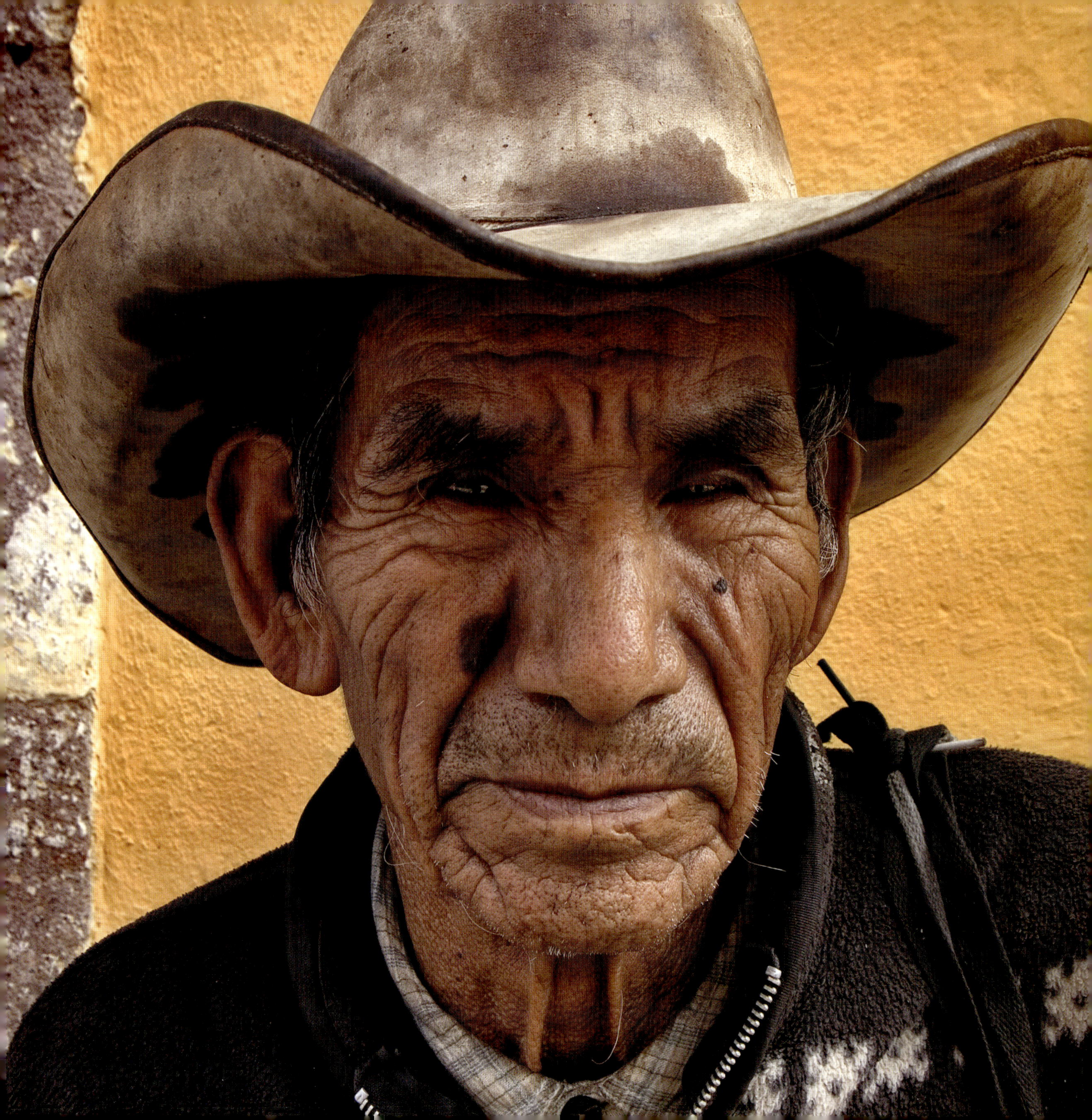

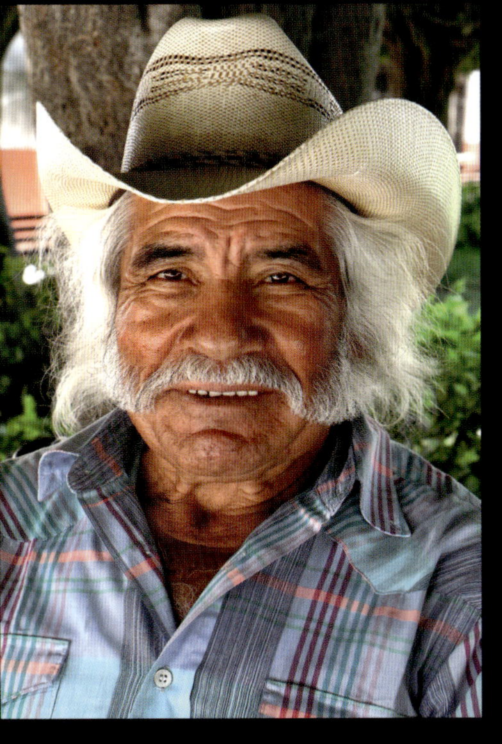

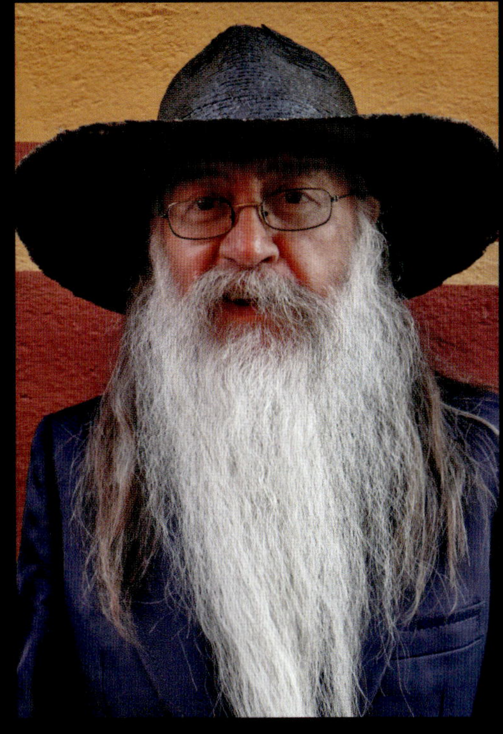

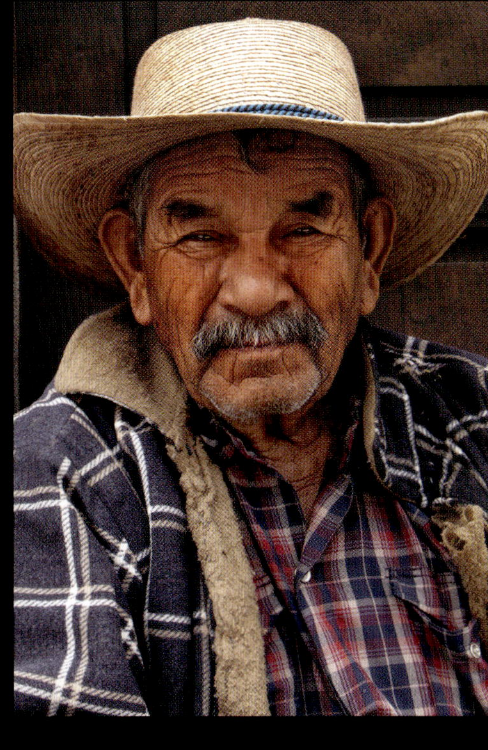

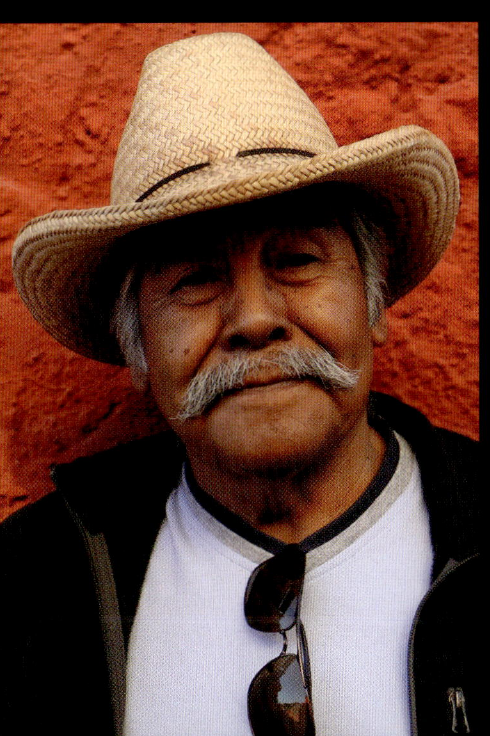

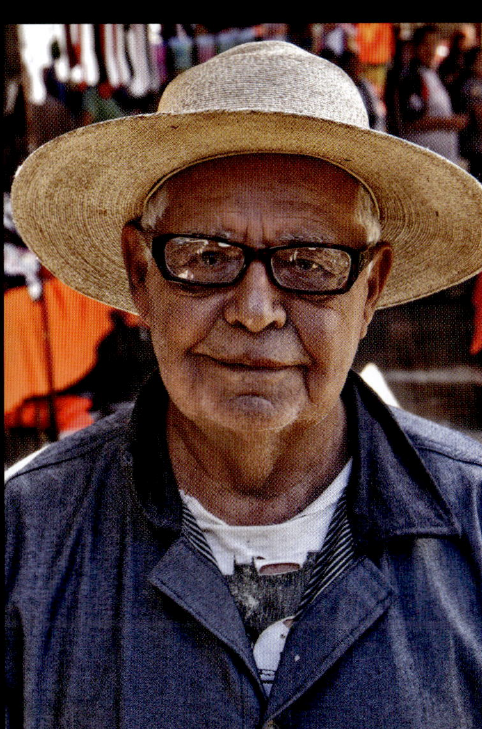

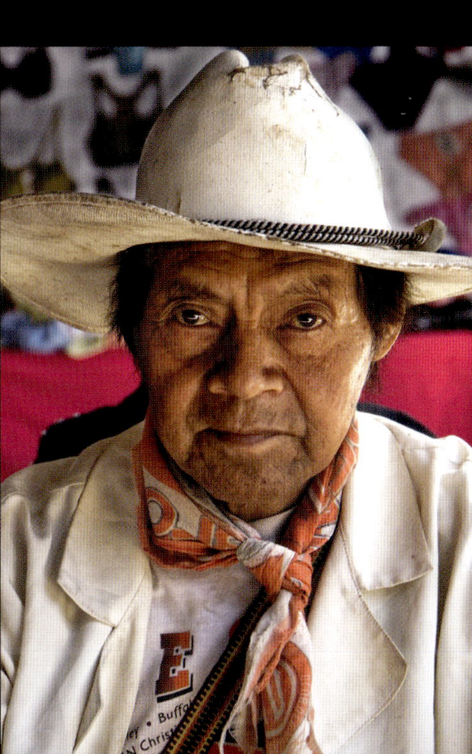

All faces are as old as the world. —Picasso

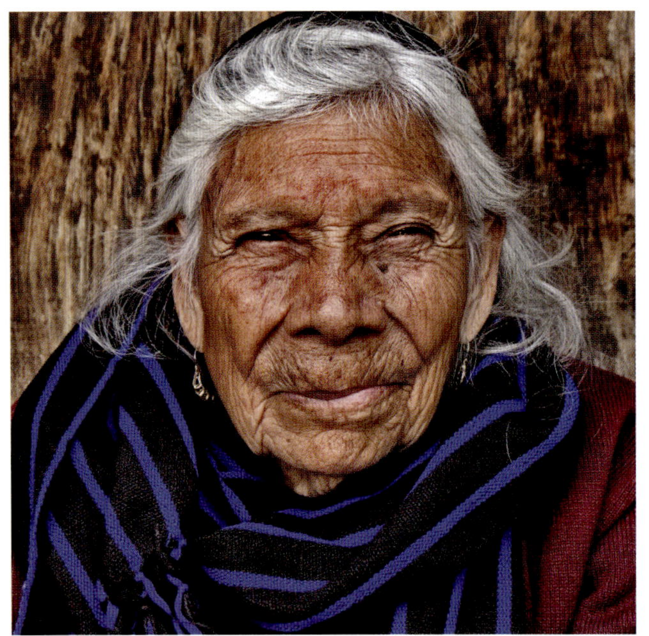

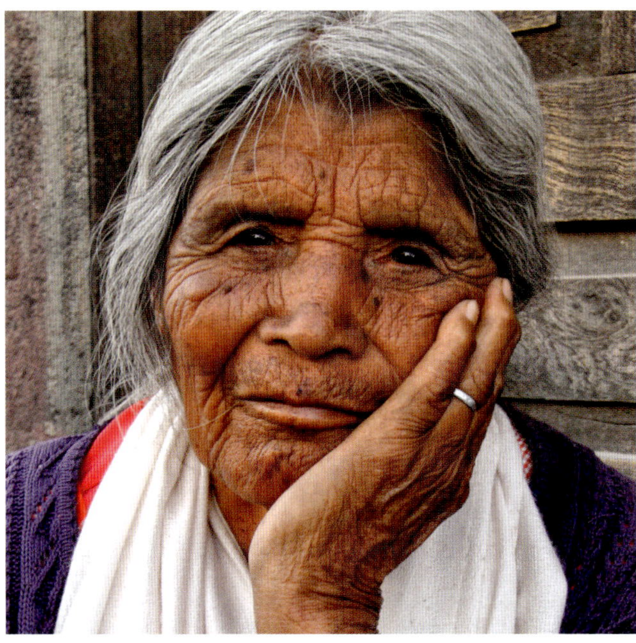

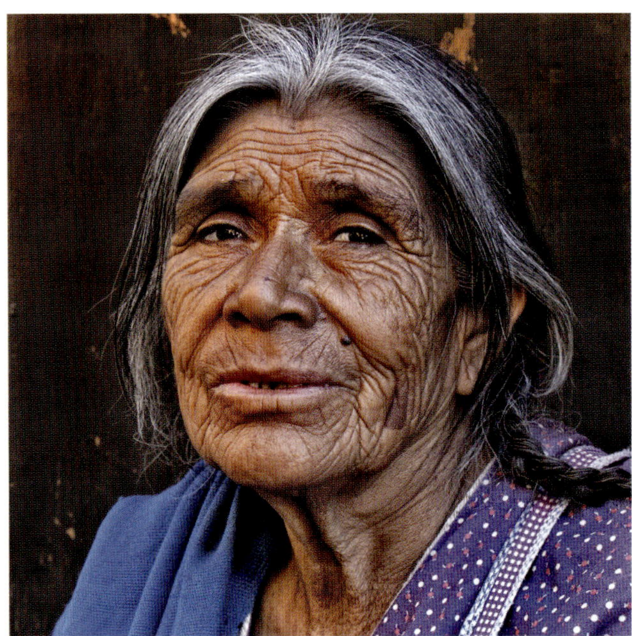

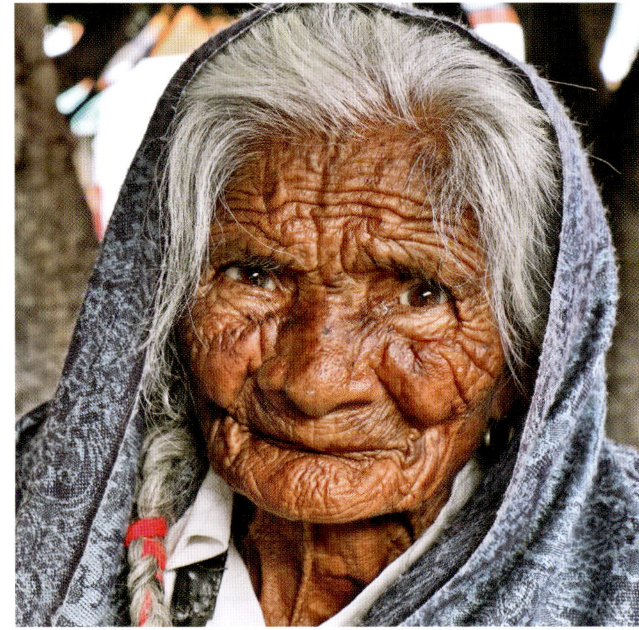

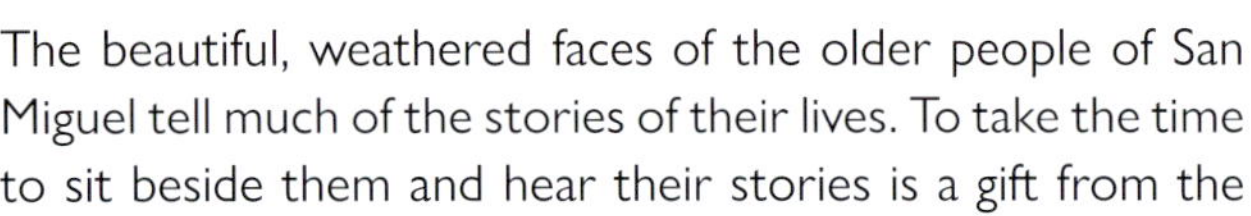

The beautiful, weathered faces of the older people of San Miguel tell much of the stories of their lives. To take the time to sit beside them and hear their stories is a gift from the past from people who have seen and learned much to teach us. These people are the iconic remains of a generation that will soon be lost, and it is a pleasure to come to know them.

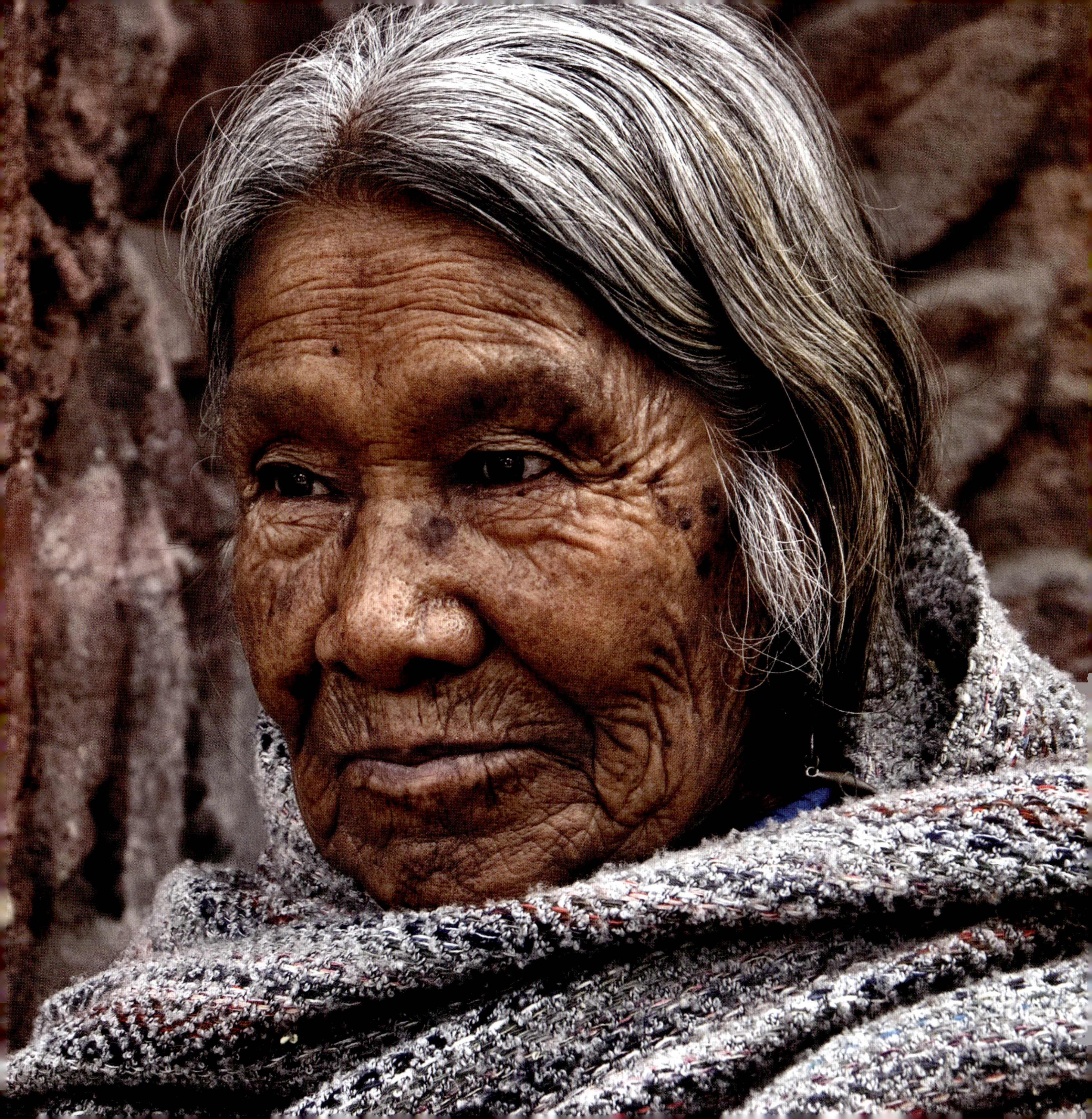

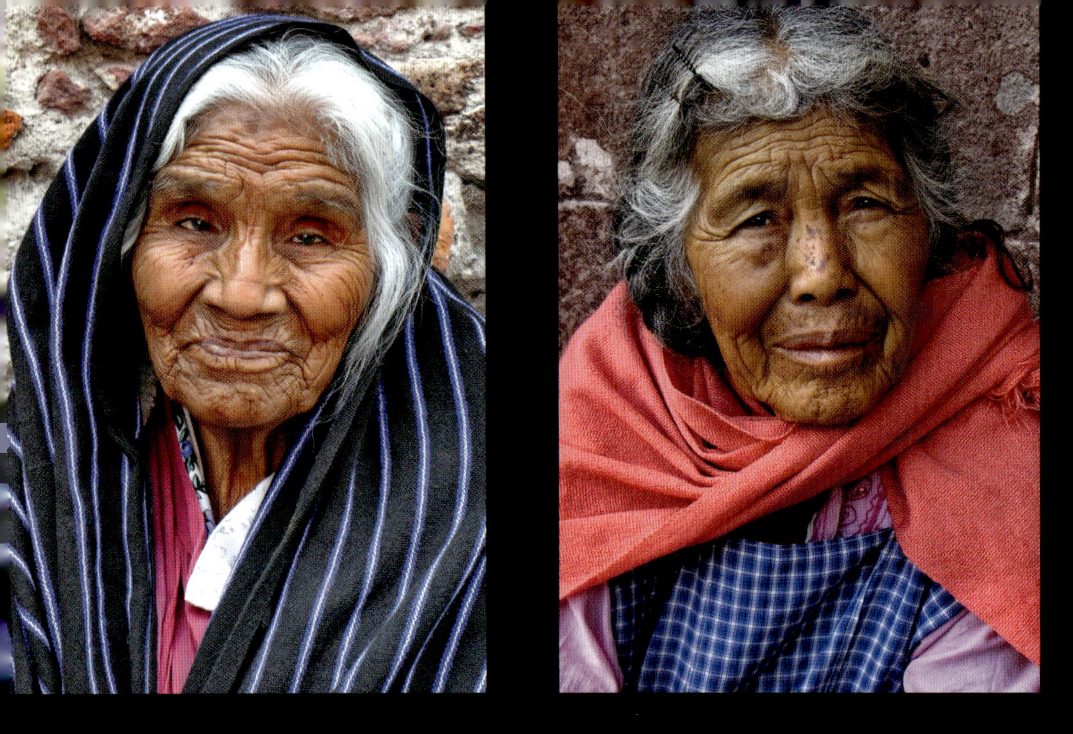

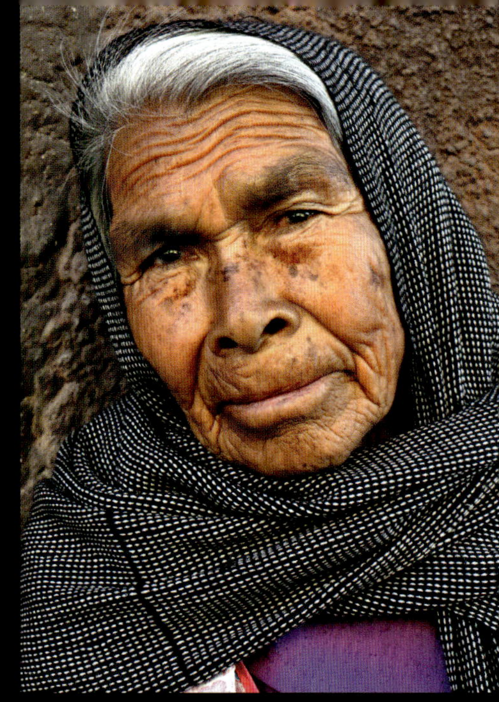

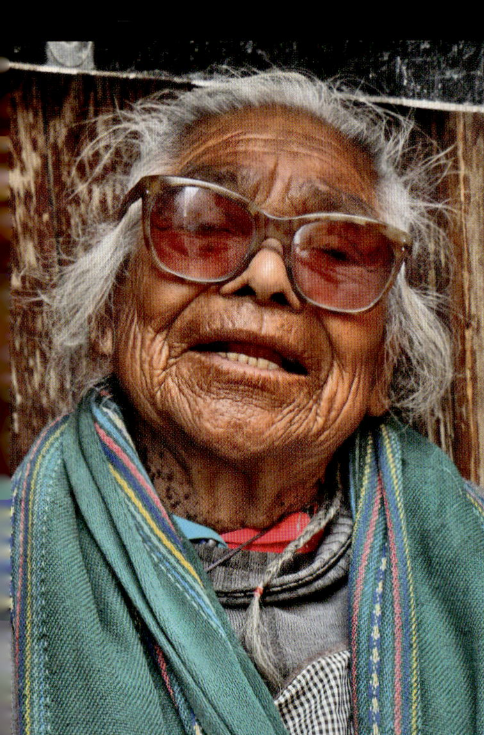

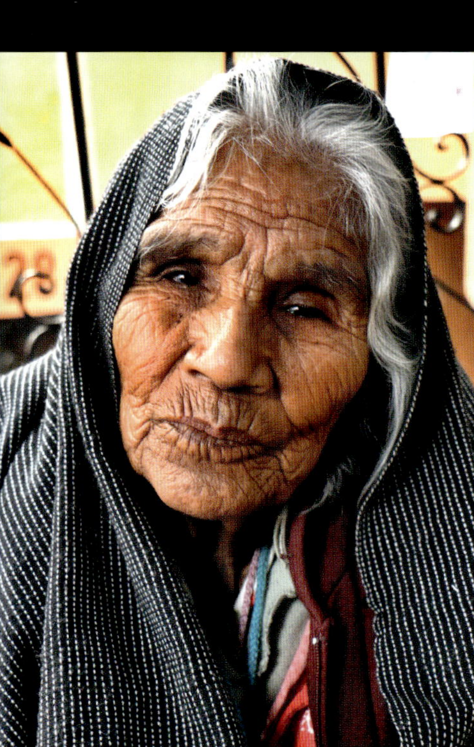

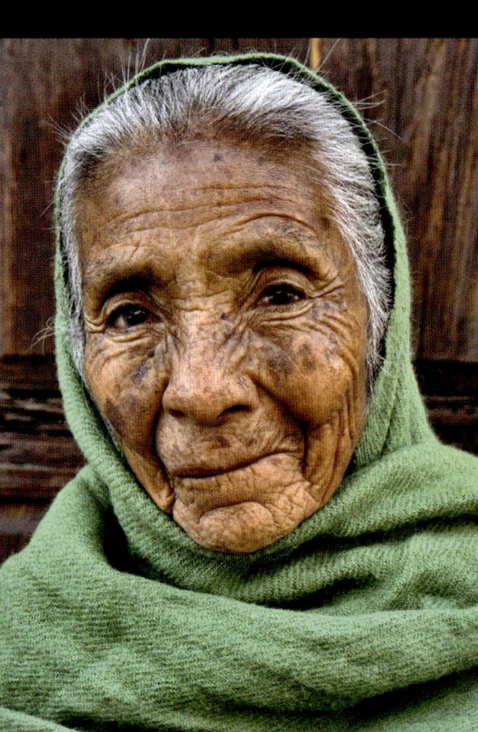

Age has no reality except in the physical world. The essence of a human being is resistant to the passage of time. Our inner lives are eternal, which is to say that our spirits remain as youthful and vigorous as when we were in full bloom. —Gabriel García Márquez

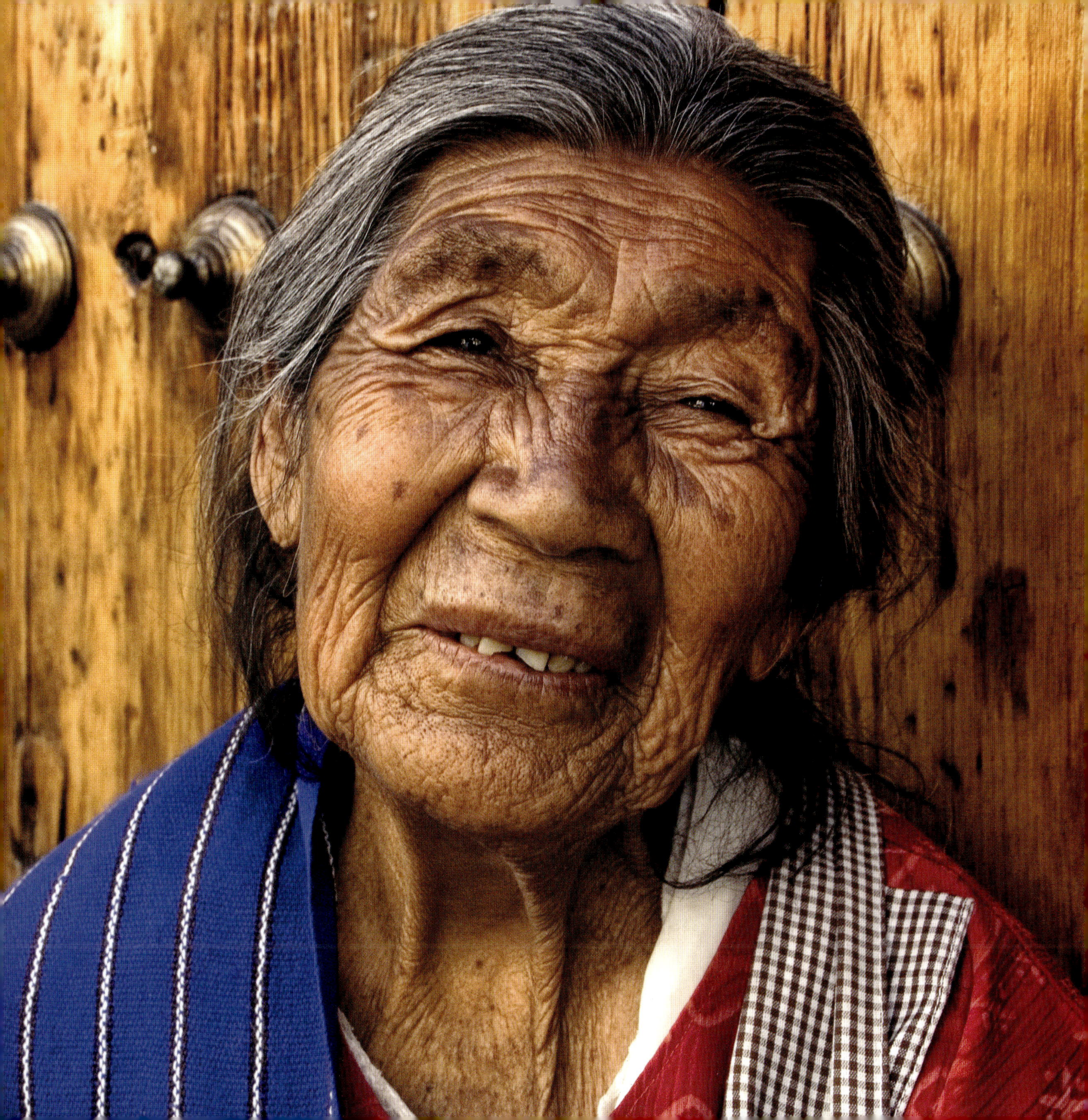

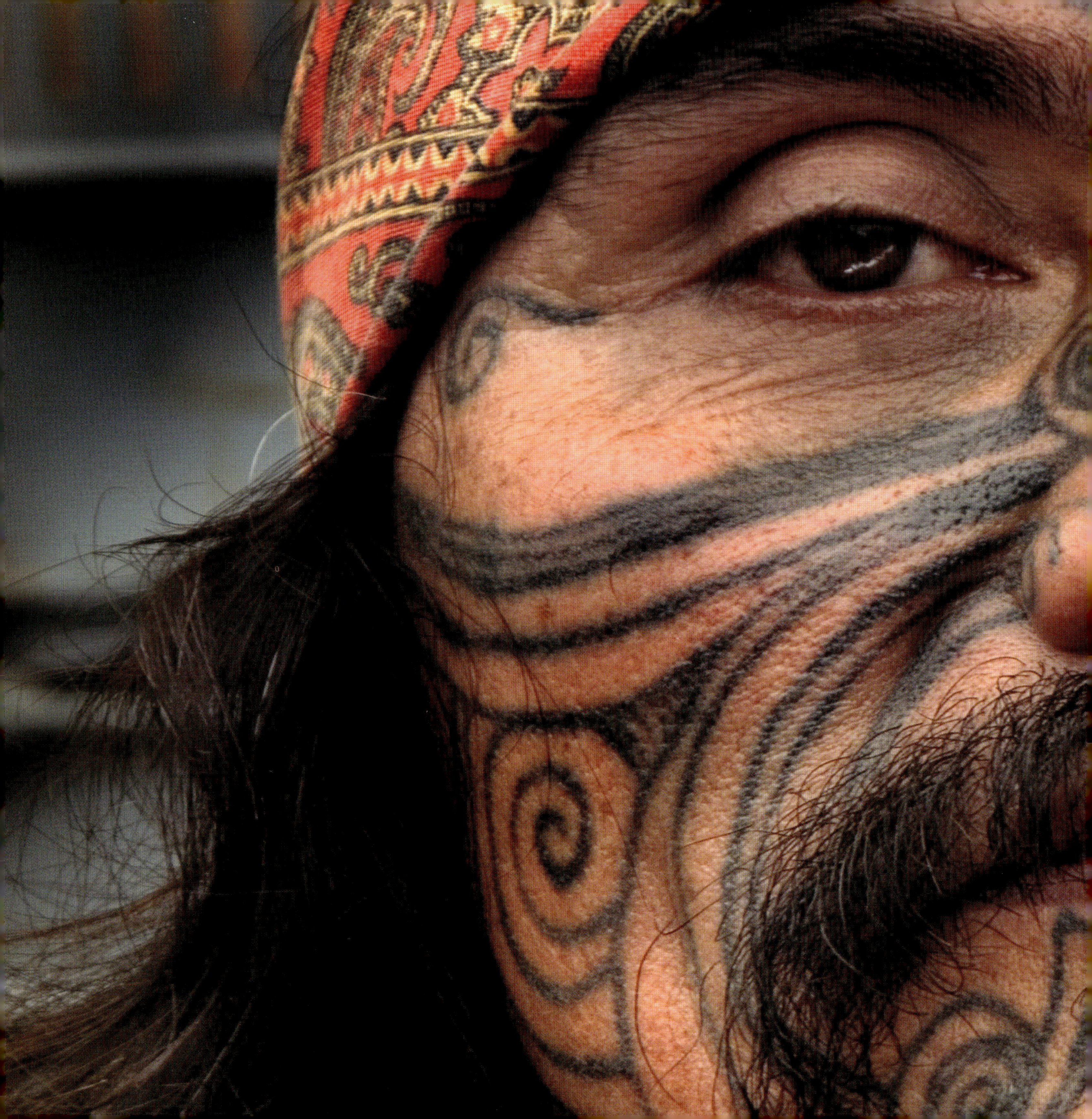

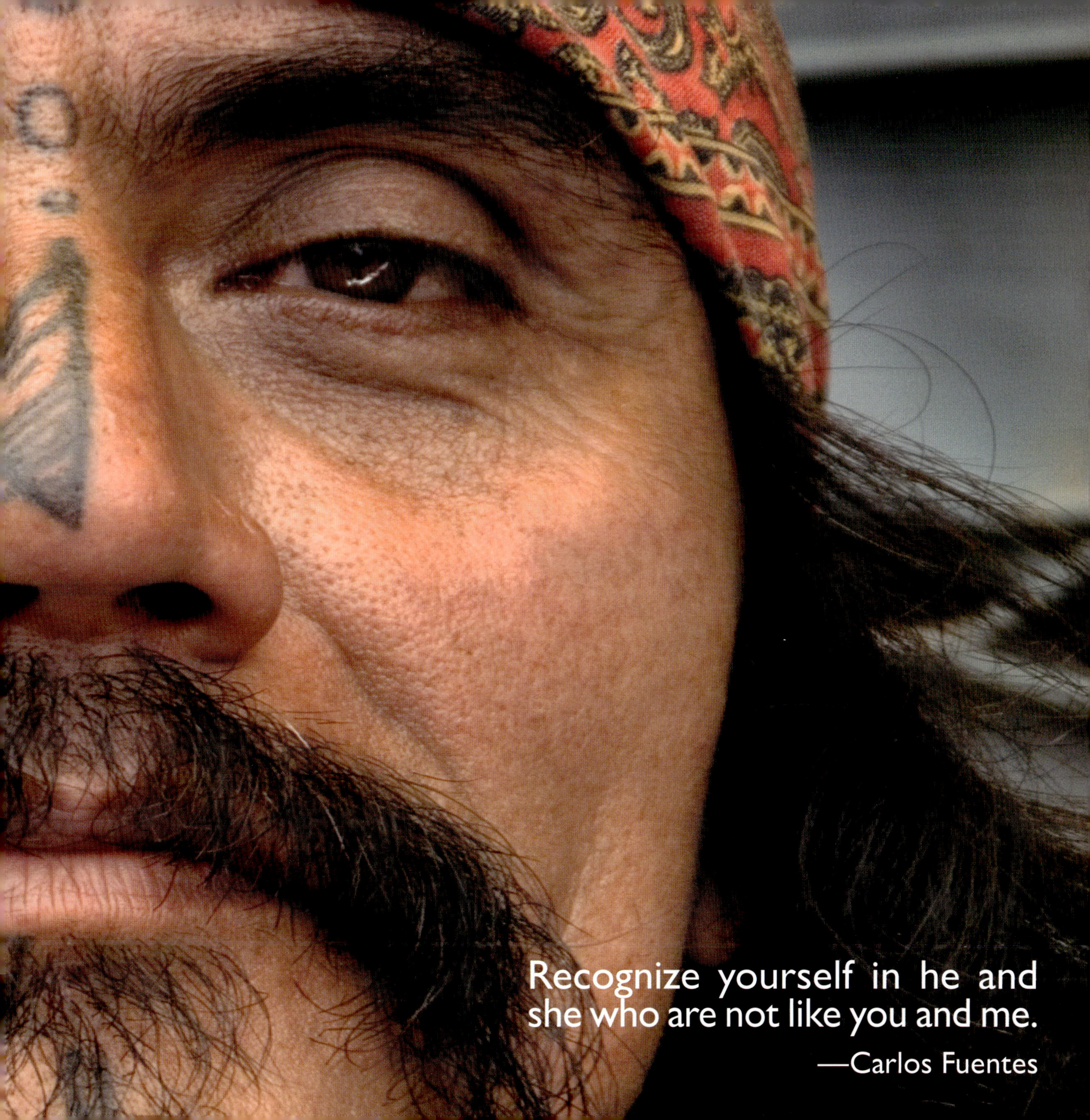
Recognize yourself in he and
she who are not like you and me.
—Carlos Fuentes

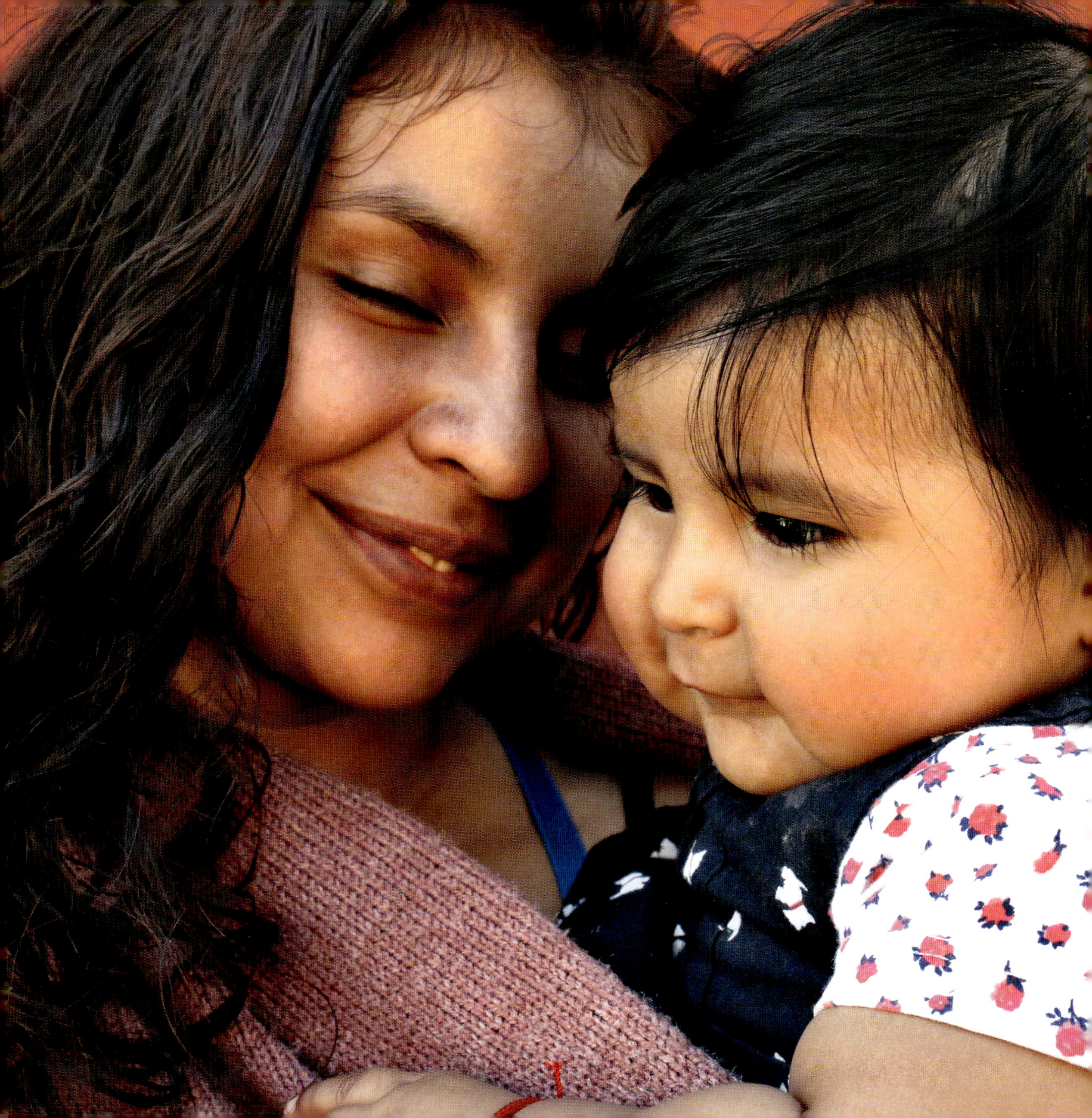

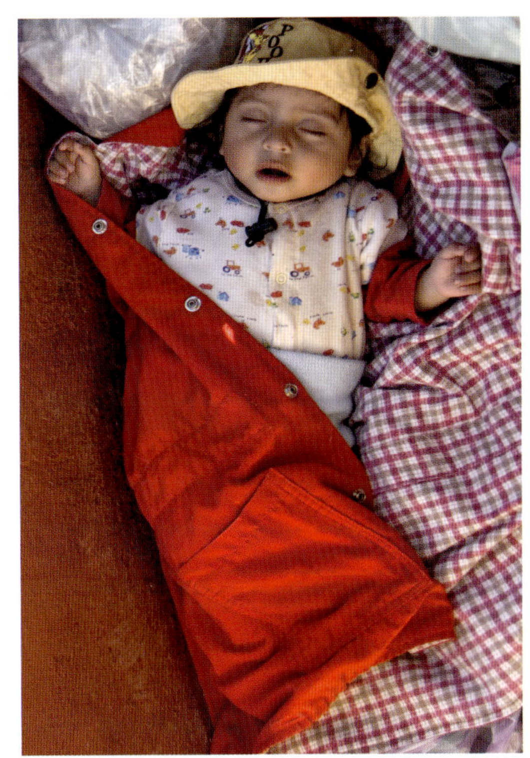

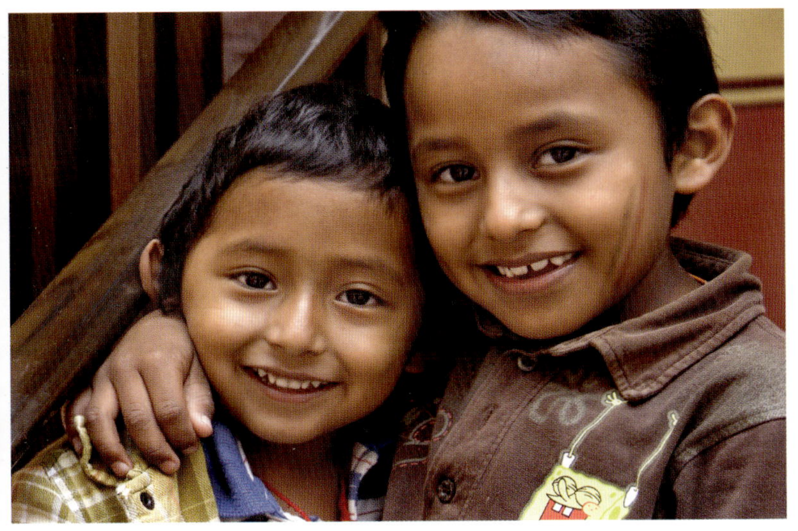

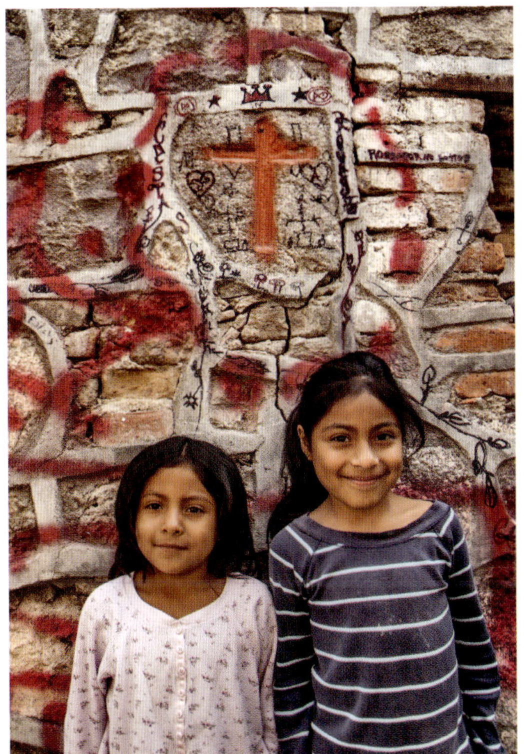

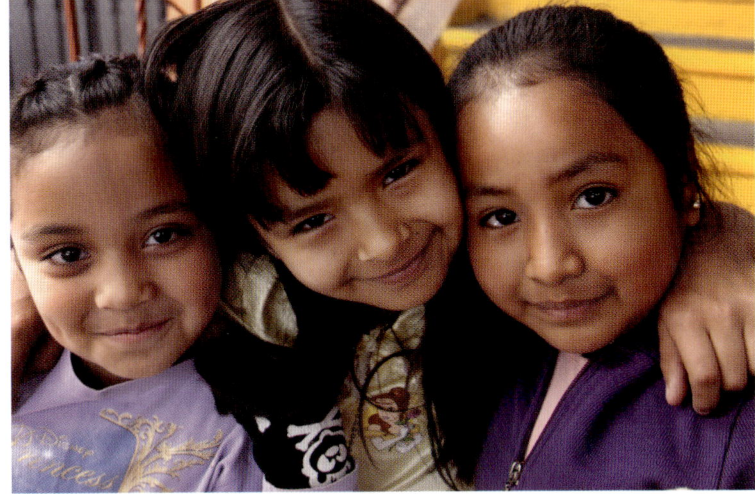

If I knew that today would be the last time I'd see you, I would hug you tight and pray the Lord be the keeper of your soul. If I knew that this would be the last time you pass through this door, I'd embrace you, kiss you, and call you back for one more. If I knew that this would be the last time I would hear your voice, I'd take hold of each word to be able to hear it over and over again. If I knew this would be the last time I see you, I'd tell you I love you and would not just assume foolishly you know it already. —Gabriel García Márquez

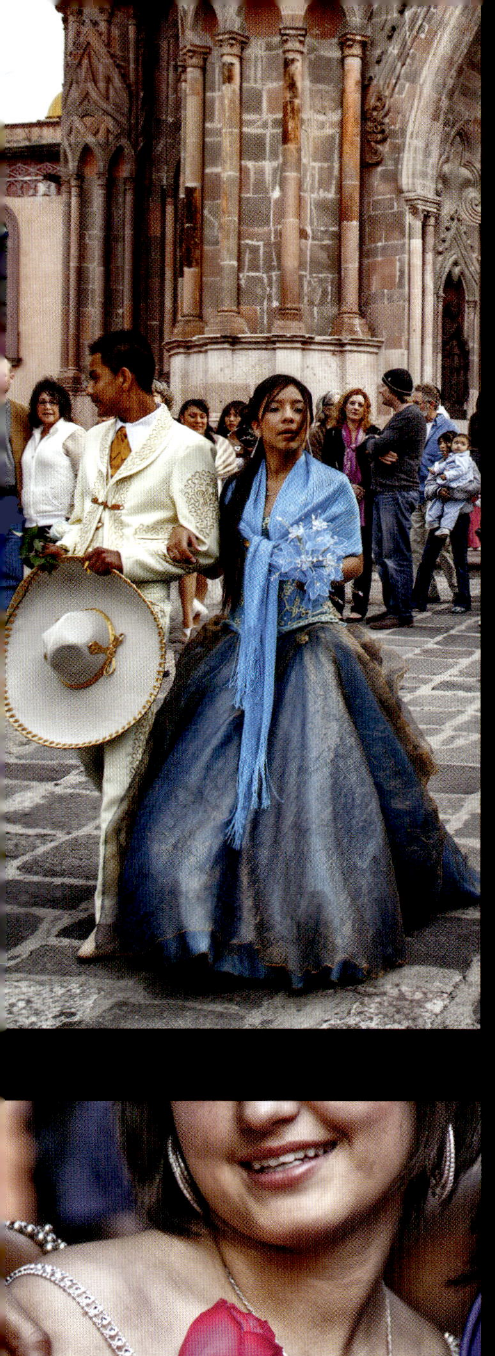
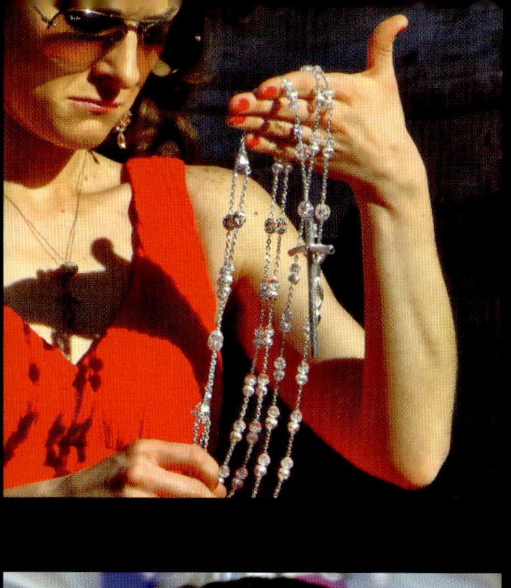
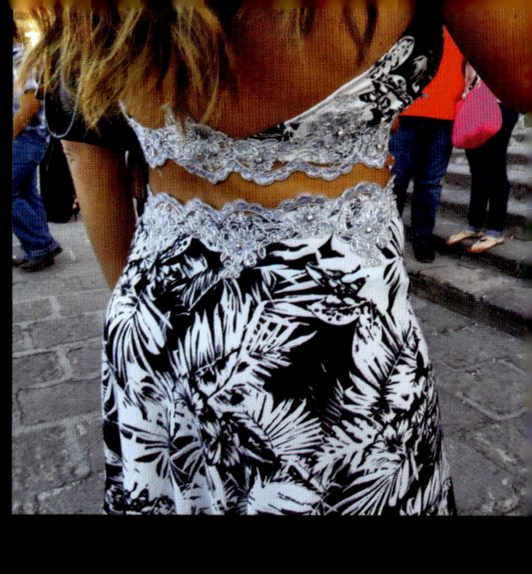
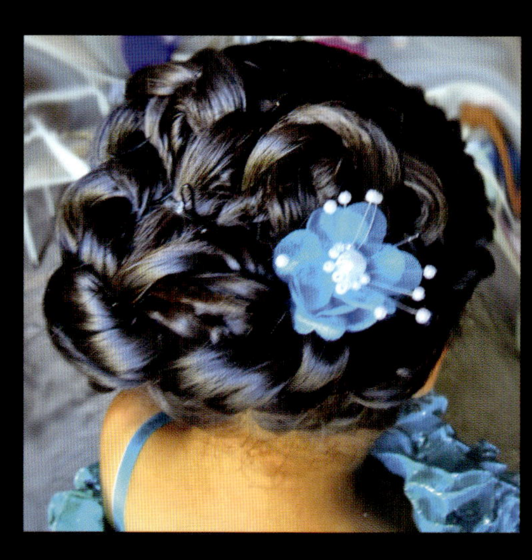
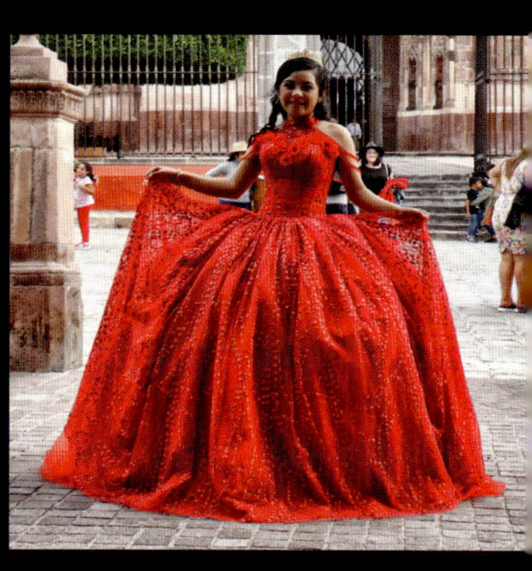
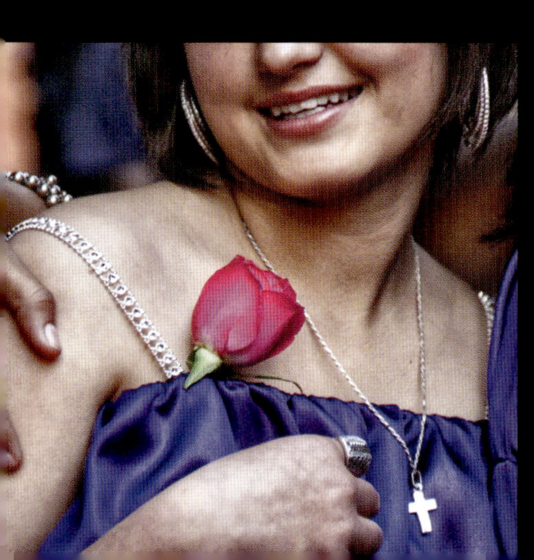
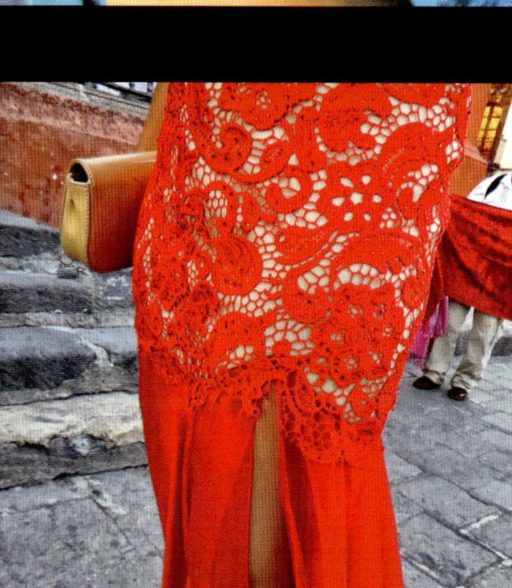
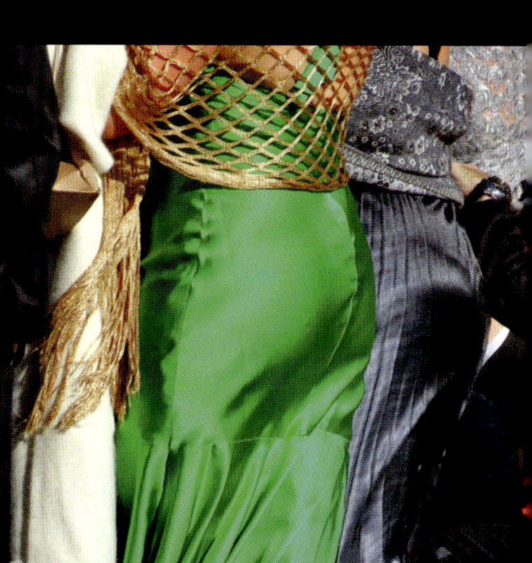

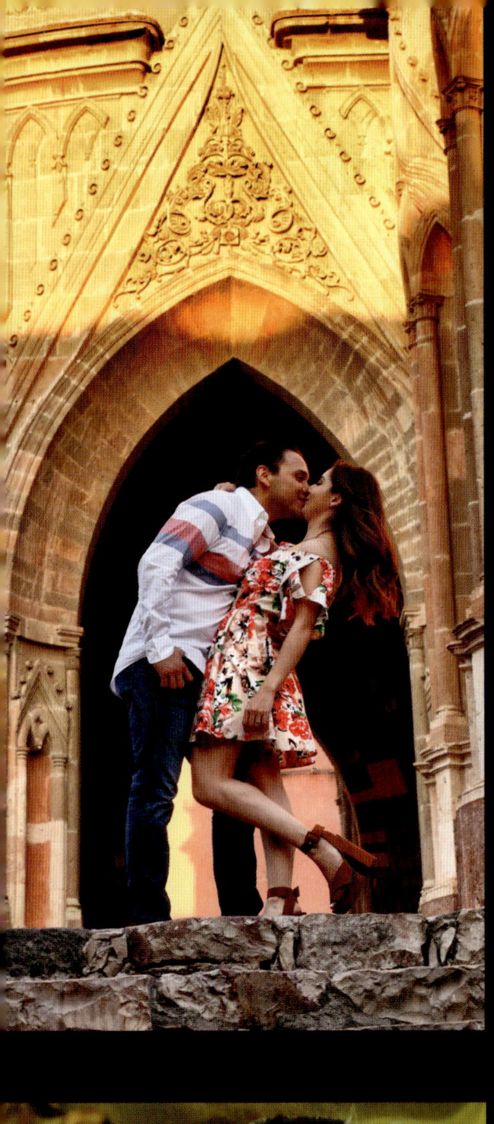

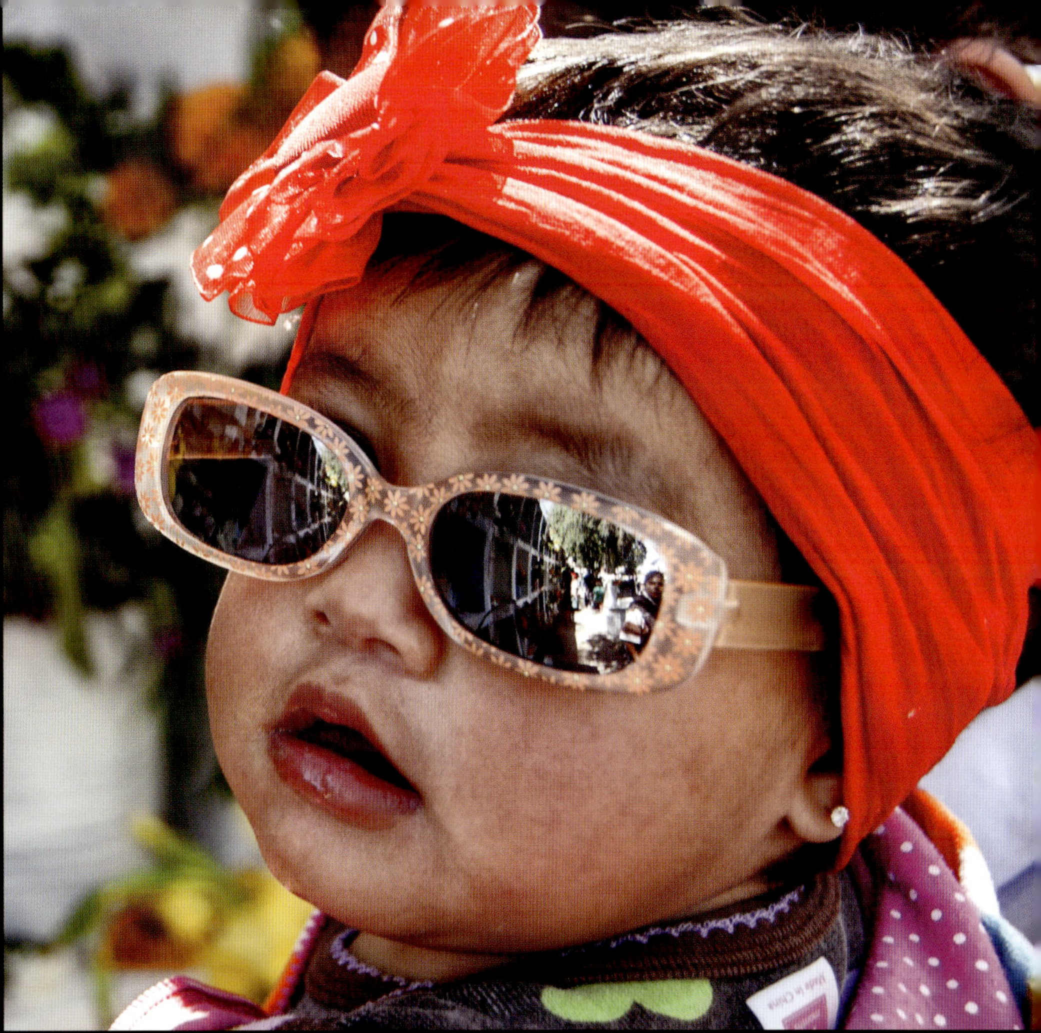

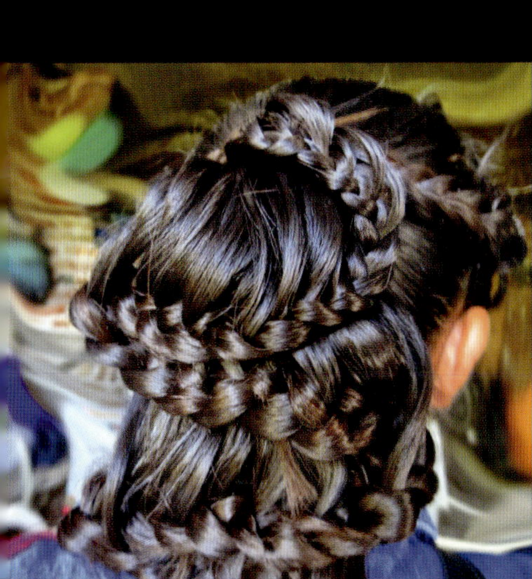

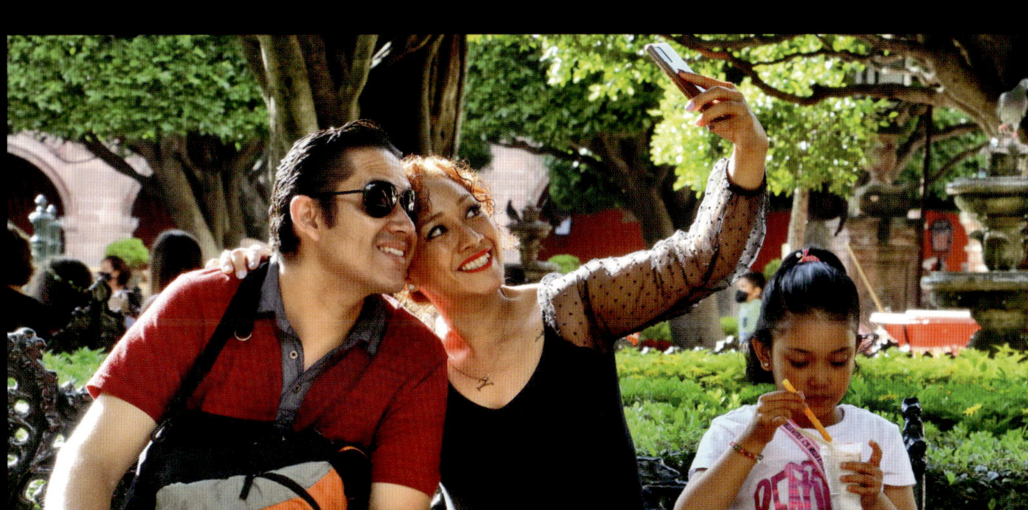

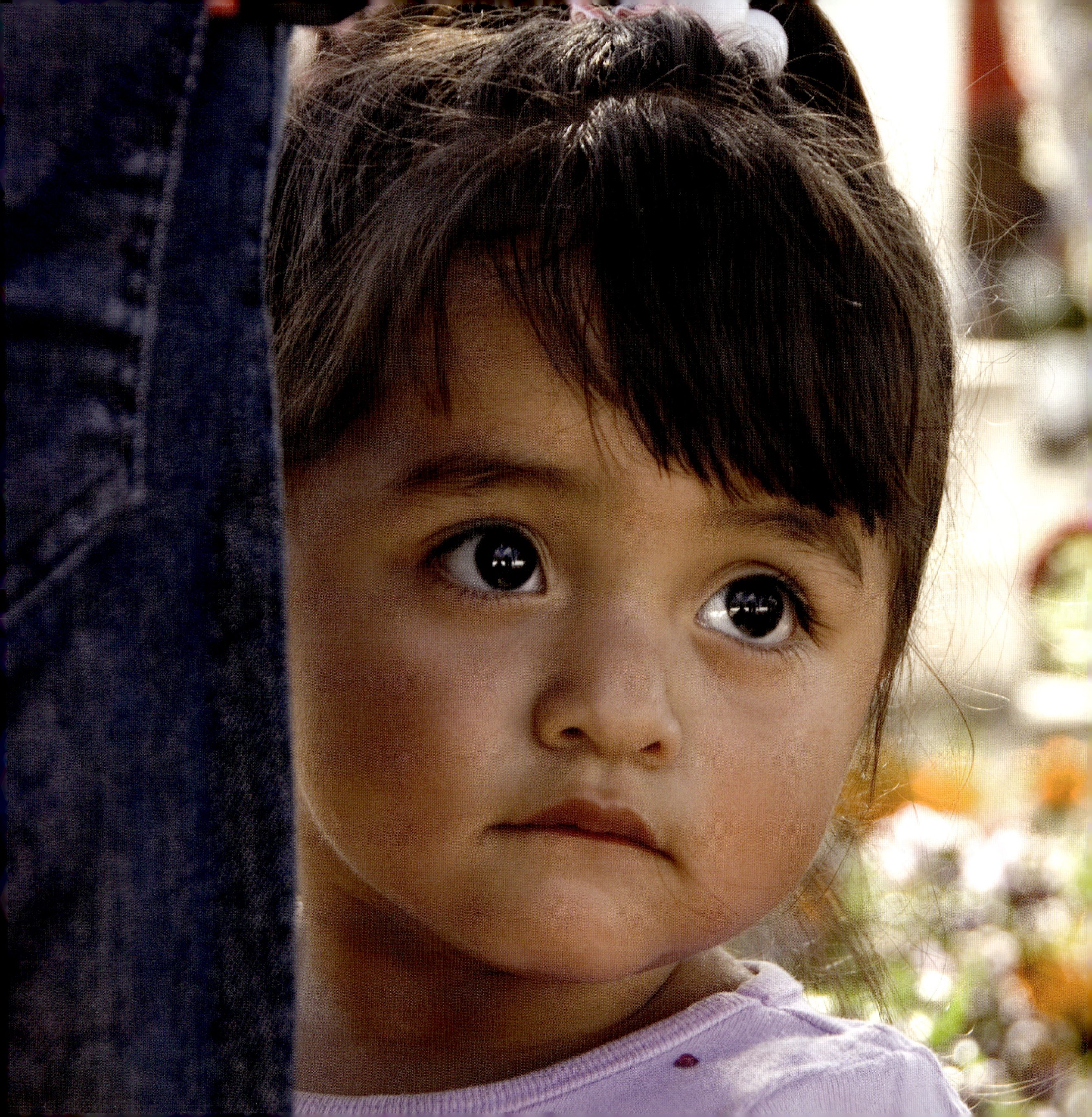

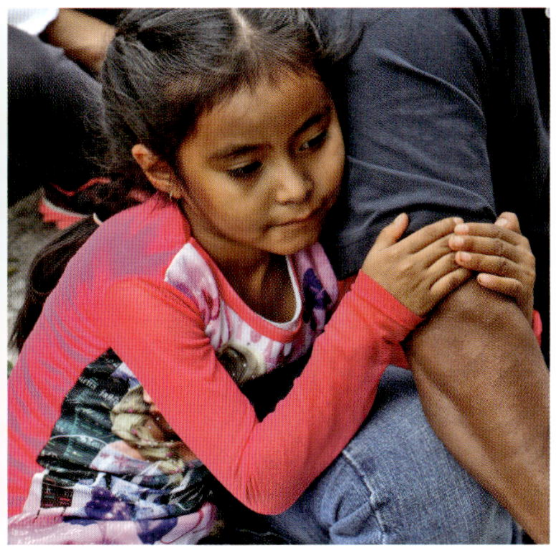
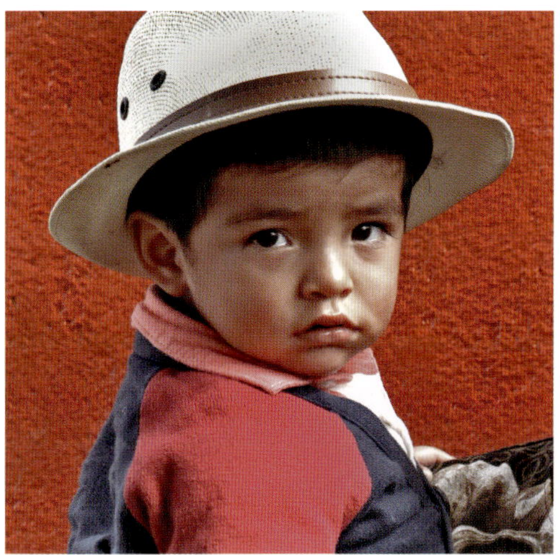
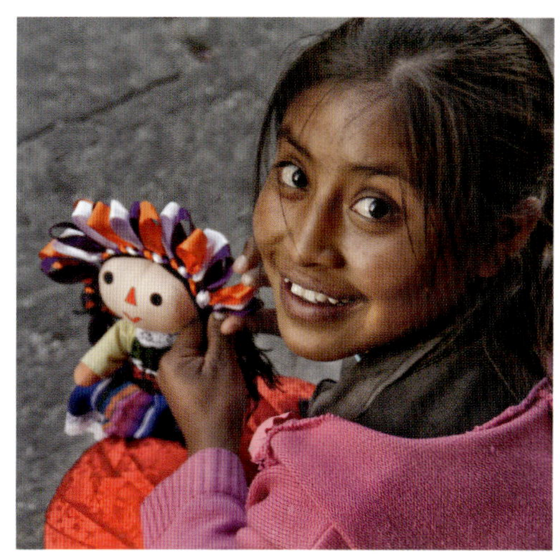
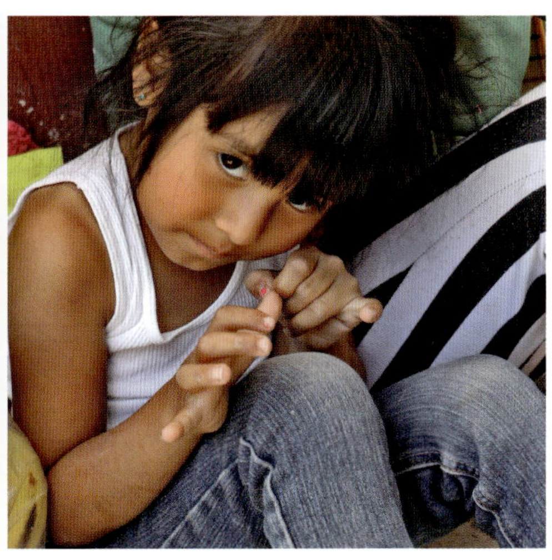
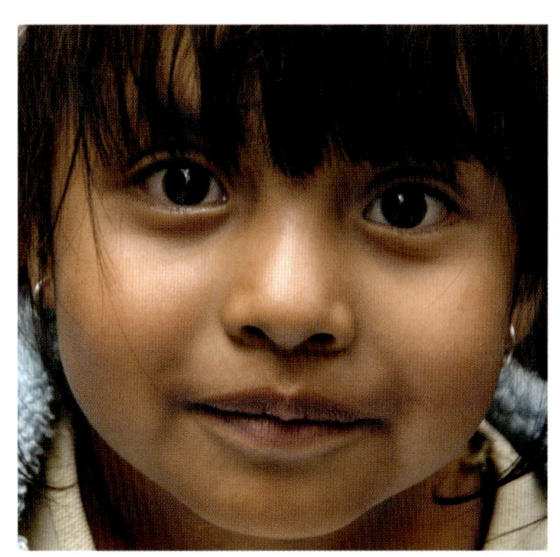
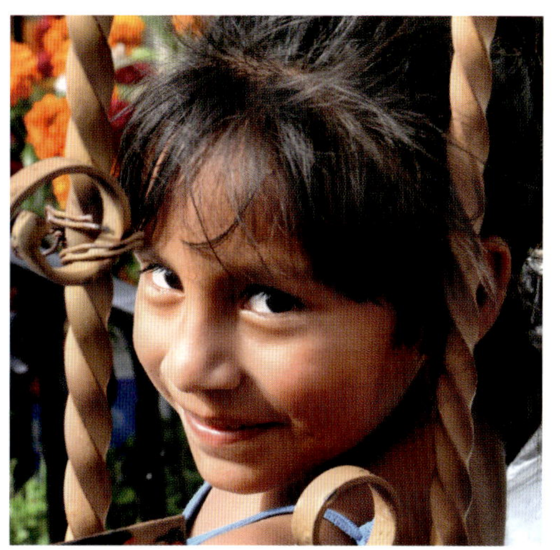
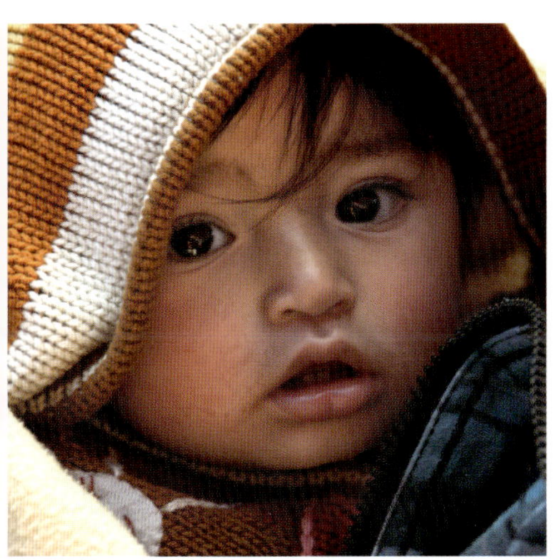
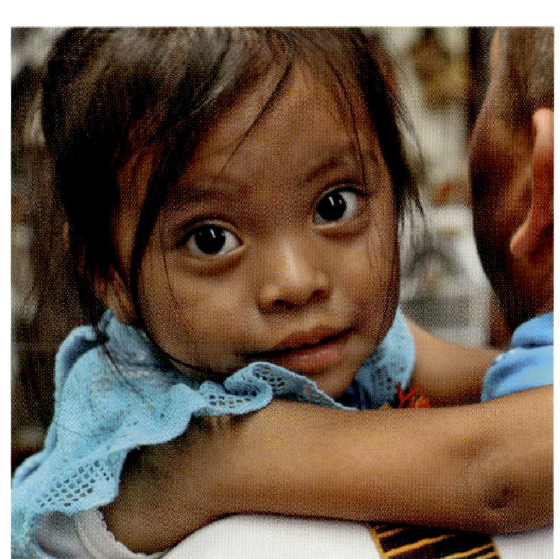
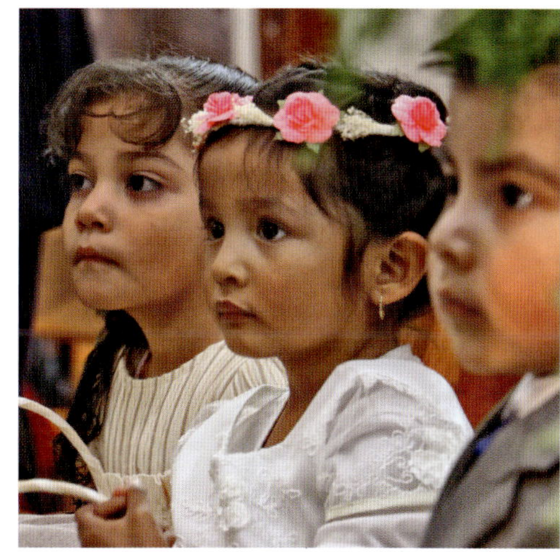

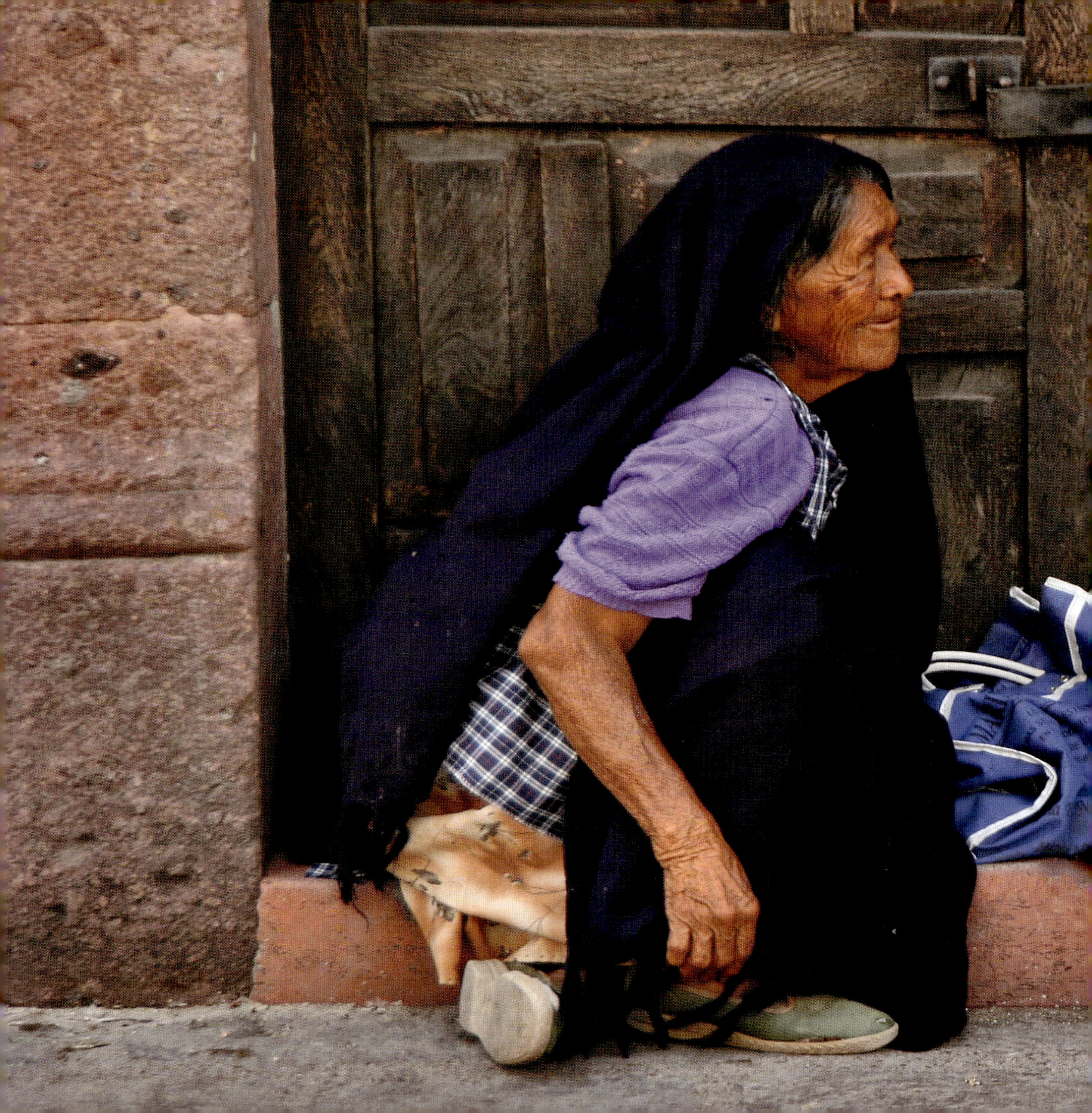

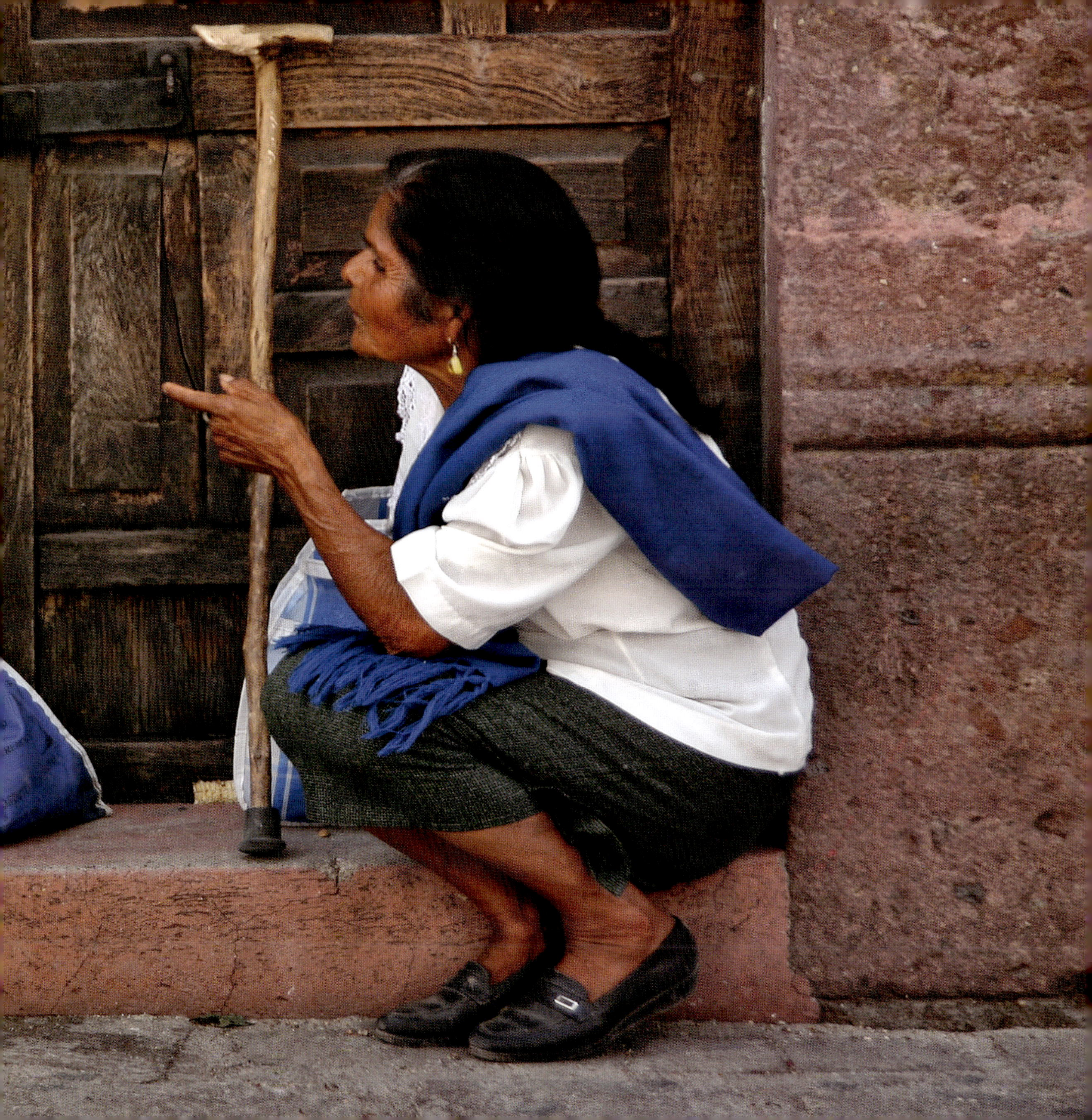

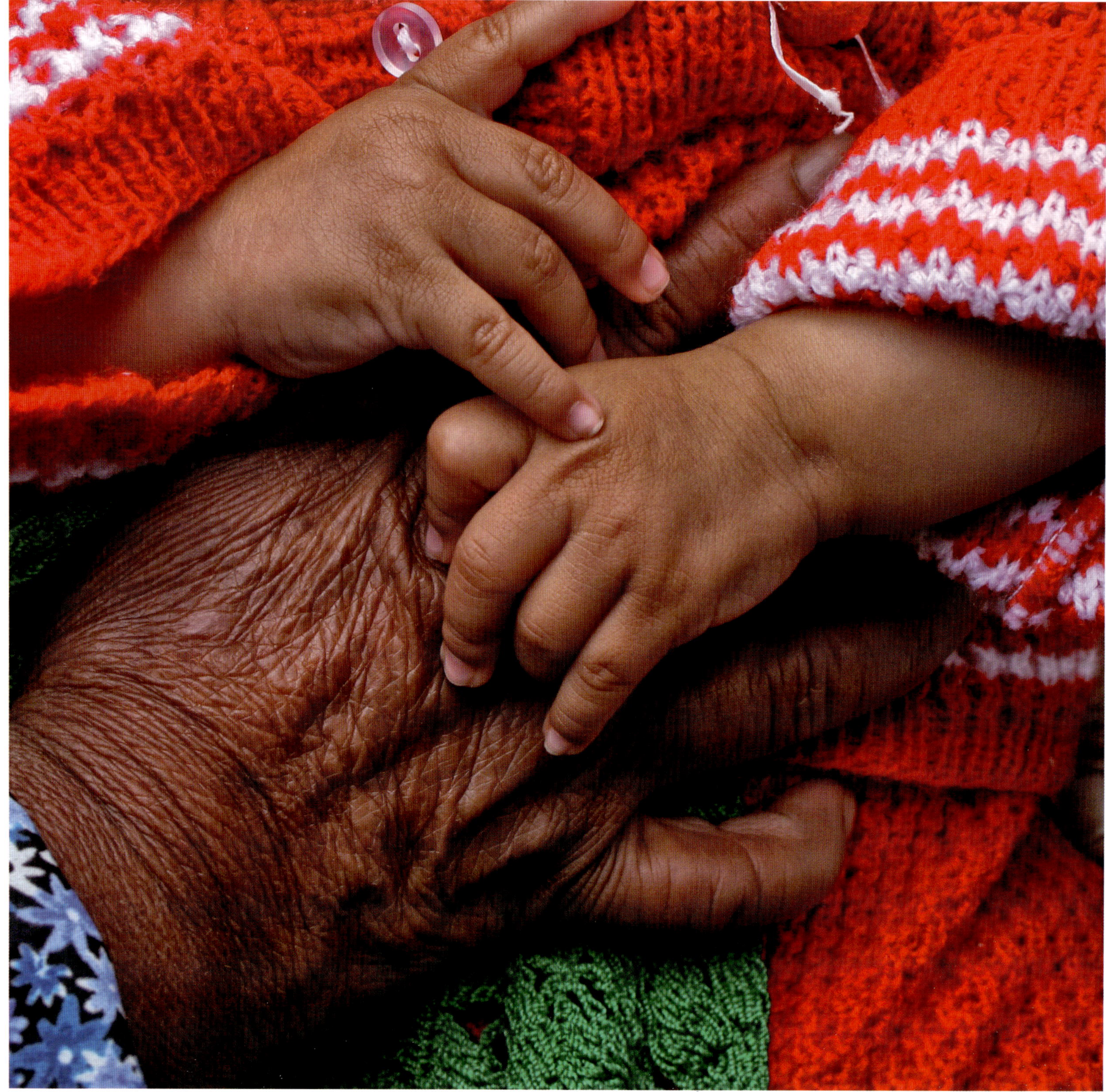

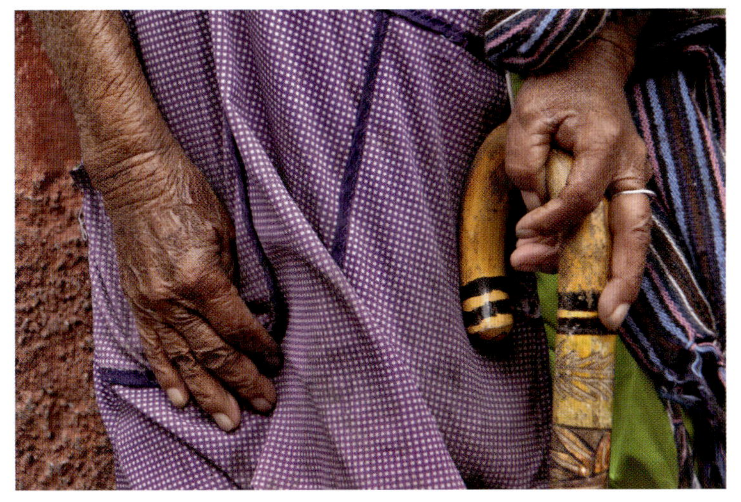
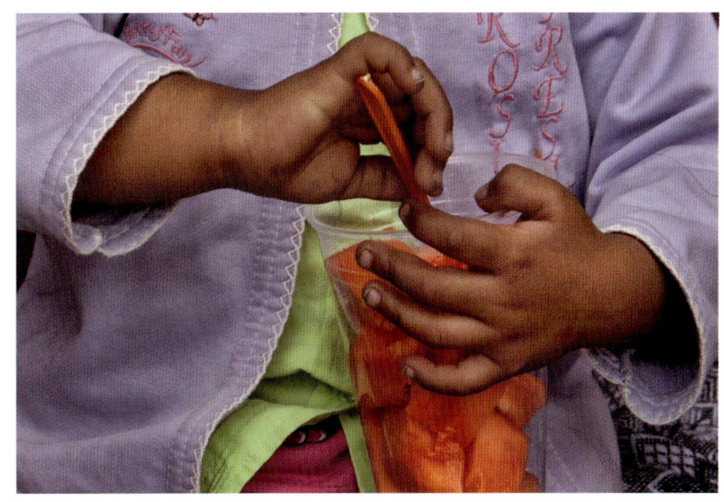
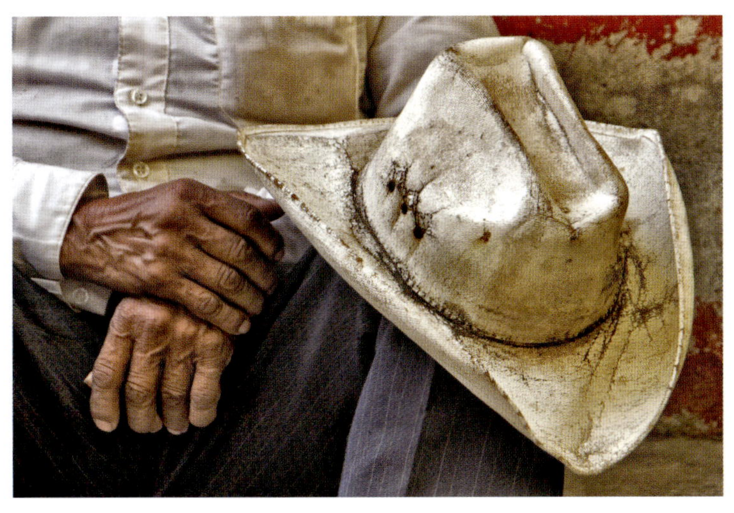
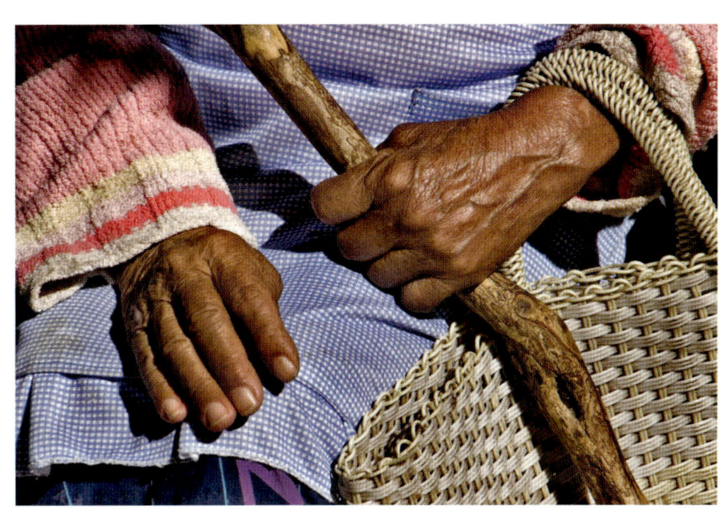
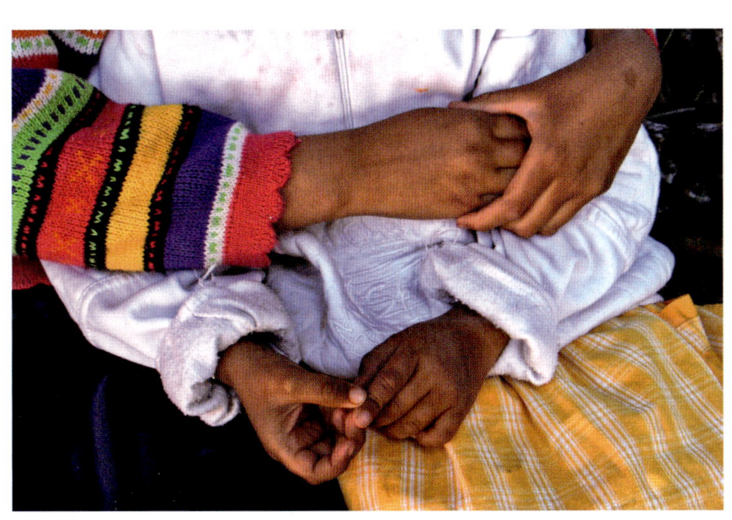
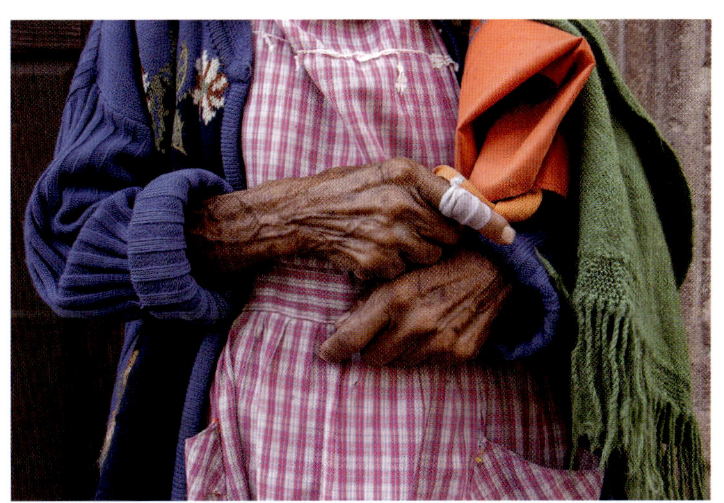

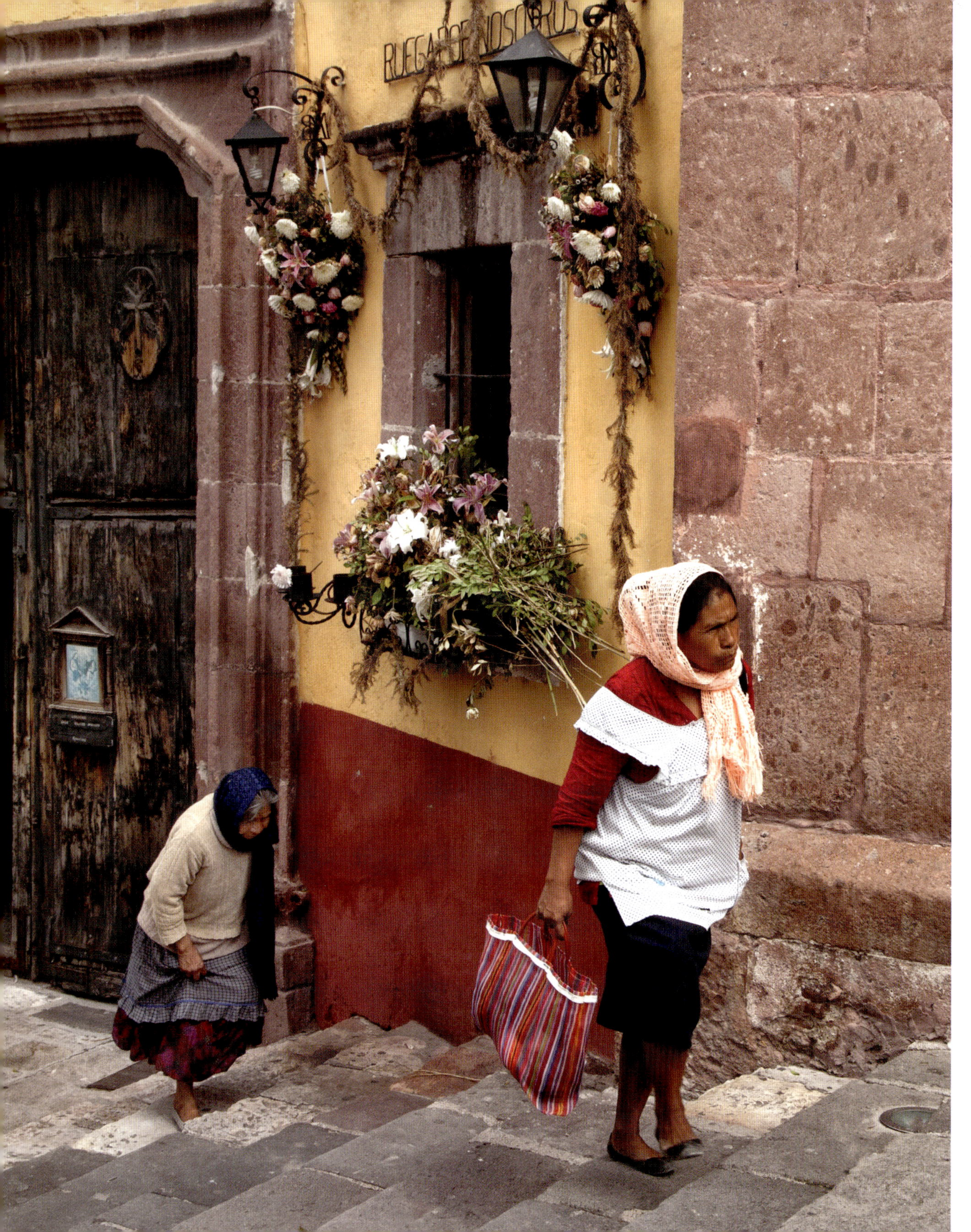
RUEGA

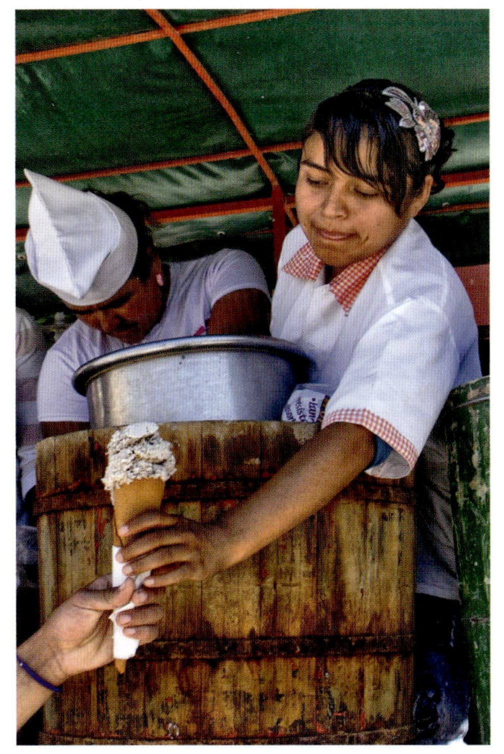

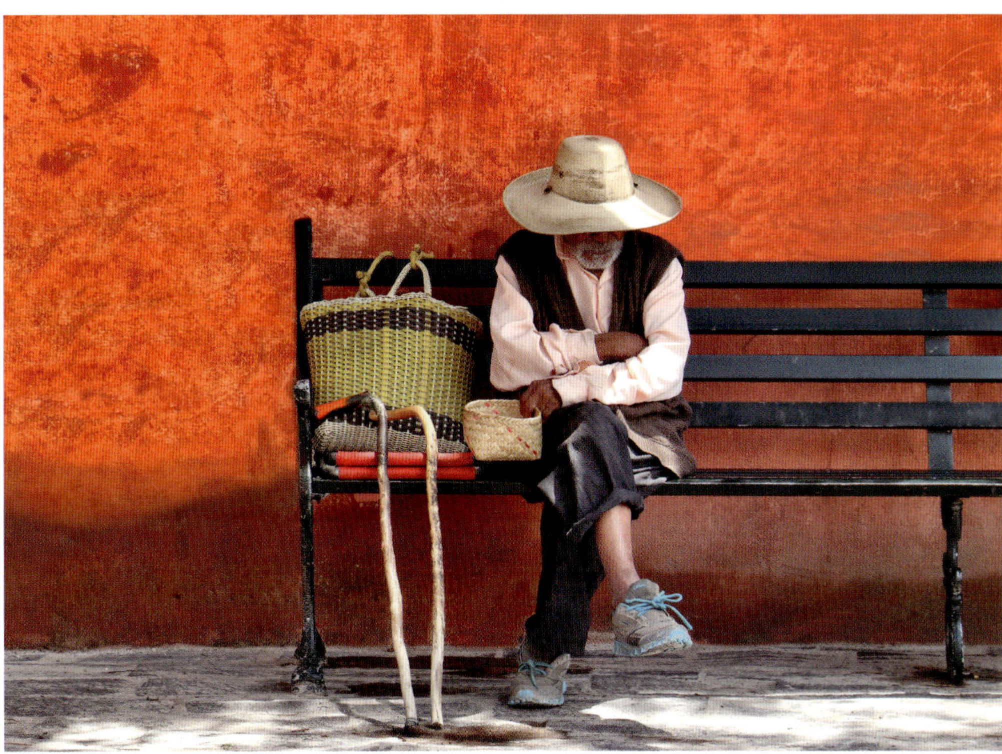

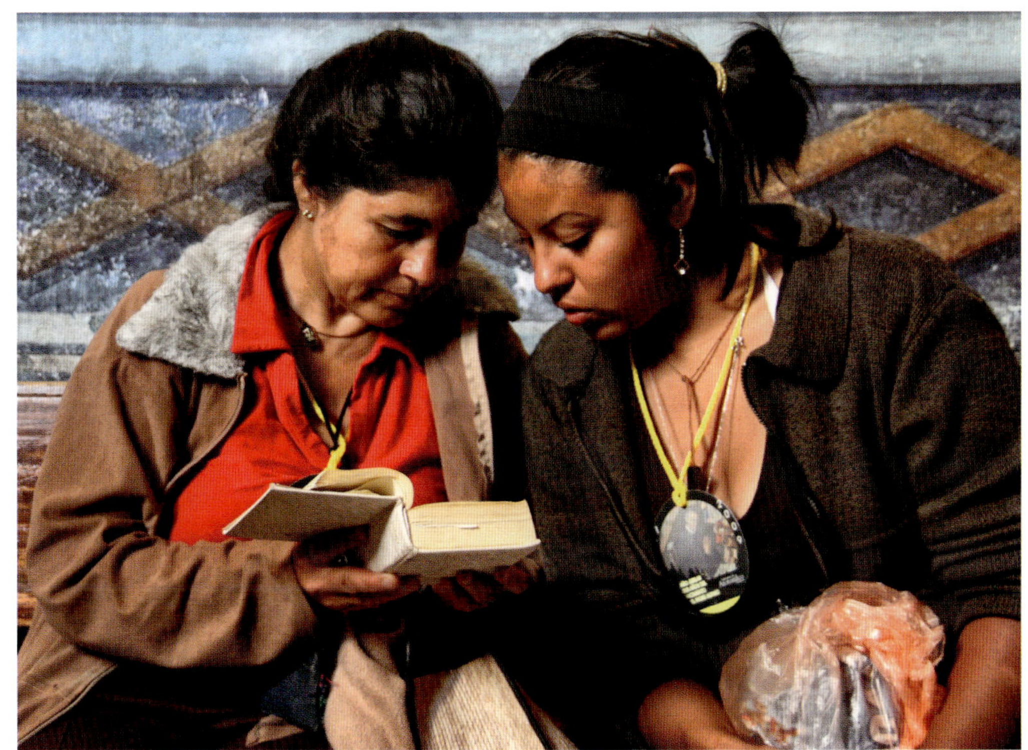

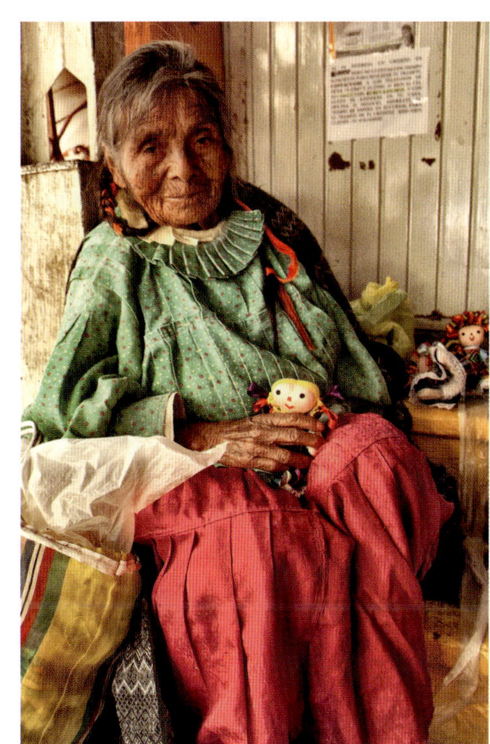

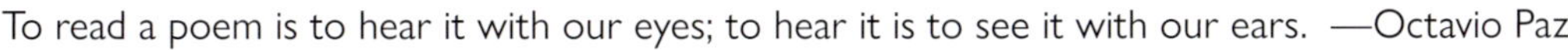

To read a poem is to hear it with our eyes; to hear it is to see it with our ears. —Octavio Paz

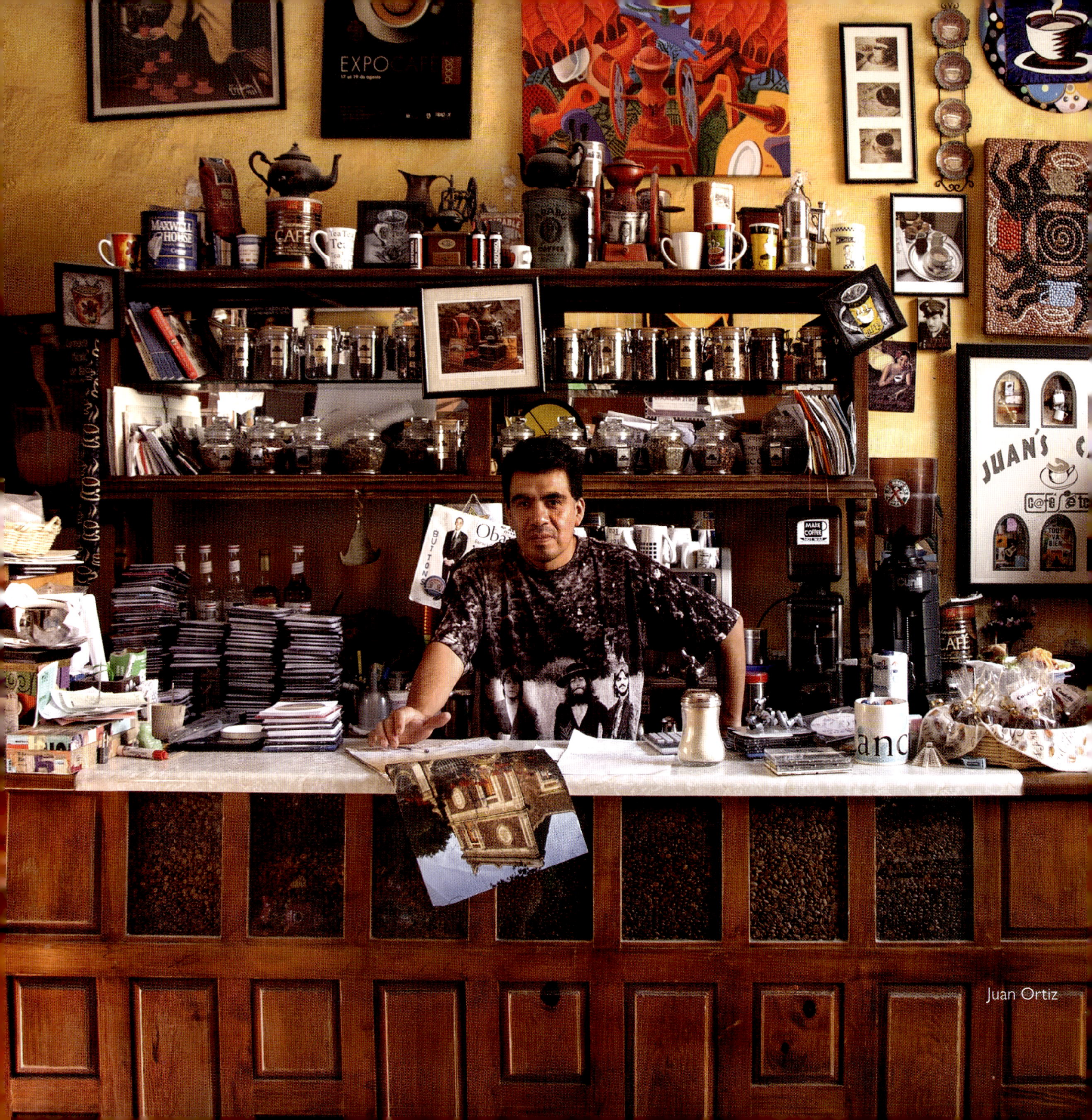

Juan Ortiz

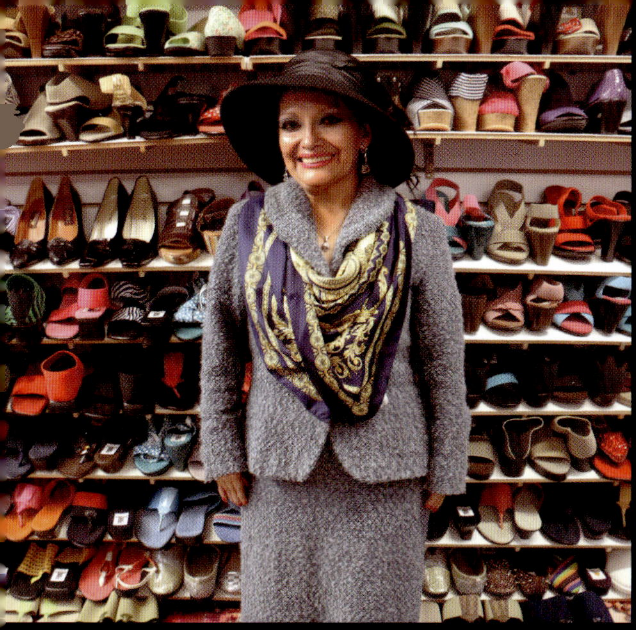

Doña Martha López

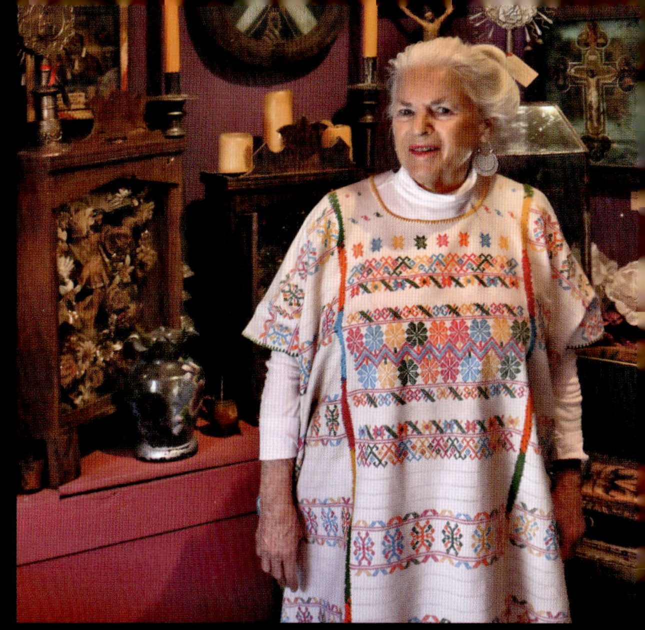

Evita Avery

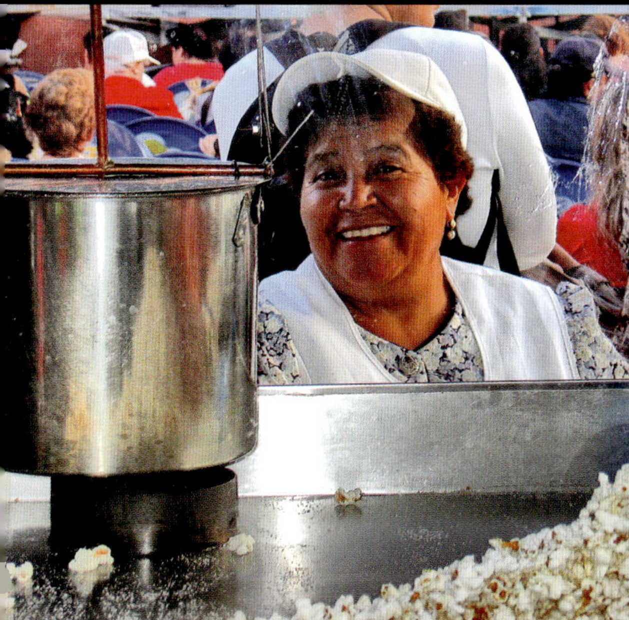

Margarita Luna Espinosa

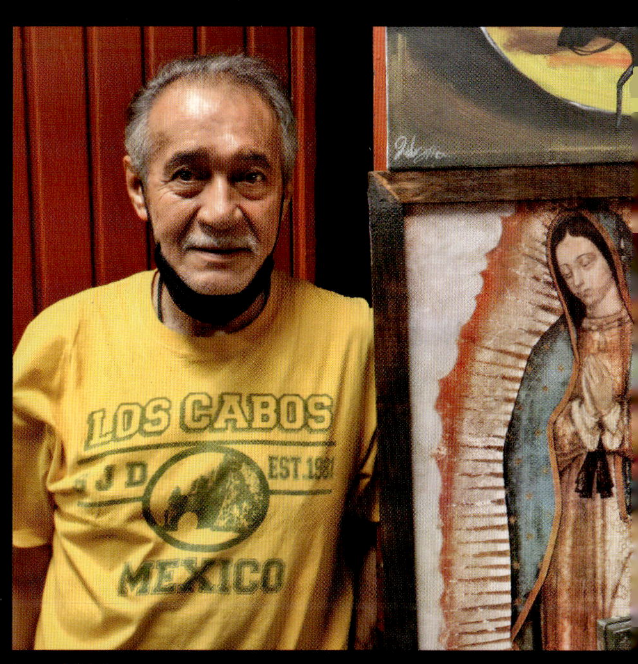

Jose Valderrama

Regardless of the size of the city or town where men or women are born, they are, in the end the size of their work, the size of their will to enlarge and enrich their brothers. —Ignacio Allende

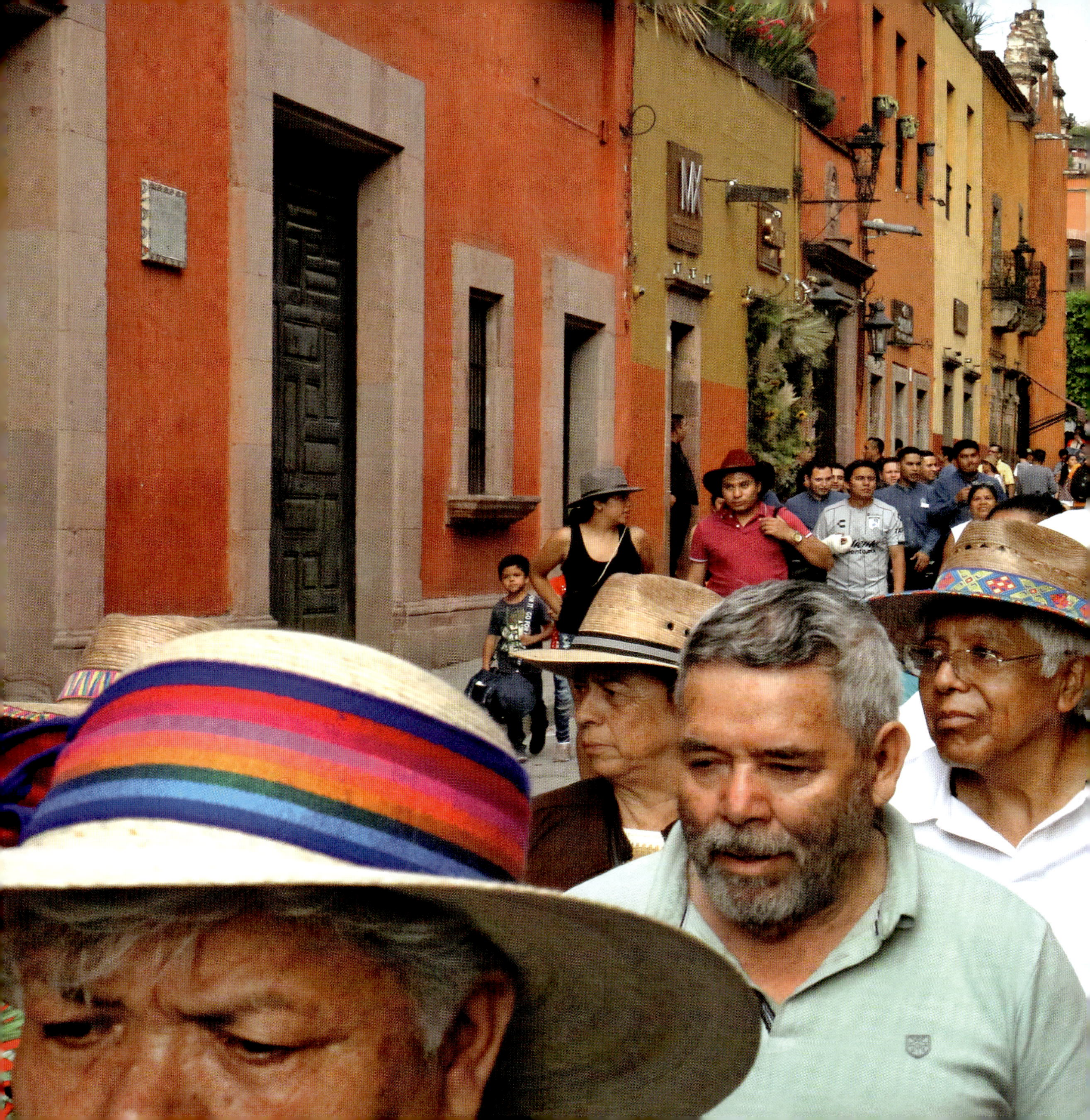

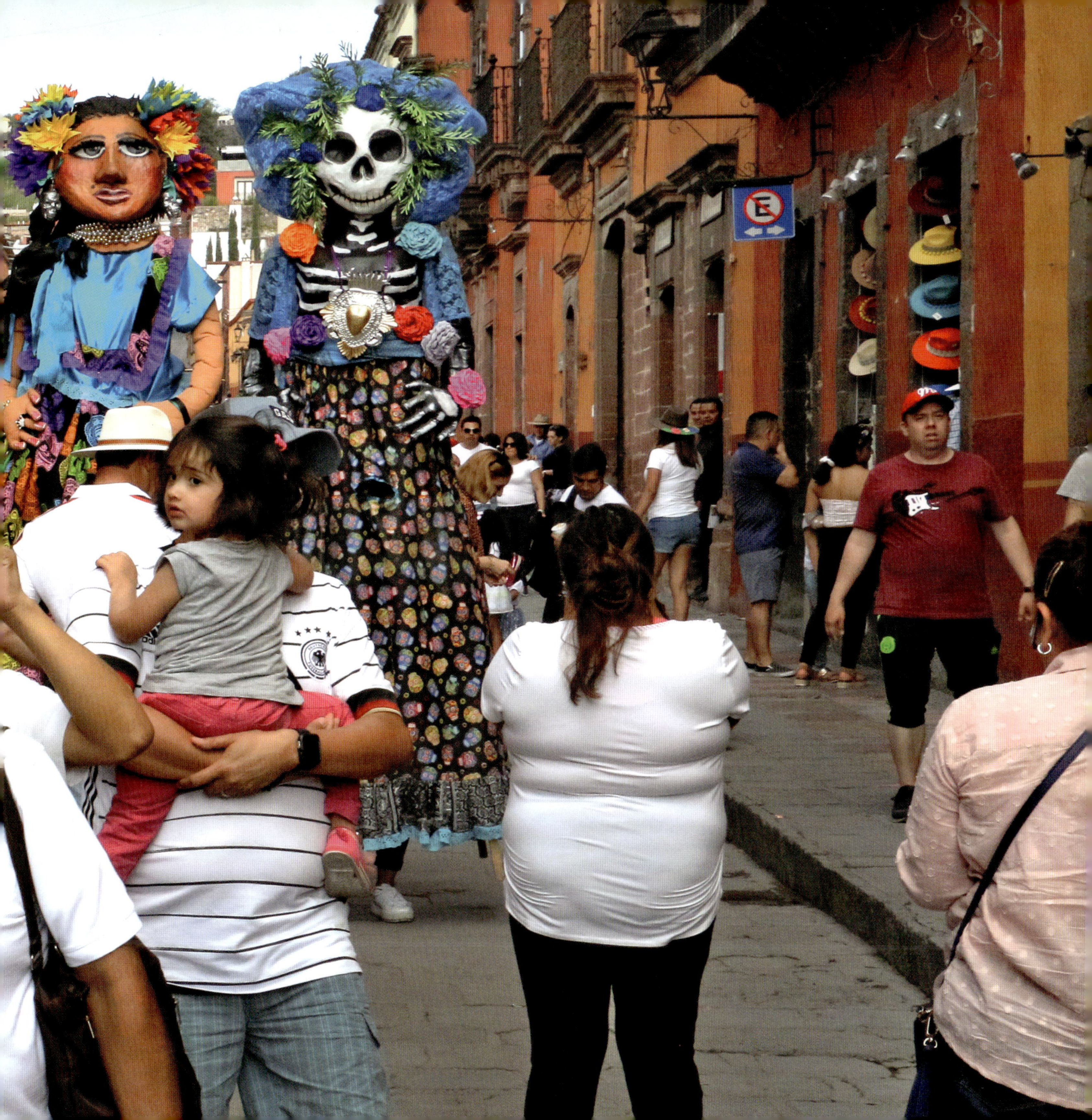
E

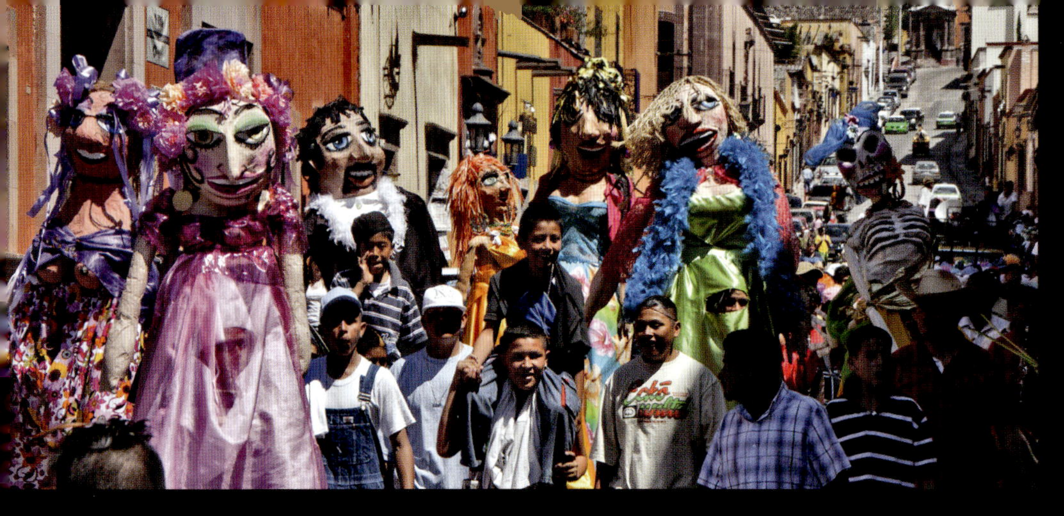
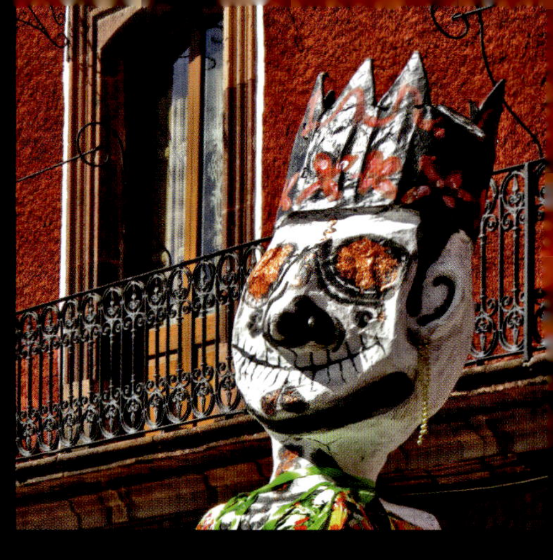
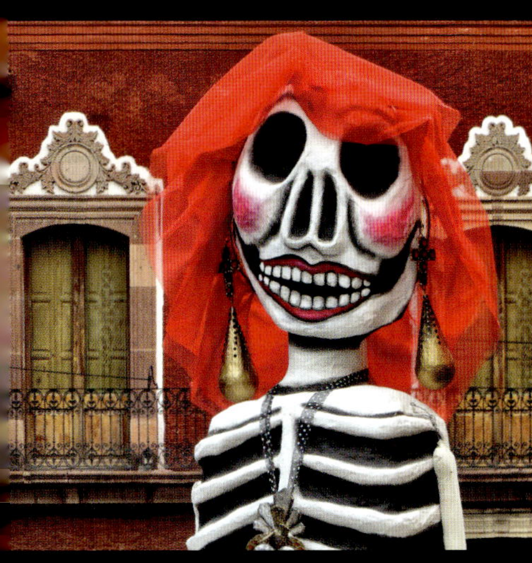
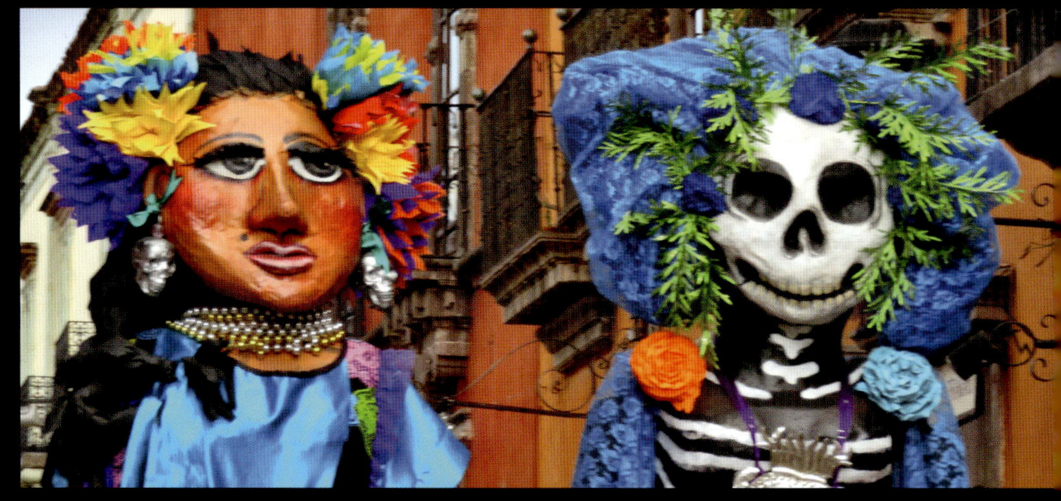
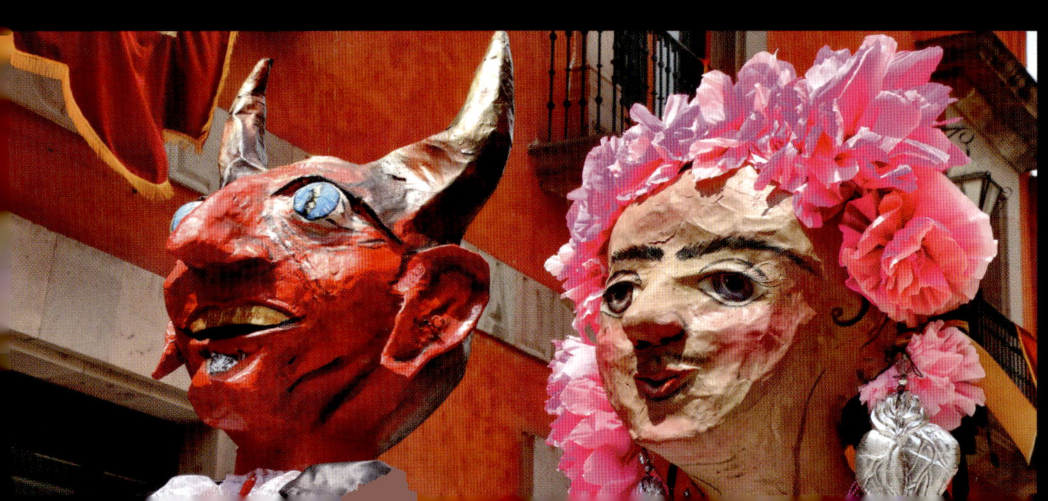
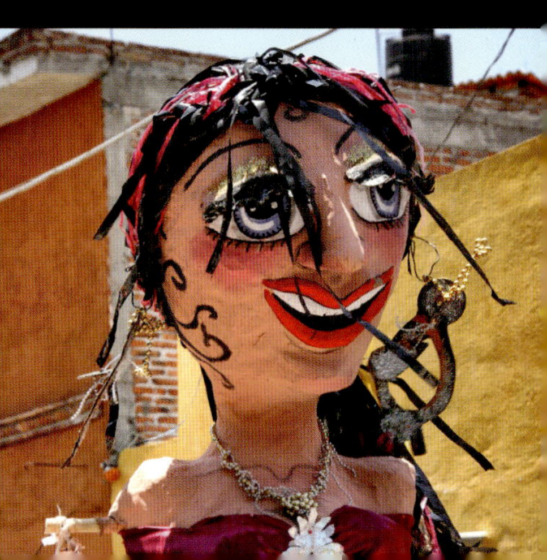

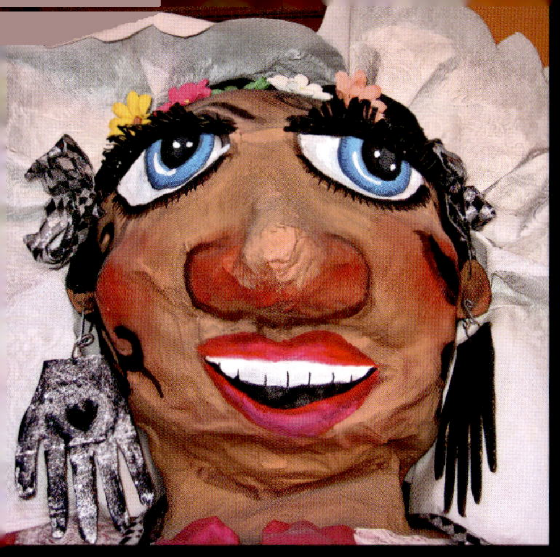

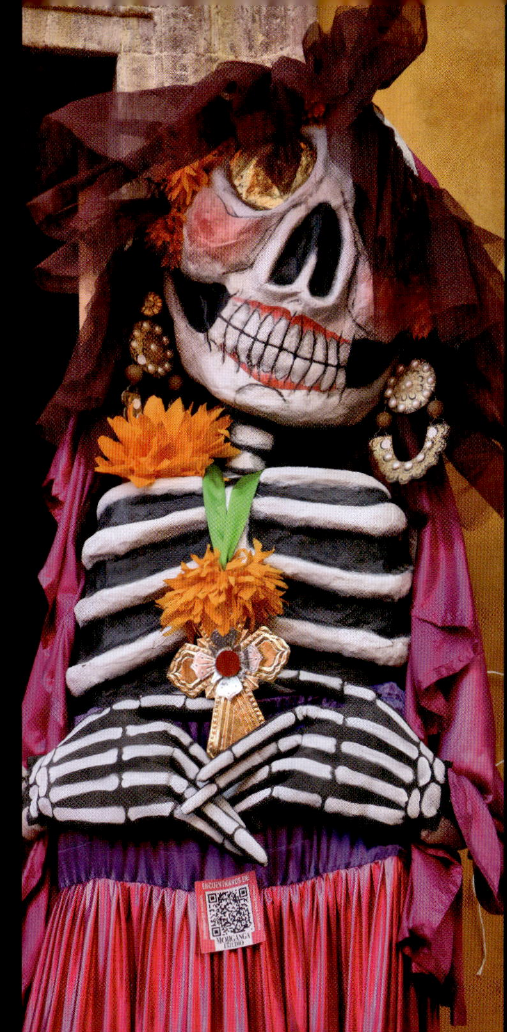

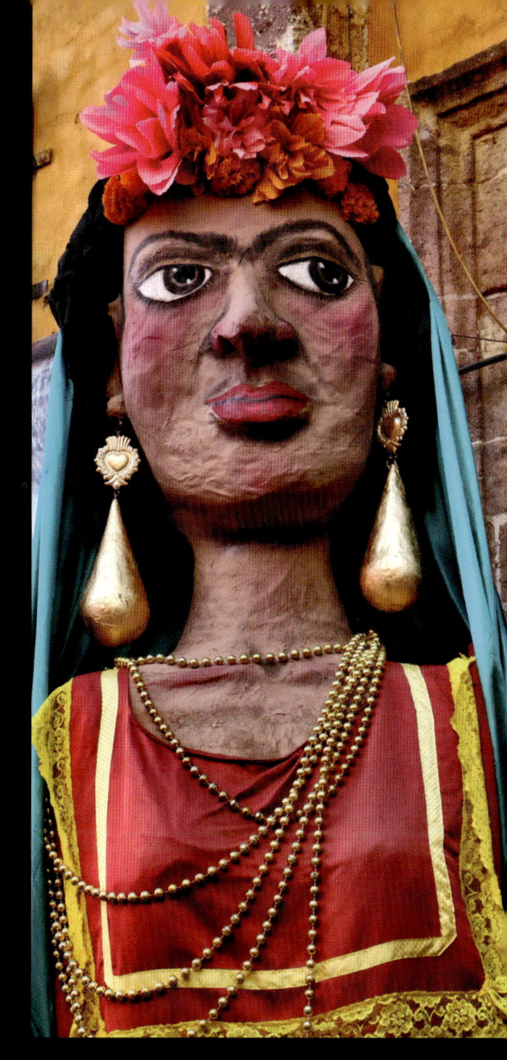

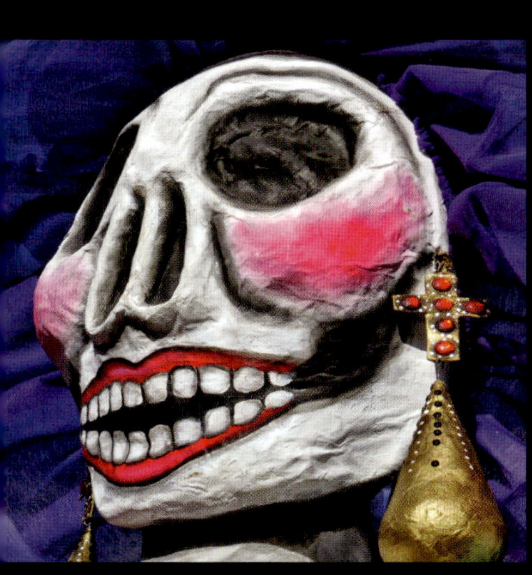

The art of papier-mâché, called cartonería in Mexico, vas introduced by the Spaniards some 400 years ıgo, though the art dates to China, 2,200 years ago. Mexican artisans use cartonería to make piñatas, anciful creatures, masks, and dolls, and it is often ısed as an inexpensive way of creating sacred figures n churches. Larger-than-life papier-mâché figures n colorful dress wander and dance in the streets of San Miguel and accompany most celebrations. These mojigangas, also called catrinas during Day of he Dead, were originally created to be destroyed during the burning of the Judases. In San Miguel, hese mojigangas are part of the general population nd spend their time celebrating with everyone else.

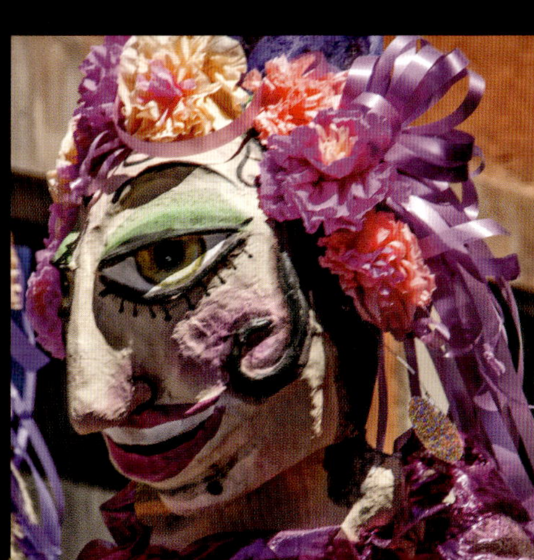

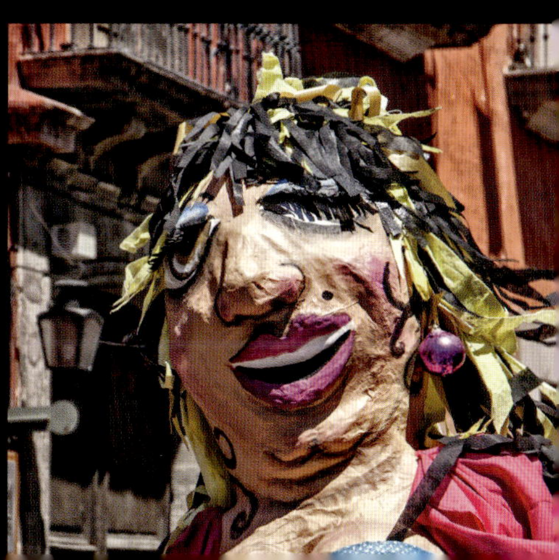

Architecture

At 6,200 feet in altitude, the sharp, clear lines of shadows embellish the colorful walls of San Miguel with layers of patterns cast from exquisitely carved stone moldings, ornate lanterns, balconies draped in greenery. Lime-washed colors glow in the sunlight as though they are illuminated from within. San Miguel has a complex mix of centuries of architectural styles, protected by the National Institute of Anthropology and History. Declared a National Monument in 1926, San Miguel's historic center has long been protected from modern intrusions such as traffic lights, billboards, neon signs, and most fast-food franchises. When San Miguel was declared a World Heritage site by UNESCO in 2008, the protected Centro was expanded.

Ancient stone walls are draped with bougainvillea; cobblestone streets lend an old-world clatter to passing vehicles; intricately carved stone churches grace every neighborhood, the music of their bells adorning every hour. The main square, the Jardín, is the center of life, its shady benches always filled, the balloon sellers adding colorful bouquets to the swirl of humanity. Birds twitter in the carefully shaped trees, fountains cool the air, and mariachi music wraps around lovers kissing on the benches or dancing in the plaza. The newspaper seller, the shoeshine man, the horse-drawn wagon selling homemade ice cream, children gleefully running . . . this dance of life plays out every day in this Jardín, so exuberant, so alive with life, what life can be when a community and the families that make it come together in the simple joys of visiting with friends, sharing gossip, and watching children play.

Spanish colonial architecture, often named Mexican baroque, is a fascinating, unique style. Sitting quietly observing the moldings, one can almost feel the flow of Moorish traditions from North Africa into southern Spain, then across the ocean to mix with local materials and Indigenous masons to become what it is here in San Miguel, luscious in color, texture, shadow, ornate moldings, and balconies. Most of the old walls are stone or adobe, plastered over and colored with "cal," lime wash colored with natural pigments. The result is walls that are bold yet soft, feeling almost alive to the touch. Cantera, a volcanic stone that can be found throughout the country in shades of gray to black, pink, orange, lavender, lime green, white, and brown, is the material of choice for carved moldings that grace nearly every building.

Facades are further decorated with potted plants along the roofs, garlands of flowers around doorways, and exquisitely ornate balconies. Decorative light fixtures cast wild shadows; crosses or small statues crown peaks or corners. Under an ancient buttress of the San Francisco church, it is still possible to see some of the original geometric painting that once covered the church. The buildings change as the sun casts living shadows that tell the time of day and year. Decorations are hung and removed in a regular rhythm of festivities. The walls of San Miguel embrace their inhabitants with warmth and beauty, celebrating holidays with them, echoing the music of life within every home, reflecting the love the inhabitants feel for these walls.

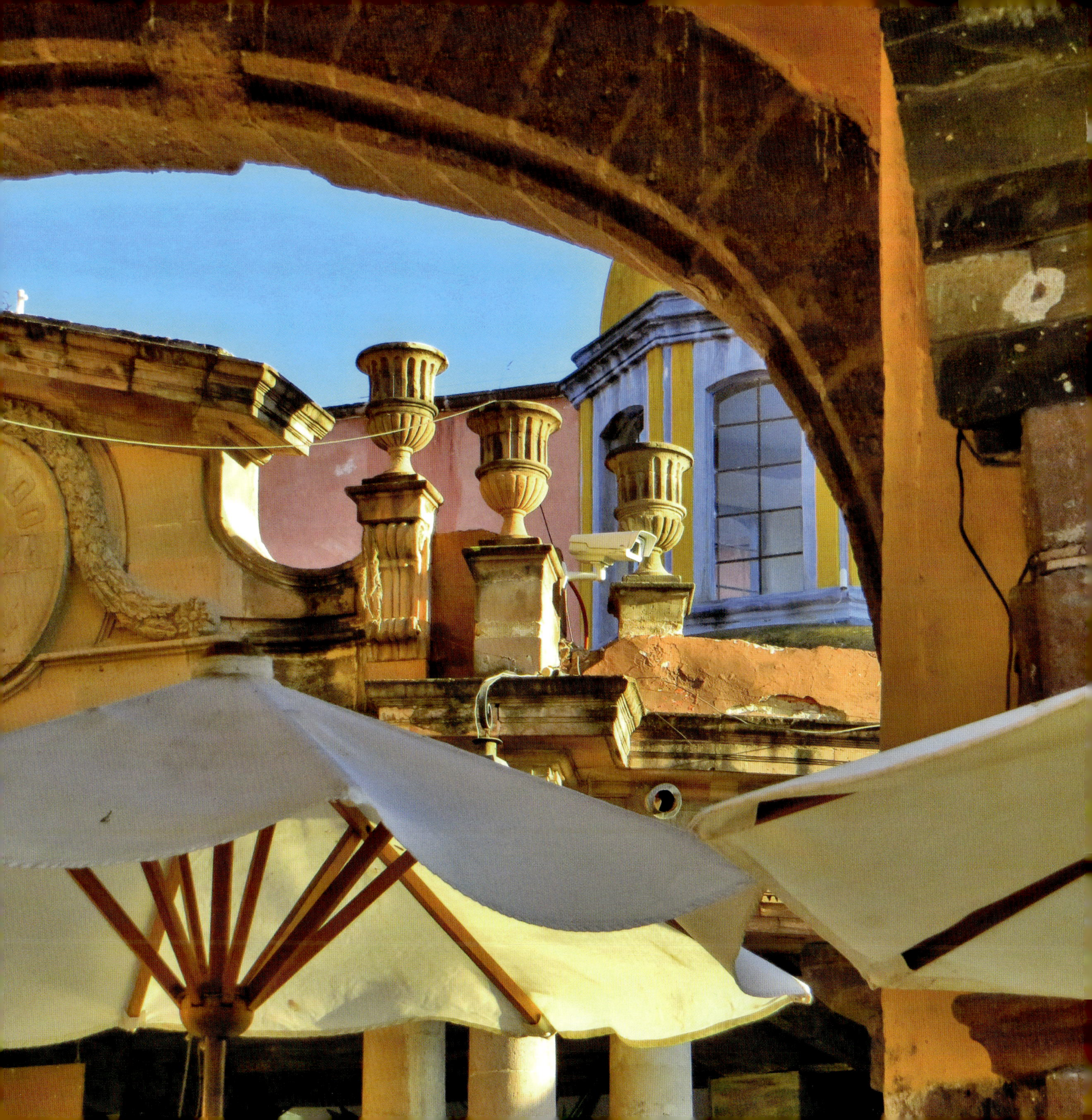

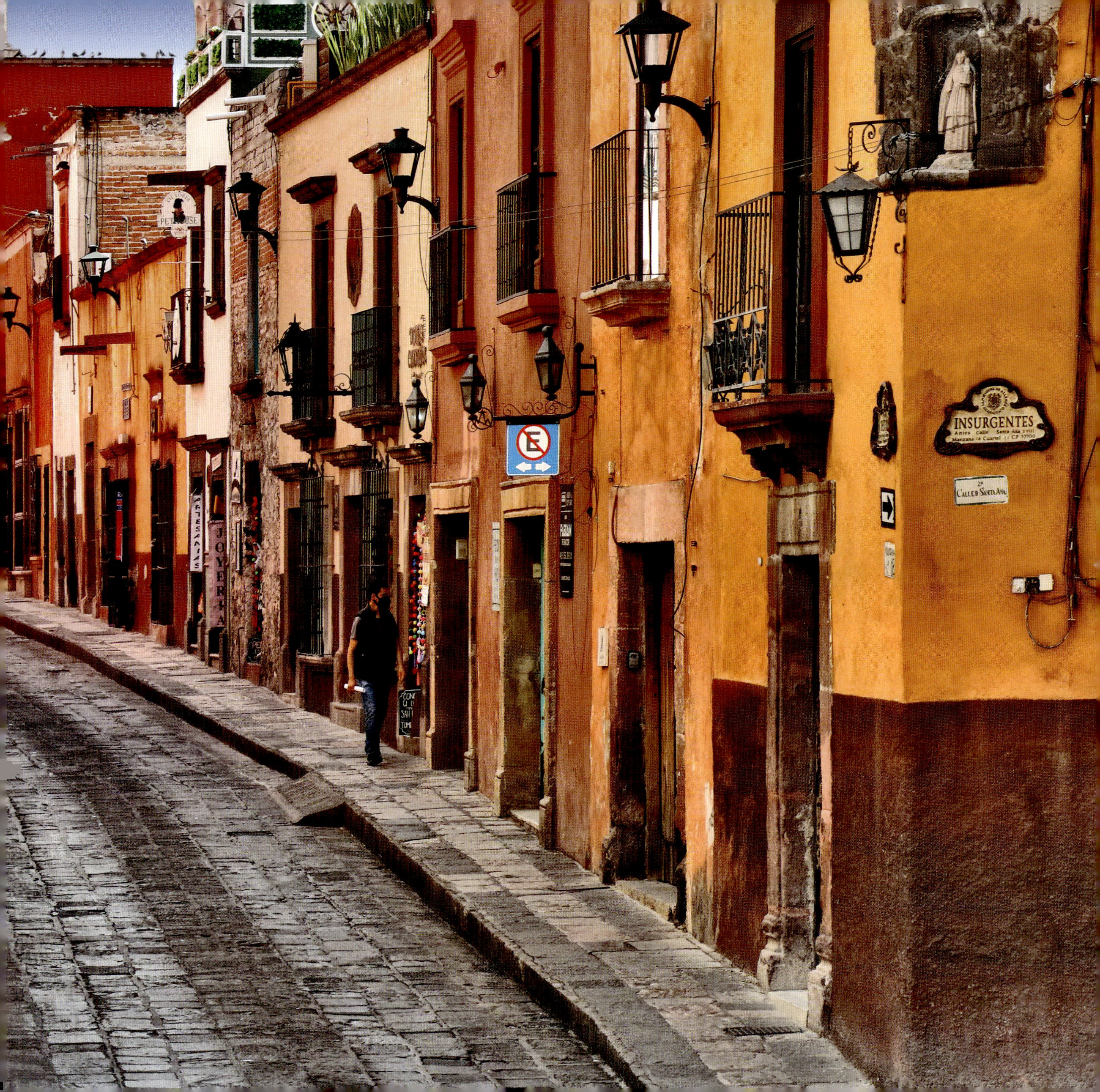
INSURGENTES
2ª
CALLE D SANTA ANA
JOYERIA

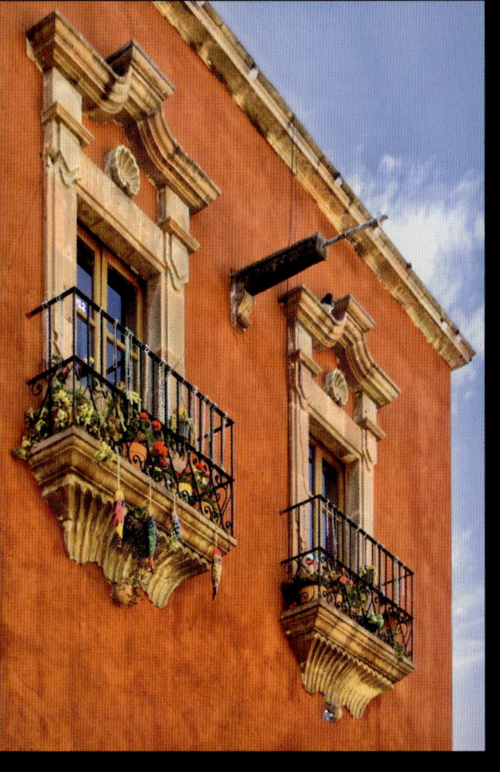

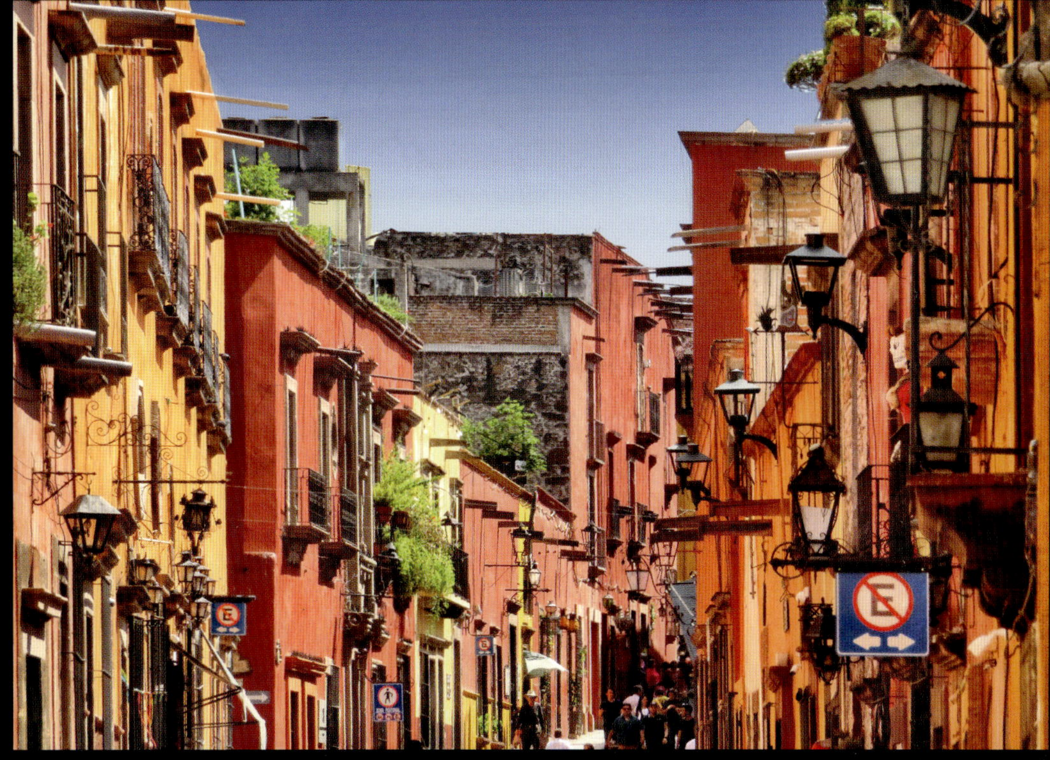

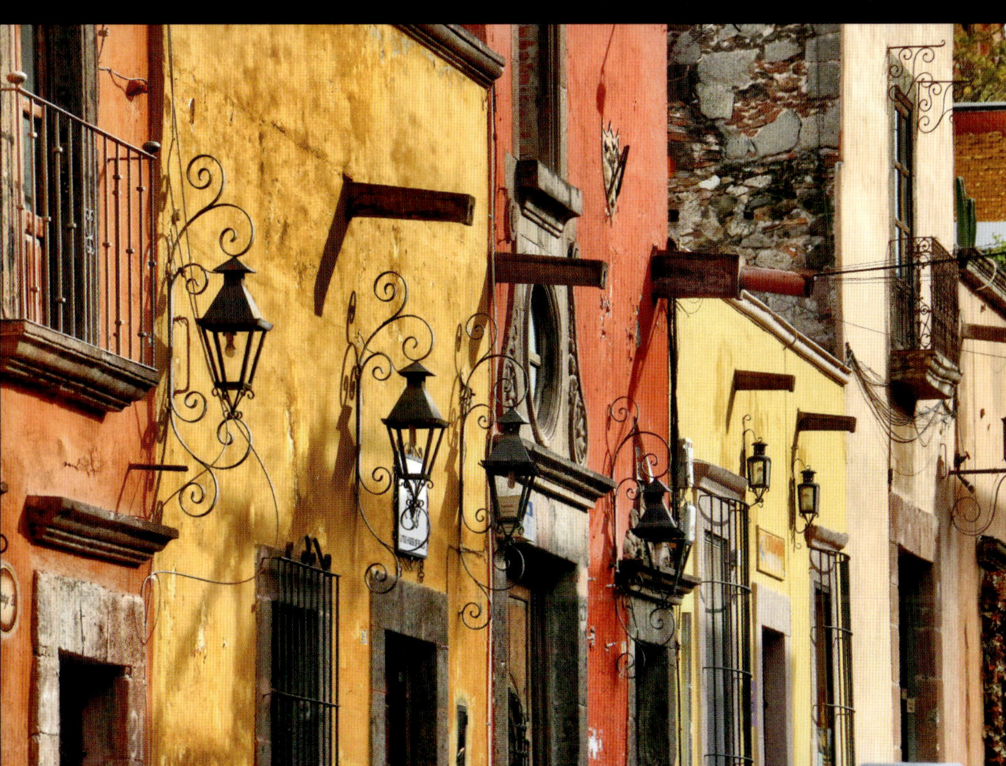

PLAZA
SAN
FRANCISCO

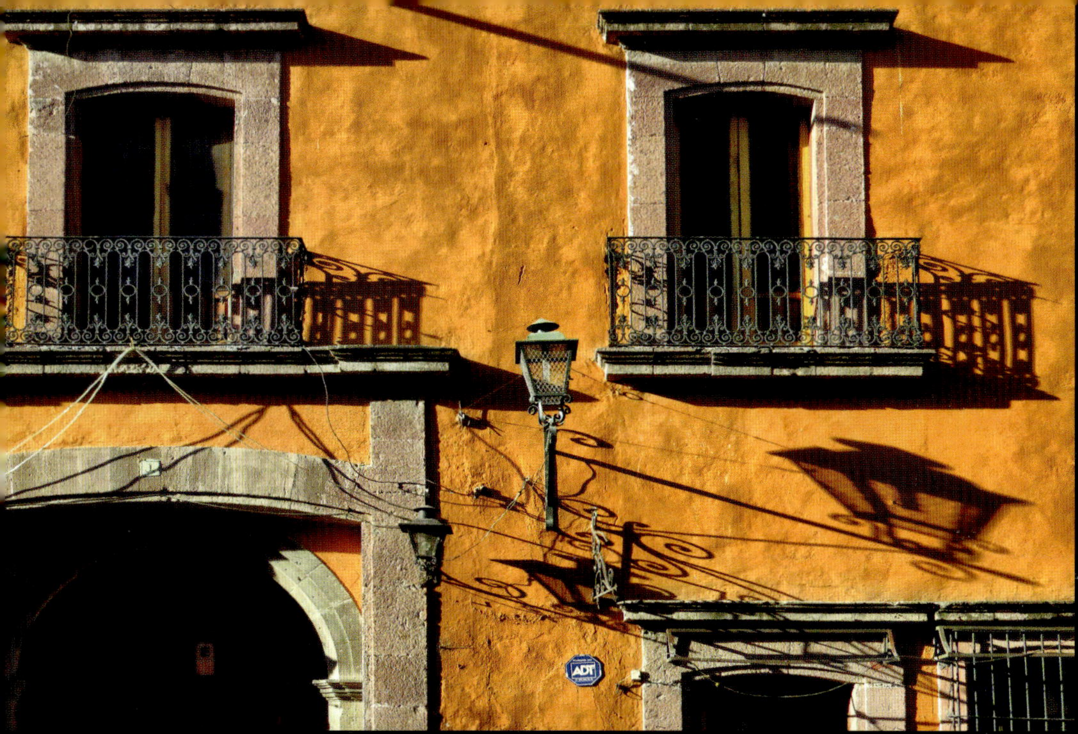

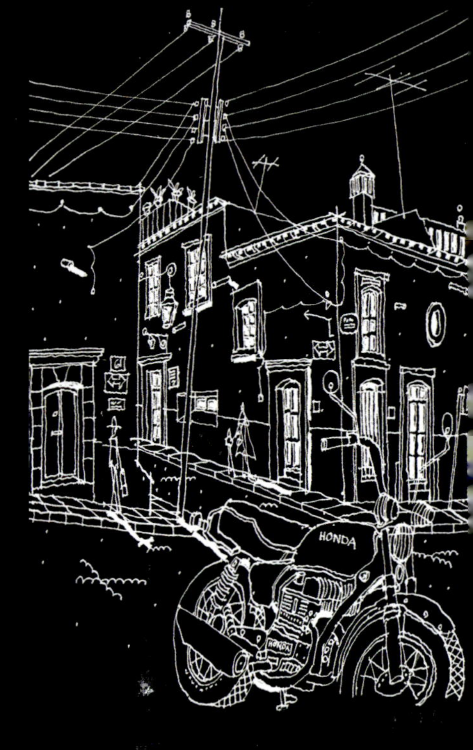
HONDA

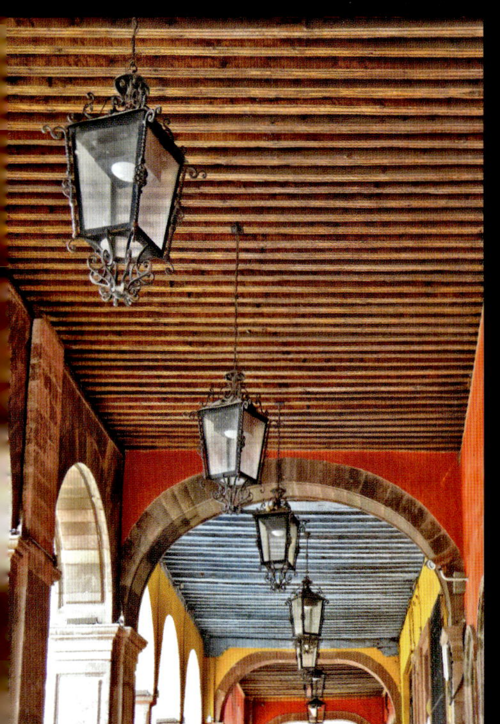

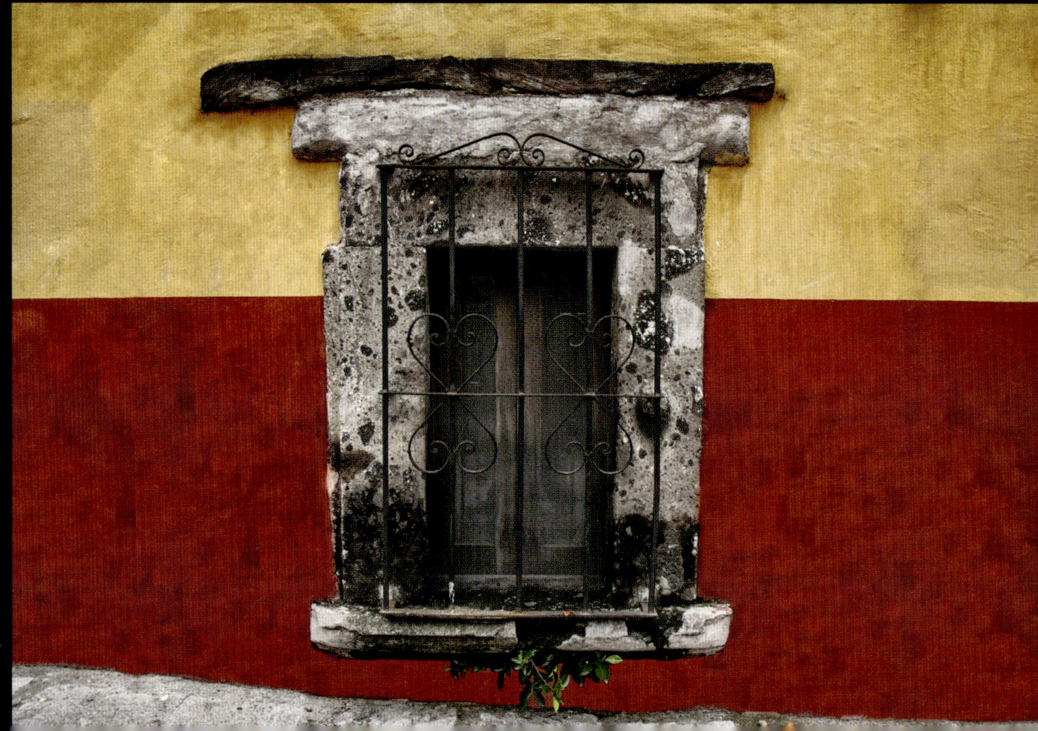

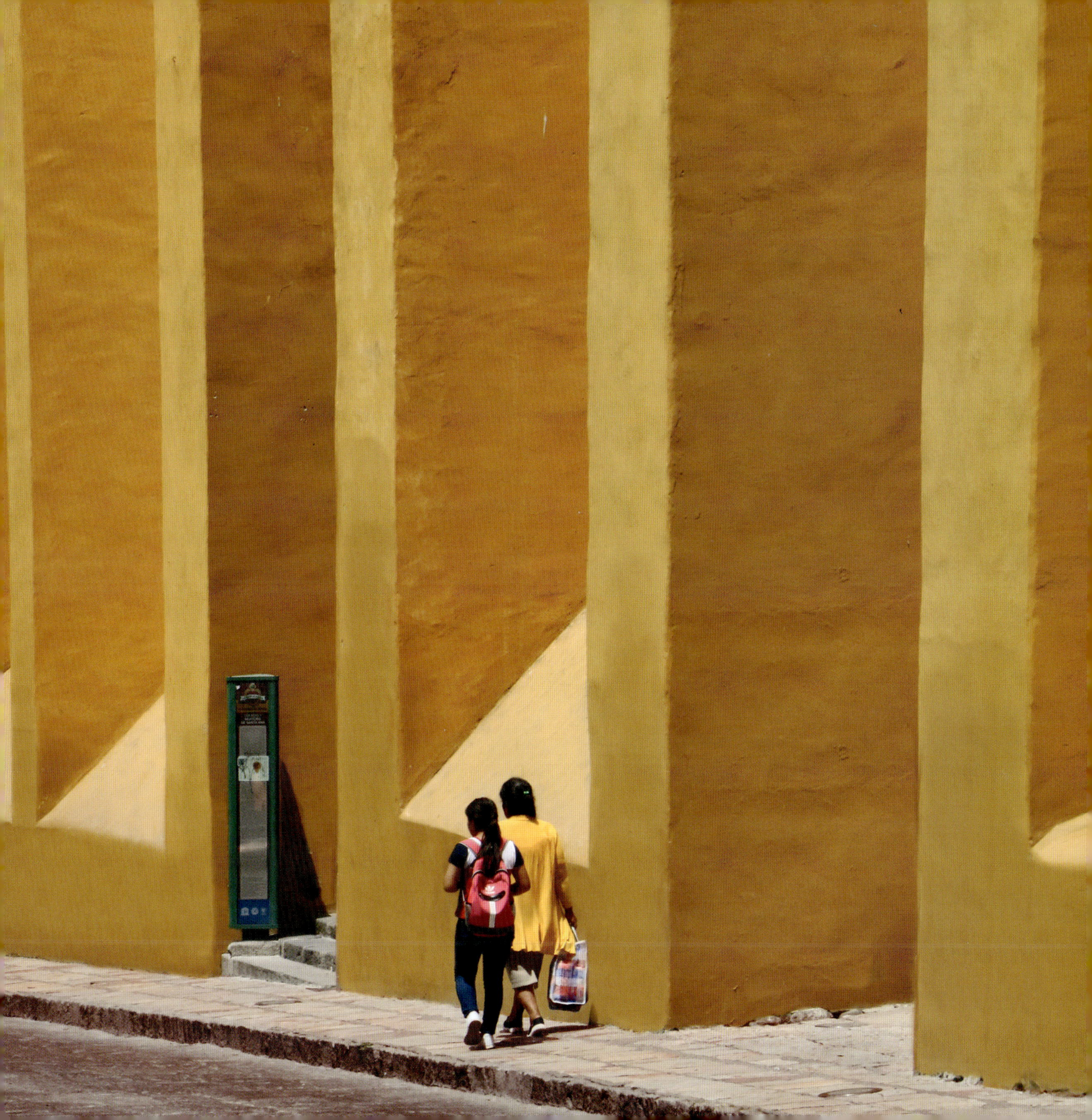

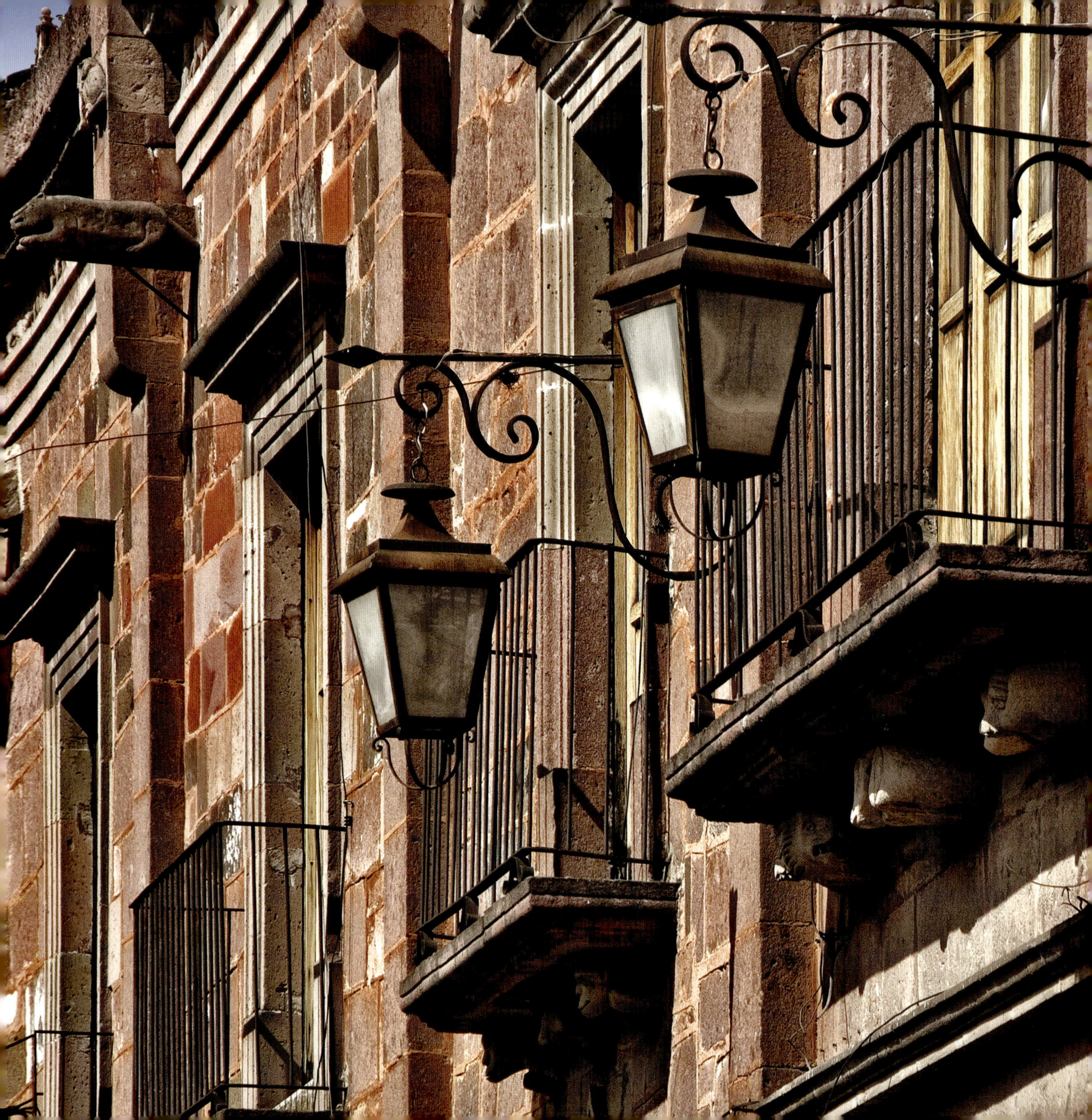

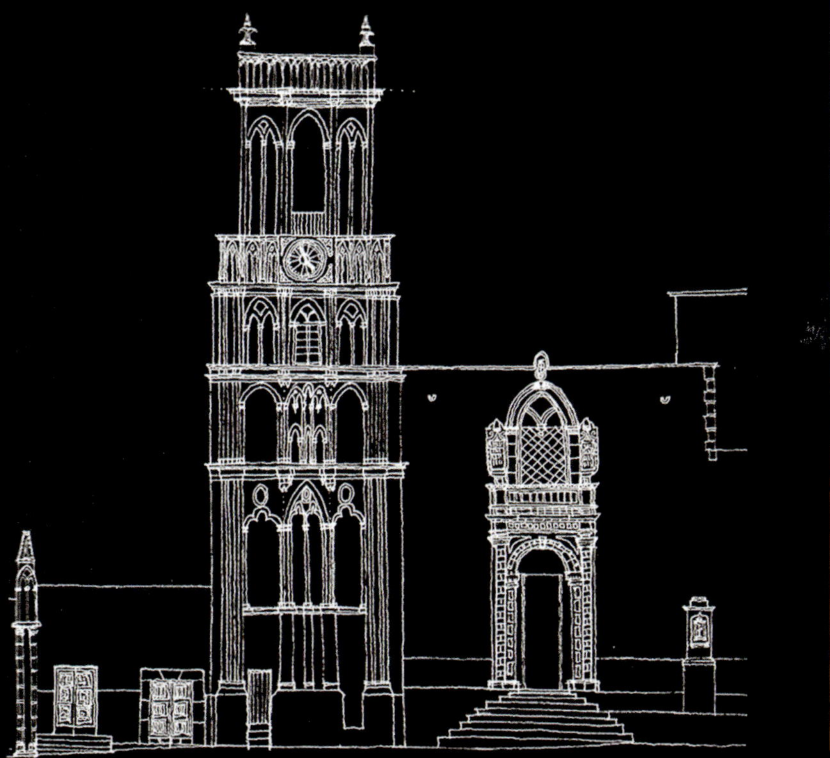

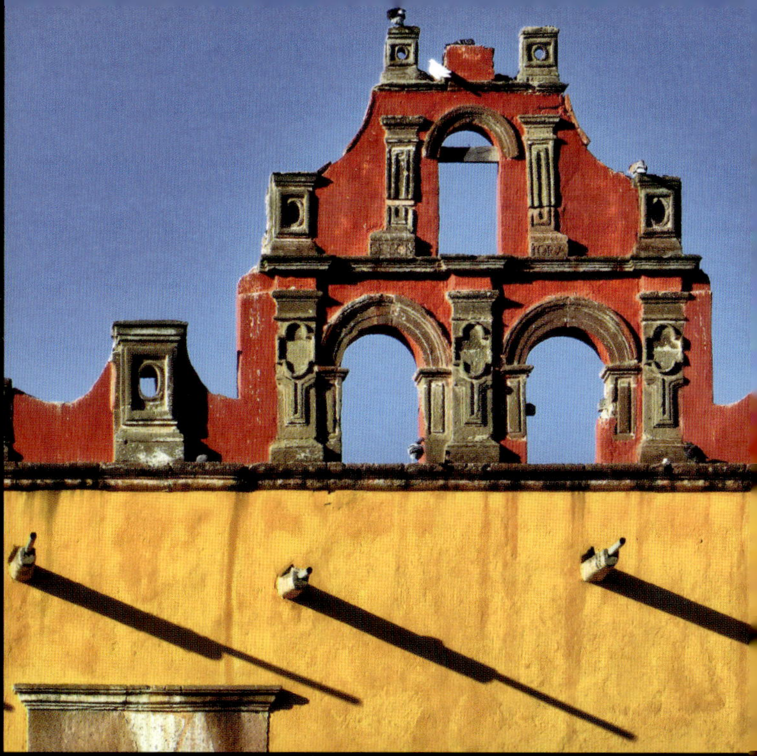

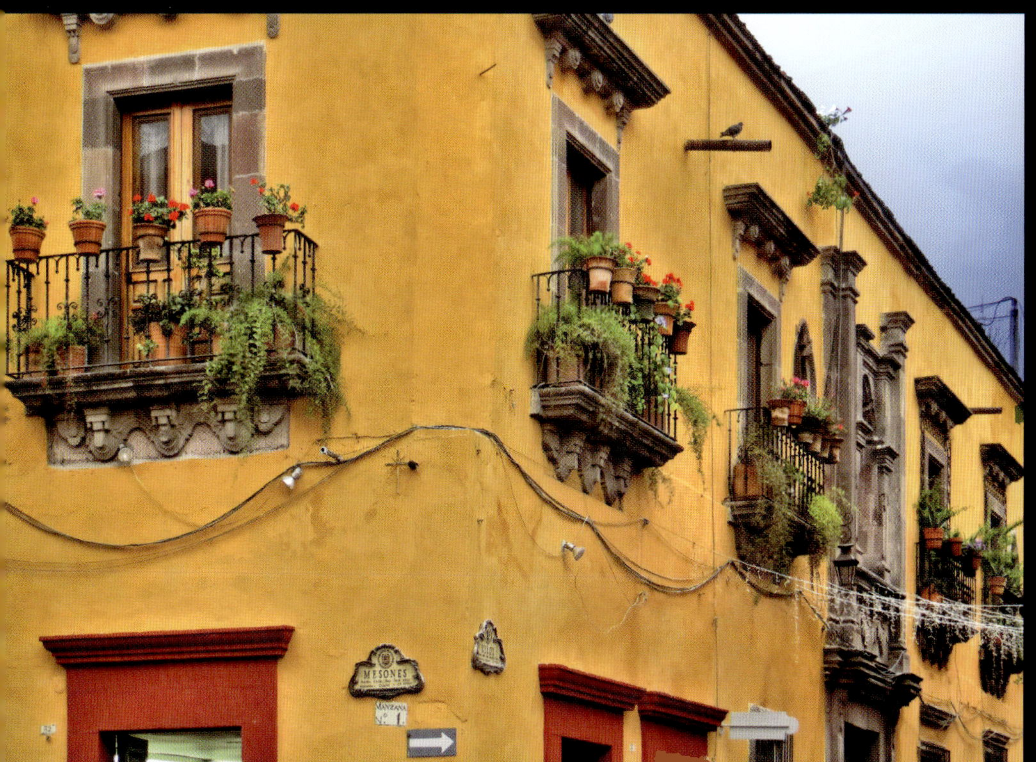
MESONES
MANZANA
Nº 1

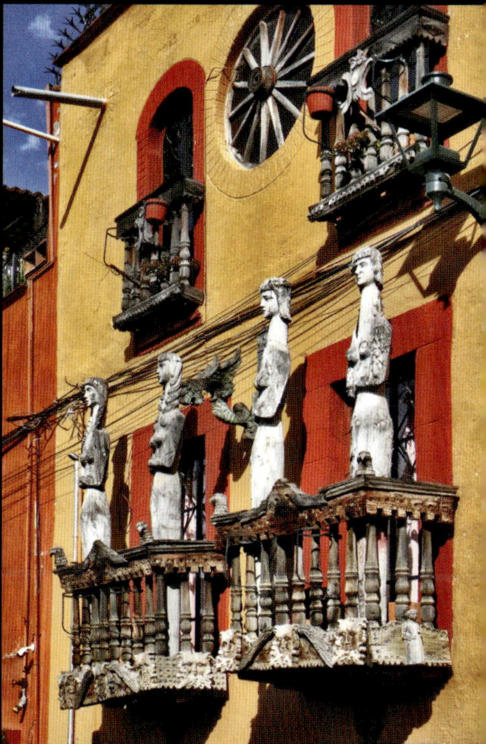

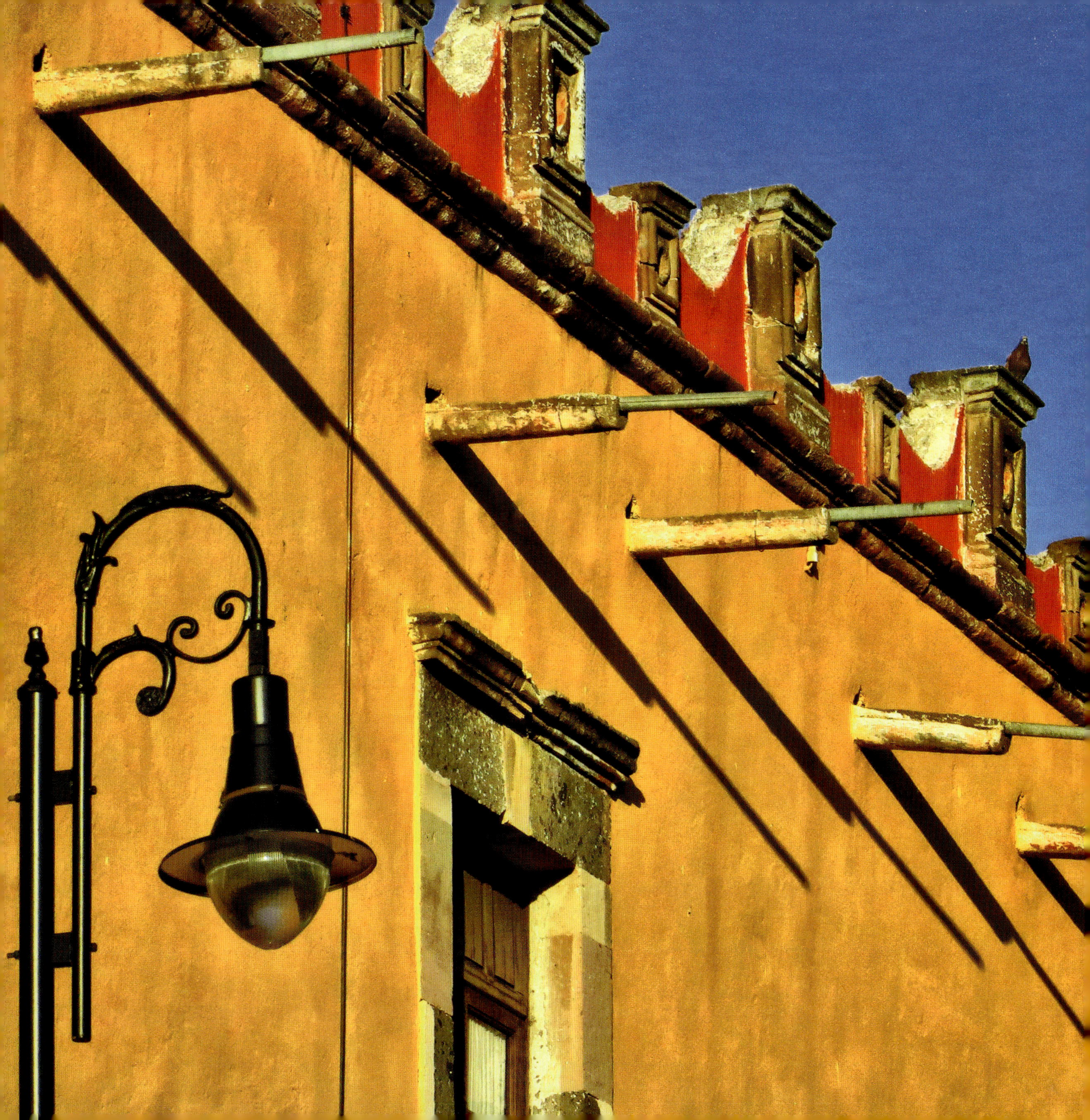

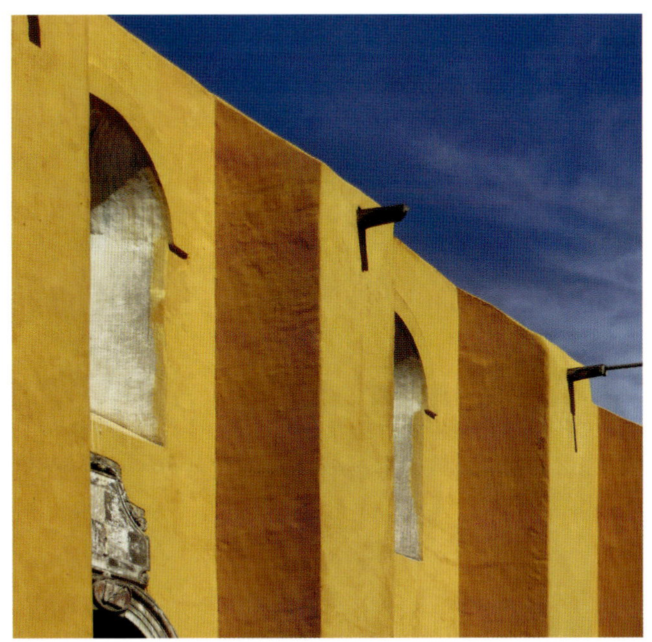

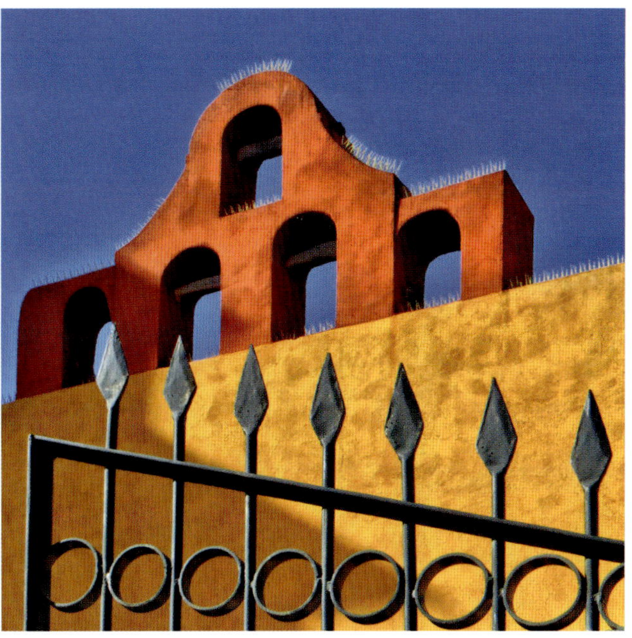

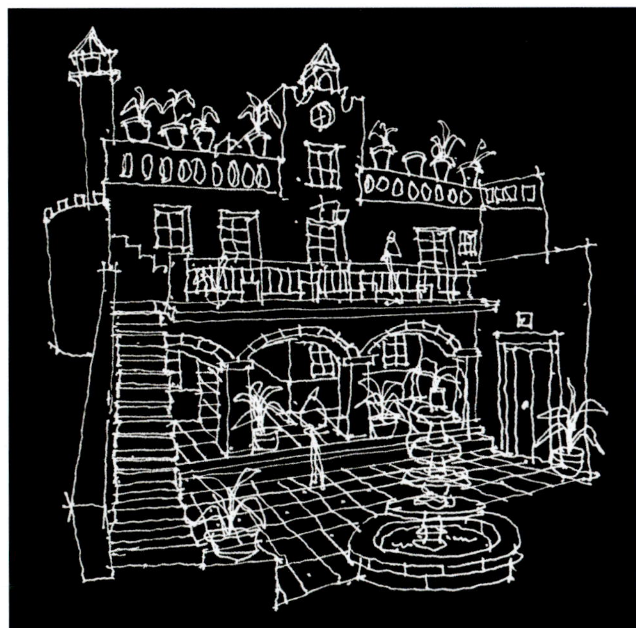

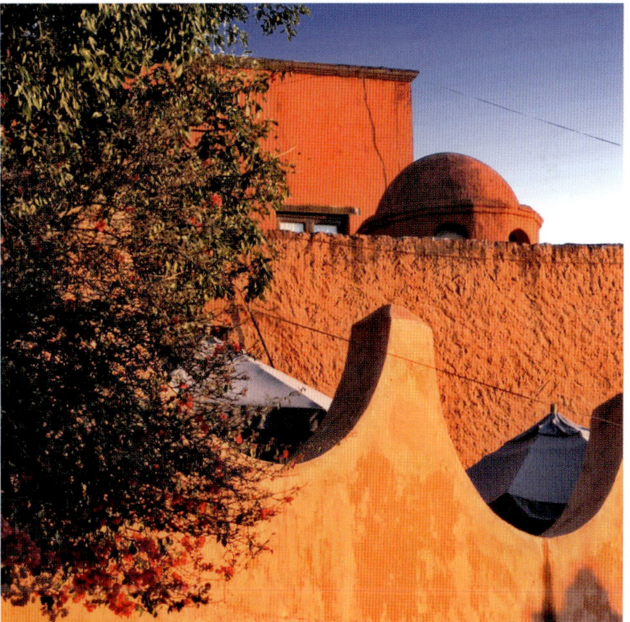

Cal, made of powdered limestone, mineral salts, and natural pigments for color, is mixed with water, then brushed by hand onto walls to form a skin that glows, as though illuminated from within, due to myriad tiny crystals. It feels warm to the touch as though alive, it is antibacterial and nontoxic, and its naturally mottled appearance is appropriate to the age of the buildings onto which it is lovingly applied.

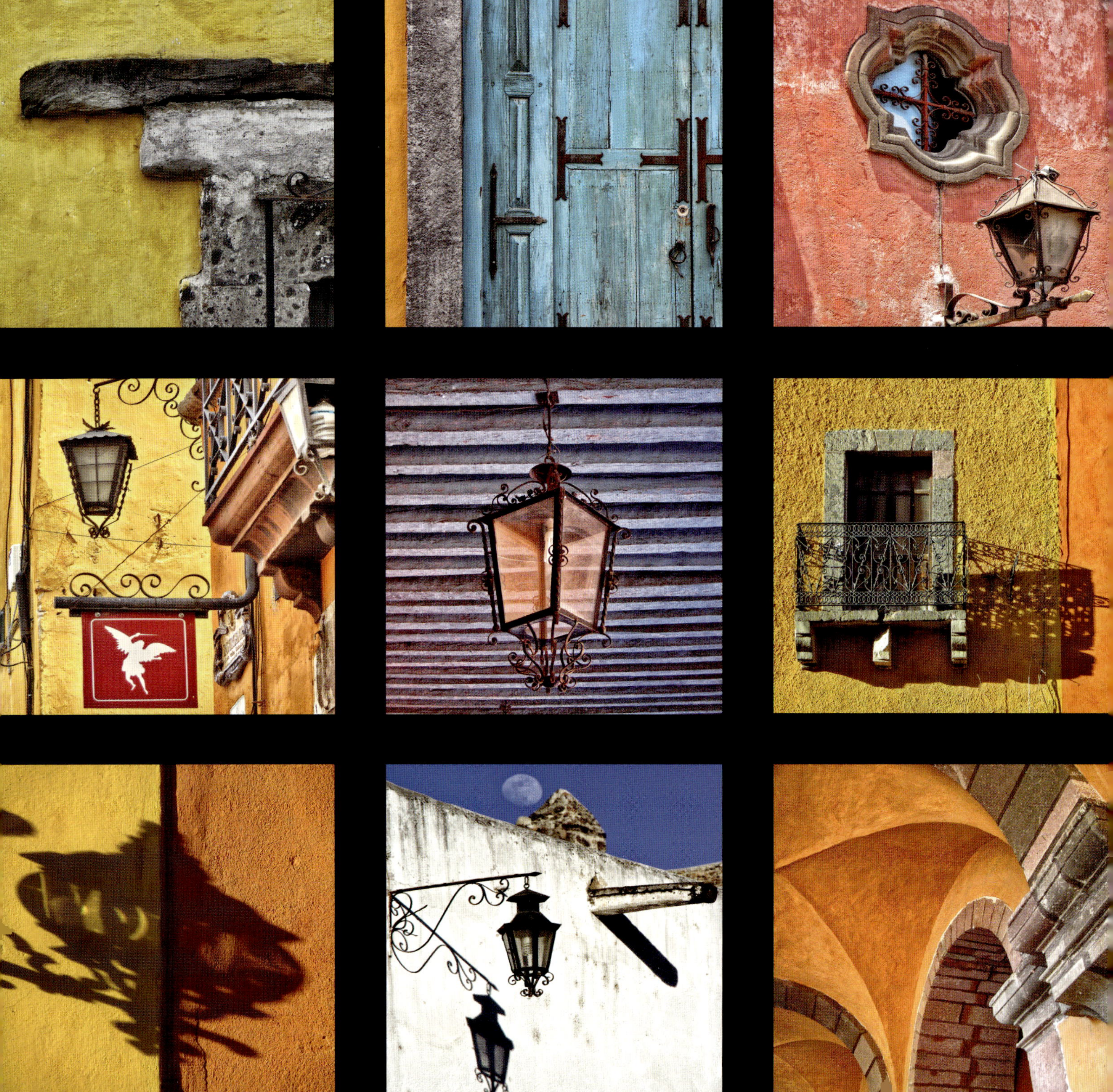

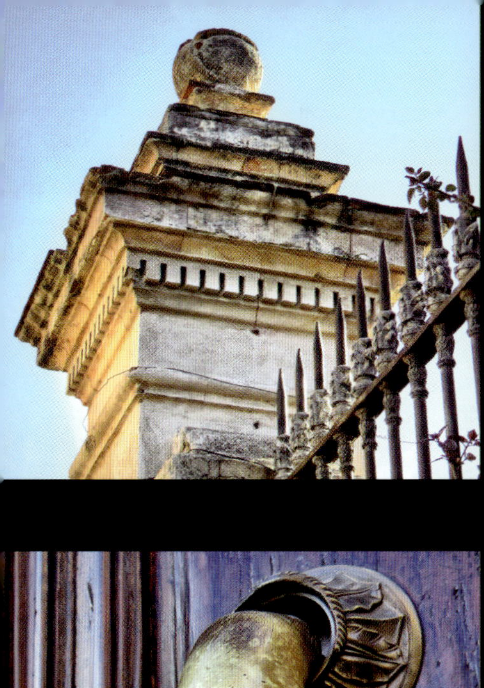

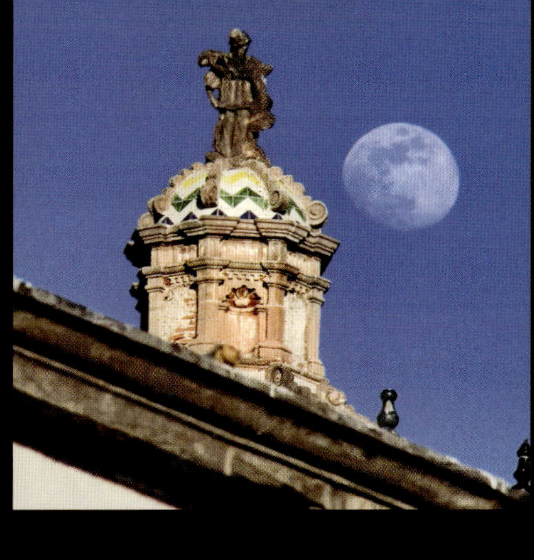

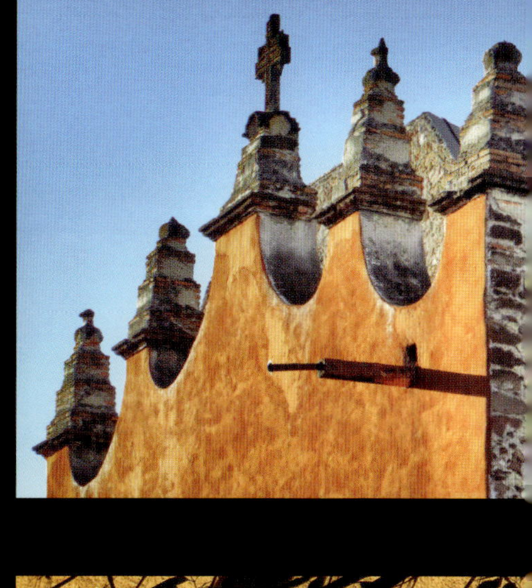

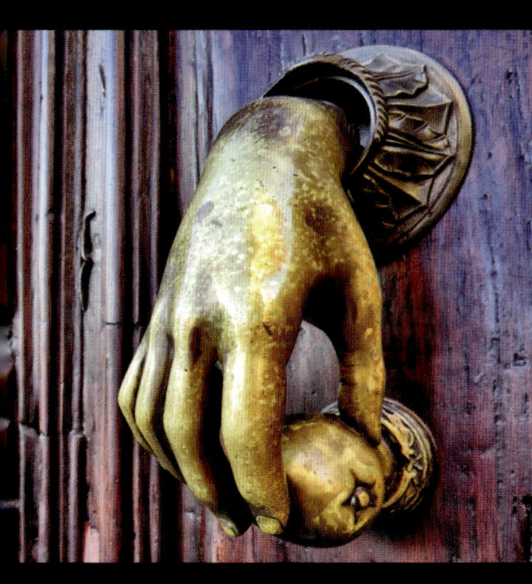

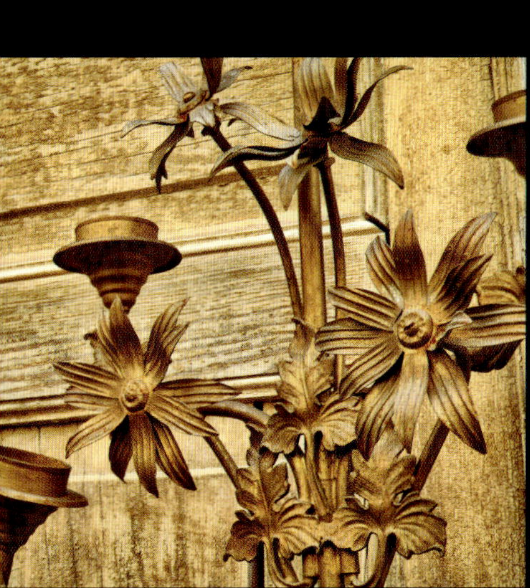

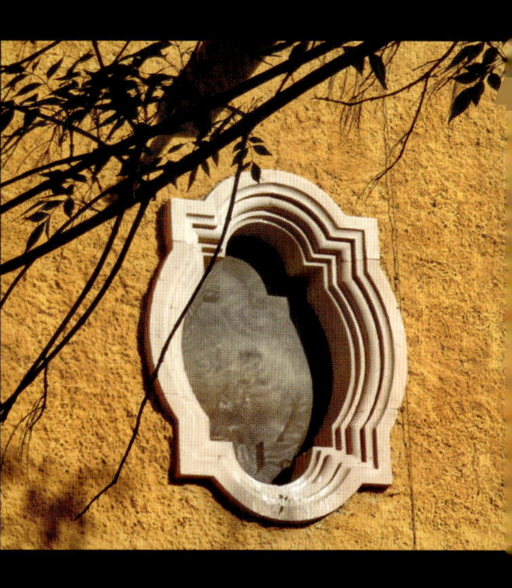

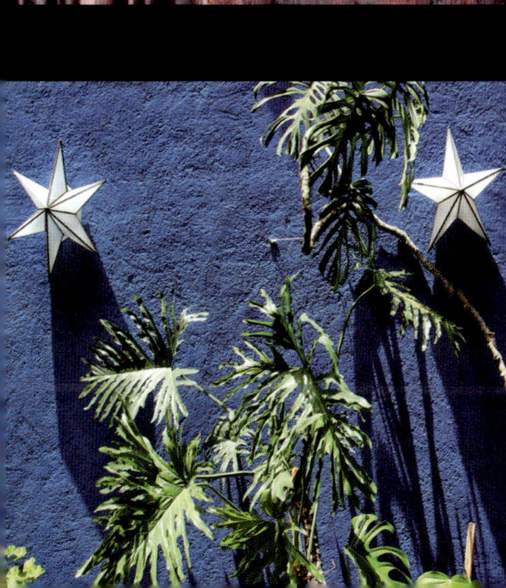

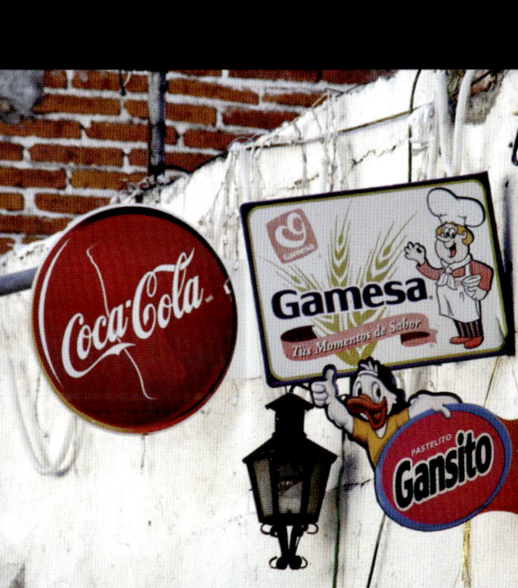
Coca-Cola
Gamesa
Tus Momentos de Sabor
PASTELITO
Gansito

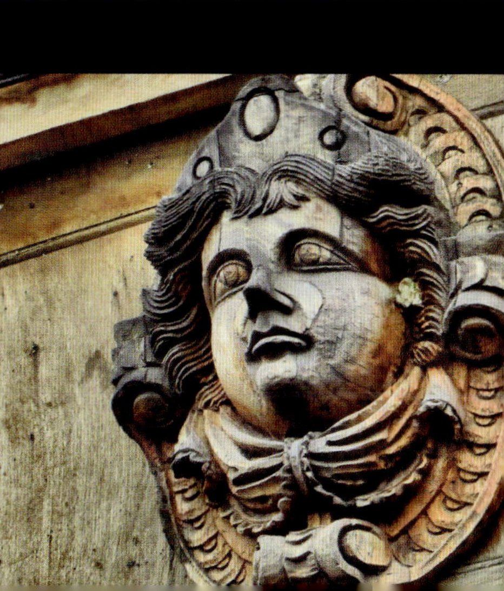

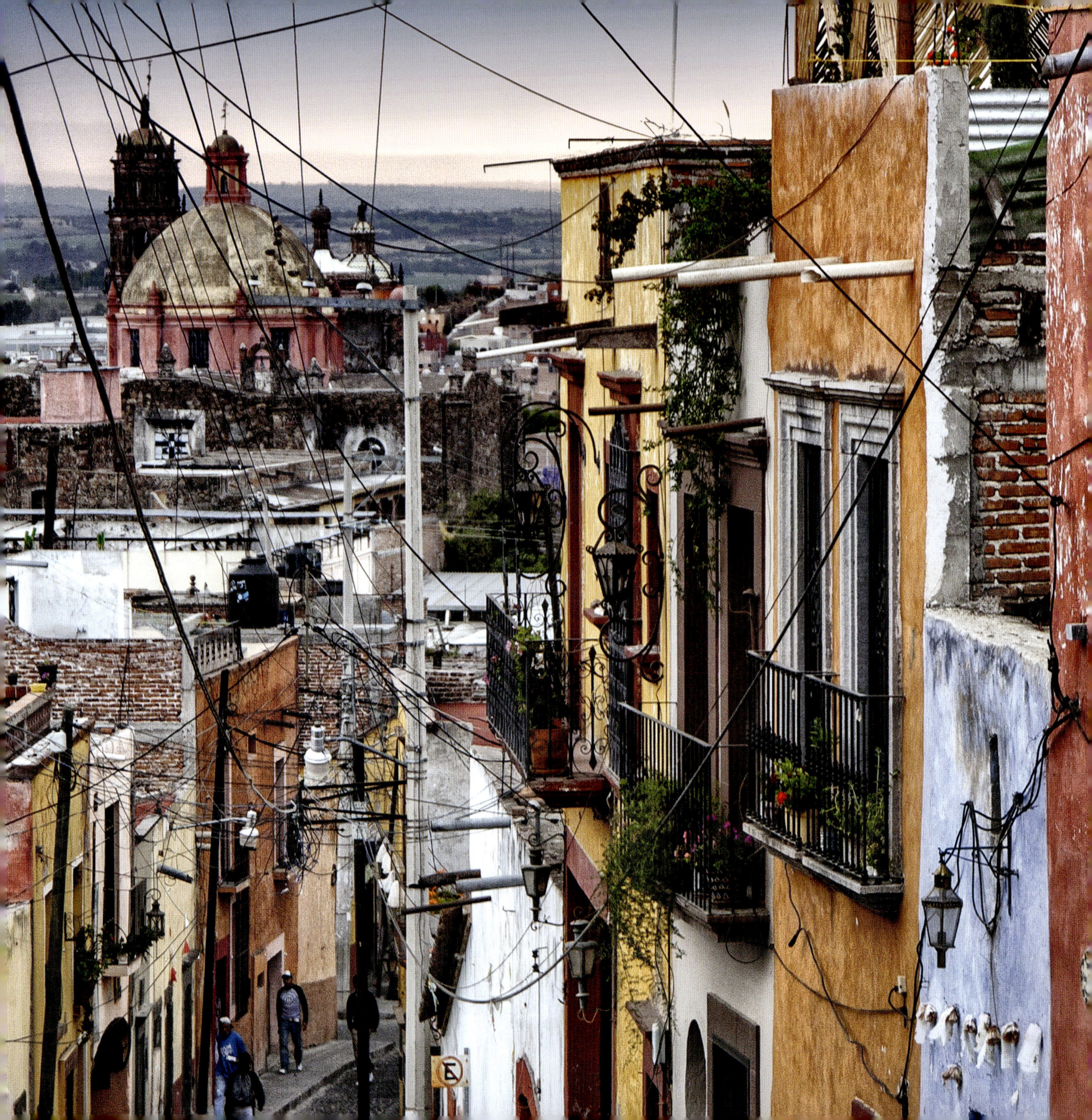

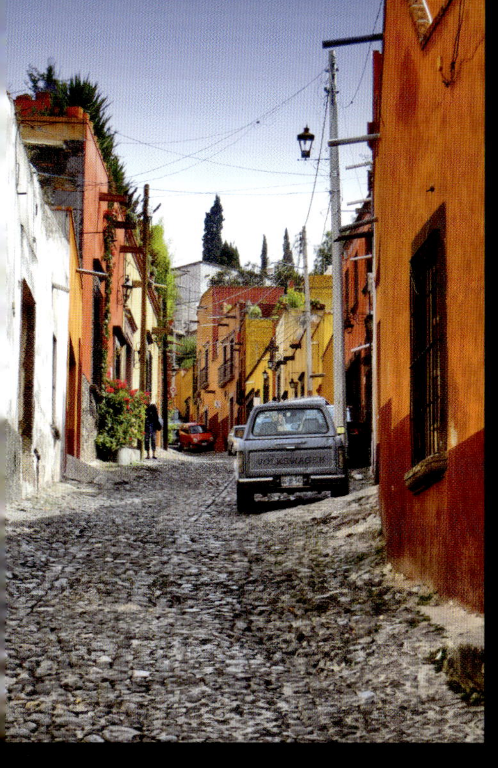
VOLKSWAGEN
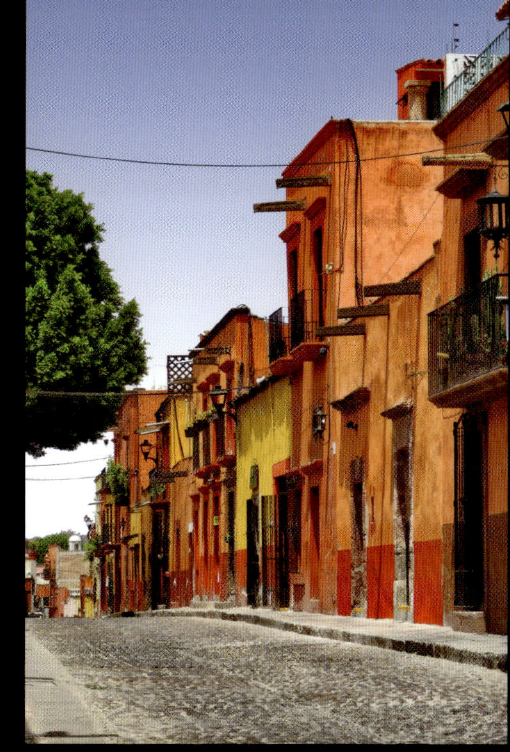
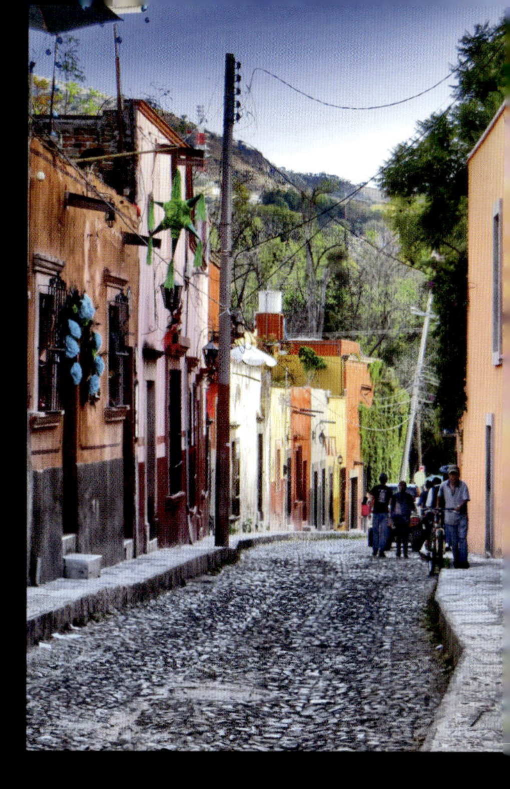
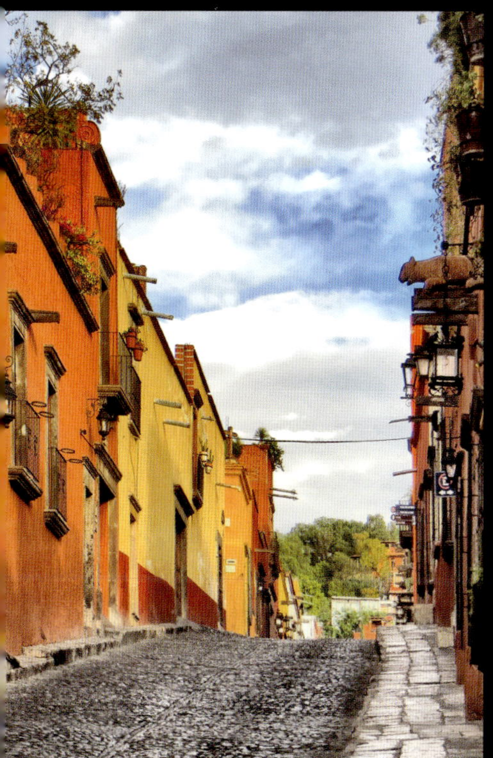
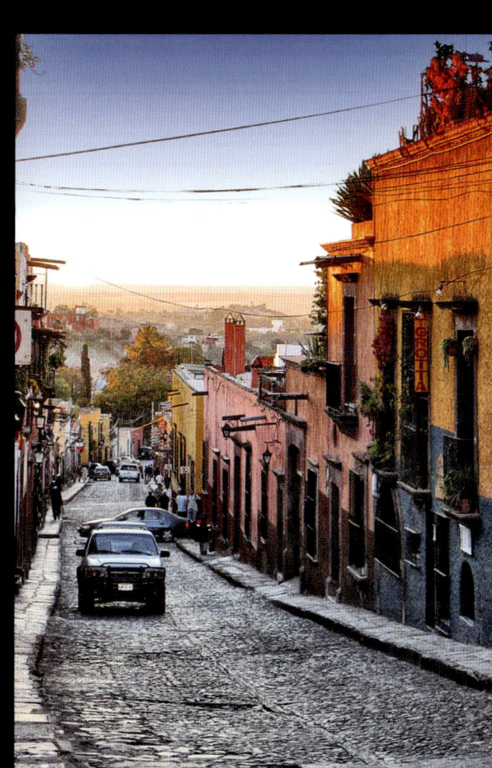
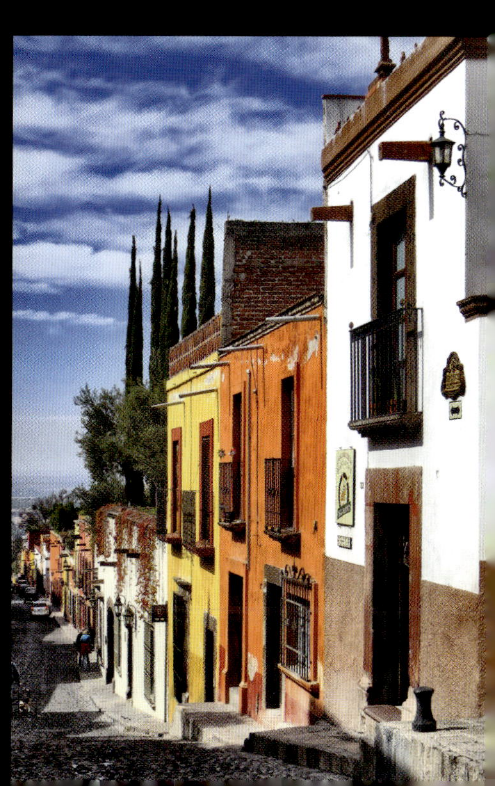

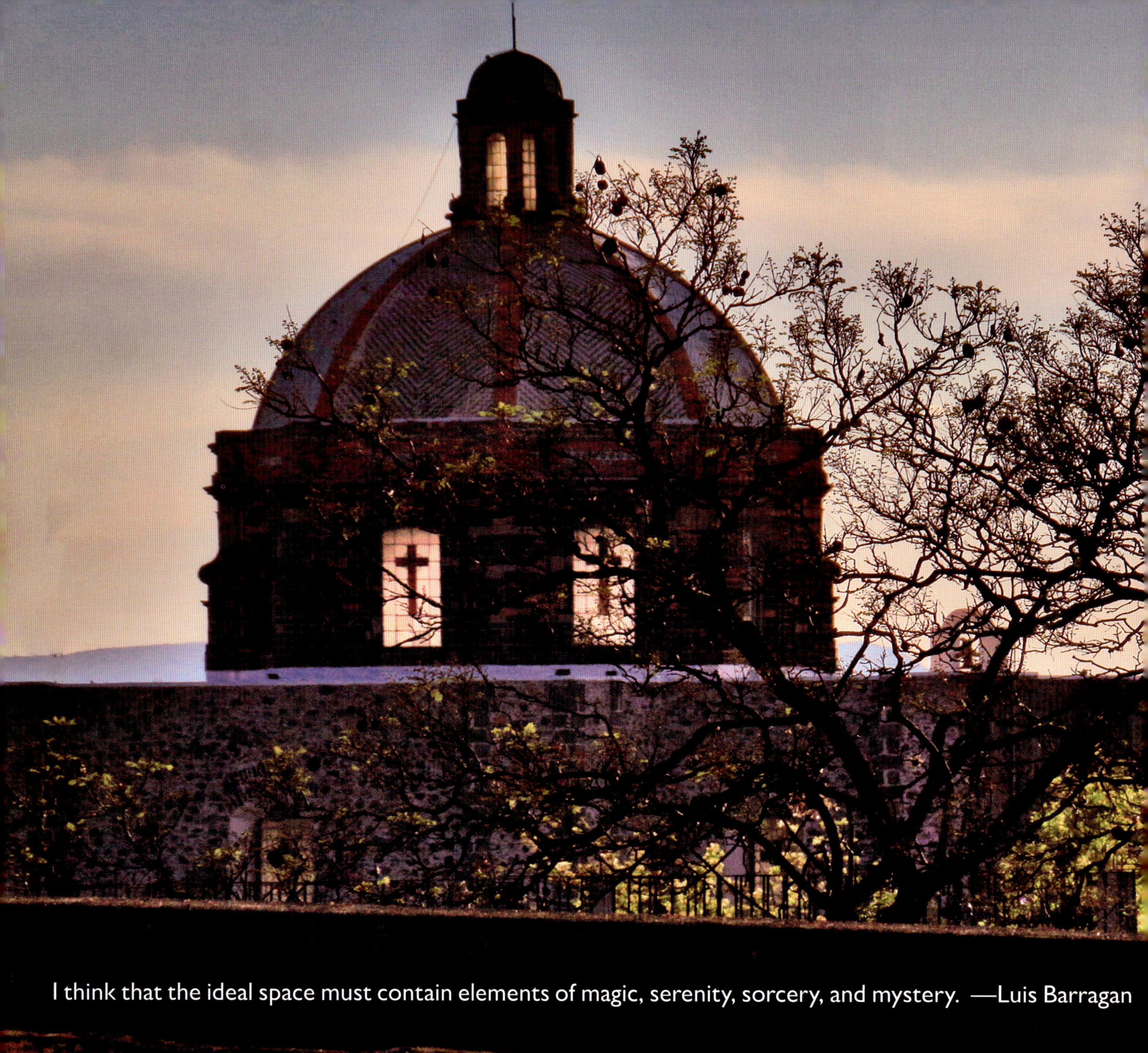

I think that the ideal space must contain elements of magic, serenity, sorcery, and mystery. —Luis Barragan

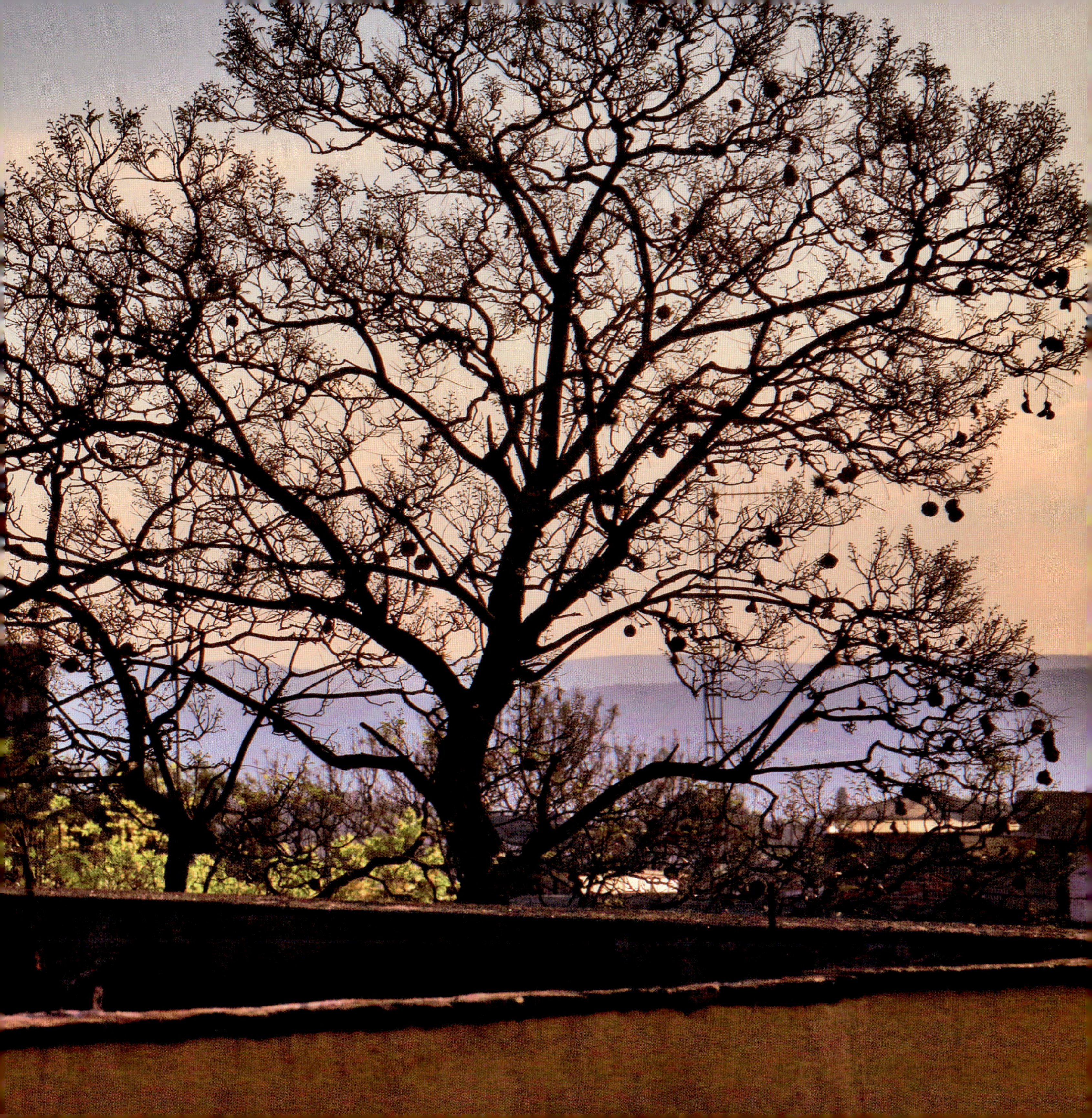

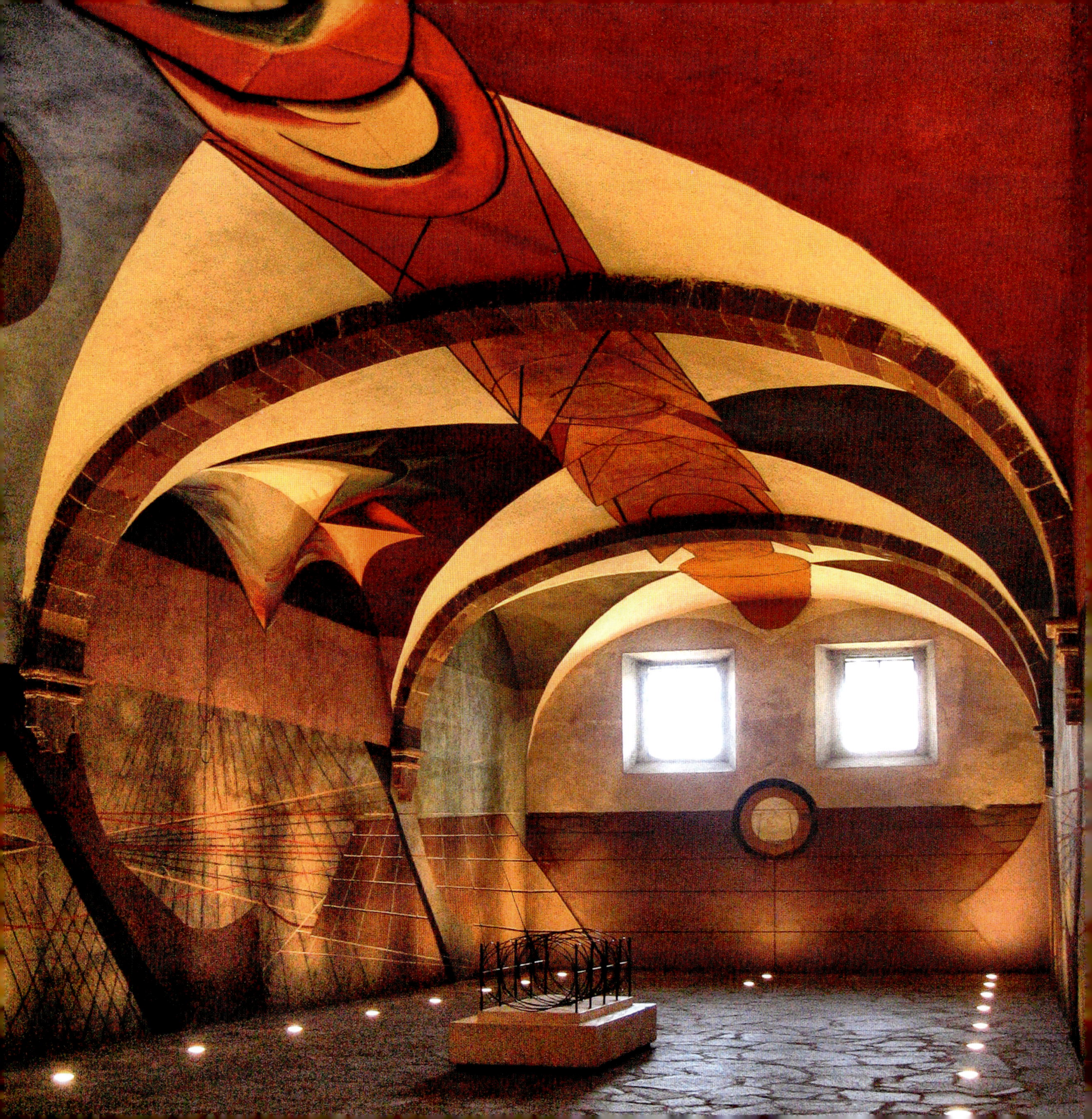

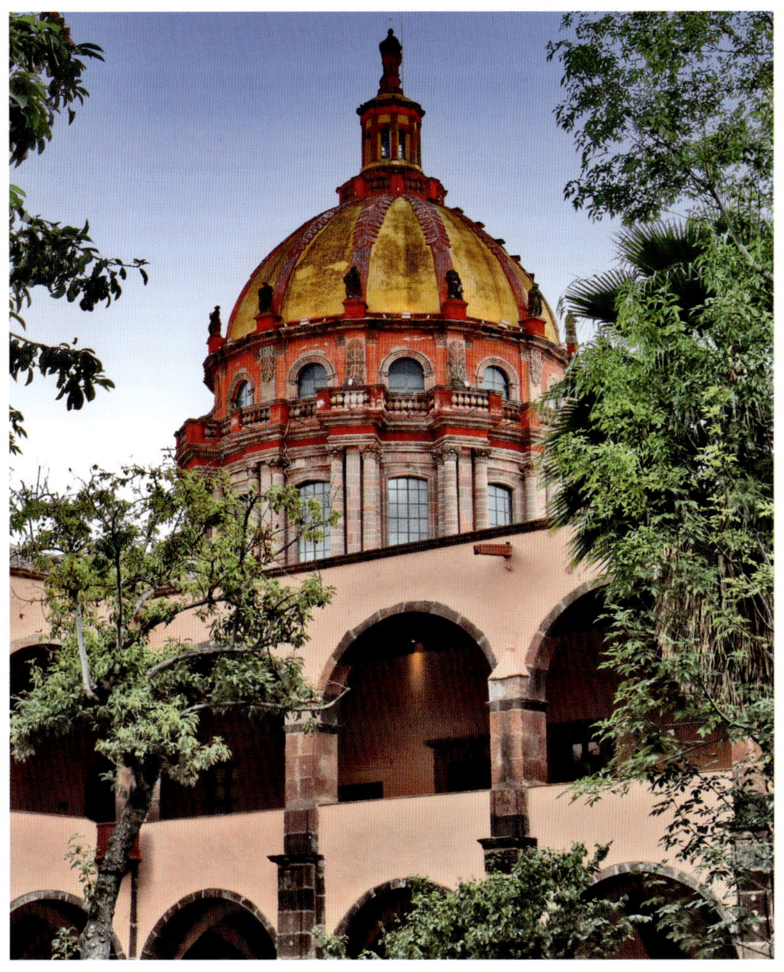

The elegant dome of Las Monjas towers over its neighbors and marks the western edge of the immediate "Centro." Part of this former convent became the "Bellas Artes," one of the two art schools that were part of San Miguel's rebirth after its decline following closure of the Guanajuato silver mines. A young American, Stirling Dickinson, found San Miguel in a state of disrepair and abandon in 1937, yet the beauty of this place caught his heart. He later recounted, "I thought, My God, what a sight! What a place! I said to myself at that moment, I'm going to stay here." Dickinson stayed until his death in 1998 and is credited, along with Felipe Cossío del Pomar and Enrique Fernández Martínez, with San Miguel's rebirth into an international art destination. Within a few months of his arrival, Dickenson opened the Escuela Universitaria de Bellas Artes in the languishing former convent, recruiting hundreds of young US servicemen to study under the GI Bill. The Bellas Artes continues as an art center with classes, exhibitions, and lectures.

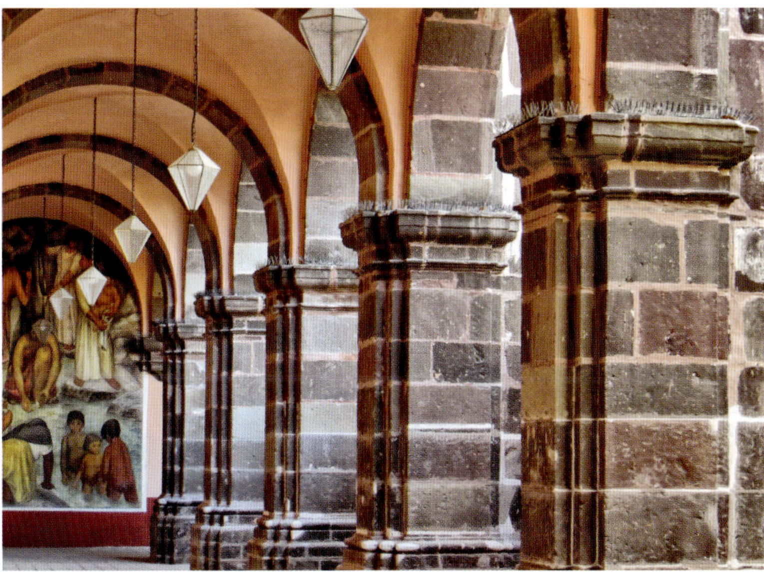

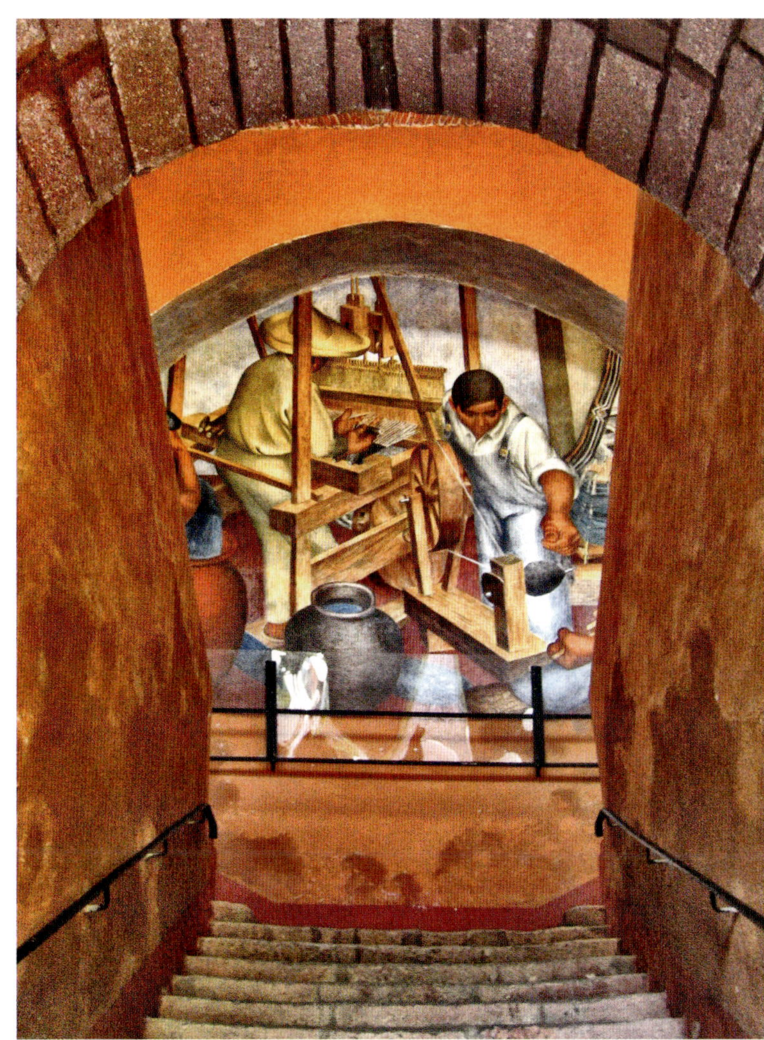

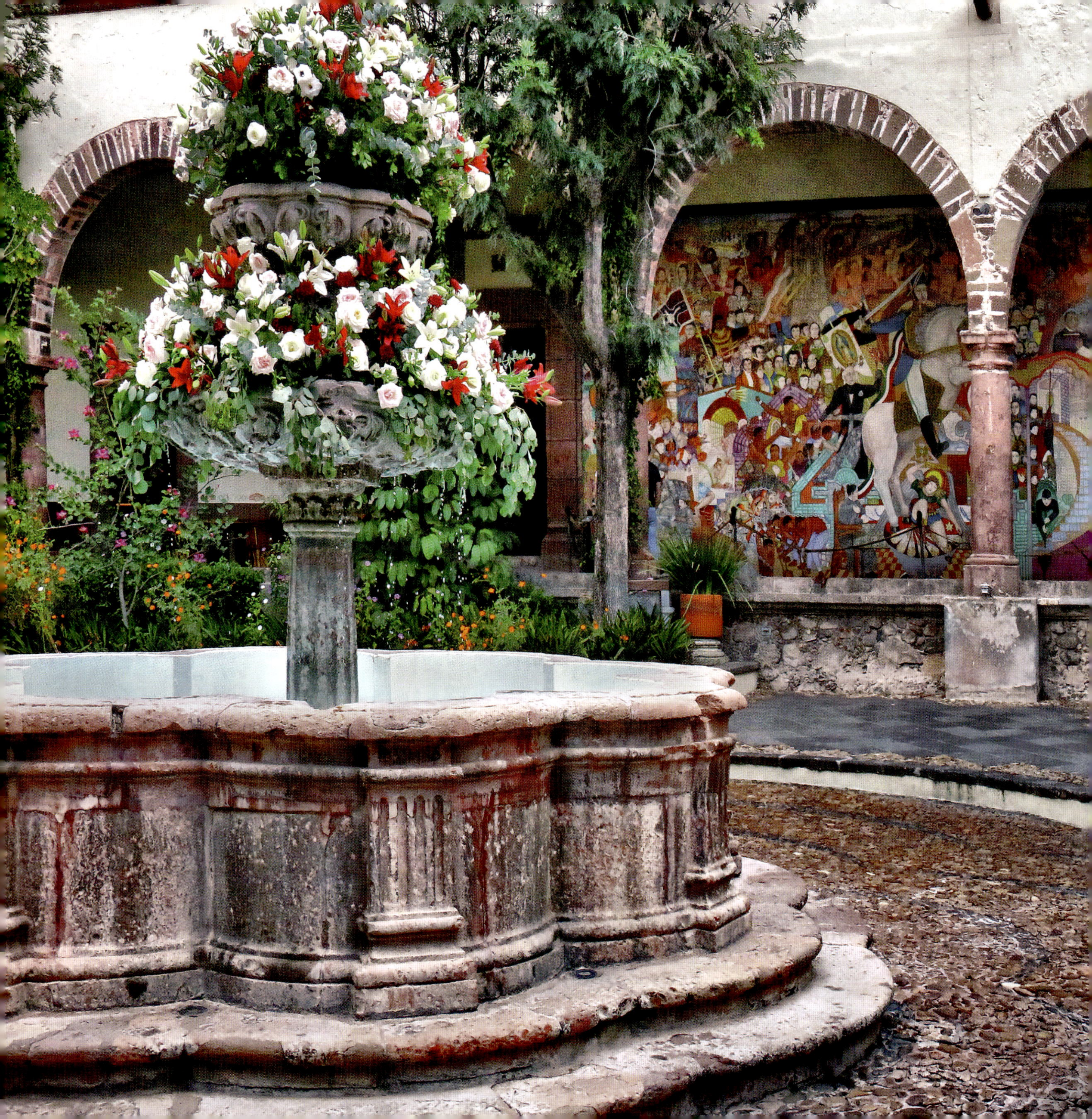

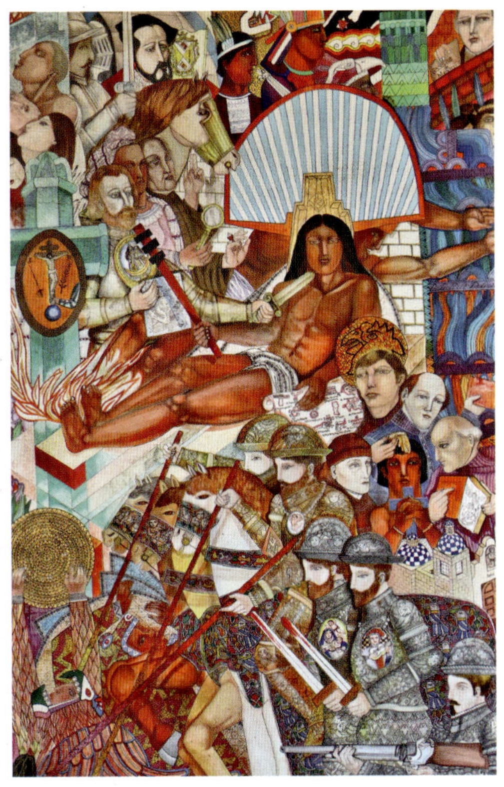

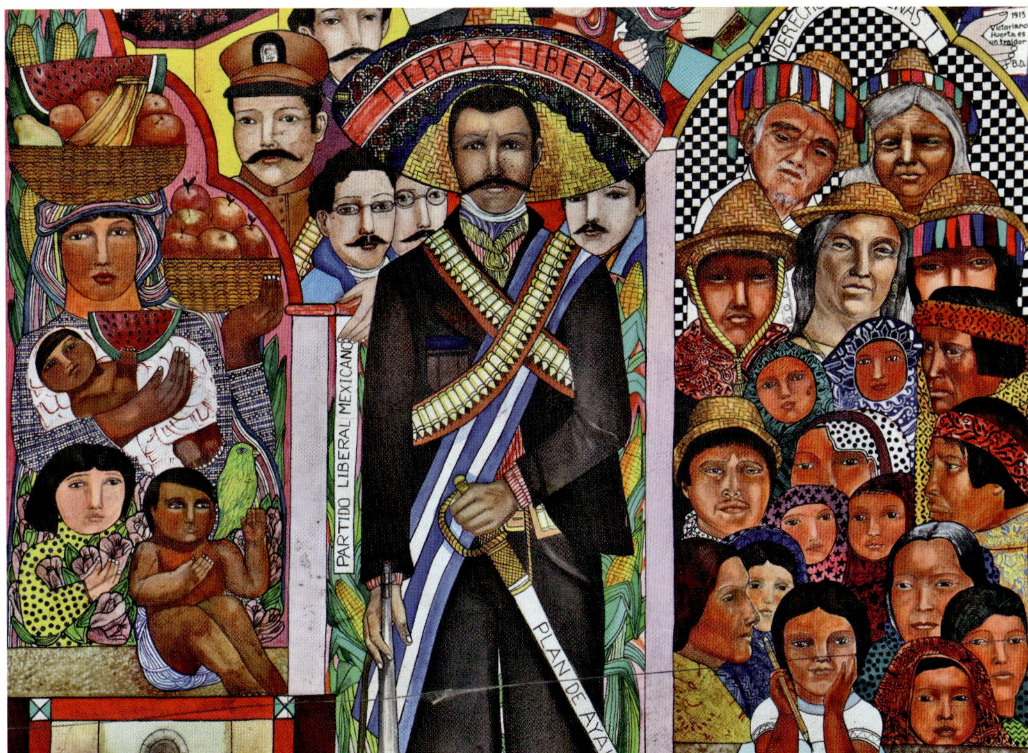

Located just a few blocks from San Miguel's center, the Instituto Allende is housed in a sprawling mansion that was home to the Canal family. A massive stone facade and enormous entry doors lead to a colonnaded courtyard with intricate stone fountain and mural-covered walls. With the Instituto joining the Bellas Artes in San Miguel's renaissance, students flocked from all over the world, including post-WWII US servicemen. The school flourished, attracting well-known Mexican muralists such as David Alfaro Siqueiros and Beat-era writers such as Jack Kerouac. Classes and workshops are available in painting, drawing, sculpture, ceramics, weaving, jewelry, photography, batik, lithography, papermaking, etching, monotype printing, and silkscreen, as well as language and art history. The Instituto and the openings it hosts are part of the core of San Miguel's art scene.

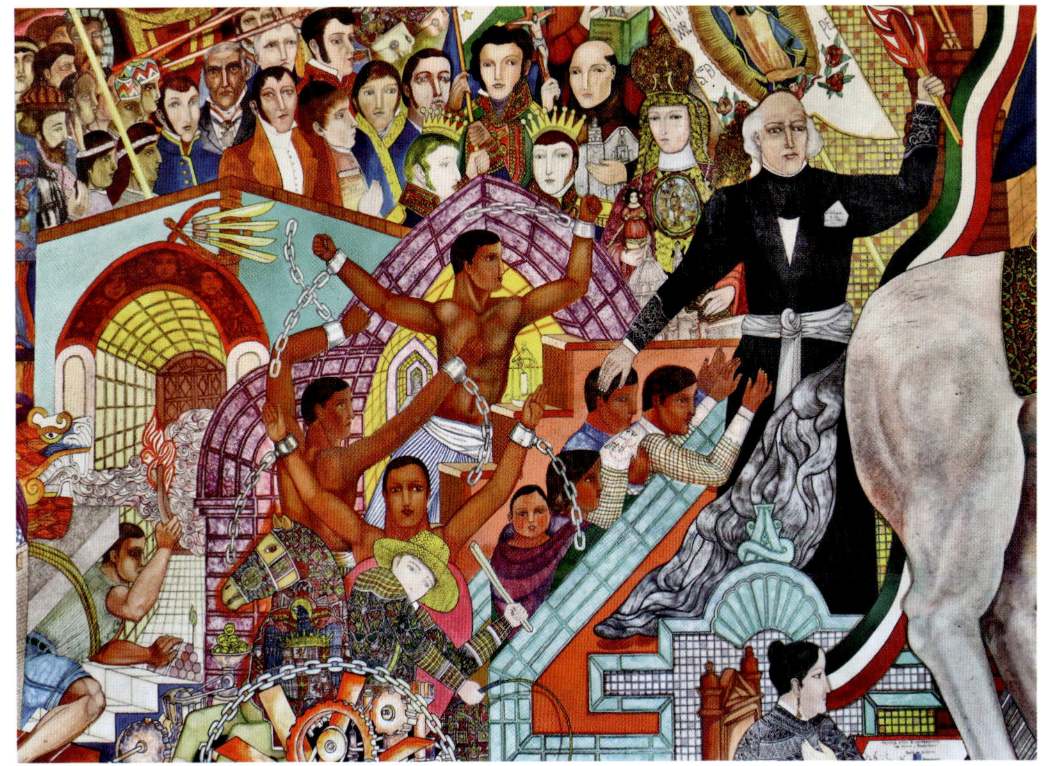

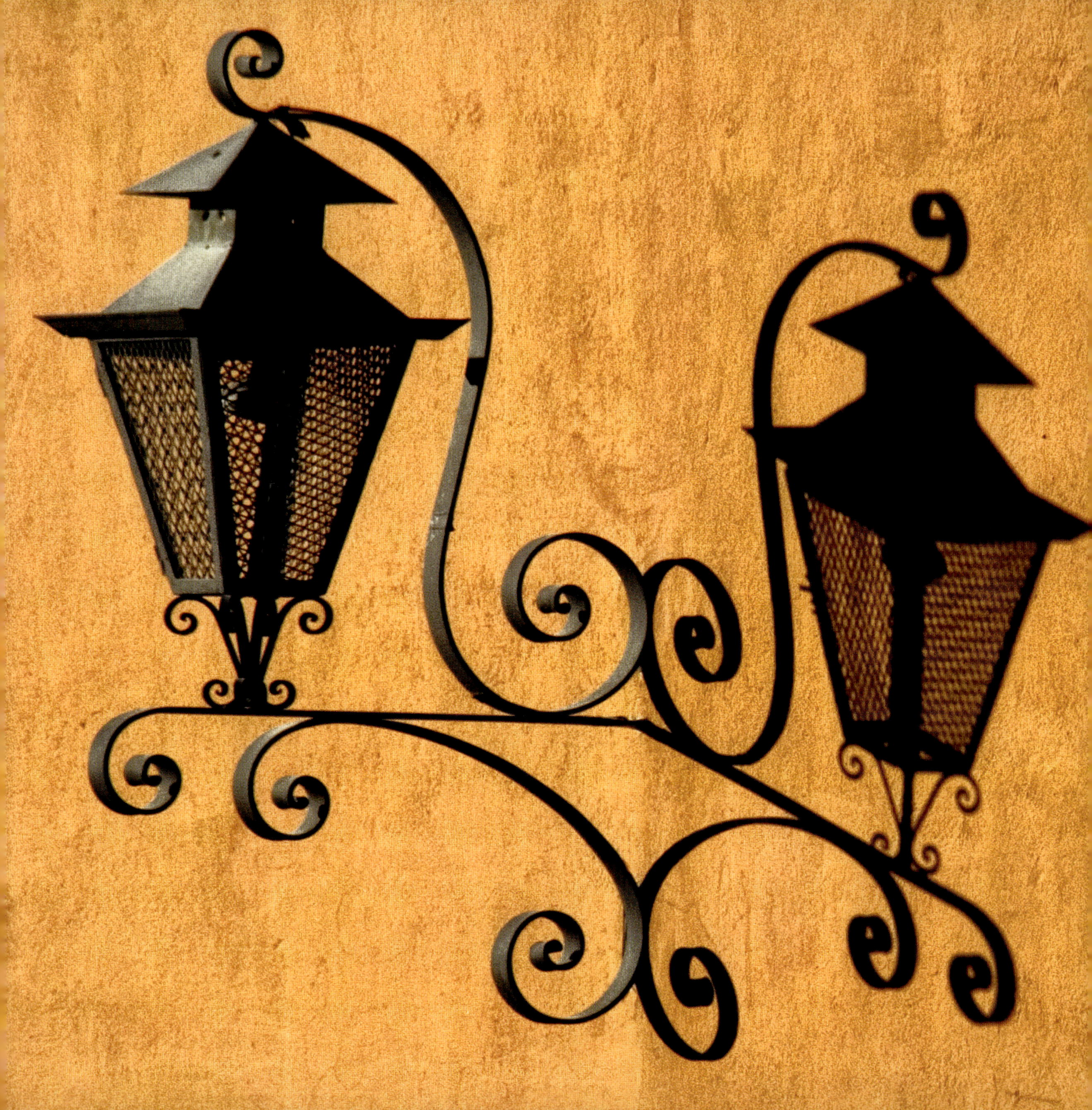

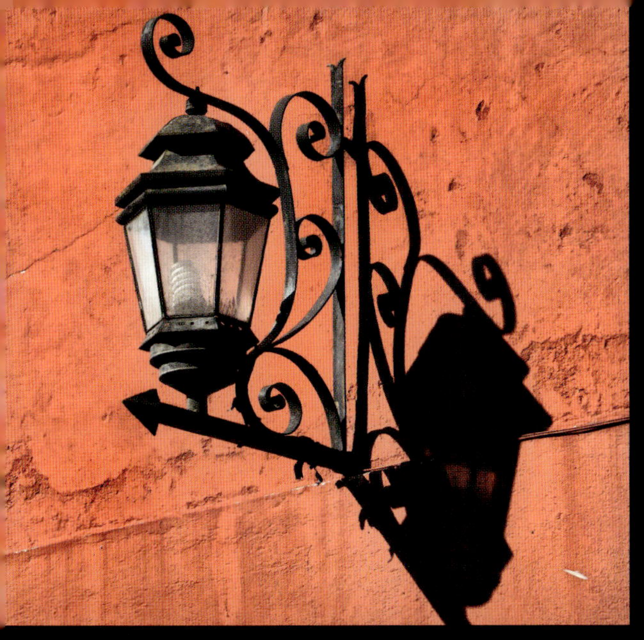

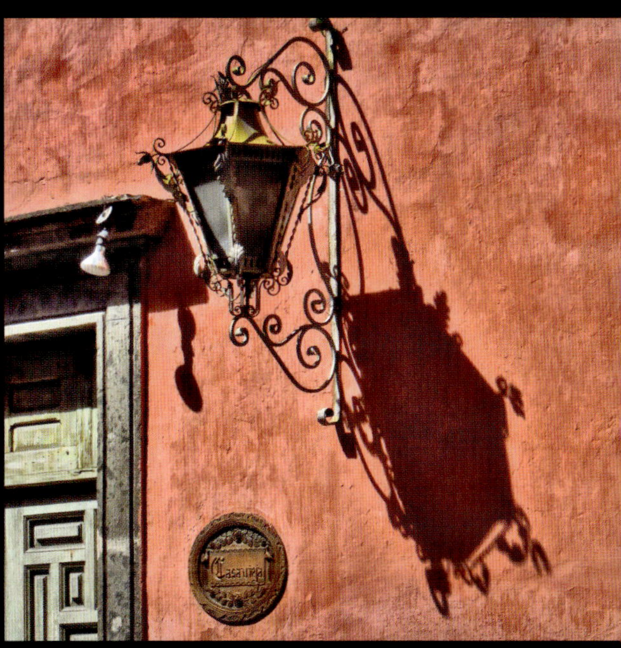

Establish beautiful masses, present pleasing contrasts. Lighting effects will offer sufficient variety. The hours of the day and night alone present so many possibilities. What diversity, when the rising sun spreads its shadow over the earth! What flickering effects when the moon traces labyrinths of light on the building. – Claude Nicolas Ledoux

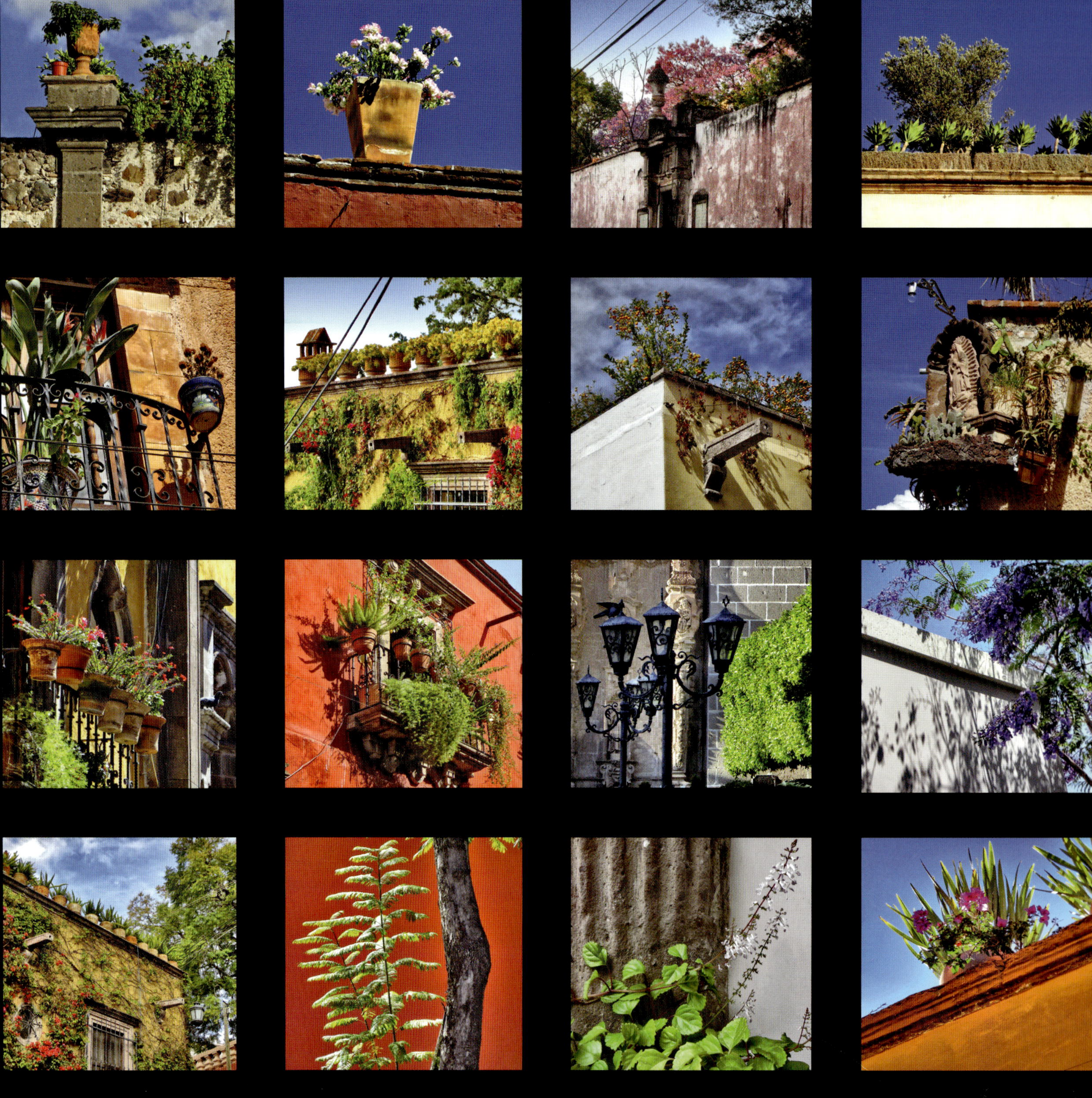

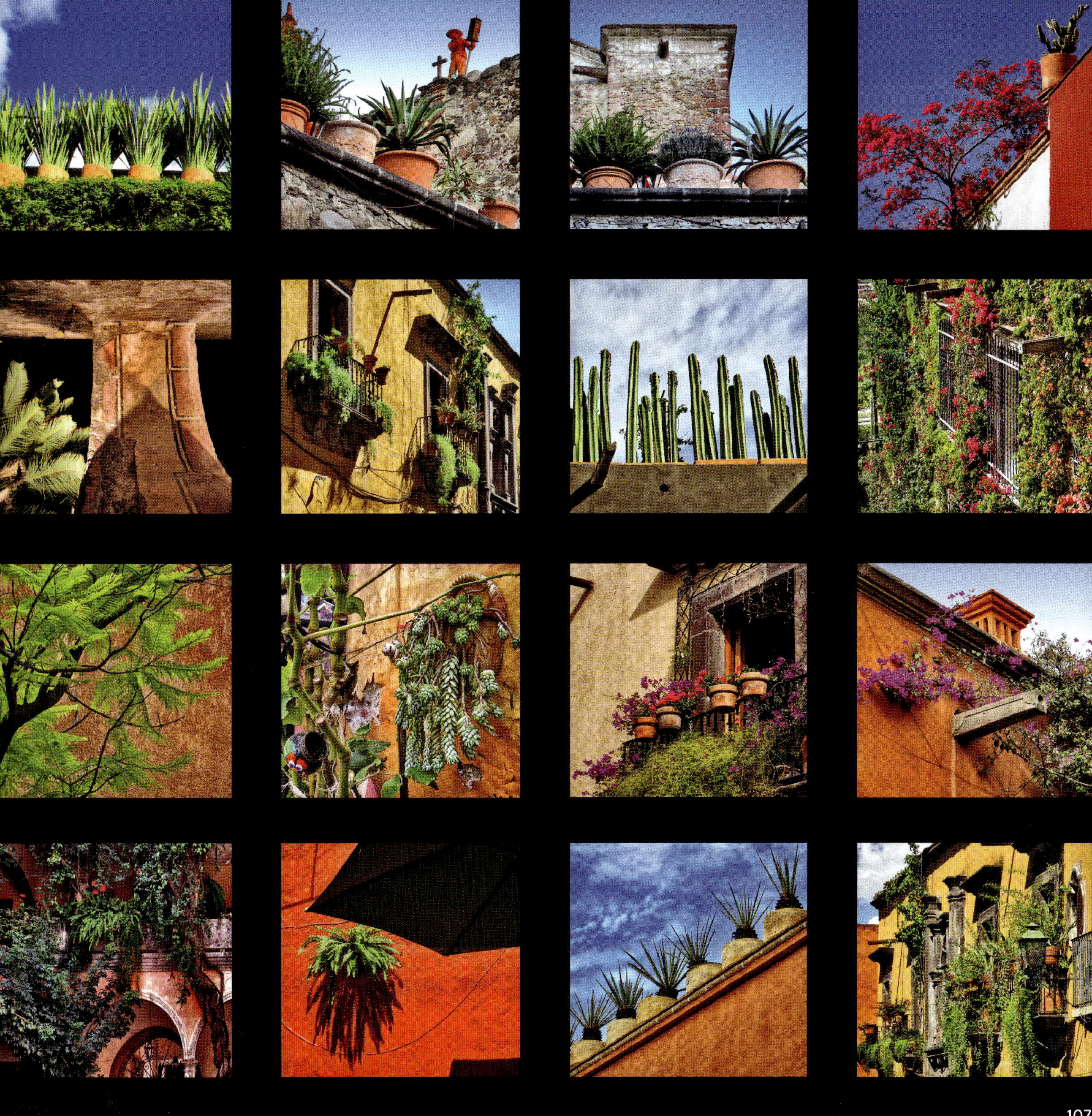

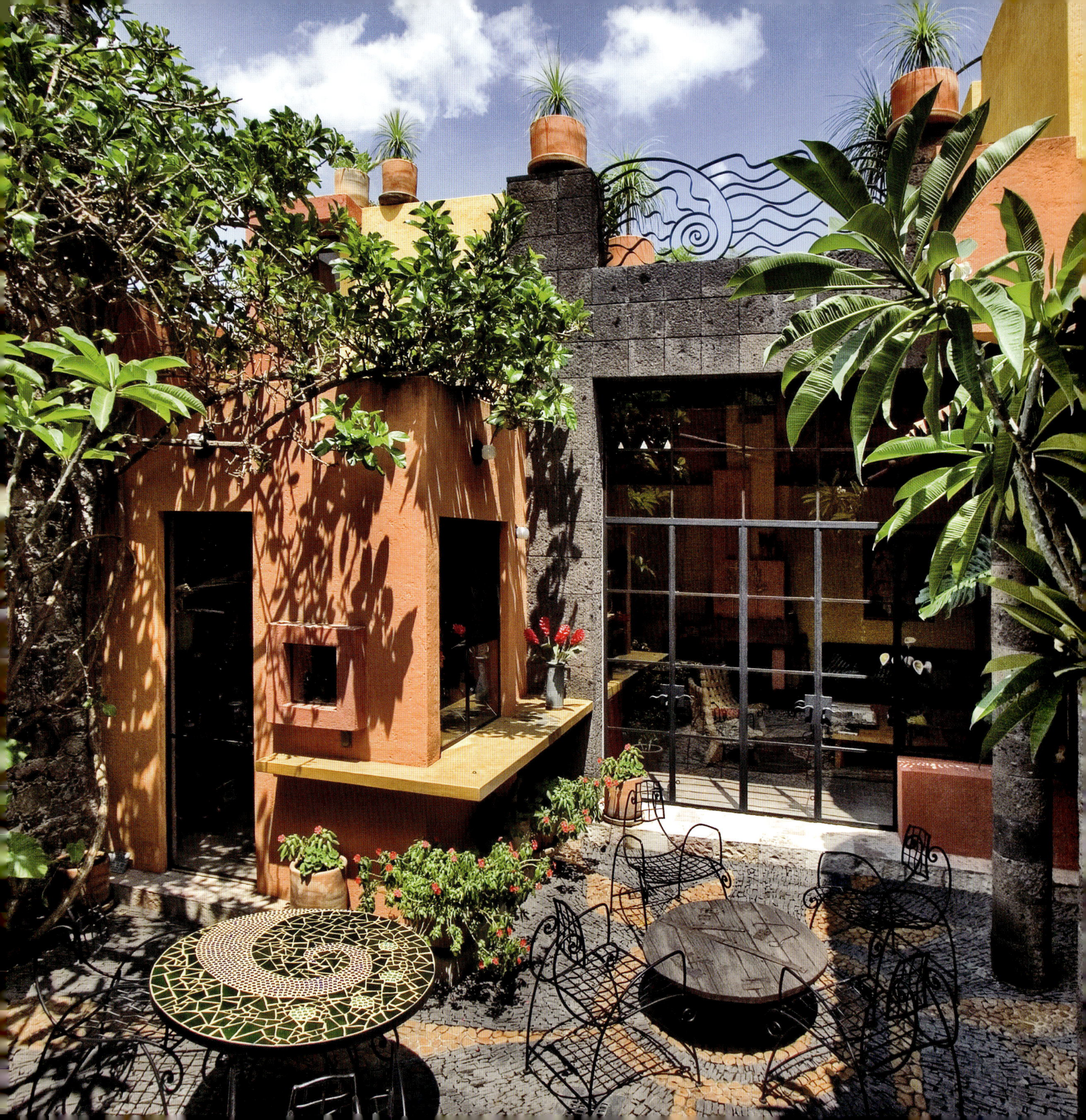

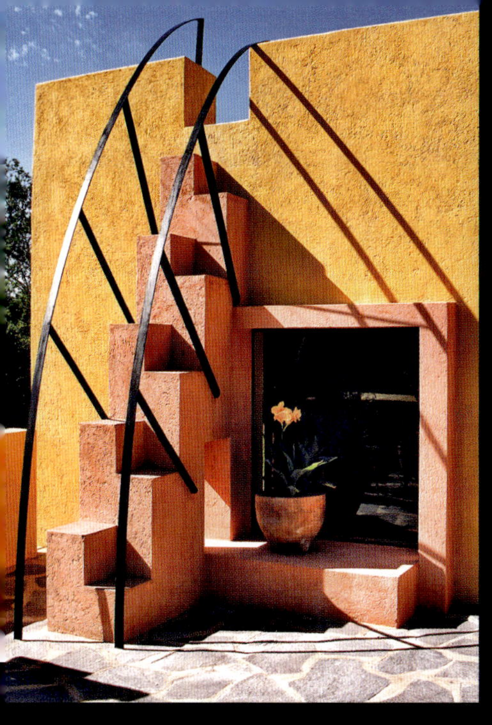

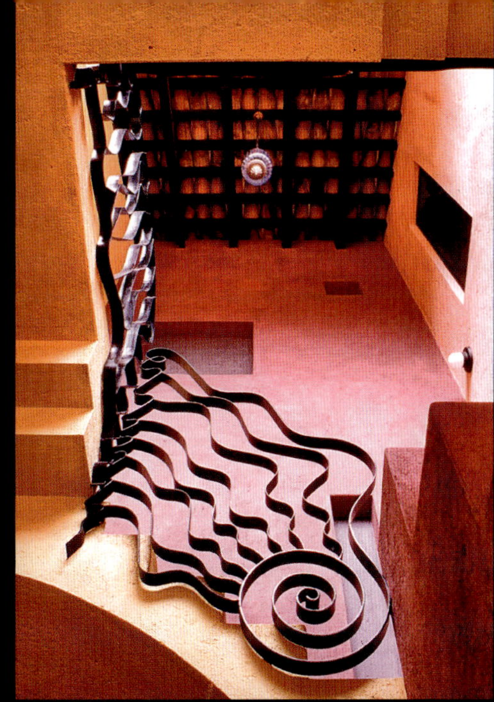

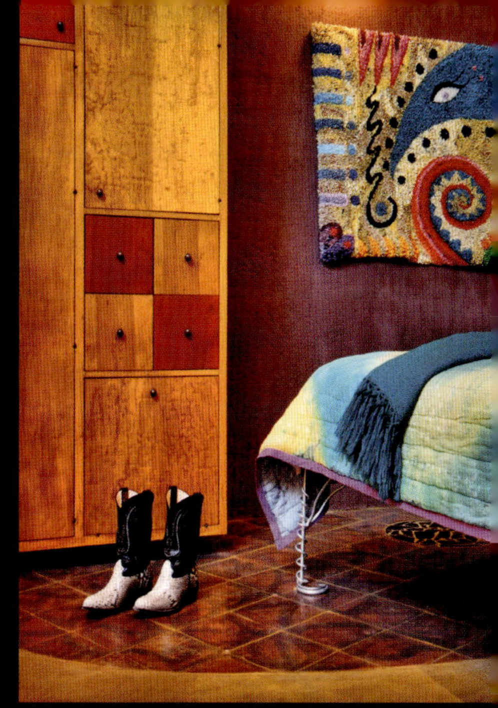

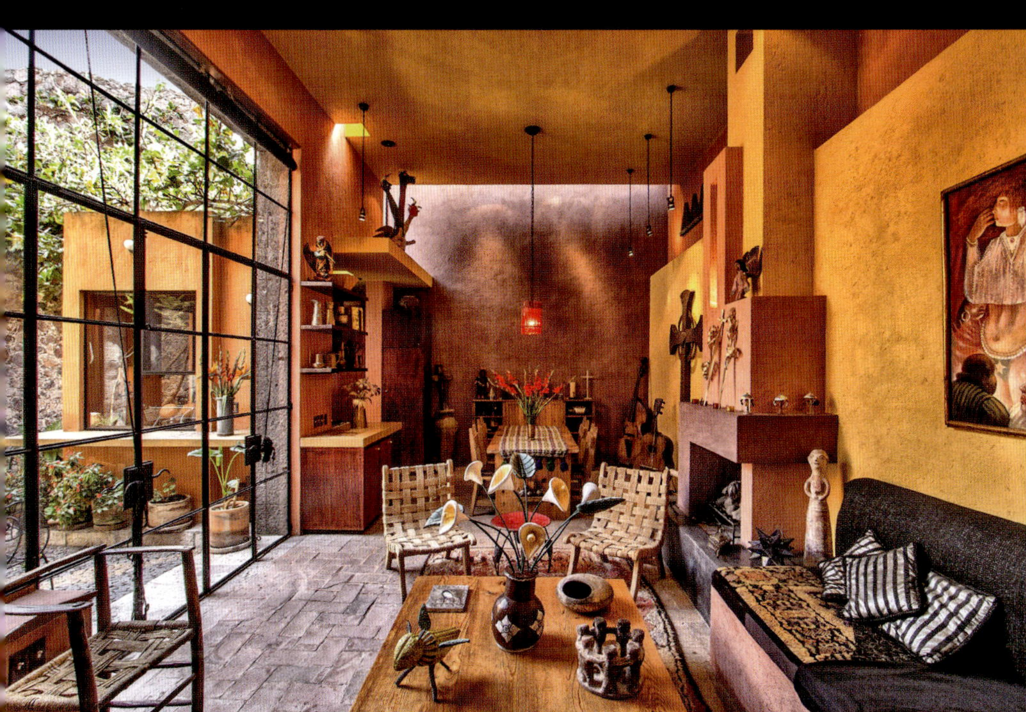

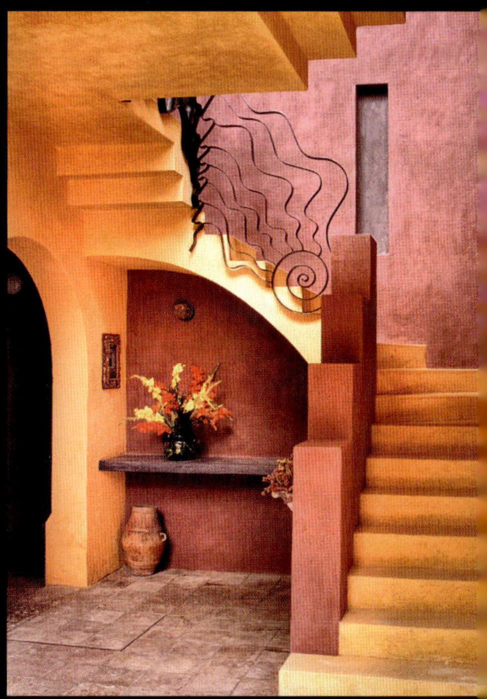

Working as an architect in San Miguel has been an honor and a gift. To have worked with the amazing men of my construction team, their passion for the art of building and their willingness to figure out how to build things they have never imagined, has given my work a voice it could never find in the US. House + House Architects is a bridge between a historic past and a respectful, sustainable future, between what has been and what is to come

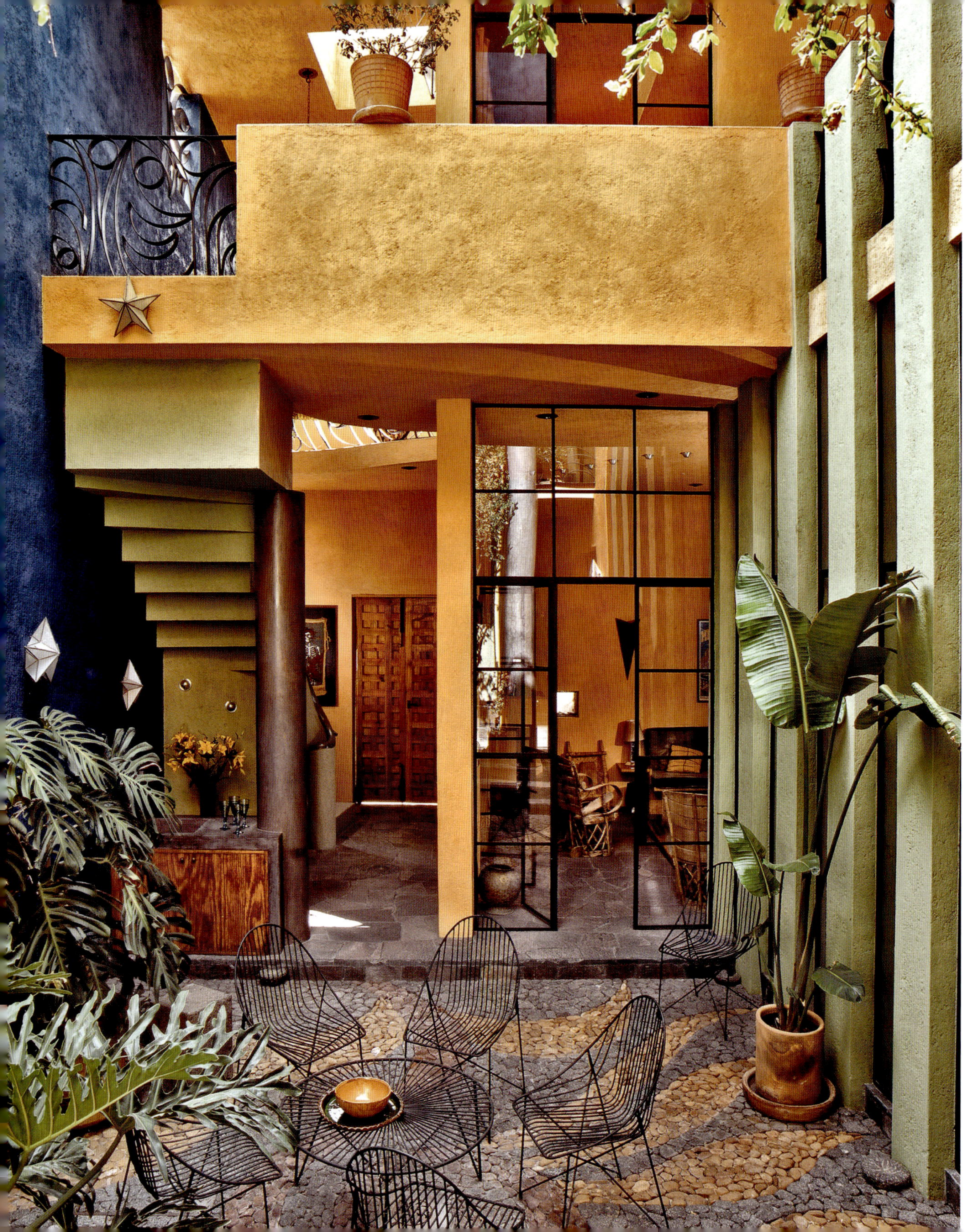

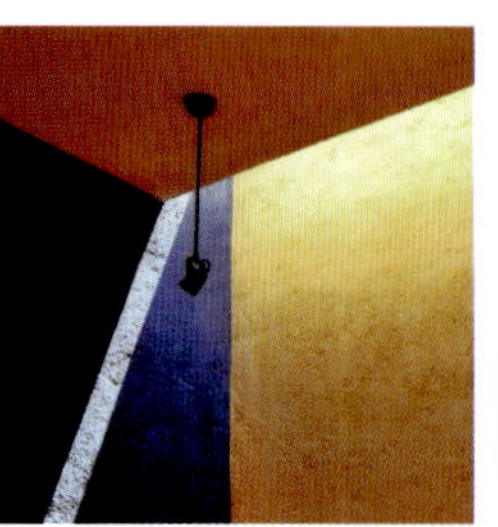
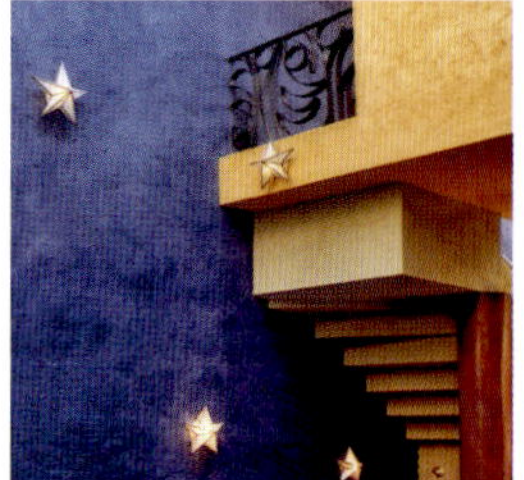
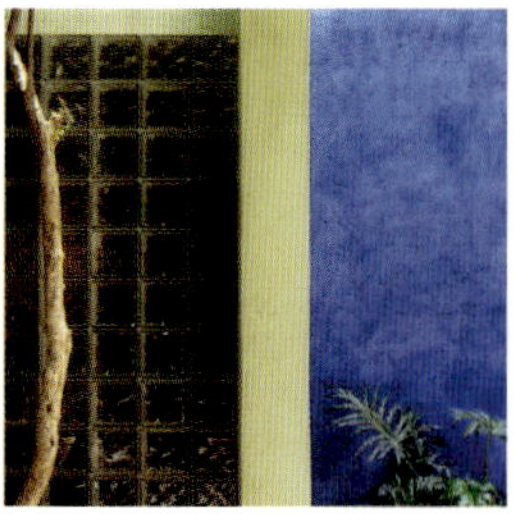
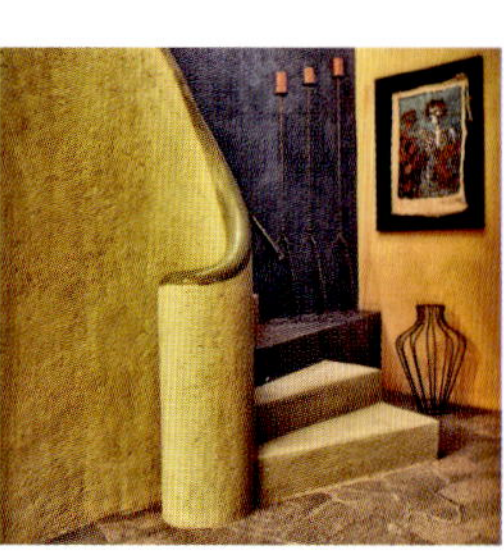
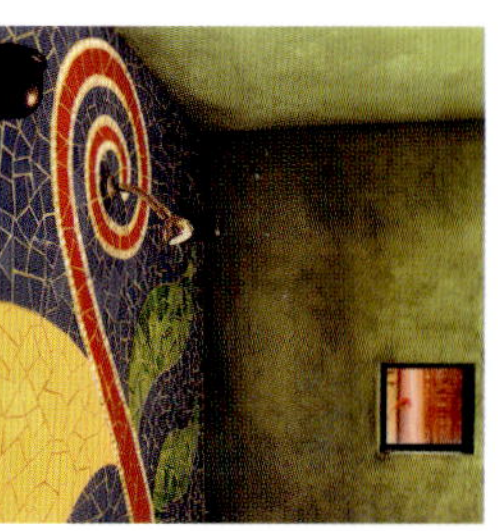

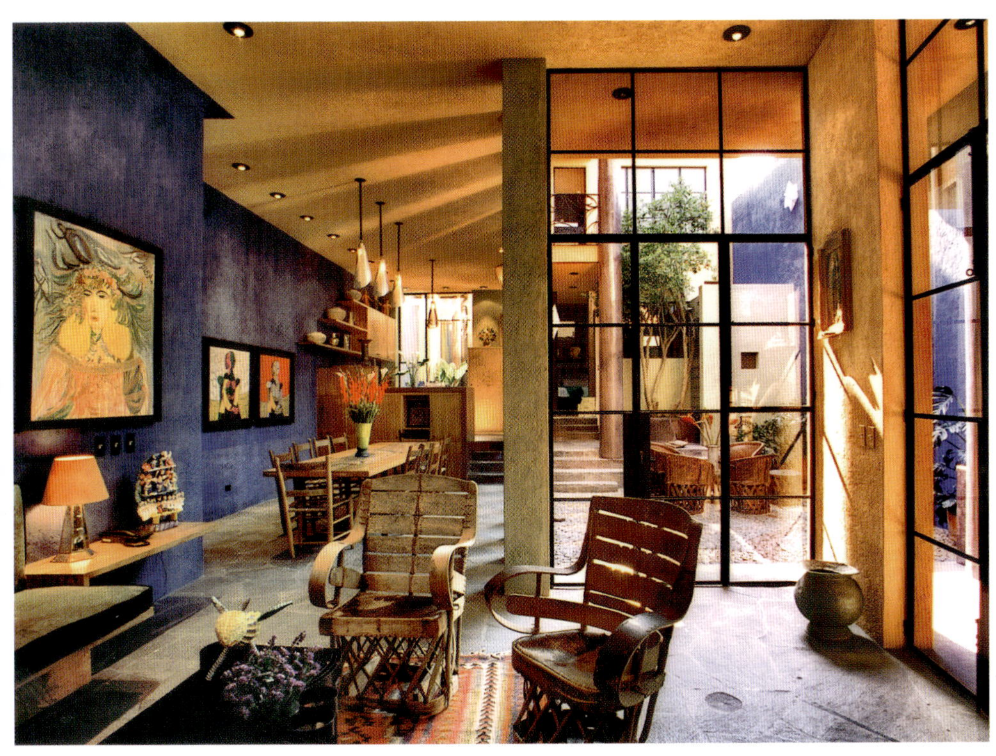

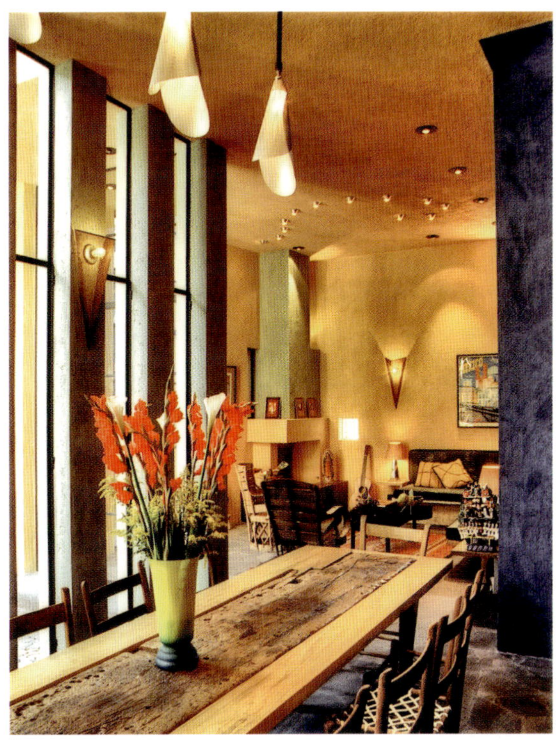

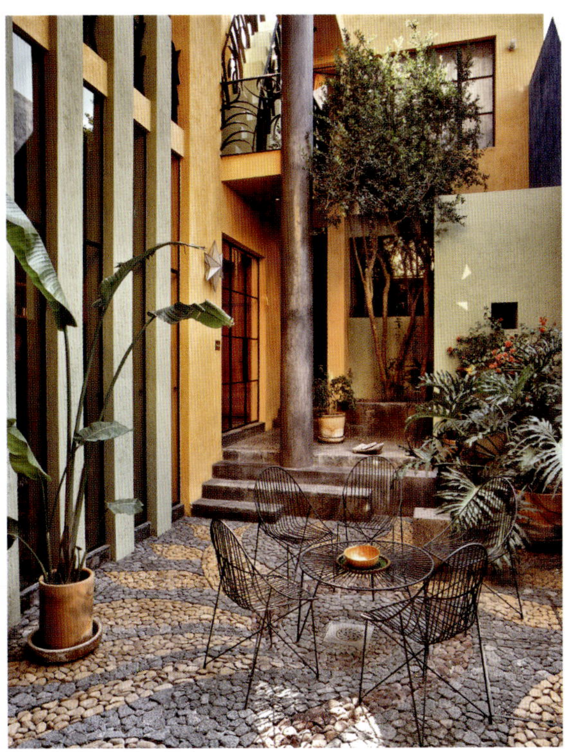

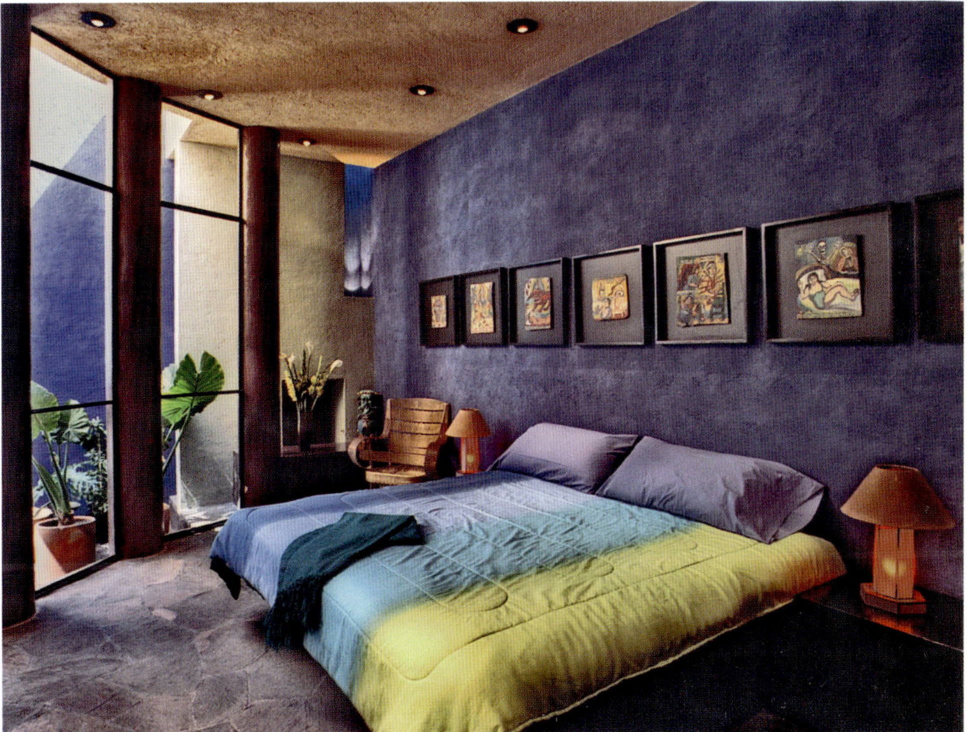

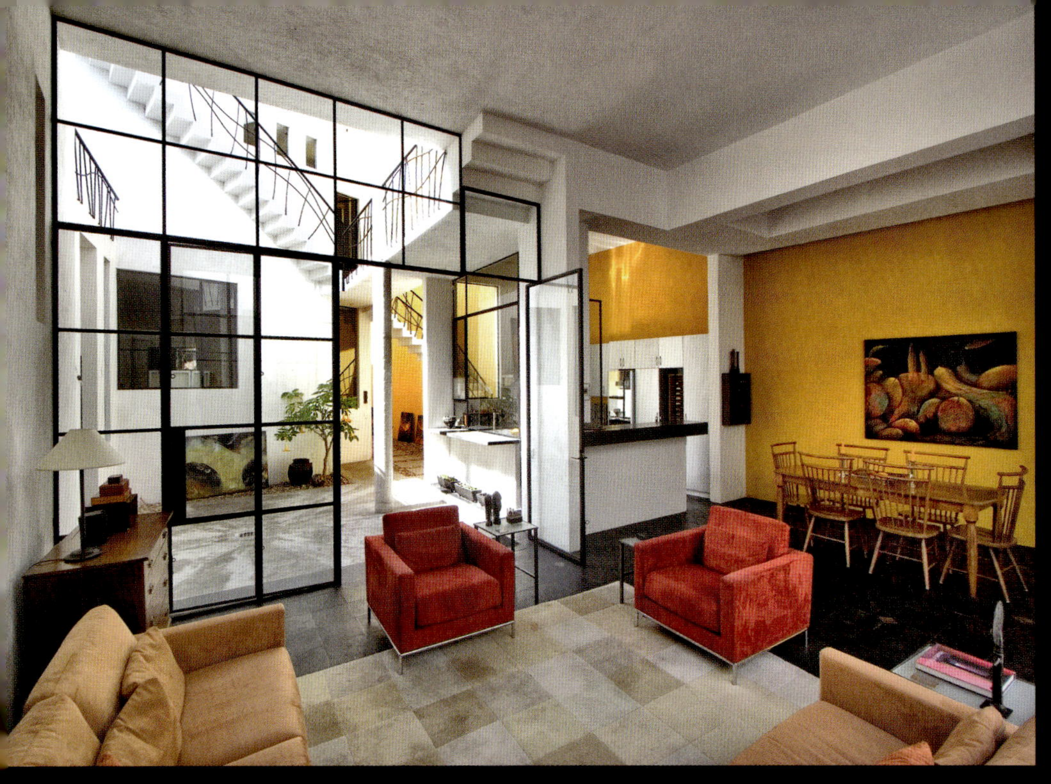
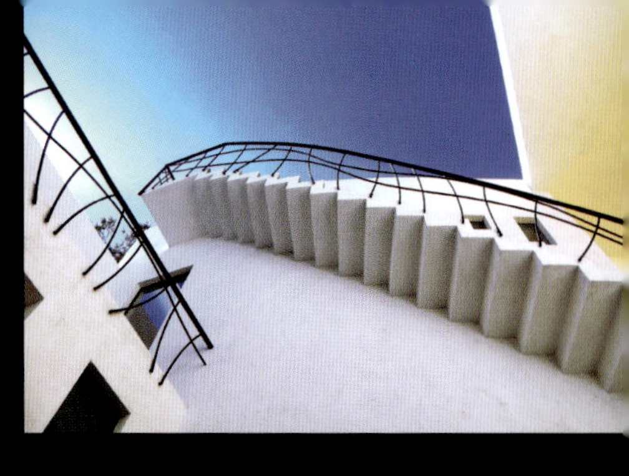
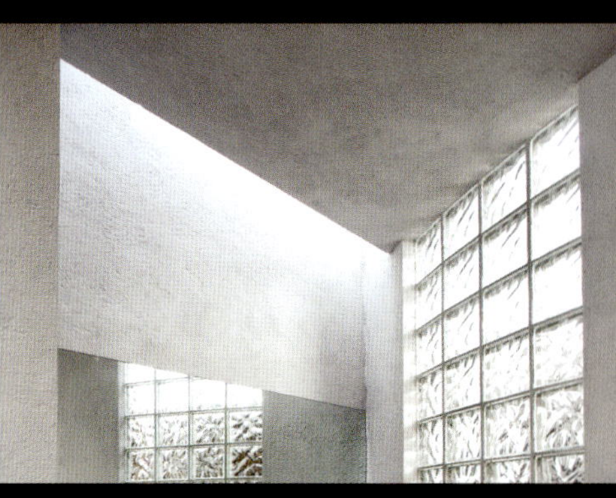
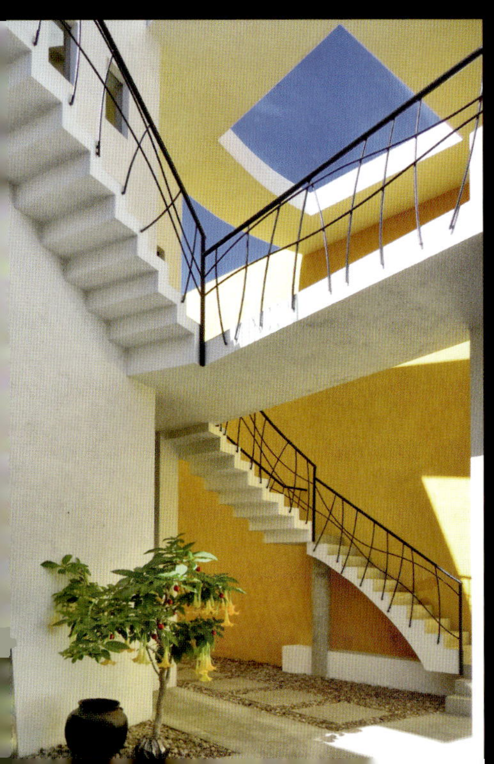
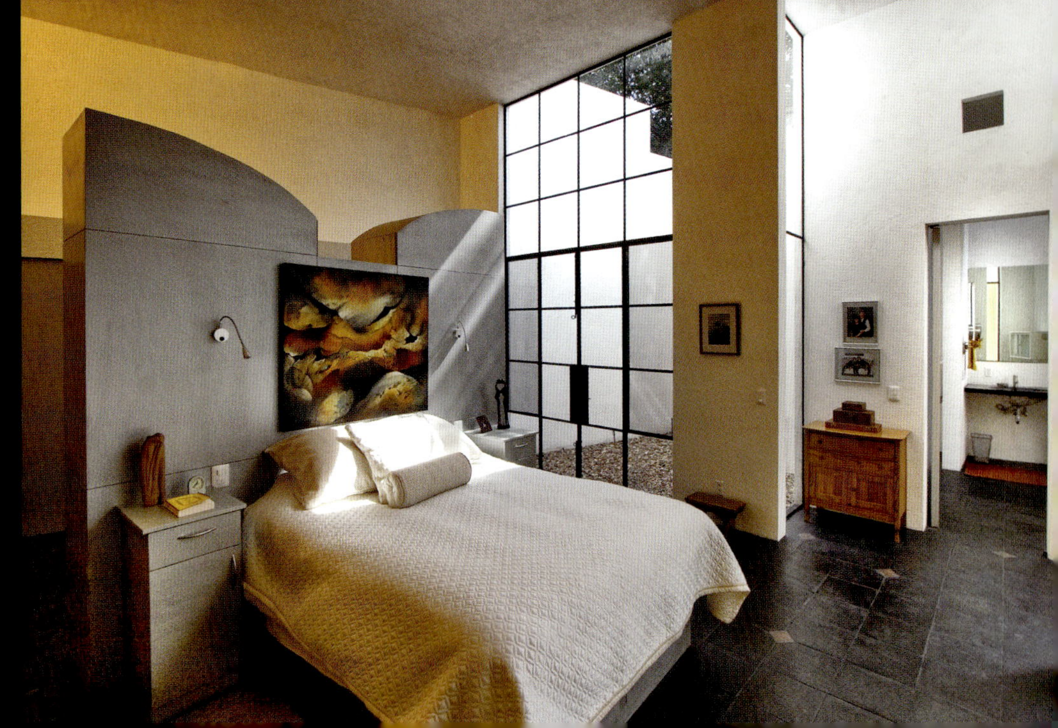

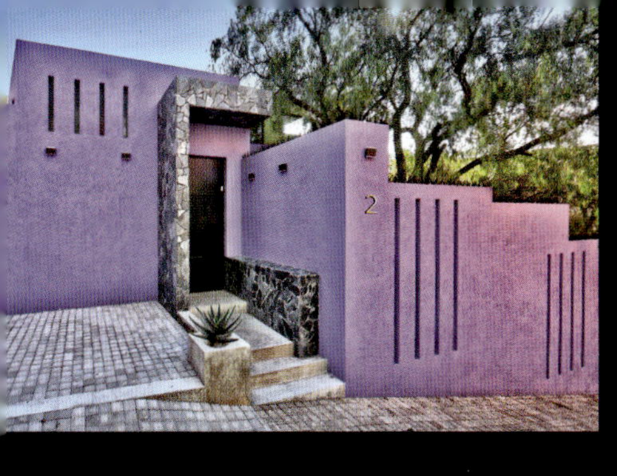
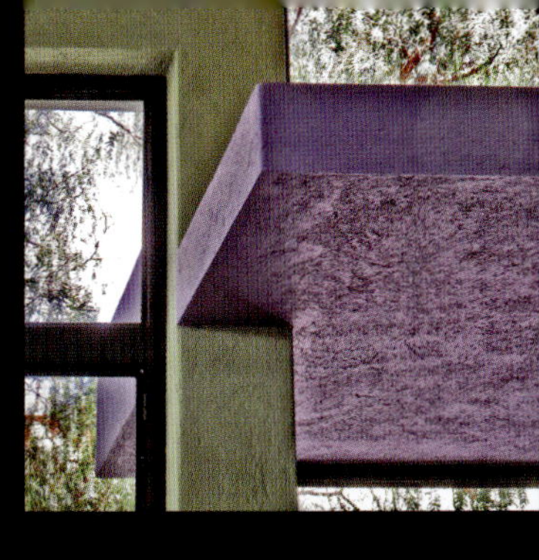
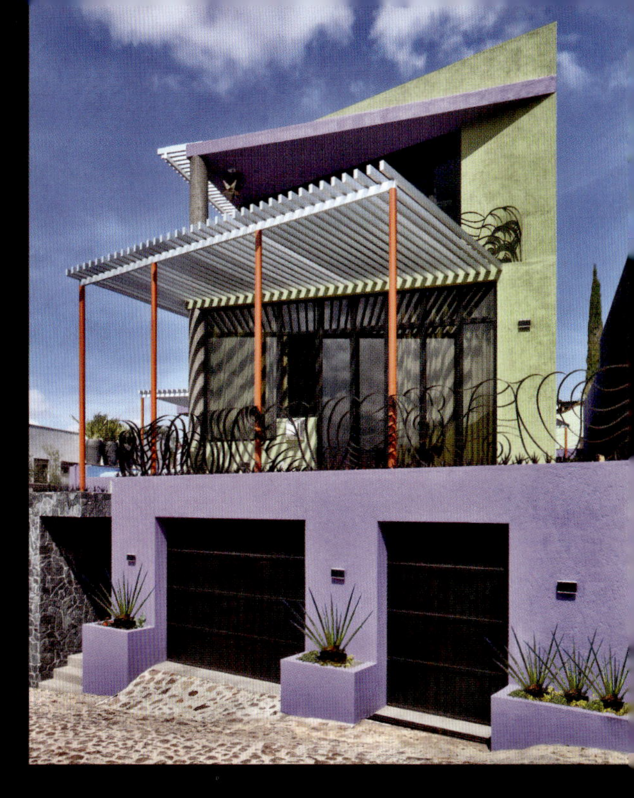
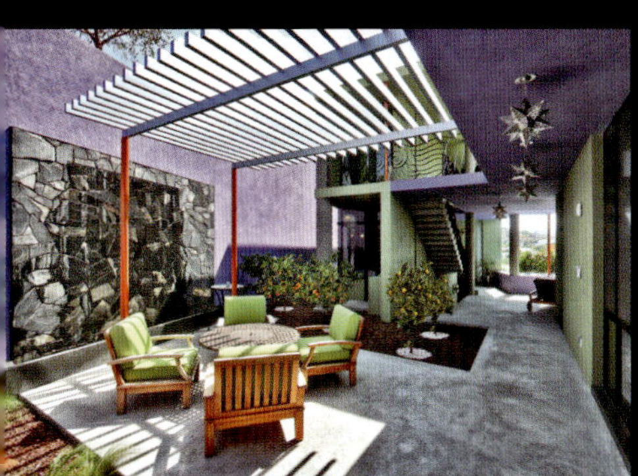
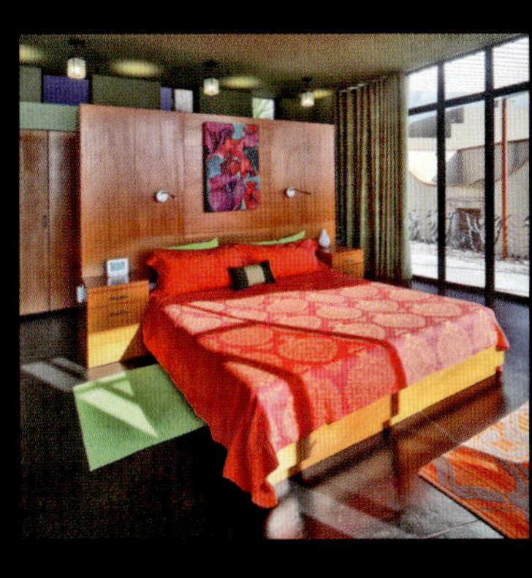
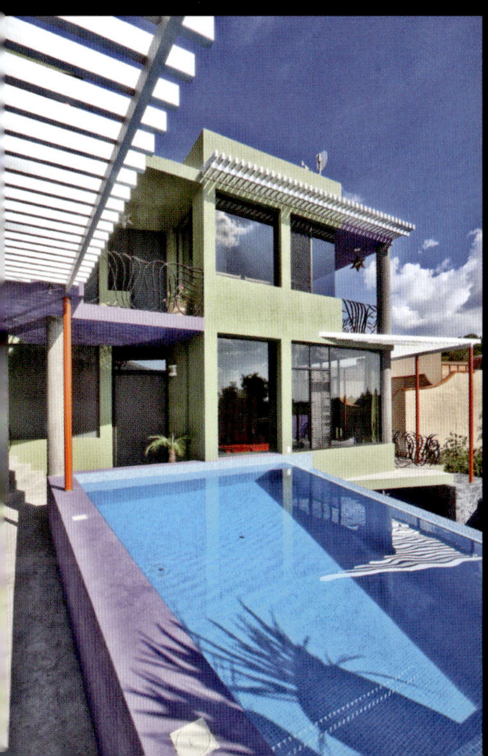
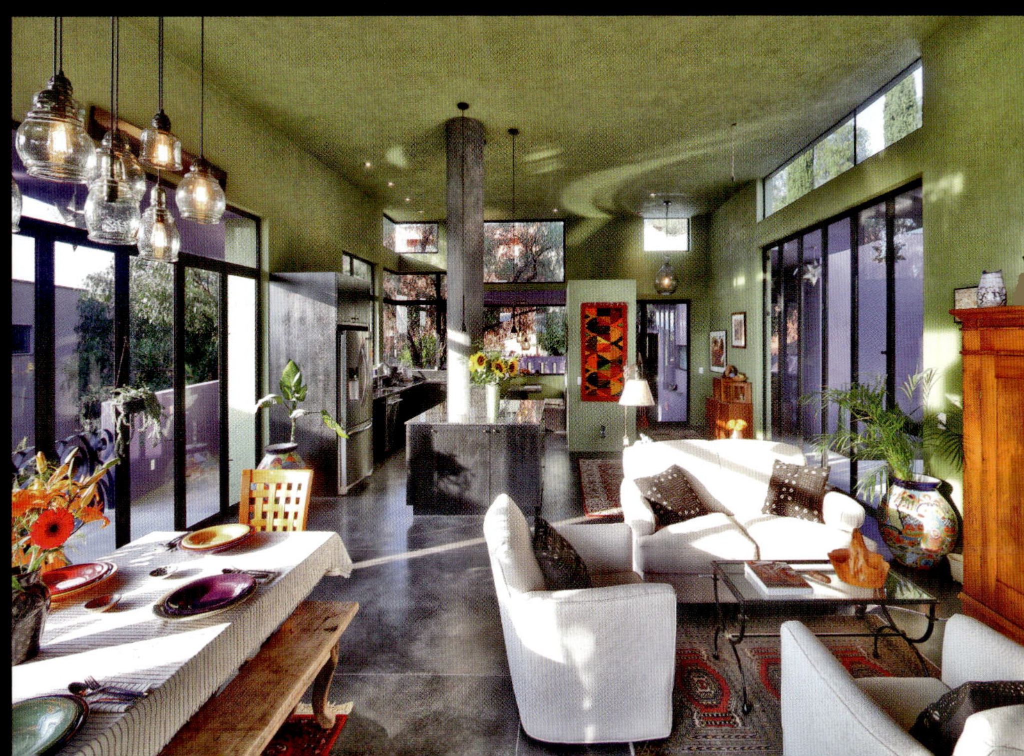

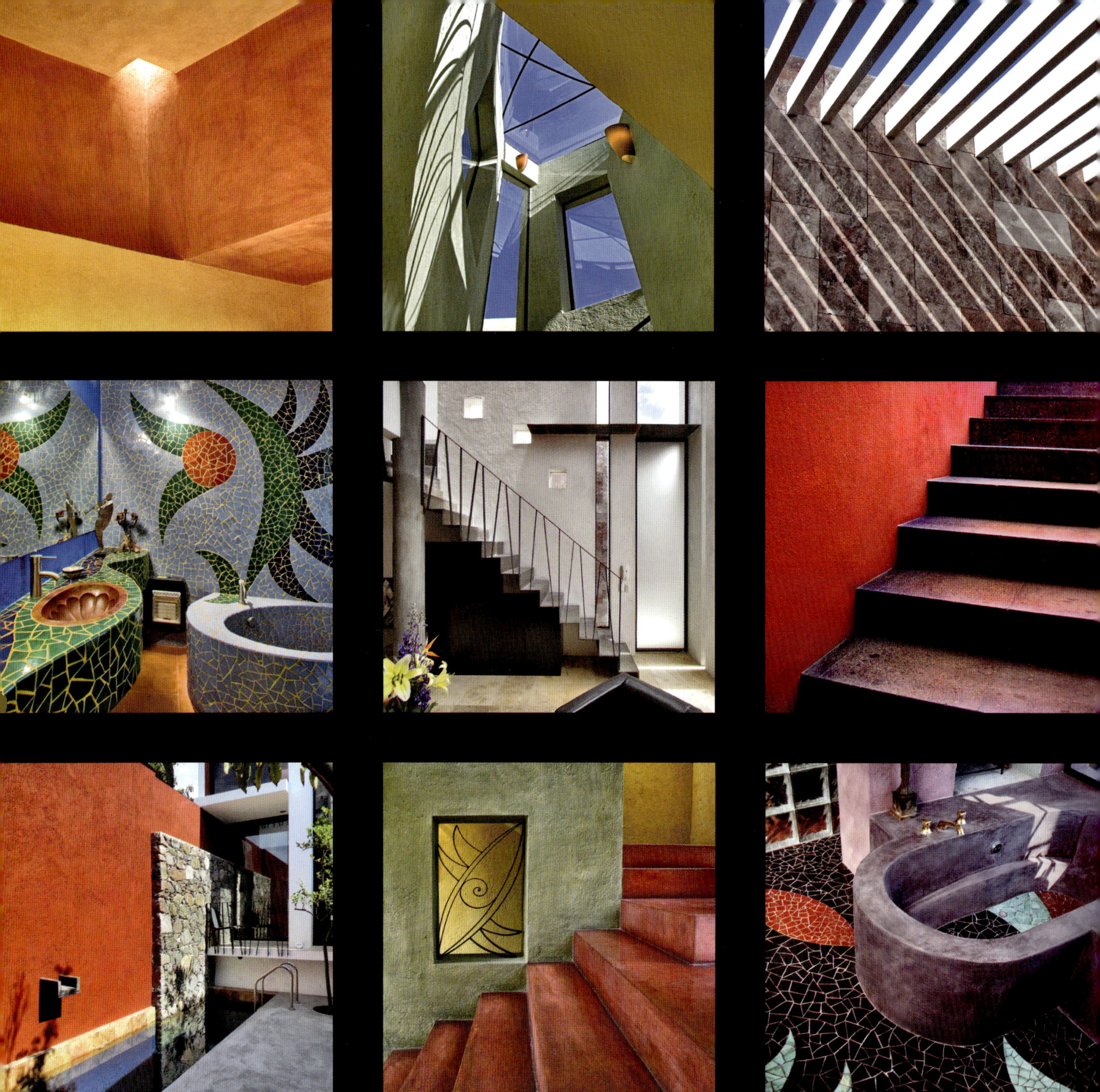

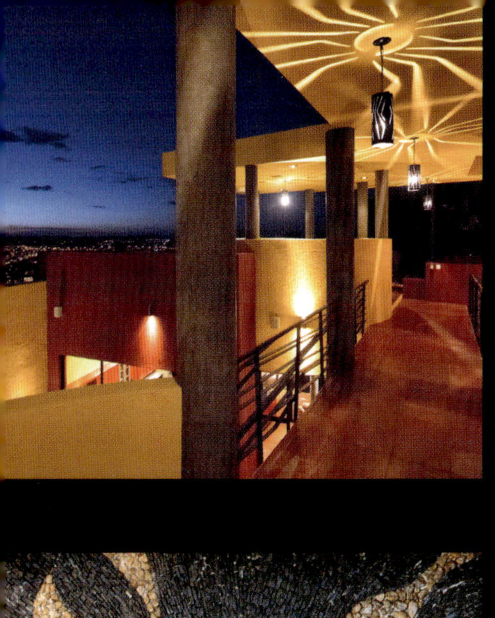
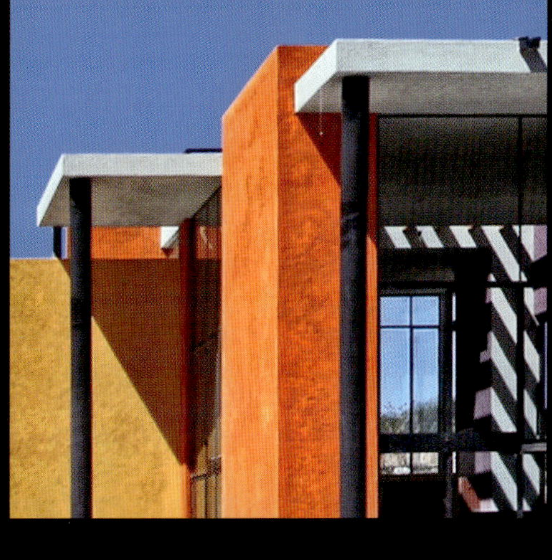
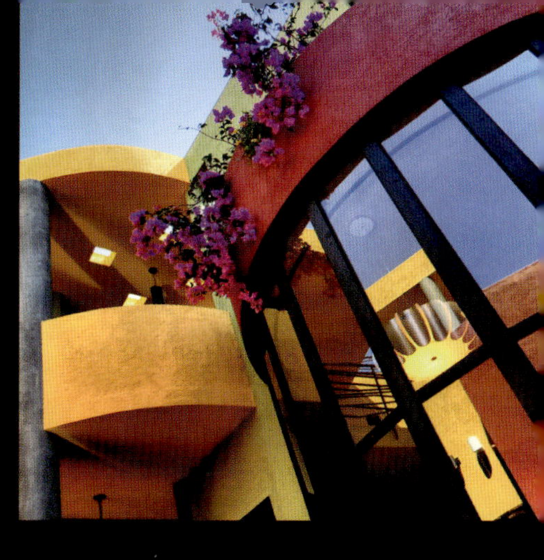
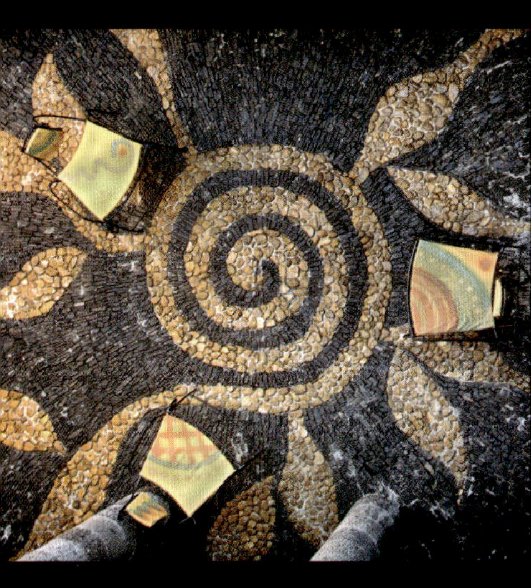
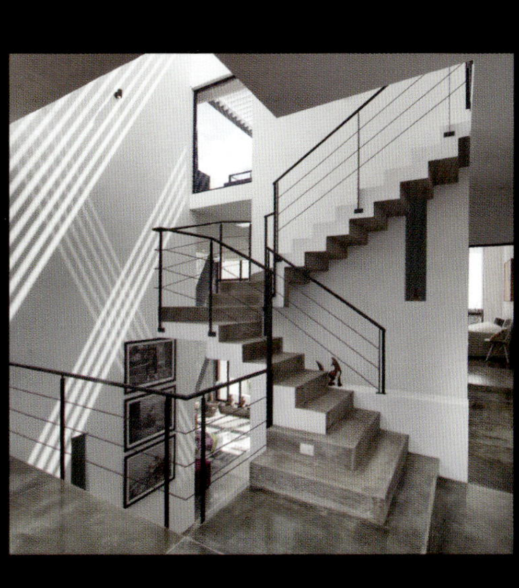
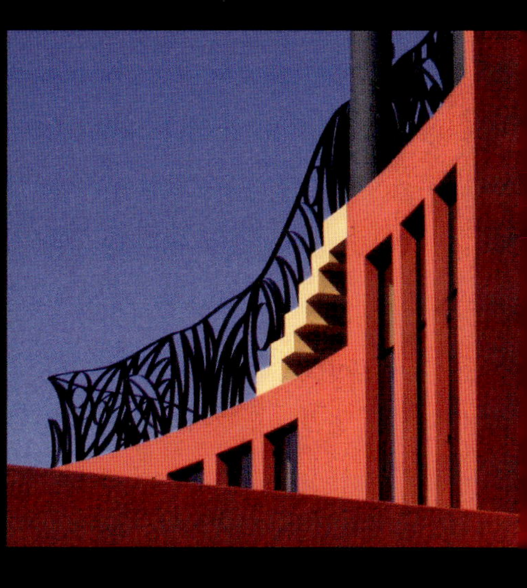
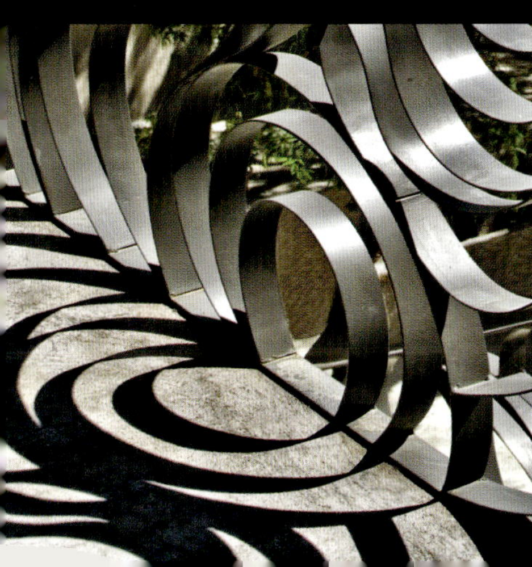
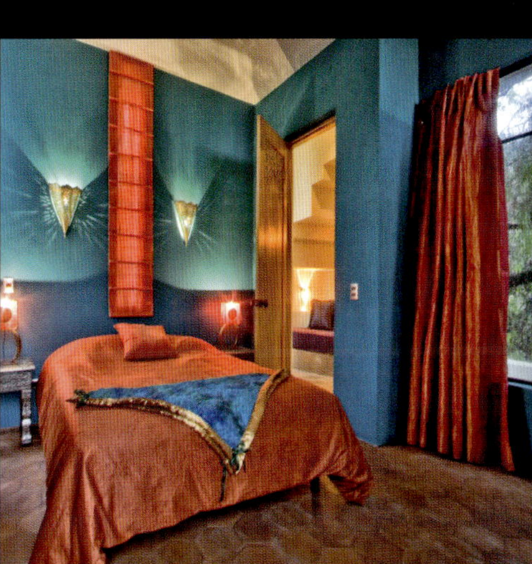
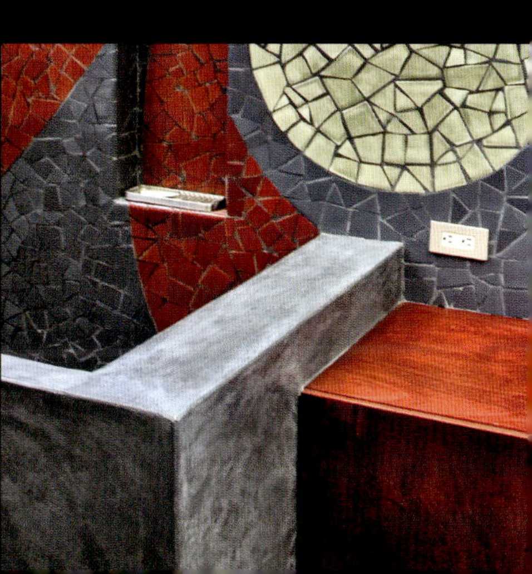

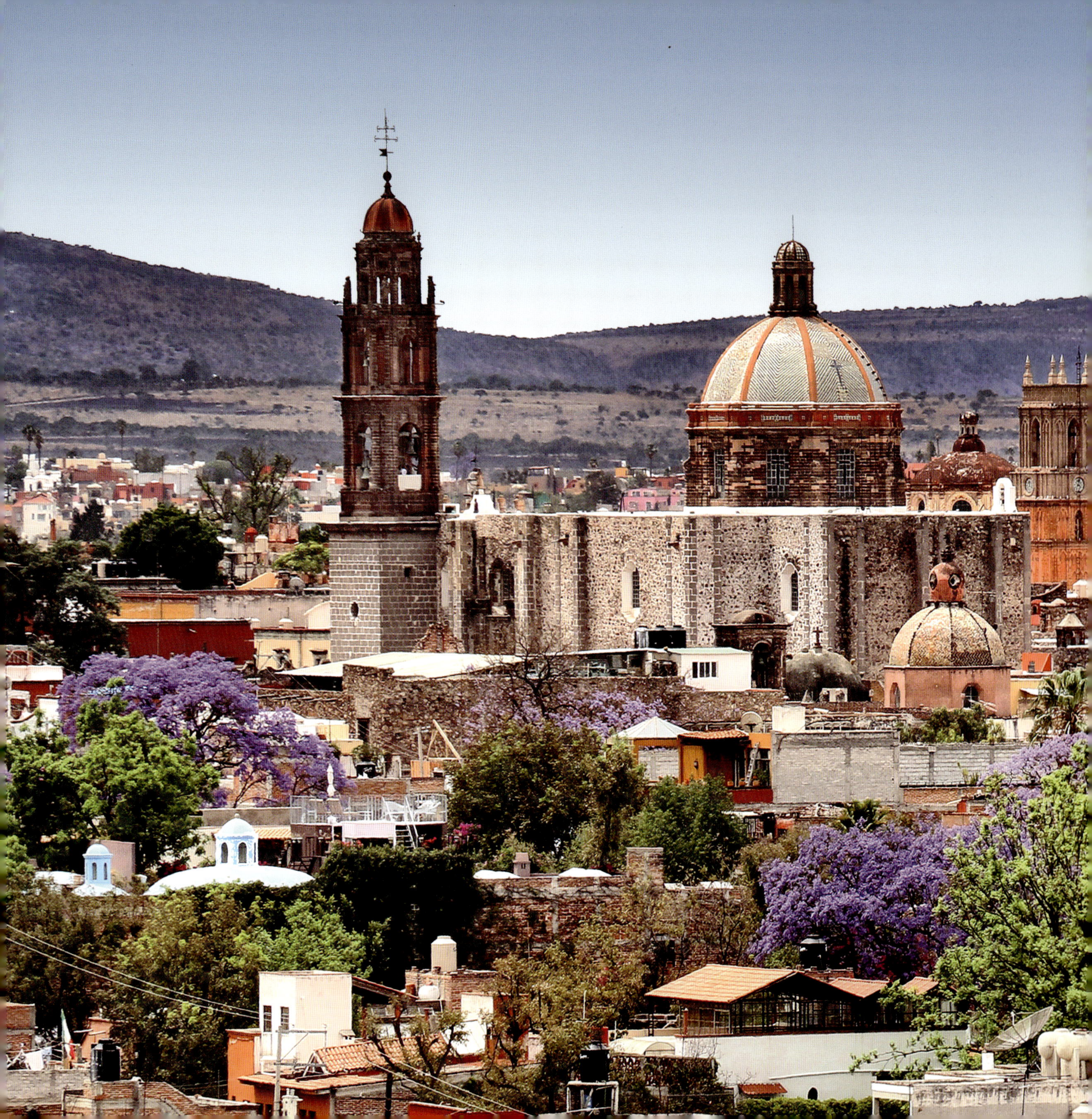

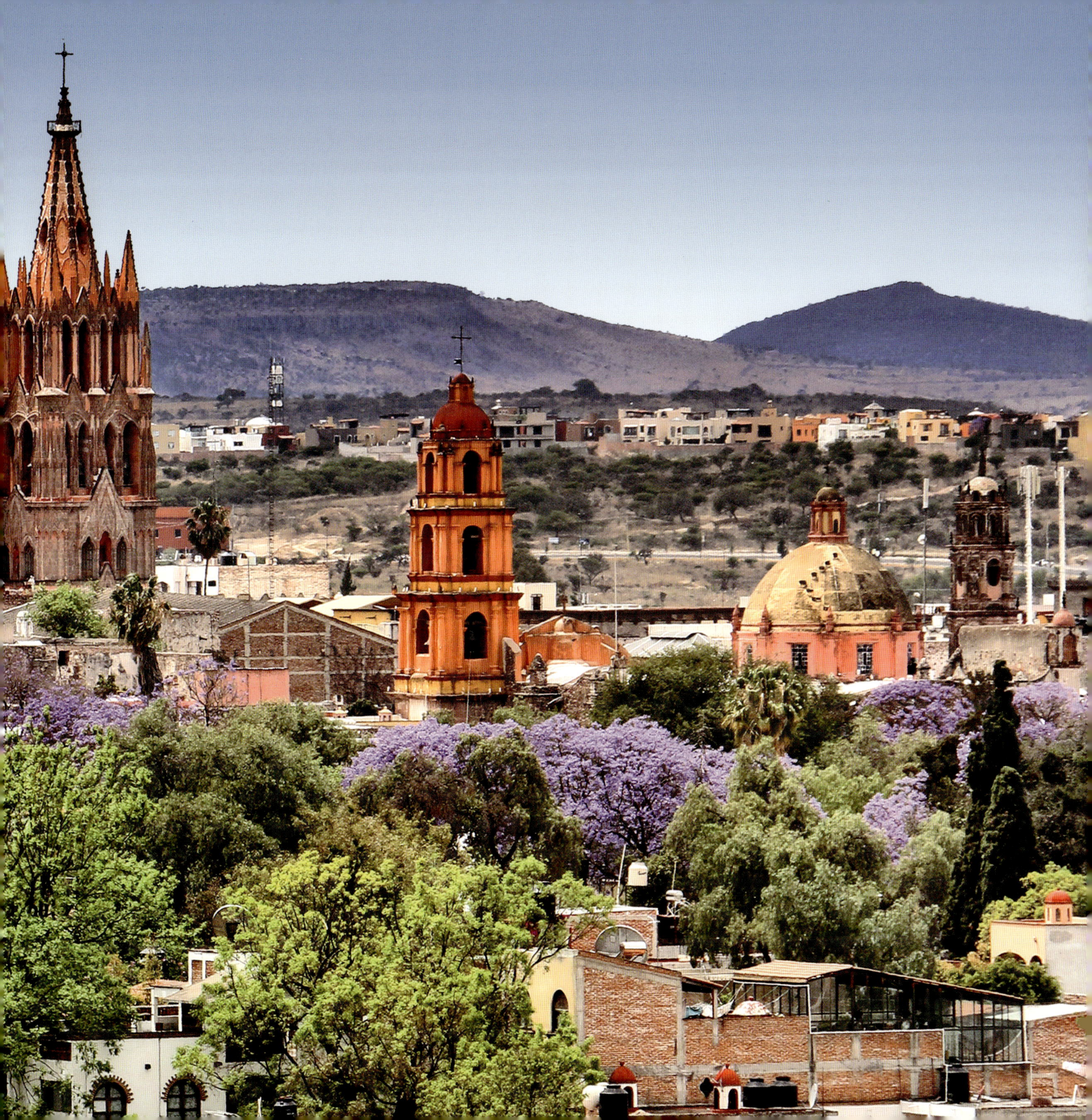

Festivals

San Miguel was once admonished for having an excess of festivities. Celebrations abound, yet after centuries they have lost nothing of their depth or meaning and are deeply rooted in the fabric of this place and in the hearts of these people. Mexico's tumultuous history is multilayered, a mix of many different Indigenous peoples and those who came after the conquest. The region around San Miguel was never conquered; it was absorbed in the aftermath of the conquest. Because of this, San Miguel exists in both worlds, that of before the conquest and that of after, and this has been a crossroads for centuries. The Indigenous roots of this place live on, some parts as yet largely undisturbed by the passage of time; the Spanish who arrived after the conquest live on in the mixed blood of their descendants. The harmony between these worlds is in no way more evident than in the town's celebrations.

El Señor de la Conquista: This is an Indigenous celebration that, when it could not be quelled by the Catholic Church, was embraced into the hybrid faith that exists in San Miguel. In honor of Christ of the Conquest, people come from surrounding communities to dance in front of the Parroquia. These dancers, concheros, wear traditional clothing and dance tirelessly all day in early March in this blended ceremony that commemorates Jesus, Mary, and oppression by the Spanish.

Dia de los Muertos: During the last week of October, altars are prepared in homes and businesses to honor those who have passed on. With love and remembrance, colorful with decorations and flowers, these altars tell the stories of their lives by the photos and objects placed there. Sugar figures represent favorite foods, pets, flowers, sports, and anything the departed loved; and the stories shared within families ensure that the new generation will know those who came before. On November 1 and 2, families move to picnics at the cemetery, surrounded by music from mariachis. Celebrations conclude with face painting and outrageous clothing as Catrinas stroll through the Jardín, representing death and the soulful way in which Mexicans face it.

Dia de Independencia: The call for freedom from Spanish colonial rule began in the early morning of September 16, 1810. Ignacio Allende held dances in his family home on the main square, where he and Father Hidalgo from nearby Dolores met secretly with fellow conspirators to plan their revolt. Their "Grito," or call to freedom, is celebrated every year when the president of Mexico rings Father Hidalgo's bell, now on the Presidential Palace in Mexico City, in memory of this Cry for Freedom and of all those heroes who fought to gain it.

Dia de los Locos: The origin of this celebration is not known, but it is said it began with town gardeners performing dances for San Antonio de Padua during the days before the harvest. Curiosity among those who came to watch these lunatics, or "locos," prompted the gardeners to dress up to scare off the crowds so they could dance in peace. Dia de los Locos is now an enormous celebration of finding the strength to let go of the constraints of normal life and find inner peace in the madness and chaos of life.

The "excess of festivities" continues and is one of the reasons to love San Miguel.

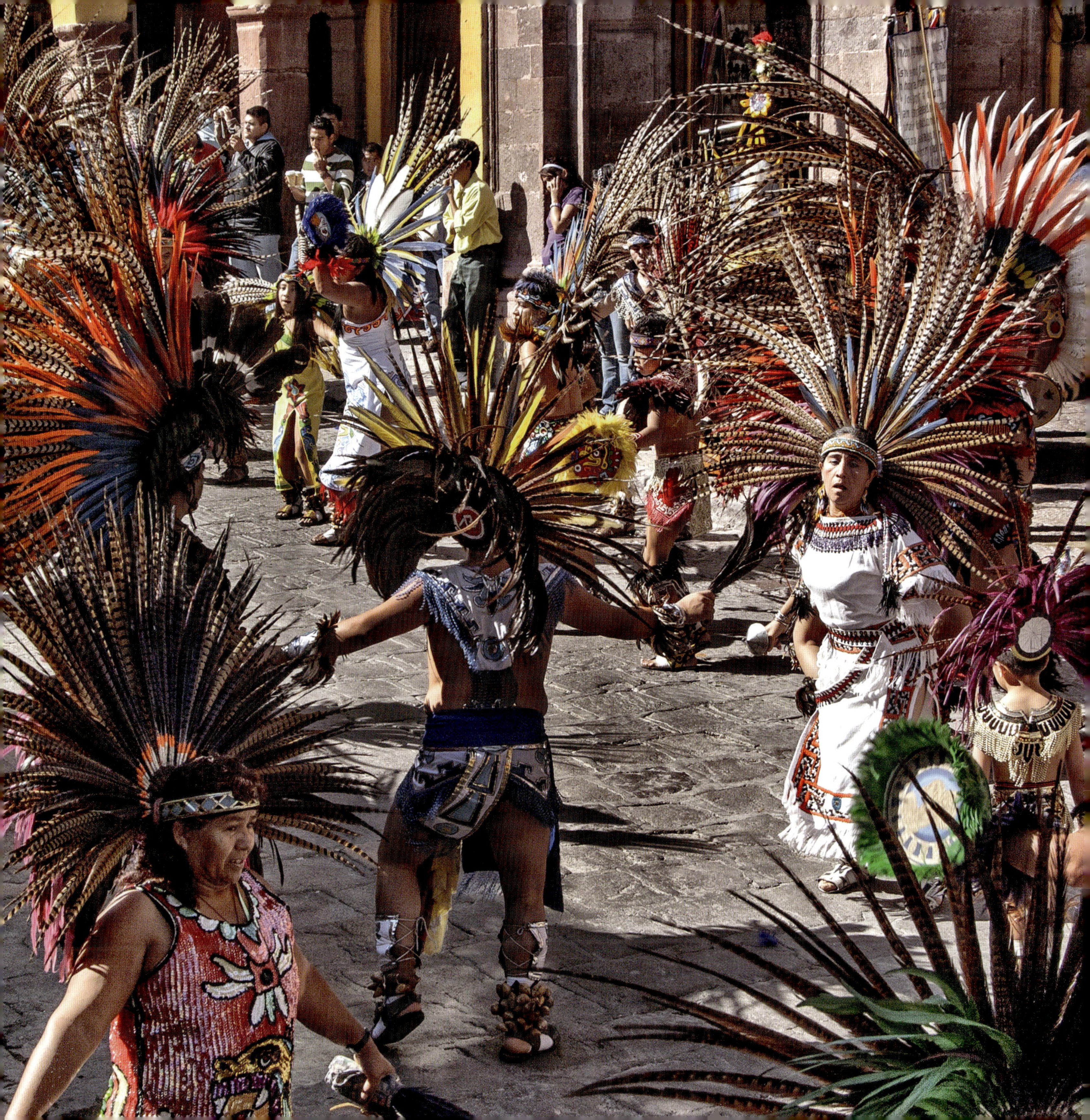

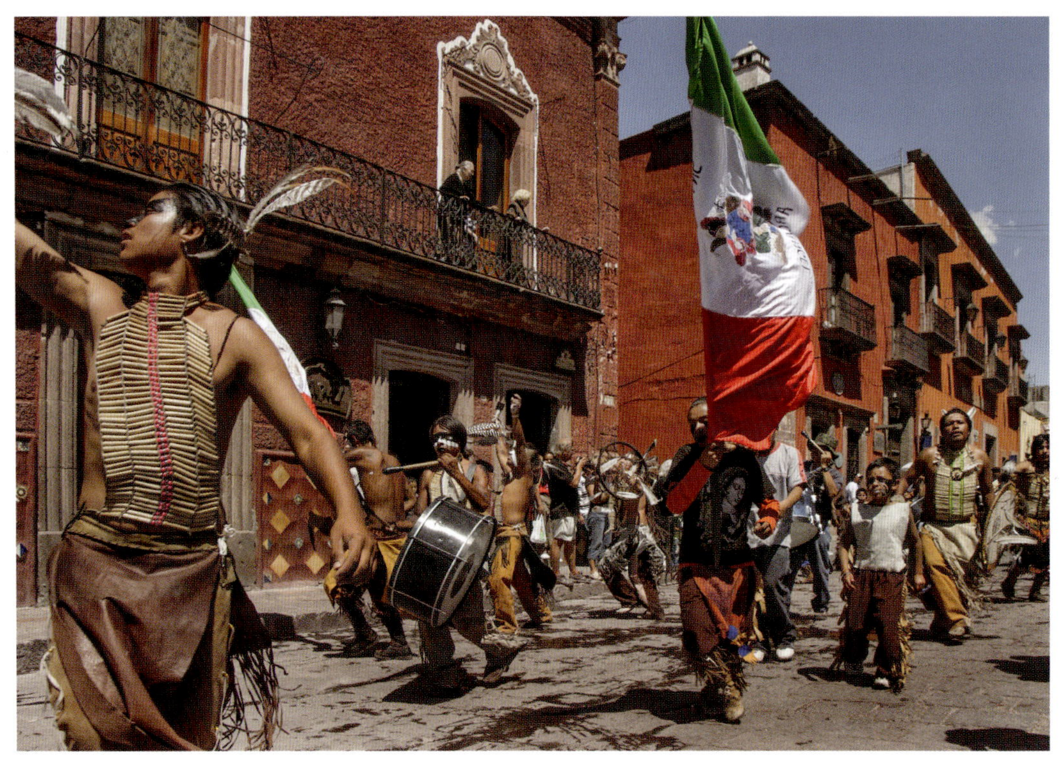
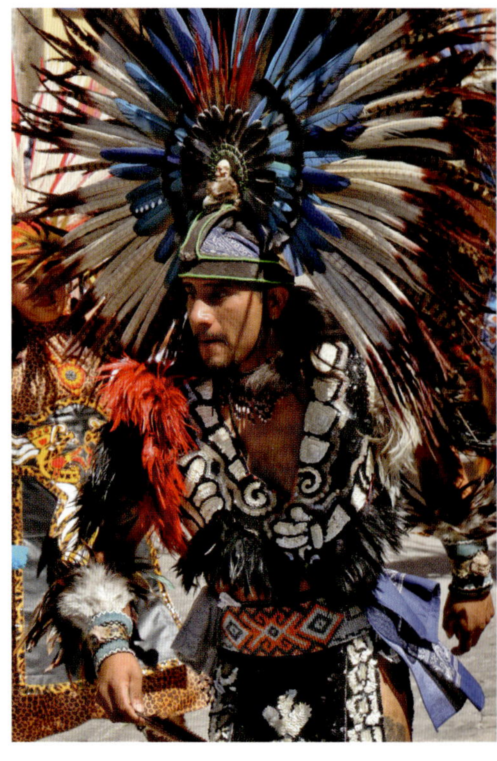
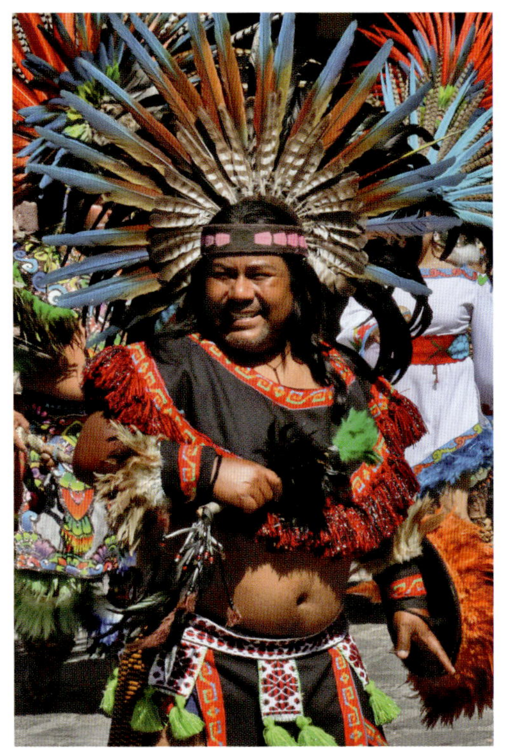
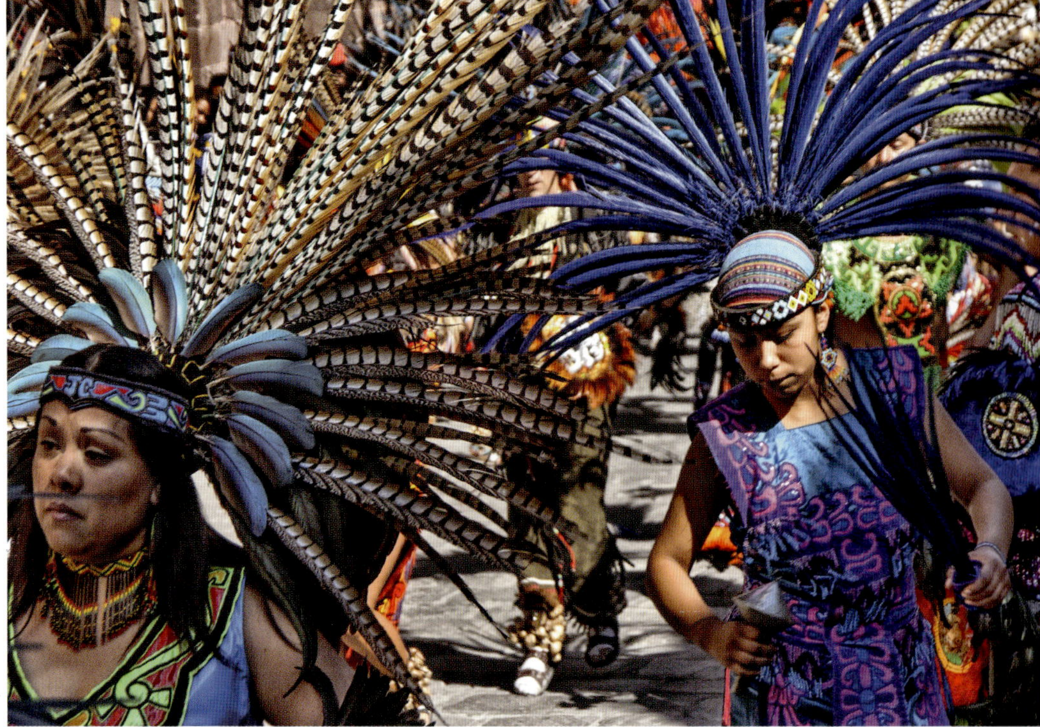

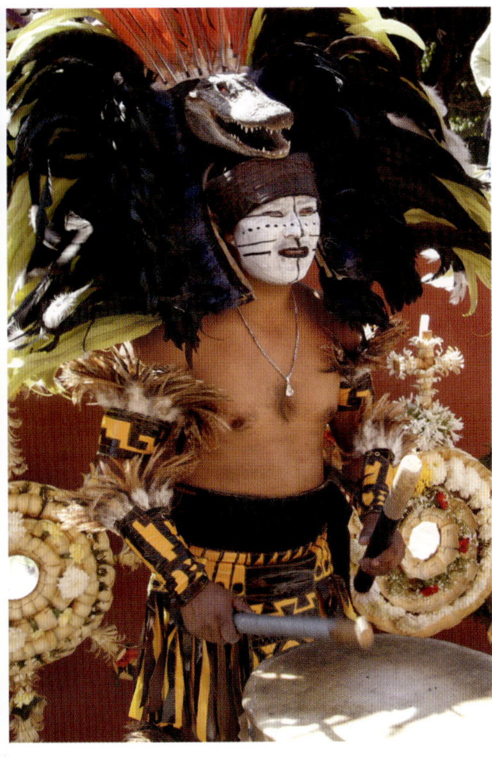

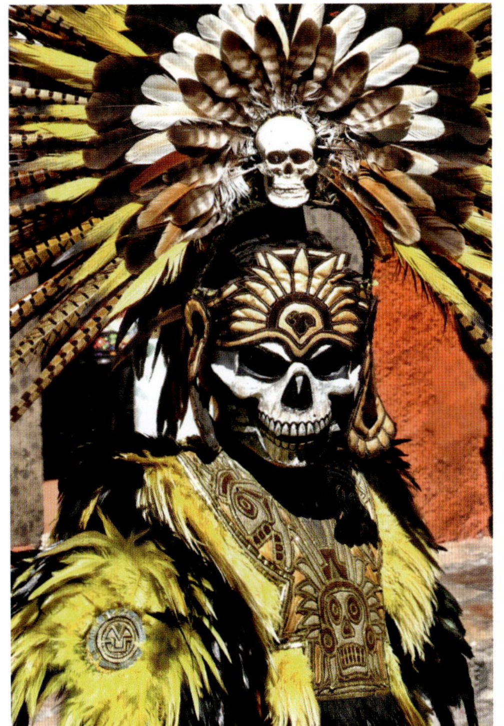

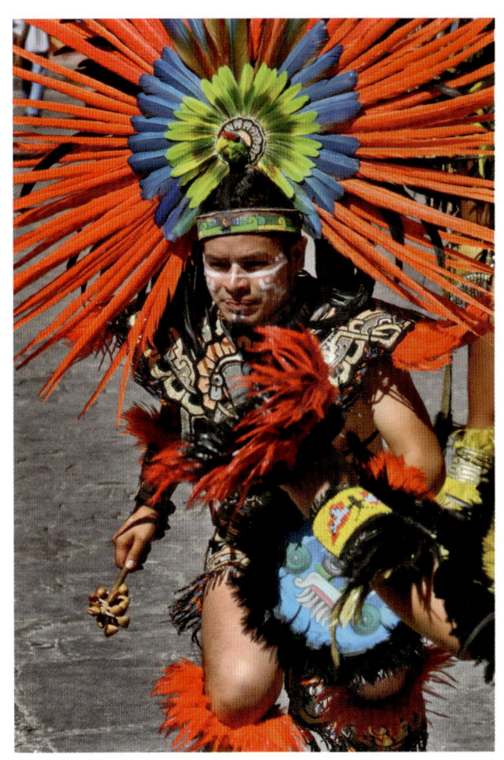

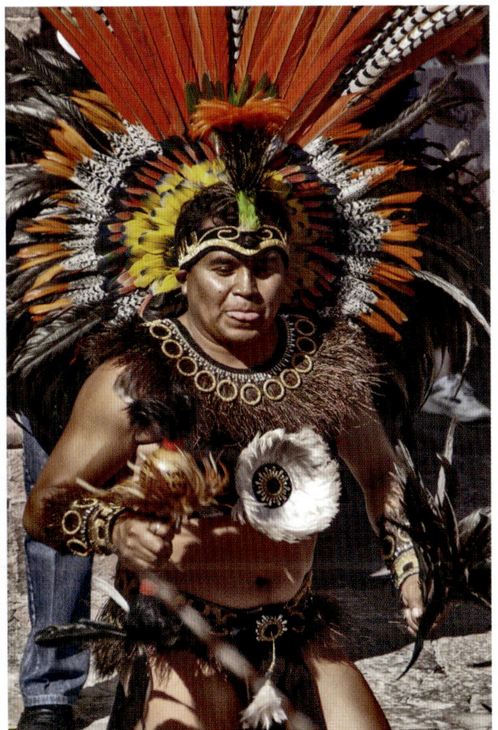

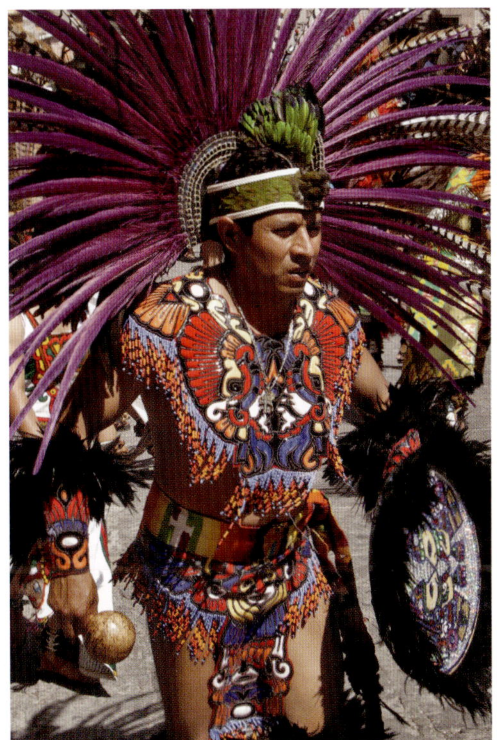

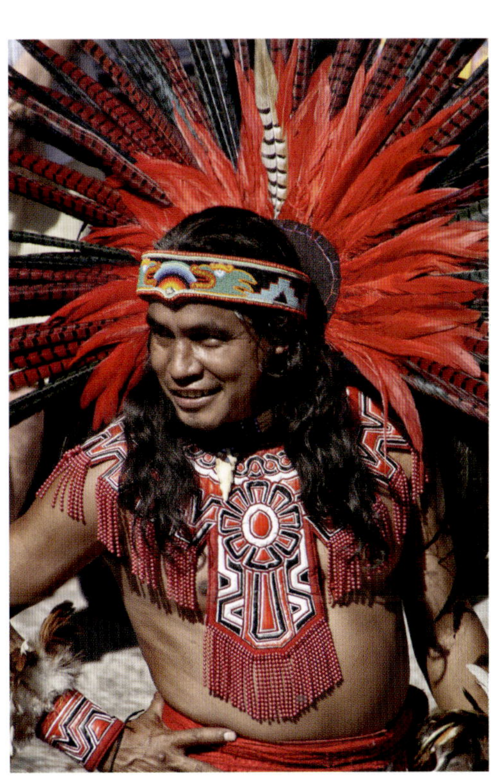

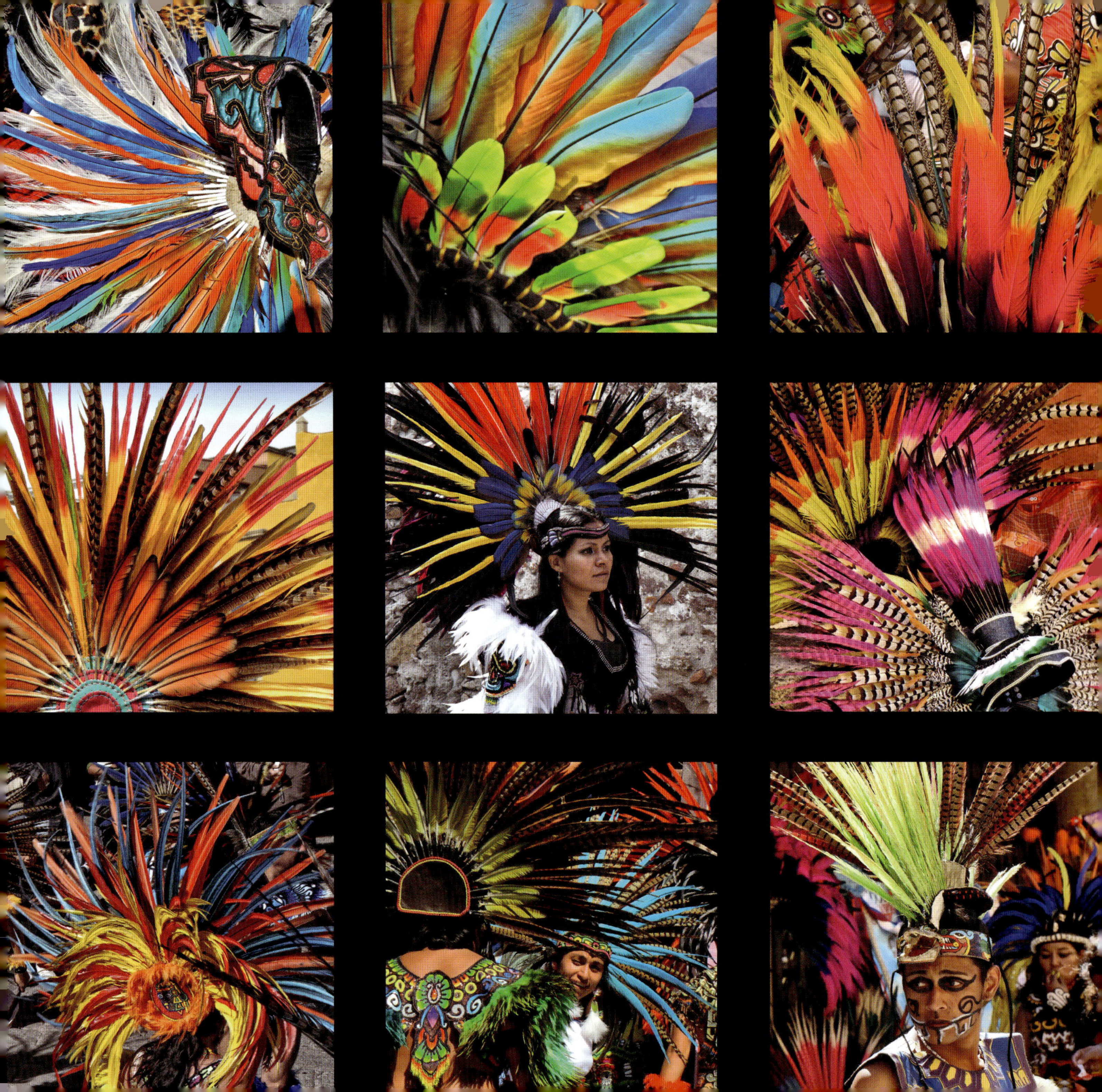

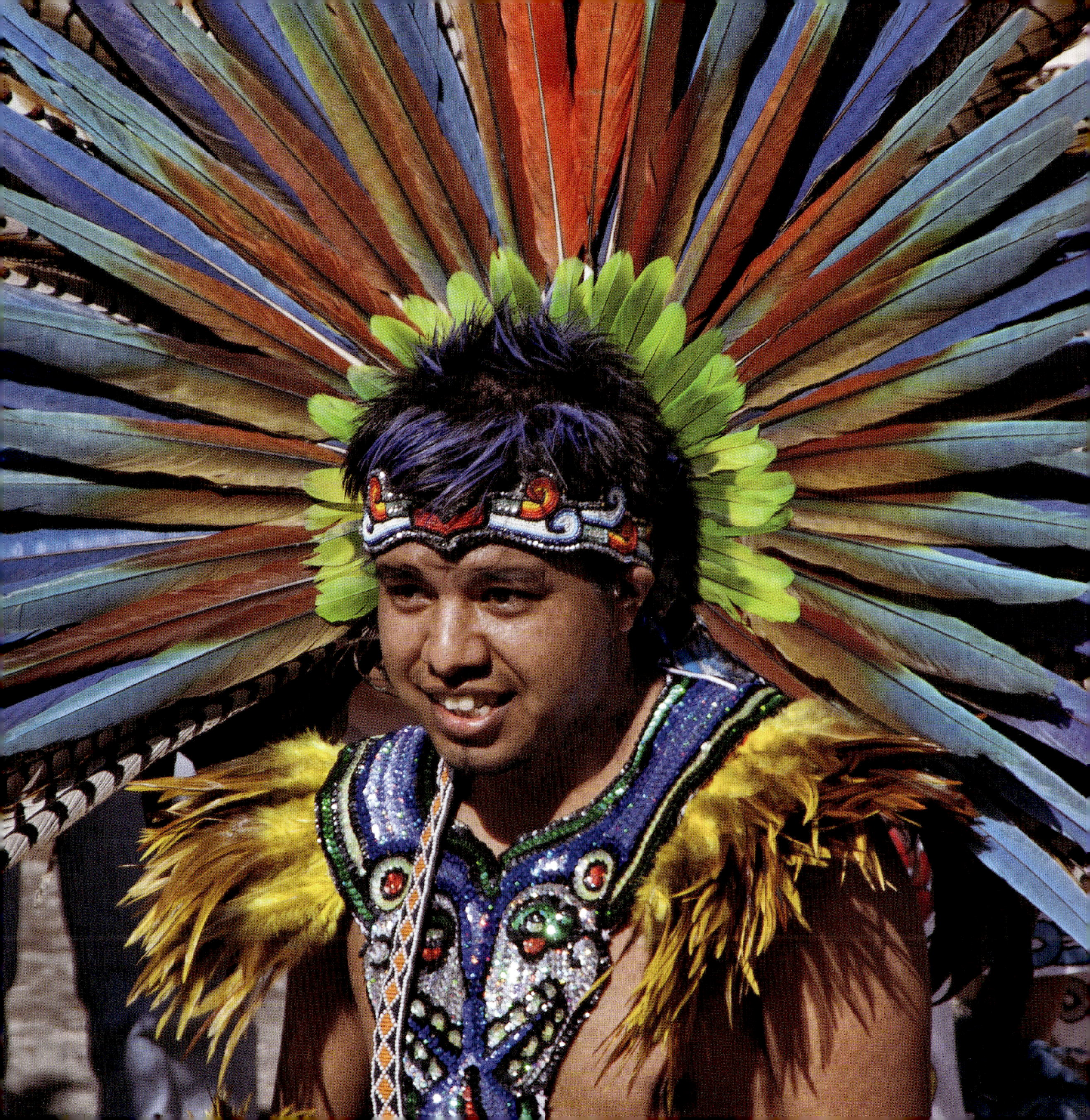

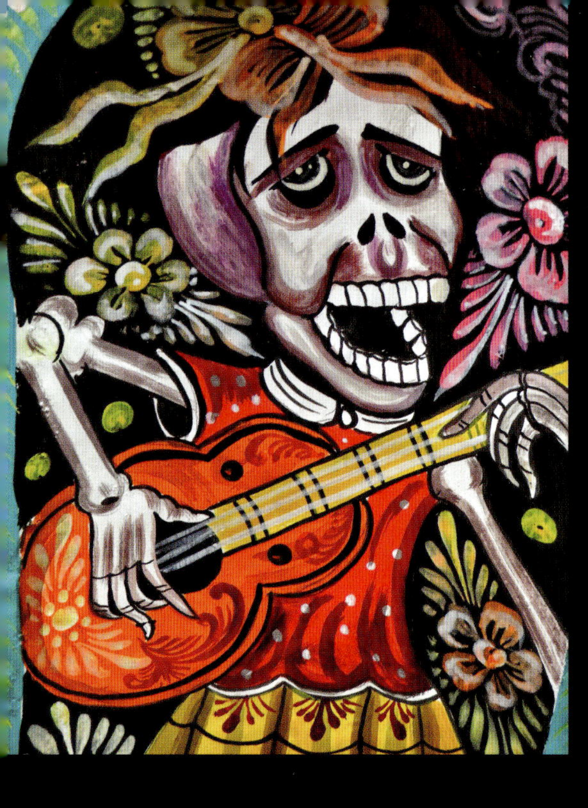
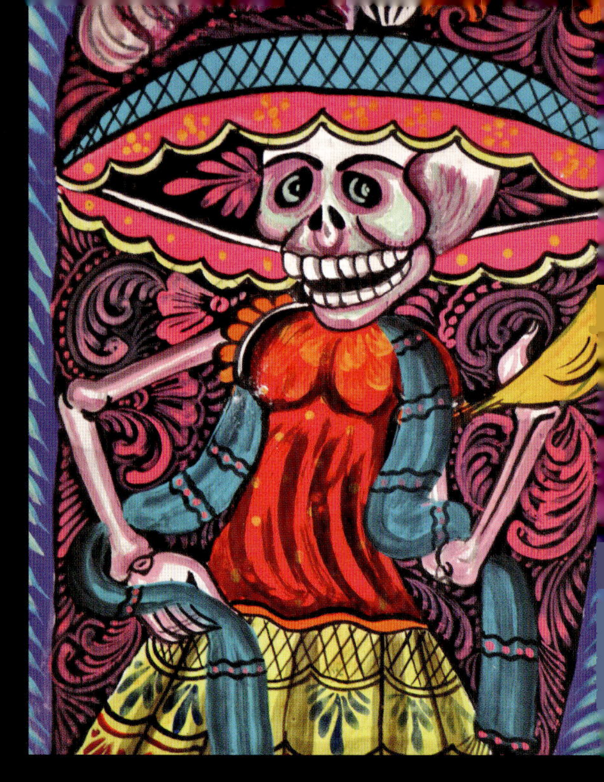
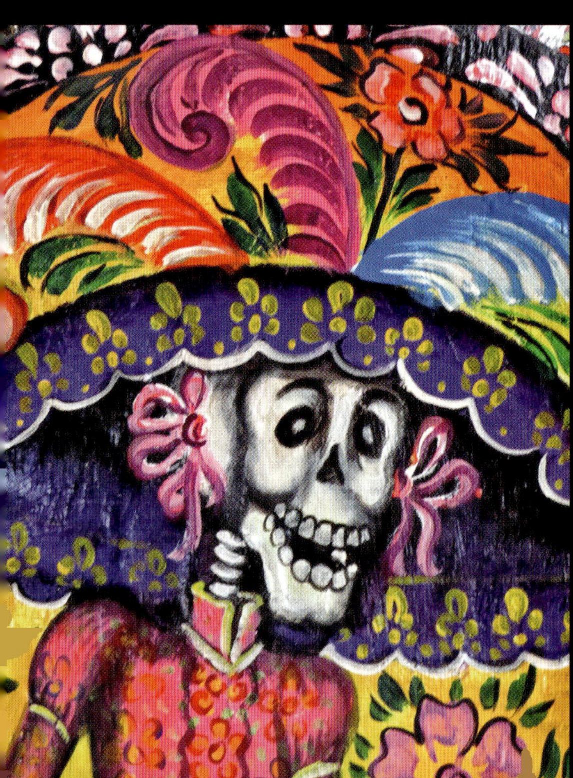
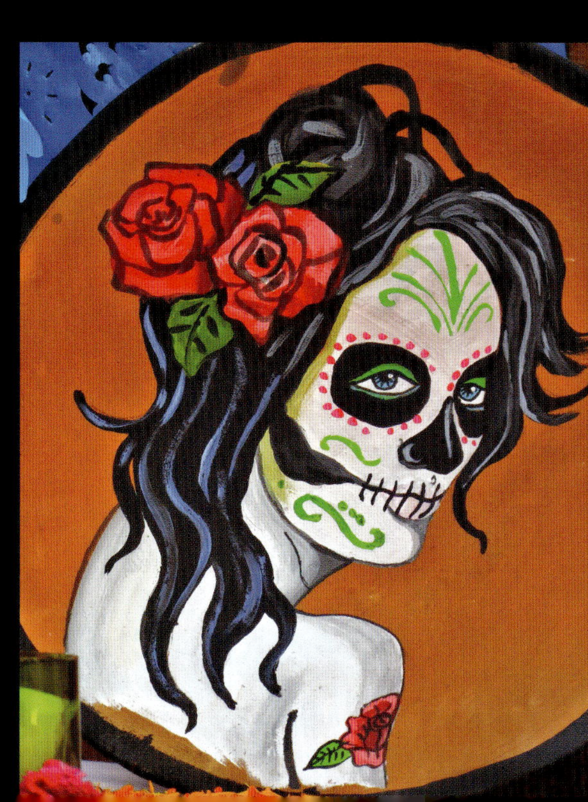

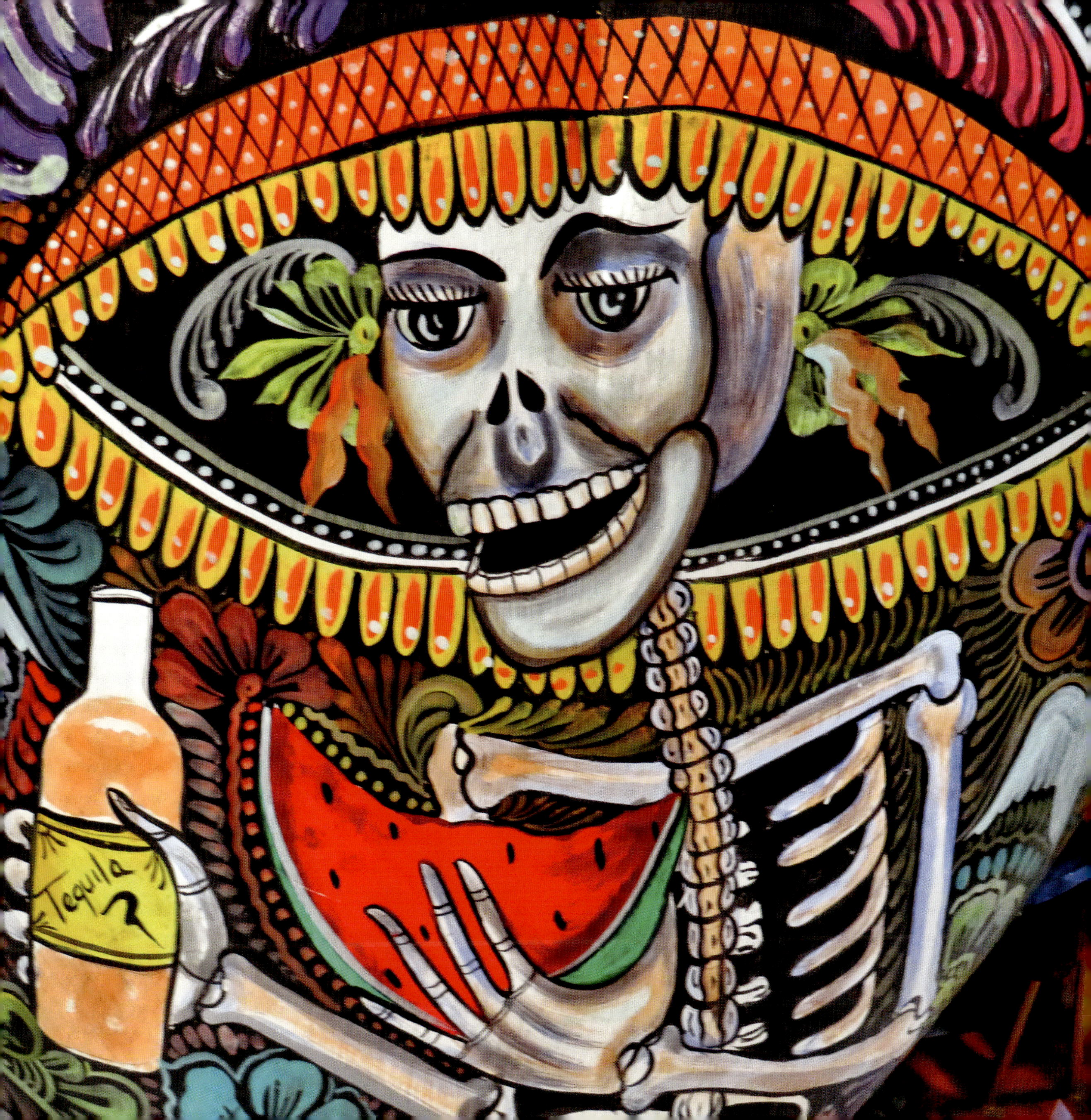
Tequila

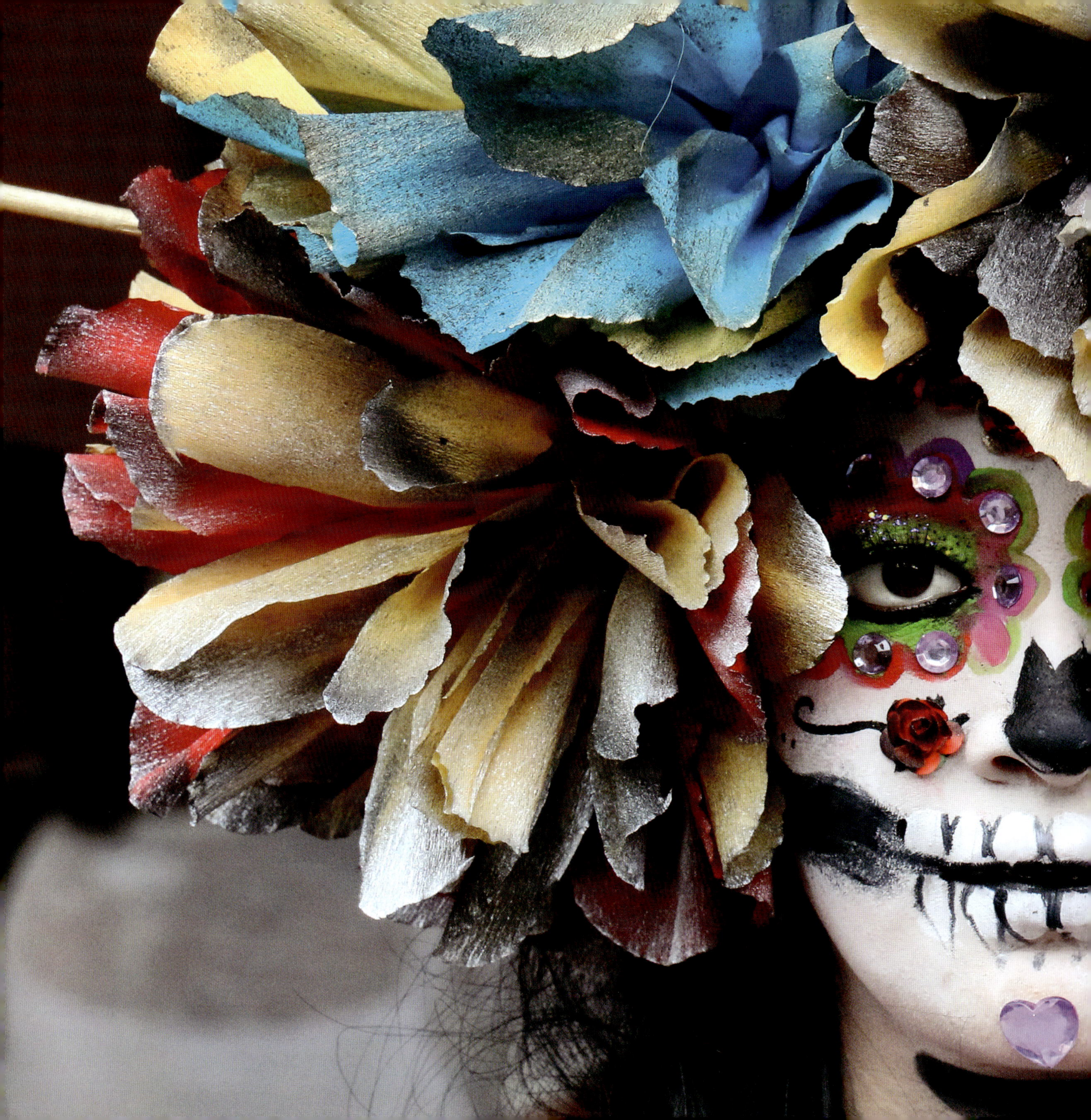

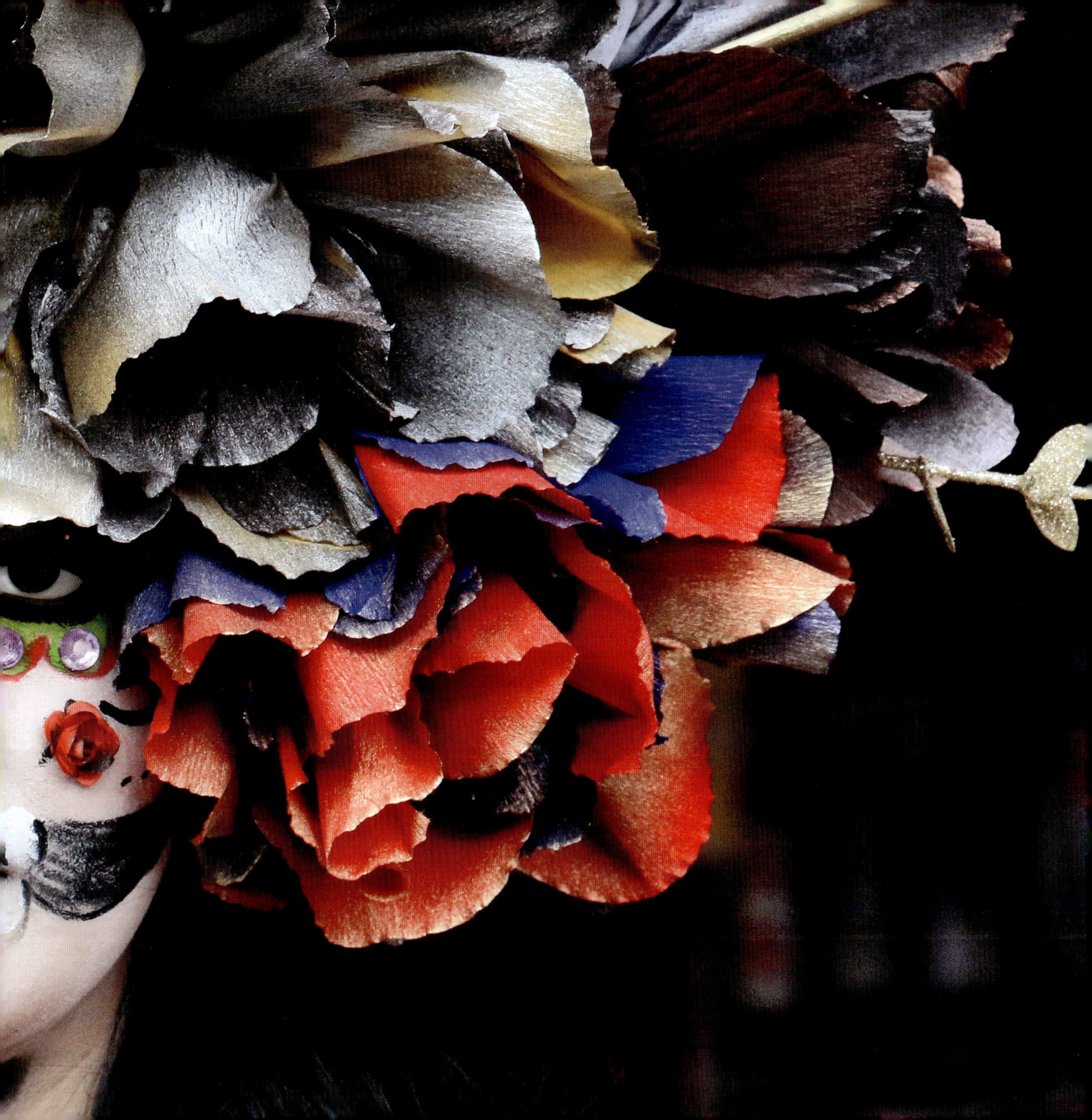

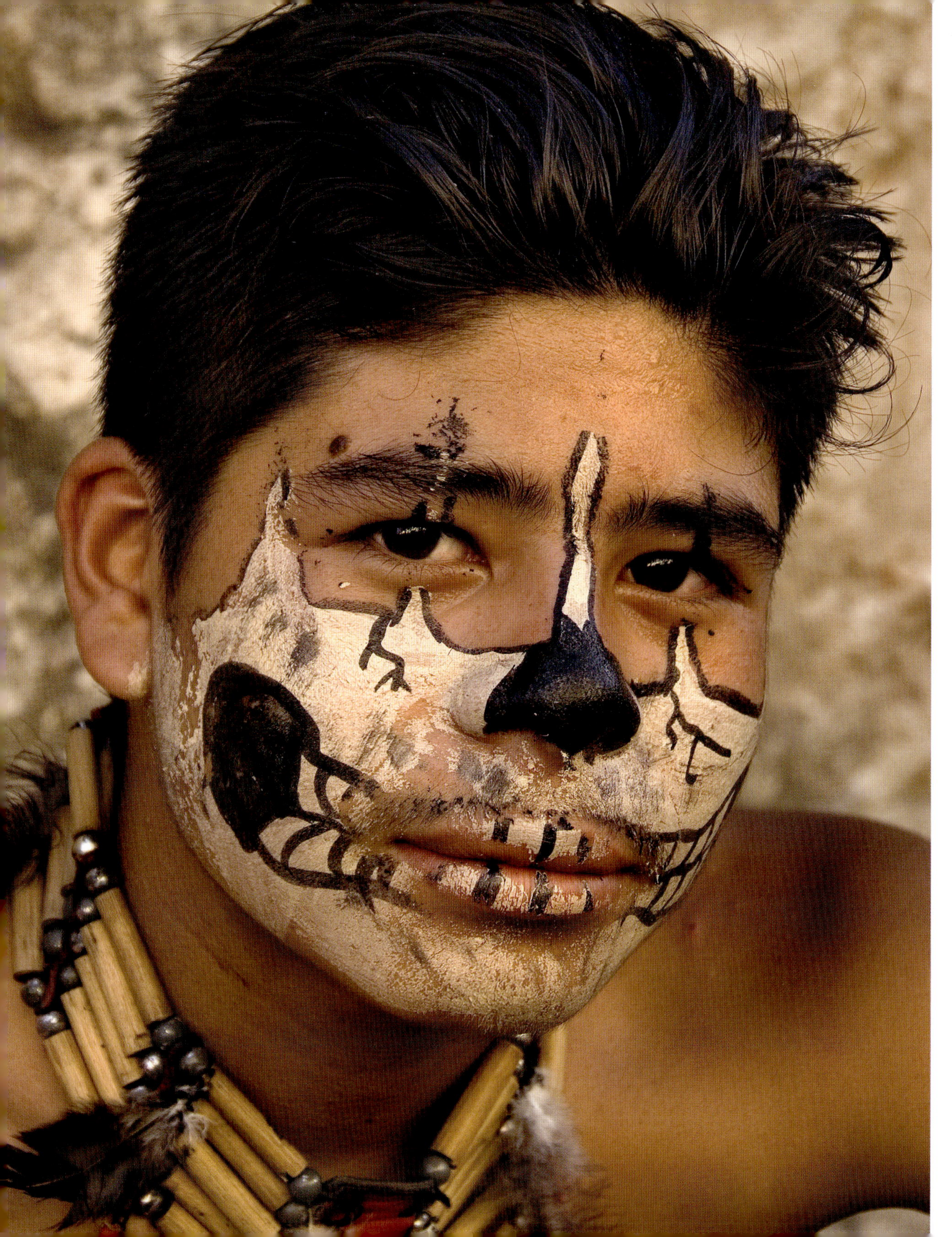

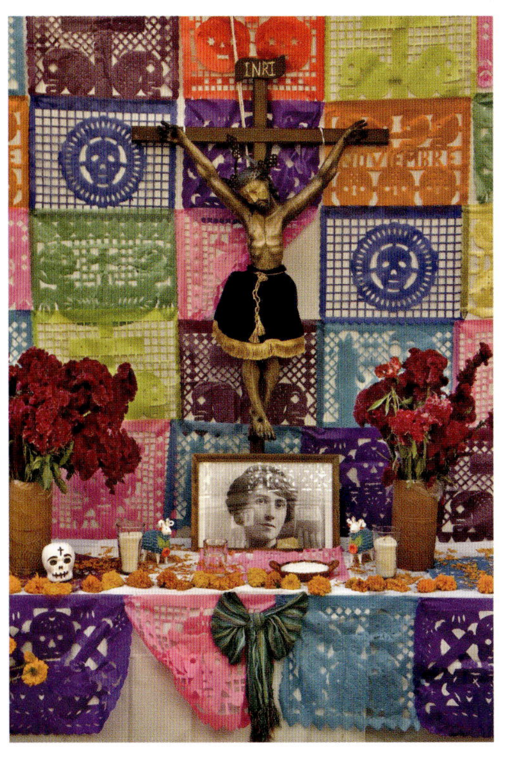
INRI

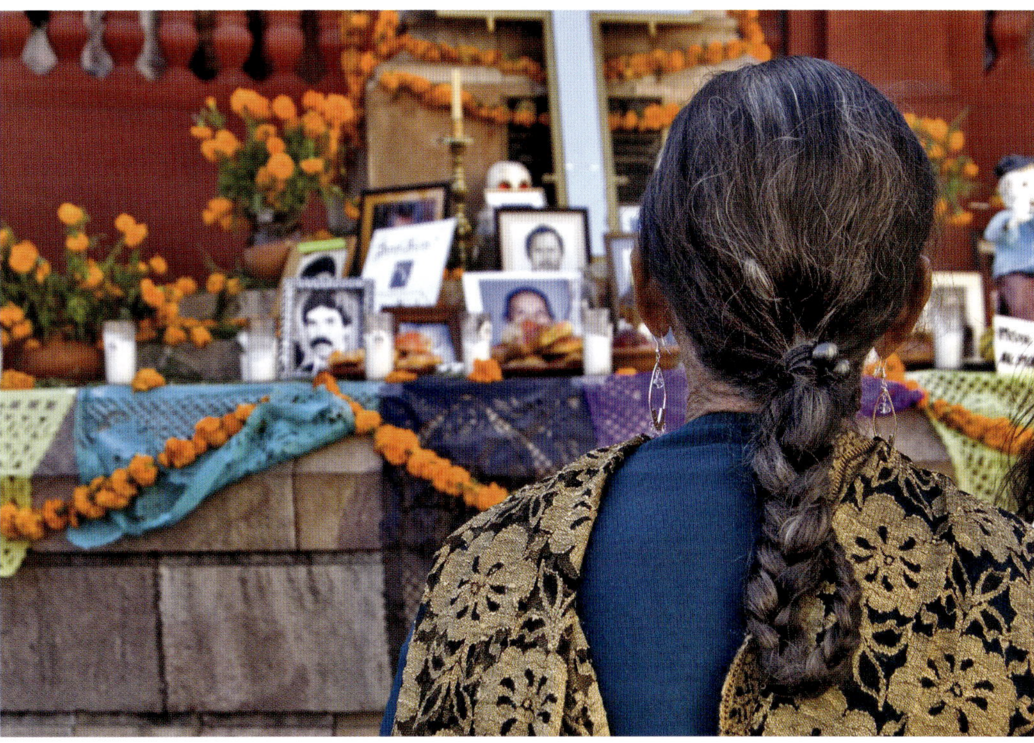

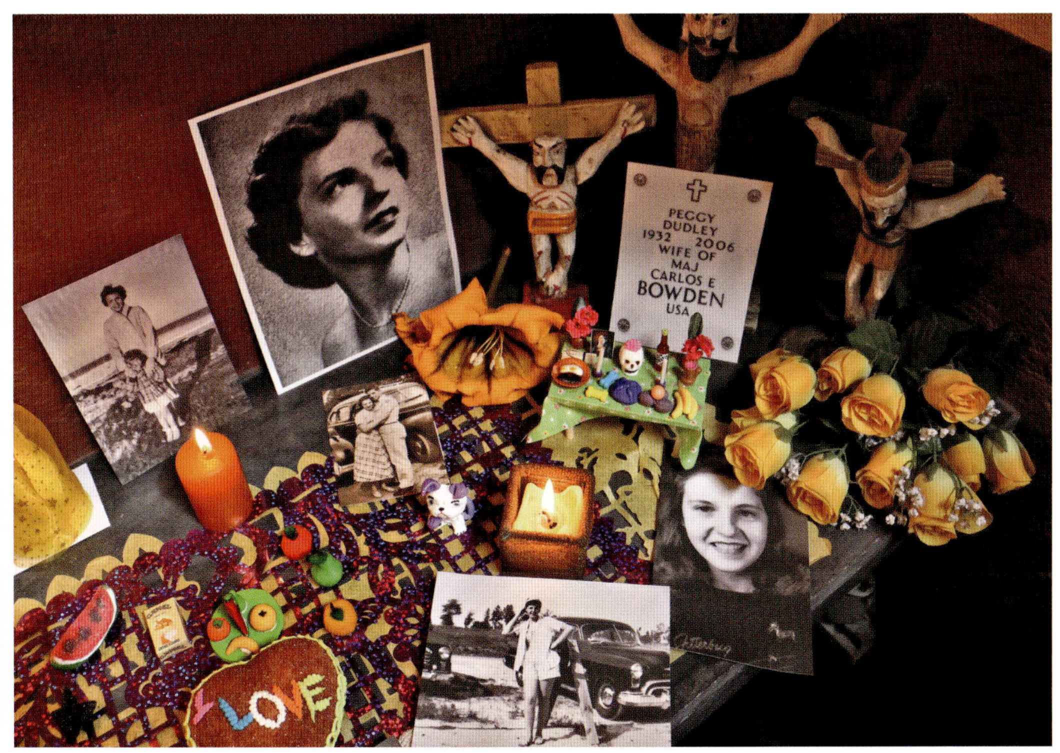
PEGGY
DUDLEY
1932 2006
WIFE OF
MAJ
CARLOS E
BOWDEN
USA
LOVE

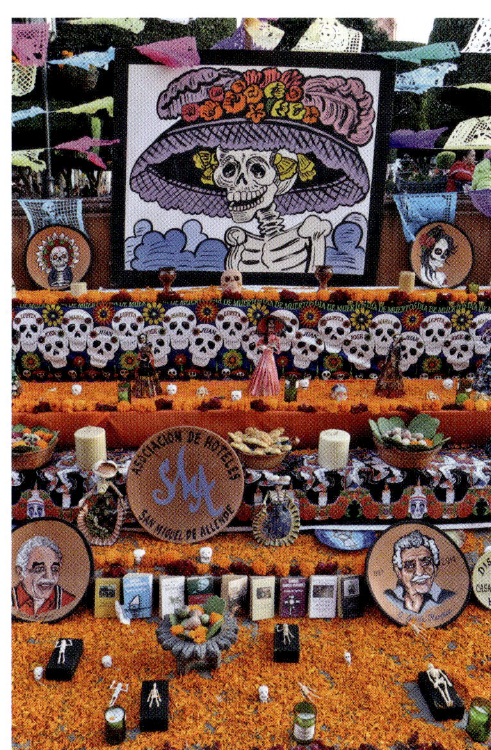
ASOCIACION DE HOTELES
SMA
SAN MIGUEL DE ALLENDE

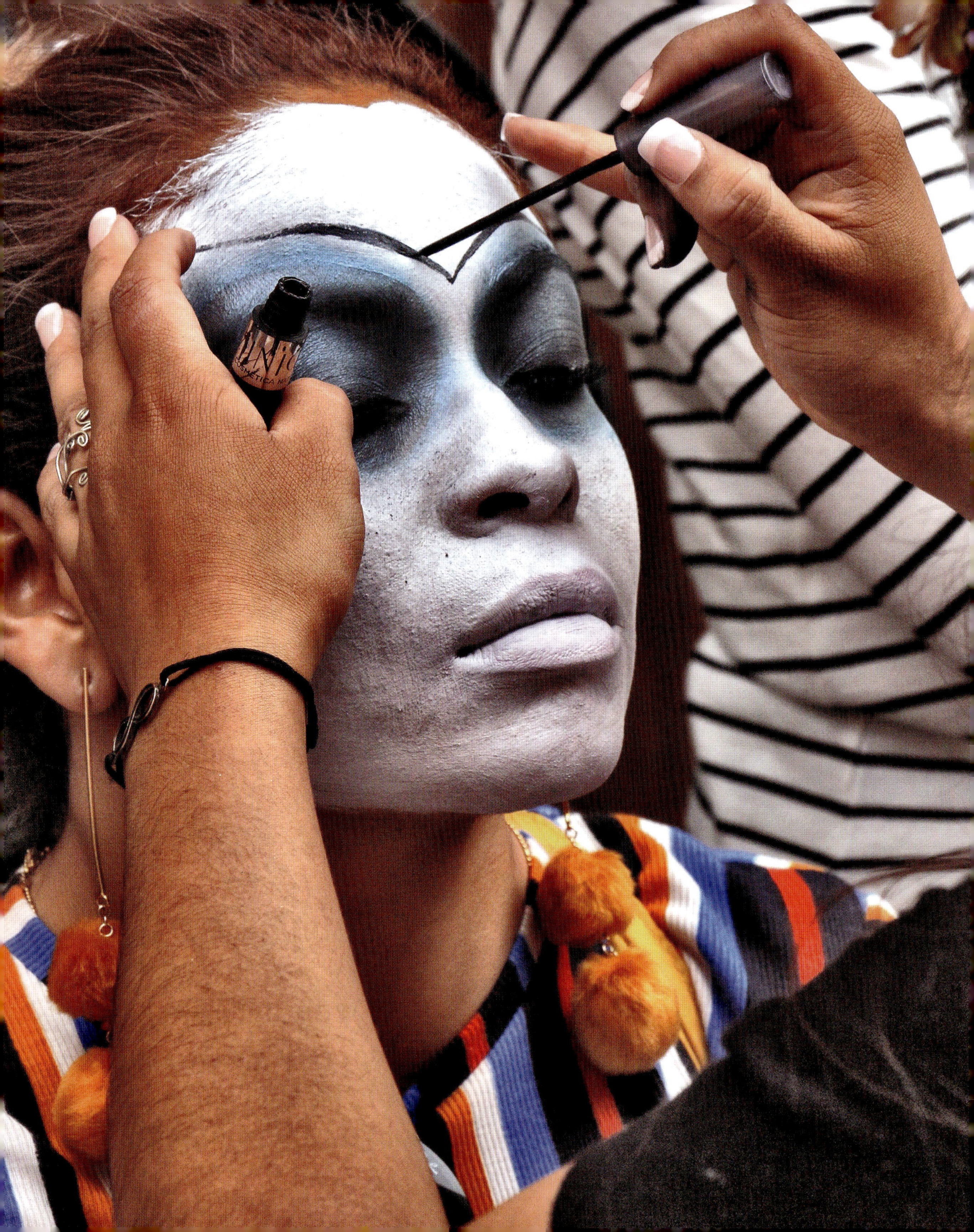

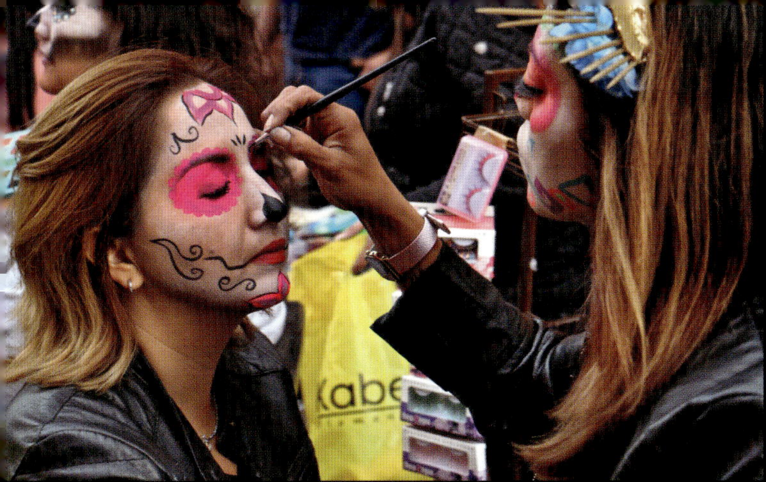

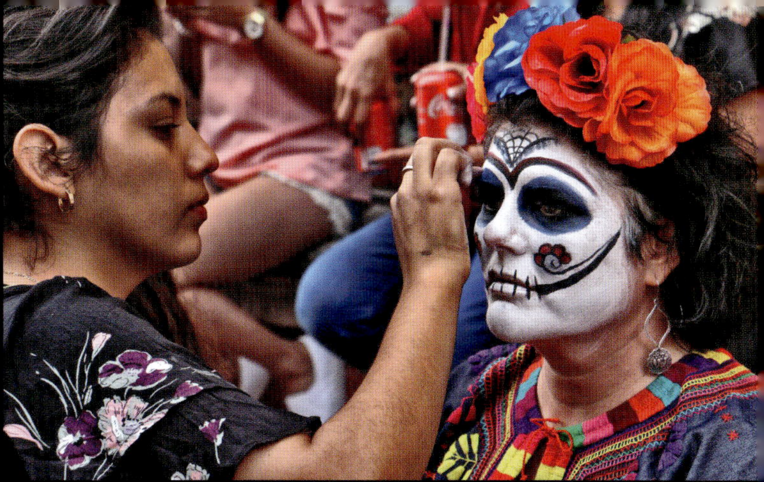

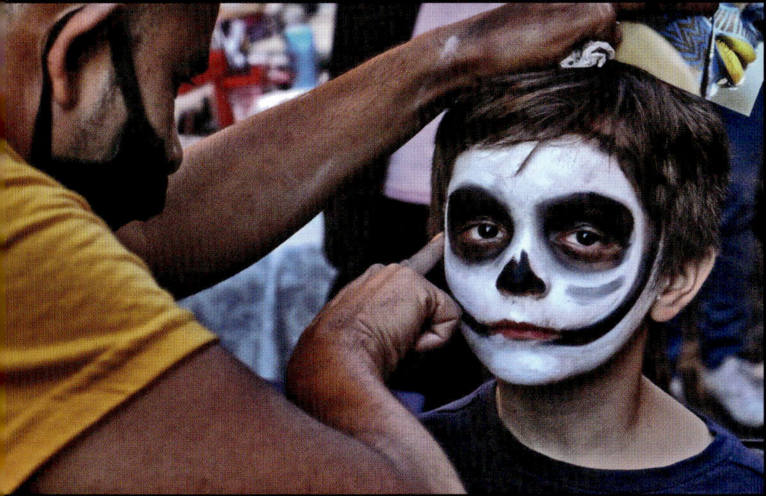

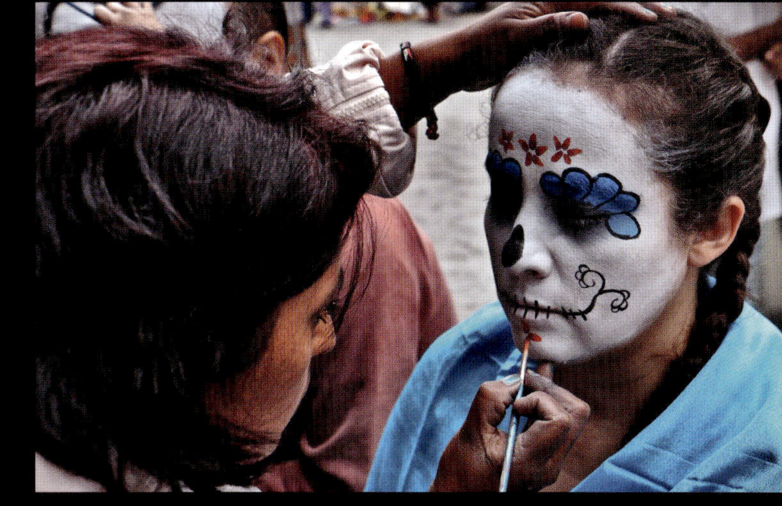

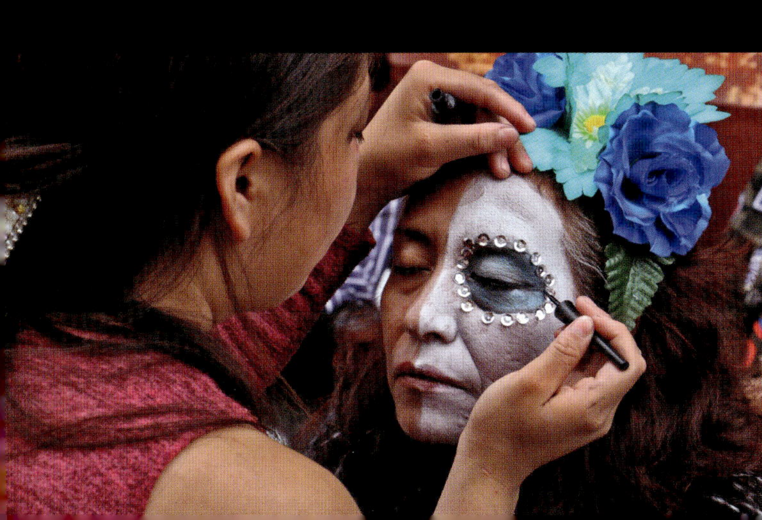

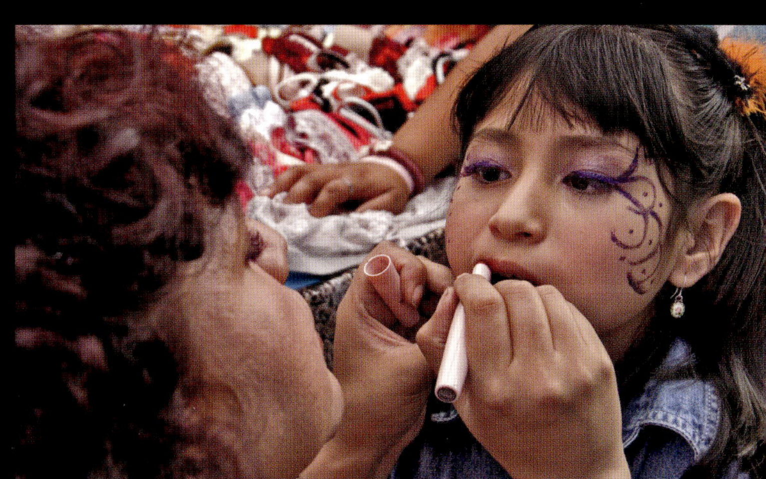

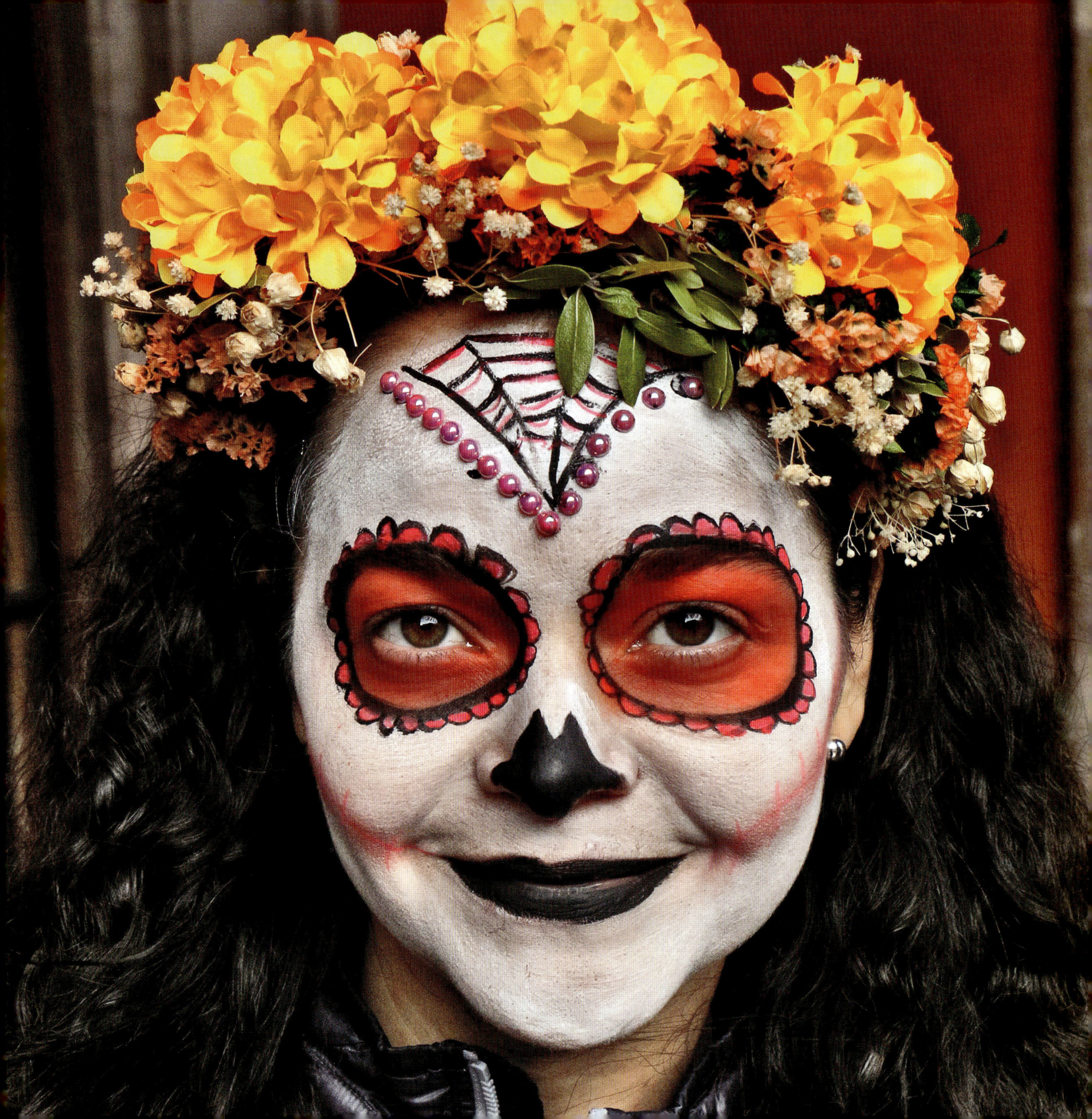

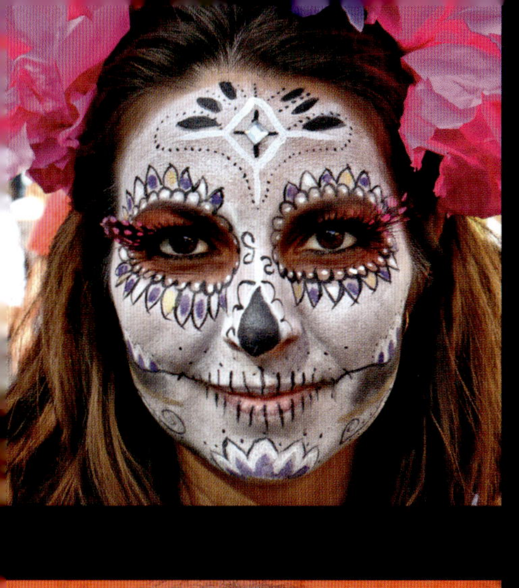
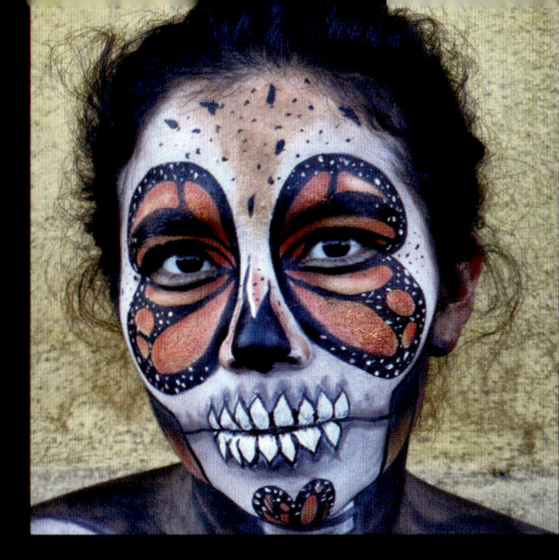
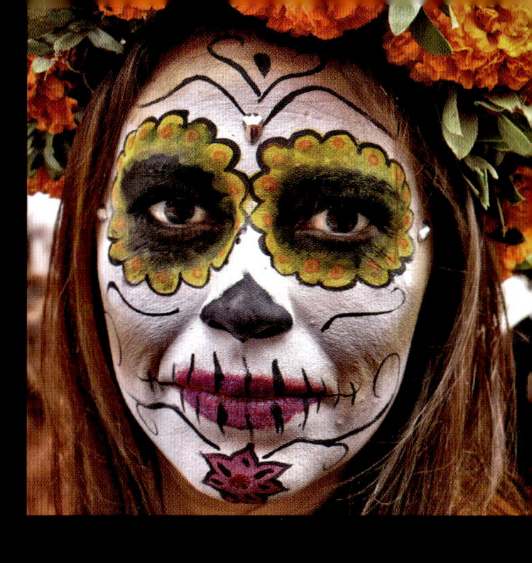
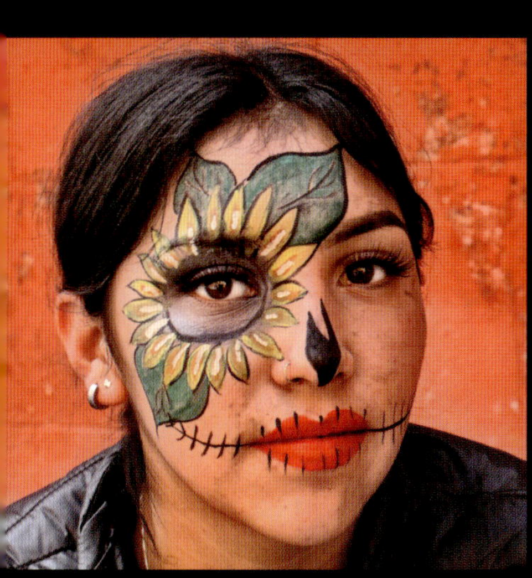
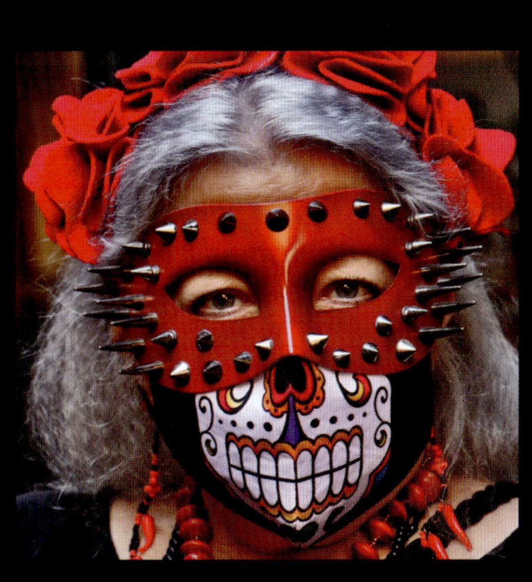
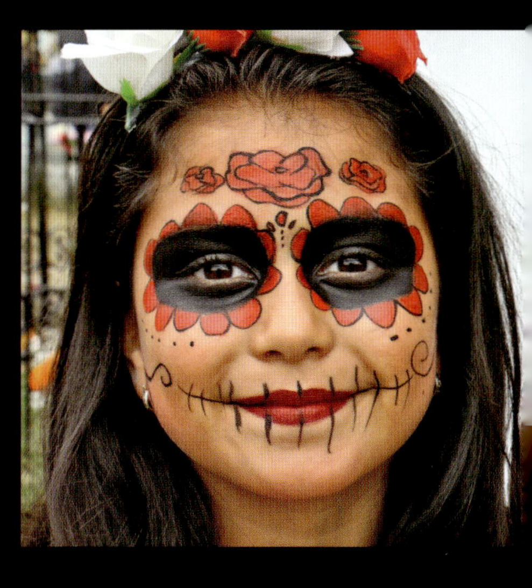
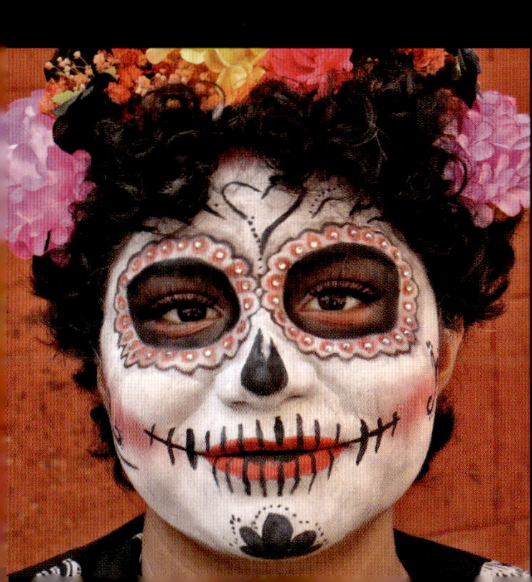
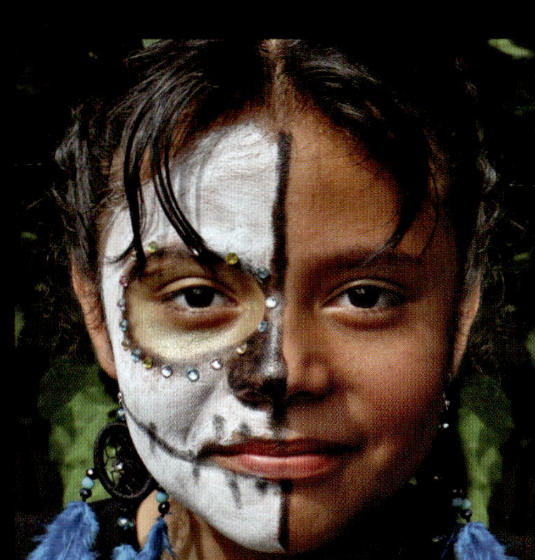
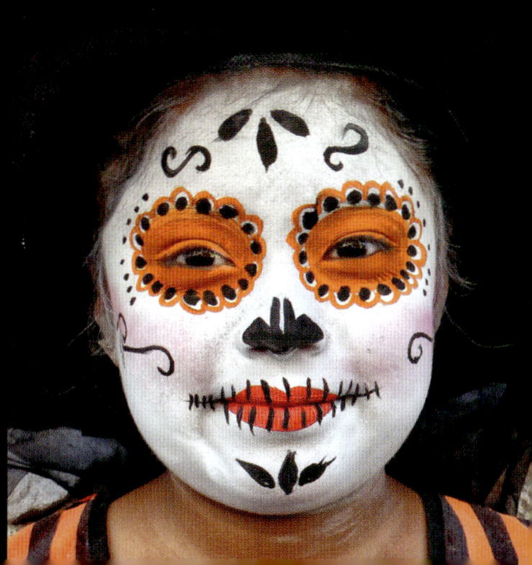

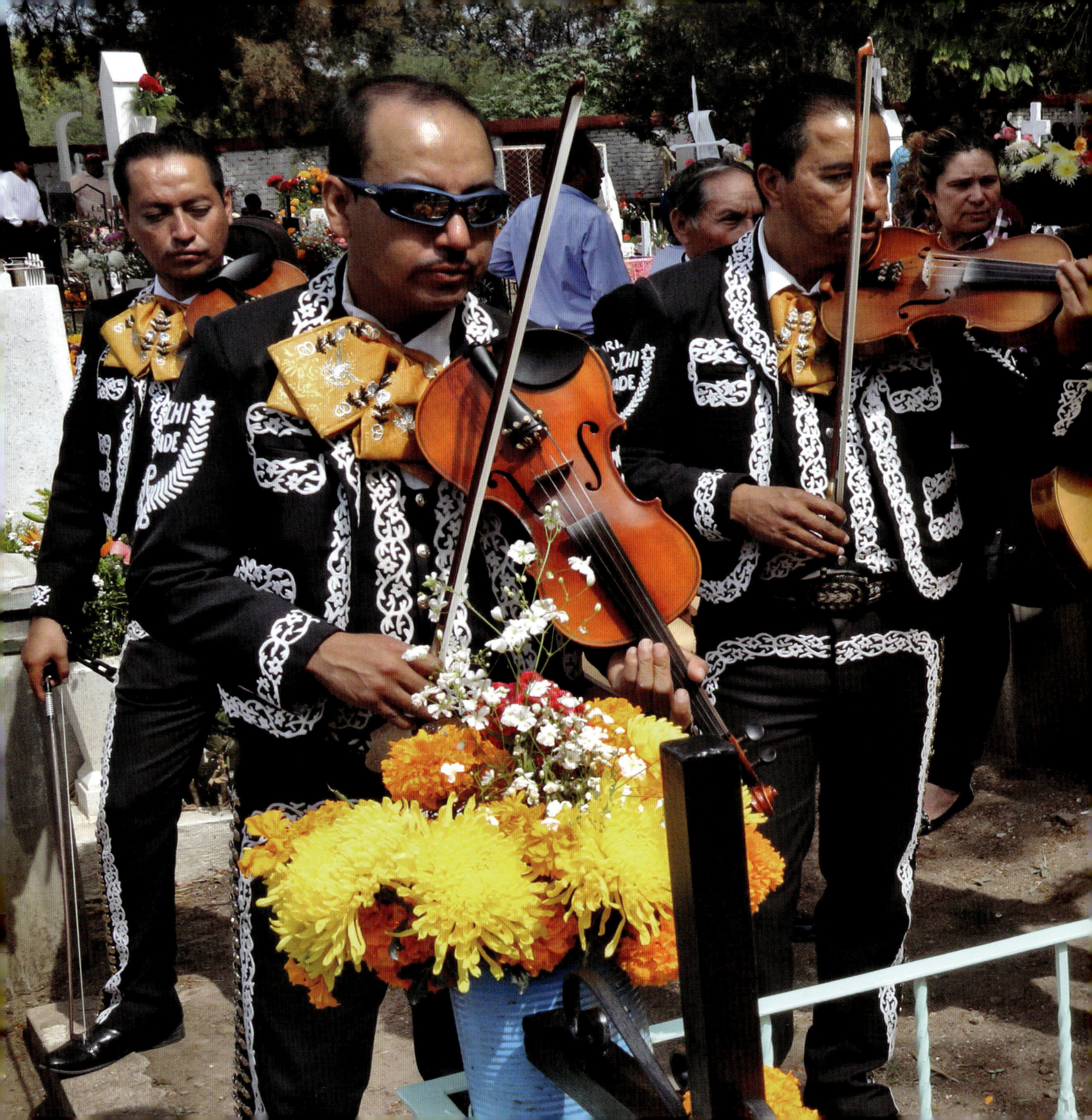

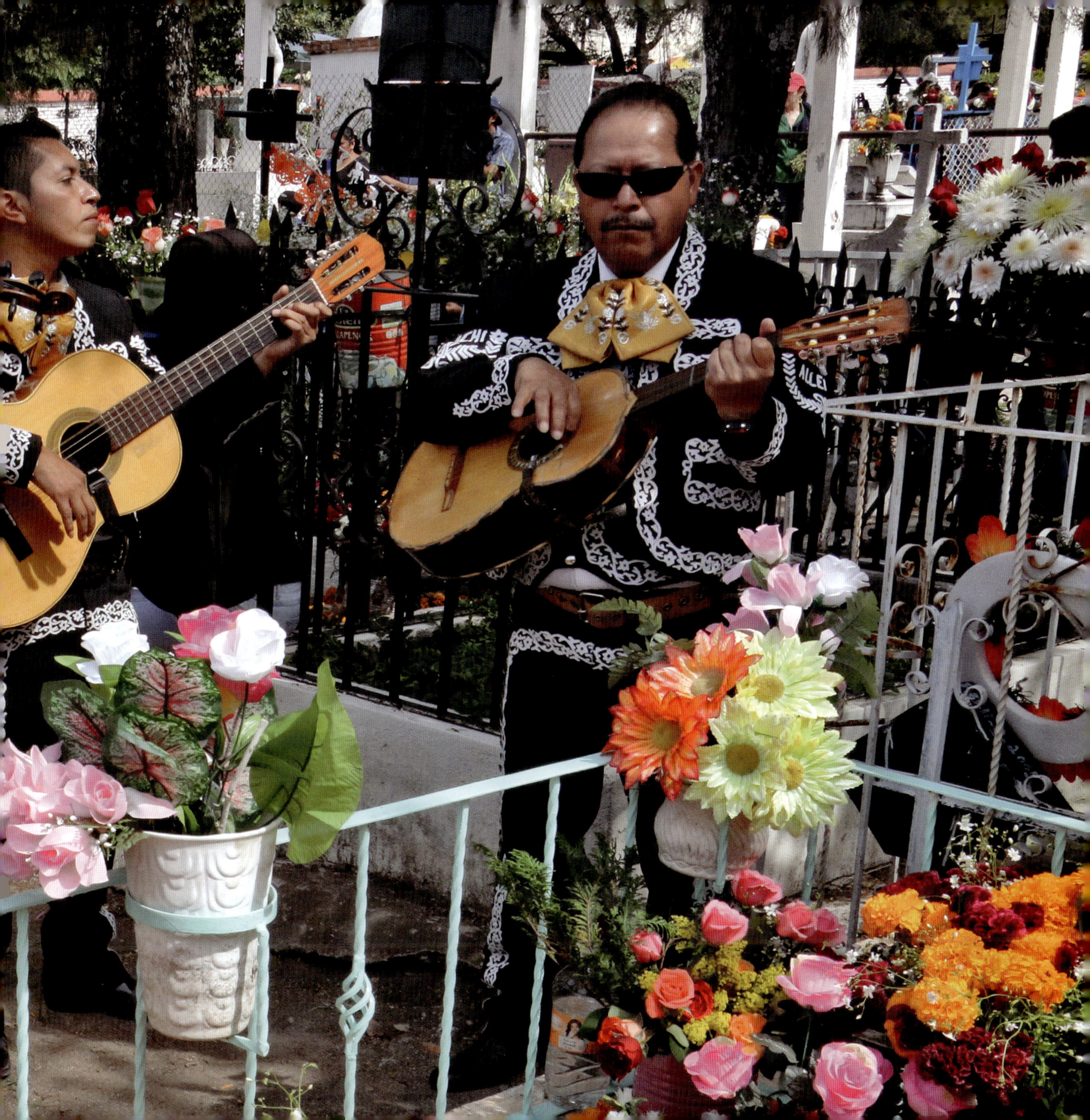

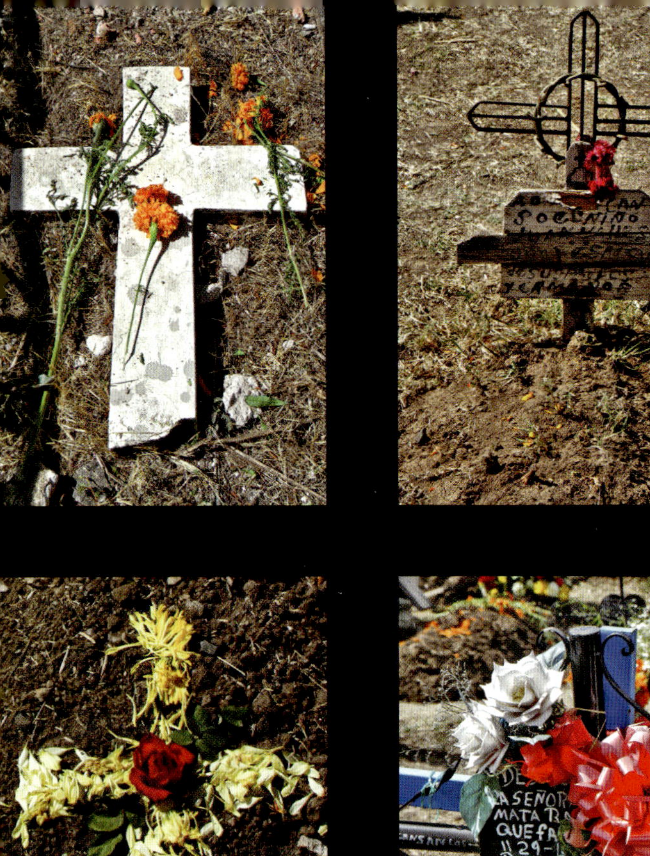
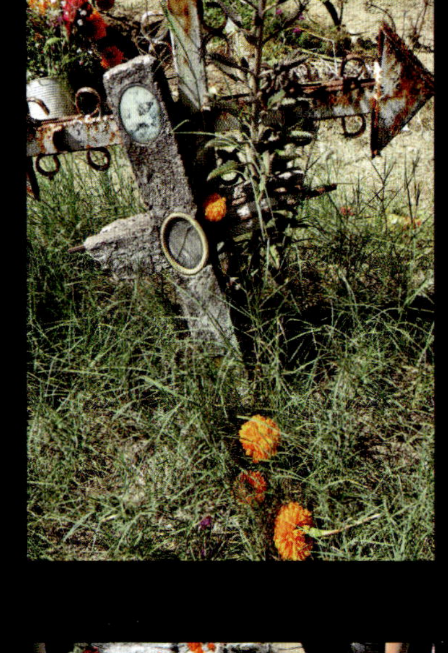
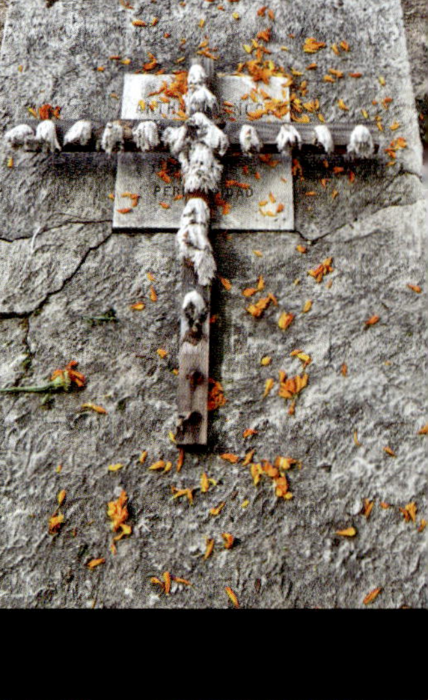
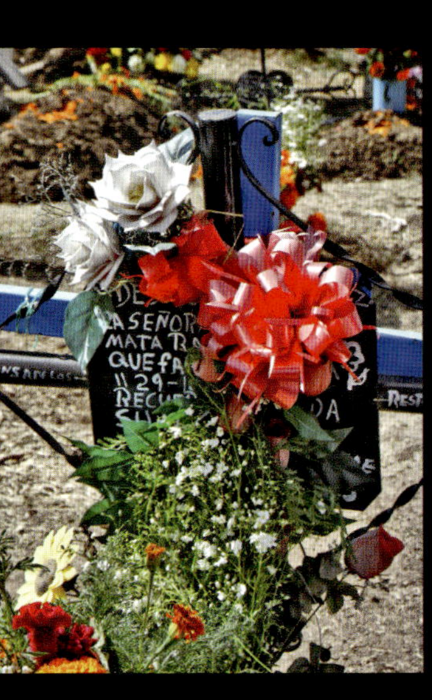
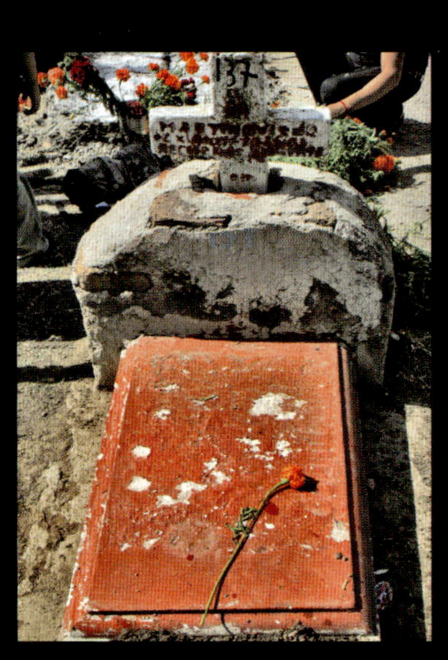
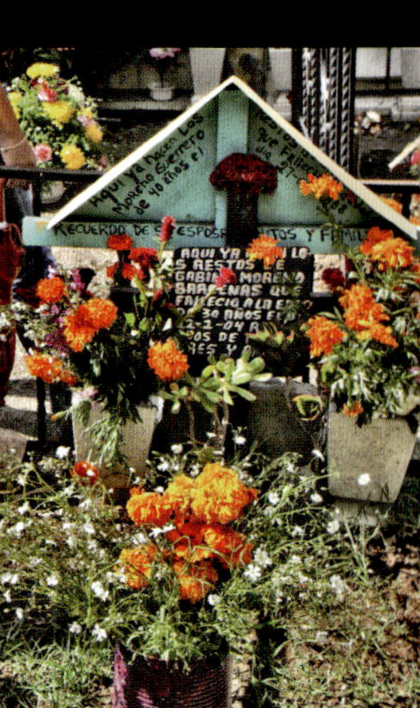
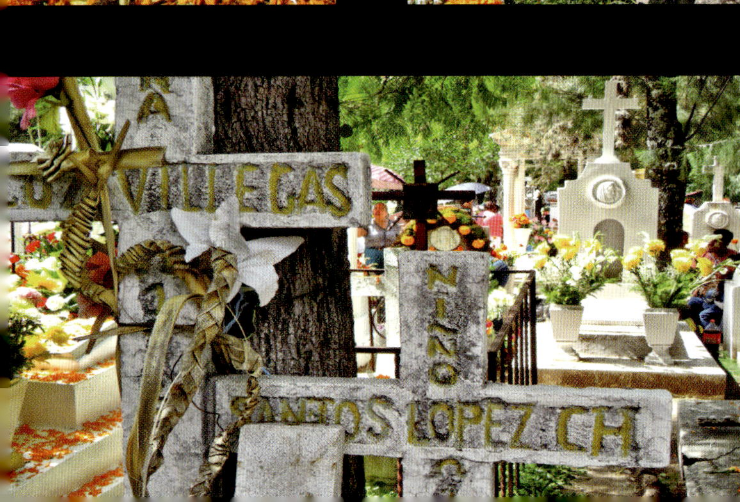
VILLEGAS
NIÑO
SANTOS LOPEZ CH
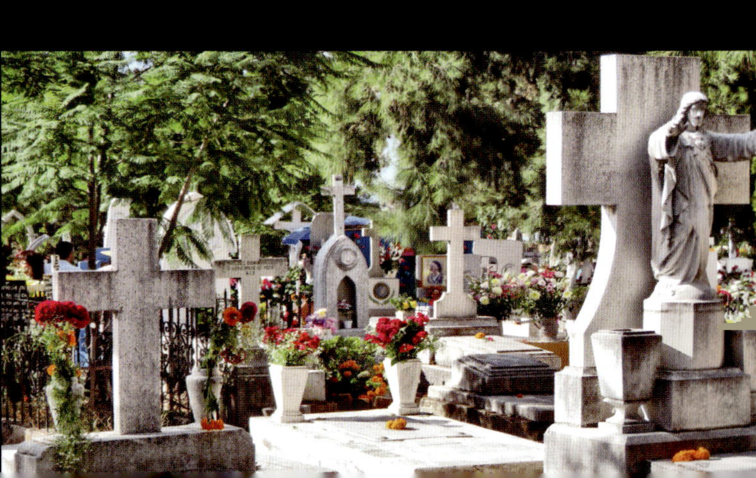

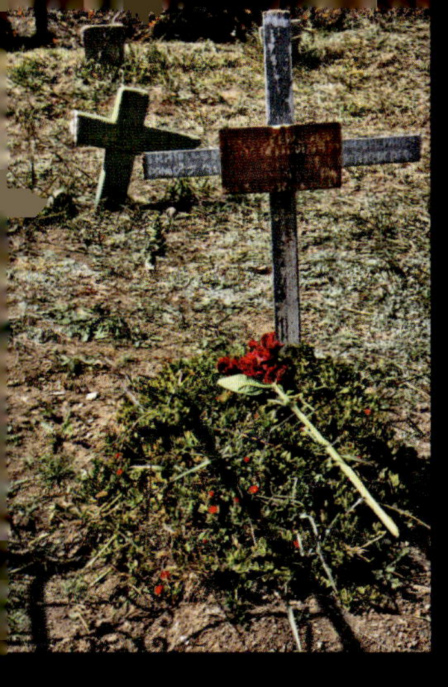
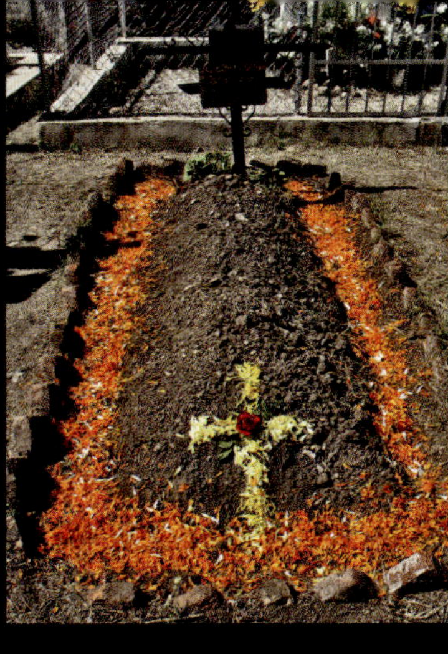
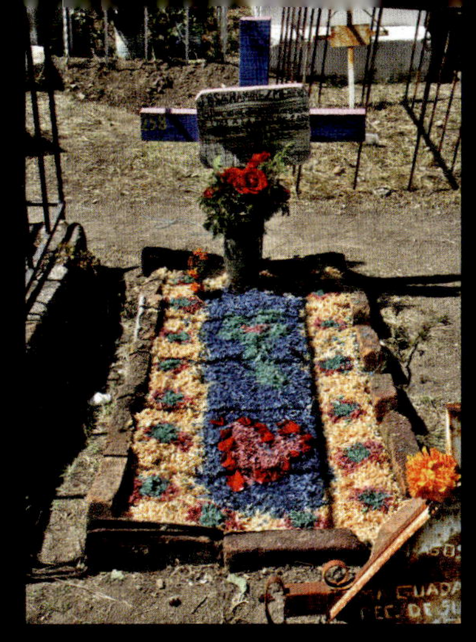
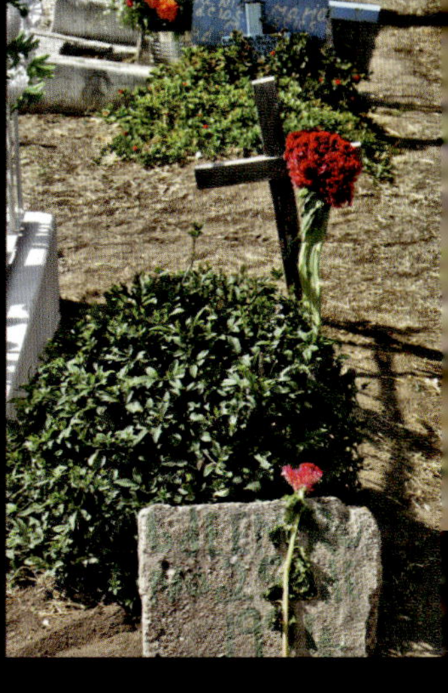
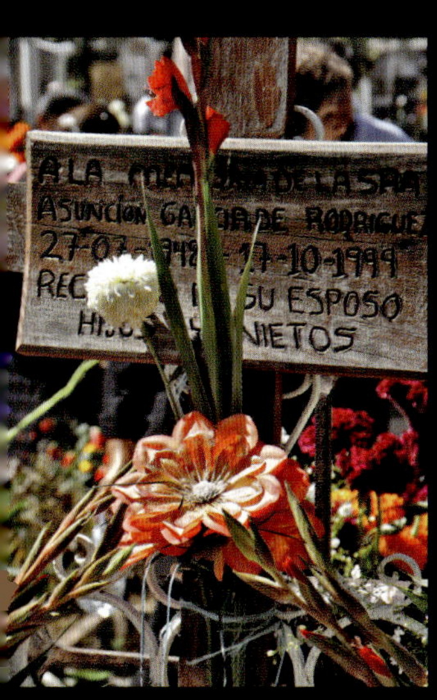
SU ESPOSO
NIETOS
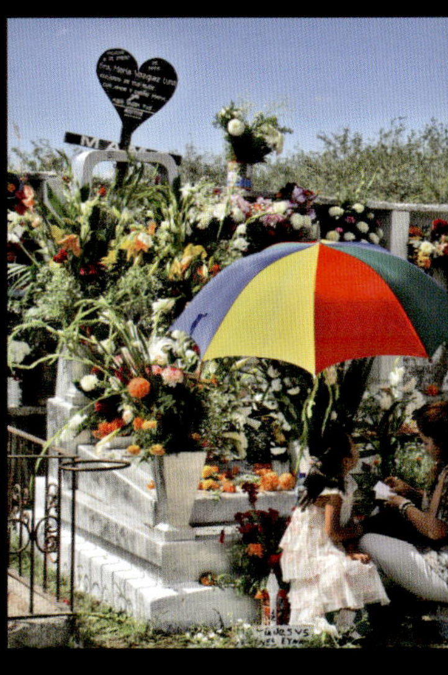
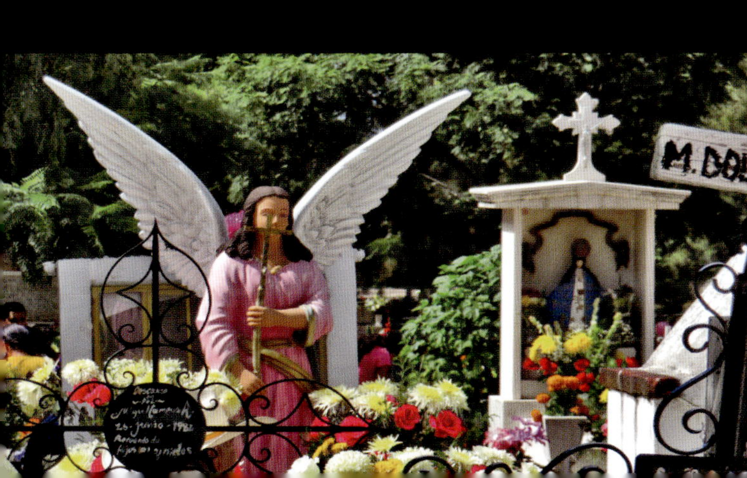
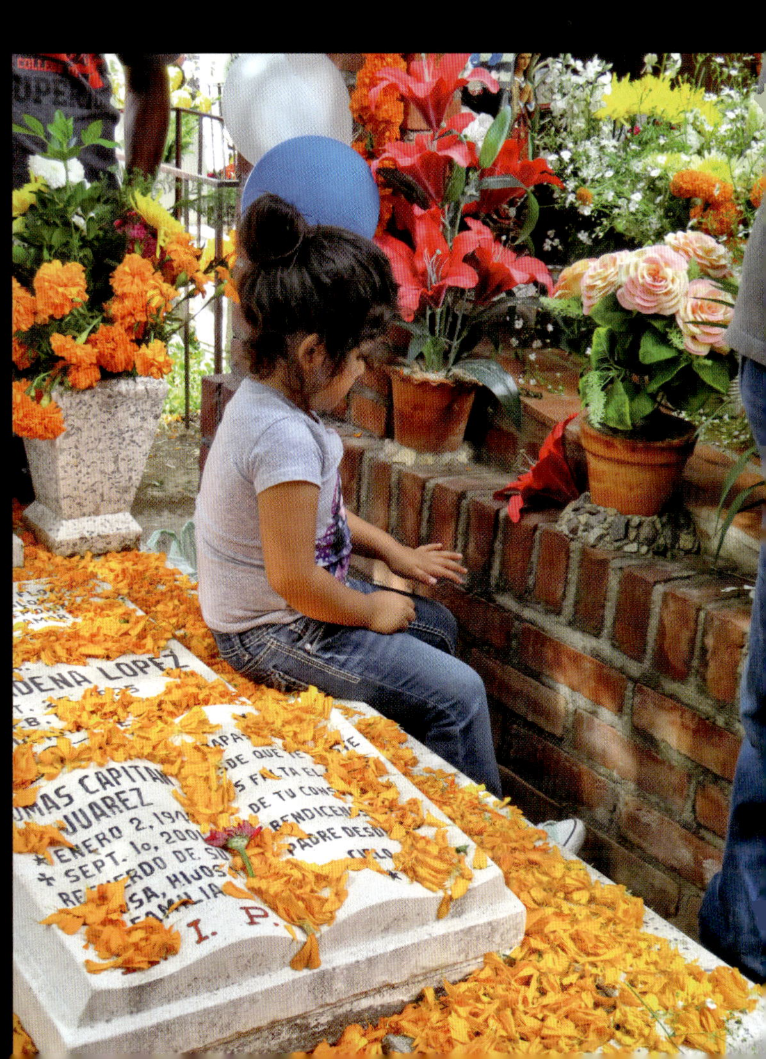
LOPEZ
JUAREZ
I. P.

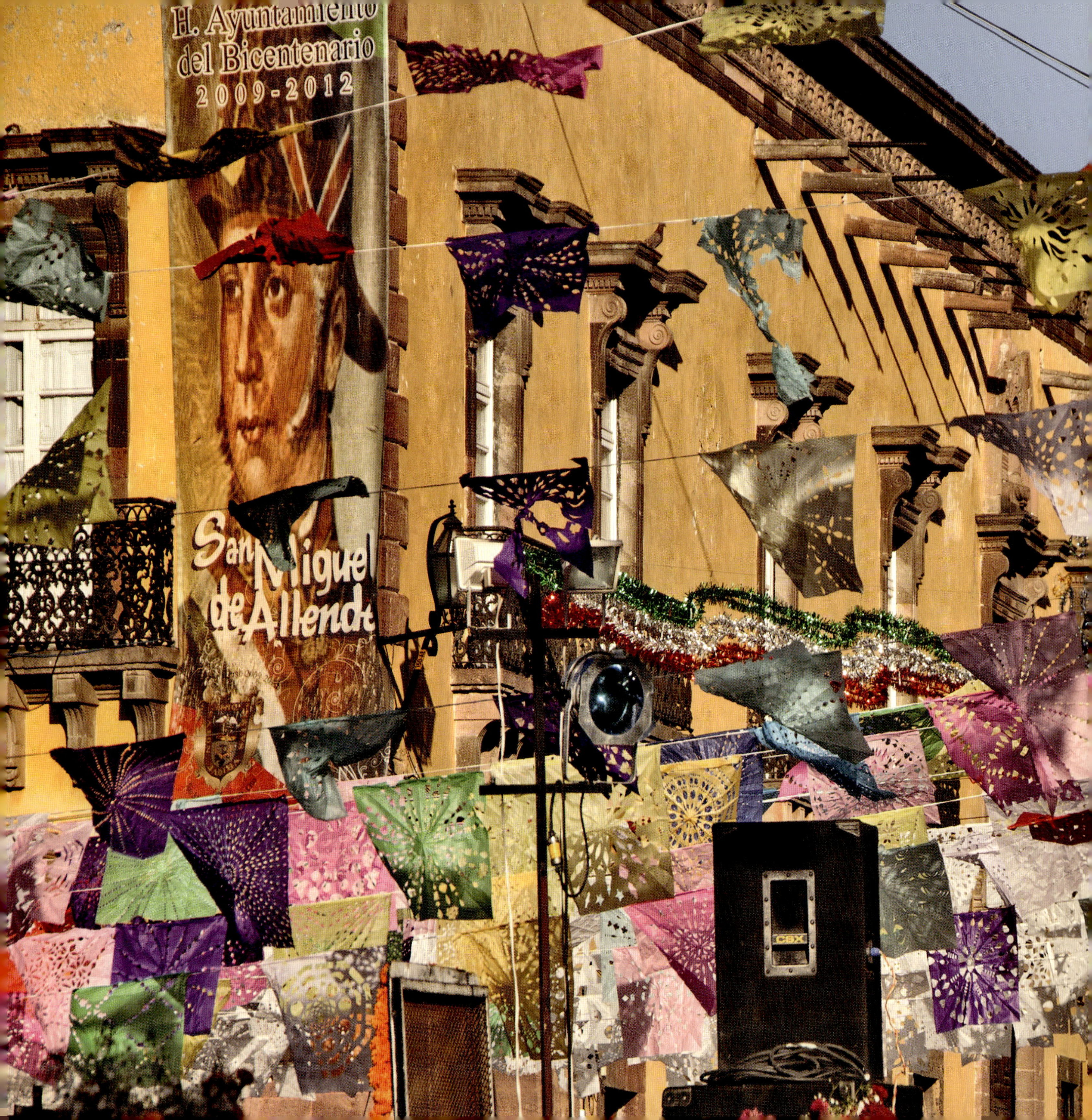
H. Ayuntamiento
del Bicentenario
2009-2012
San Miguel
de Allende

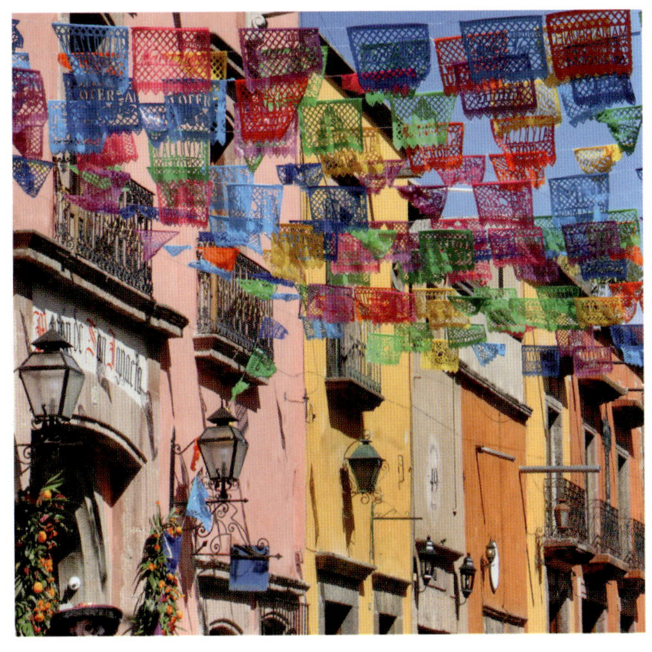
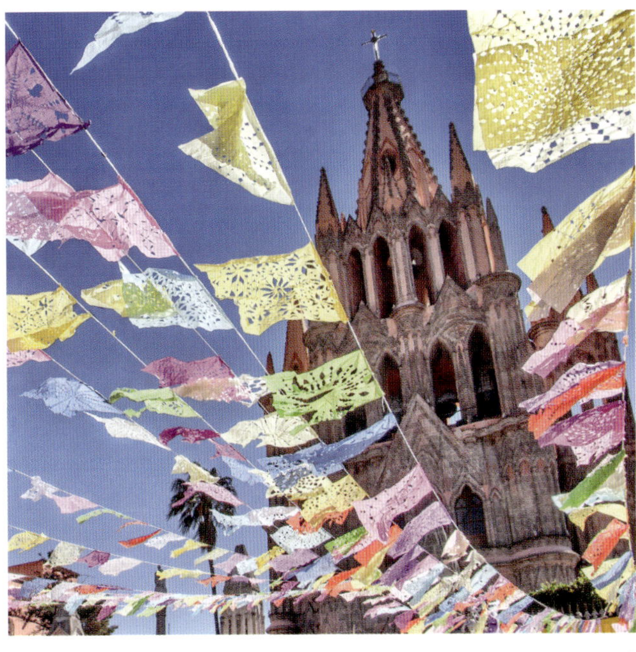
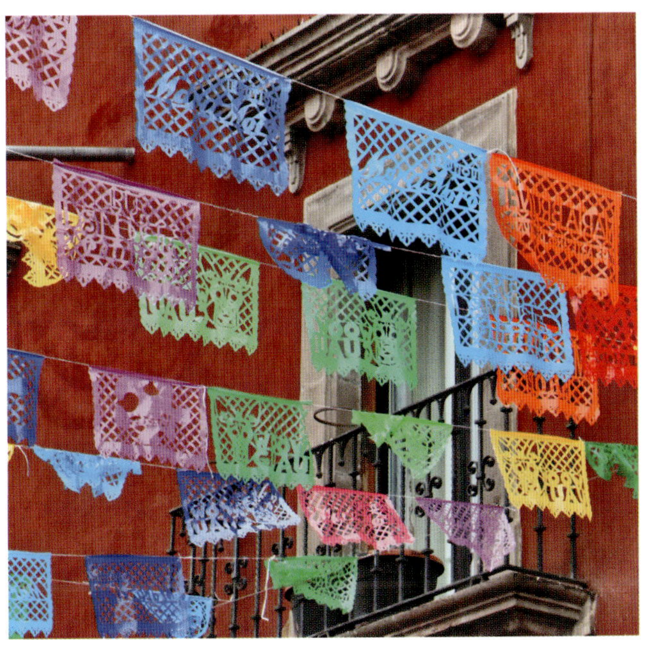
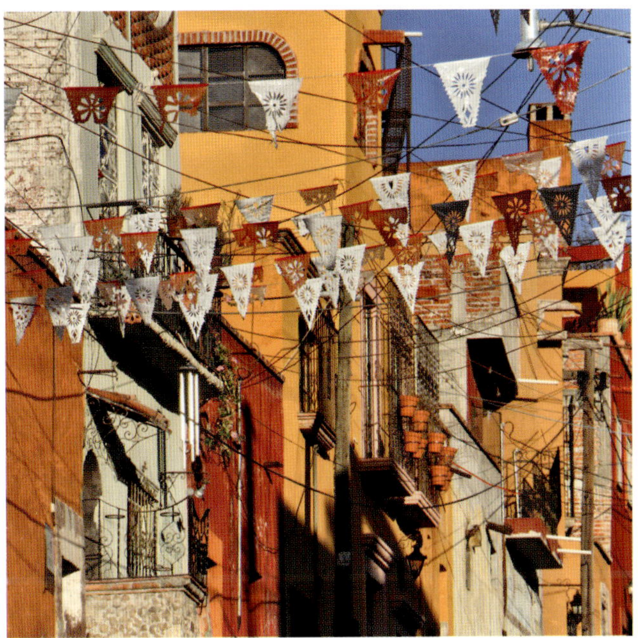

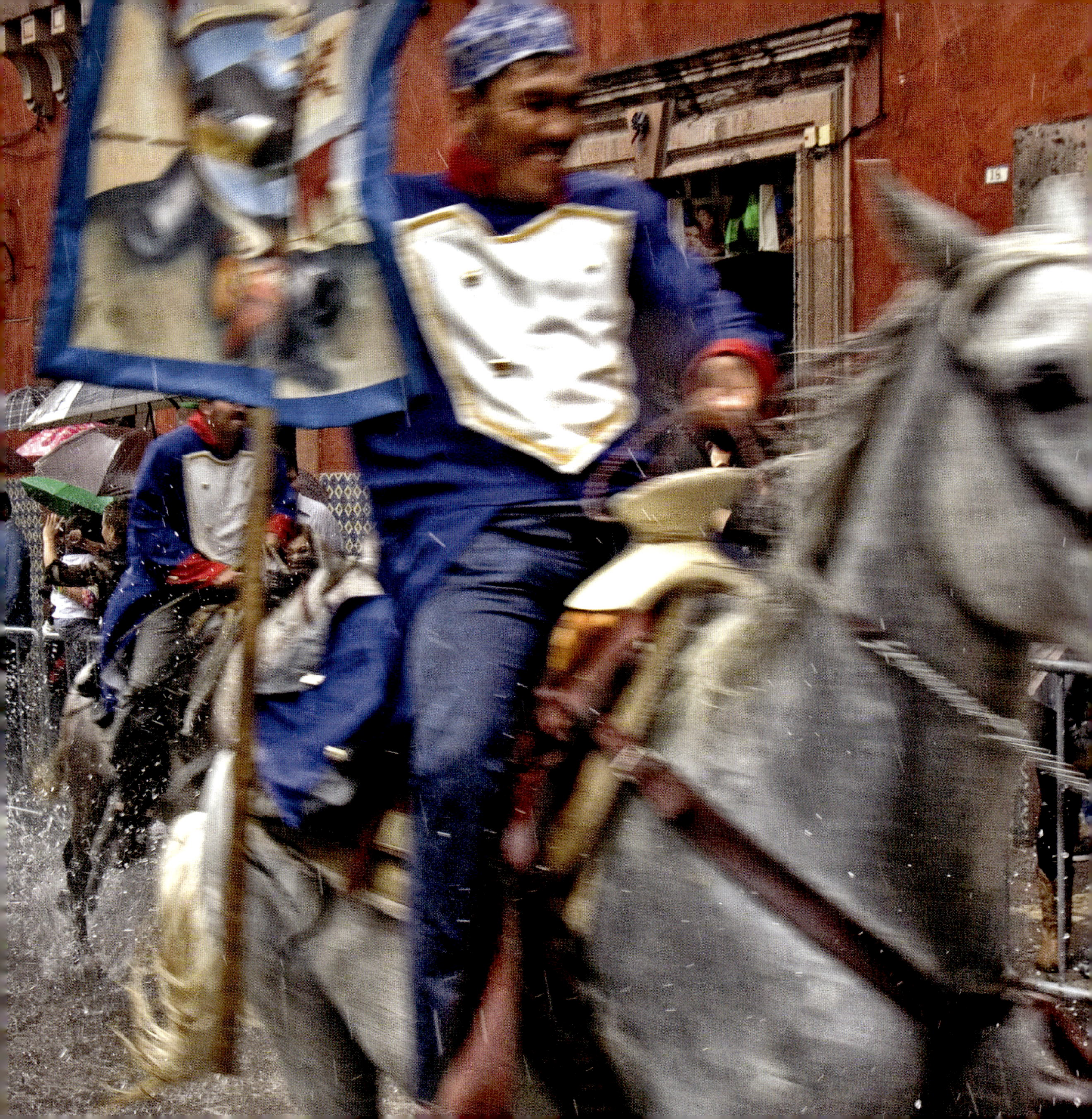

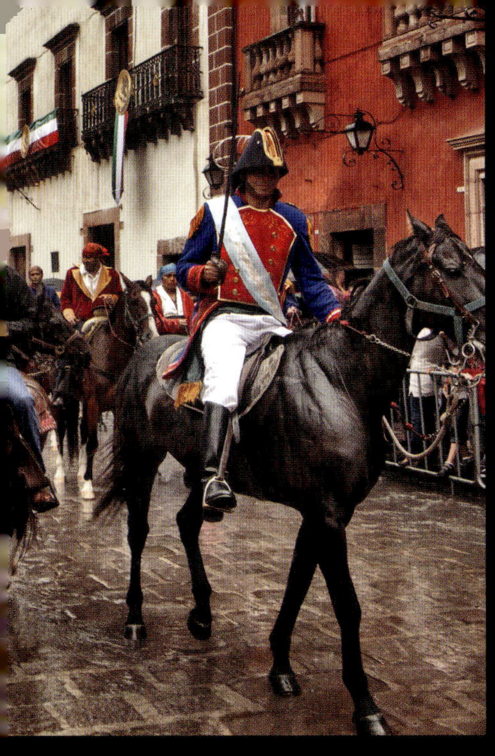

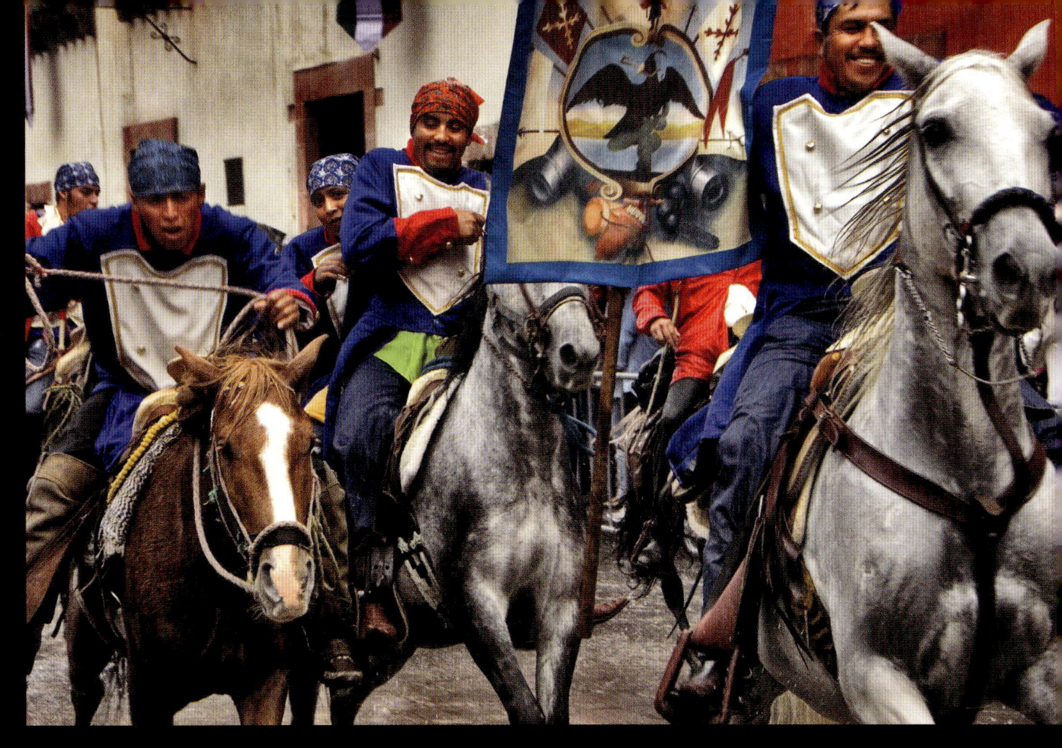

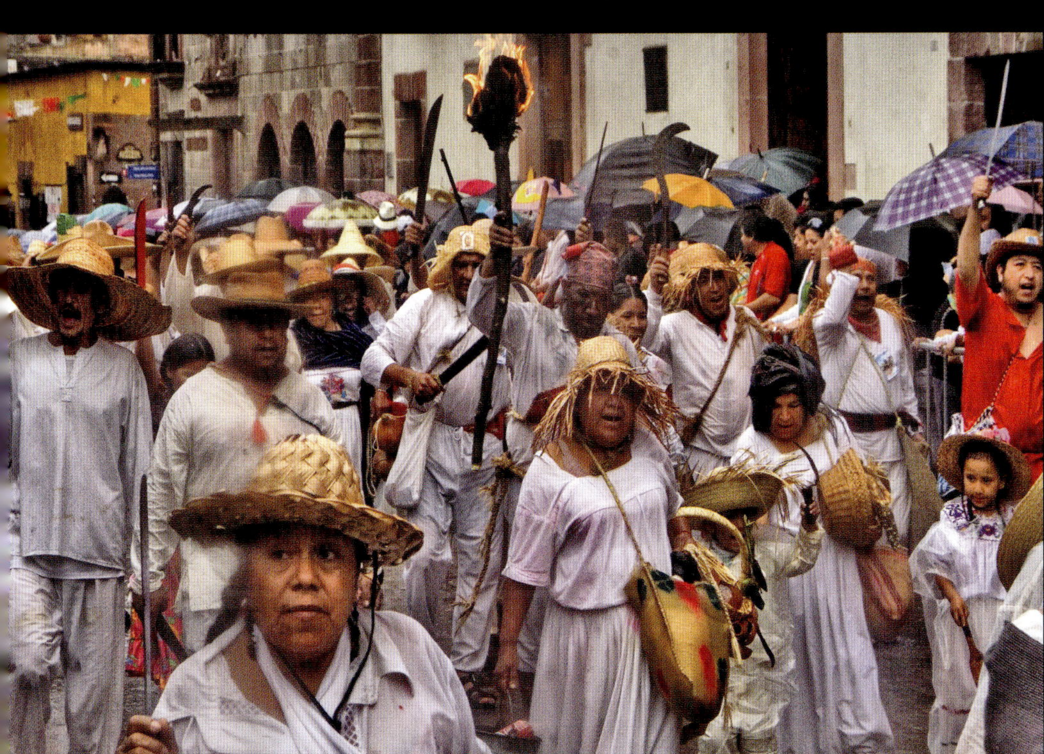

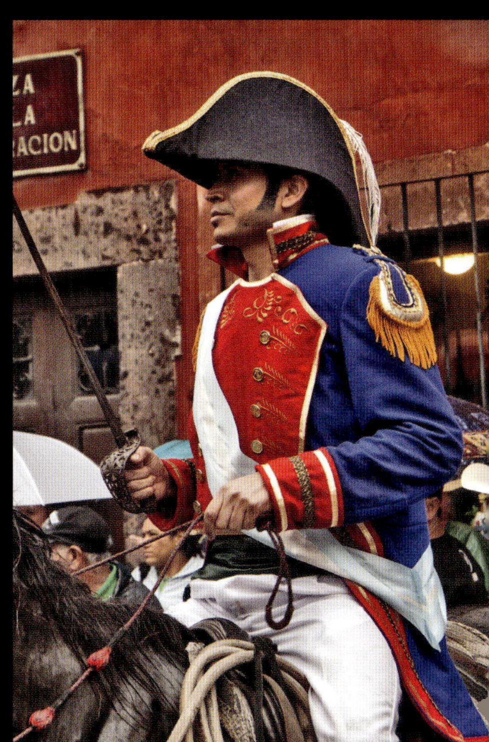

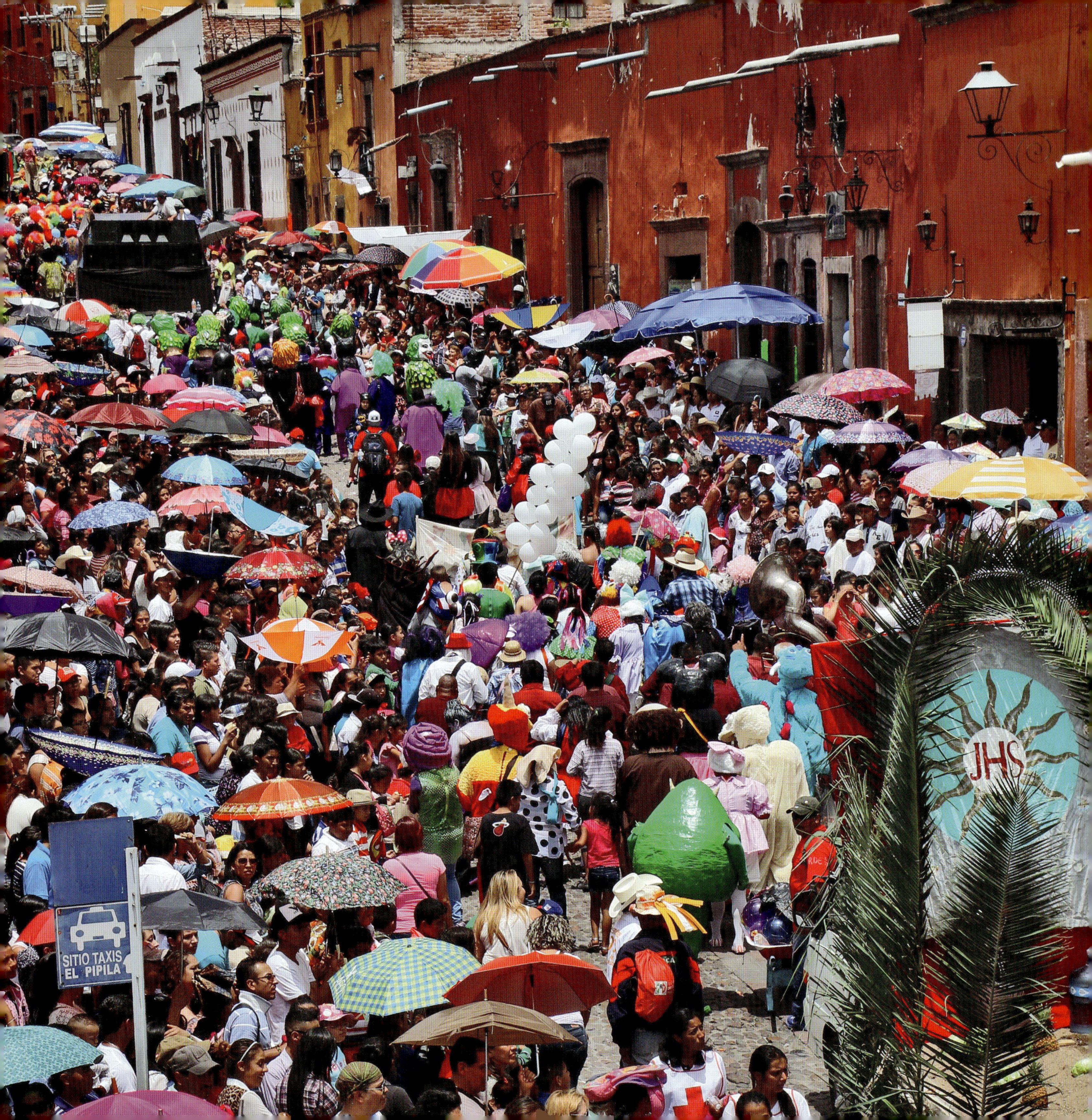
SITIO TAXIS
EL PIPILA
JHS

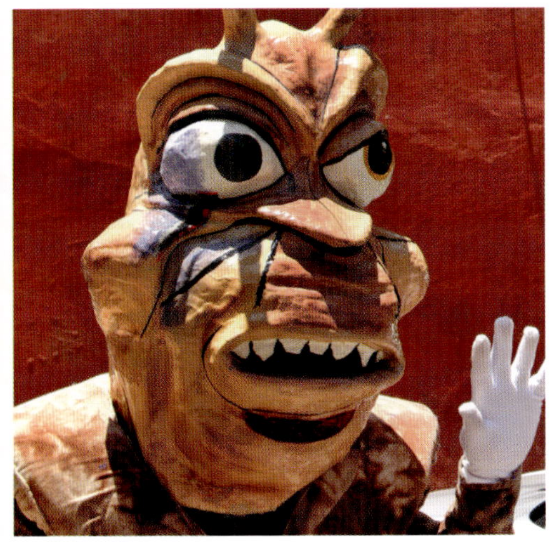
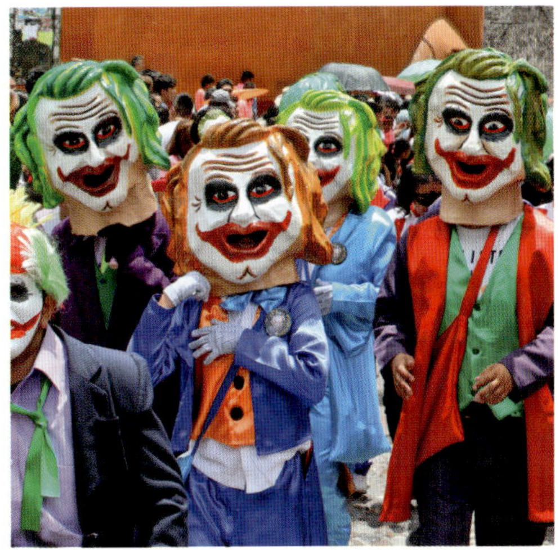
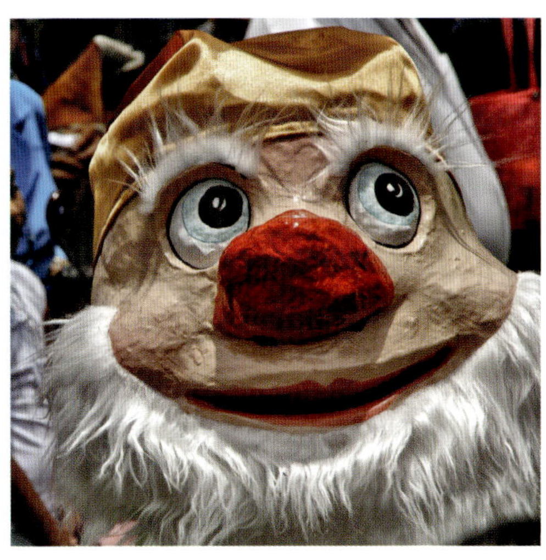
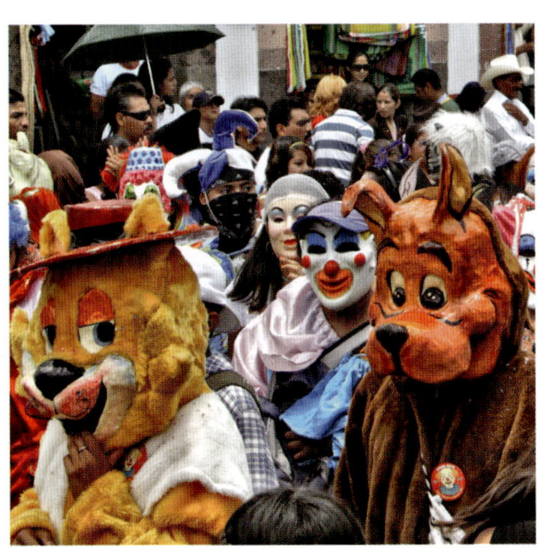
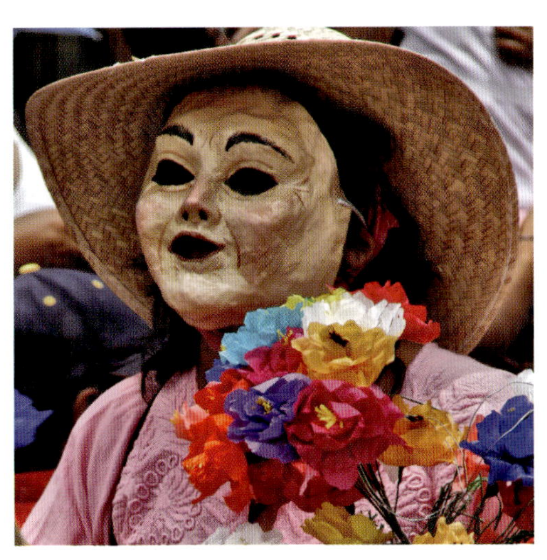
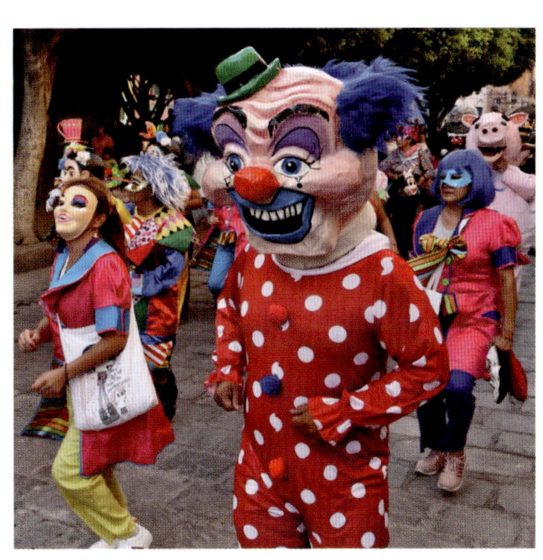
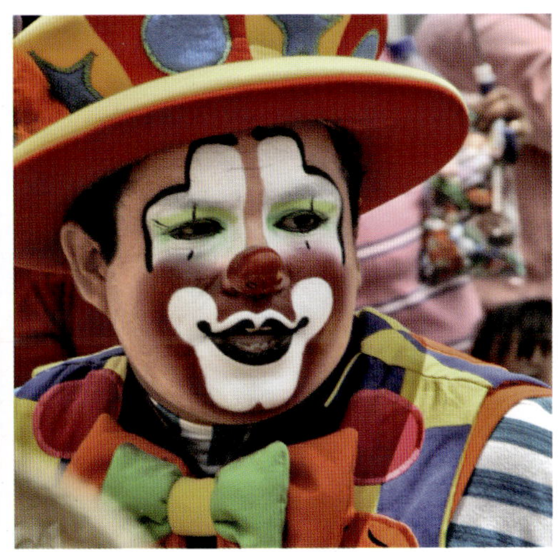
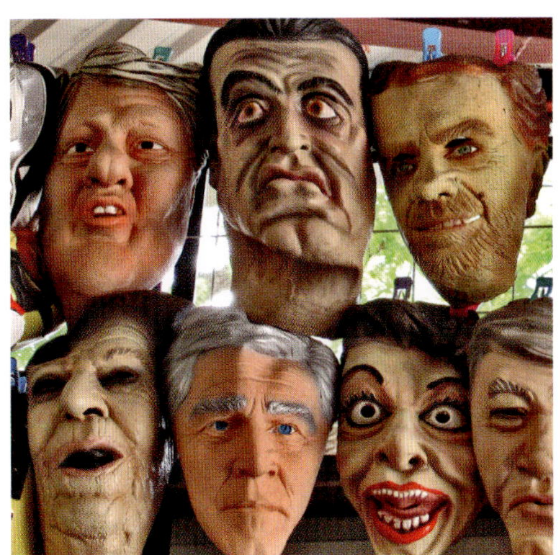
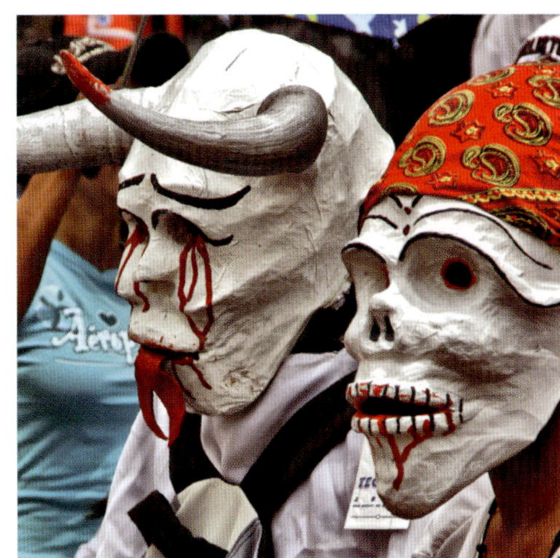

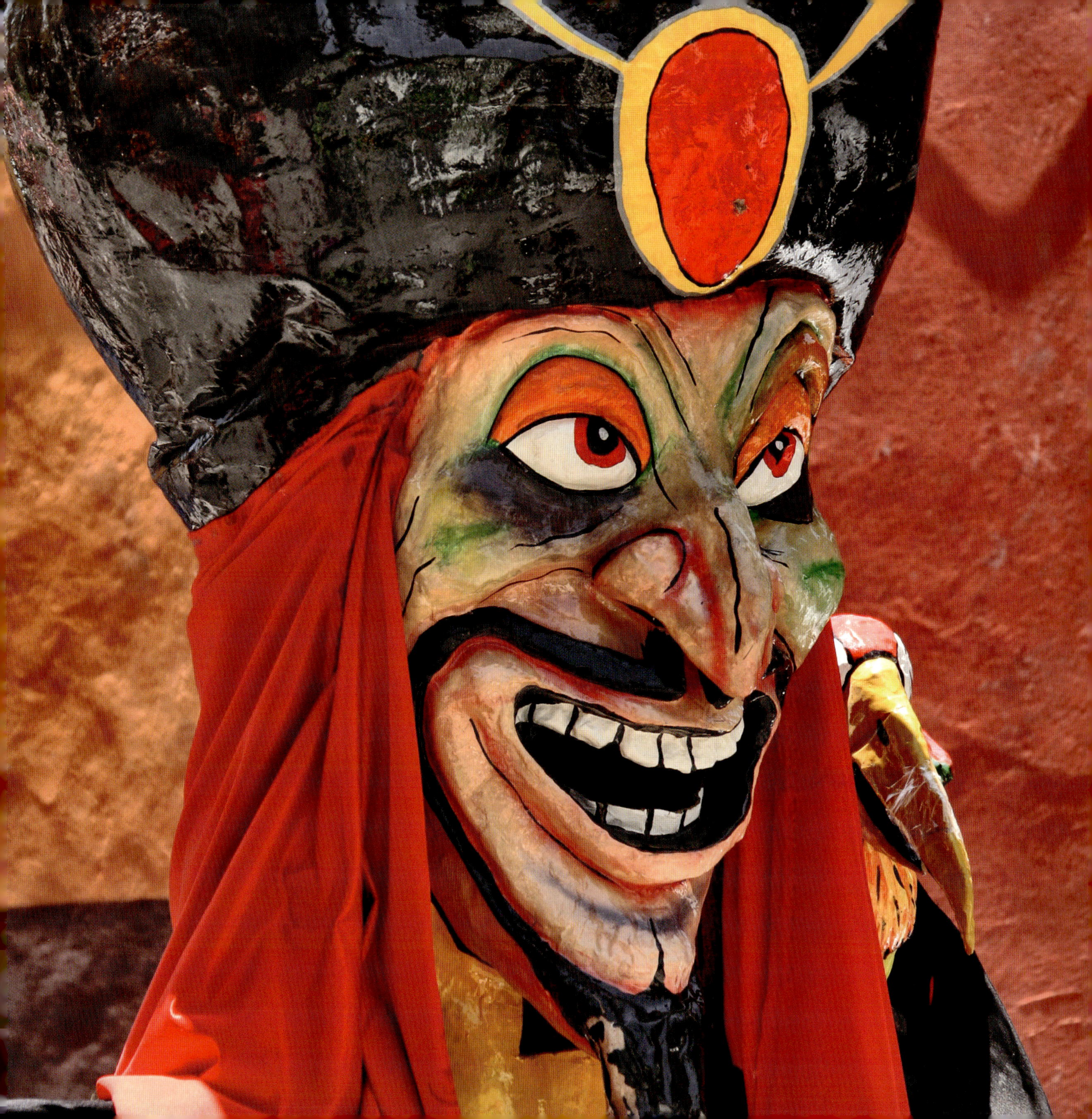

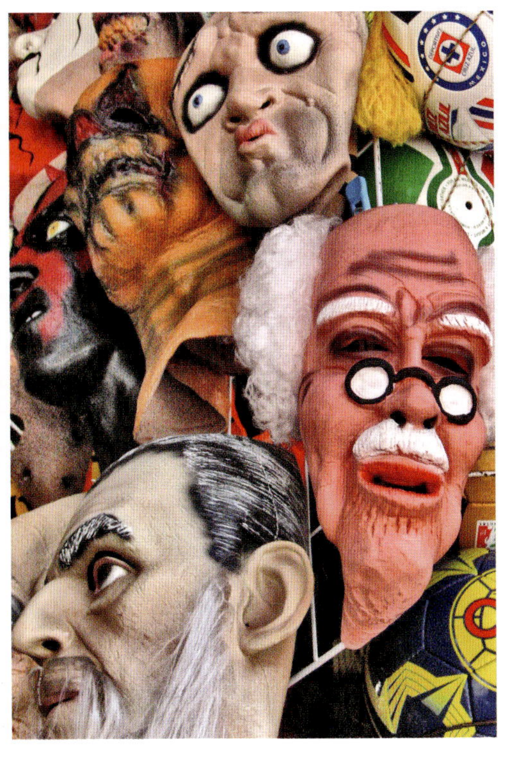

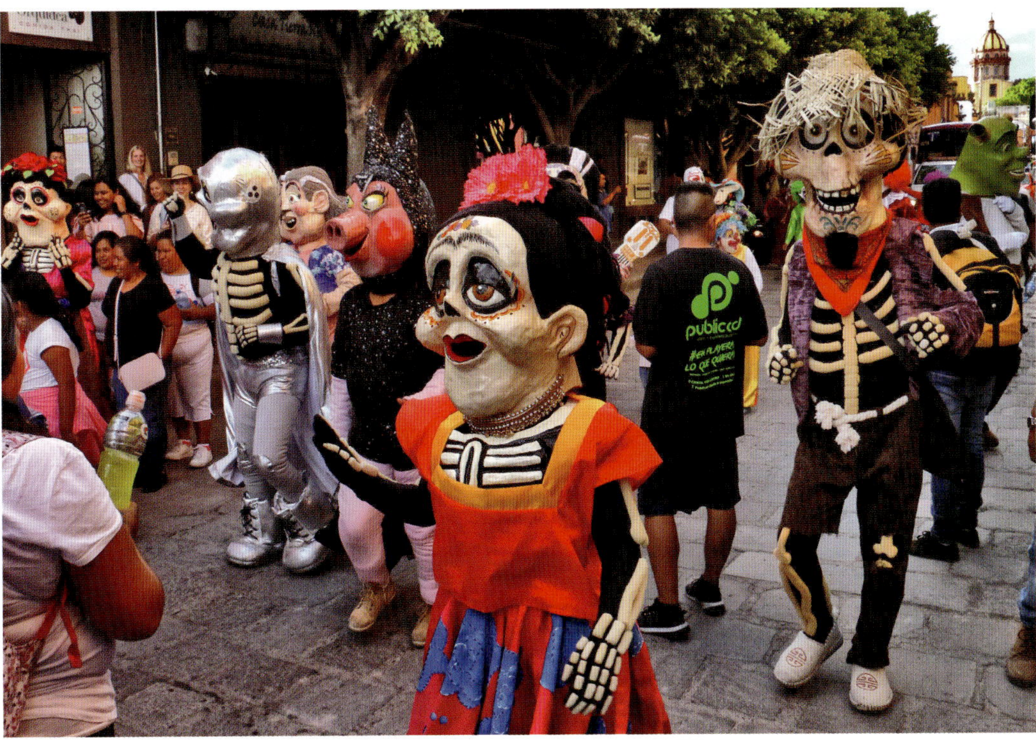

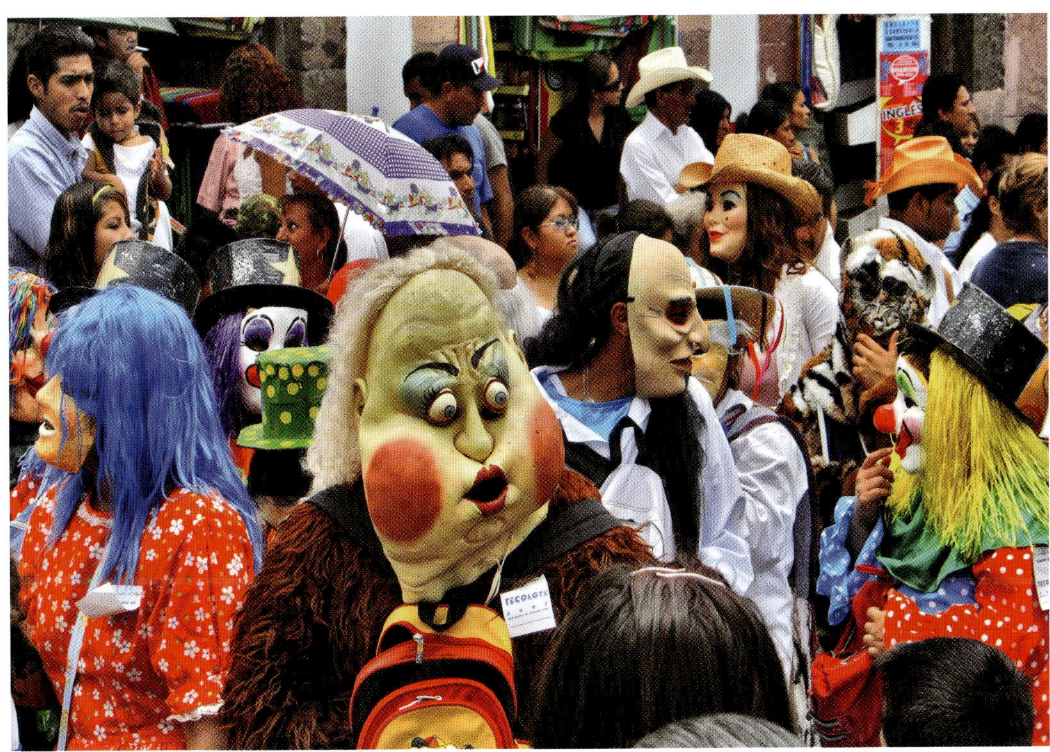
INGLÉS

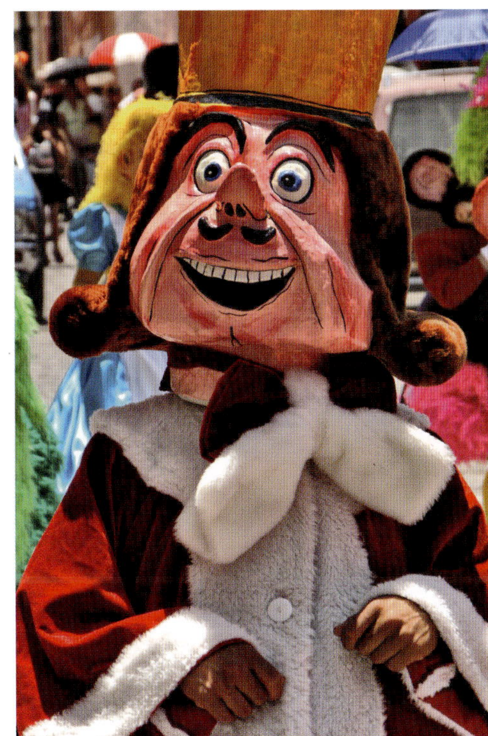

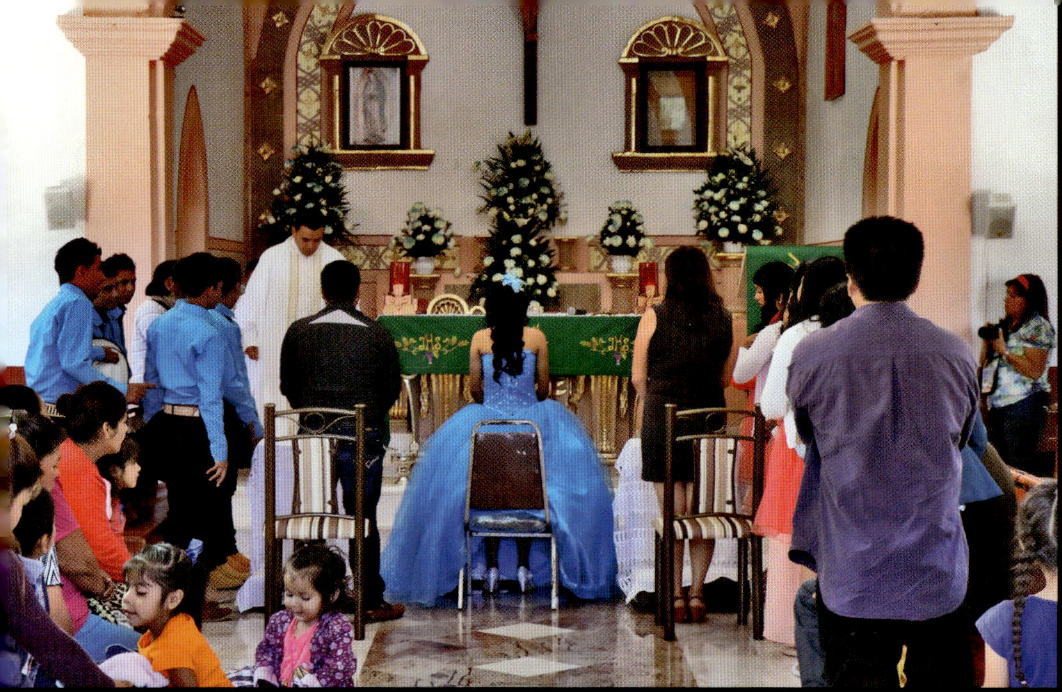

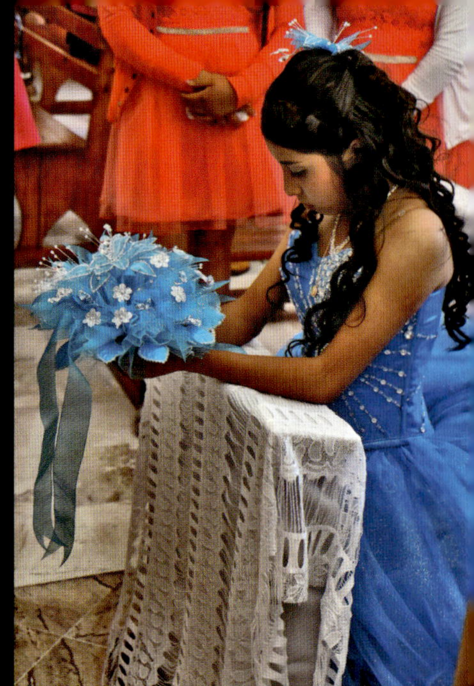

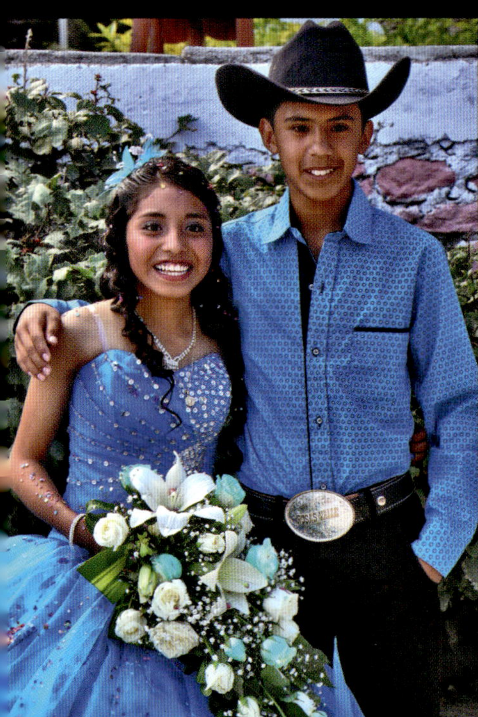

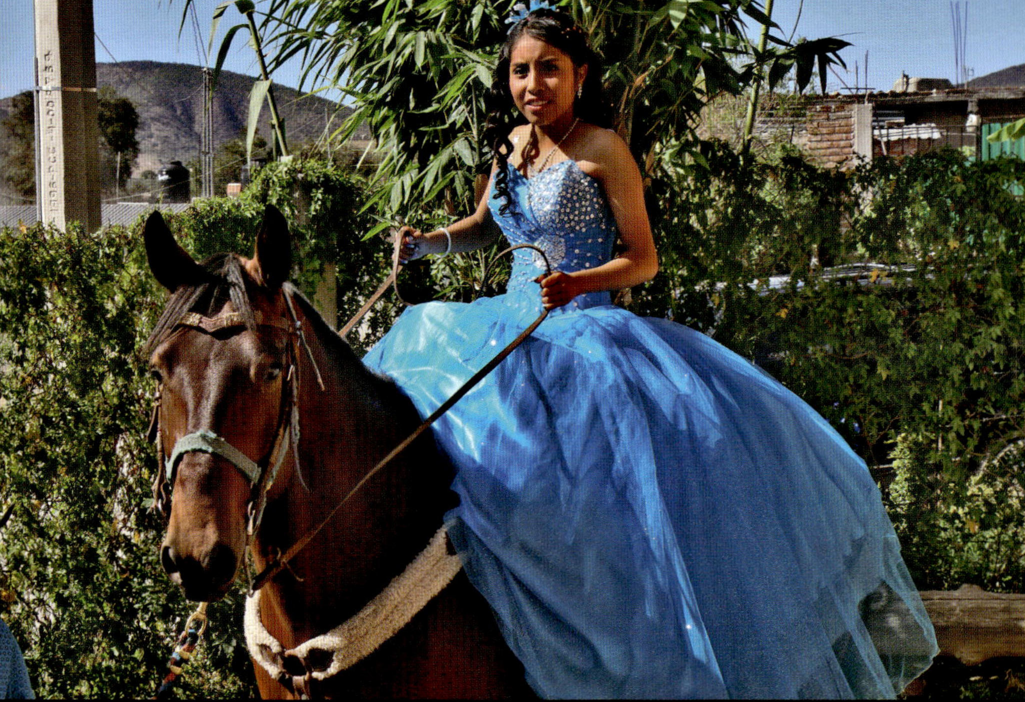

From the comforting support of her honor court, to the changing of her shoes from those of a child to those of a woman, to her dance with her father, the quinceañera ritual, which celebrates the transition to woman hood, is one of the most beautiful traditions in Mexico.

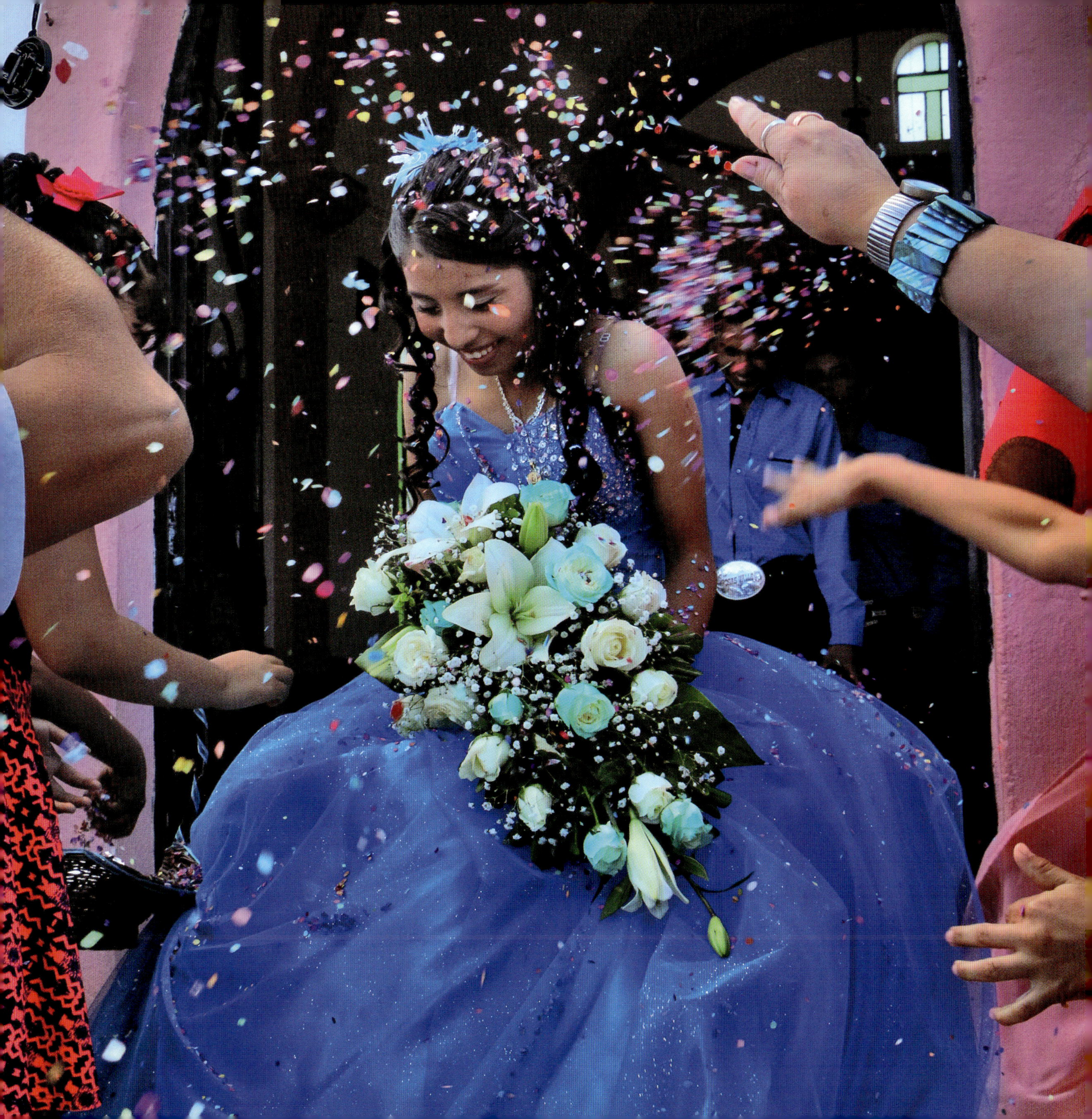

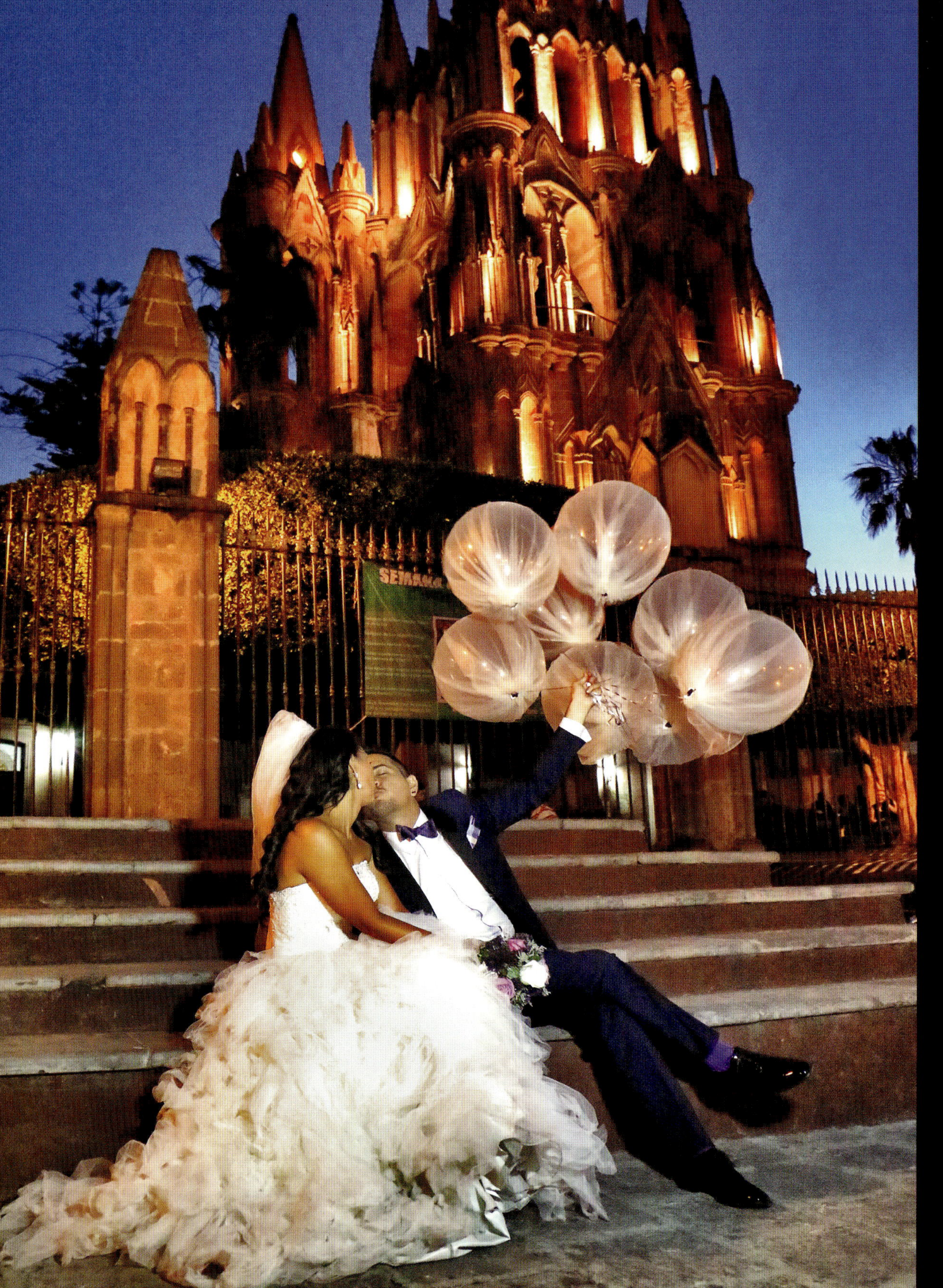

Love is not seen, it is felt, and even more so when she is with you.
—Pablo Neruda

One thing I can swear: I, who fell in love with your wings, will never want to cut them off.
—Frida Kahlo

A world is born when two kiss.
—Octavio Paz

To be totally, completely, absolutely in love, you have to be fully aware that you are also loved, that you also inspire love.
—Mario Benedetti

Marriage is the only war in which you sleep with the enemy.
—Mexican proverb

To be with you or not to be with you is the measure of my time.
—Jorge Luis Borges

In a kiss, you will know everything that I have kept quiet.
—Pablo Neruda

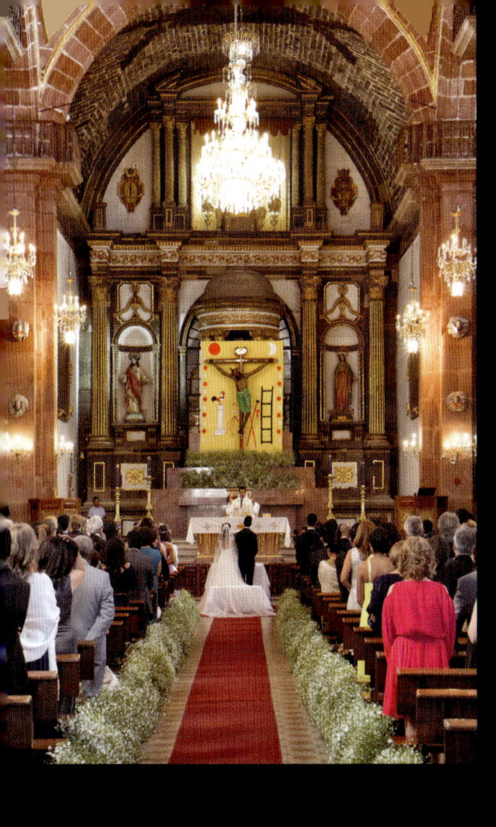
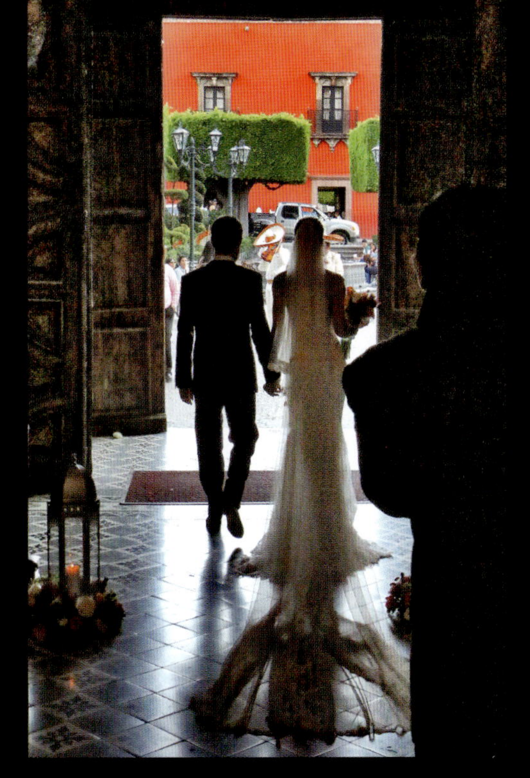
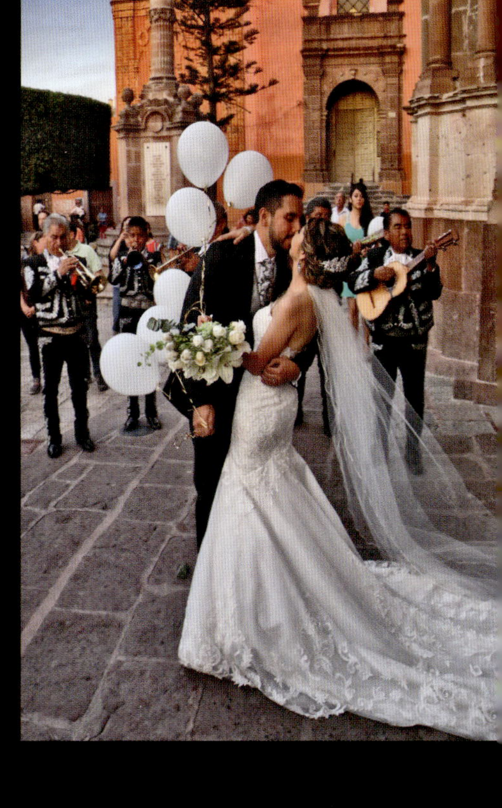
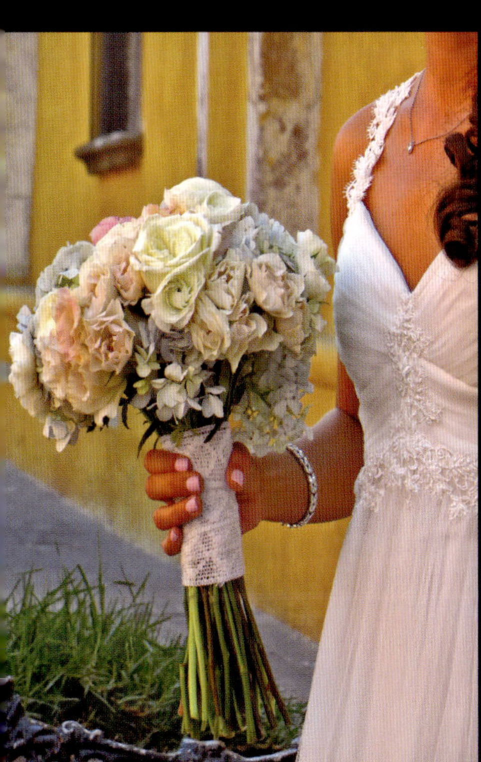
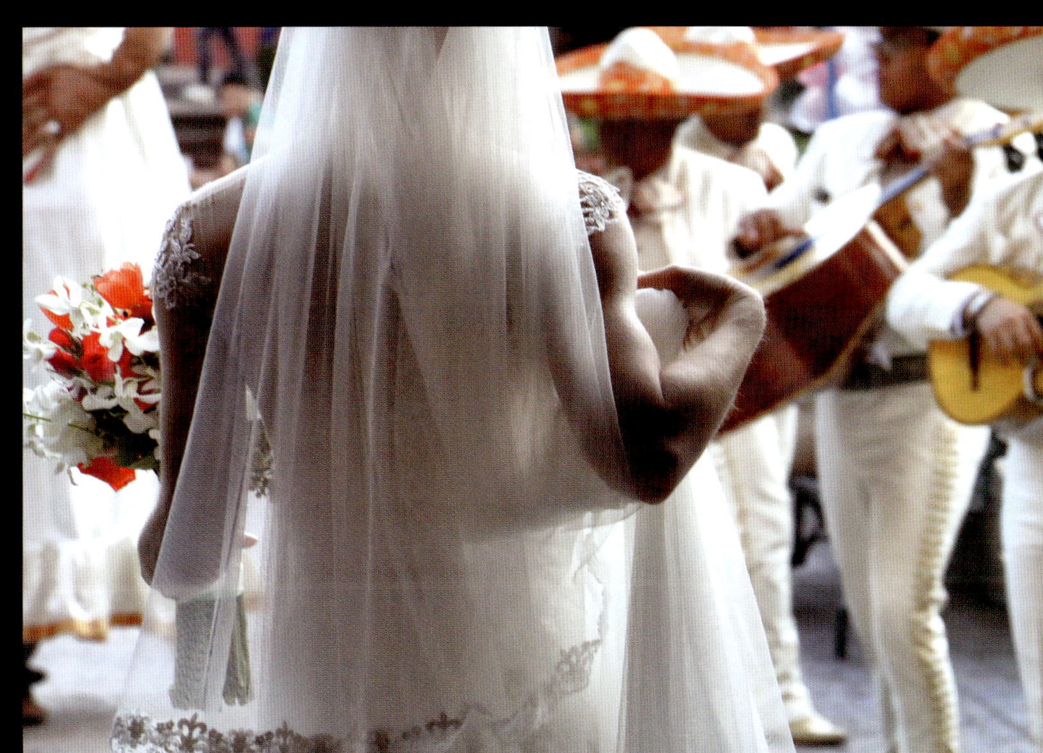

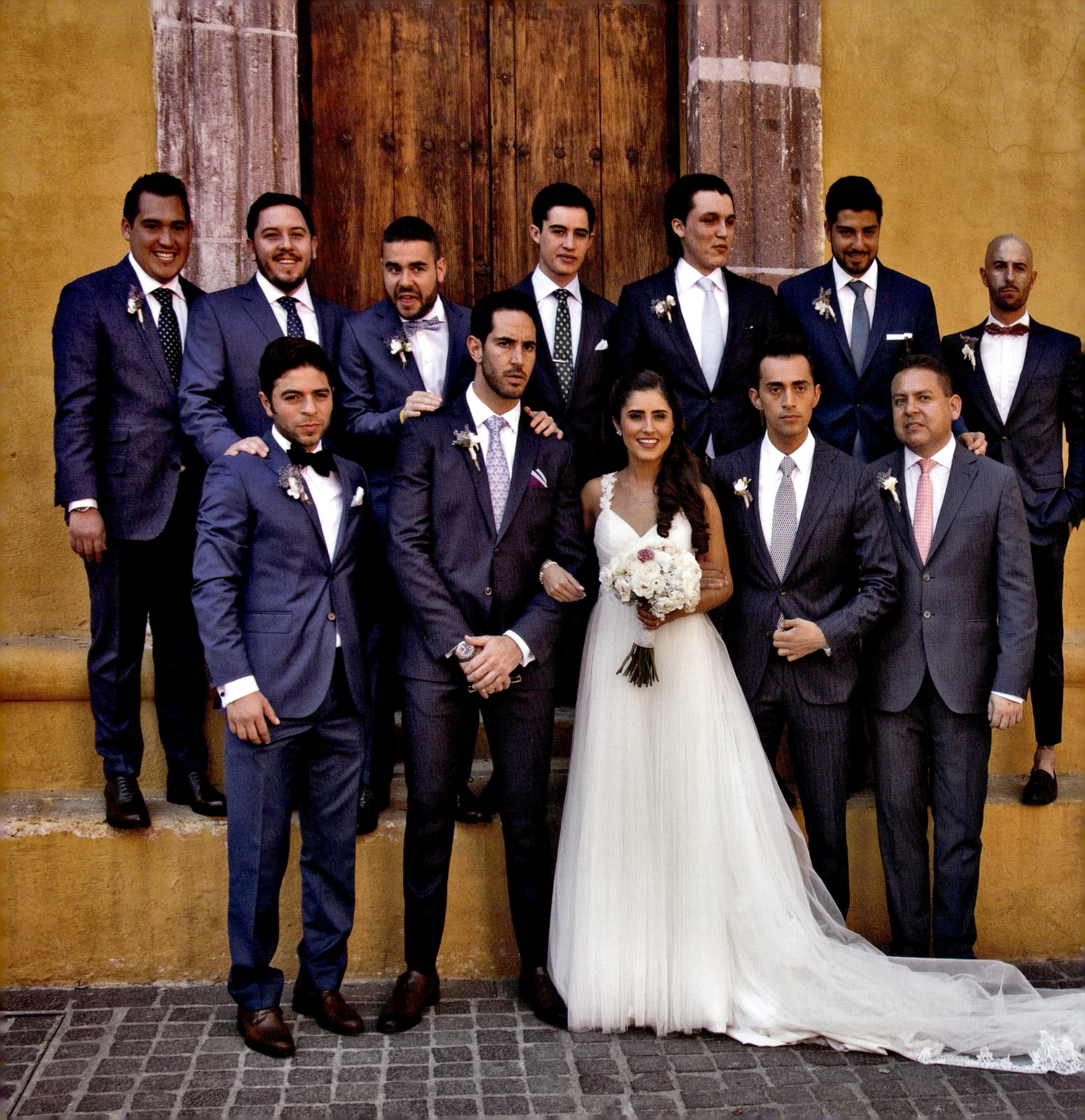

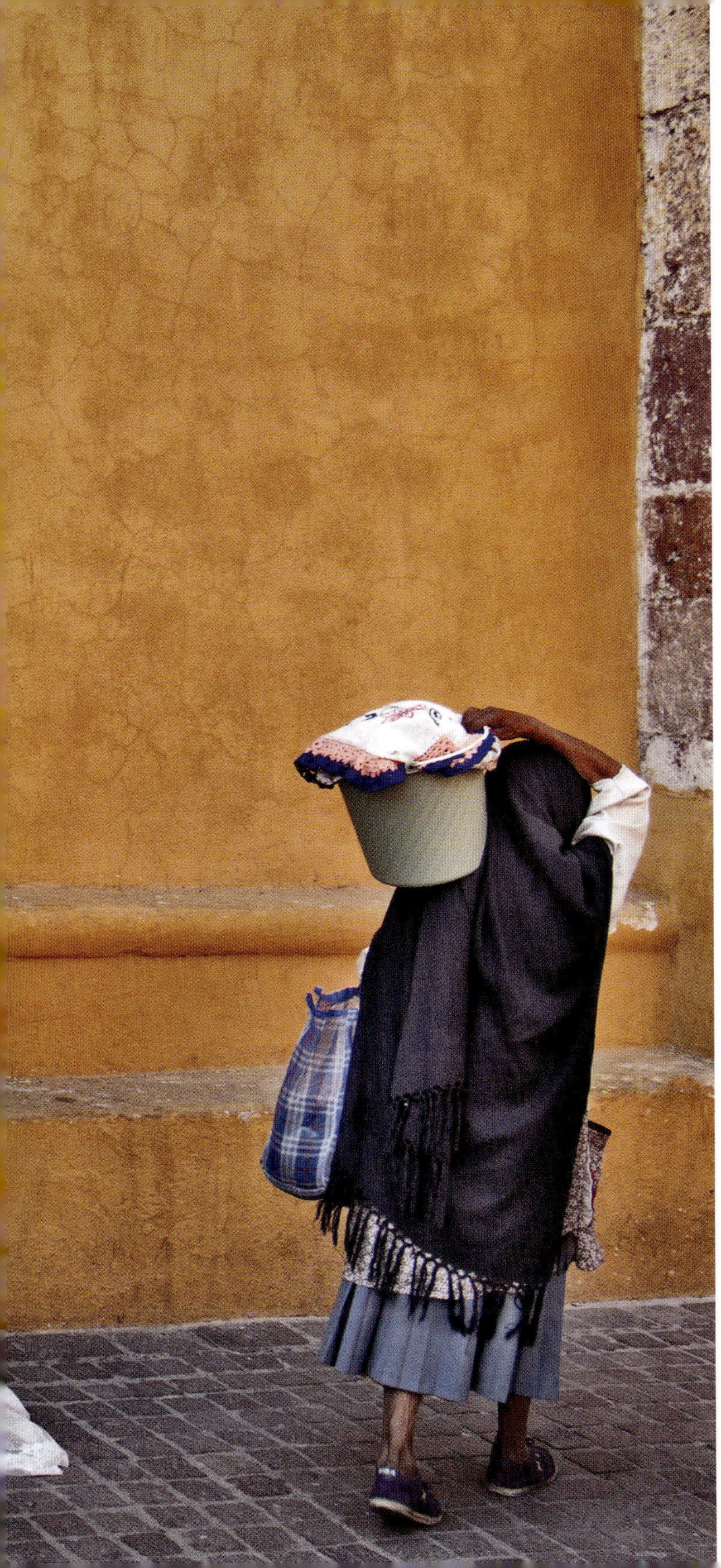

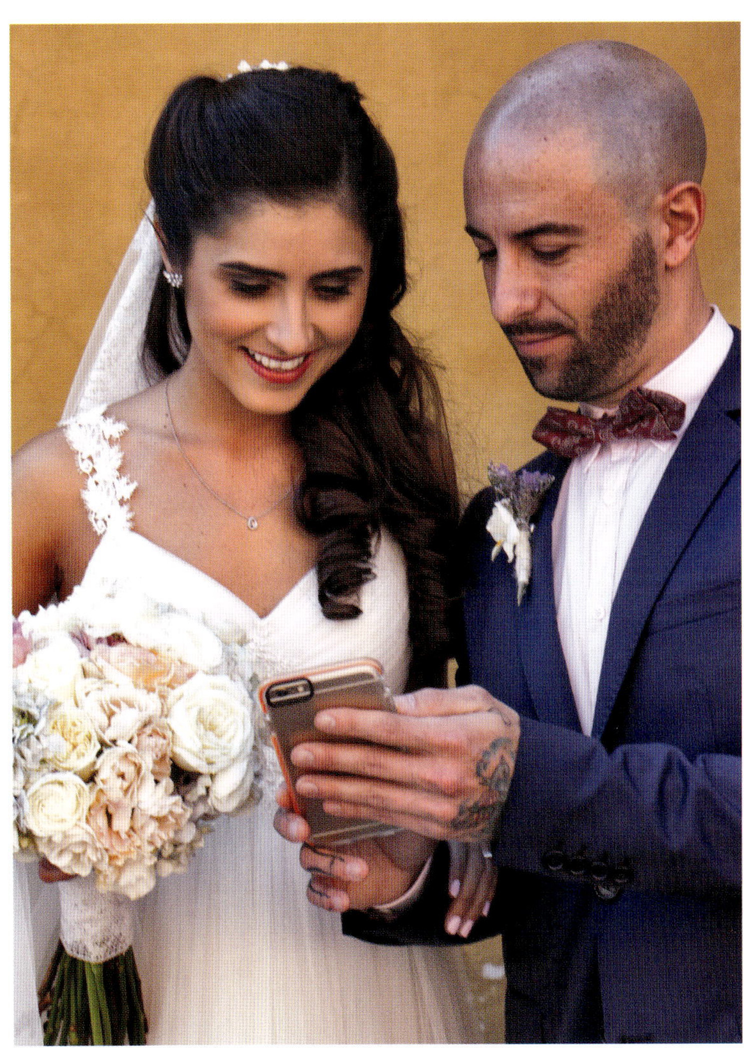

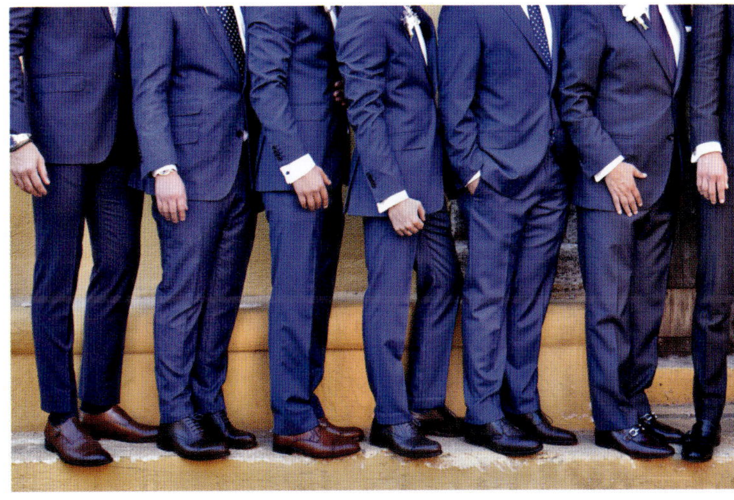

The Arts

San Miguel may have been born as a stopover place for wagons filled with silver on their way from Guanajuato to Veracruz and Spain; no one could have anticipated what an art mecca it would grow into. In the 1700s, San Miguel was larger than any city in North America, including New York, and nearly as large as Barcelona, but after closure of the silver mines a declining population by the 1900s left the town a shadow of its former self without even a passable road to get there. It all changed with the arrival of one young man from Chicago. A fascinating series of events brought Stirling Dickinson to San Miguel in 1937. Like many who have come after him, he came looking for a quiet place to finish writing a book. He immediately fell in love with Mexico and with San Miguel and stayed.

Highly educated, from a family whose comings and goings were chronicled in the society pages, Stirling and friend Heath Bowman were looking to finish their third book, *Death Is Incidental*, about the Mexican Revolution, when they came to San Miguel. Within ten days Stirling bought the home he would live in until his death in 1998. He was instrumental in reviving part of an abandoned convent into an art school and was appointed director of the Bellas Artes in 1938. Later, he moved on to help create the Instituto Allende, working with José Mojica, Felipe Cossío del Pomar, and Enrique Hernandez Martinez. A WWII veteran himself, he actively promoted the schools for veterans to study under the GI Bill. These two world-renowned art schools and the many charitable organizations Dickinson founded set the tone for the rebirth of San Miguel as an artists' haven. Today there are countless artists, photographers, musicians, and writers from all over the world who call San Miguel home, and with this an influx of art lovers. Whether it is Indigenous traditional craft in open-air markets, exceptional fine art in elegant galleries, music, dance, theater, or film, all manner of the arts flourish in San Miguel.

There are numerous galleries, studios, workshops, and classes in every kind of artistic endeavor. A former textile factory, the Fabrica la Aurora, is a huge complex of art where frequent gatherings bring people from all over the world. The quality of the art, the depth of meaning behind the art, and the sheer quantity of art in San Miguel qualify it as an art destination, whether it is to create it, enjoy it, or buy it.

There are few towns in the world that support the arts as beautifully as San Miguel. The stunning 150-year-old Angela Peralta Theater hosts musicians that may be on a world tour, stopping in New York, Paris, Rio de Janeiro, and San Miguel. Stages or enormous screens are regularly set up in the plaza between the Jardín and the Parroquia to present world-class performances or for international film and music festivals that host not only the music or film, but the creators as well, so they can share their processes and dreams with the audience. The renowned San Miguel Writers' Conference draws poets and writers from around the globe.

The quality of these creative outlets is unexpected in a town of this size anywhere in the world. To find it in a small town in the middle of Mexico is both a surprise and a delight.

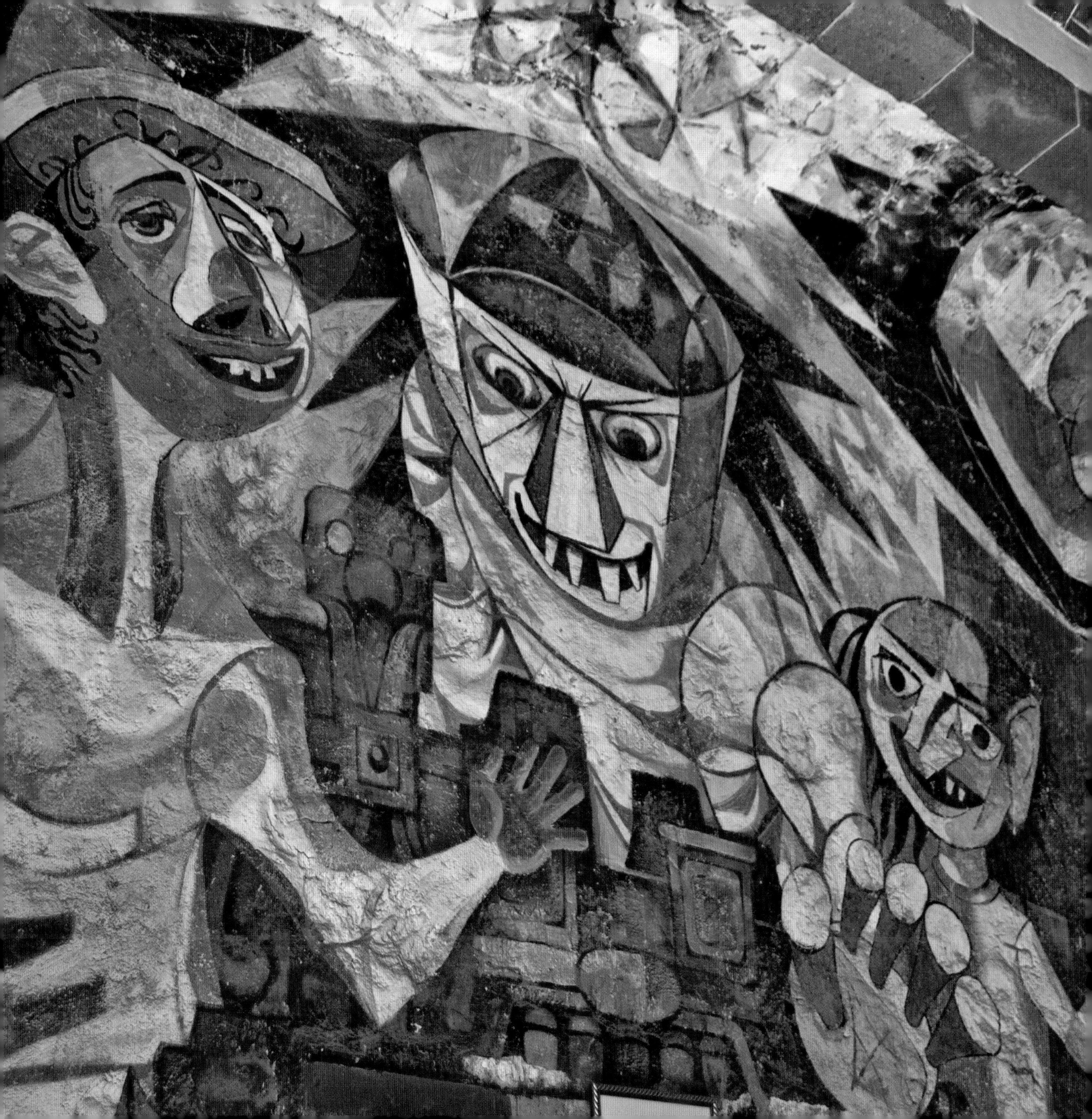

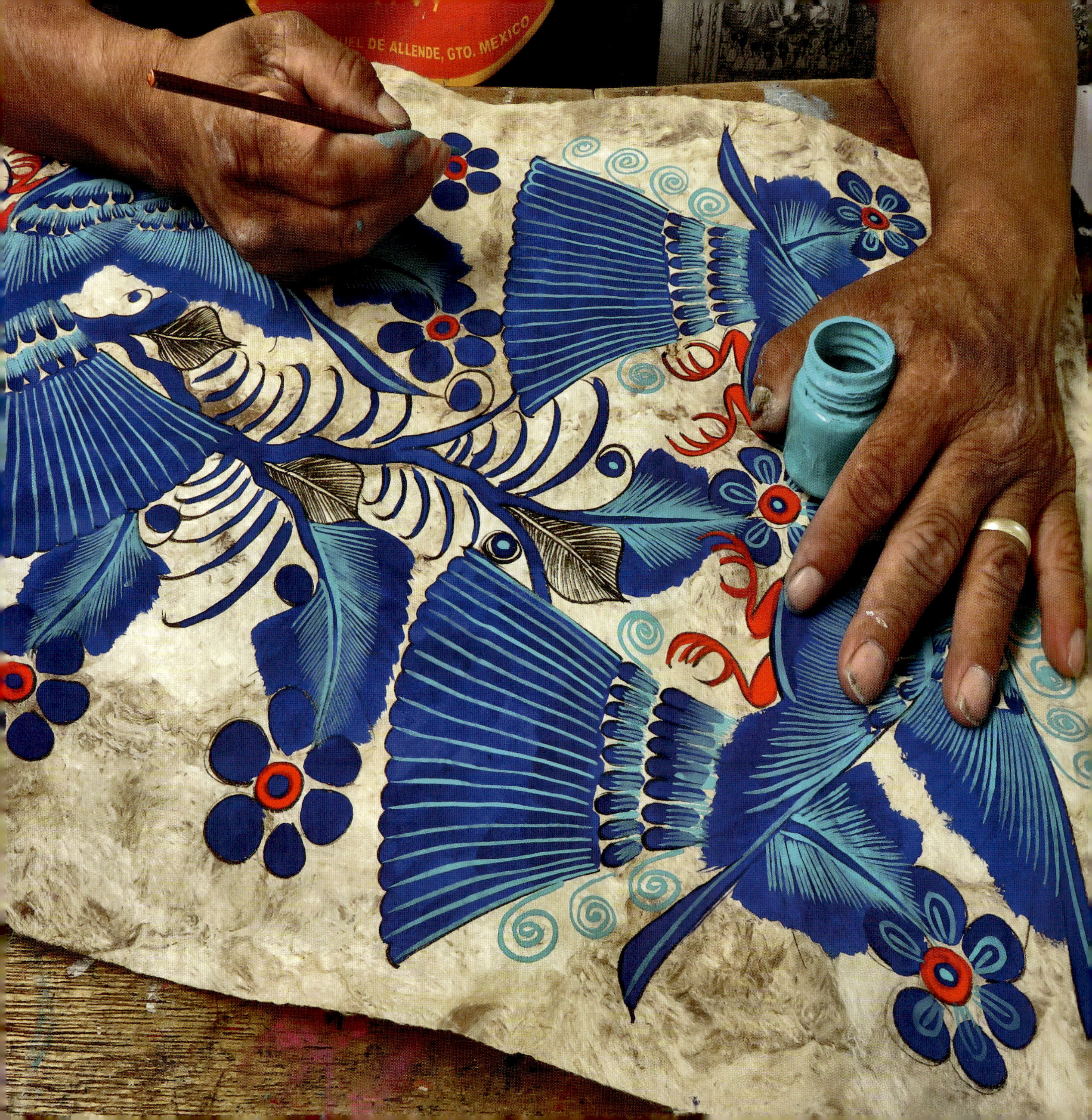
DE ALLENDE, GTO. MEXICO

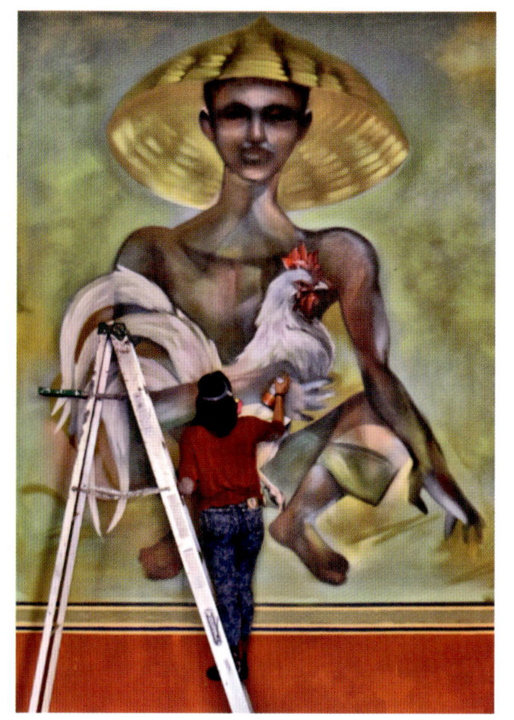

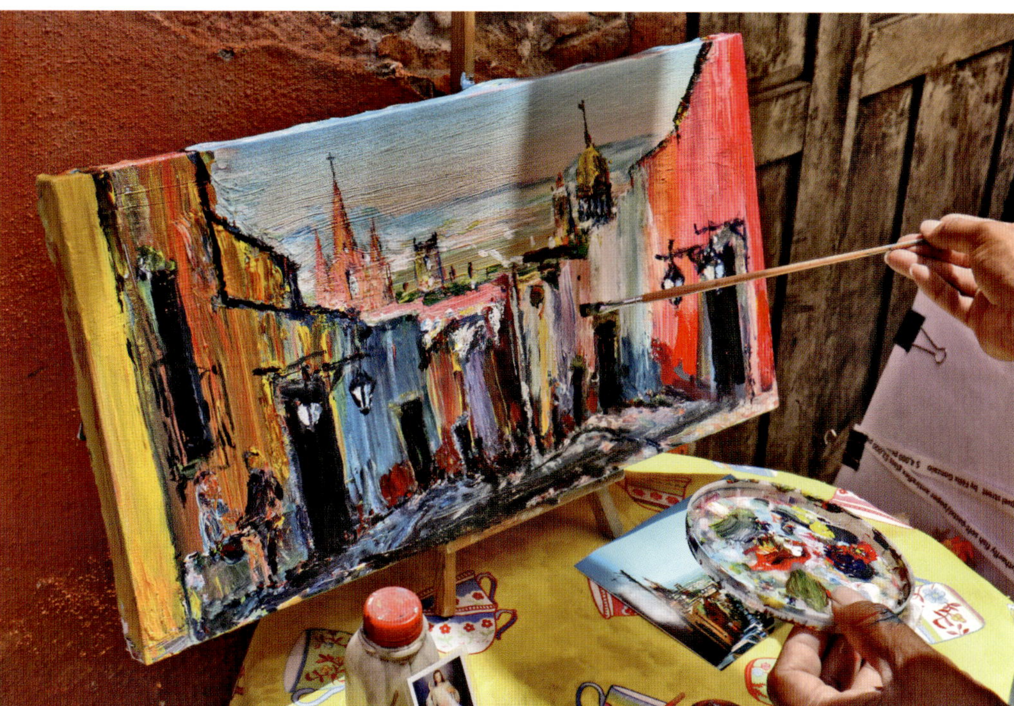

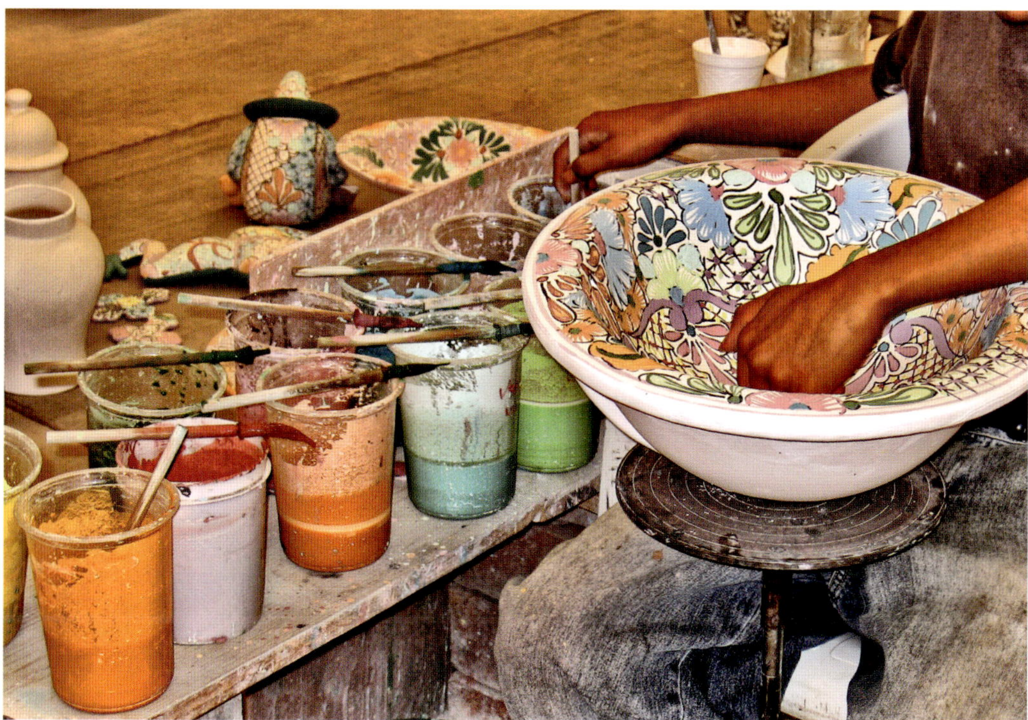

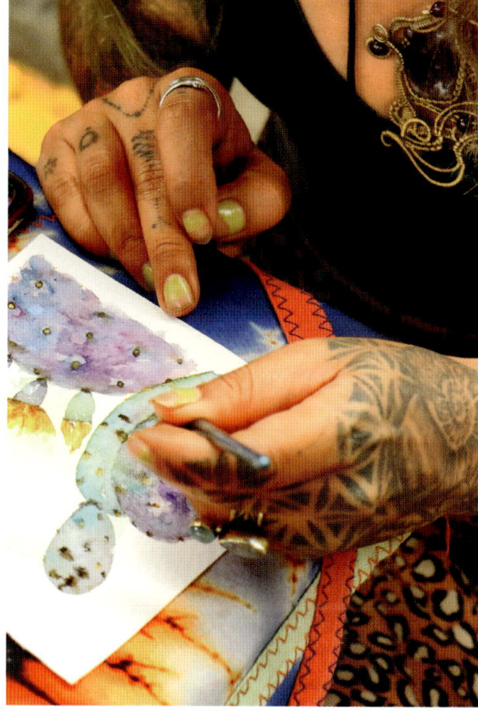

The artist is a receptacle for emotions, regardless from whether they spring from heaven, from earth, from a scrap of paper, from a passing face, or from a spider's web. —Picasso

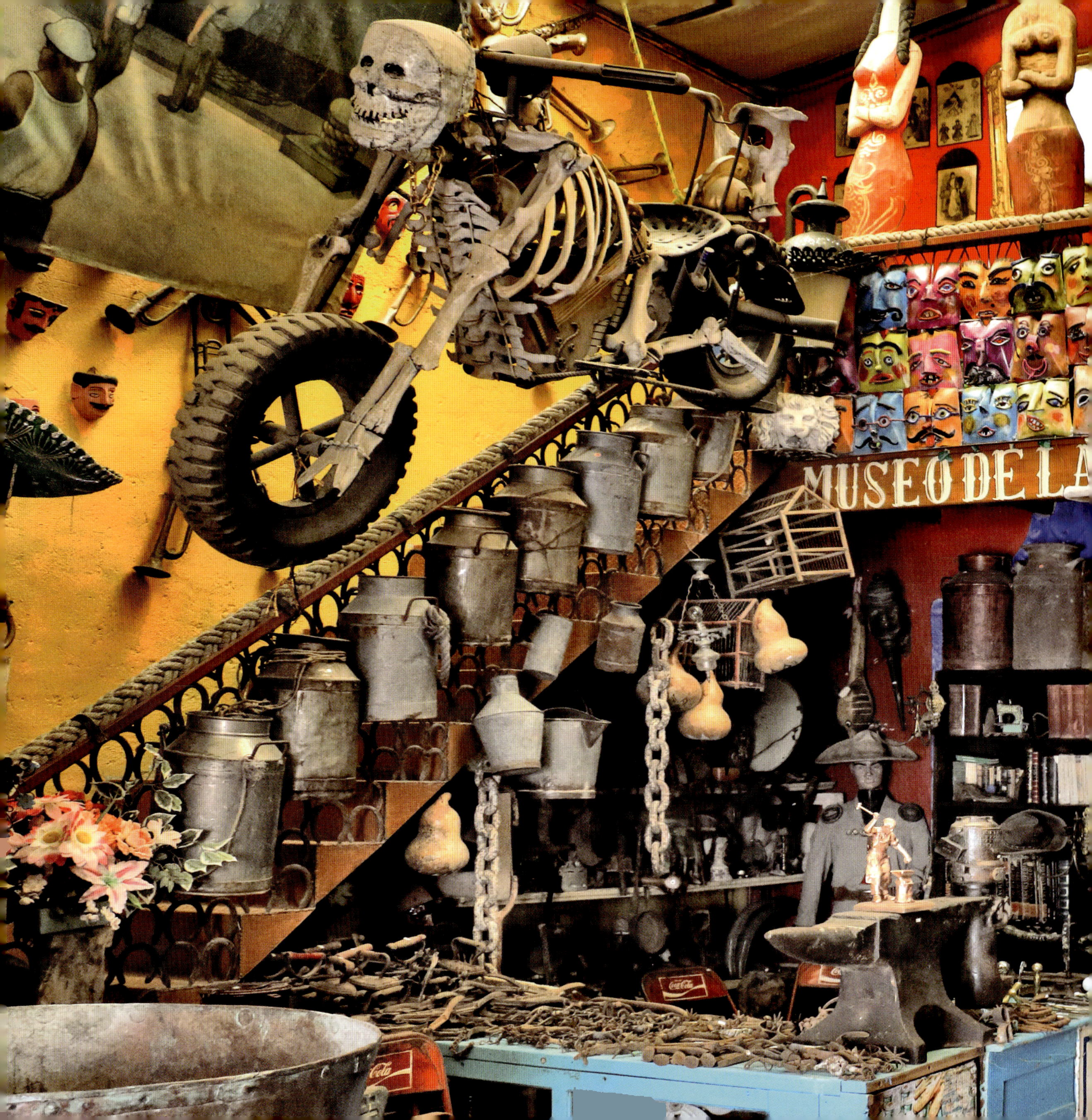
MUSEO DE LA
Coca-Cola

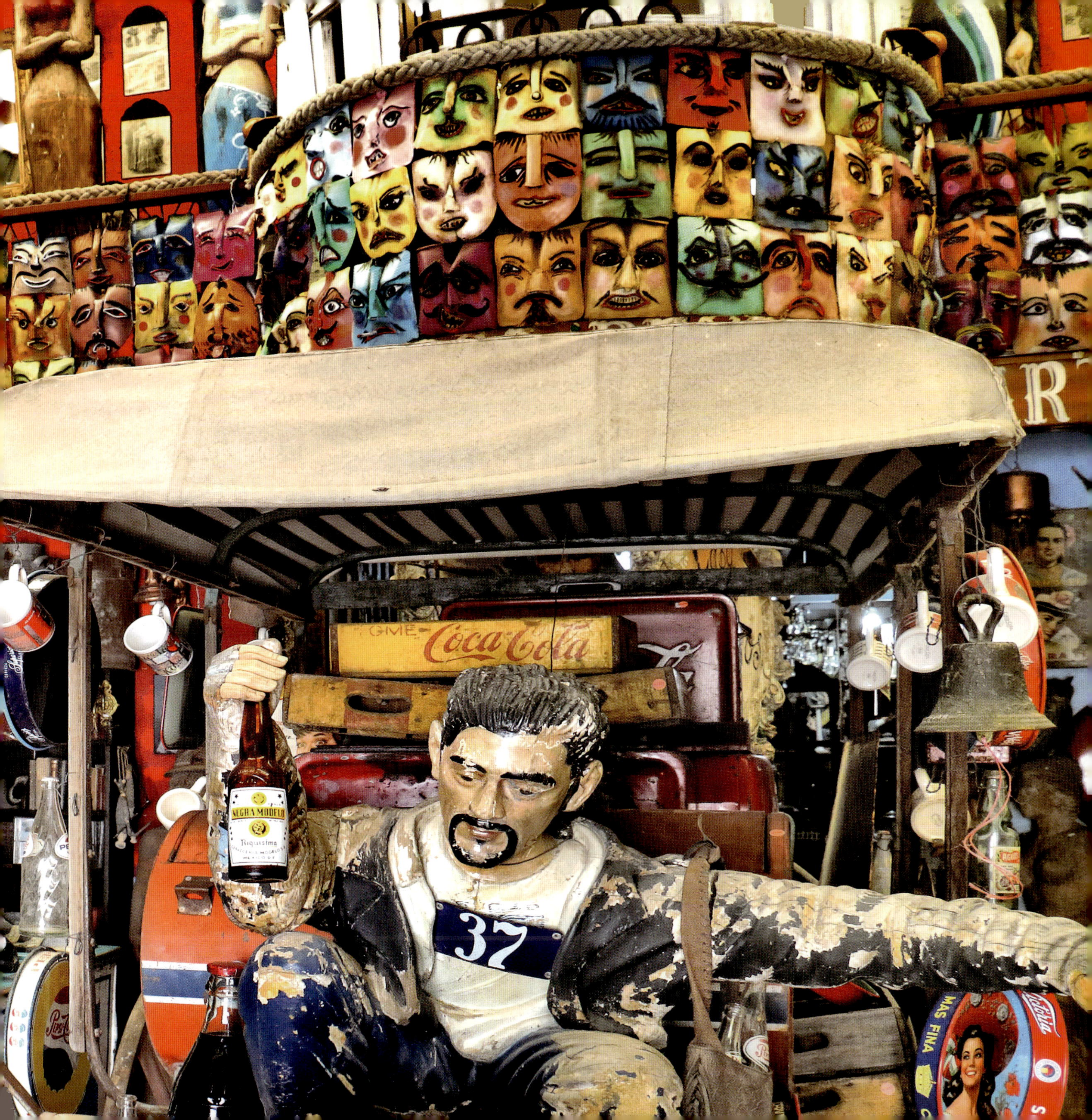

Coca-Cola
NEGRA MODELO
37
MAS FINA

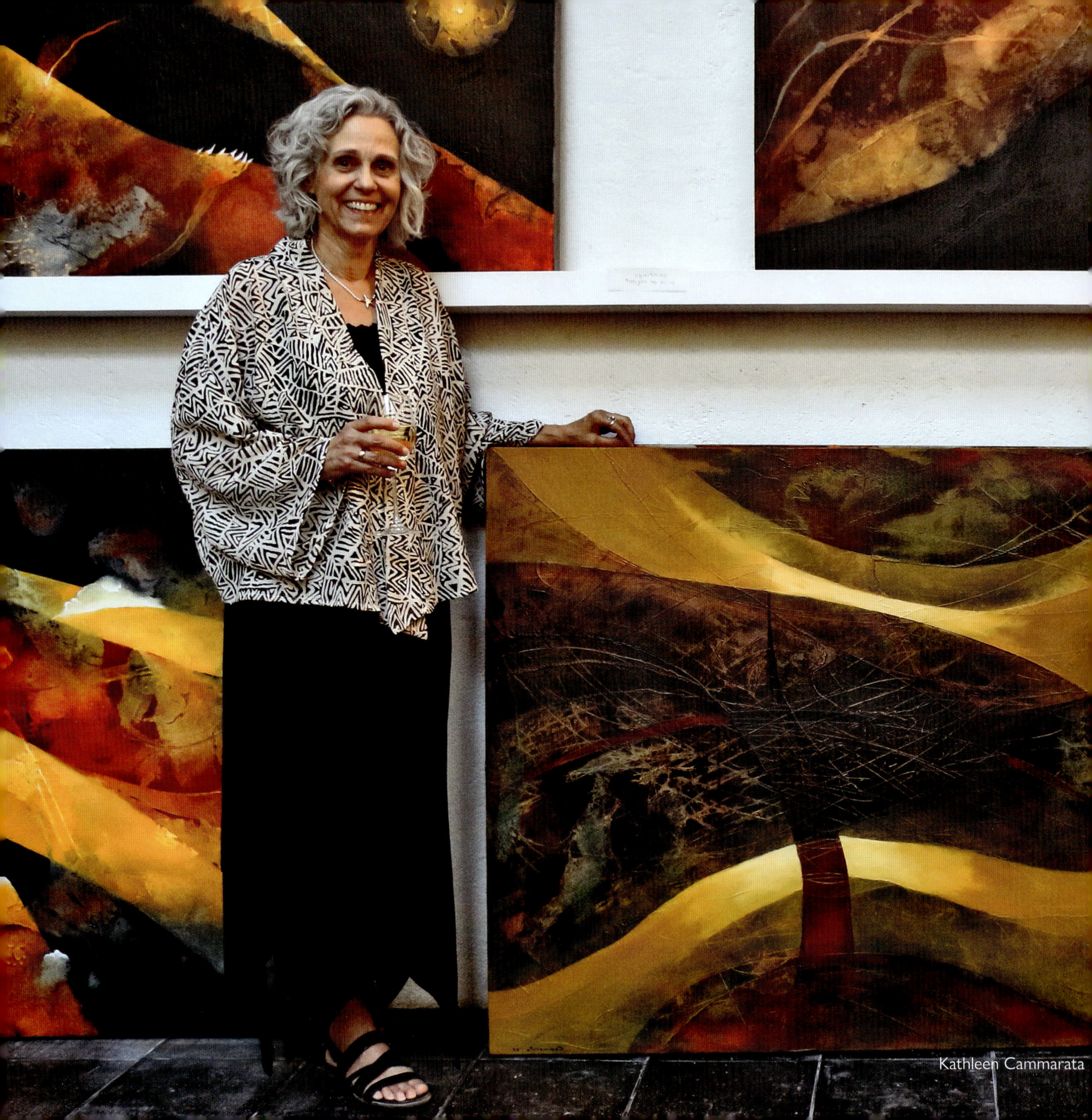

Kathleen Cammarata

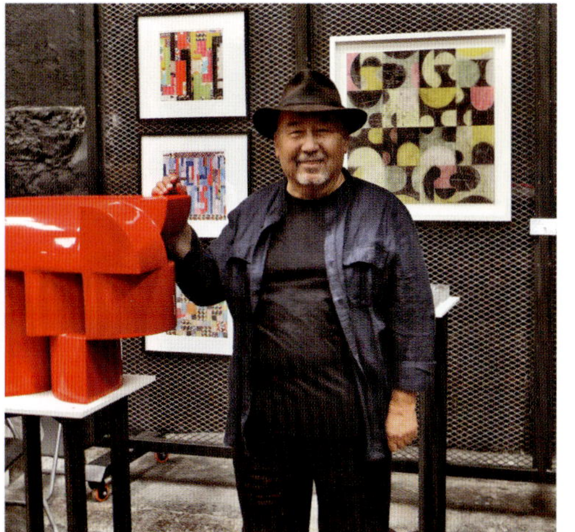
Alberto Lenz

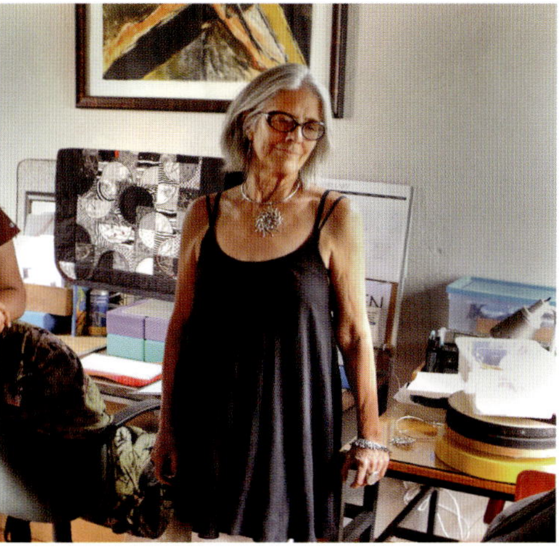
Karen Wight

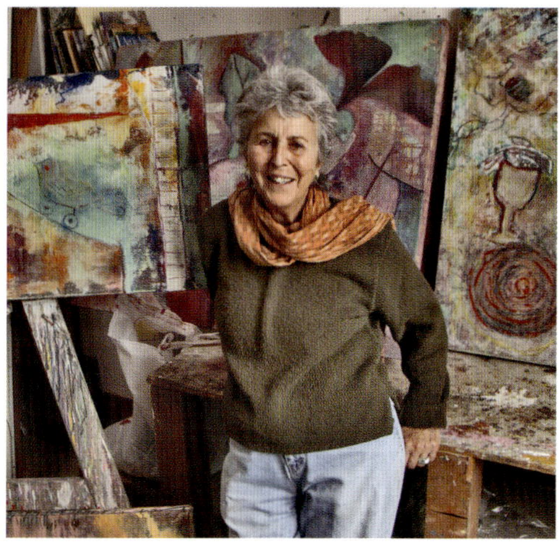
Gerry Gill

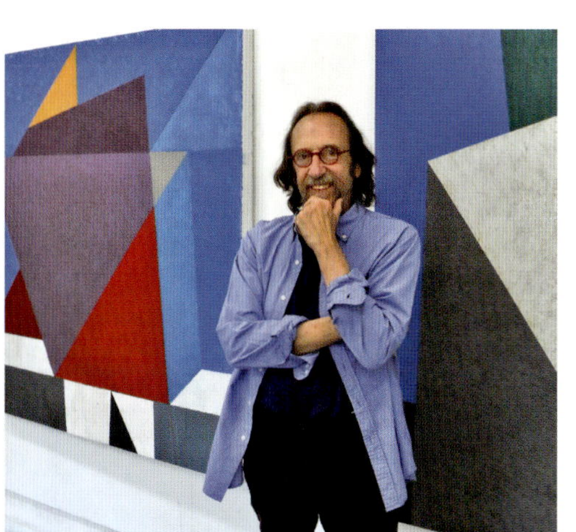
Gene Johnson

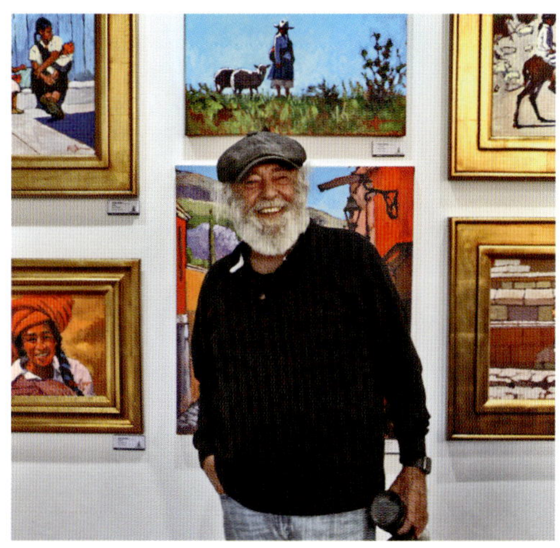
Daniel Ruffert

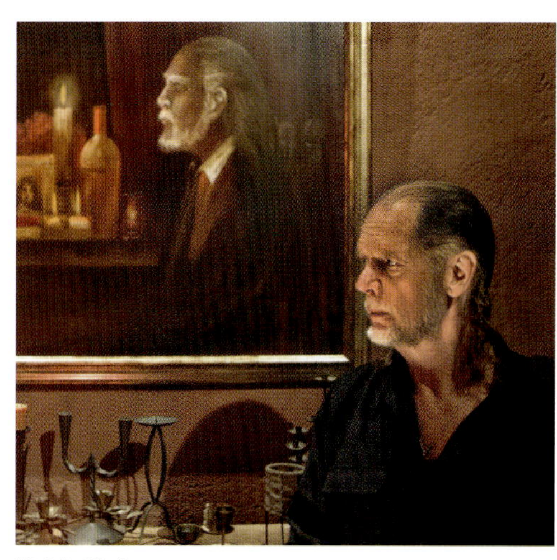
Keith Keller

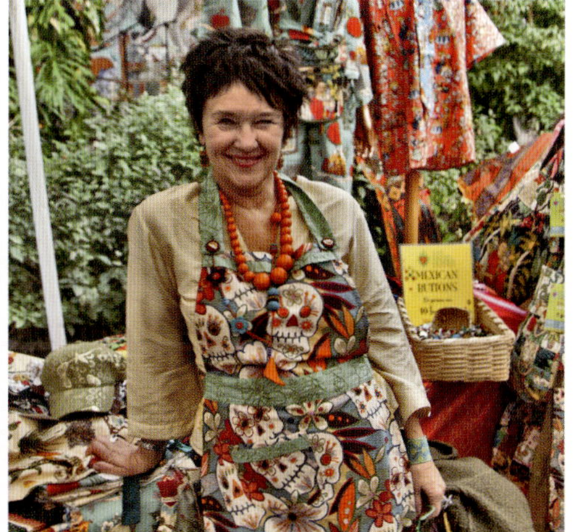

Patrice Wynne

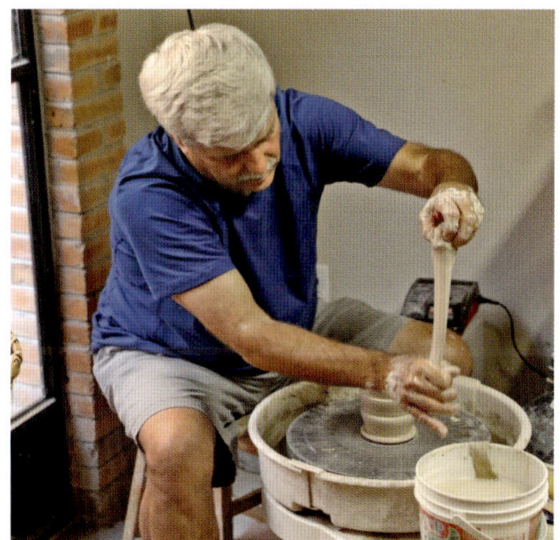
Joe Molinaro

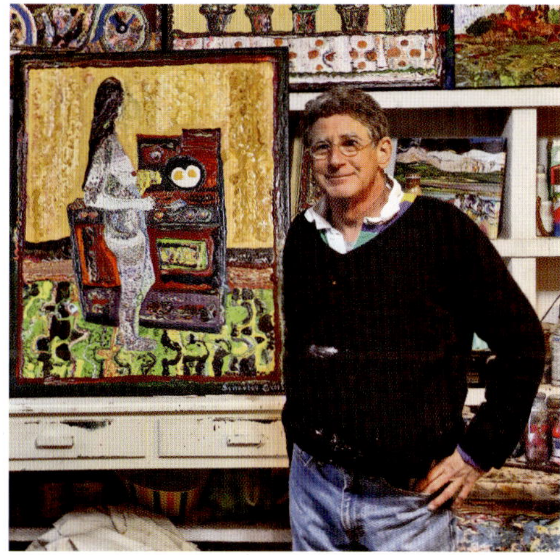
Jon Schooler

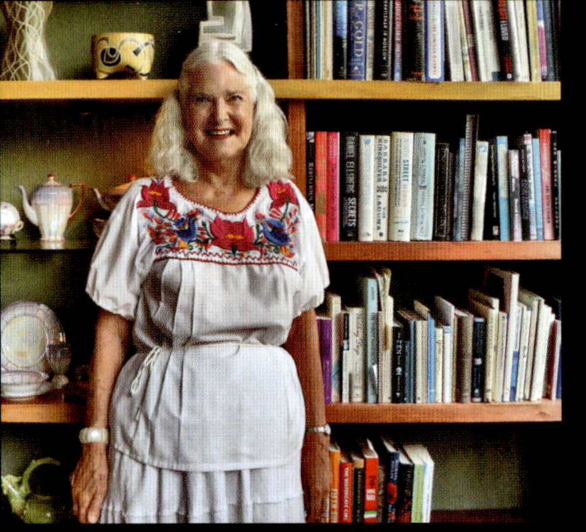
Susan Page

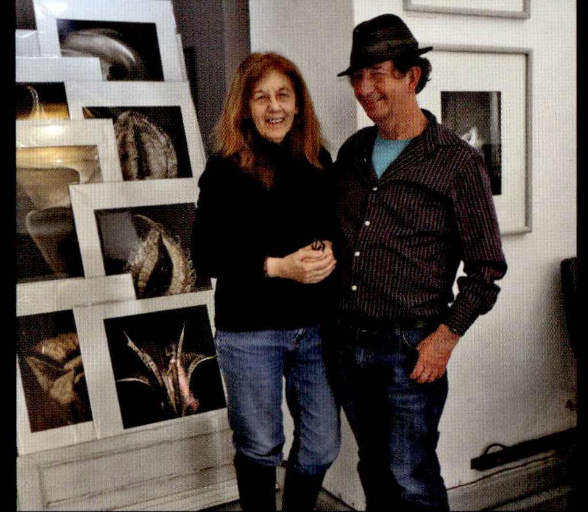
Jo Brenzo & Gregory Berkowitz

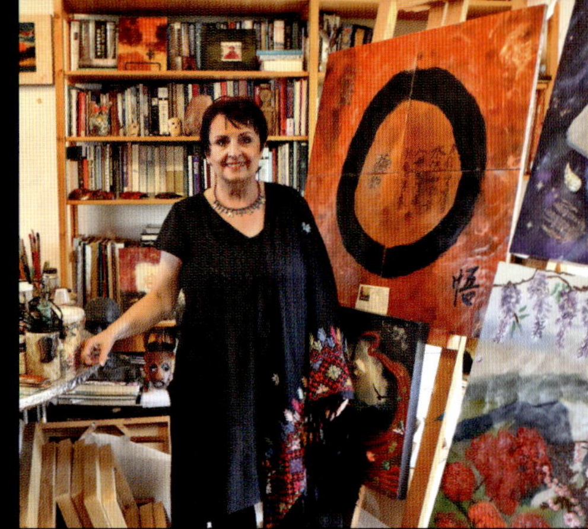
Dawn Gaskill

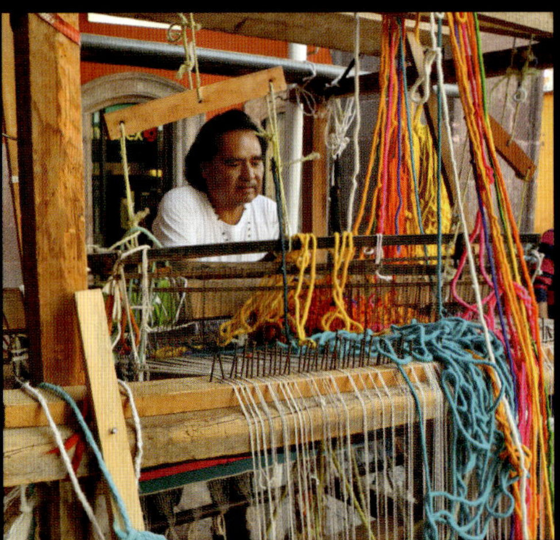
Ramiro Miranda

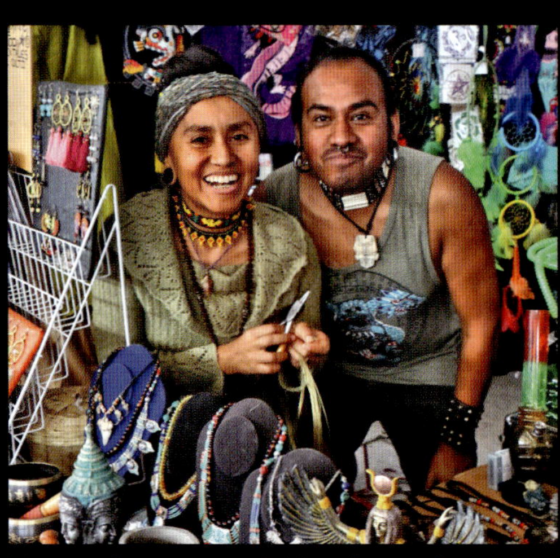
Yesenia Garcia Leon & Noe Castro Sosa

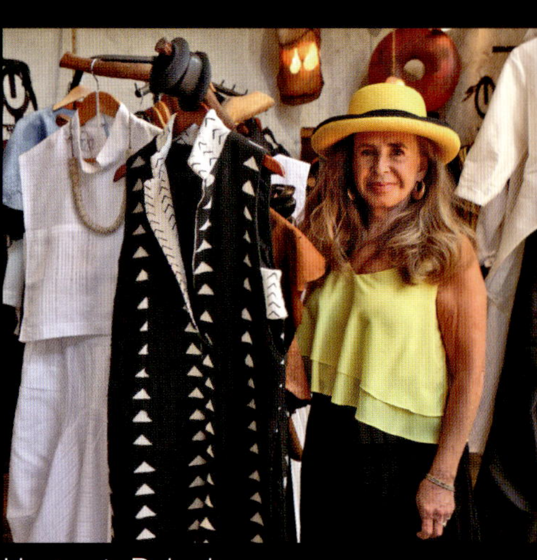
Hortensia Delgado

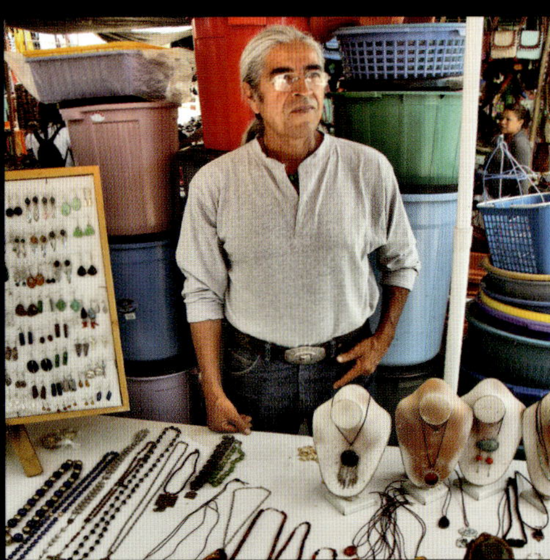
Ismael Hernandez

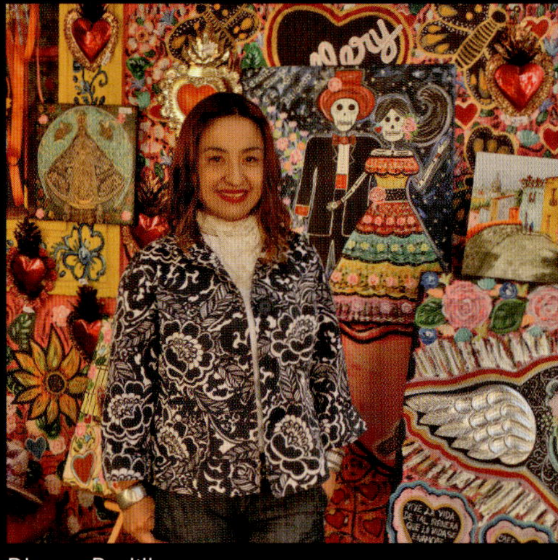
Blanca Badillo

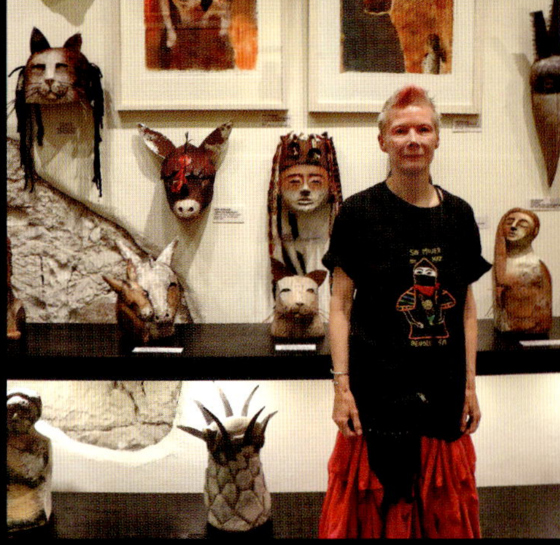
Jane Bingham

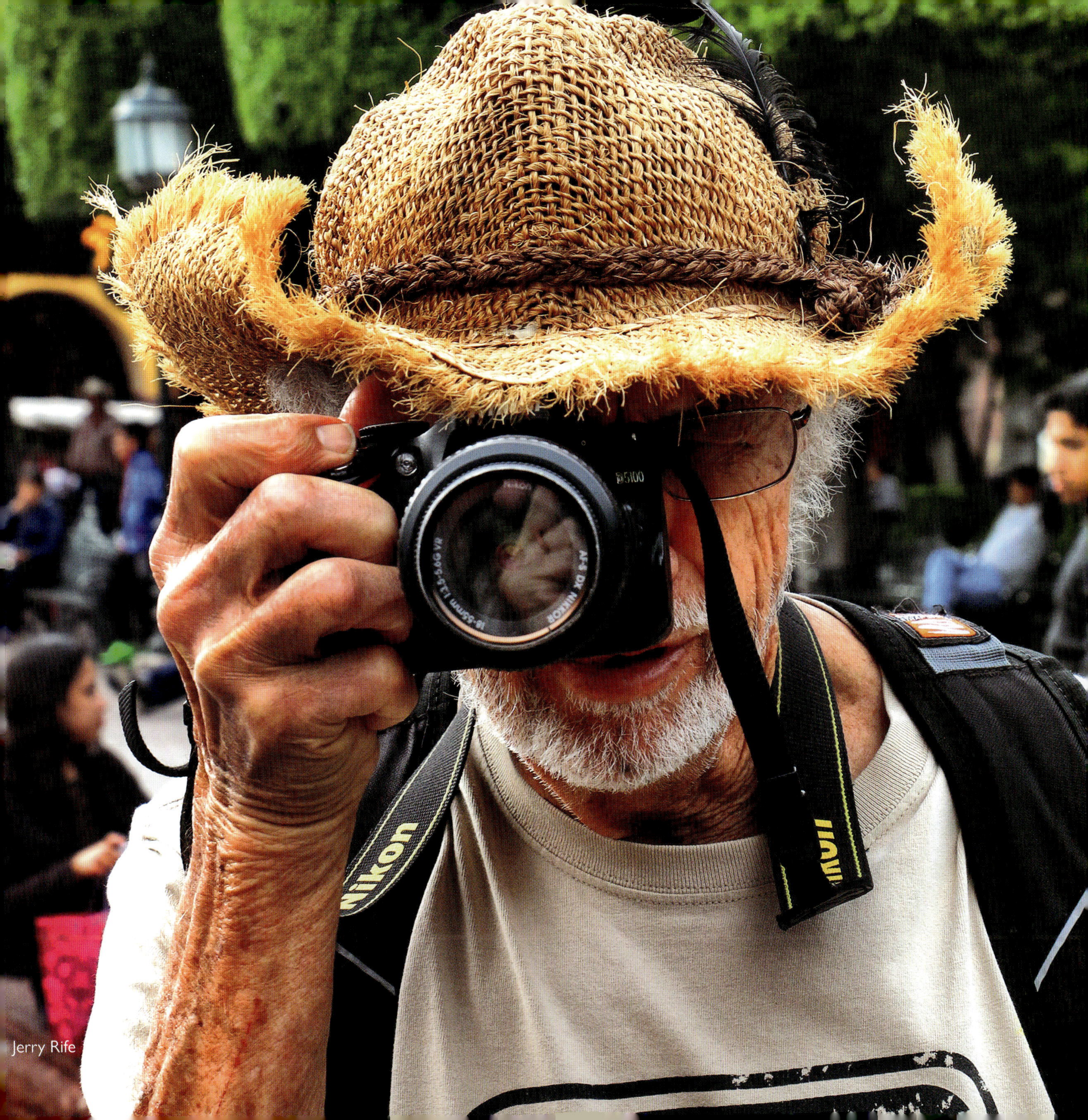

Jerry Rife

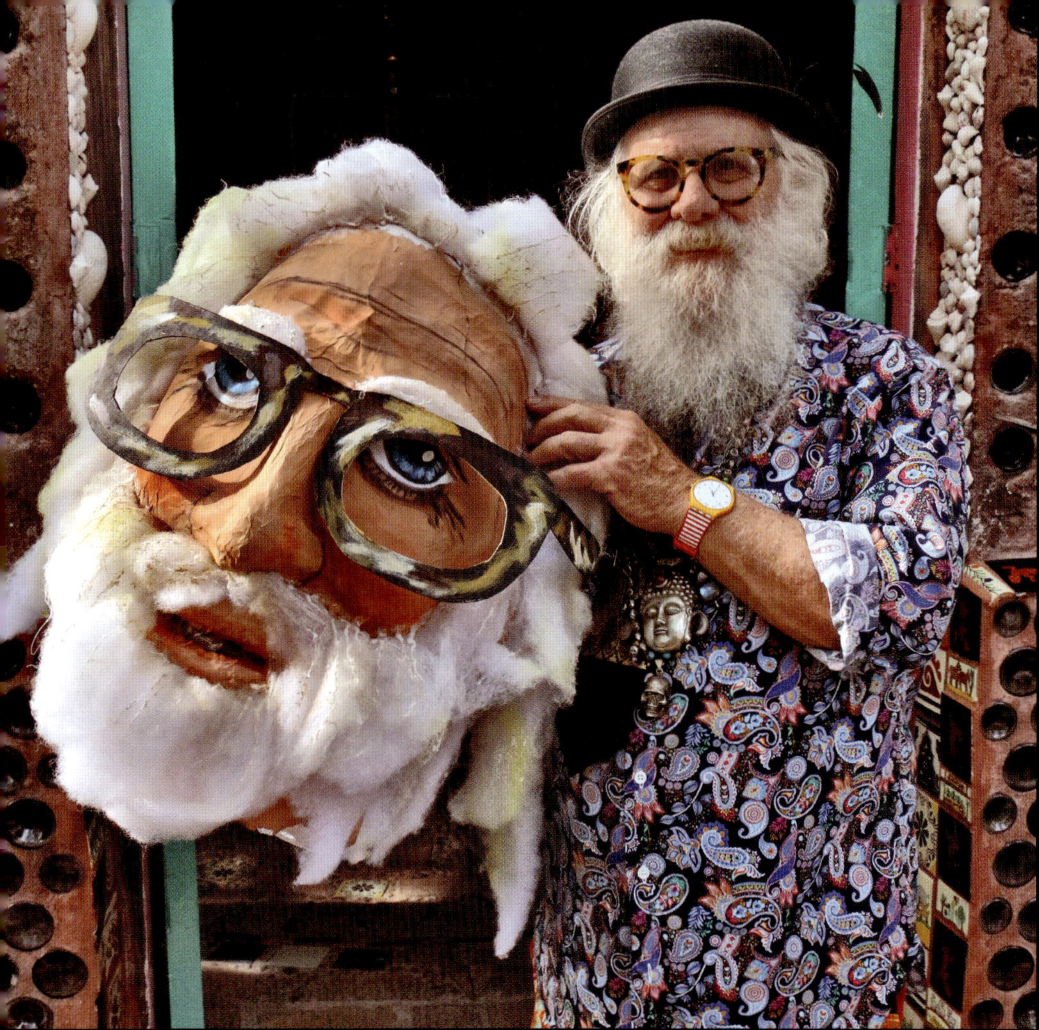

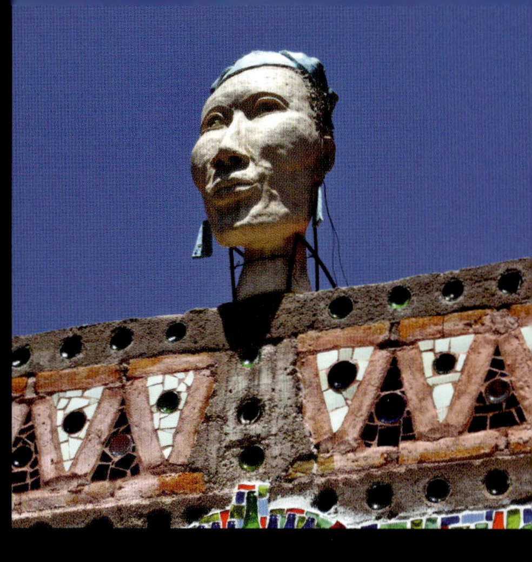

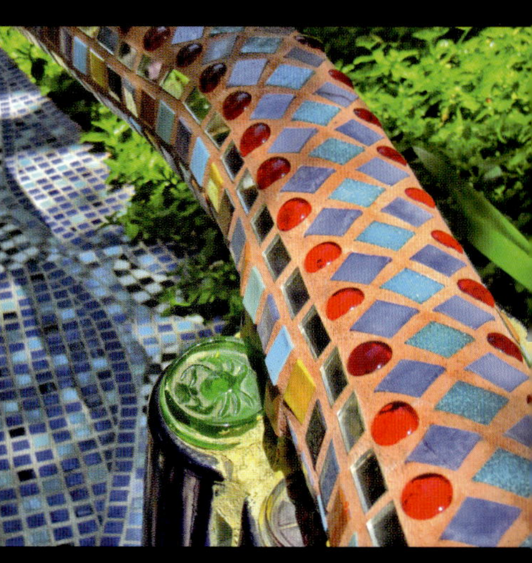

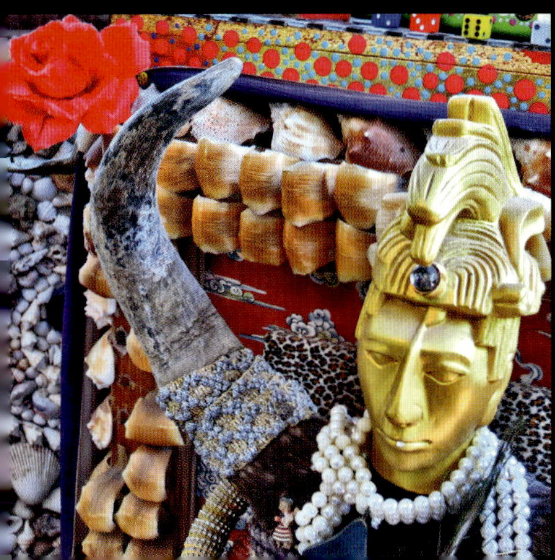

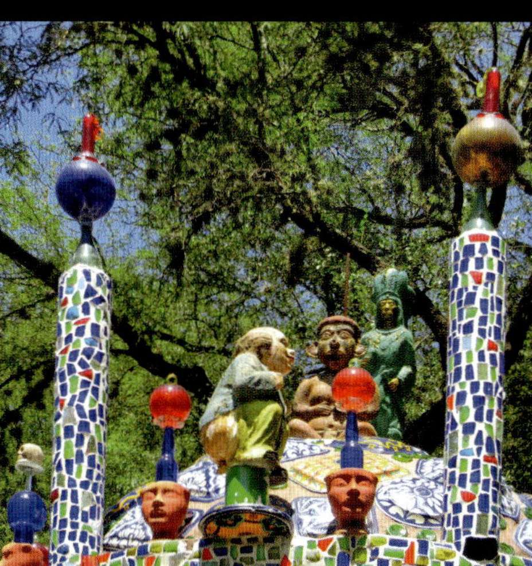

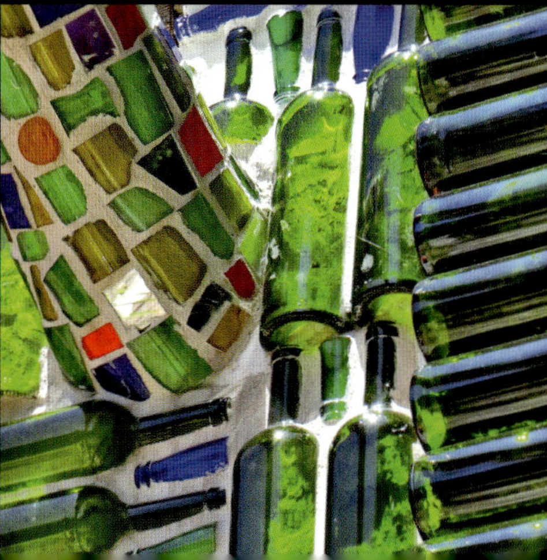

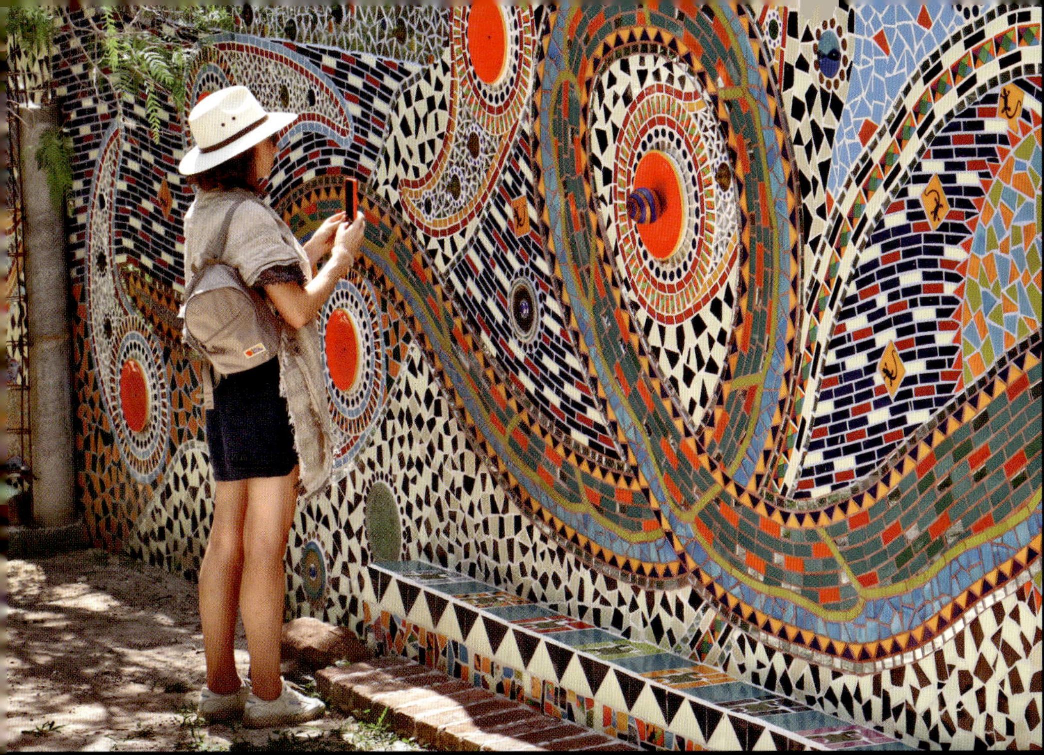

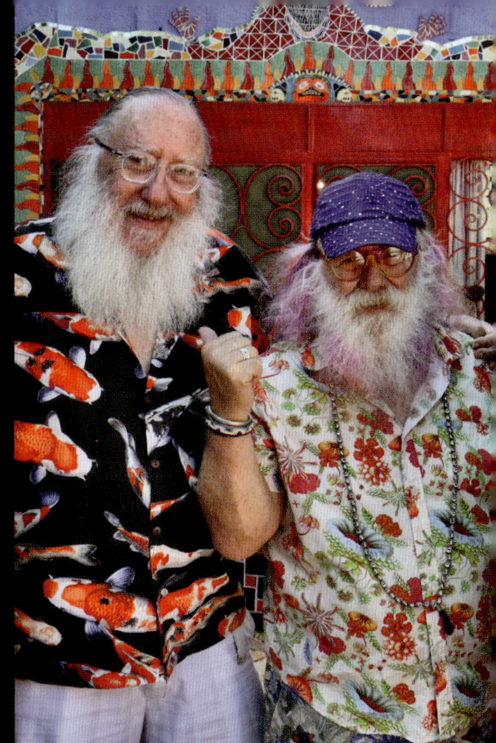

Anado McLauchlin and Richard Schultz built the Chapel of Jimmy Ray in 2012 as a gallery within their compound La Casa de las Ranas, the House of the Frogs. In the quiet community of La Cieneguita, just a few miles outside San Miguel, in a tranquil garden setting, an amazing collection of handmade, broken-tile, mosaic-decorated structures is an oasis of art that hosts a multitude of events celebrating the joy and meaning of art, dedicated to "the Outlanders of the world, those who have chosen the road less trodden" (Anado McLauchlin).

Anado McLaughlin's life was dedicated to his and to others' art, celebrating in every manner the ideas of making, questioning, and finding new truths.

What I do on a poetic, metaphorical level is try to combine all of the different belief systems and all of those spiritual roads, and to show that in reality, there is only one road.
—Anado McLauchlin

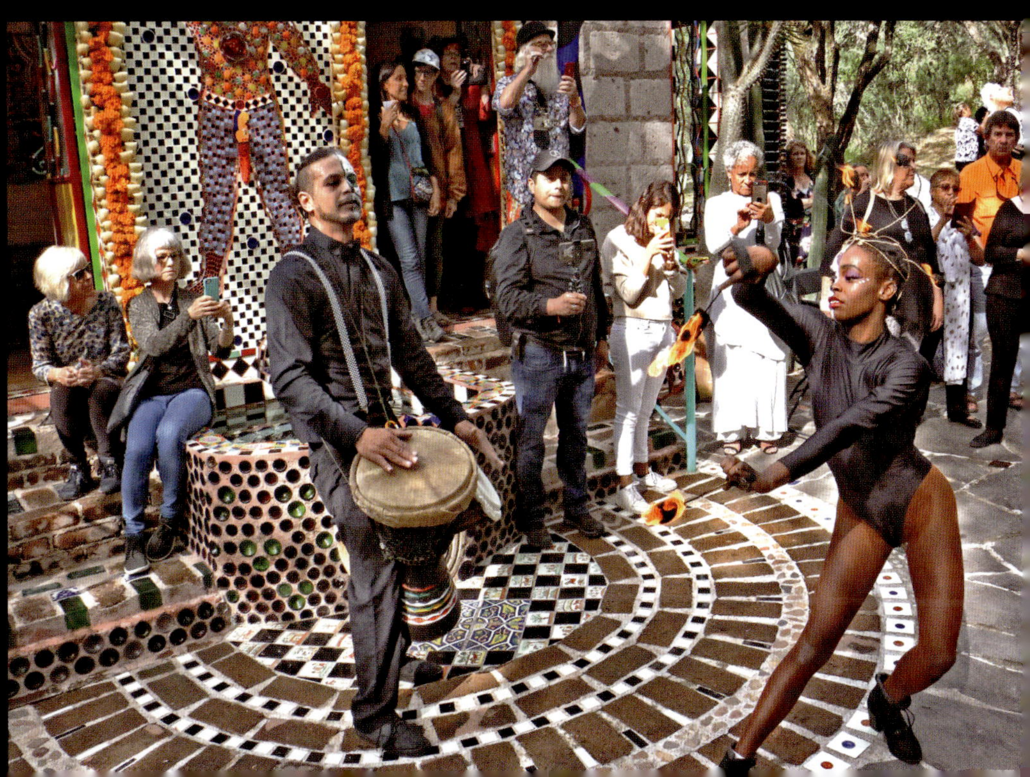

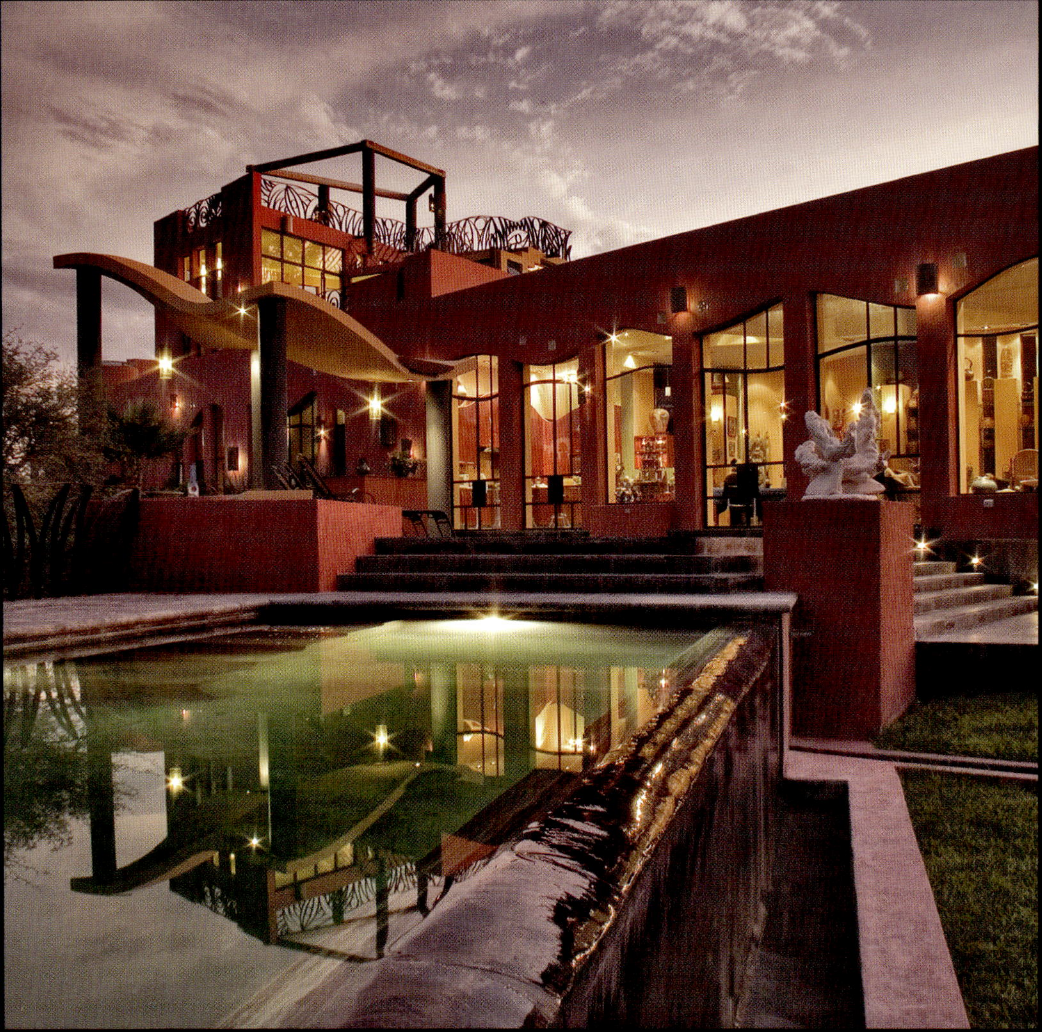

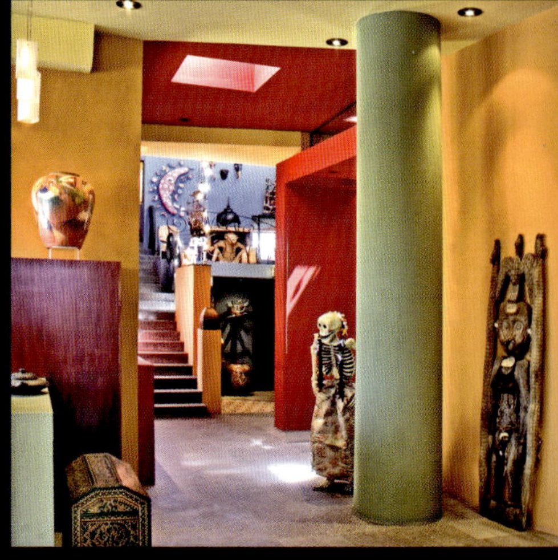

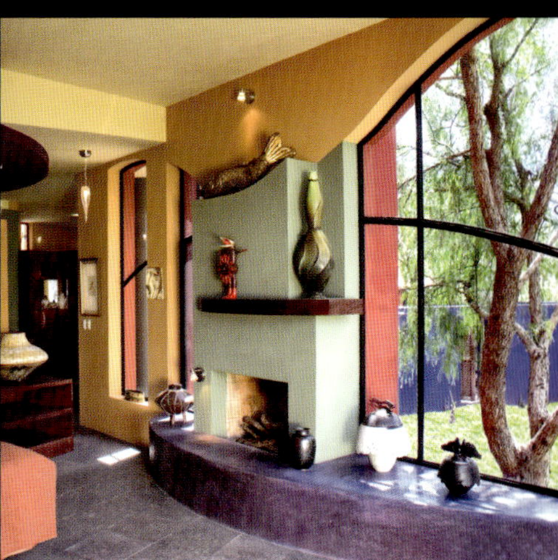

Gallery owner Mayer Shacter brings over fifty years of experience as a collector, dealer, and ceramic artist to his passion for Mexican folk art at his Galería Atotonilco, just a few minutes north of San Miguel. When he and his wife, writer Susan Page, bought an abandoned furniture factory surrounded by ancient mesquite trees, they had no idea how much their lives would change and their dreams evolve. Mayer has since become one of the preeminent experts on Mexican folk art. Every piece in the collection has been hand-selected by Mayer, himself a ceramic artist whose career flourished for twenty-seven years before he gradually began dealing in fine antiques and midcentury modern furniture. His eye for beauty, innovation, and top-quality craftsmanship is highly refined, and he finds the best artists working today, then purchases their finest work, often commissioning pieces, so many of the items in the gallery are unique. Mayer shares his knowledge and stories freely, having traveled all over Mexico with Susan in their pursuit of undiscovered artists whose work deserves support. "One of the great pleasures of this gallery," says Mayer, "is my ability to support talented artists and their families and to help keep alive one of the richest traditions of Indigenous art anywhere on the planet." Galería Atotonilco has been praised as the finest collection of Mexican folk art in Mexico.

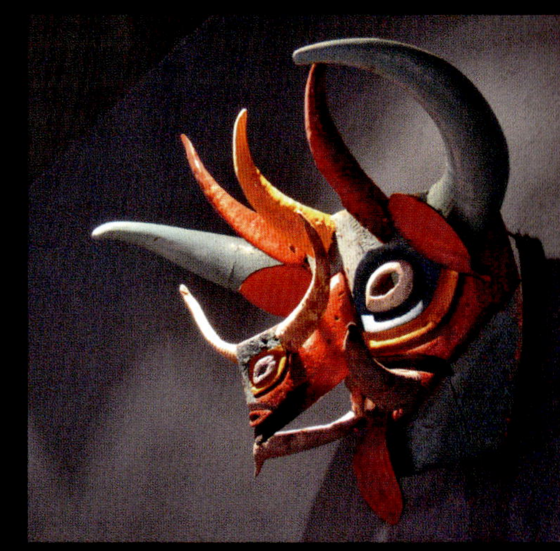

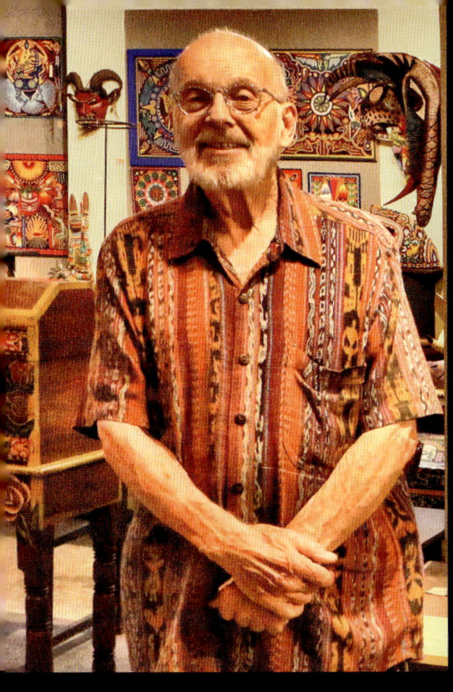
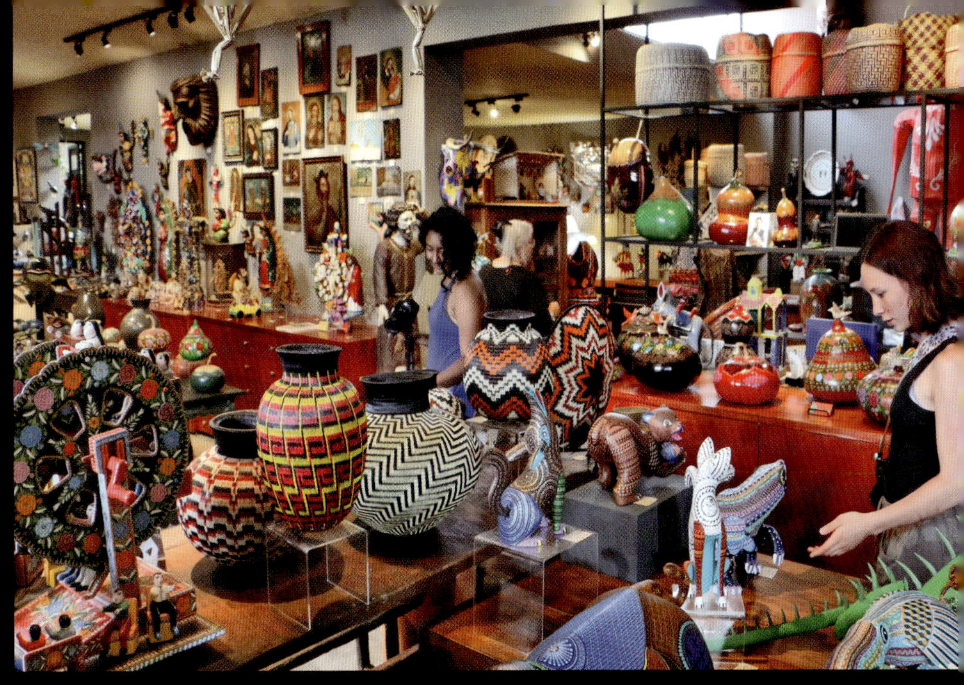
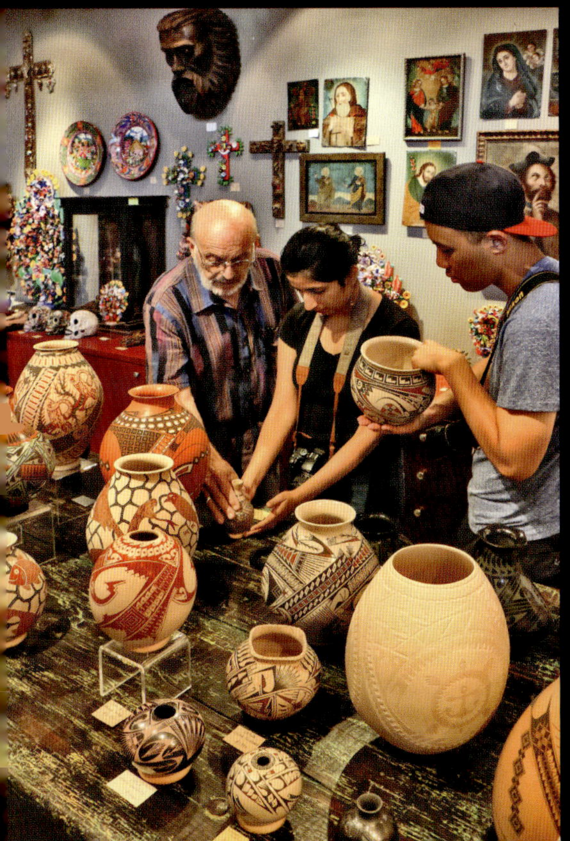
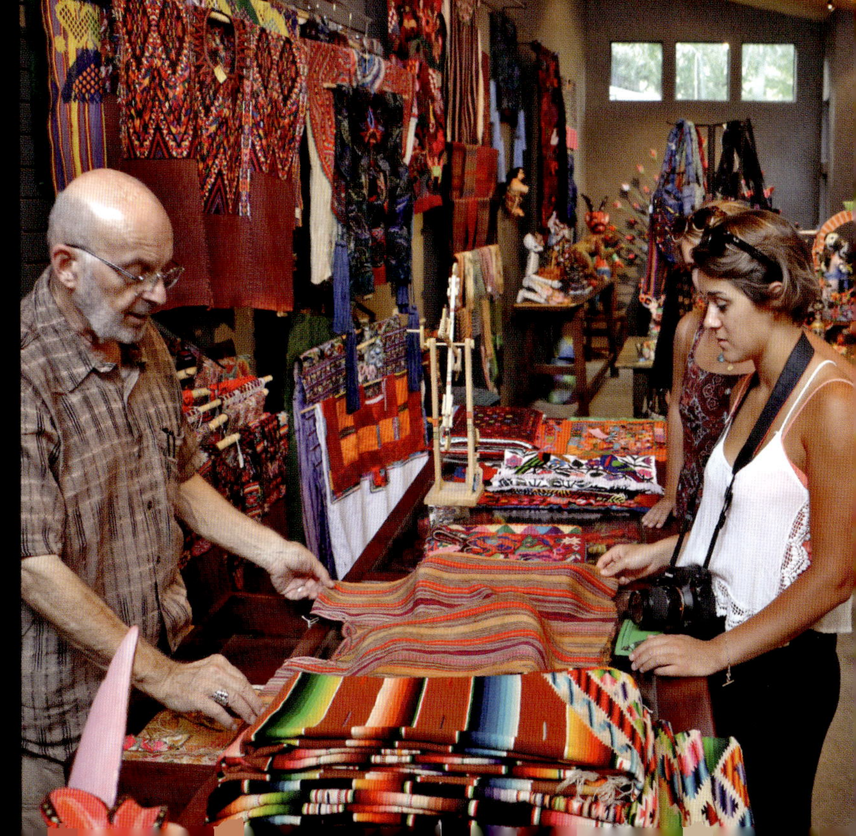

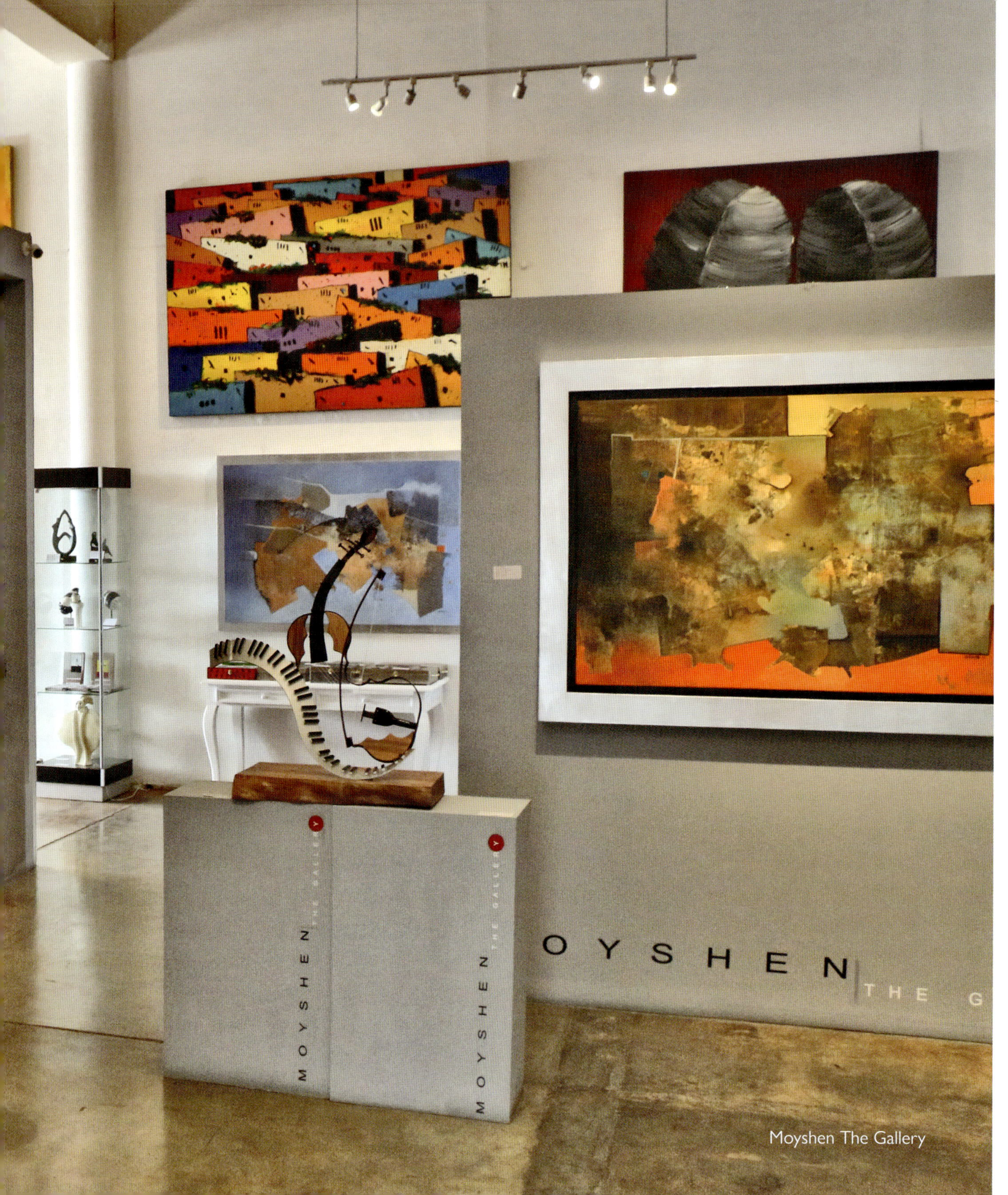

Moyshen The Gallery

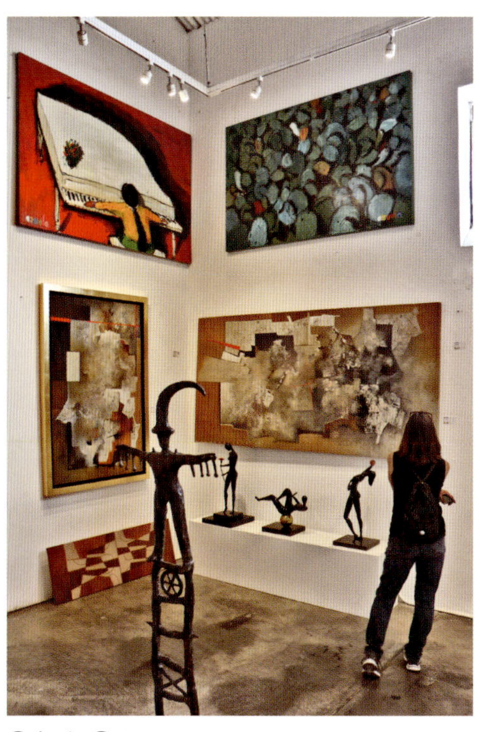

Galería Guiness

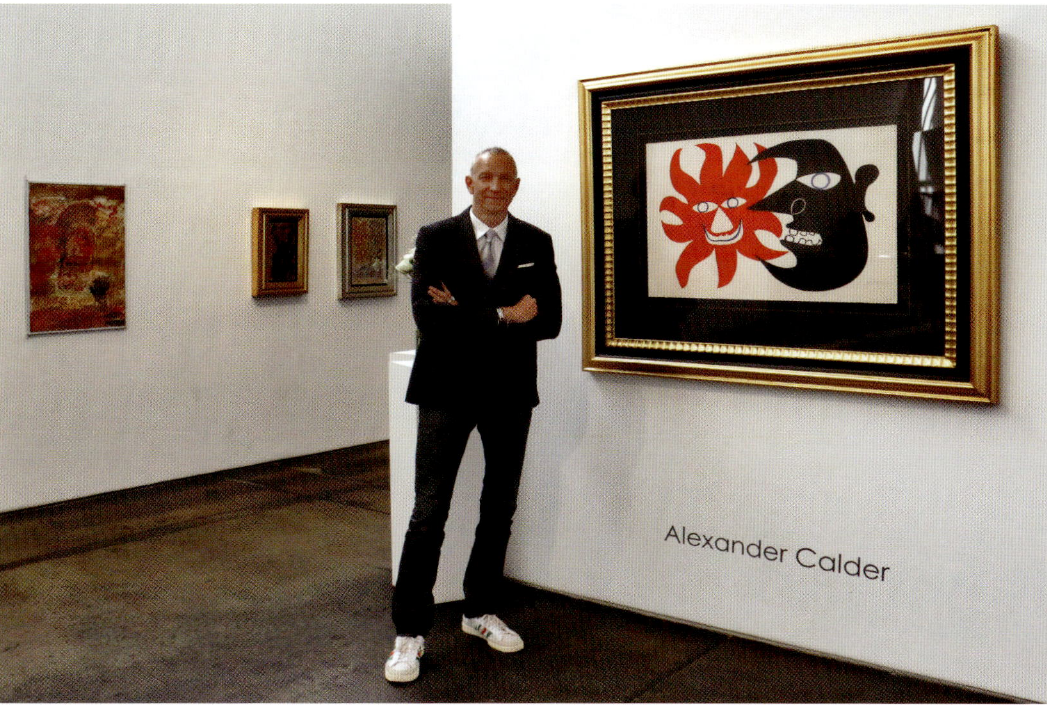

Skot Forman Gallery

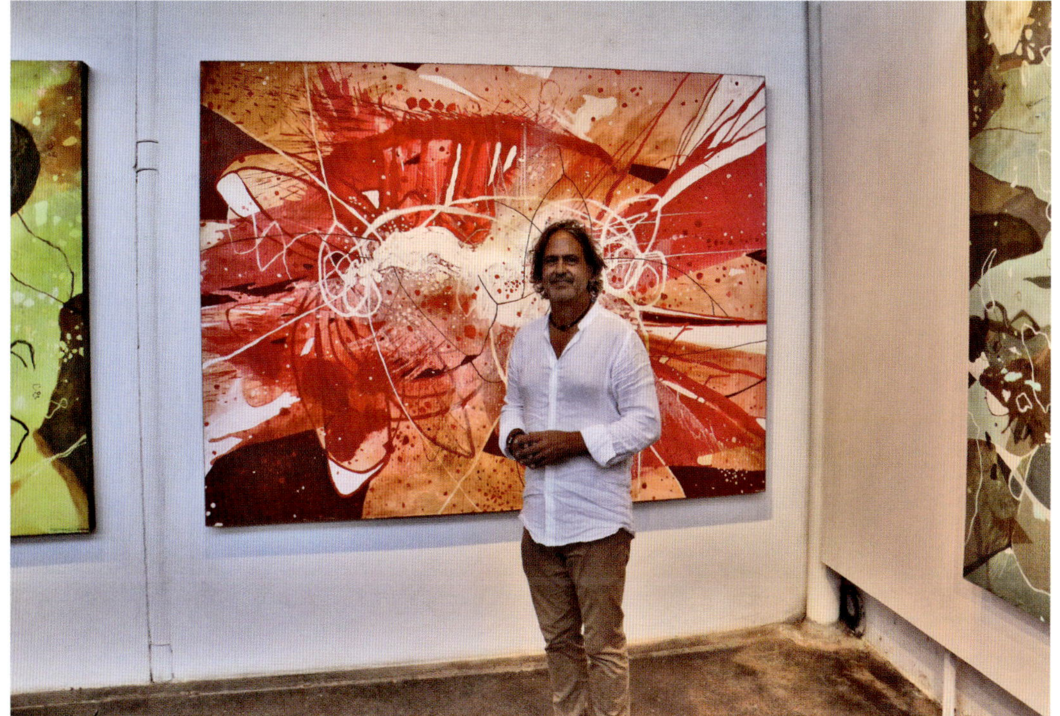

alQuimia4 Galería

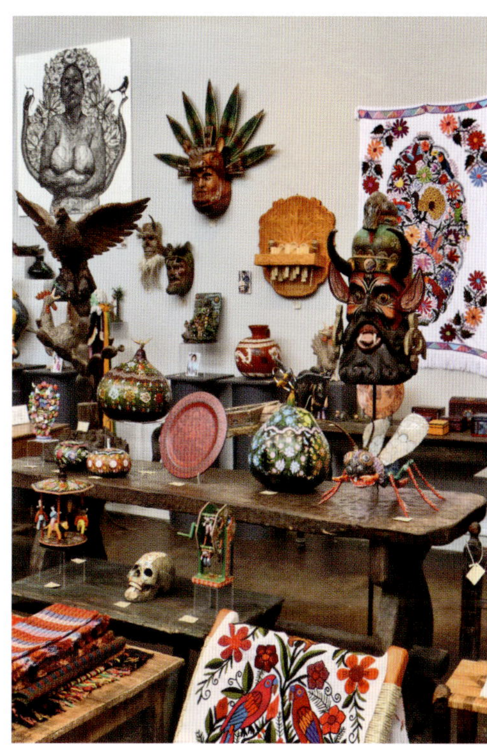

Galería Atotonilco

Colleen Sorenson is a tile and ceramic artist from Texas, whose interest in graffiti as a serious art form led her to create Muros en Blanco. The quiet Colonia Guadalupe neighborhood was little visited until Colleen's efforts convinced authorities to permit more than 140 murals by local, national, and international graffiti artists. This put Guadalupe literally "on the map." Officially declared an art district, Muros en Blanco, through Colleen's efforts, has given voice to artists whose work was considered defacing and illegal.

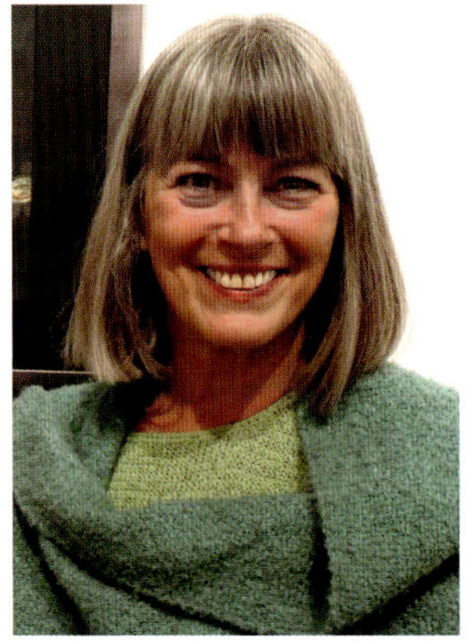

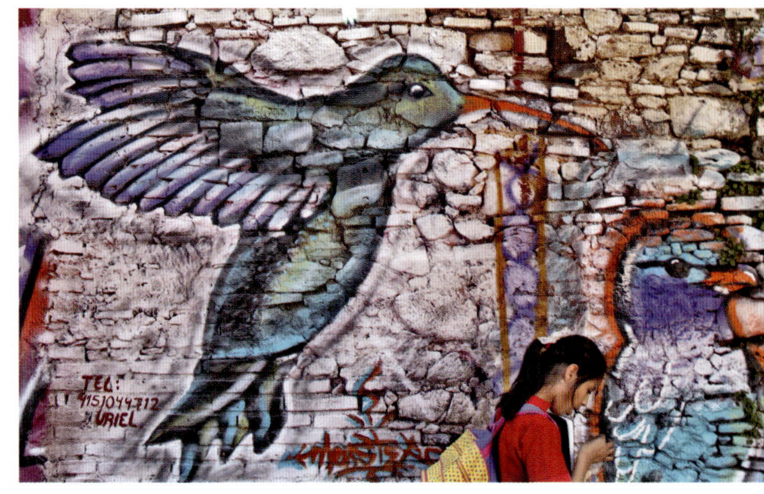

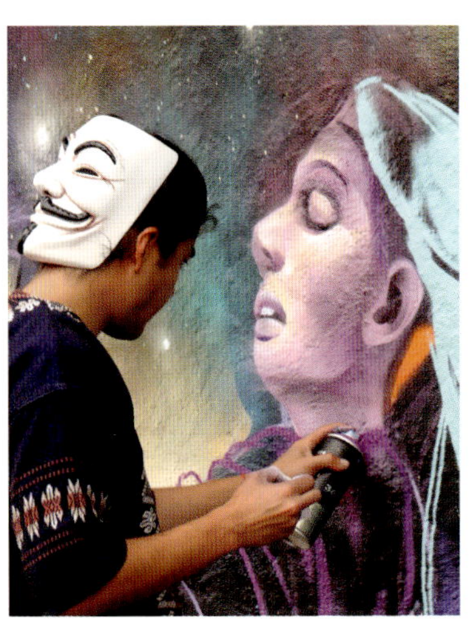

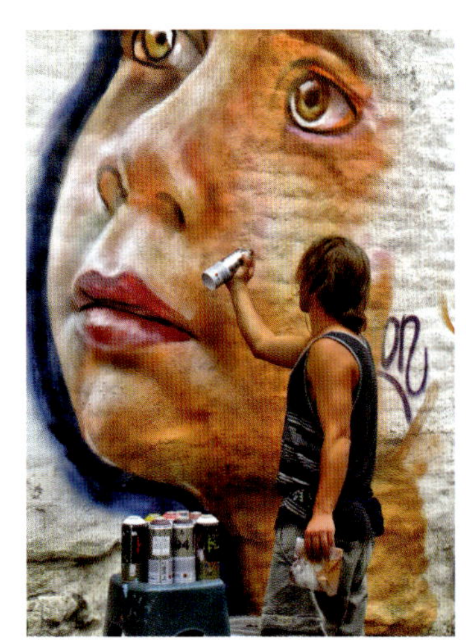

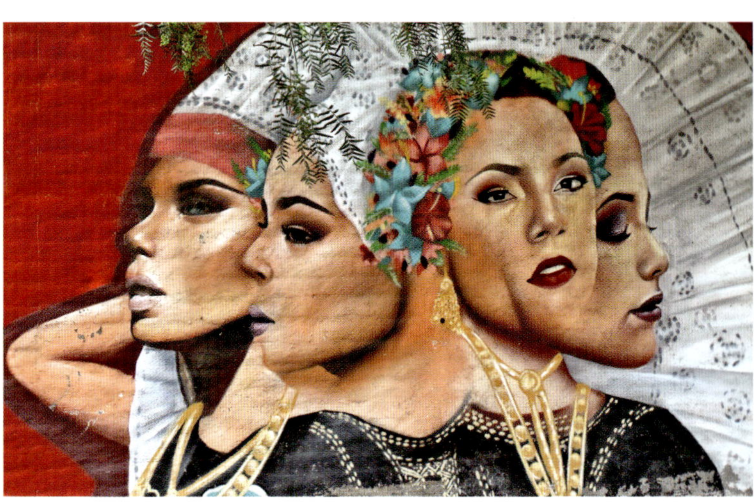

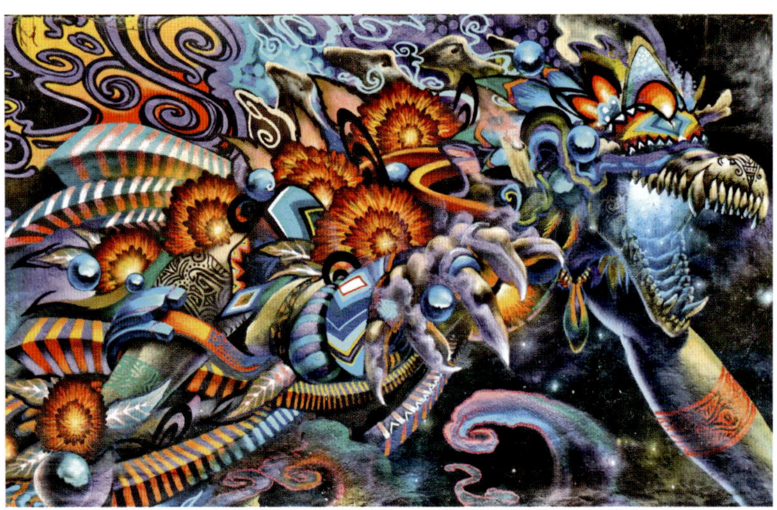

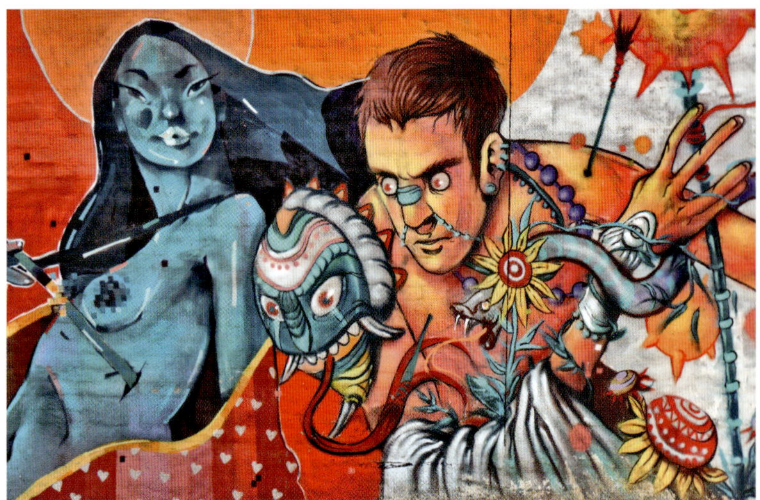

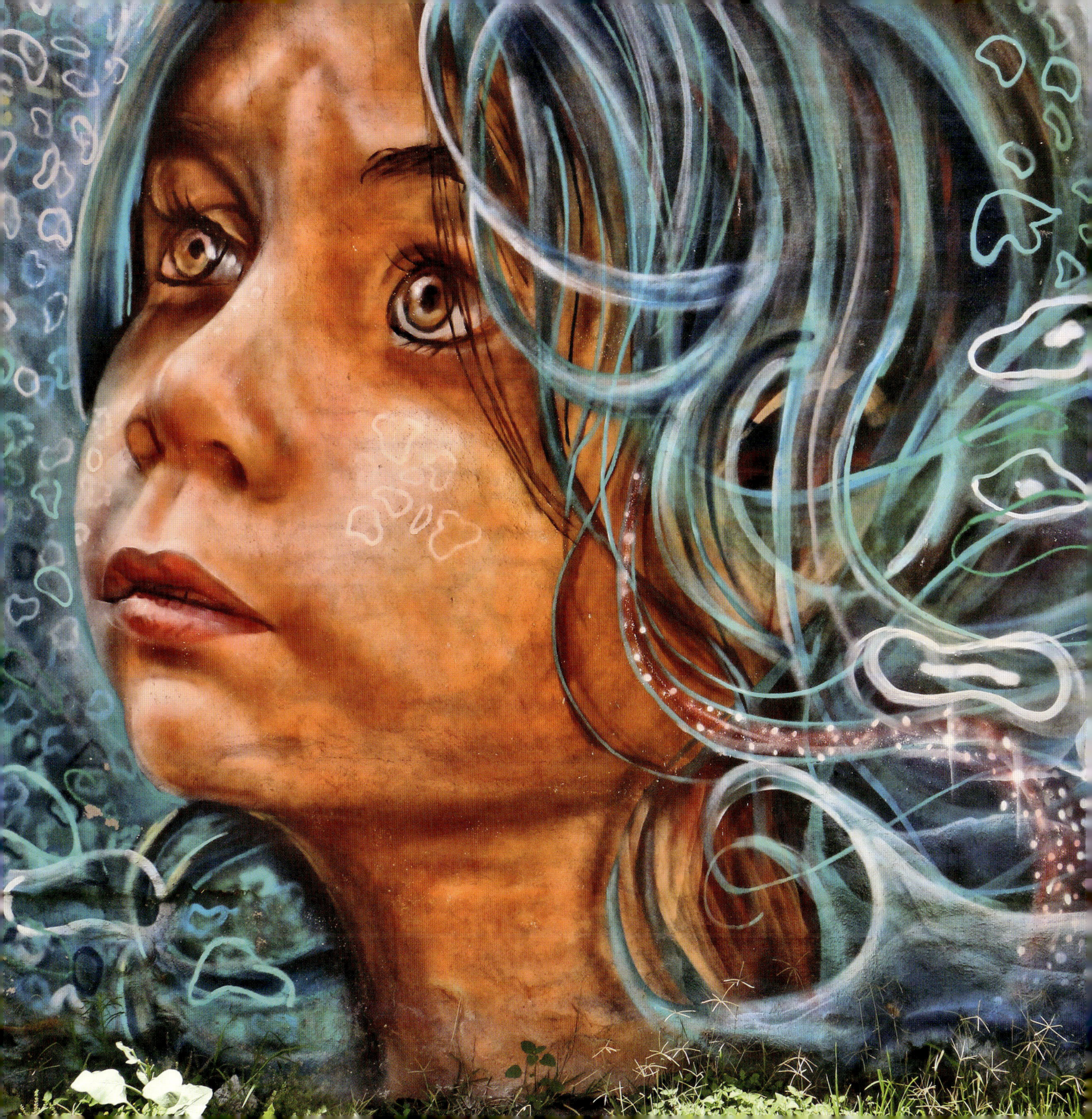

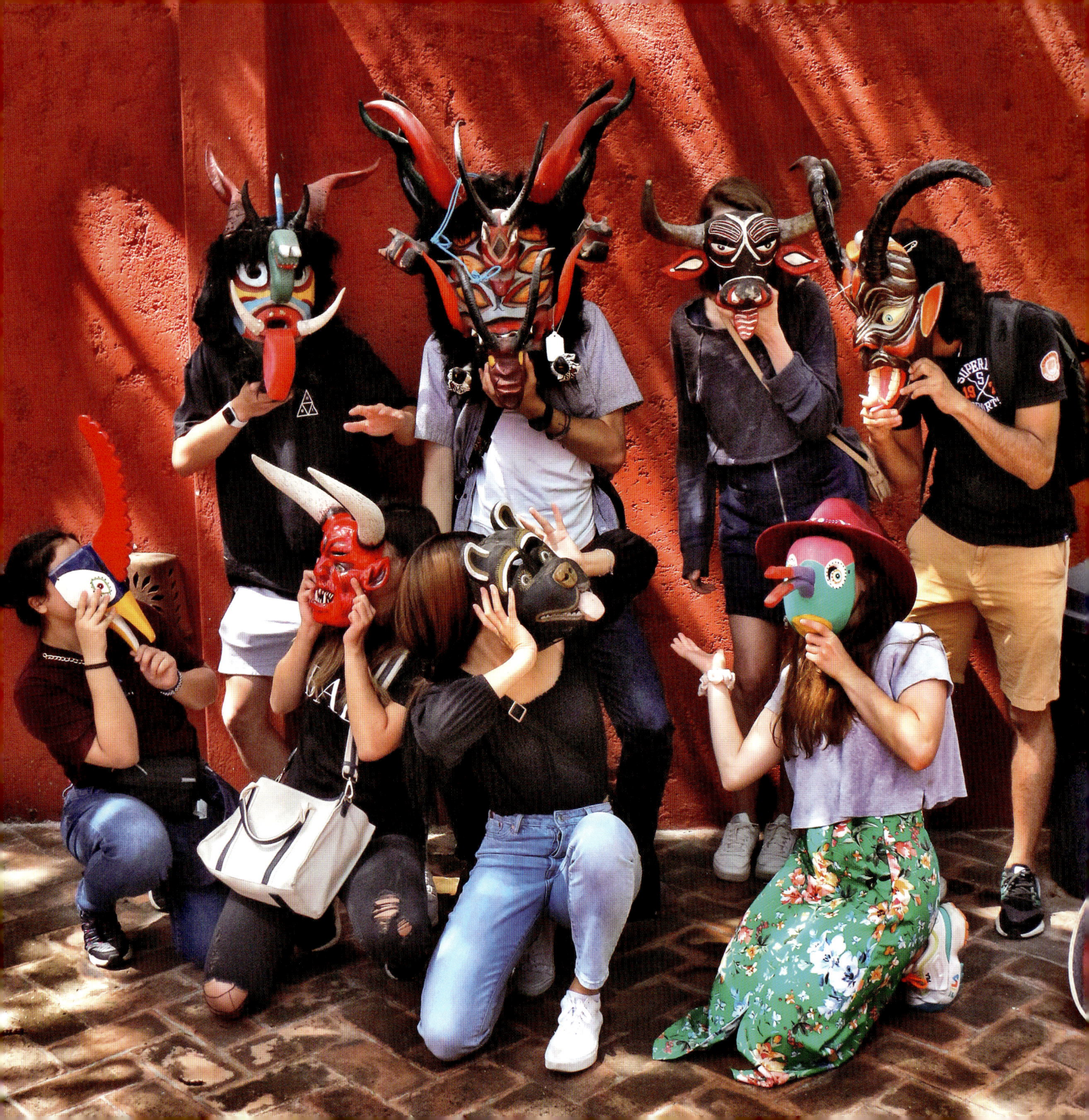

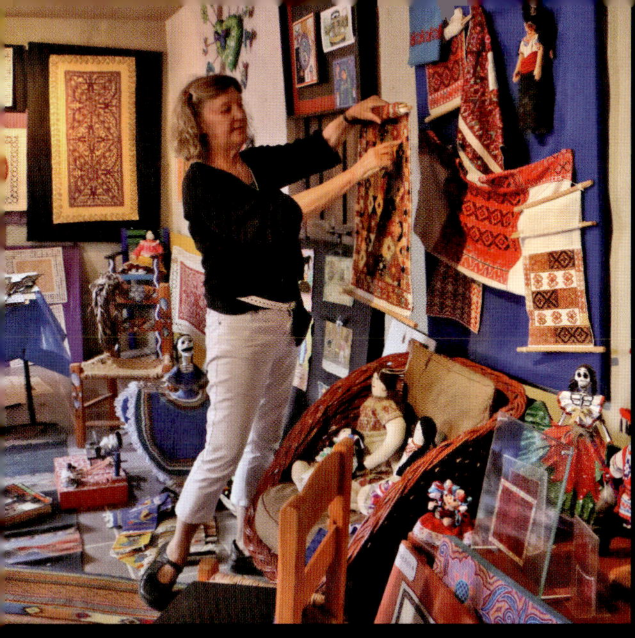

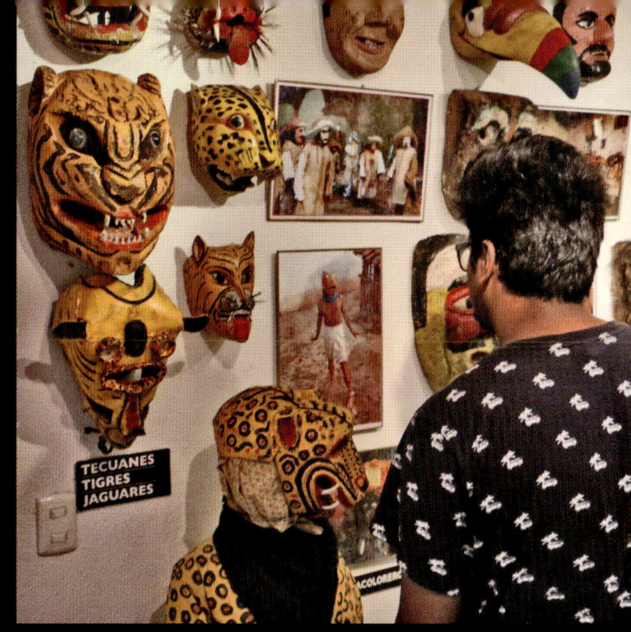

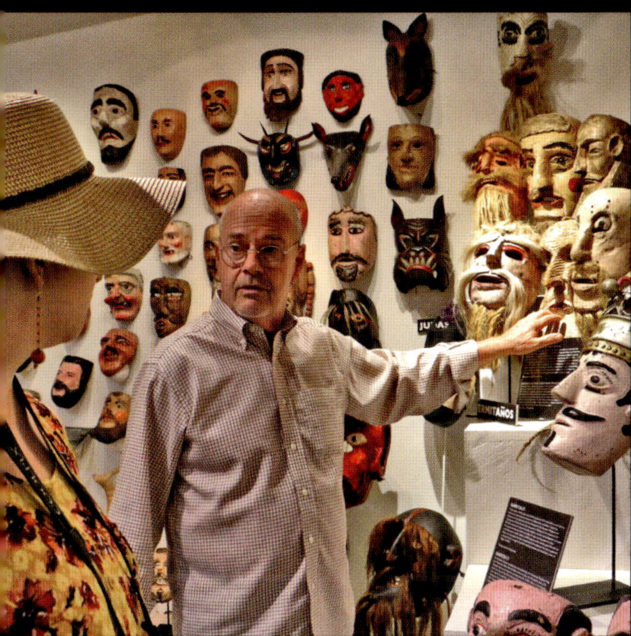

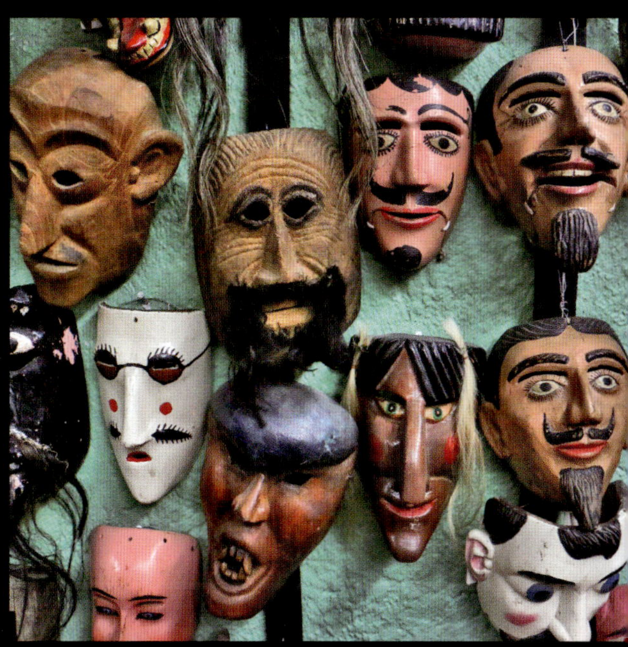

Bill LeVasseur and his wife, Heidi, have spent twenty-five years acquiring more than 500 Mexican ceremonial masks for their museum Another Face of Mexico, and for the folk art gallery that is part of their home and Casa de la Questa B&B. Their passion for Mexican craft, traditions, and culture is felt in their willingness to share all that they have learned on their quest throughout Mexico to find, celebrate, and preserve Indigenous traditions and ways of life.

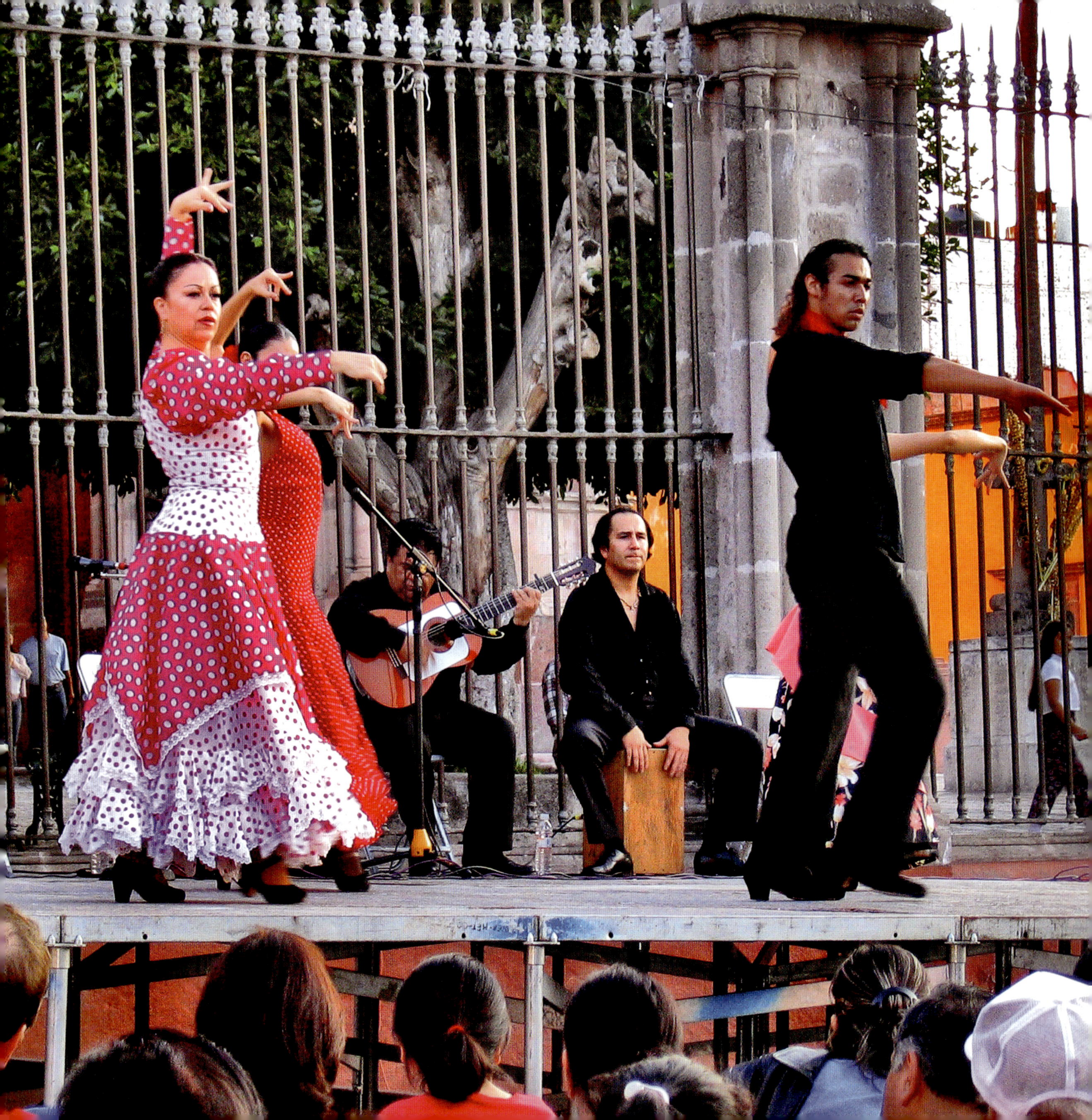

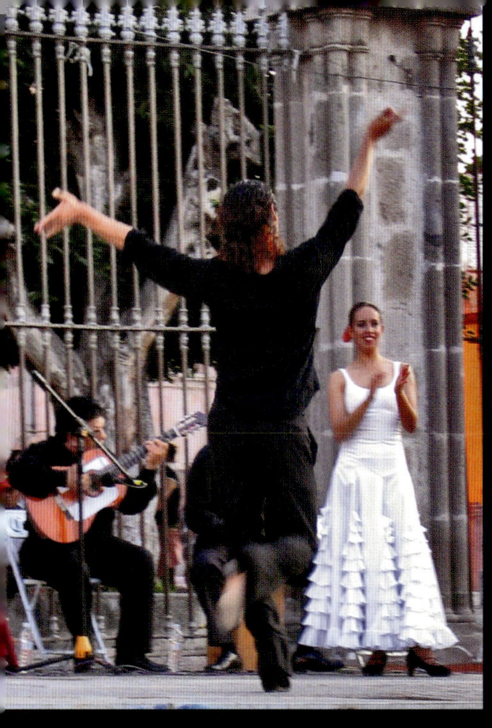

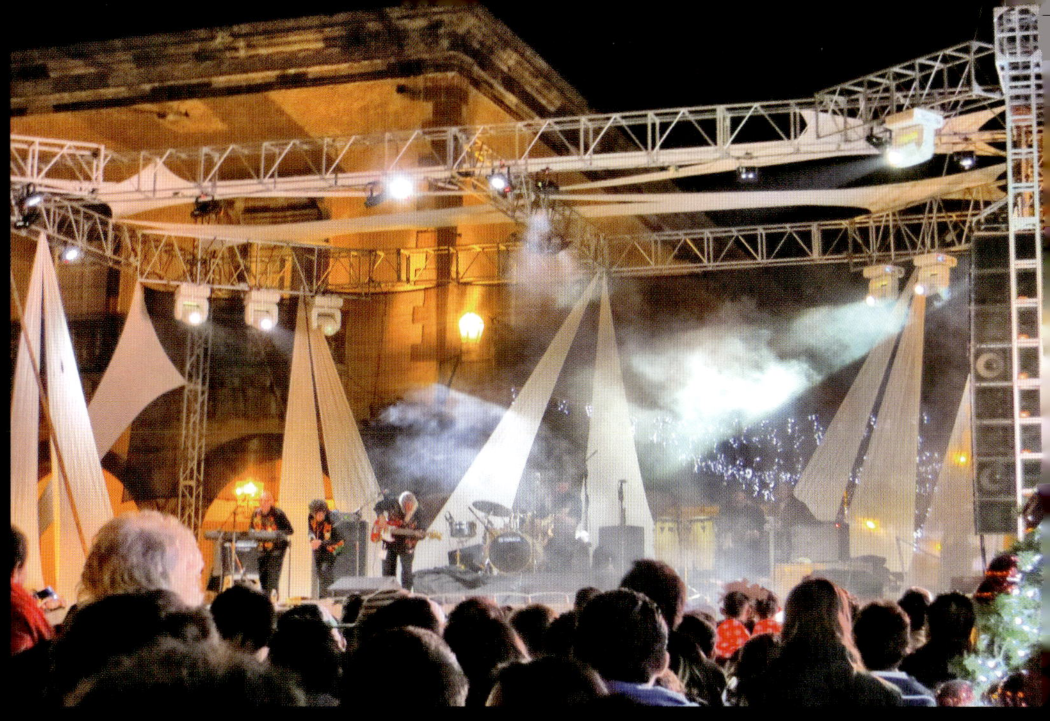

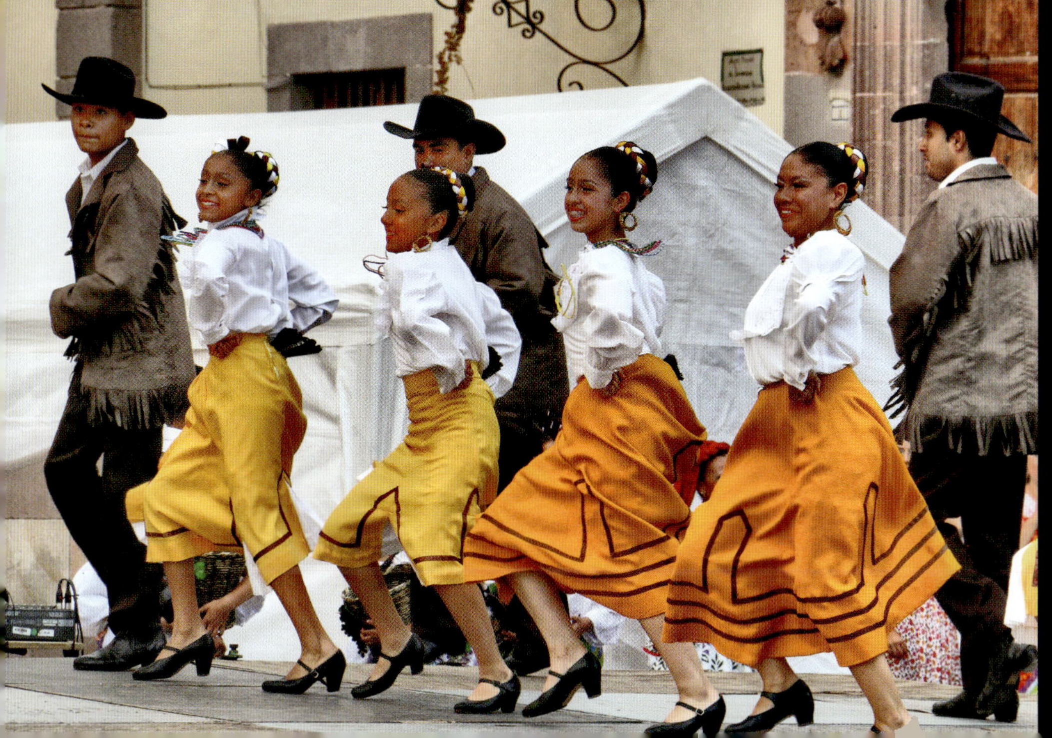

Dance flows through life in San Miguel in intimate and bold ways. It is common at a Spanish guitar concert, or even in restaurants, for dance to erupt among the audience, so overcome with passion that they dance in aisles or between tables, often moving onto the stage, so filled with ecstasy that they must dance. Performances of traditional folk dance in its many forms are common in San Migue whether in theaters or on grand public stage. in the plaza between the Jardín and the Parroquia. Traditional folk dancers swirl around each other in stories of courtship and love. Lovers on a bench in the Jardín who ask for a mariachi song are often so filled with ardo that they leap to their feet and begin dancing. Salsa and tango are danced in bars and restaurants throughout San Miguel, even in the streets, day or night. The intensity of love and courtship between couples, through dance, gives visual poetry to love and brings music to joyous life.

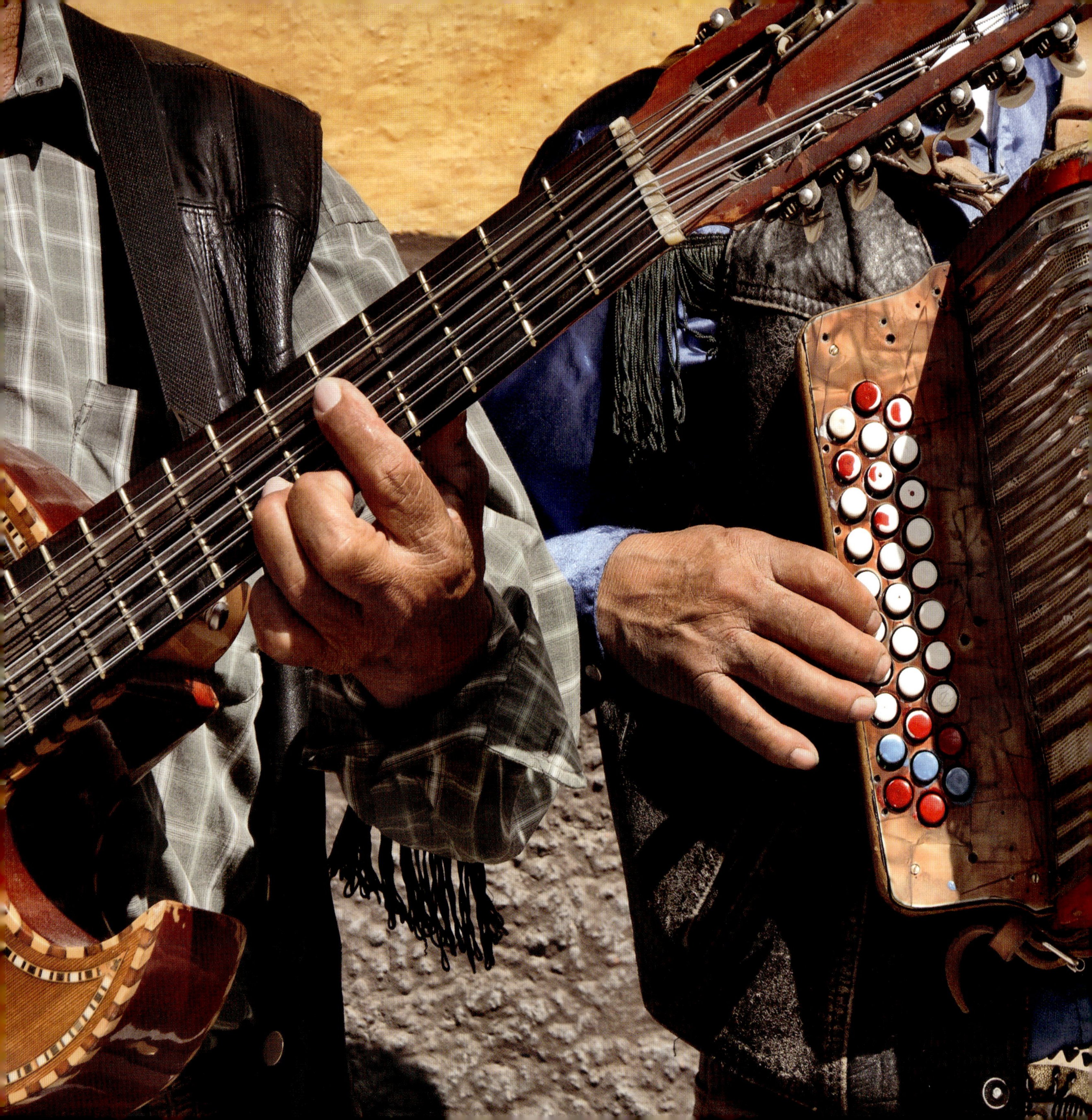

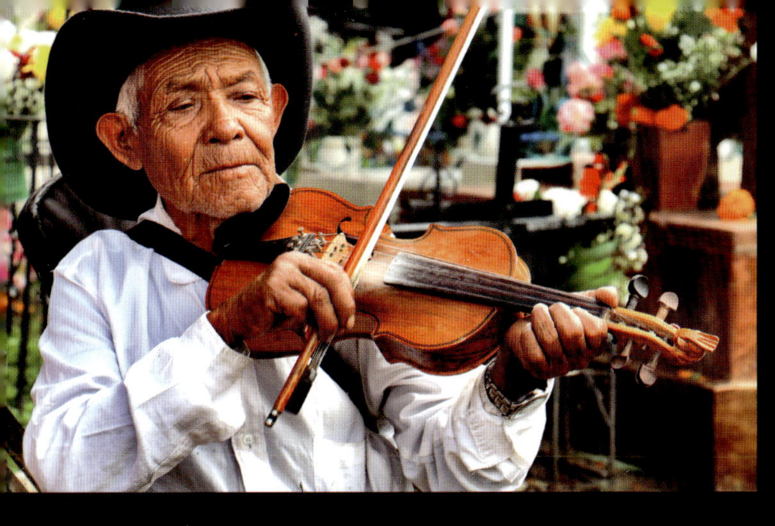

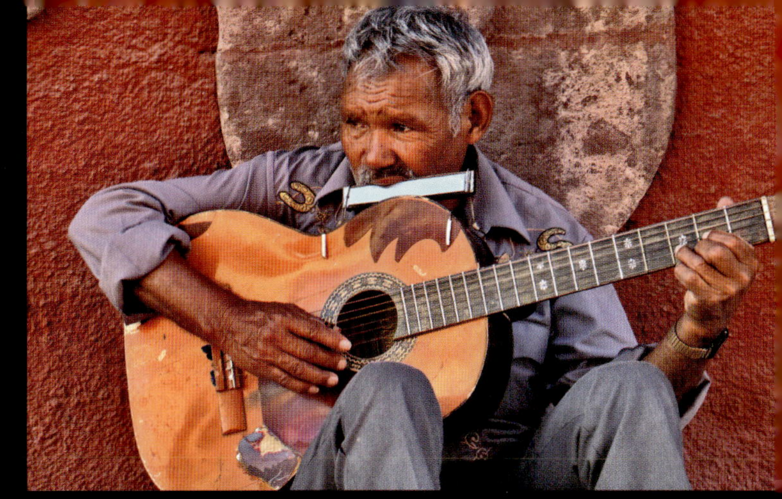

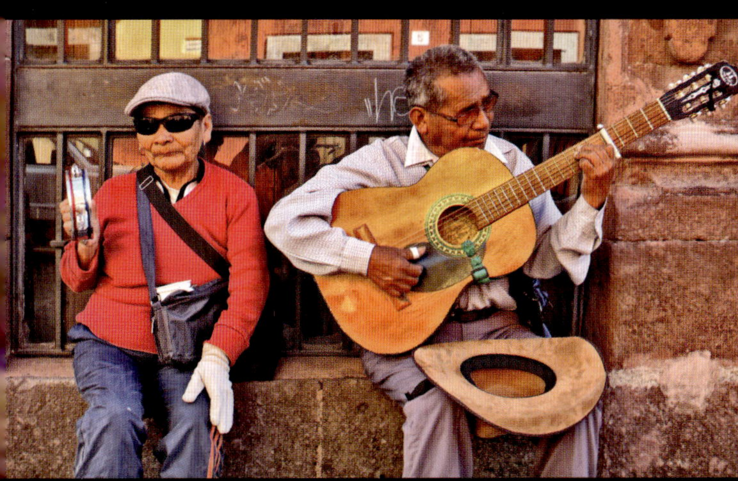

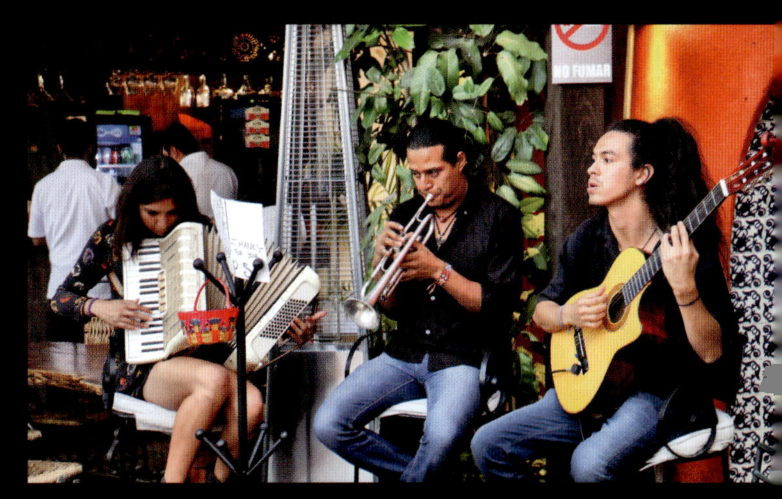
NO FUMAR

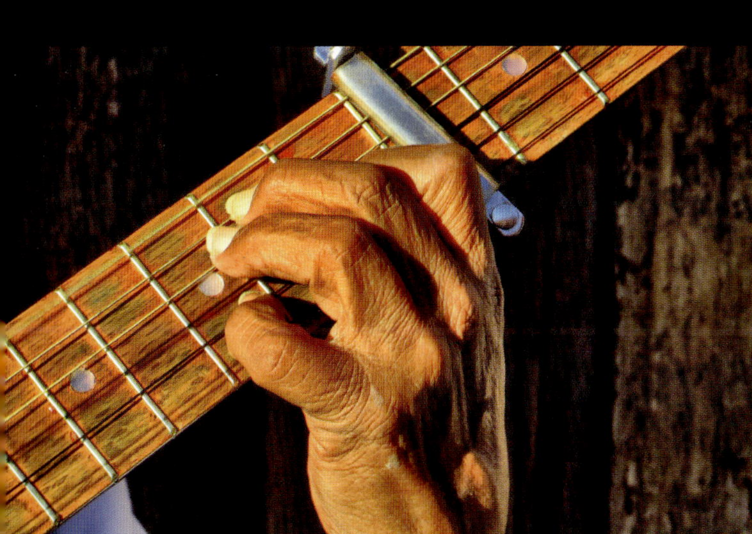

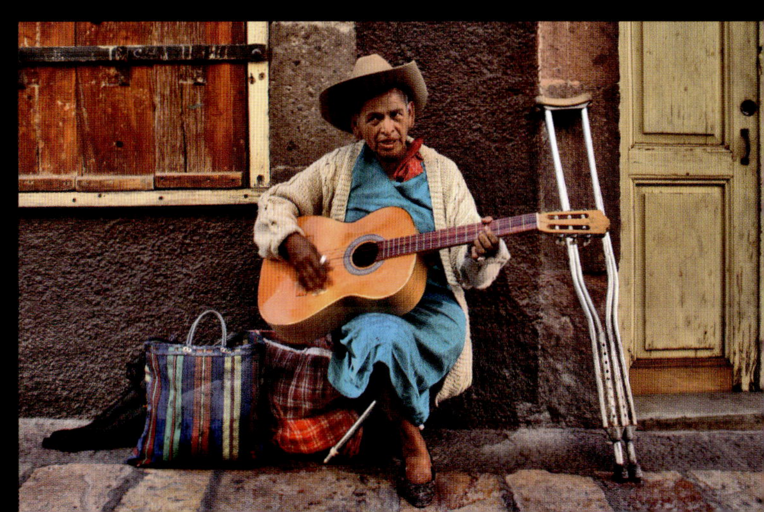

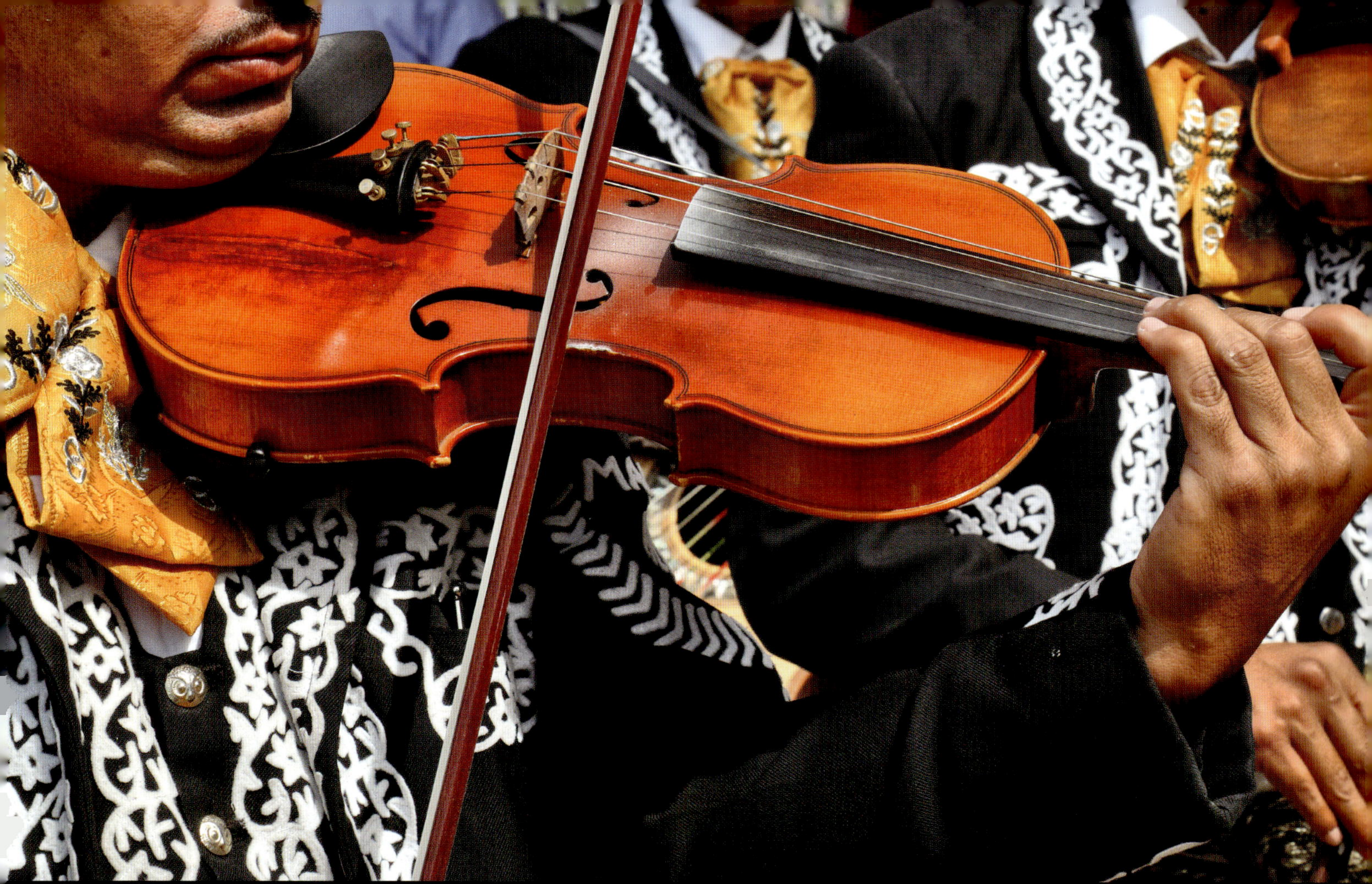

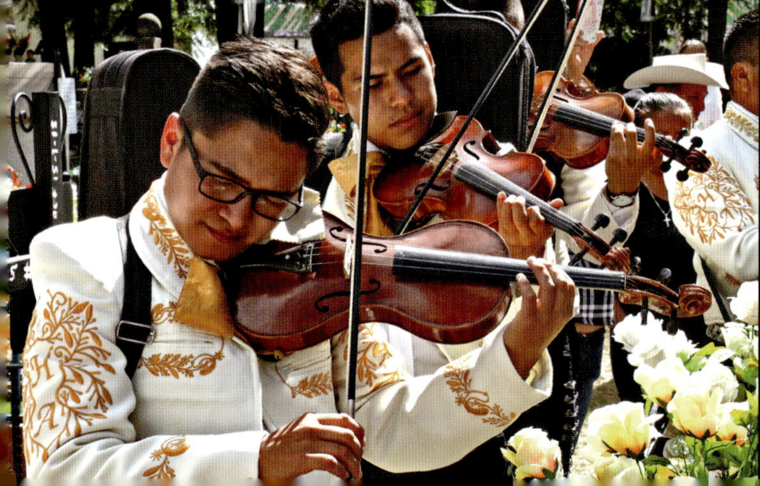
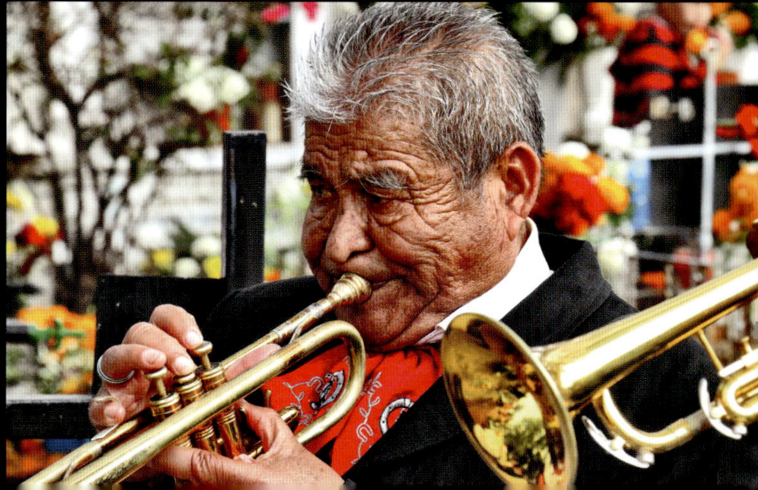

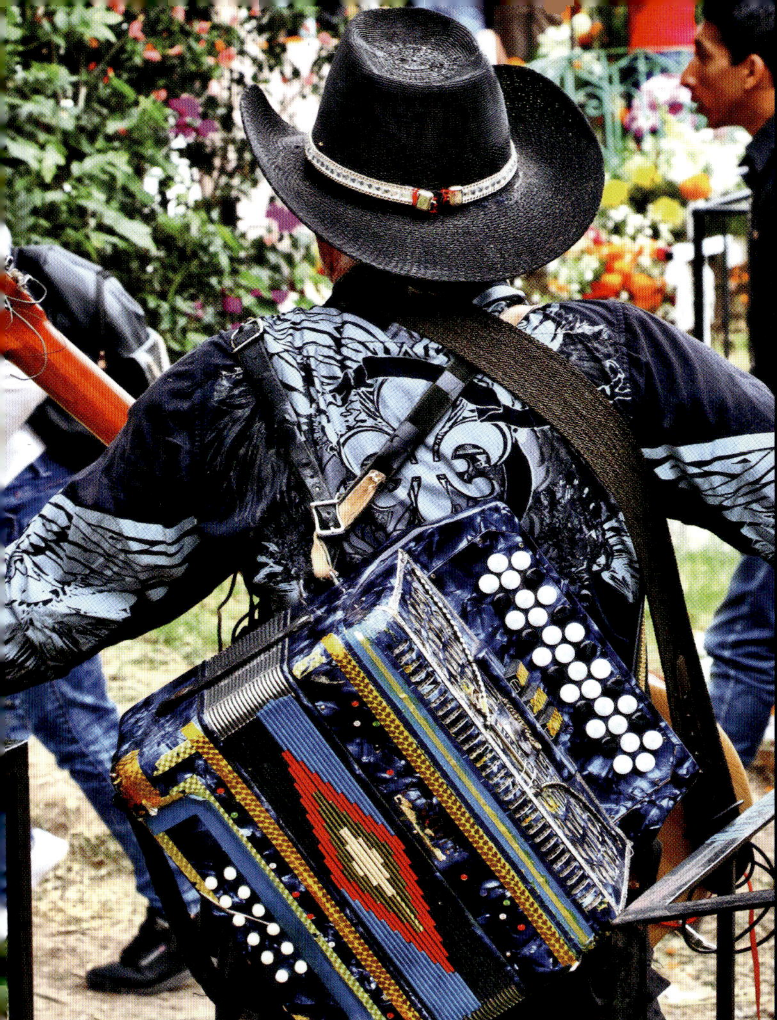

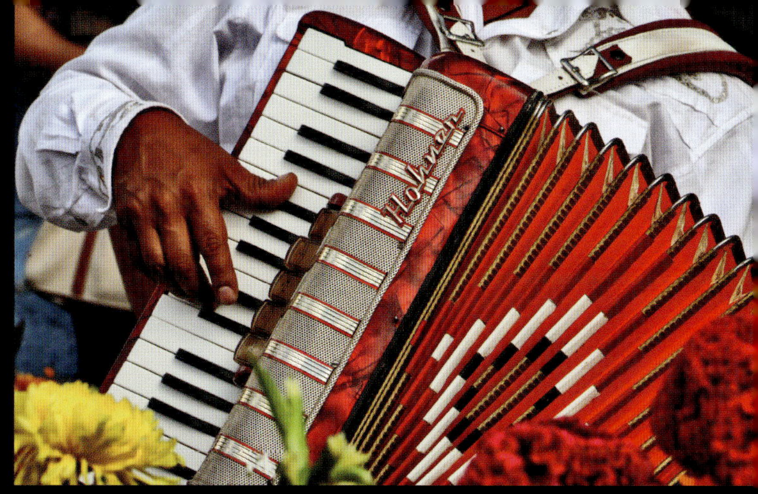

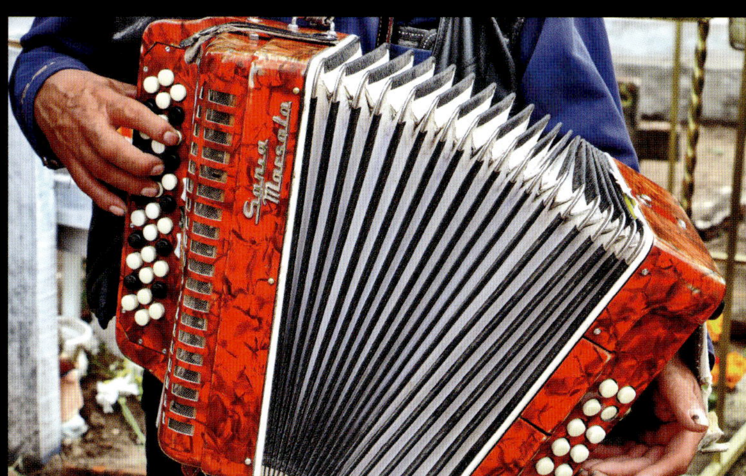

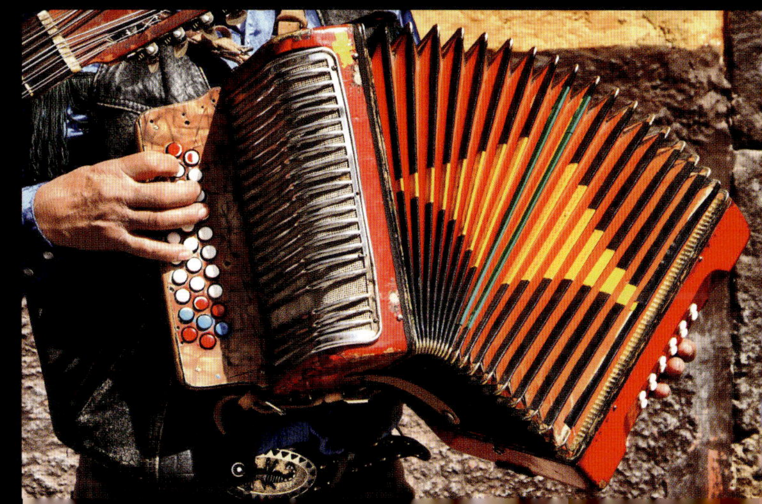

Mexican life is filled with music: in the streets, in restaurants, in squares and gardens, in courtyards and homes, and in churches. They sing of love with desperate passion, of their country and the oppression they have endured. They sing of their legends and history. Whether it is the mesmerizing sounds of classical Spanish guitar or the ever-present mariachi, whether the era of the music is from days gone by or from today, the music of Mexico is everywhere, especially in San Miguel. From a lonely soloist sitting quietly in the embrace of a doorway on a busy street, to major productions in theaters, music is central to daily life in Mexico. Every special occasion, from birth to marriage to death, is accompanied by the uniquely Mexican sounds of the mariachi. Music explodes through gigantic speakers carried on the back of flatbed trucks at processions, rattling the stone walls, calling the inhabitants to celebrate, dance, and participate in the traditions of life that sustain the rich cultural knowledge that is part of the Mexican soul.

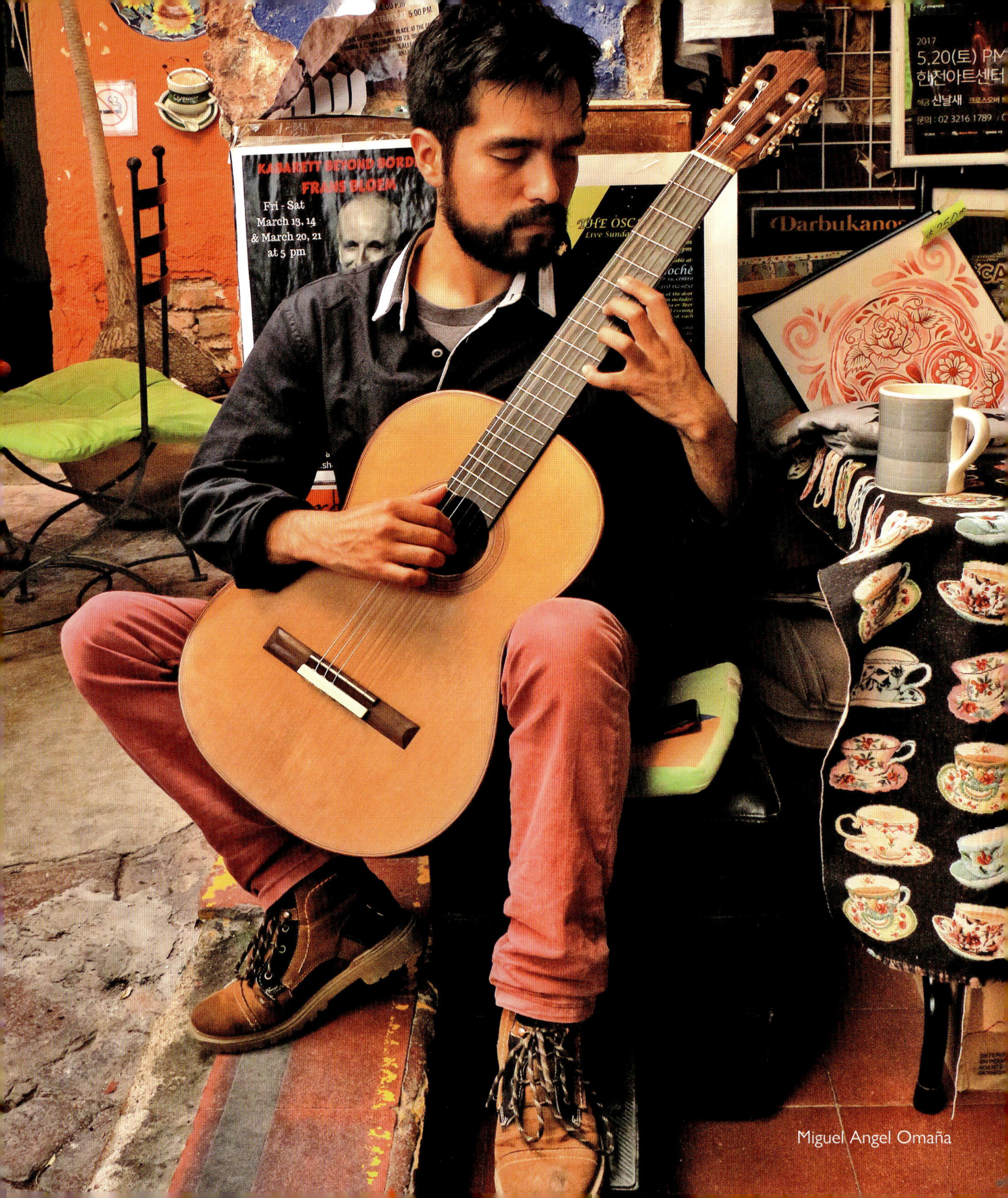

Miguel Angel Omaña

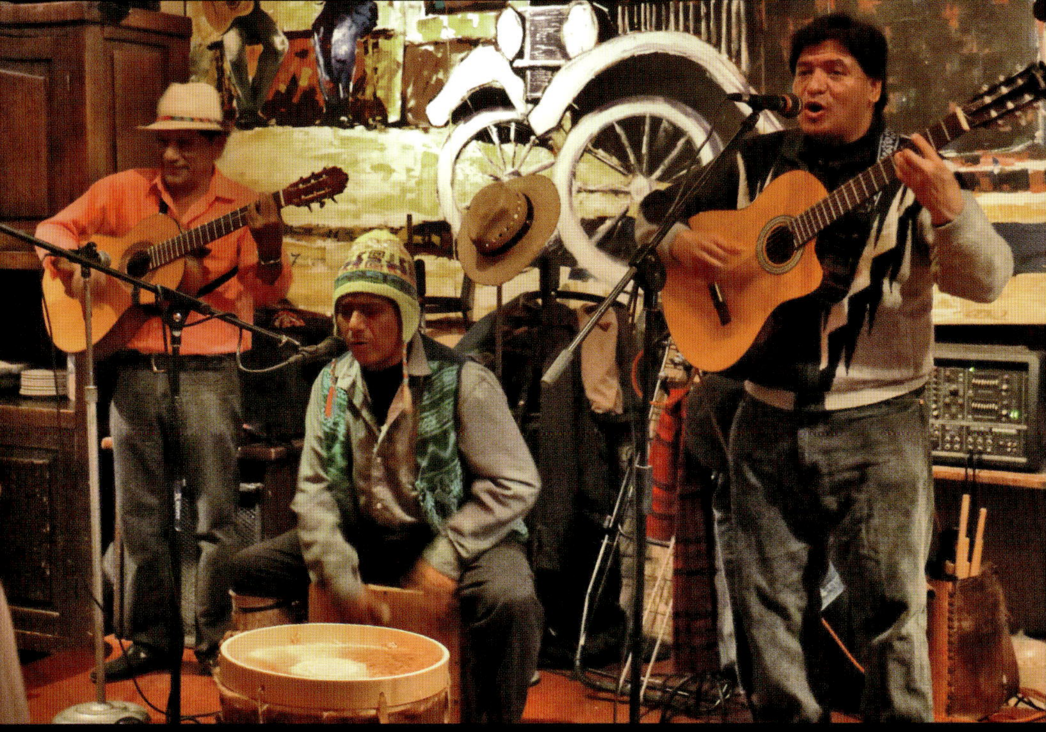

Los Garambullos

Myrna La Chanteuse

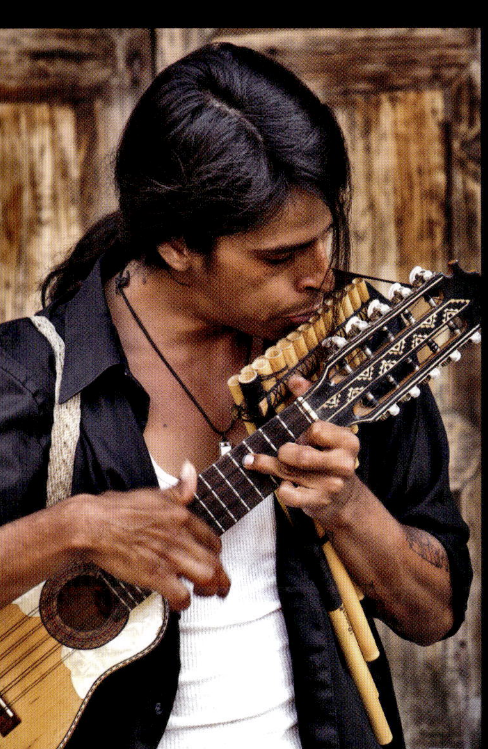

Traveling Musician

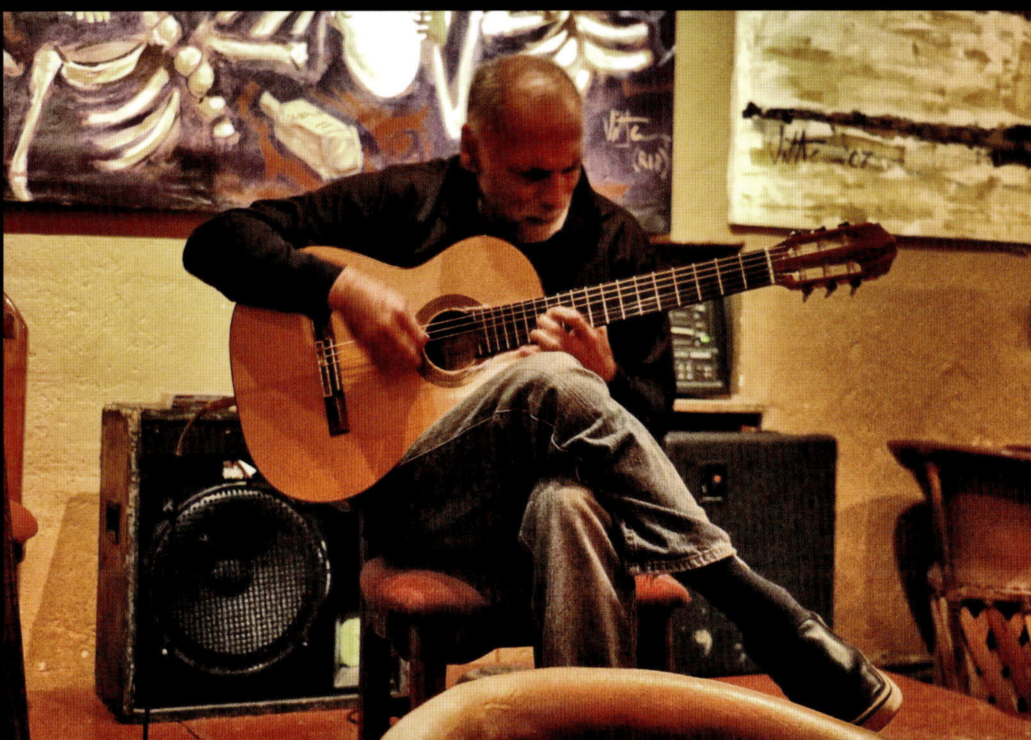

Severo Barrera

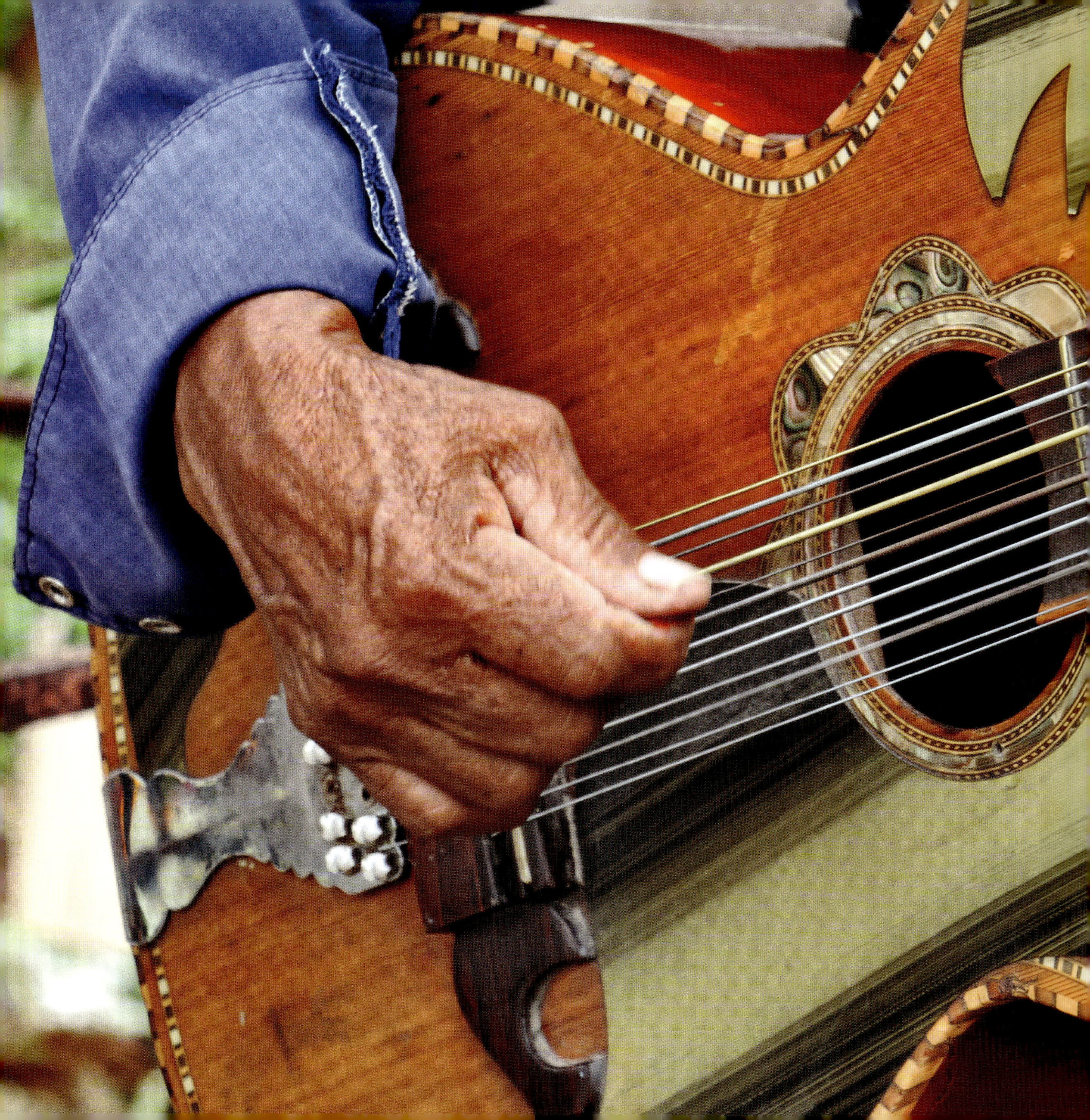

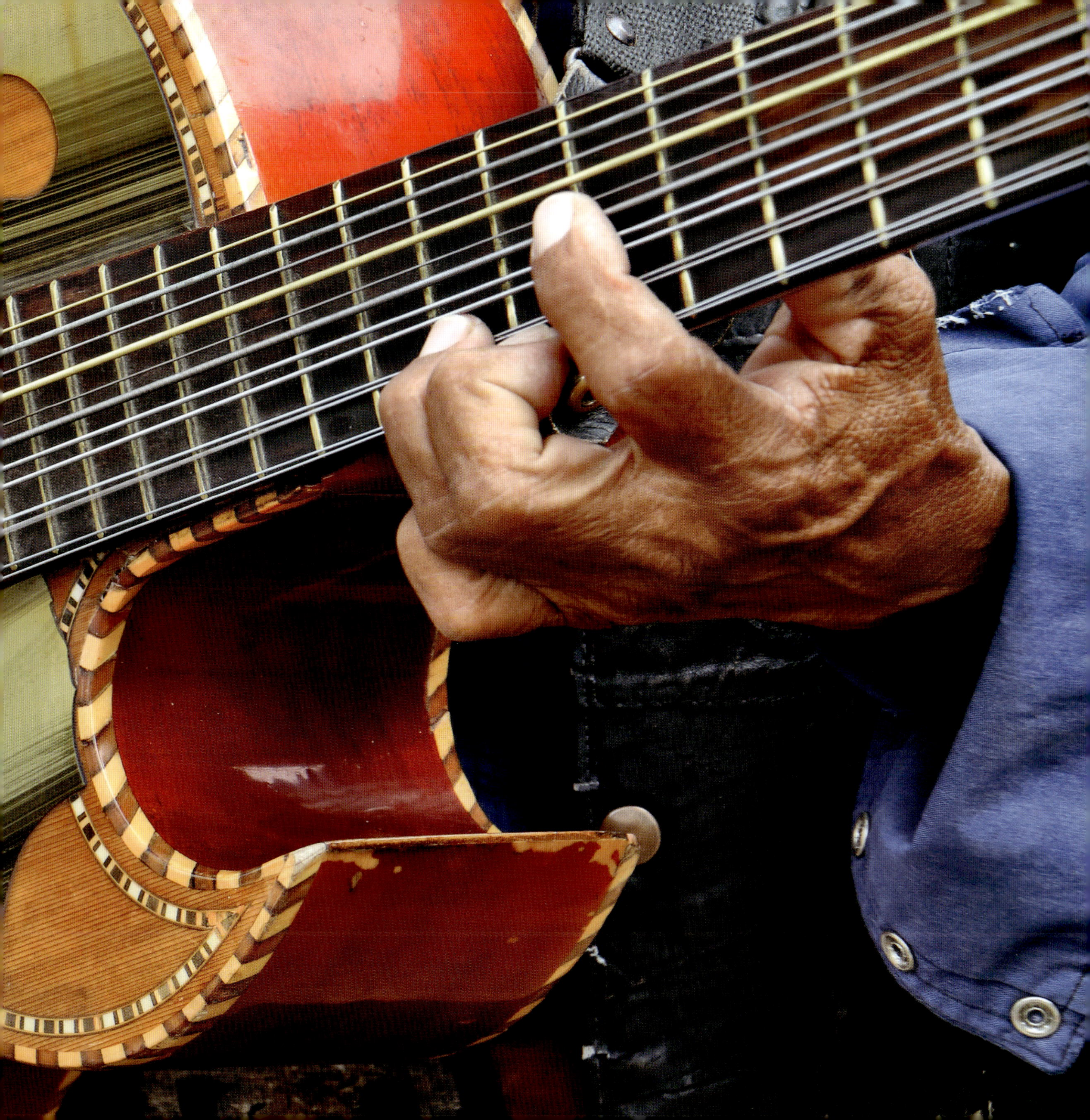

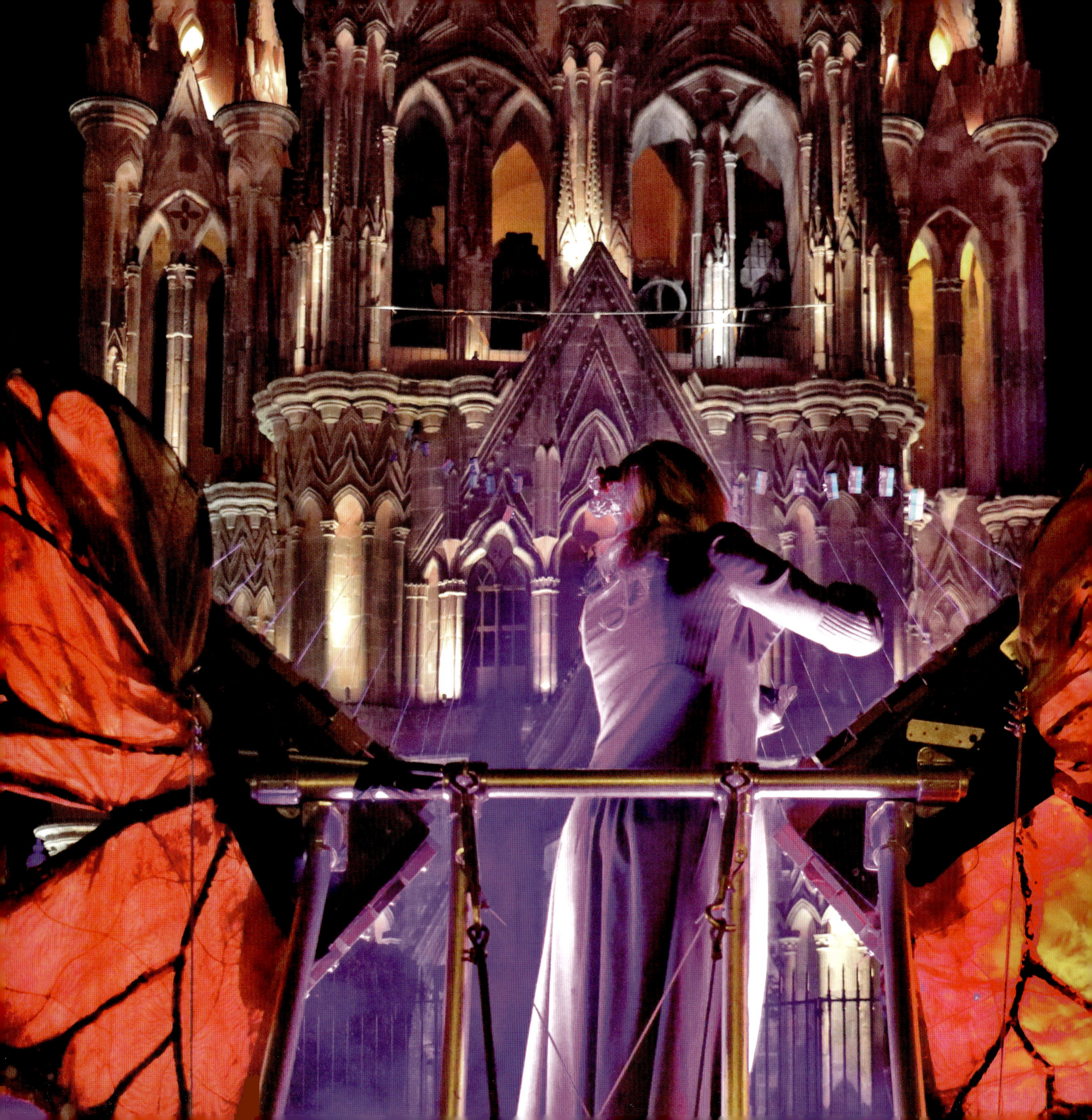

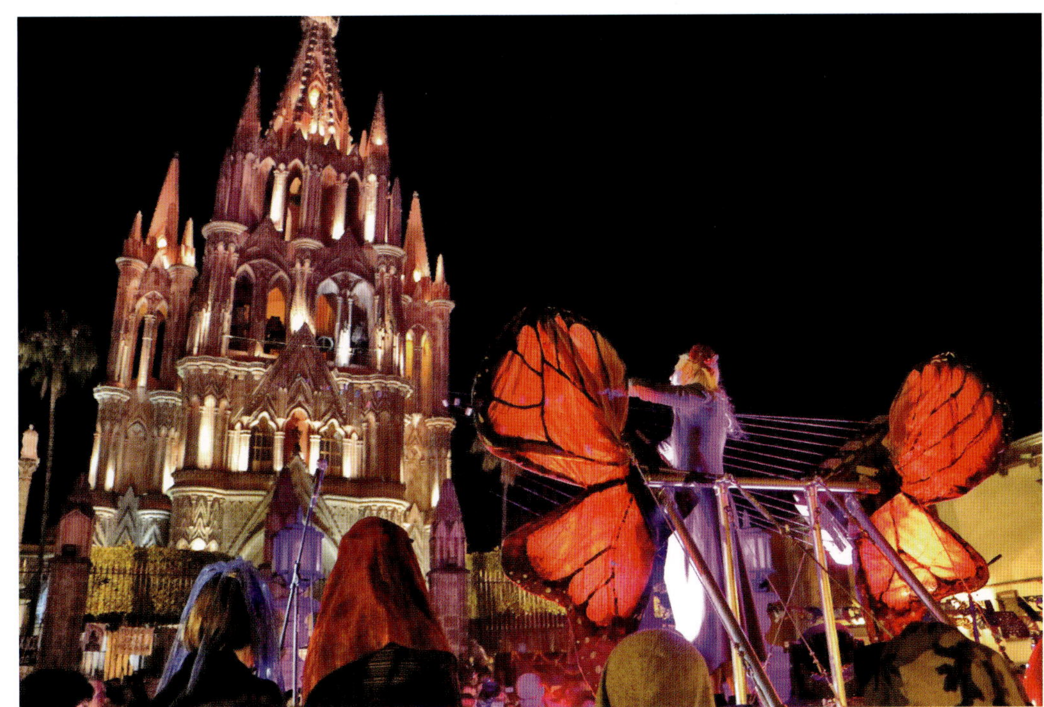

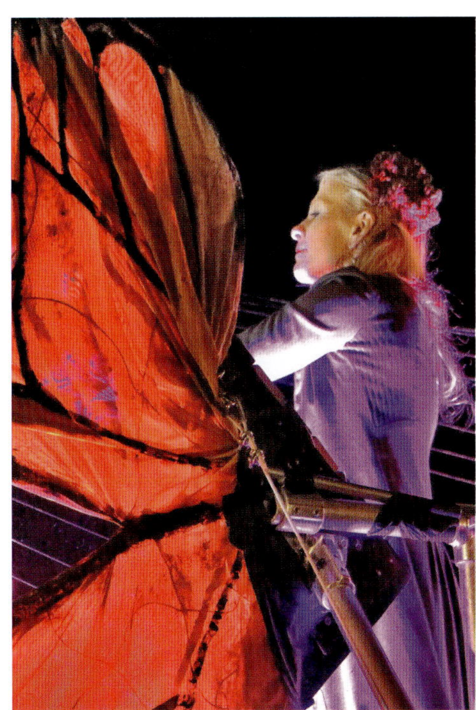

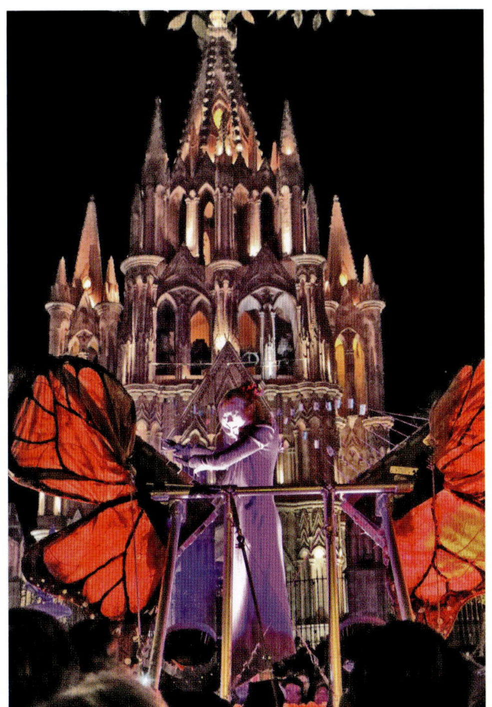

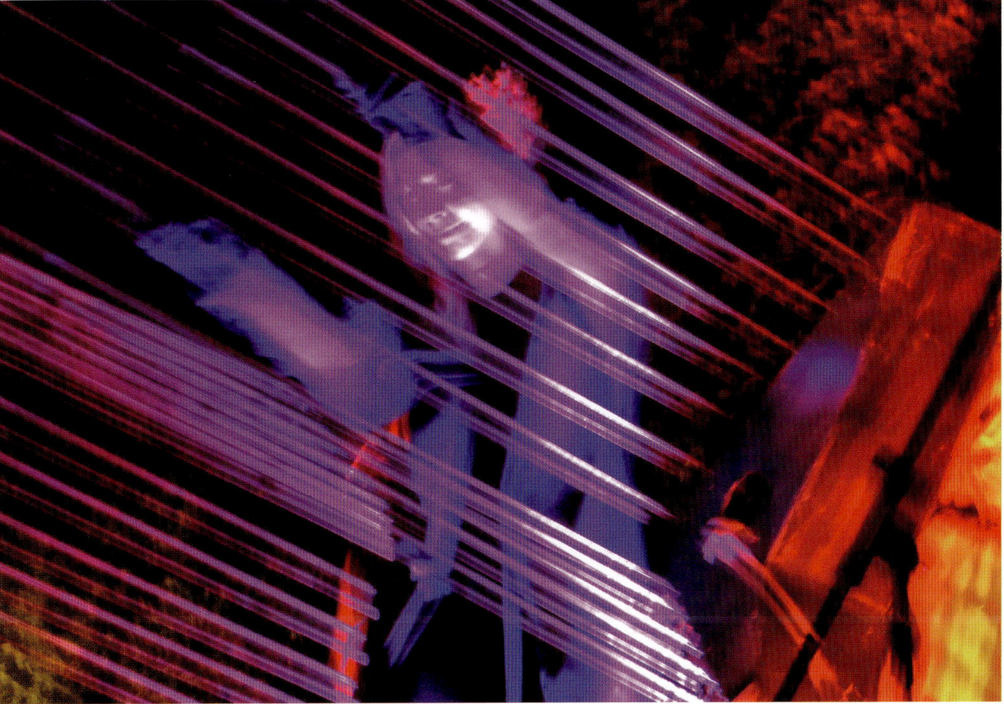

The earth harp is the largest stringed instrument in the world, developed in 1999 by William Close. For this performance in San Miguel by Andrea Brook, the strings stretched from the Jardín to the towers of the Parroquia, turning the Parroquia itself into an instrument and the Jardín into its amplifier, flooding the entire Centro with music that can only be described as the sounds of heaven.

Gardens & Plazas

The Jardín Principal of San Miguel is the beating heart of this beautiful town, which links the past and the future with the joys of life. Leafy trees carefully shaped into bold cylinders meld together to create an embracing ceiling for those seated on the many benches of the Jardín. The sounds of birds twittering in the branches, the rustle of the leaves in a gentle breeze, the soft sounds of water in the fountains, all work together to create a peaceful space in which to gather. The Jardín is quiet during the day, with single souls who watch life from a protected retreat. As the day turns to evening, more people come, then more, and more, until the entire Jardín is filled with life. Balloon sellers pace the plaza between the Jardín and the Parroquia; children toss silvery balloons into the air in rockets of glittering color. Families sit together, snacking on homemade ice cream; lovers find quiet shadows in which to share sweet kisses; adolescent boys and girls swirl in opposite directions, shy and giggling, making eye contact and eventually finding their spouse in this traditional dance of love. Special days are marked by hanging cut-paper flags or by laying carpets made of grains, beans, and colored flower petals in larger-than-life art. Altars appear and disappear for Day of the Dead; stages are set up for concerts, dances, and performances. Antique cars and bicycles gather for races or shows. Children don wings to become butterflies to mark the equinox, or angels to welcome the risen Christ.

The sounds of celebration reach from this living plaza over the colorful walls and directly into the courtyards of nearby homes, beckoning the residents with music and the promise of yet another joyful experience. The church bells of the Parroquia sound out the hours and days; the mariachi stand ready to delight with songs of love; children laugh and chase the birds; visitors pause for a photo with the church; the shoeshine man keeps everyone's shoes clean and shiny. You can buy a newspaper and read what is going on in the world, or you can sit on a bench and hear it from your neighbors. Ice cream and popcorn vendors add flavor; fountains, birds, and children add to the music.

Almost every home and certainly every church and restaurant have patios that are mini versions of the Jardín. These gardens are places to share, to celebrate in, to sit quietly in and contemplate life. Rooftops offer more outdoor experiences as gardens, studios, terraces. Music and laughter from the rooftops are accompanied by barking dogs and crowing roosters, and at night the sounds of crickets and frogs join the fray.

Parque Juárez is filled with children playing, running, climbing. During school hours, the park waits quietly, its fountains still, reflecting the sky and trees, waiting for the daily joy of children. The Plaza Cívica, with its impressive statue of Ignacio Allende, hosts fairs of every description, filled with families daily.

Trees peek over walls, balconies flourish with colorful flowers, bougainvillea climbs on stone walls, and hummingbirds flit from colorful blossom to colorful blossom, pausing in flight to study any newcomer to the area. The lushness of the gardens and plazas of San Miguel speaks of more than plantings. They are a living embrace for everyone who pauses in the busyness of daily activities to realize how precious life is, how much there is to celebrate, how fortunate we are to live in such a world of color, friendship, family, flavor, and love.

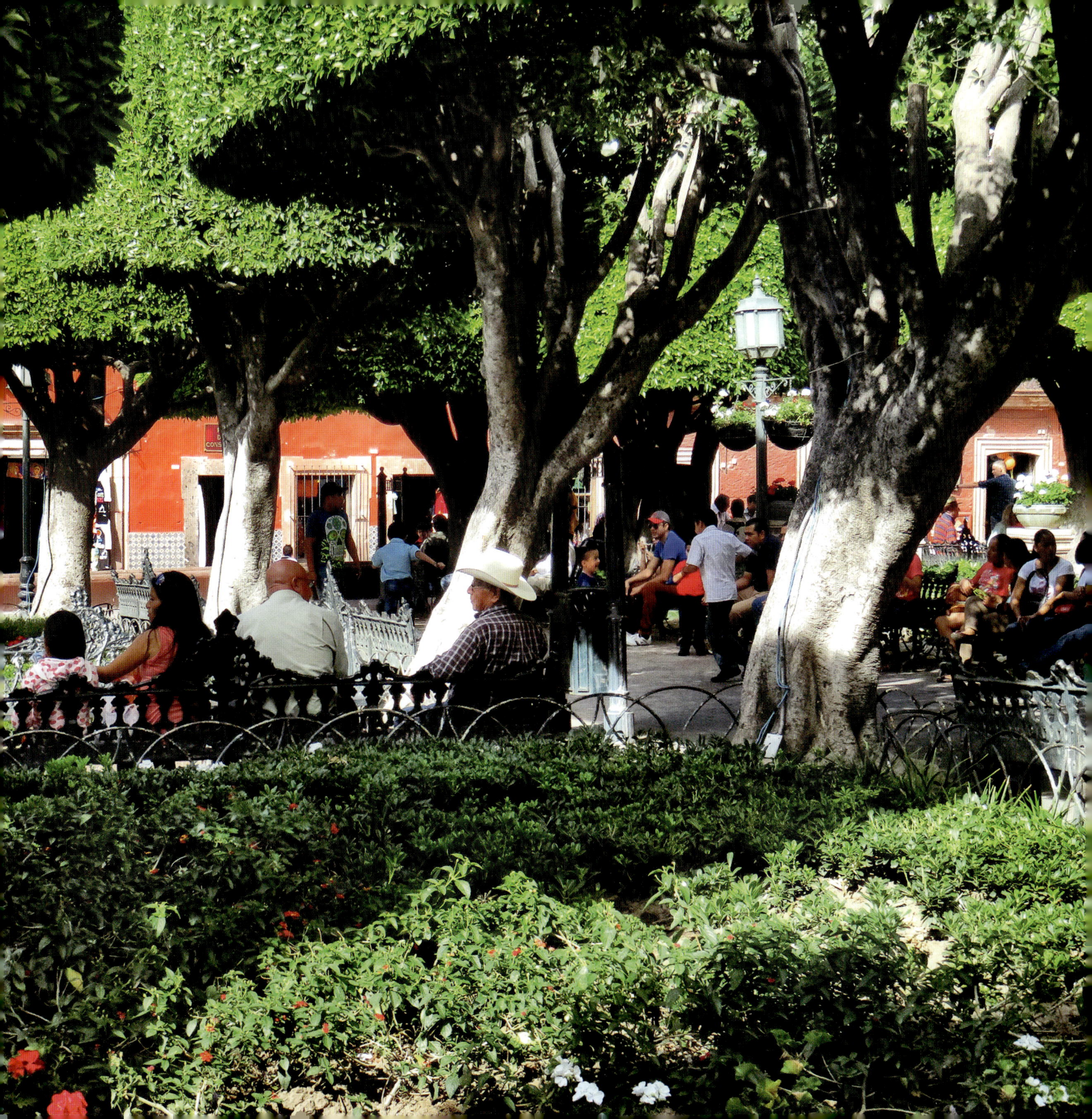

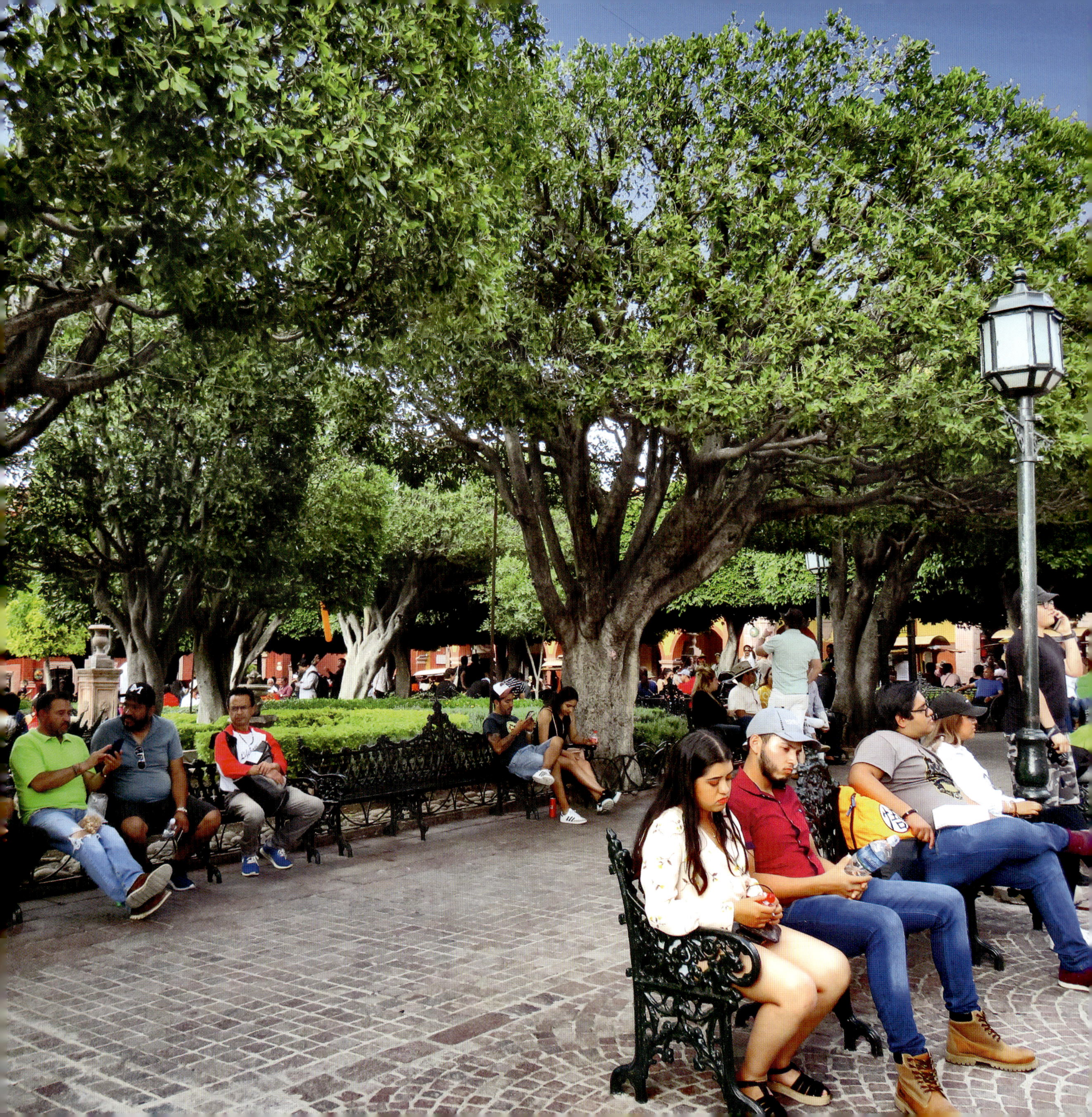

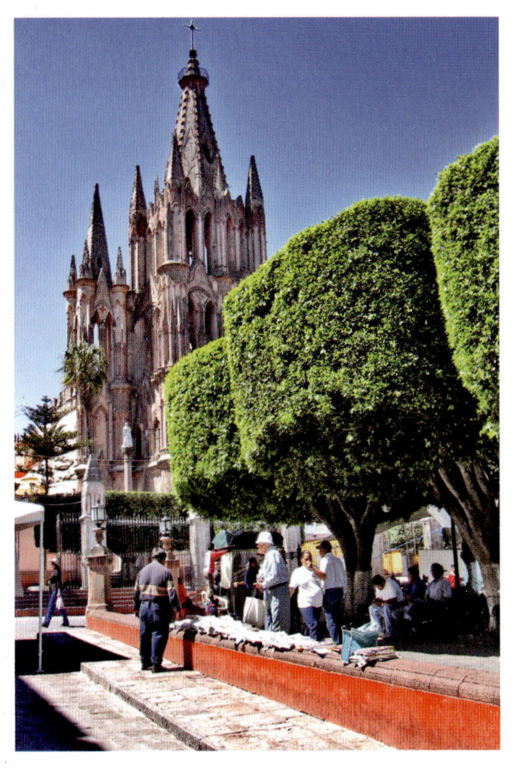
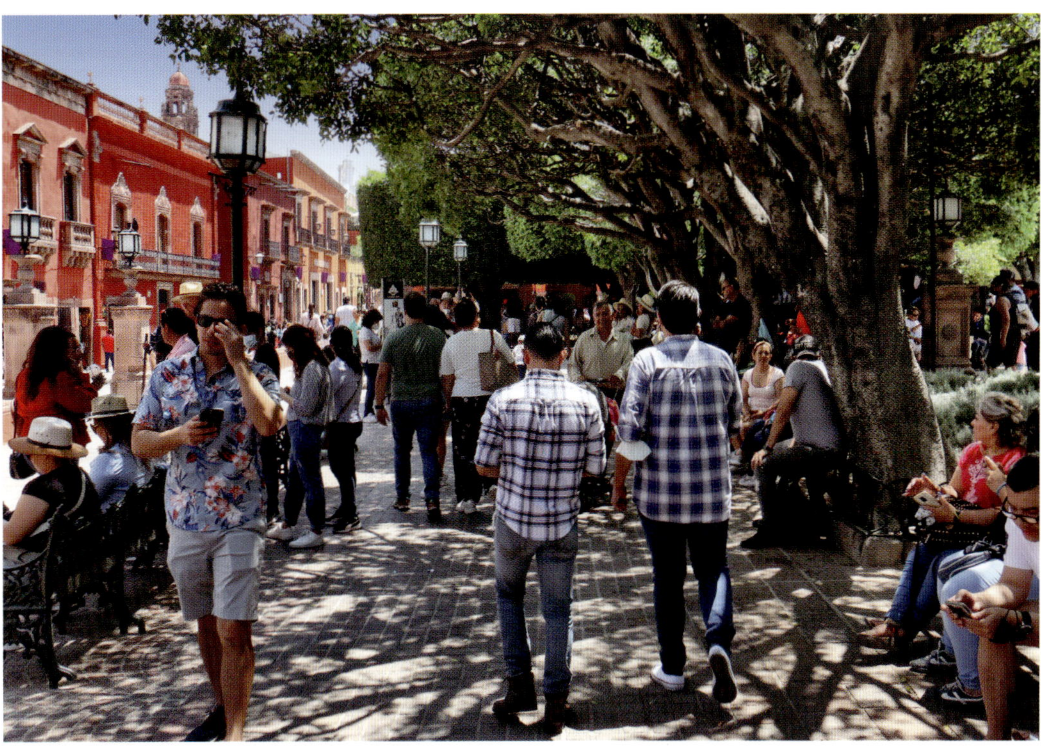
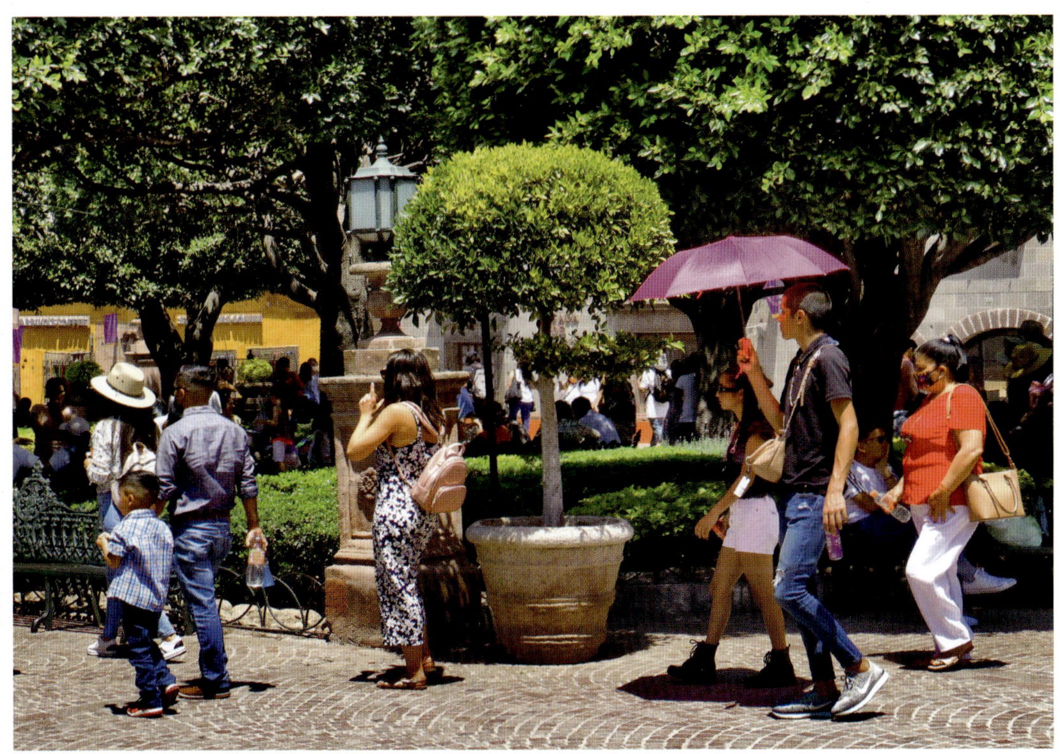
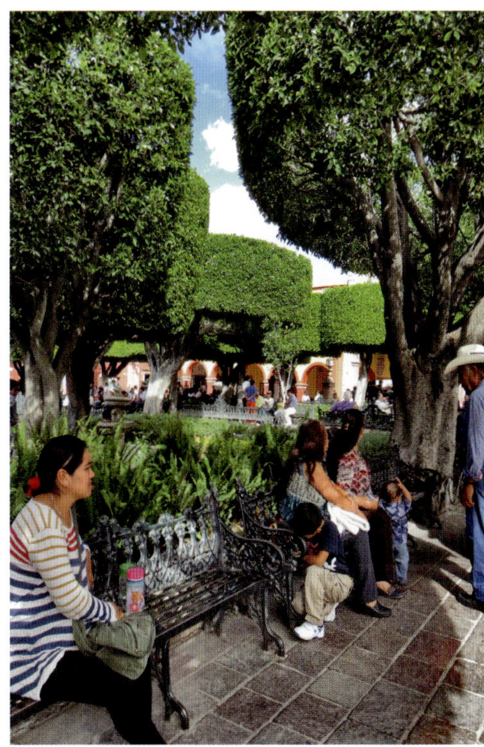

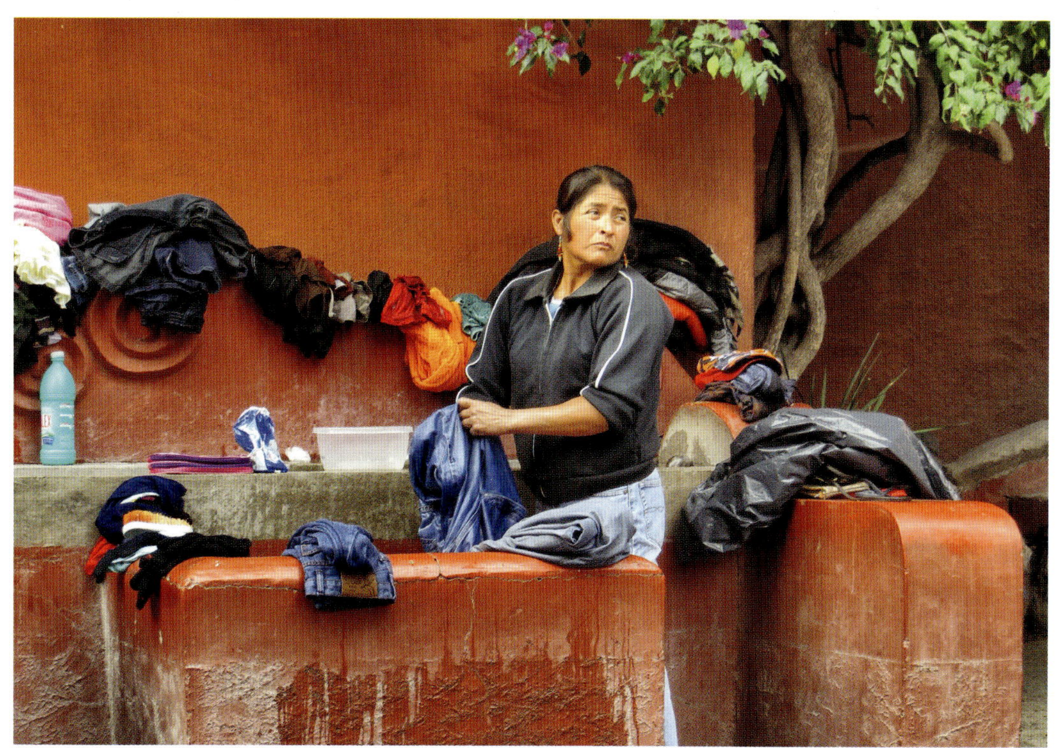

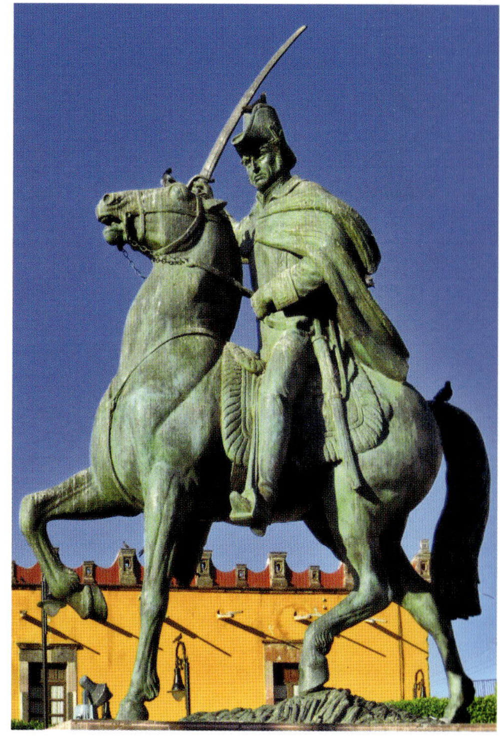

General Ignacio Allende, native son

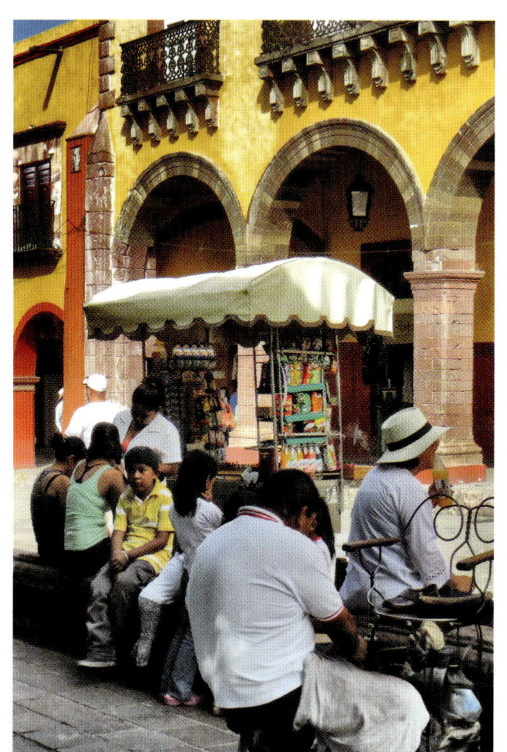

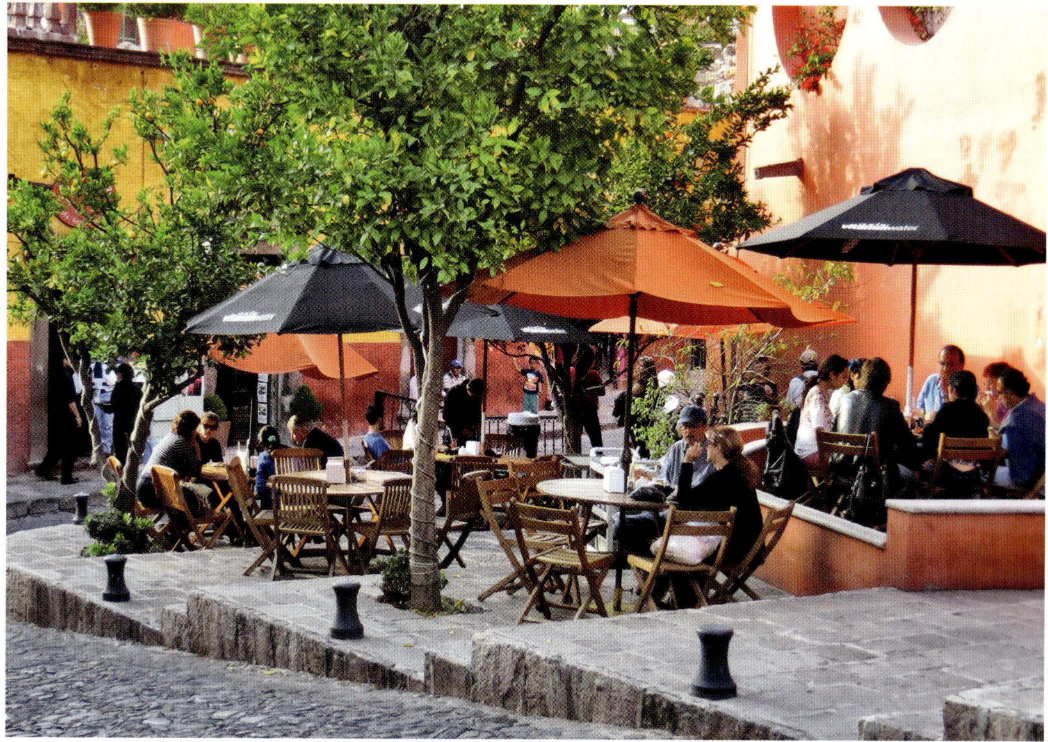

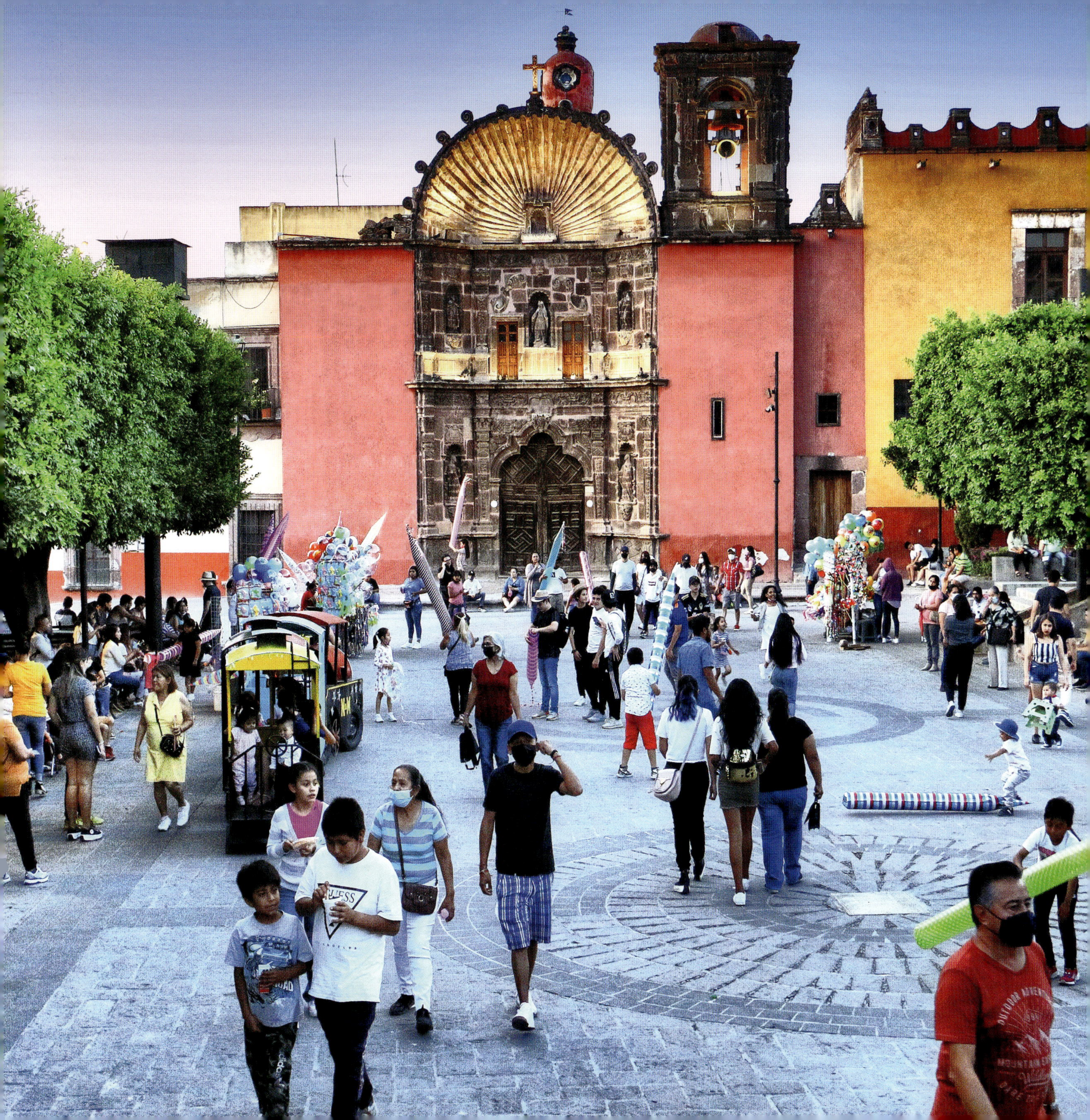

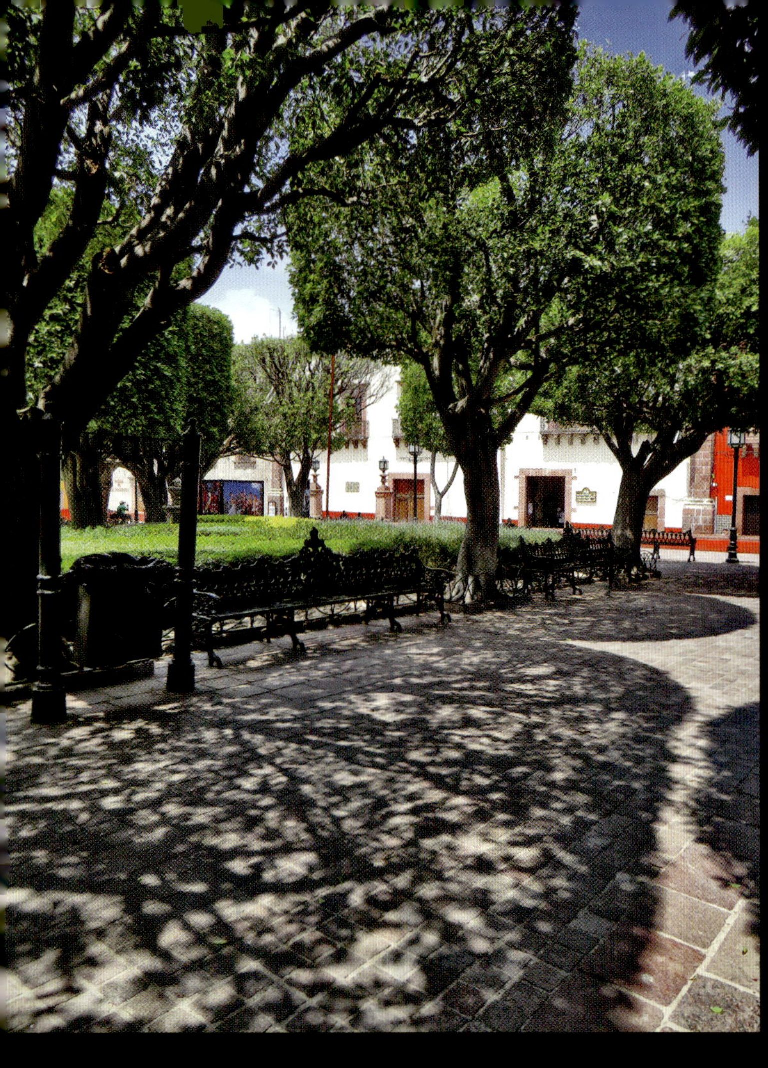
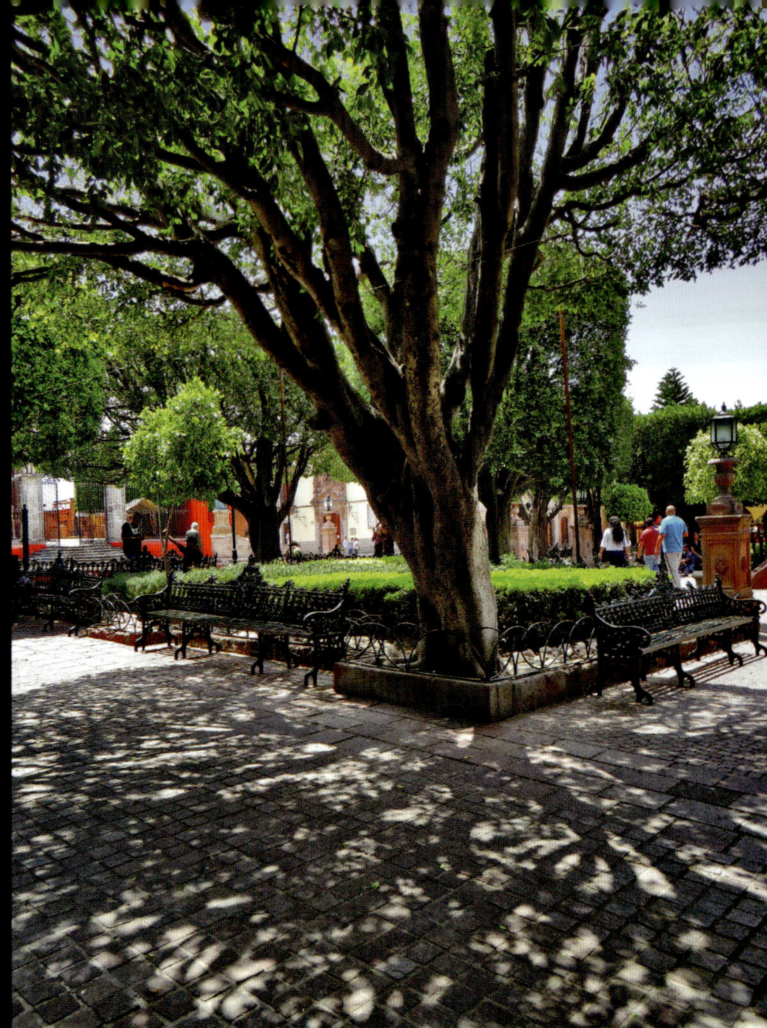
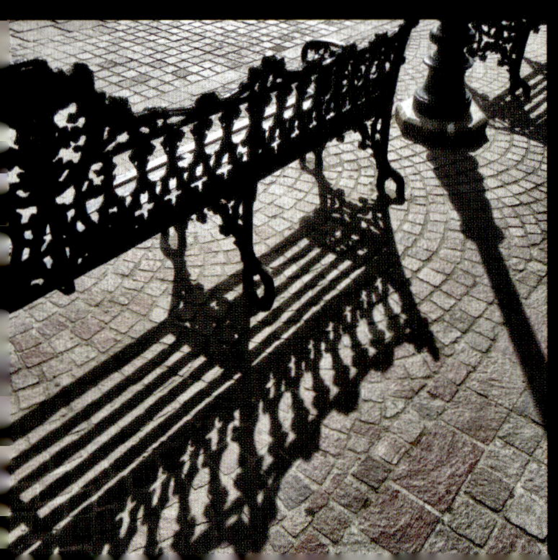
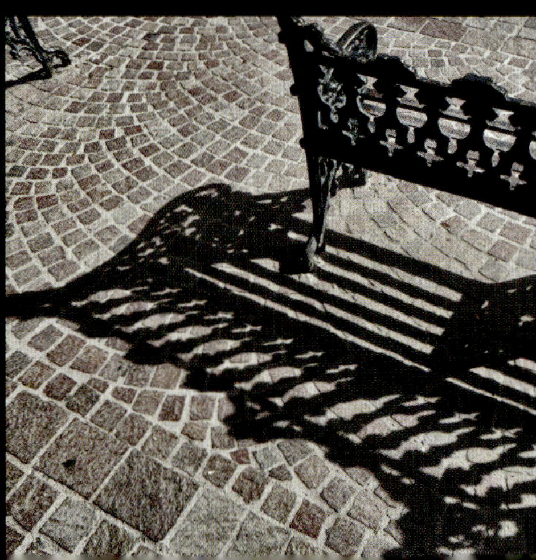
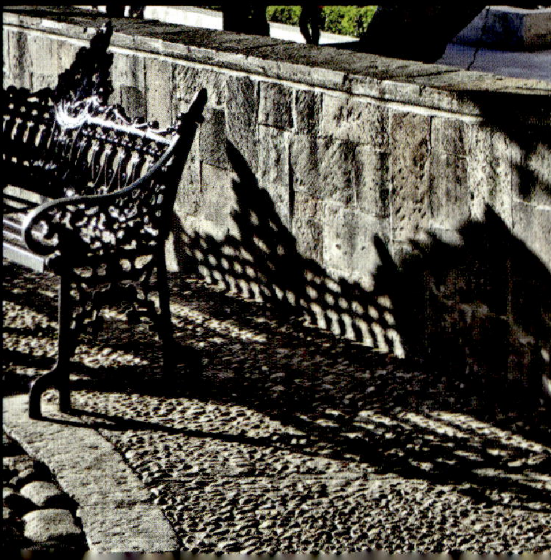

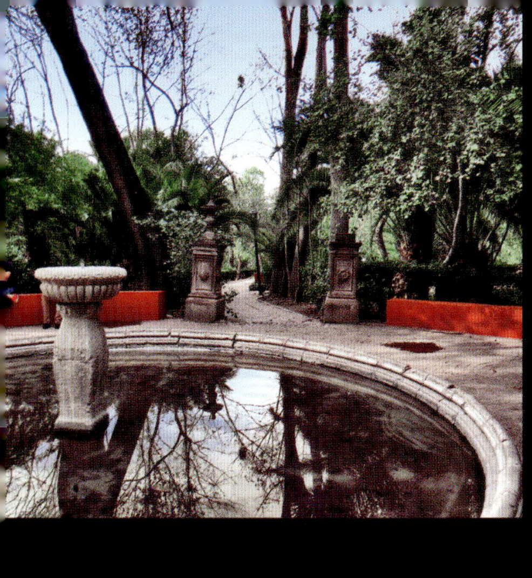
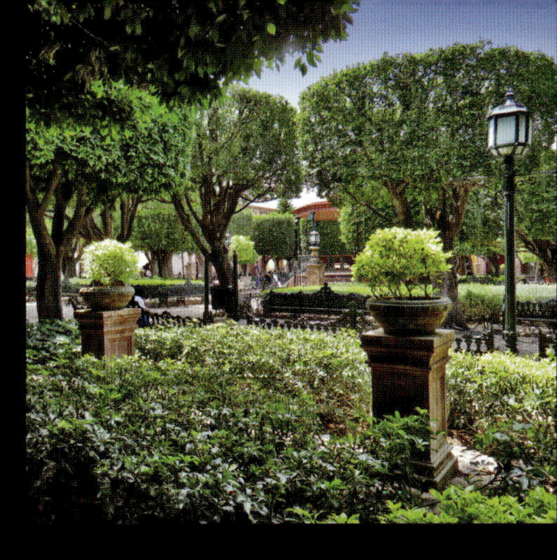
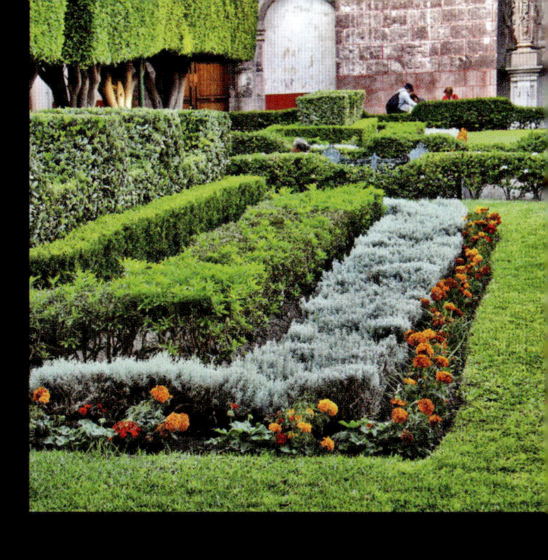
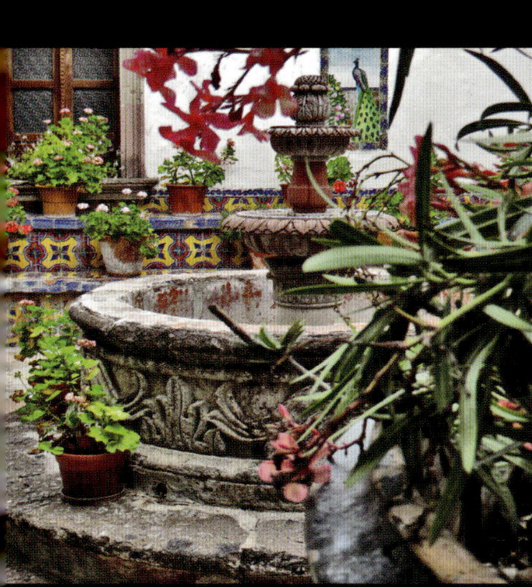
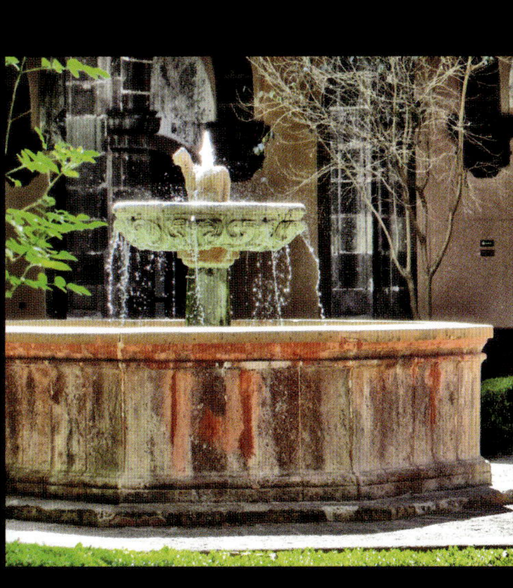
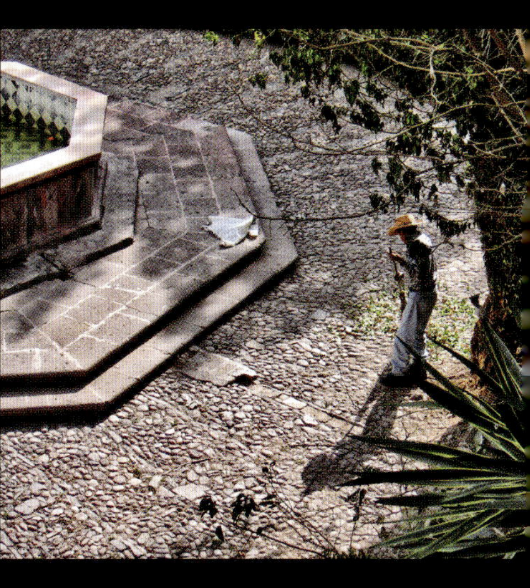
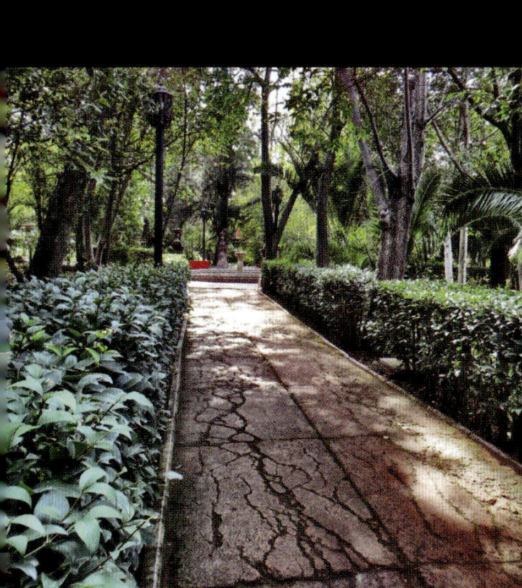
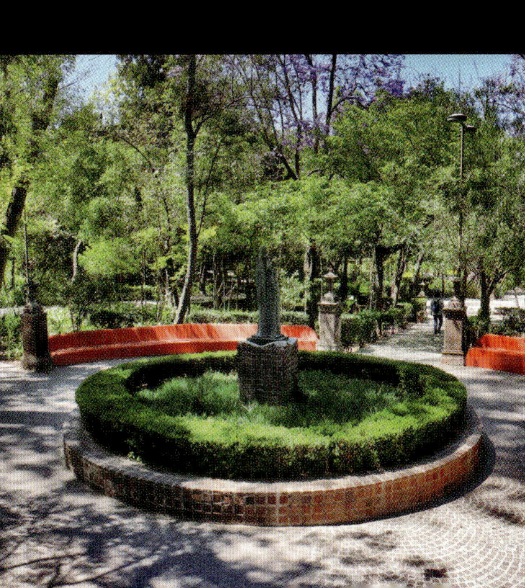
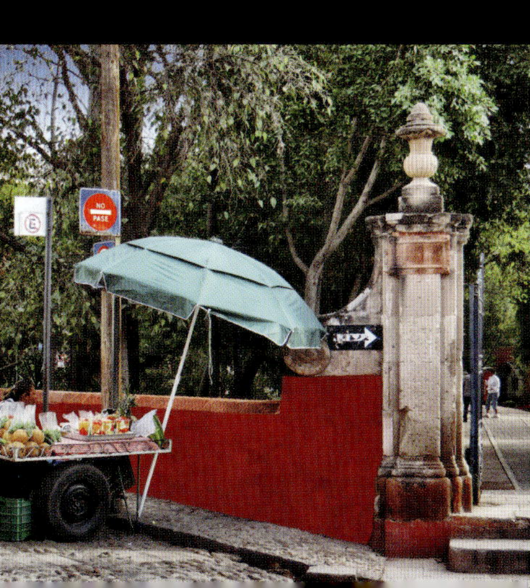
E
NO
PASE

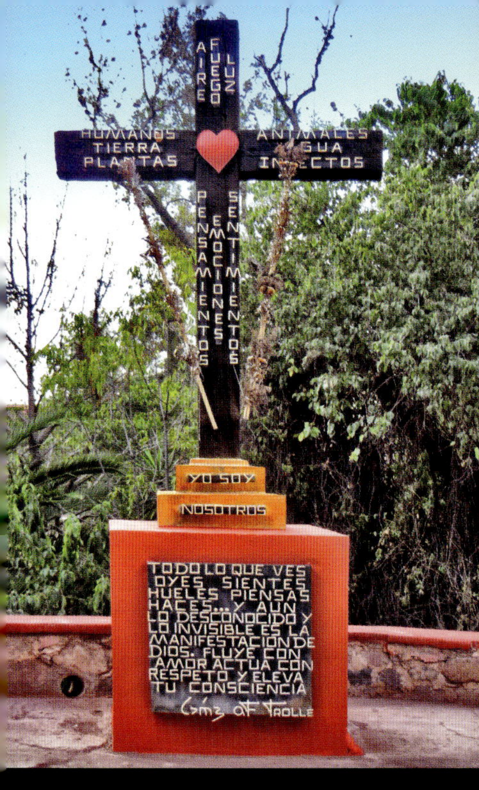

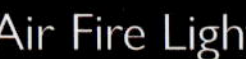

Air Fire Light

Humans Earth Plants

Animals Water Insects

Beliefs Emotions Feelings

I am we

Everything that you see, you hear, you smell, you think, you do . . . and even the unknown and the invisible is the manifestation of God.

Flow with love

Act with respect

Raise your consciousness

—Gomez Trolle

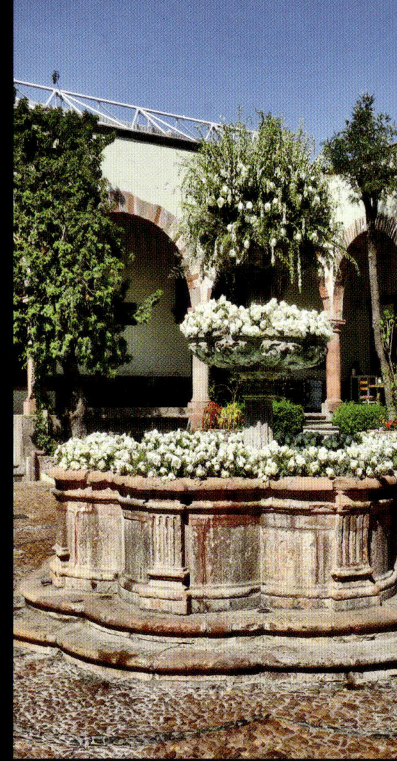

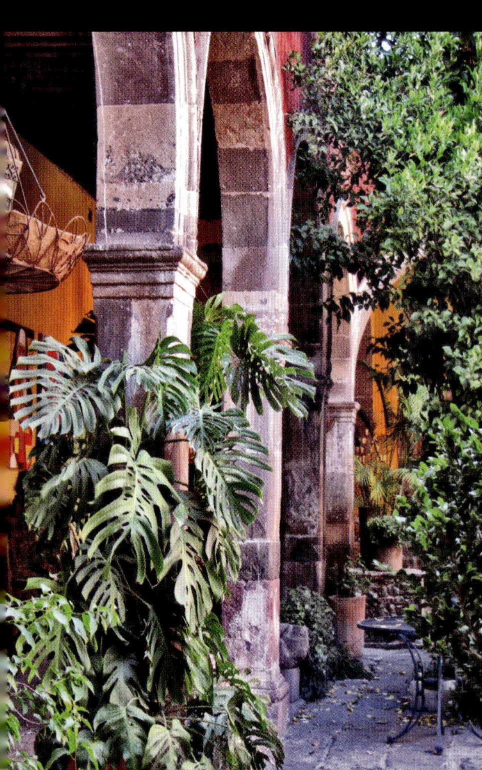

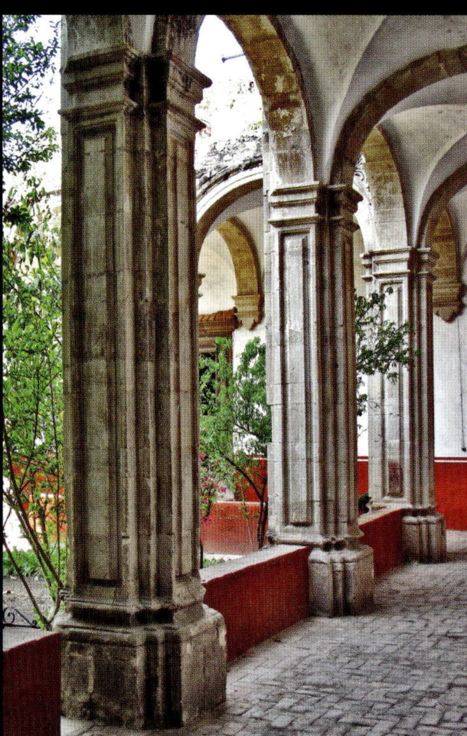

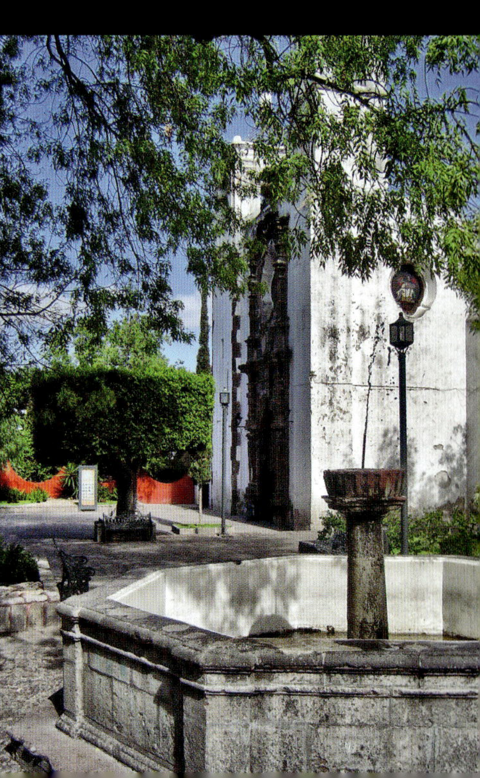

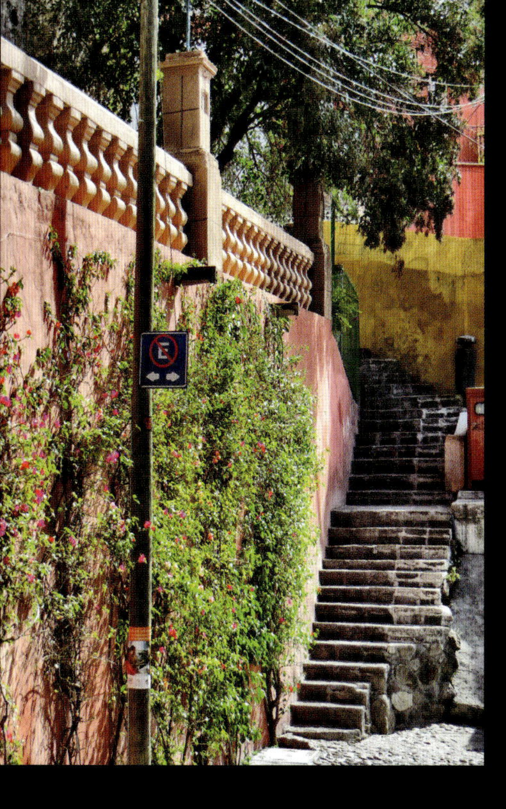

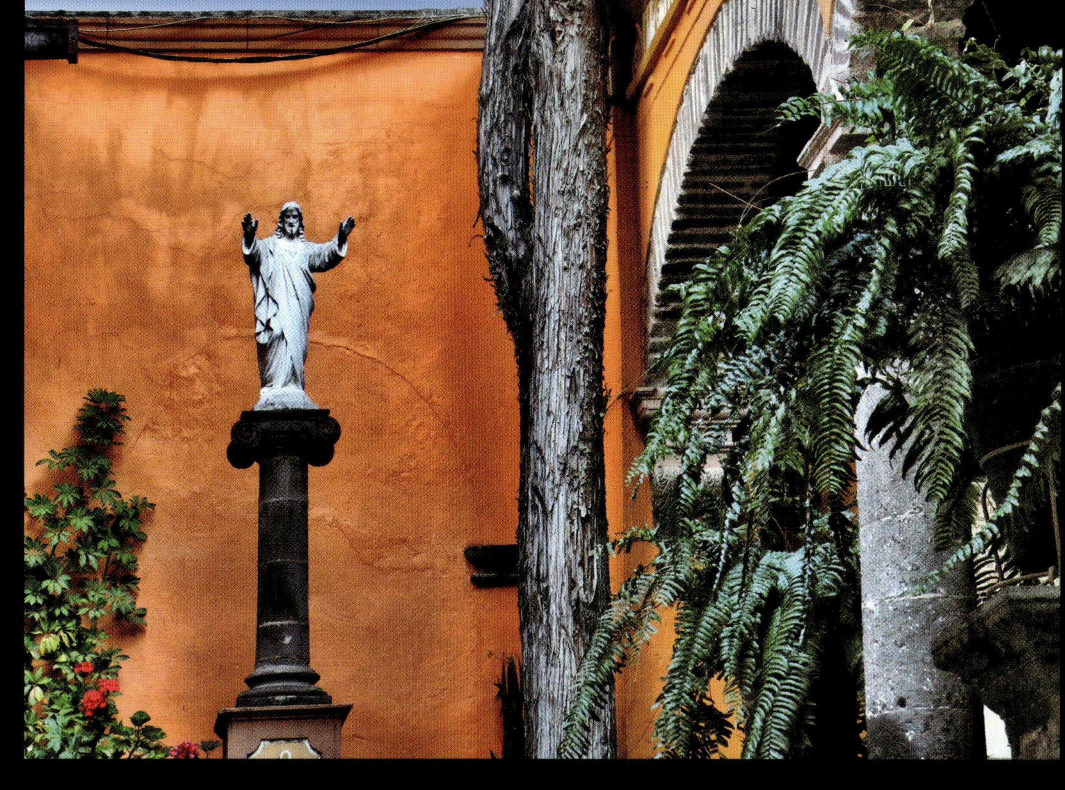

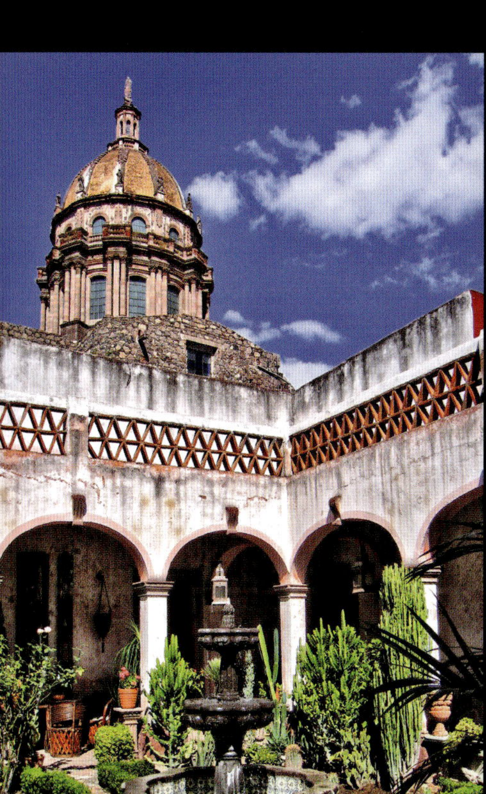

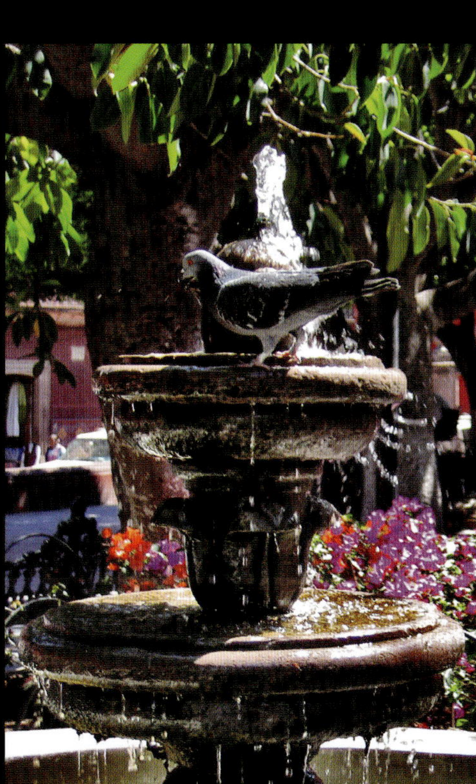

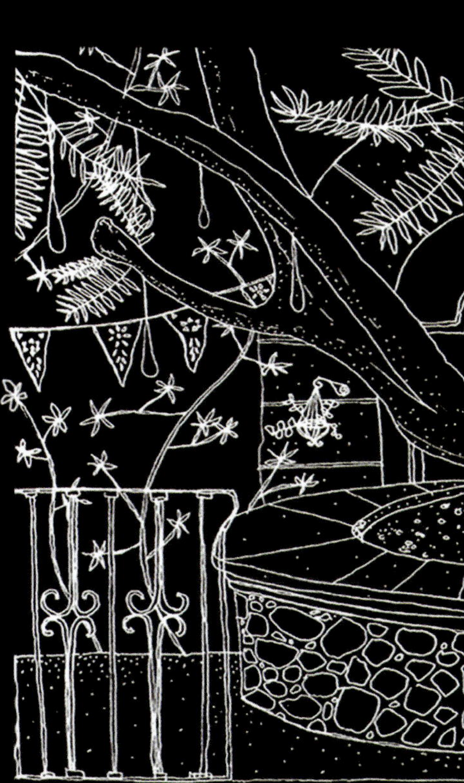

Holy Days

Holy days come frequently in Mexico, even more so in San Miguel, where many Indigenous celebrations continue as they have for millennia, blending with the Catholic faith in unique combinations of old and new ideas. As a predominantly Catholic country of deeply religious souls, Mexicans see Catholicism as part of their identity and national cultural heritage. They celebrate with passion and fervor every aspect of their faith, and they see no conflict in the practice of Indigenous ceremonies honoring God, nature, and the cosmos alongside Catholic ceremonies.

Sacred statues come out of their niches in churches, to be carried through the streets on the shoulders of the faithful. There is a feeling first, rather than a sound, to these processions, as a deep rumble vibrates the stones of the walls from chanting, singing, or enormous speakers. Solemn or gleeful music sets the tone. There may be dancers, children, and costumes. For each, the streets are hung with fluttering flags, flowers abound, and a sacred tradition is renewed and passed on to the next generation.

On Palm Sunday, the terraces in front of churches are filled with people folding palm fronds into fantastic compositions. The steady beat of Roman soldiers marching in the streets, whipping Jesus in yearly re-creations of His last days, sends the faithful weeping as though seeing His death before their very eyes. At the Sanctuario de Jesús Nazarino de Atotonilco, the Crucifixion reenactment is so real that it is as though He is suffering His death once again.

On Holy Saturday, the day between Christ's crucifixion and ascension to heaven, the church bells are silent and there is a ceremonial burning of Judas. This ritualistic burning was originally just for burning Judas in effigy. But that tradition has expanded to filling larger-than-life-size papier-mâché figures not only of Judas, but of others such as politicians, with fireworks and exploding them over the heads of those gathered in the Jardín.

Christmas Day in San Miguel is preceded by evenings of soft singing and candlelit processions as the faithful stroll the streets of each neighborhood singing the stories and prayers of Christmas. Just as Joseph and Mary were refused entry, the carolers are turned away, until they come to the one place, a different home each night, that opens its doors, inviting the procession to continue the stories of Christmas at their manger, serving a rich Christmas punch and gifts of fruits and cookies. Every home has its own manger, empty during the days before Christmas while the songs and prayers are shared; then, in celebration of the birth of Christ, each home holds a ceremonial presentation of the baby Jesus into his manger, followed by a feast to celebrate His birth.

One's saint day is often more important than one's birthday. They are celebrated with song and sweets. On certain saint days, the streets are spread with beautiful handcrafted carpets of flower petals, beans, grains, and colored wood shavings, across which the faithful carry the saint in their ceremonial rituals.

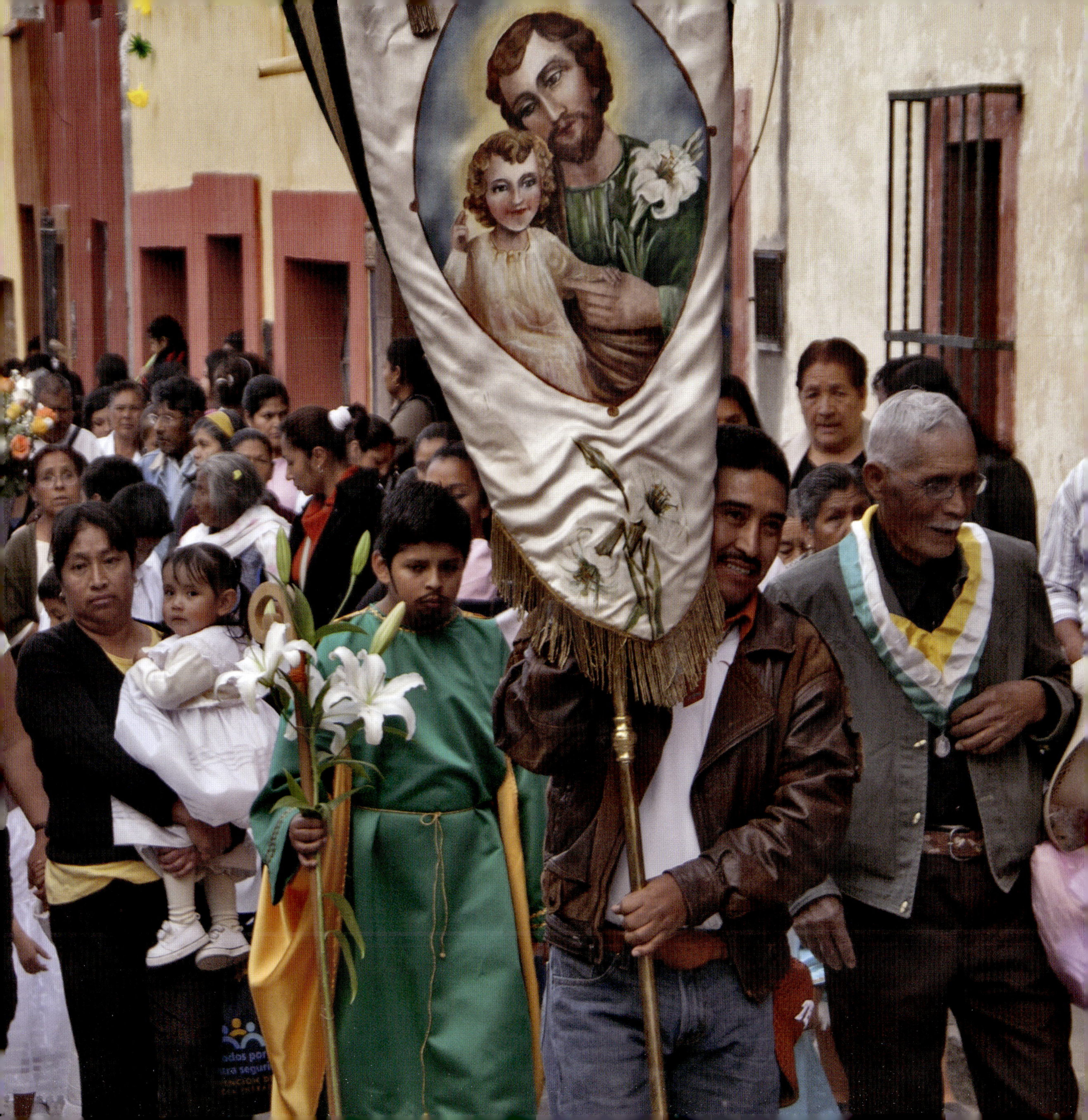

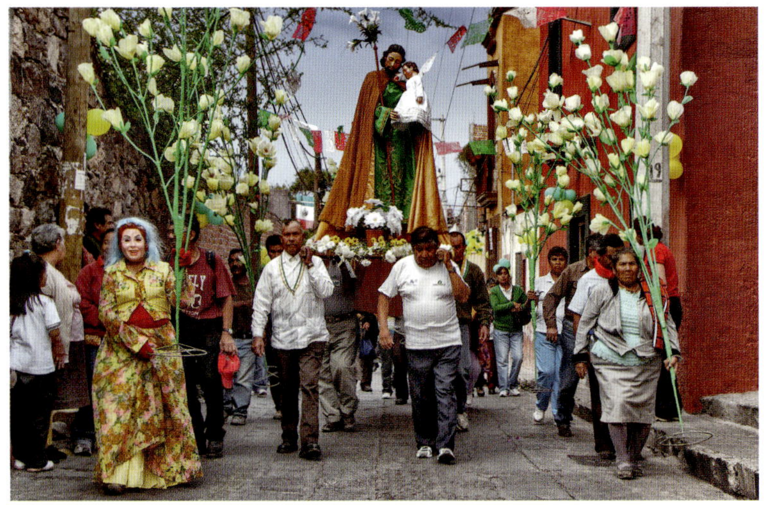

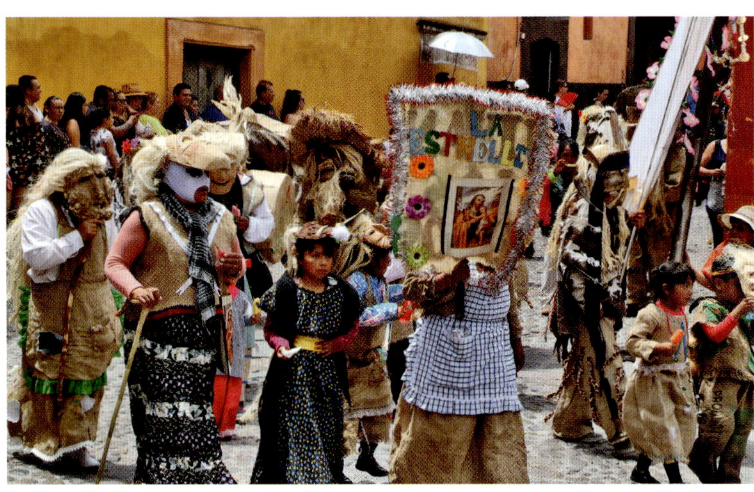
LA

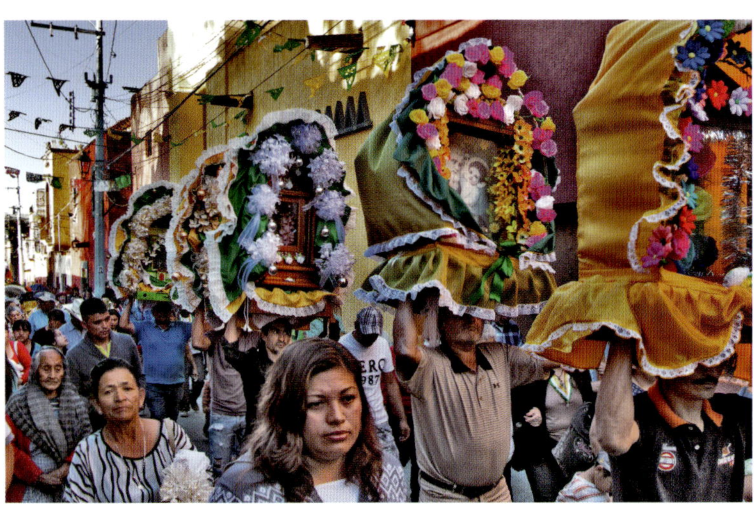

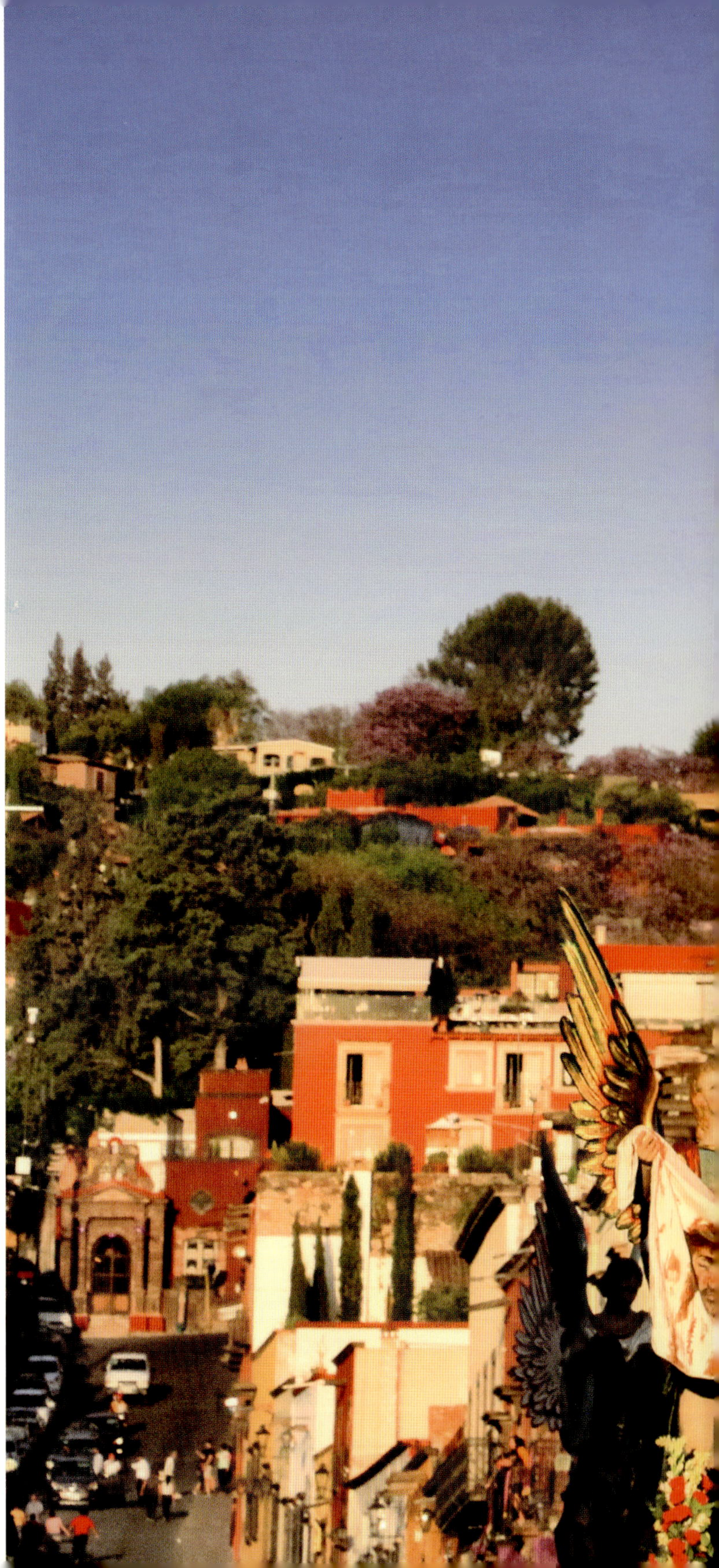

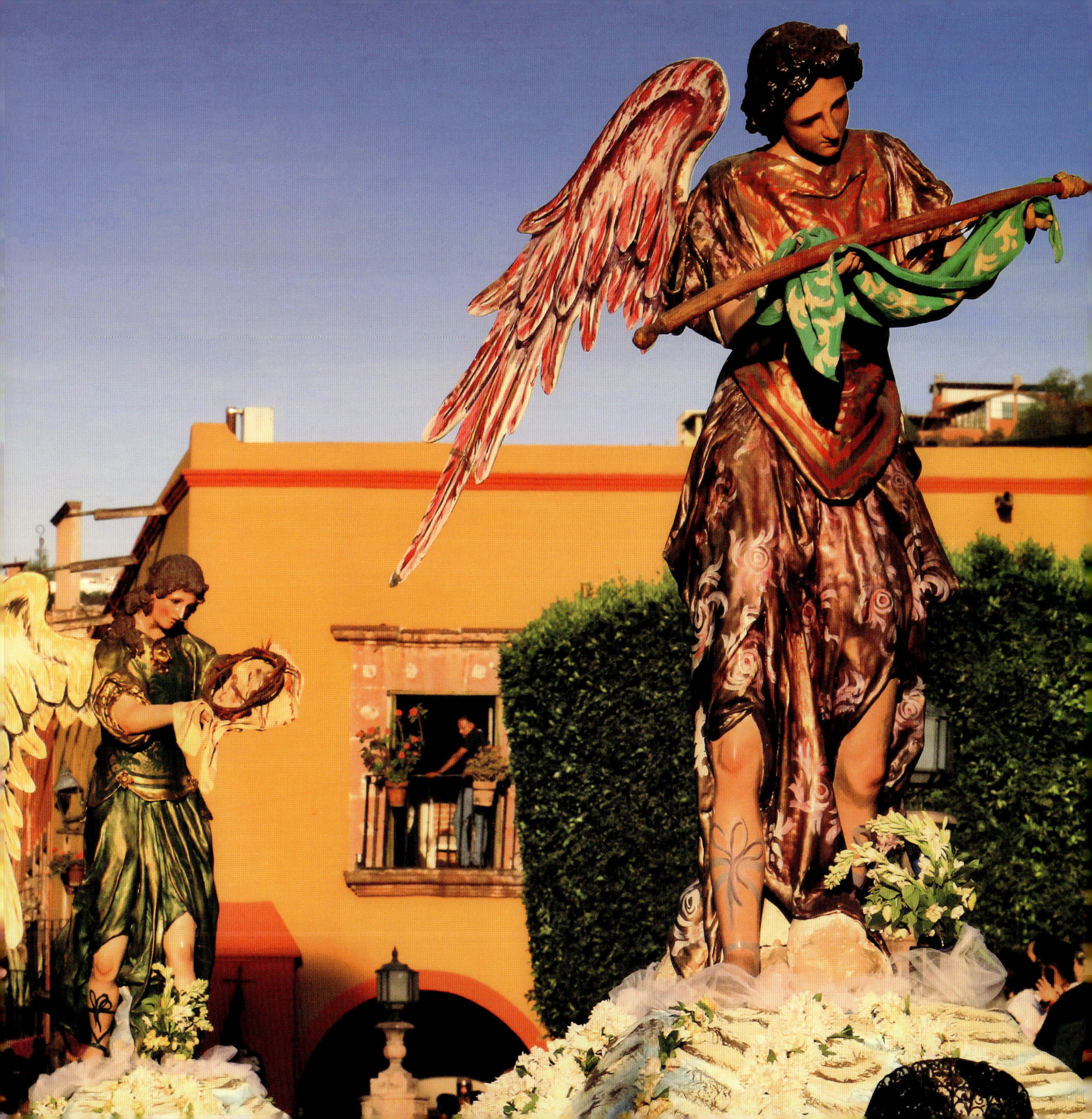

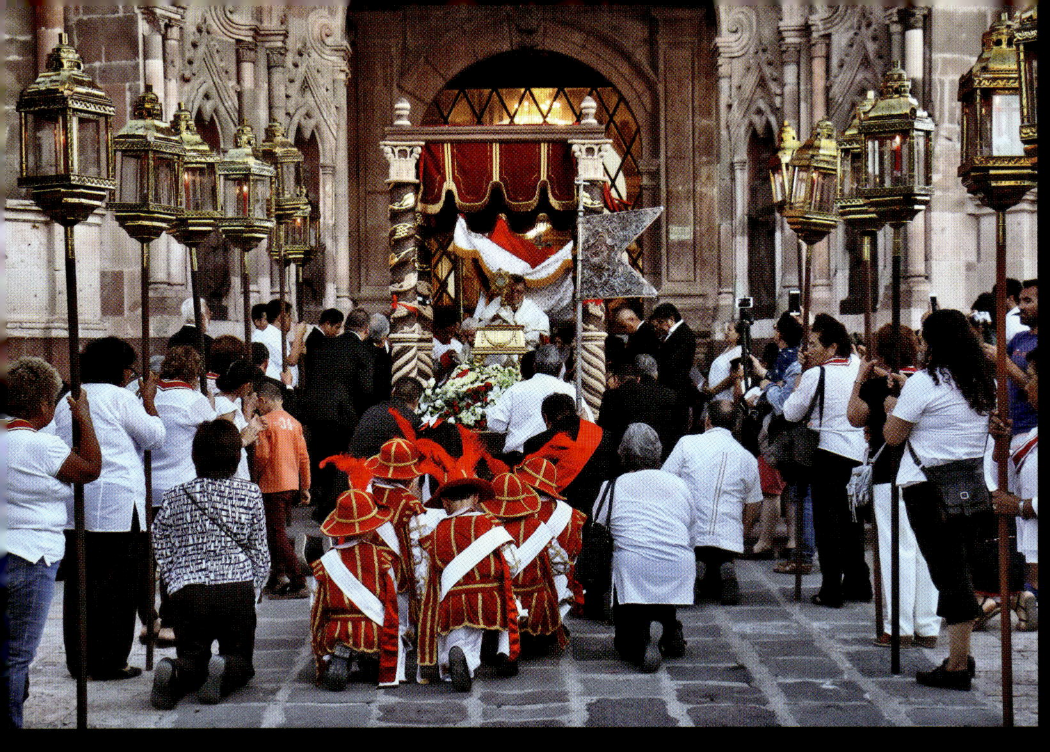
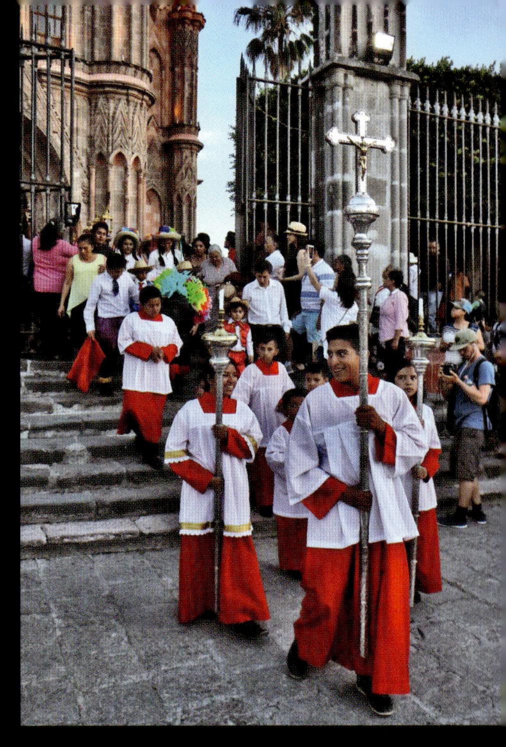
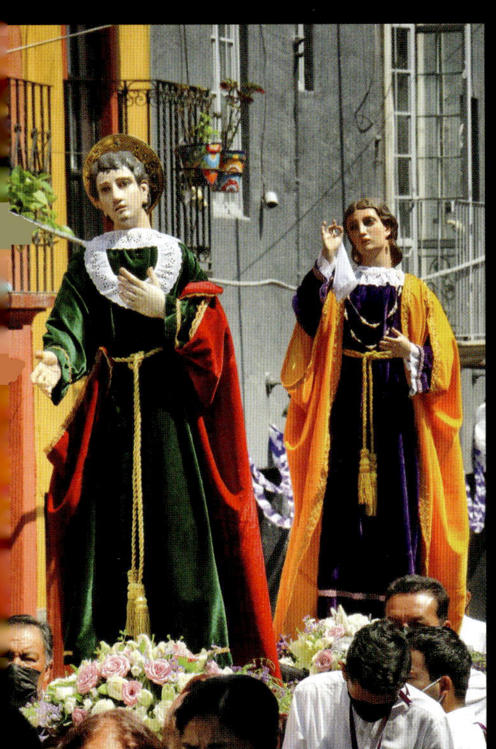
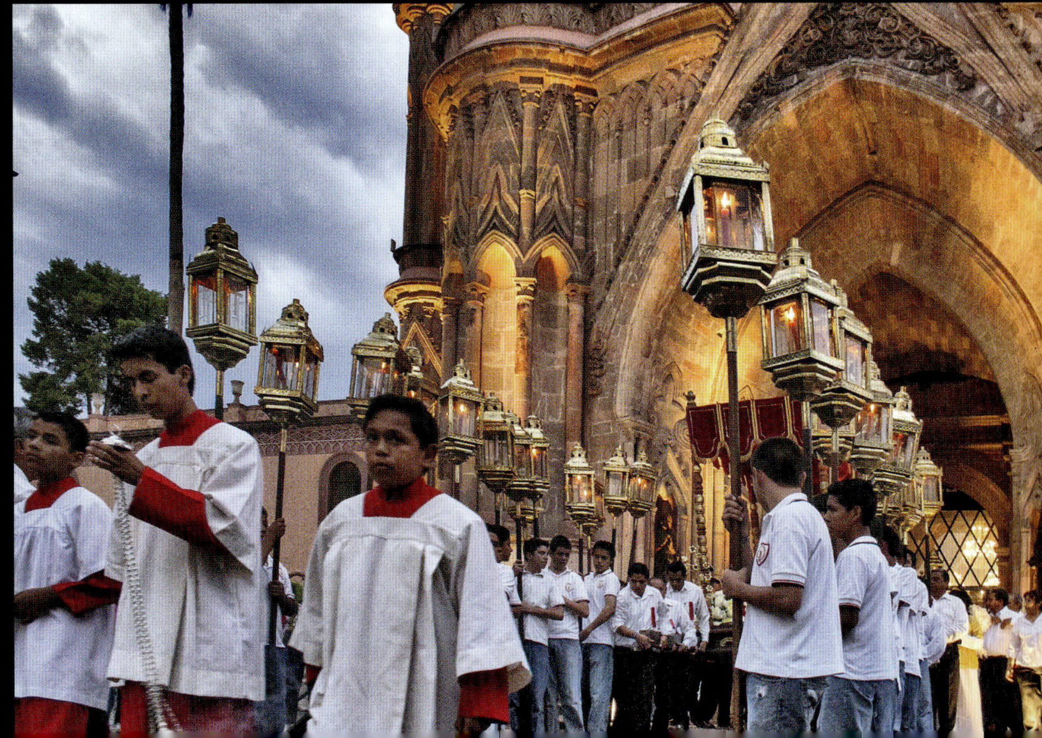

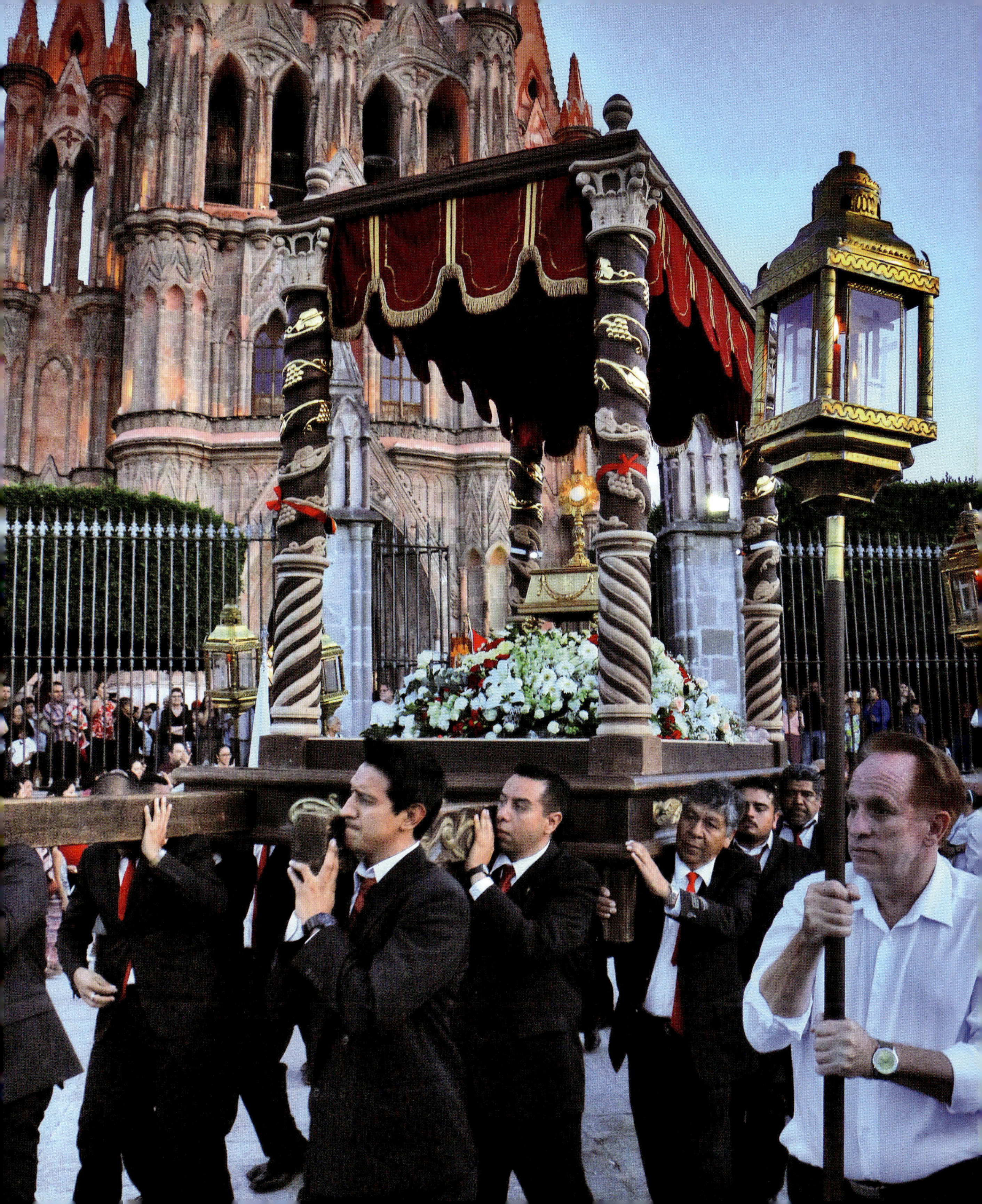

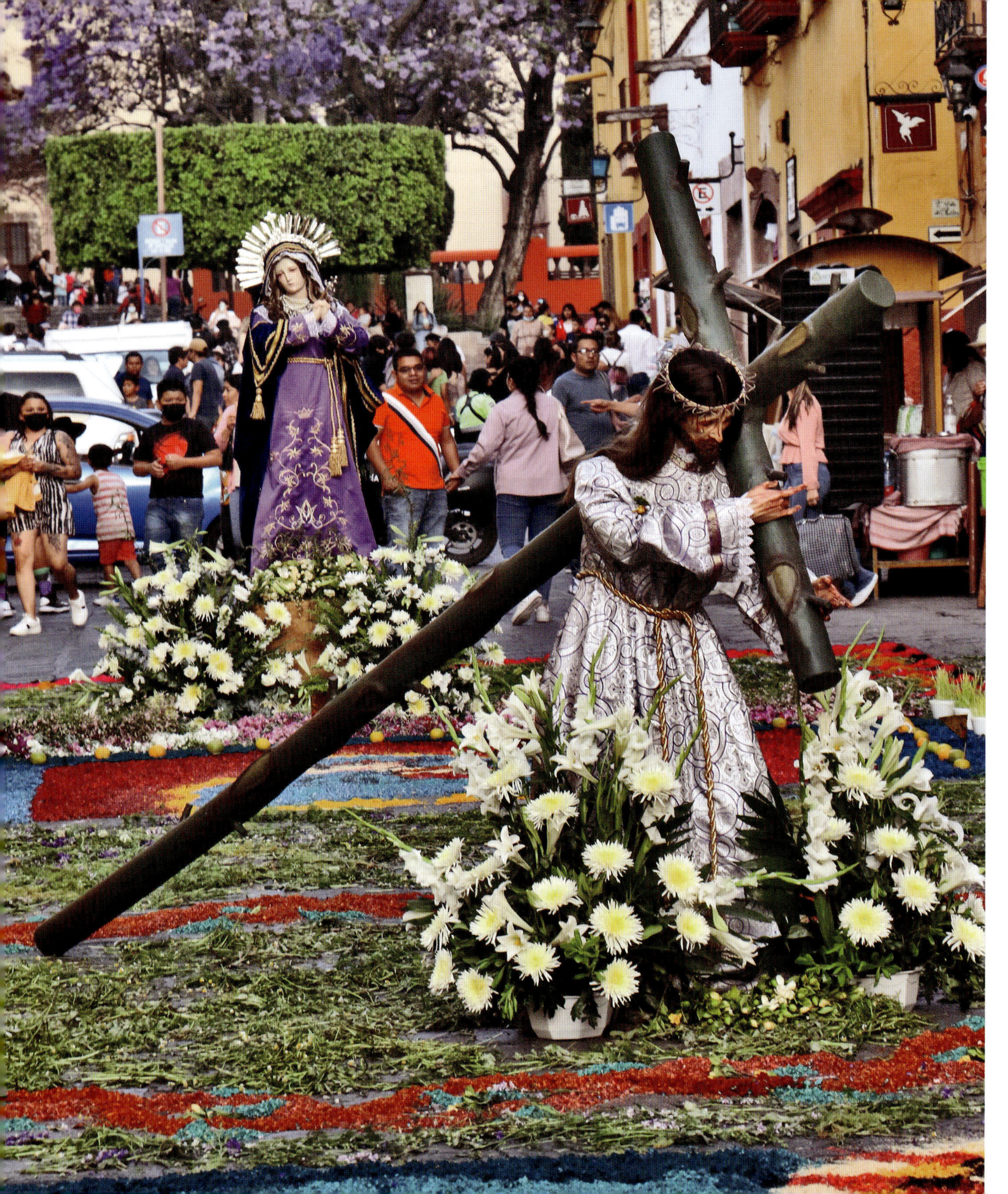

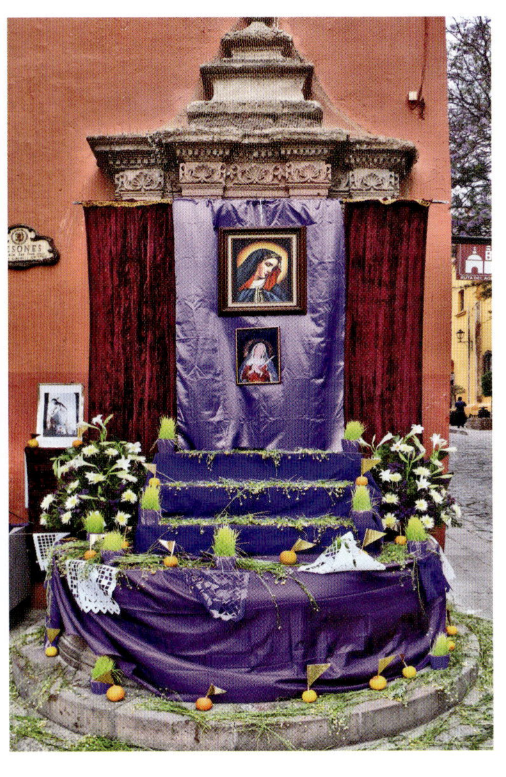

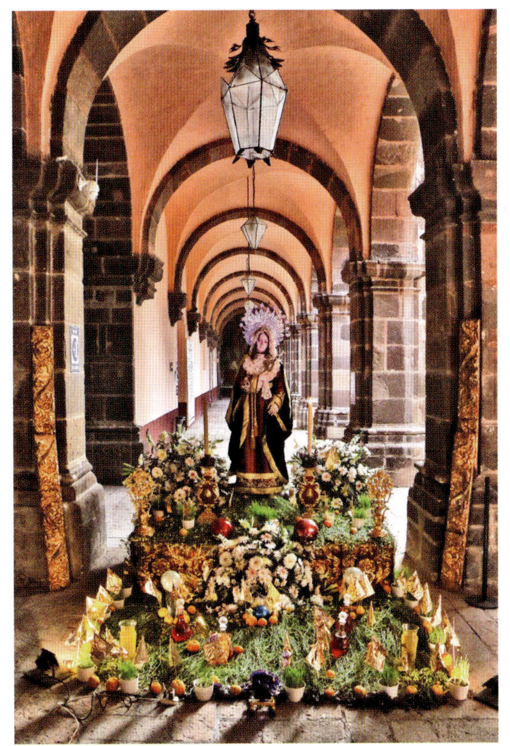

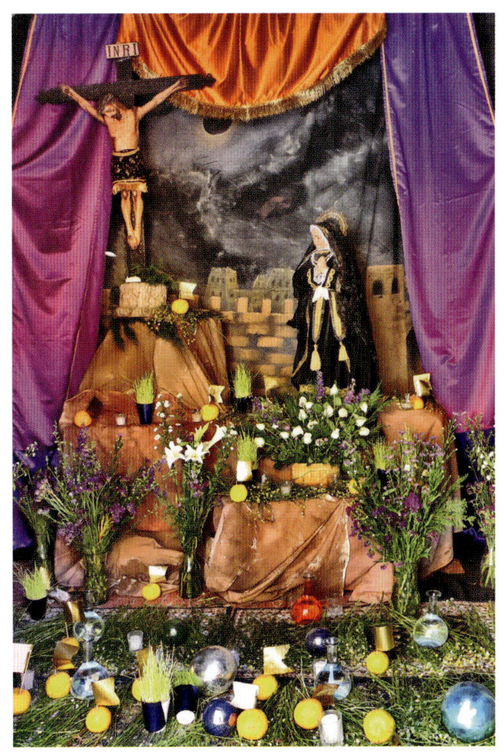
INRI

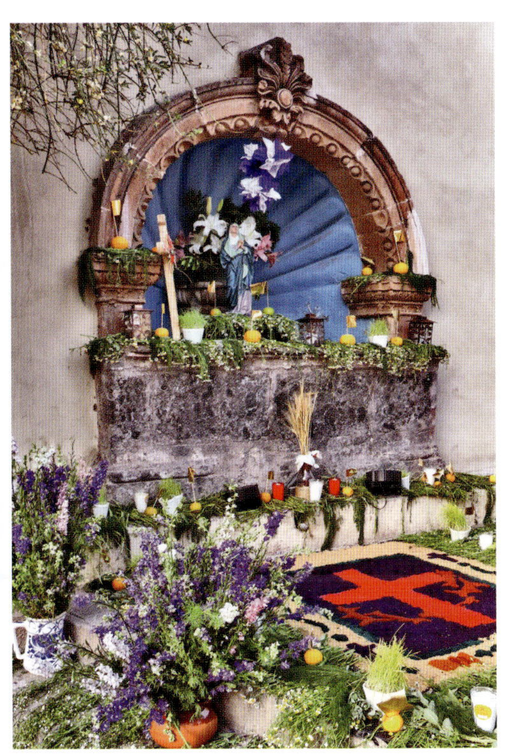

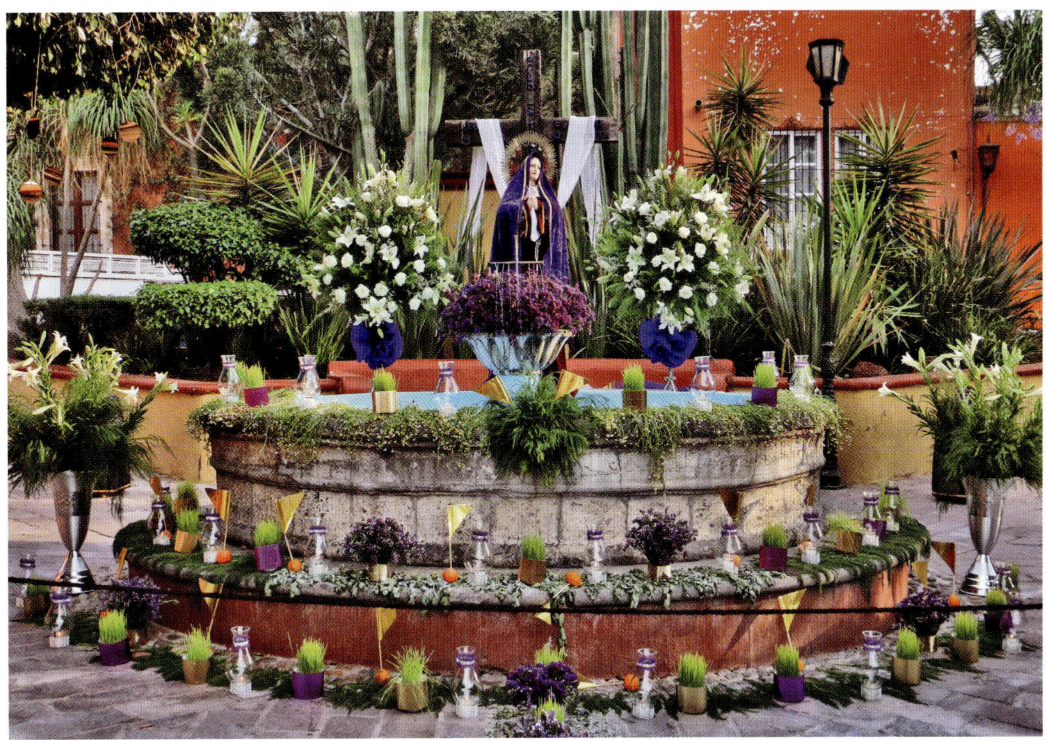

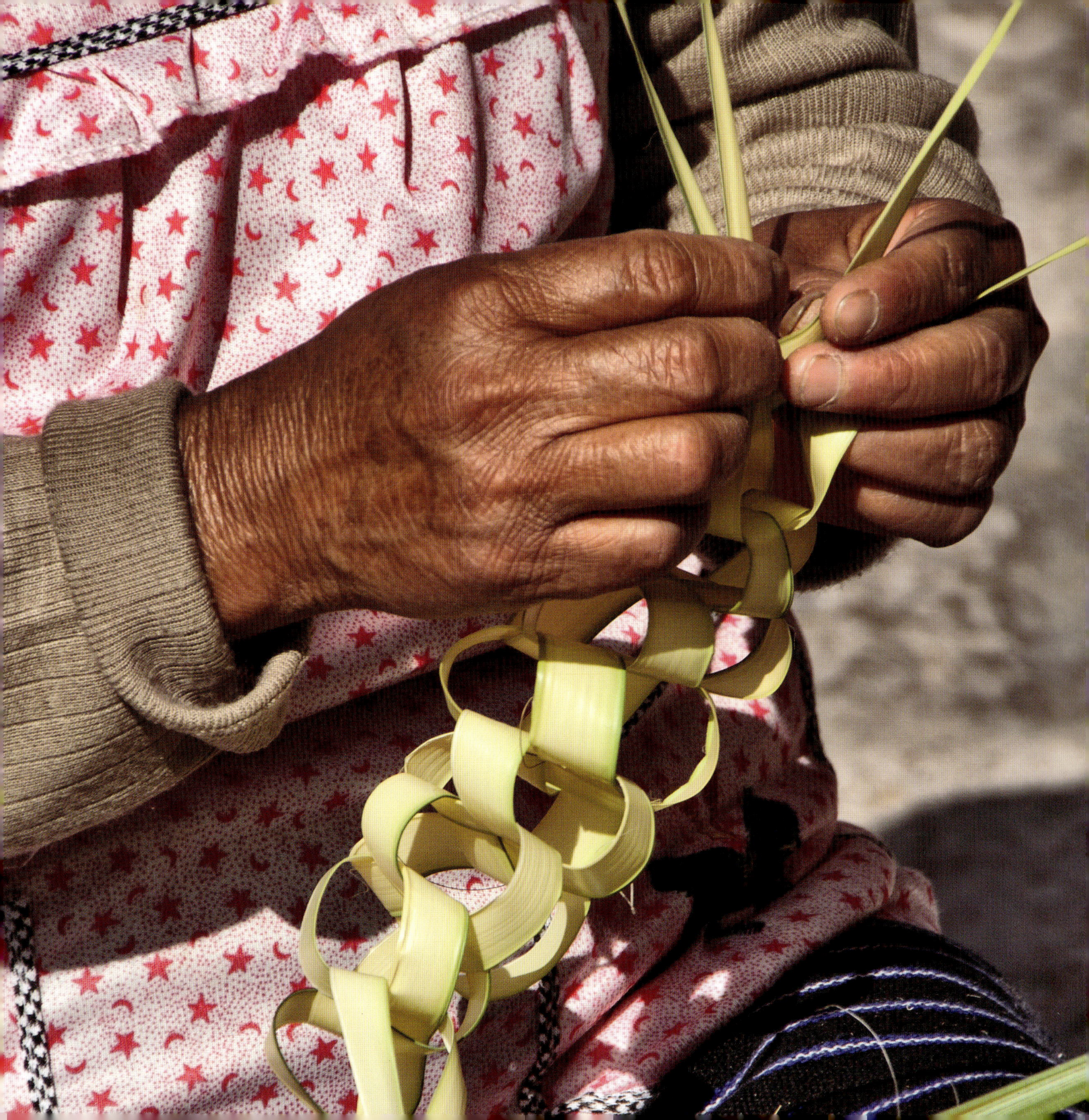

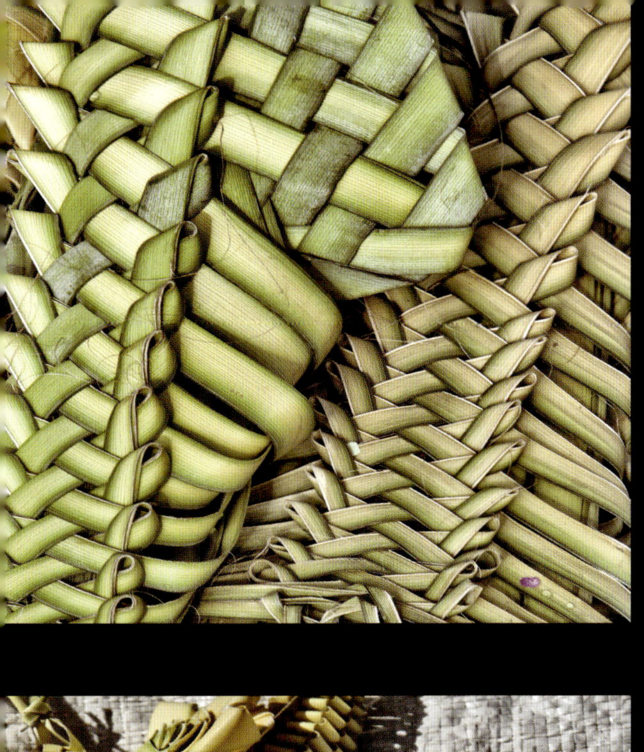
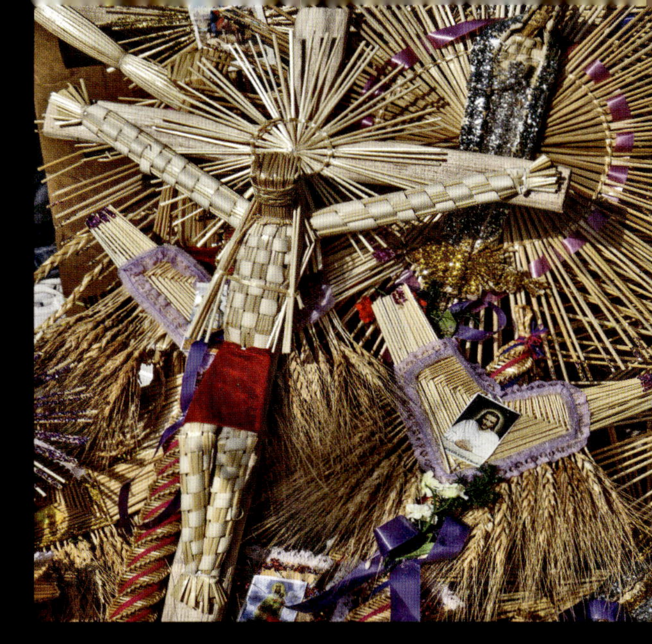
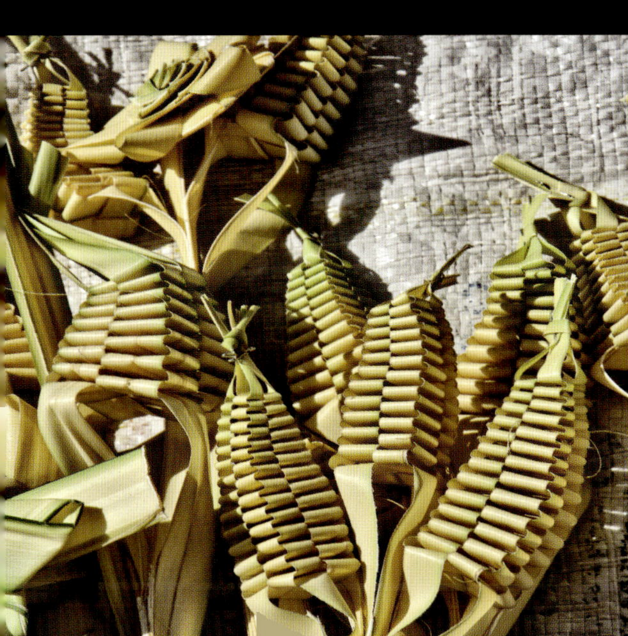
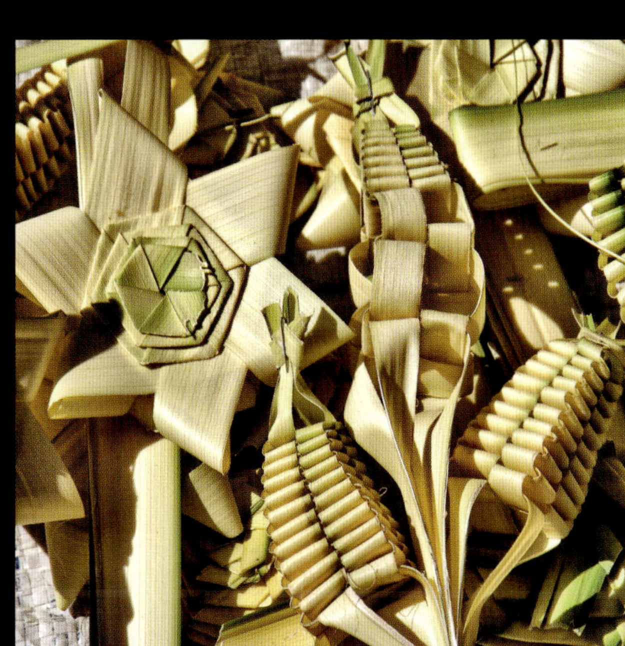

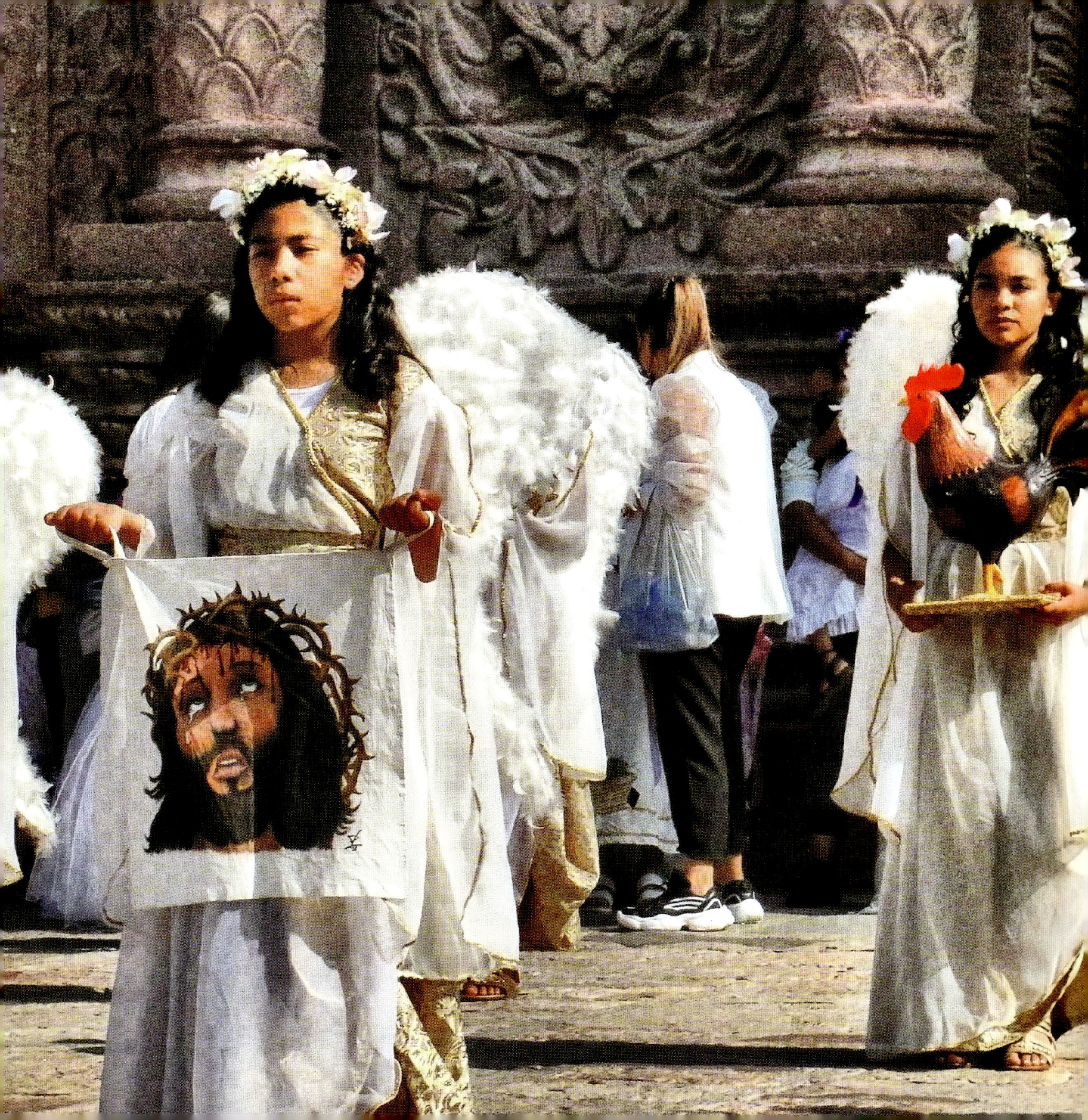

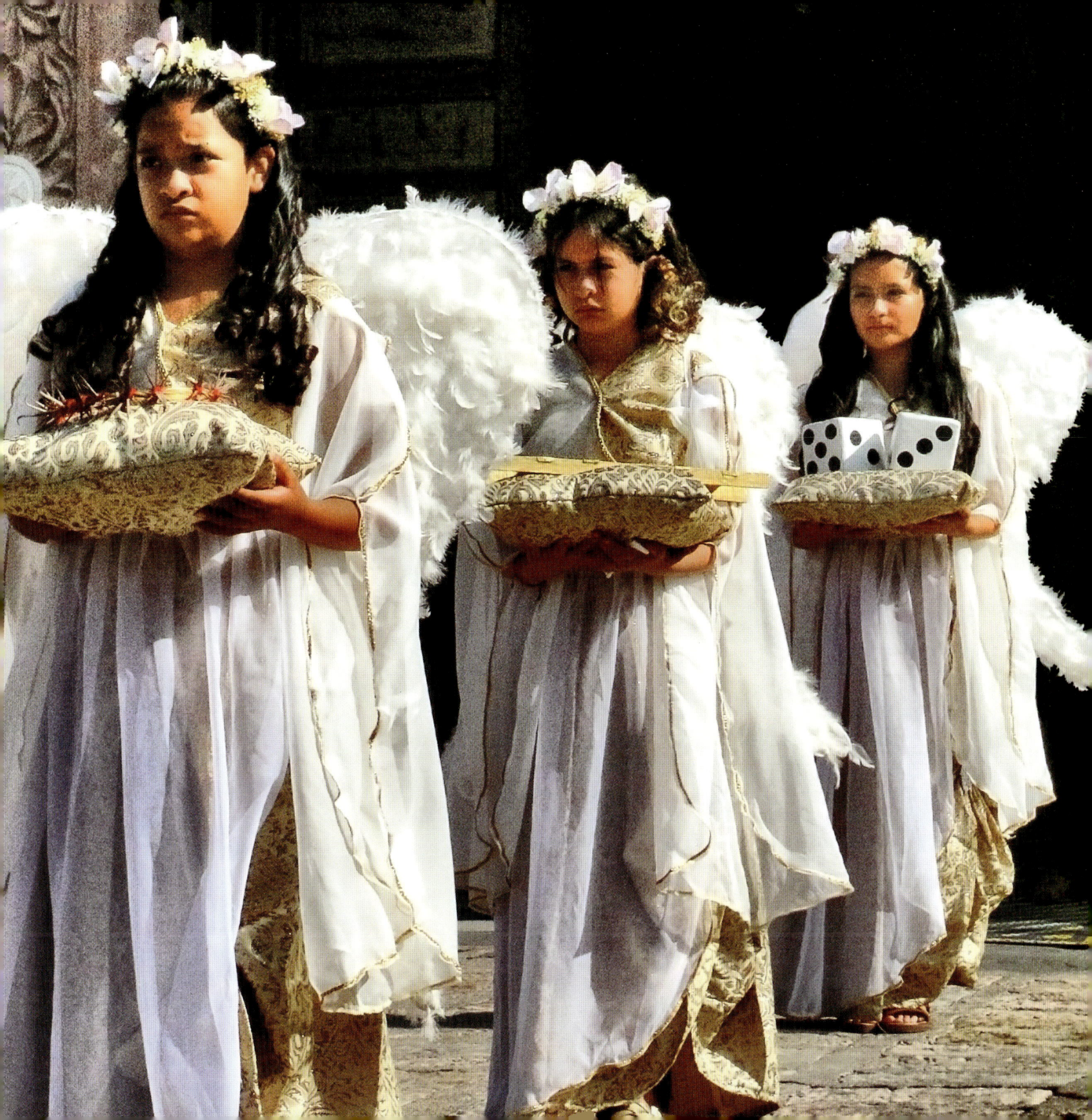

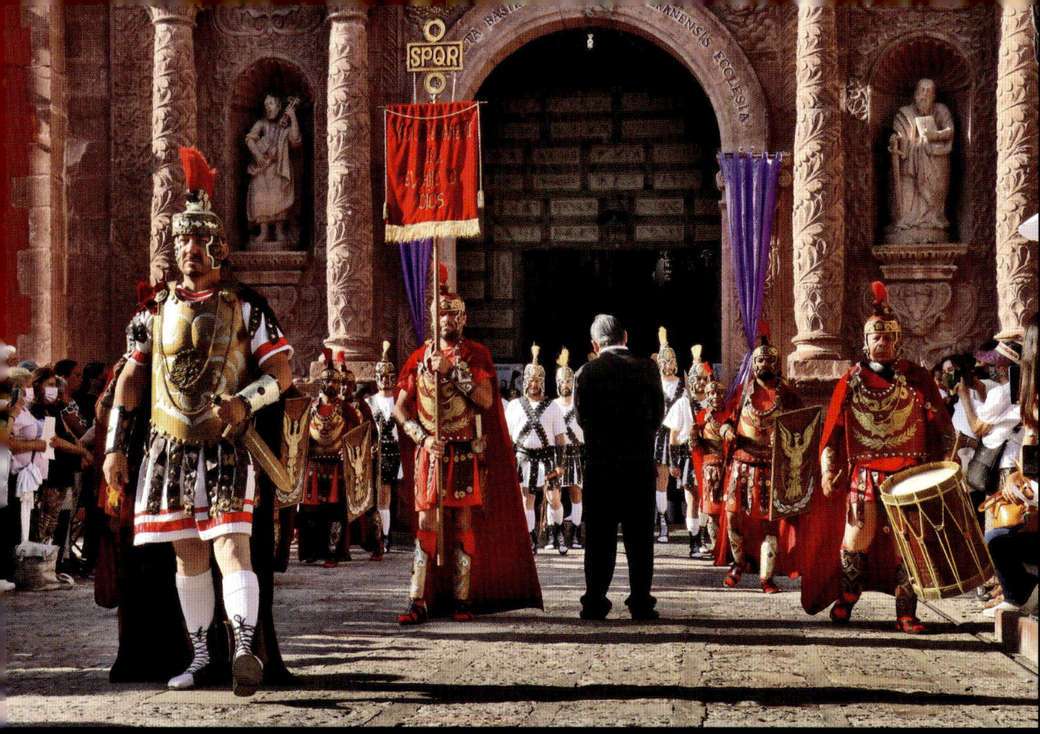

Easter is celebrated with the passion it deserves as the most important event in the birth of Christianity. Roman soldiers march through the streets and Jesus is carried in many forms whether as statues removed from their niches in churches, or as a living young man who submits to endure the torments of Jesus's final days. Streets are strewn with flowers, children in angel wings sing prayers, and women weep as Jesus dies once again for us.

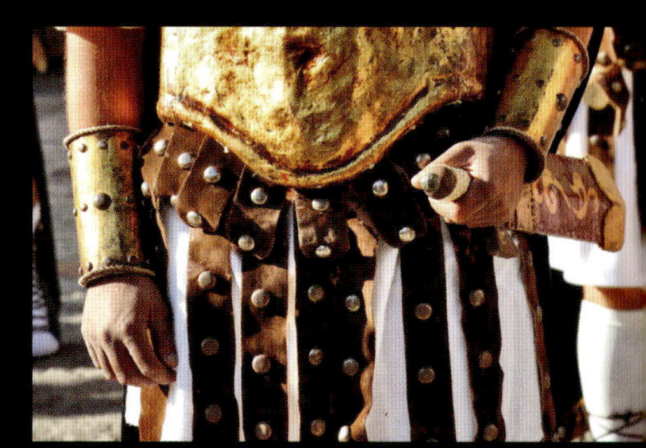

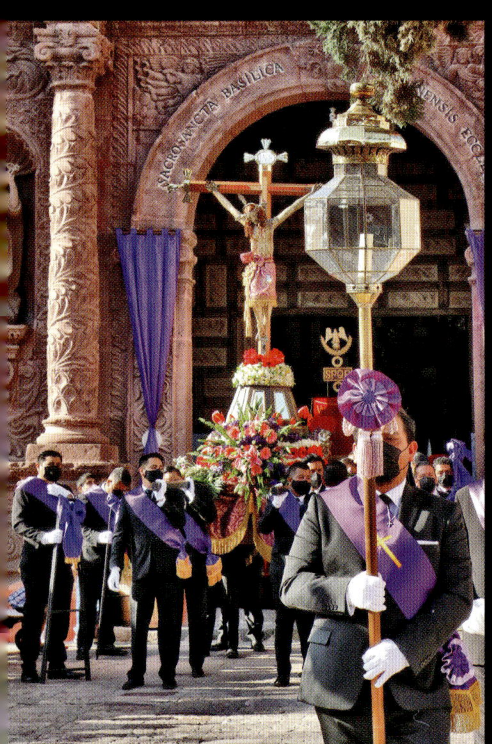

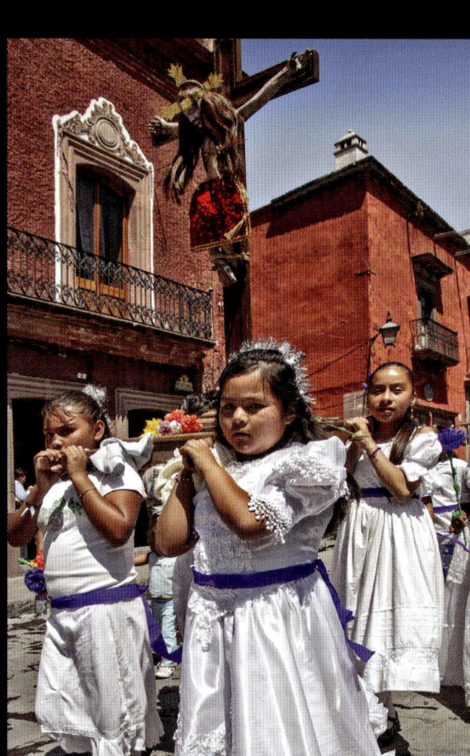

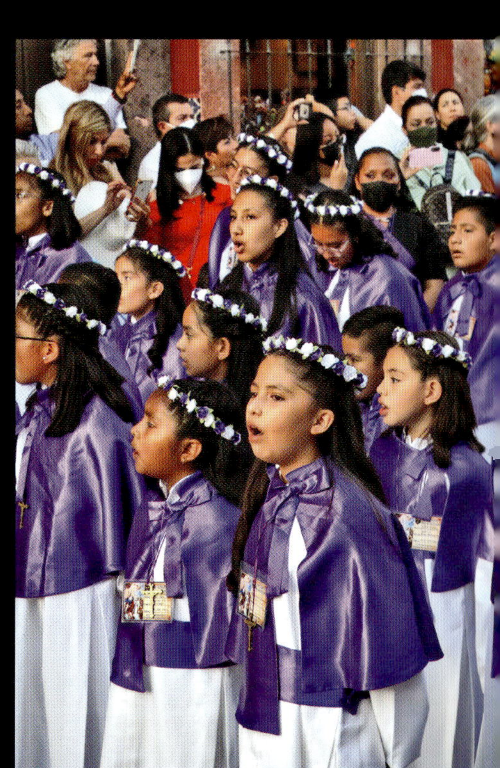

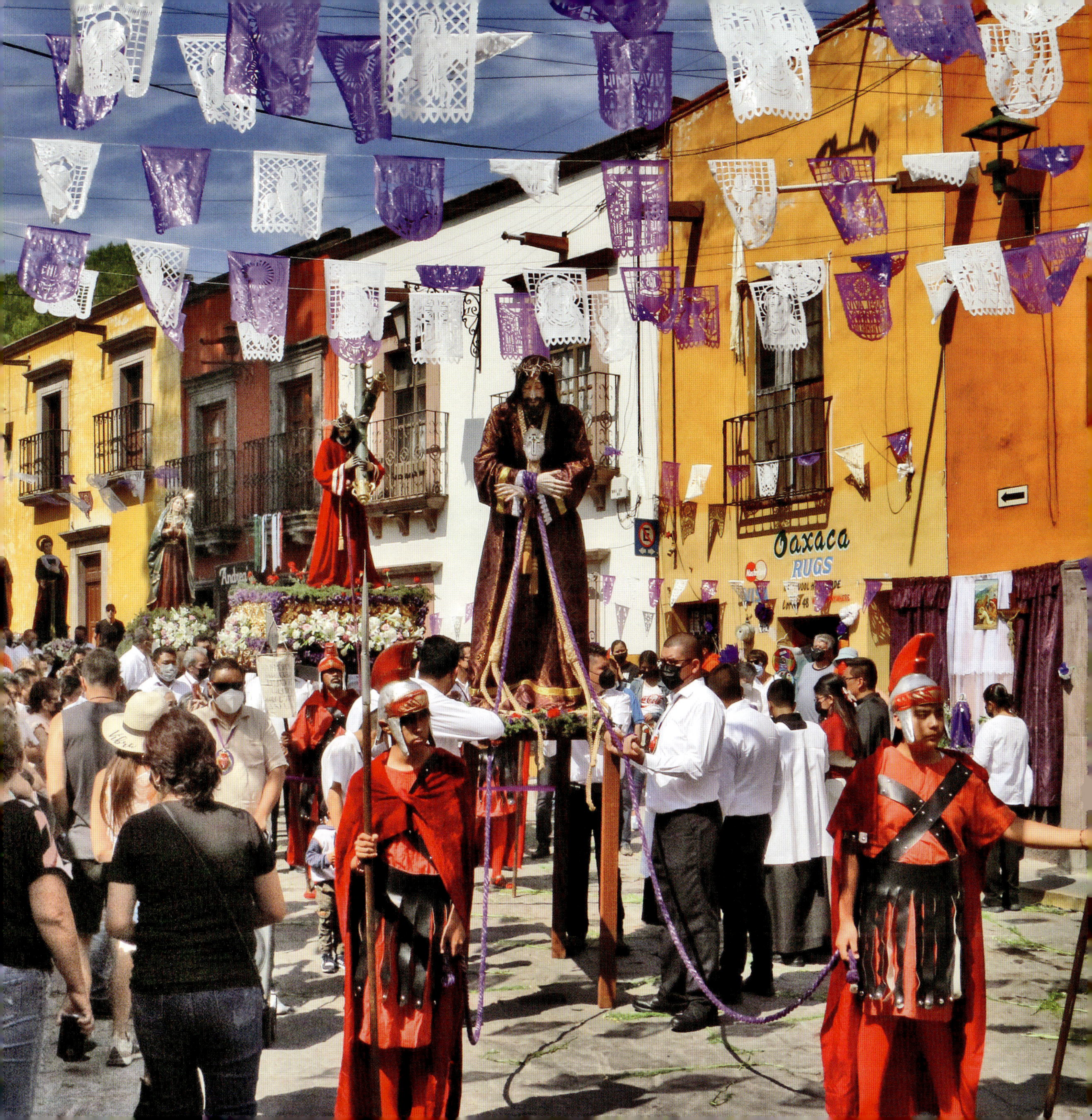
Oaxaca
RUGS

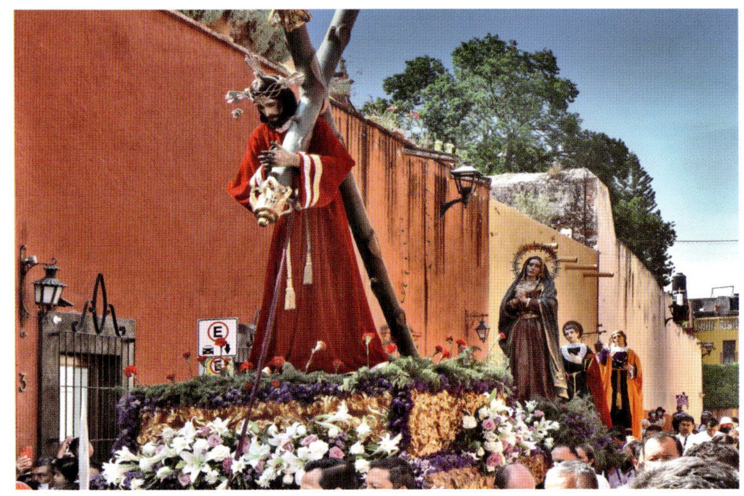

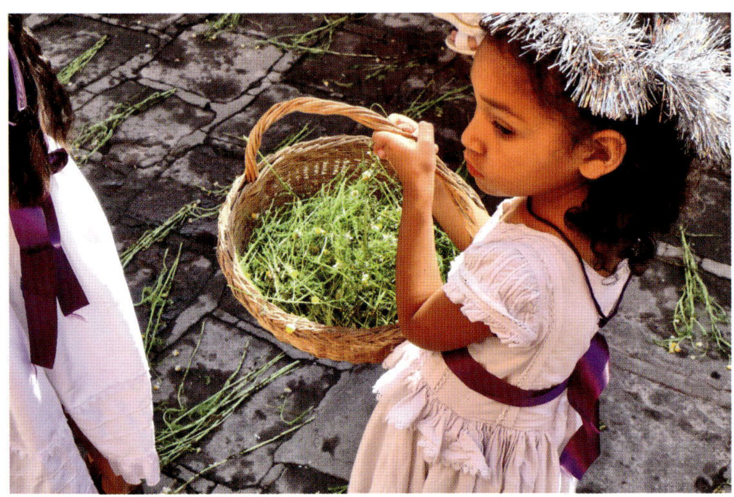

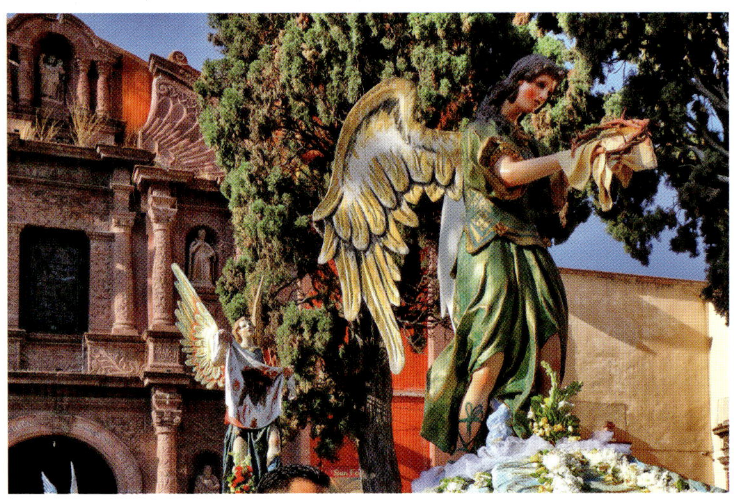

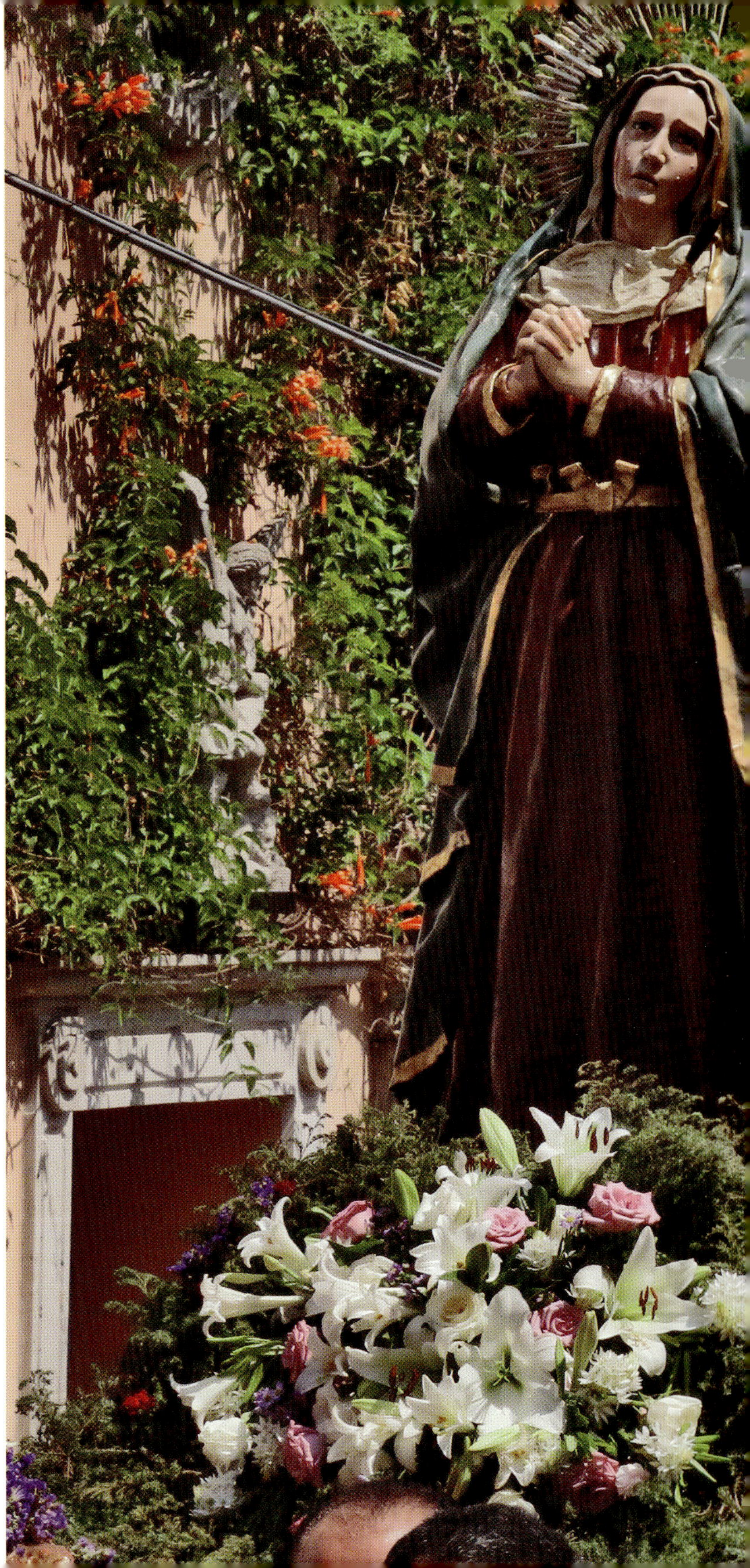

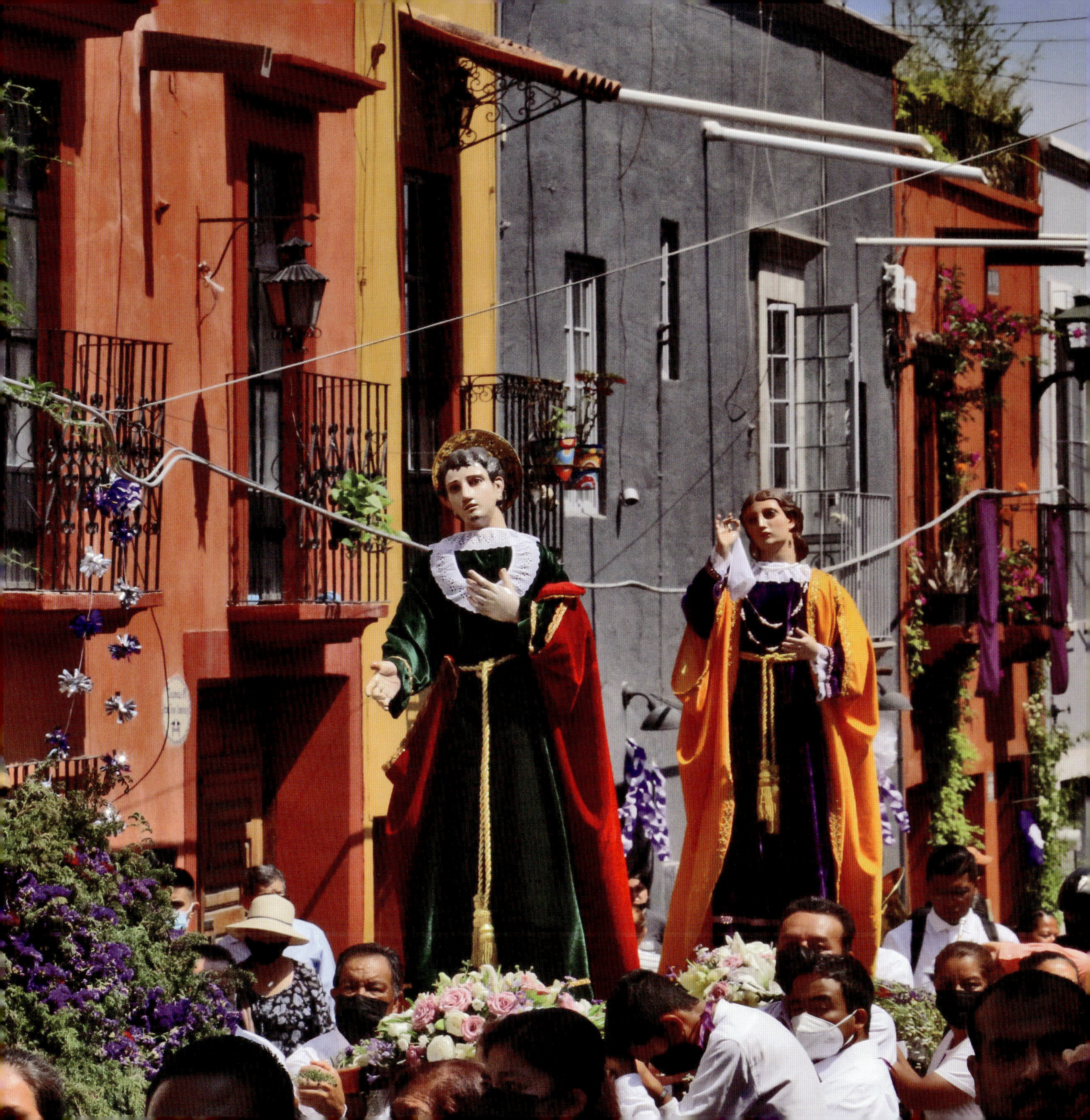

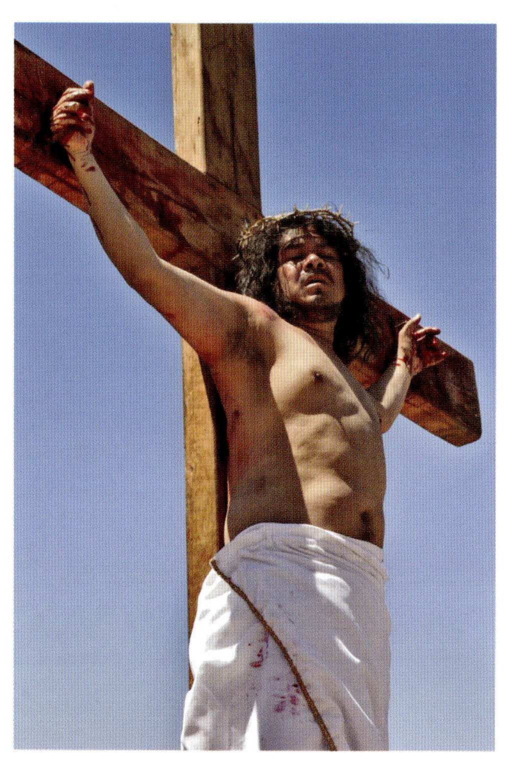
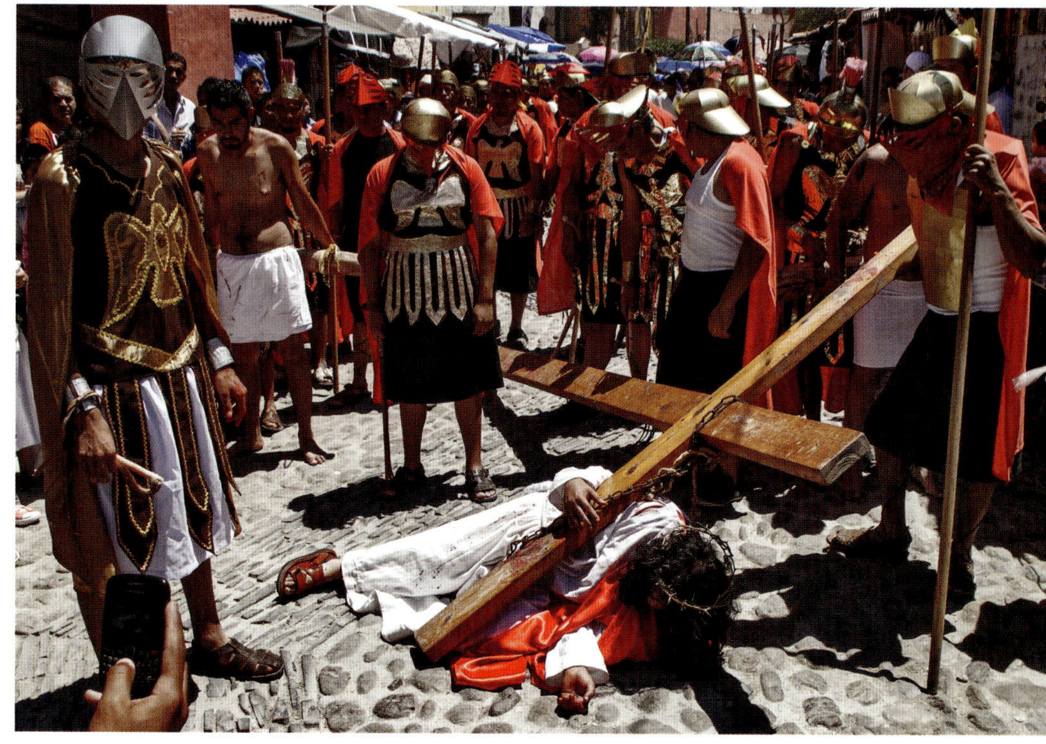
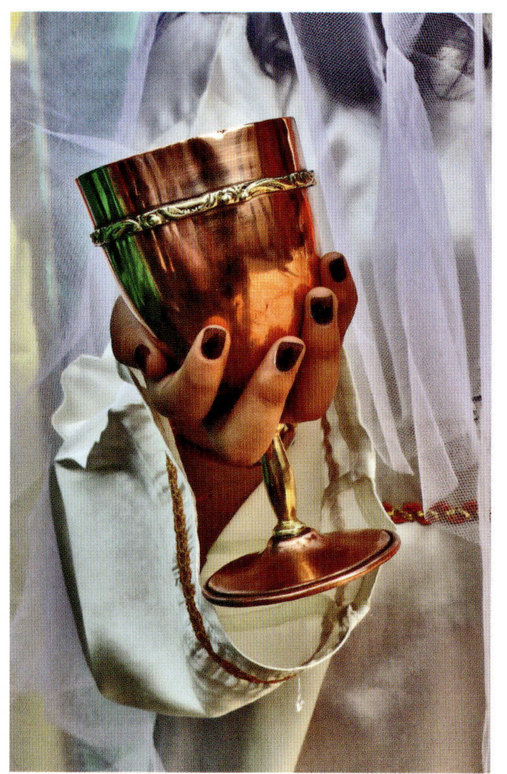
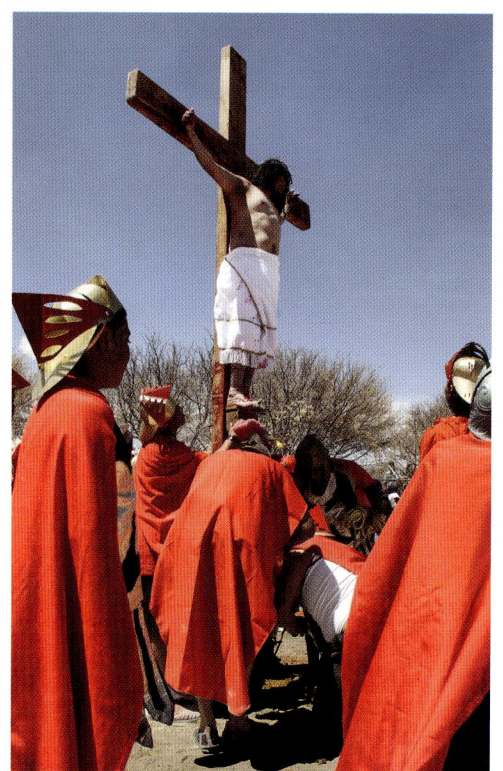
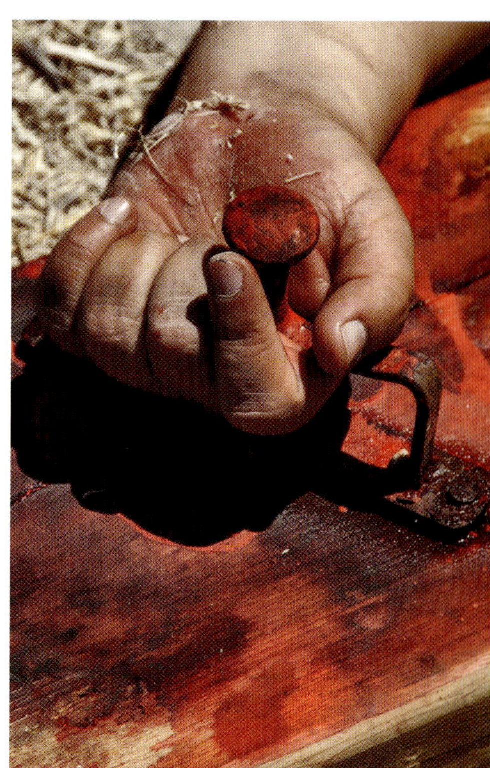

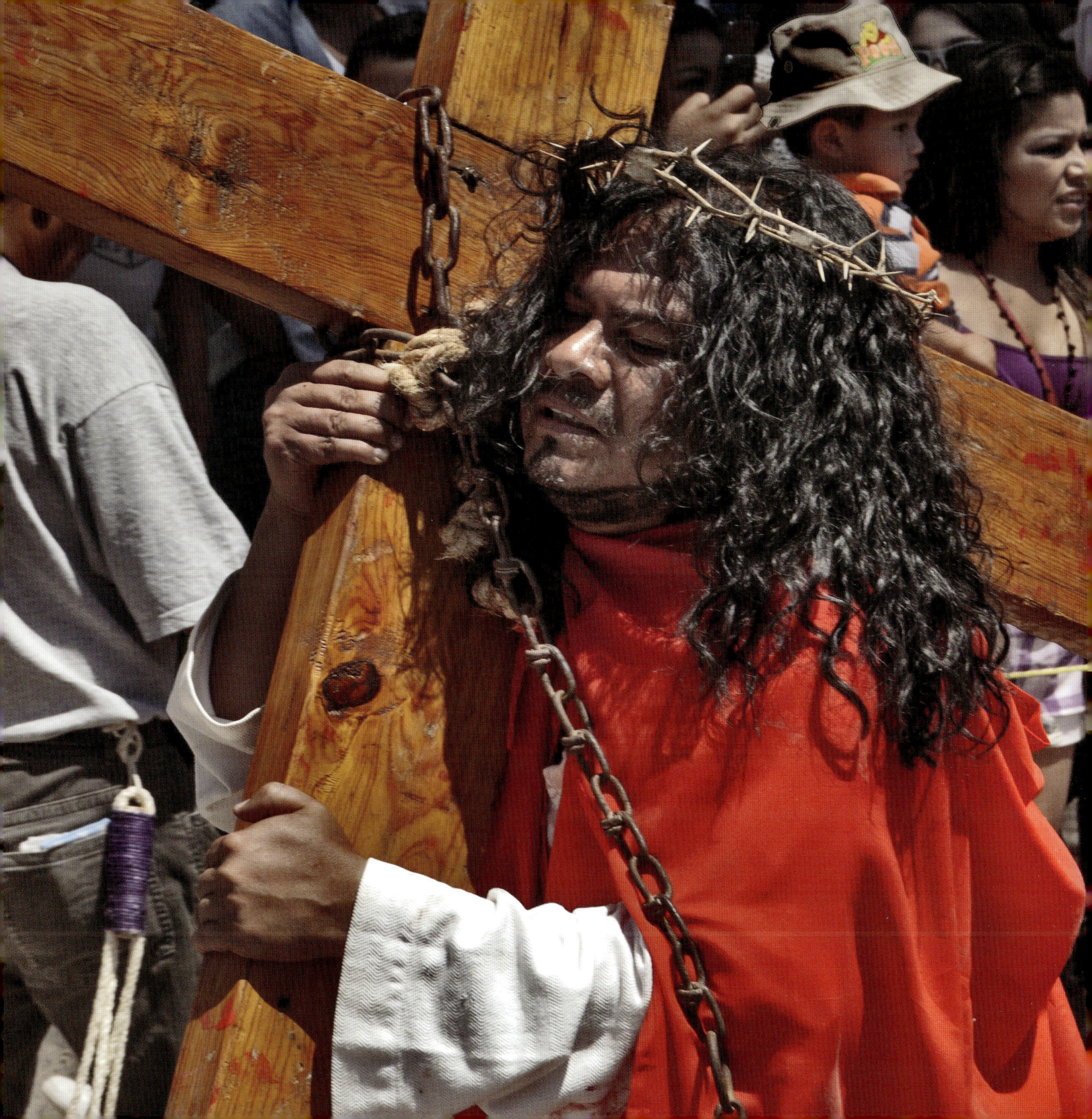

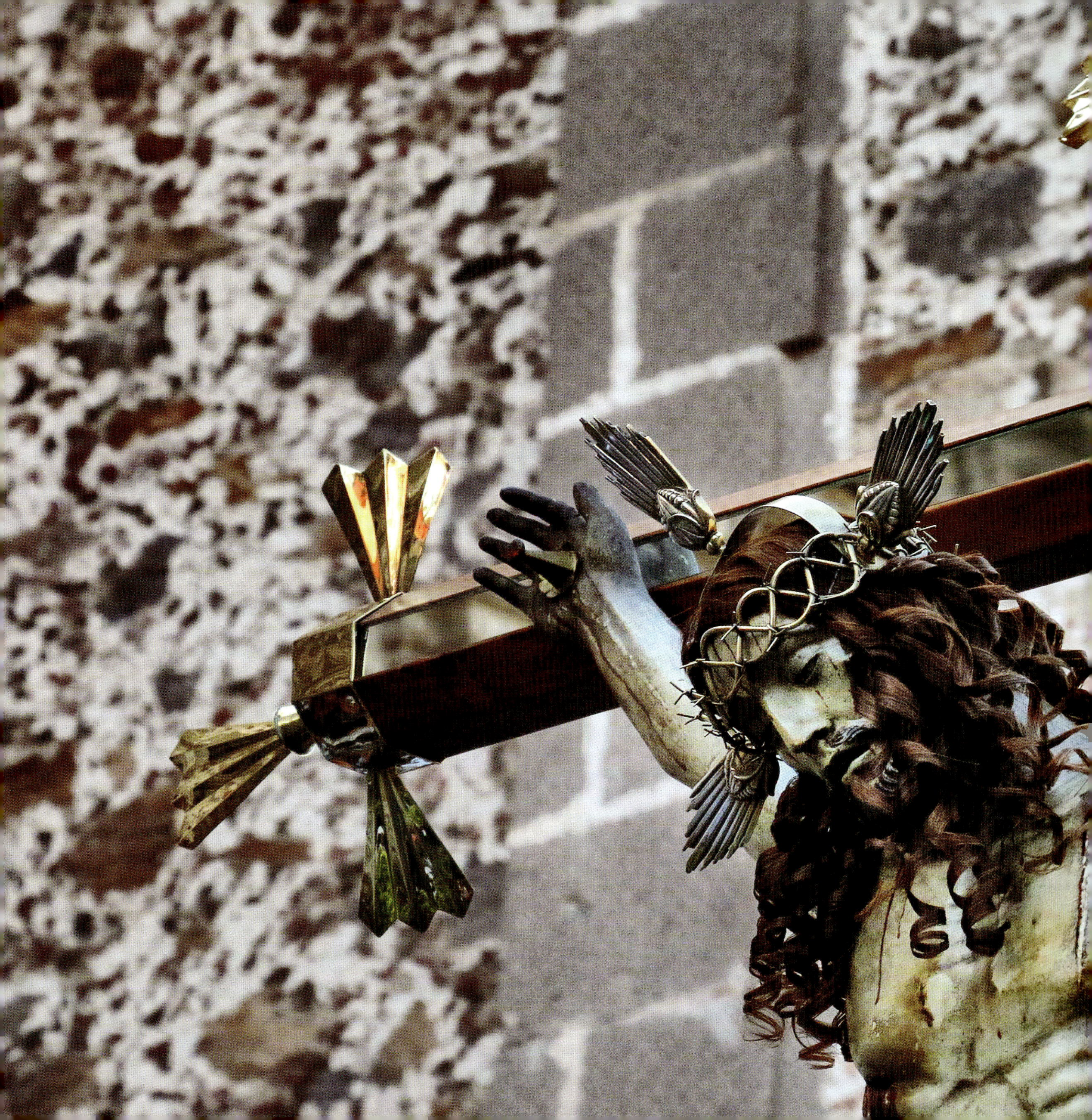

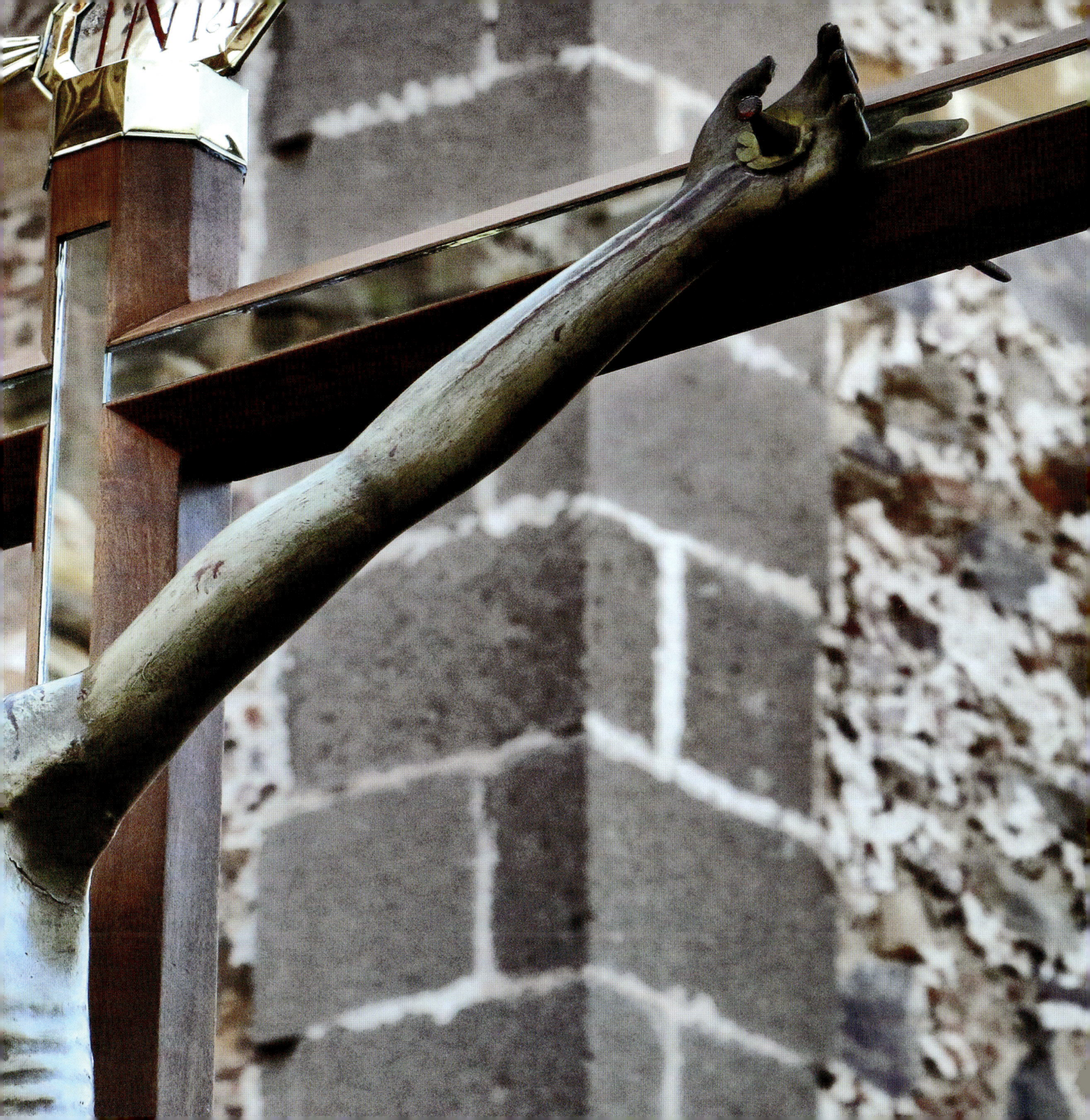

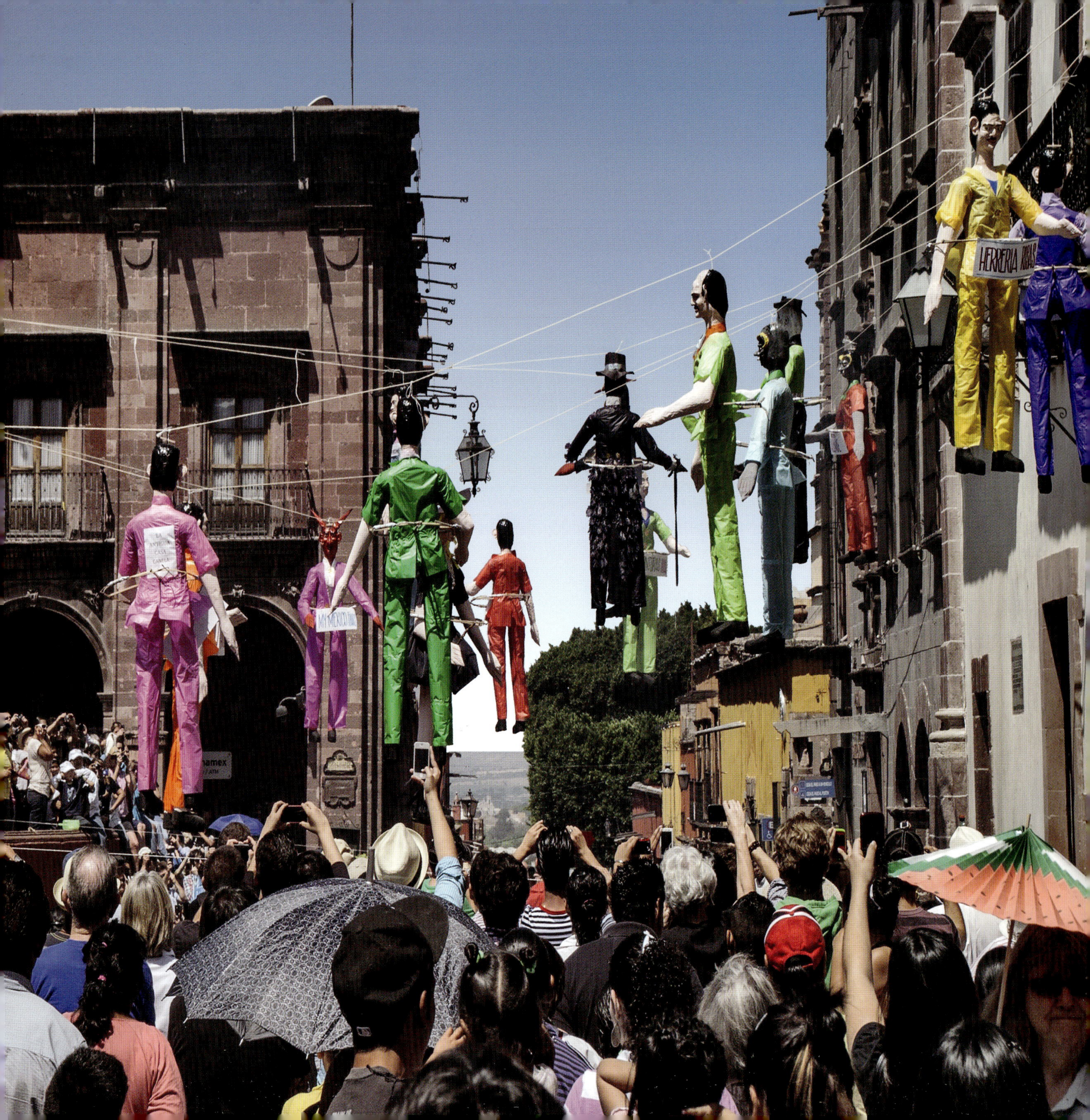
HERRERIA

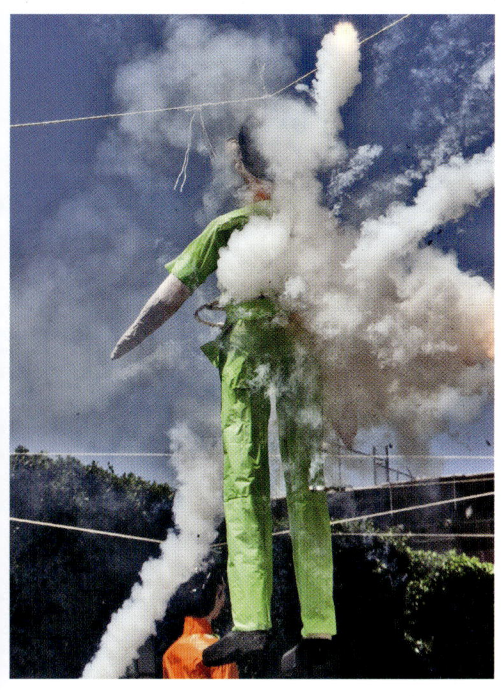

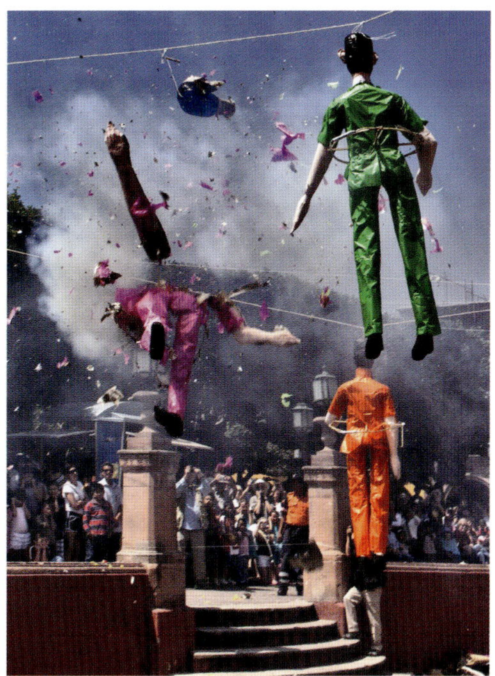

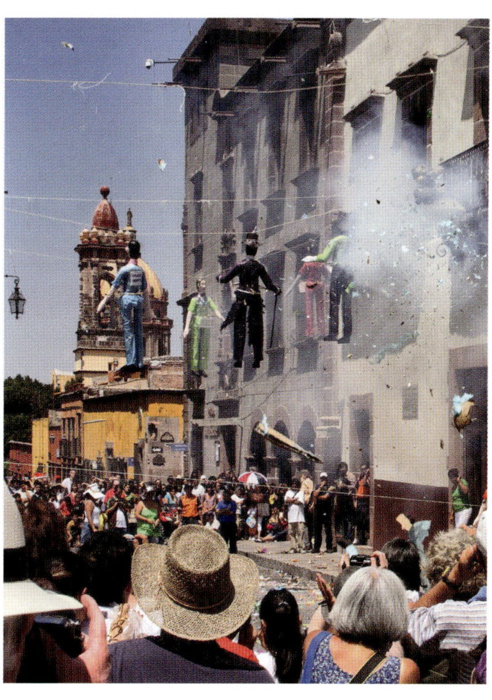

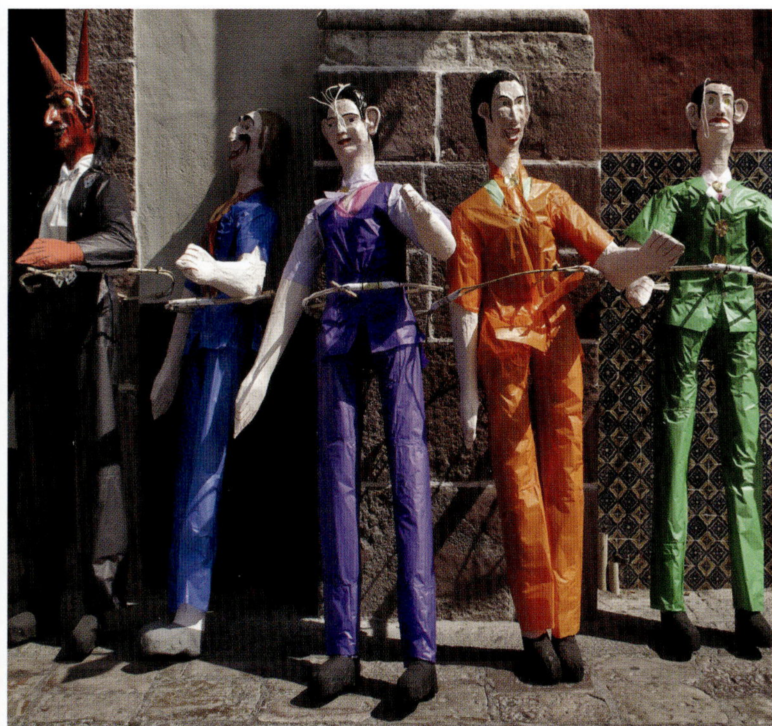

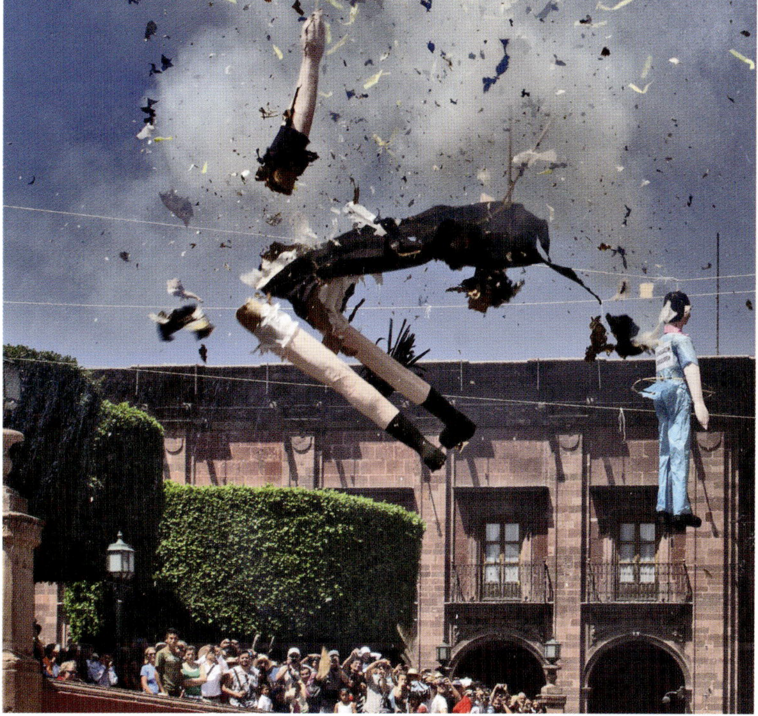

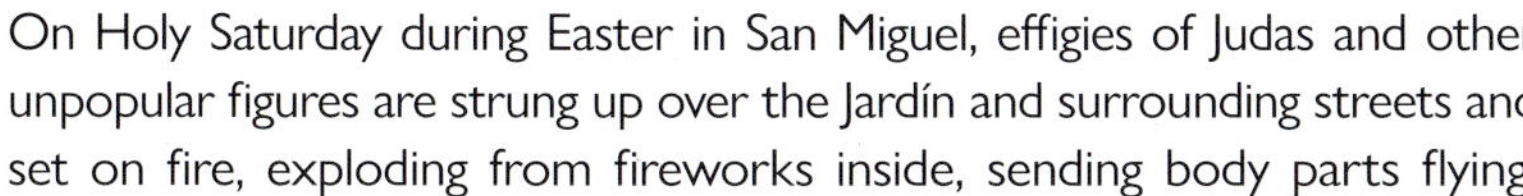

On Holy Saturday during Easter in San Miguel, effigies of Judas and other unpopular figures are strung up over the Jardín and surrounding streets and set on fire, exploding from fireworks inside, sending body parts flying.

Sometimes candies or other treats are inside, so they are dispersed into the crowds. Children and adults delight in the noisy, chaotic scene, and a moment of calm results from watching the evildoers meet their appropriate end.

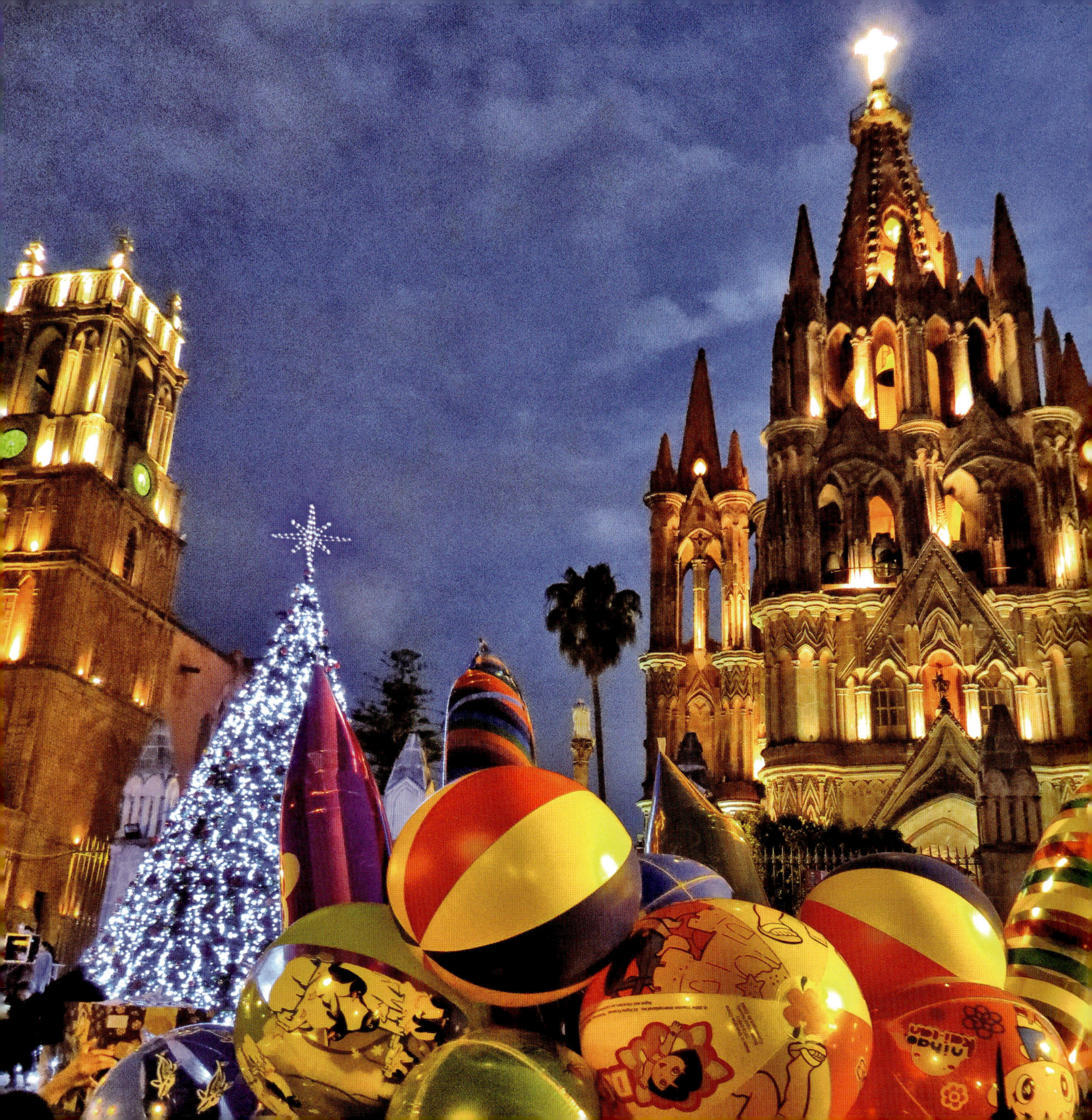

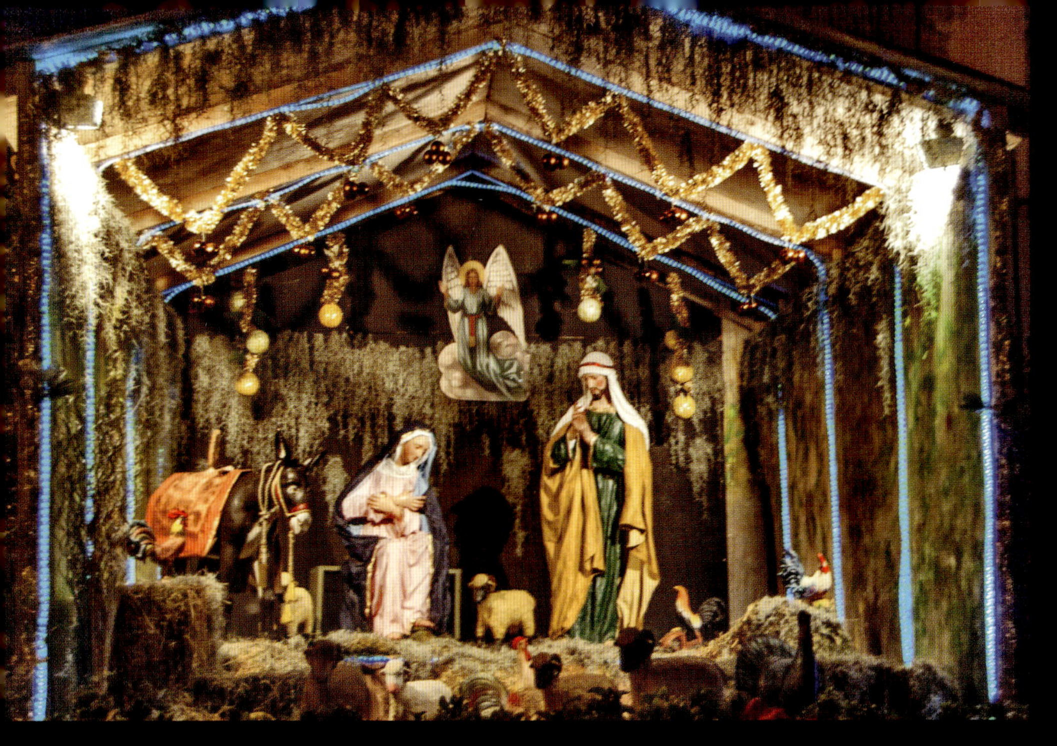
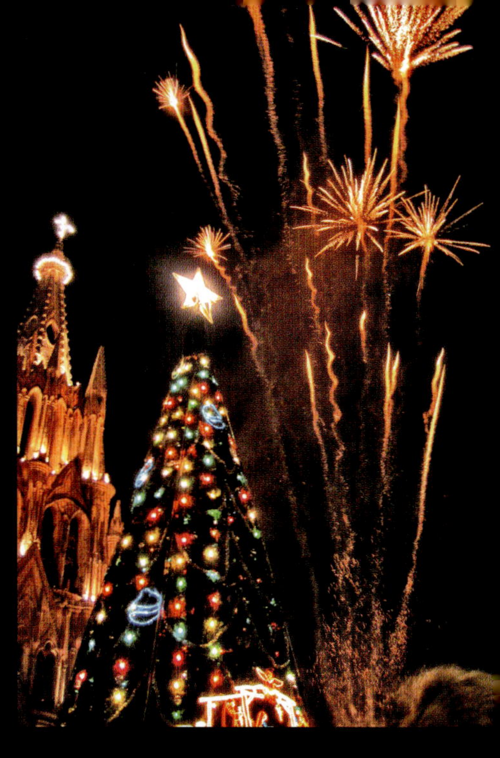
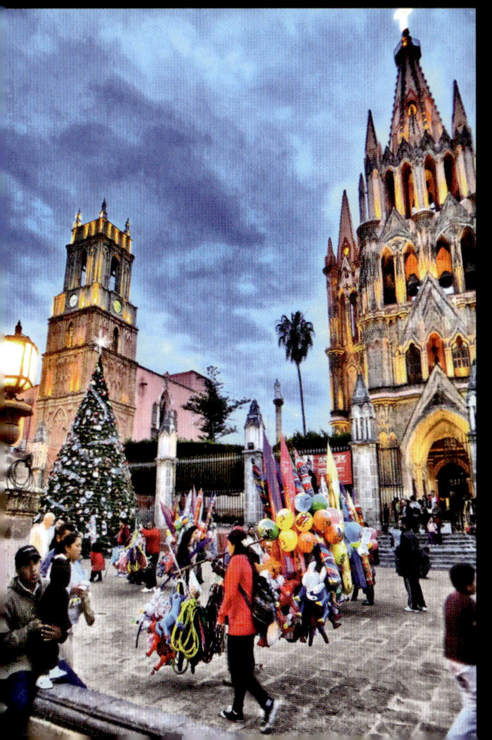
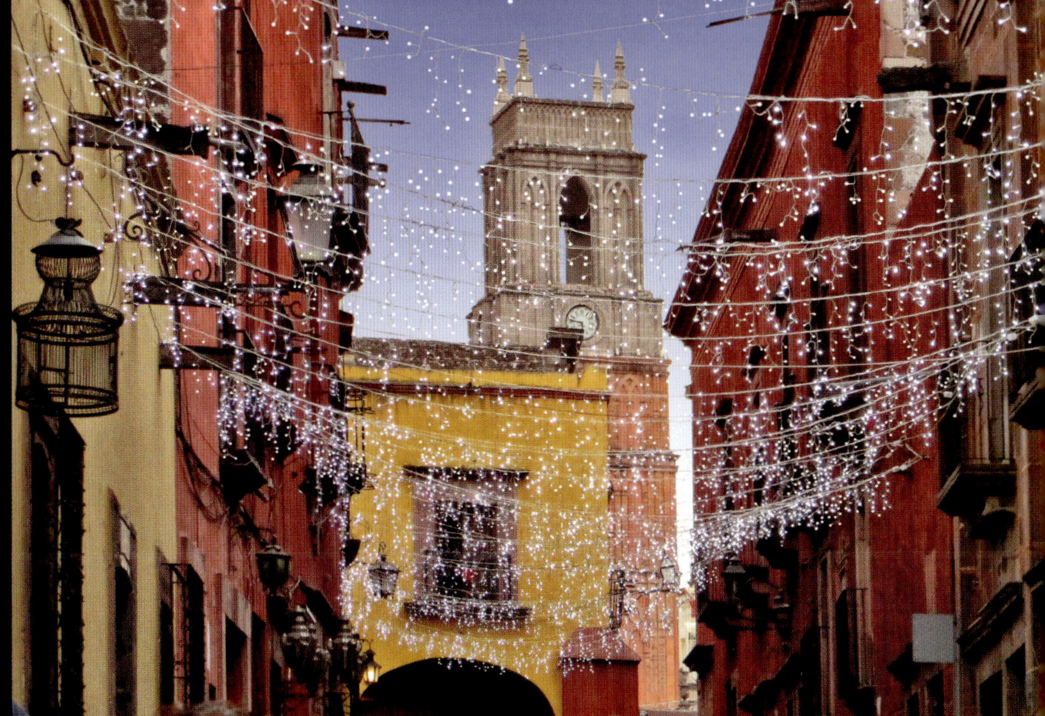

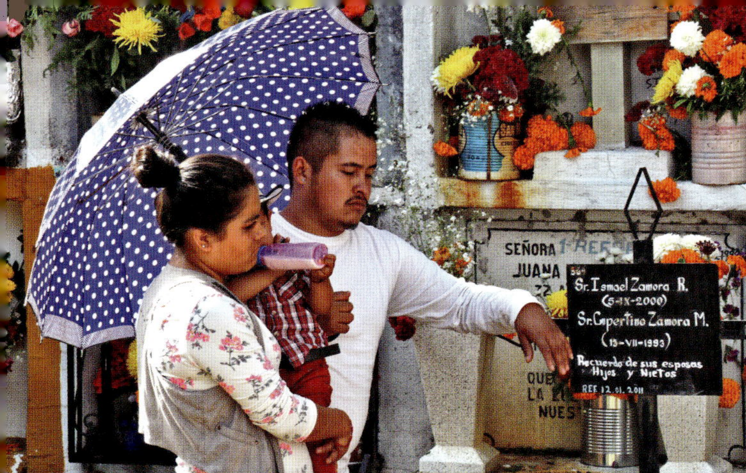
SEÑORA
JUANA
Sr. Ismael Zamora R.
(5-IX-2000)
Sr. Cupertino Zamora M.
(13-VII-1993)
Recuerdo de sus esposas
Hijos y Nietos
REF. 12. 01. 2011

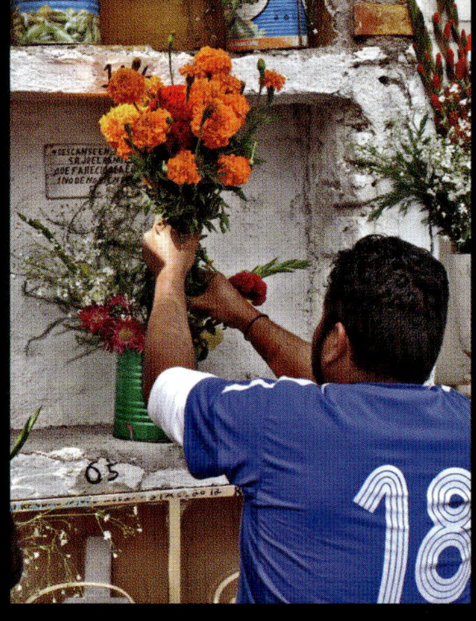

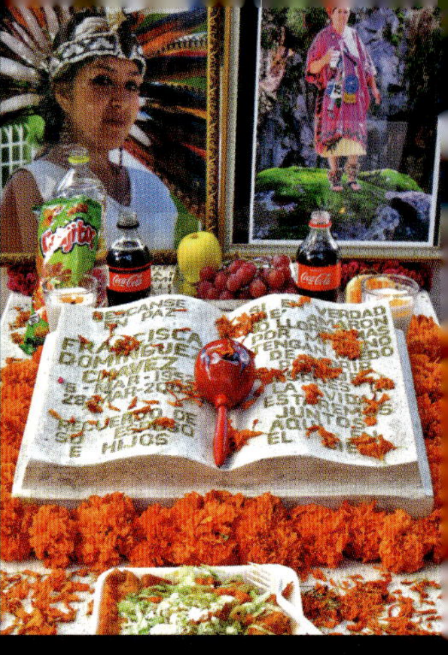

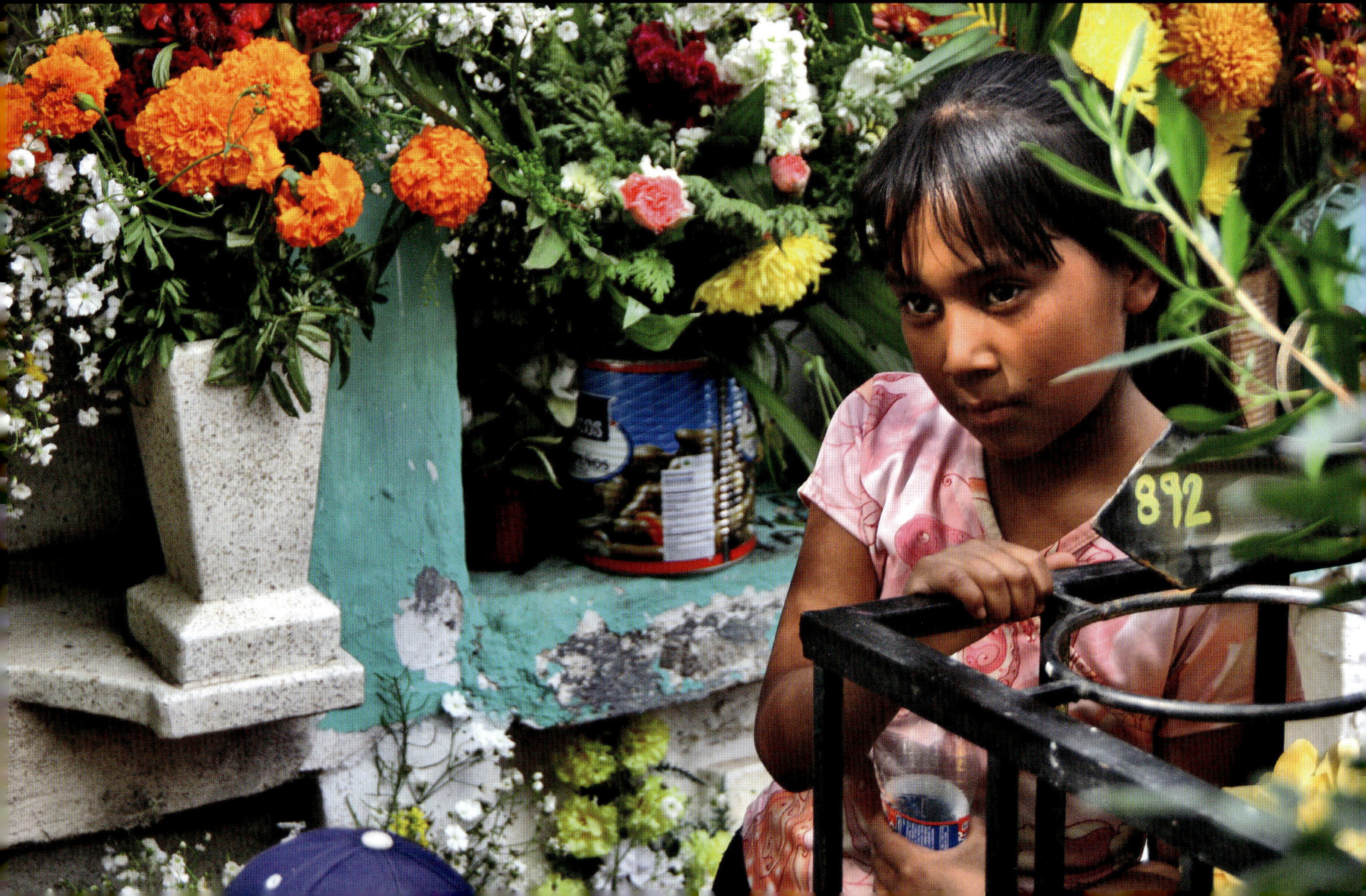

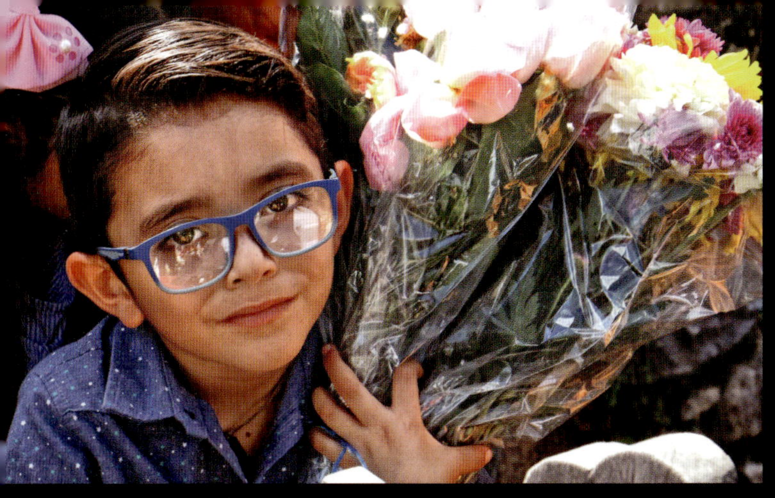

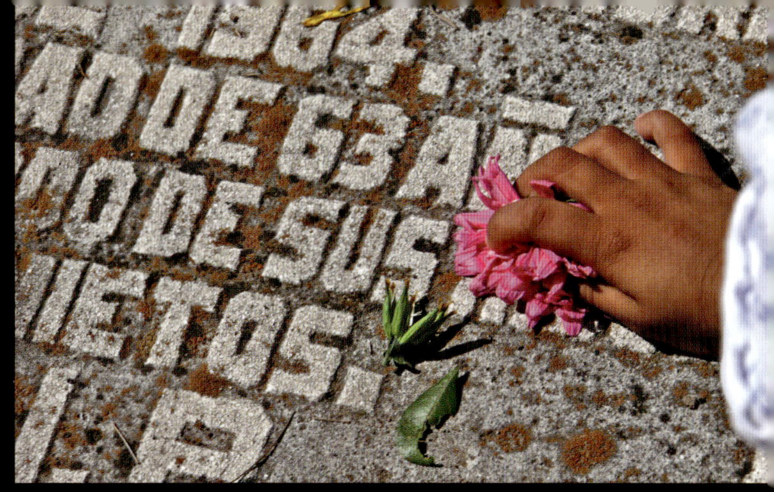

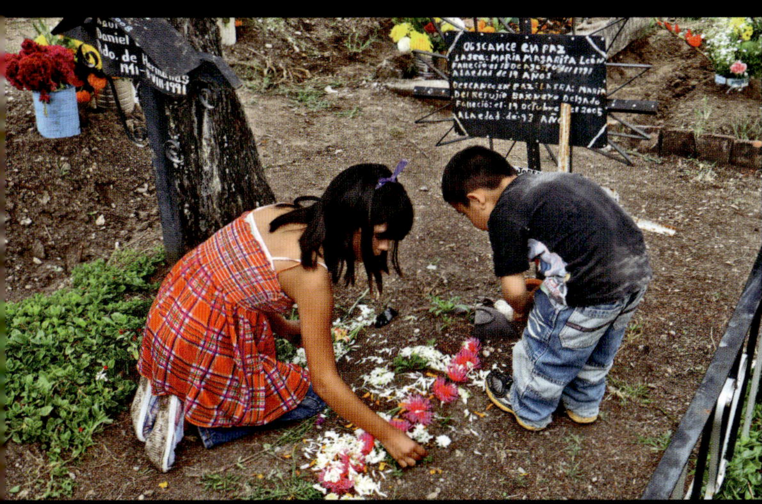

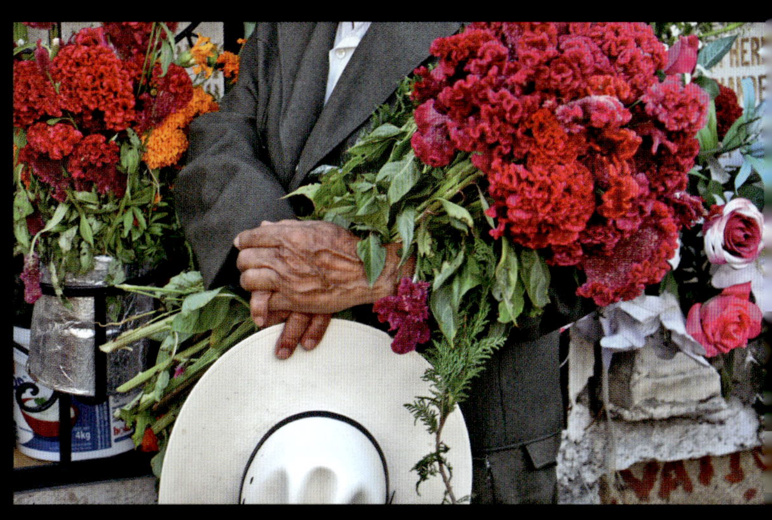

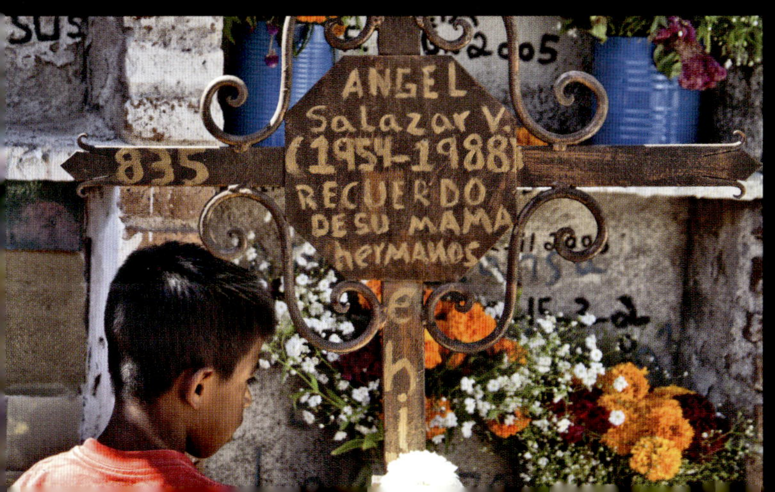

Death is a constant presence in all the world, but none have a more somber and passionate experience with death than the Mexican people. Funerals are deeply experienced with grand and solemn masses held in ornate churches, mariachi music a constant accompaniment. Long processions of friends and family slowly make their way to the cemetery behind the casket of the dearly departed in its passage on a horse-drawn wagon to the grave. Loud weeping and much hugging and consoling comfort those present as the casket is lowered into its final resting place and carefully covered. Music and food follow in a party dedicated to the dead, and then every year, during Dia de los Muertos, altars and stories bring them back to their families as the youngest learn the stories of the departed's life and come to know those who they will never meet. The ceremonies and traditions around death are one of the treasures of life, nowhere celebrated more beautifully than in San Miguel.

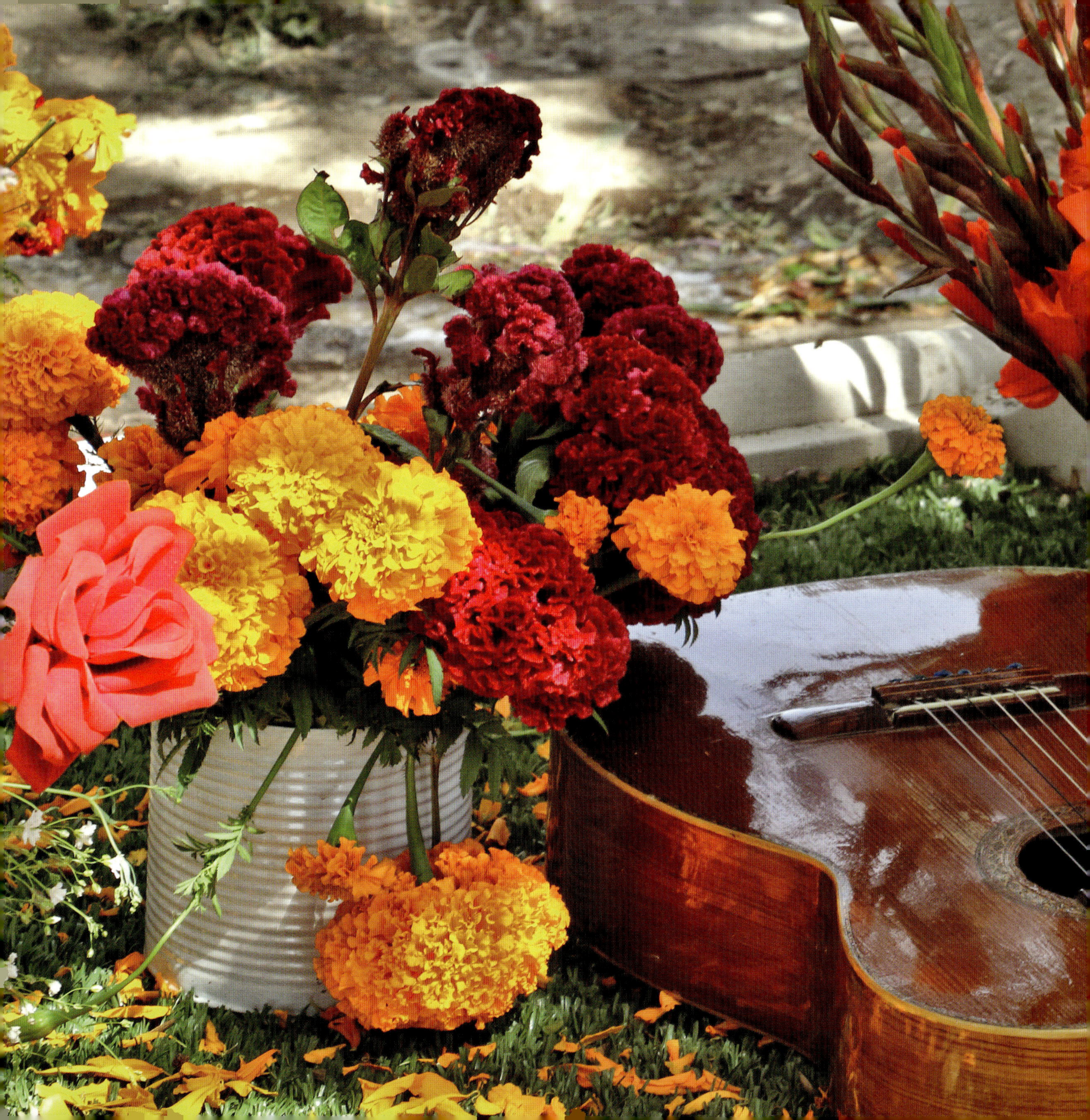

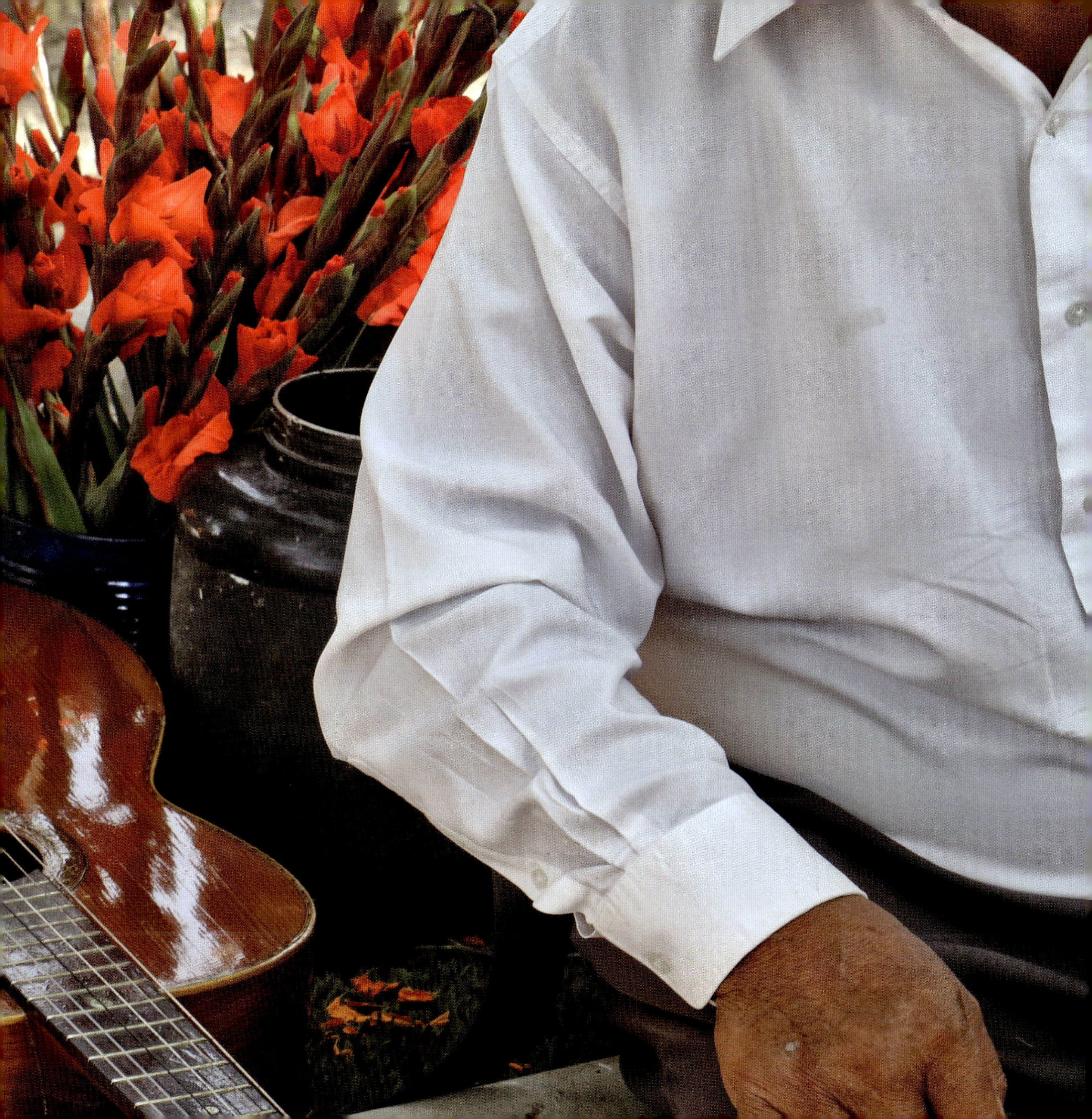

Acknowledgments

This book celebrates the beauty, history, culture, poetry, and spirit that pervade San Miguel de Allende, Mexico. As stunning as San Miguel is, it is the spirit of the generous and kind inhabitants that makes this place so precious. We are forever grateful to all of our friends and neighbors in San Miguel, who opened their hearts to us and shared their world. We hope their presence is felt in these pages.

We offer a very special thank-you to our dear friend and builder, Maestro Jose Guadalupe Gonzalez Morales, and his tireless, talented crew who have built our many projects in San Miguel. They showed us the true spirit and skill of the Mexican people.

We are forever indebted to our professors Olivio and Lucy Ferrari, Tom Regan, Gene Egger, Harold Hill, Ellen Brattan, and Charles Burchard for opening our eyes to the possibilities. Sketches in this book were done by Steven House and our CASA students Jason Andrews and Corey Akers.

We are grateful for our many friends and colleagues who have encouraged us over the years in our journeys and celebrated our exhibitions and lectures with us. Several of them were kind enough to review this manuscript and offer their advice. We offer our most sincere gratitude to Susan Page and Mayer Shacter, Jan and Jerry Rife, Jean Smith, Douglas Ward, Phil and Joanna Enquist, Frank Thoms and Kathleen Cammarata, Steven Lavine and Janet Sternberg, Paul and Carol Sundstrom, and Hartmut Gerdes.

We offer special thanks to Tony Cohan, a kindred spirit, for his encouragement, for his passion for travel and discovery, and for his thoughtful foreword, and to poet Laura Obregón Baranda, whose beautiful words on the back cover celebrate our book.

And we would like to give a very special thank-you to Cheryl Weber, Pete Schiffer, and the staff at Schiffer Publishing for their enthusiasm for this project and desire to bring this book to fruition.

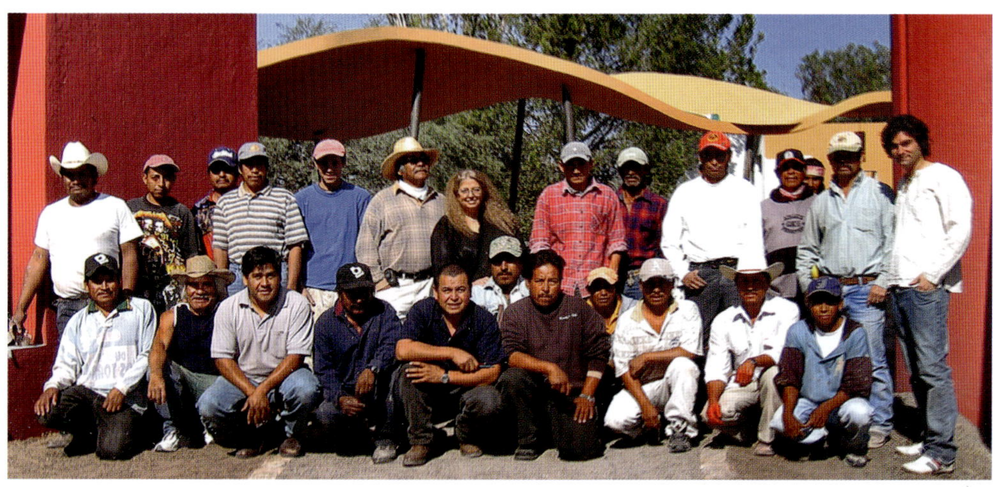

Cathi, shown centered with Maestro Guadalupe Gonzalez to her right, and their construction crew

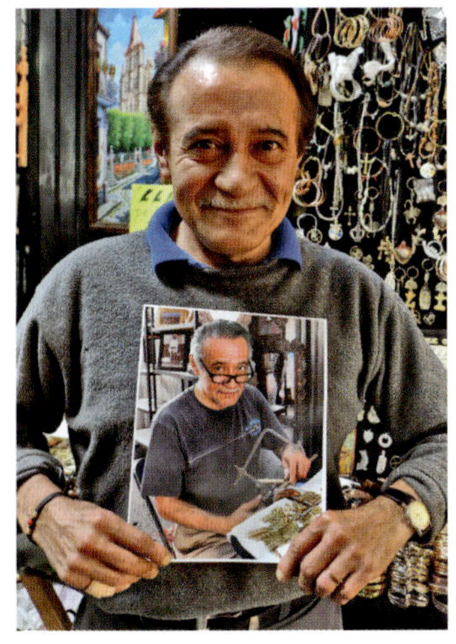

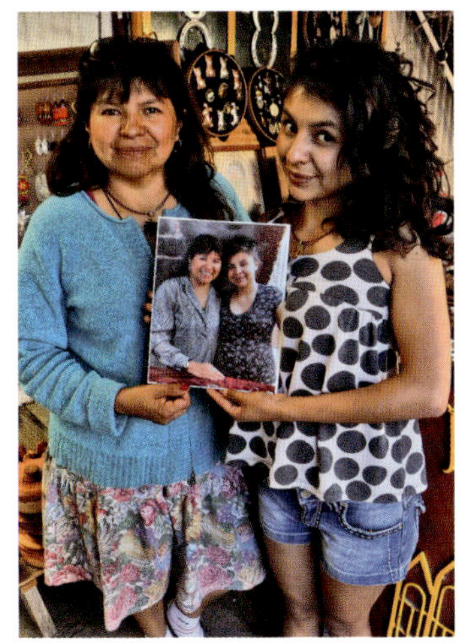

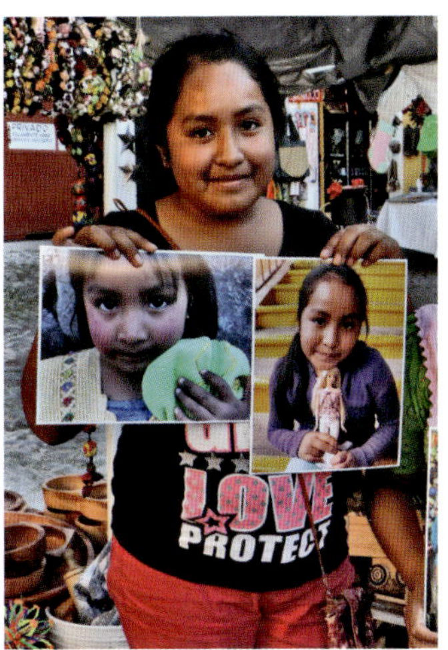

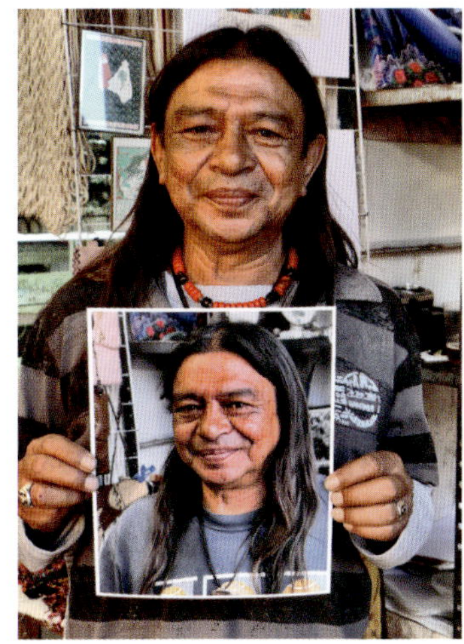

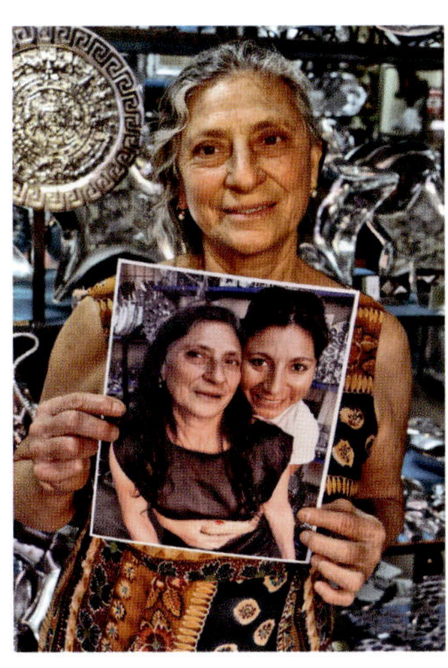

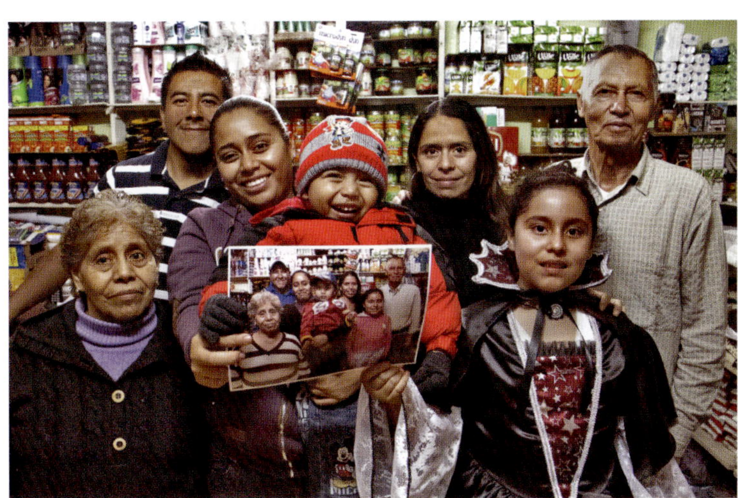

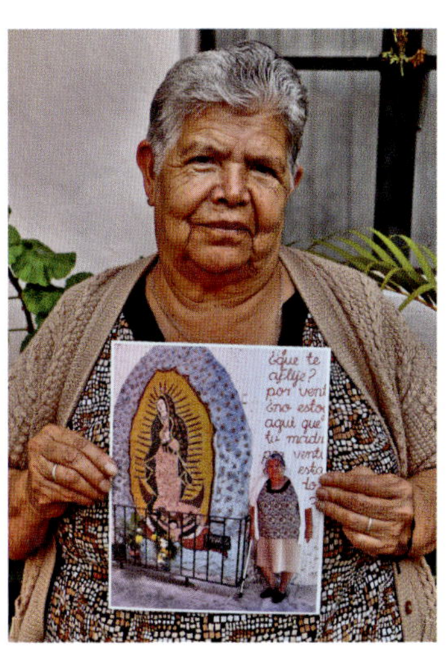

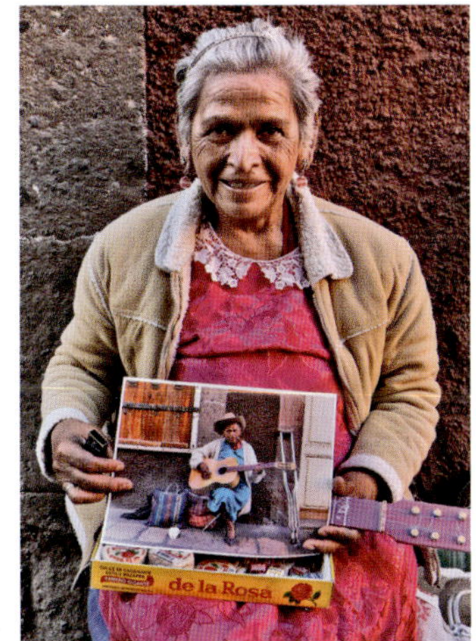

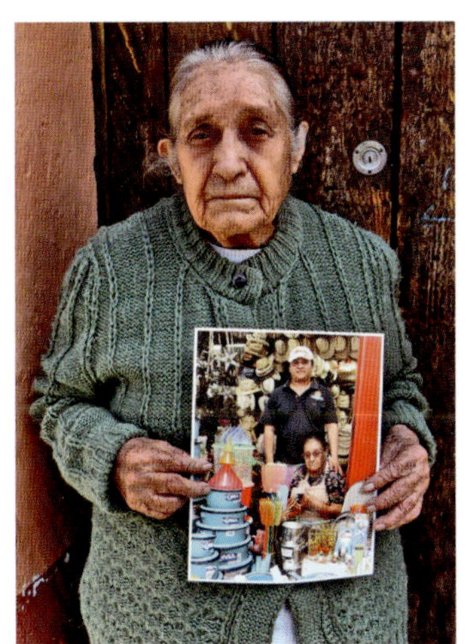

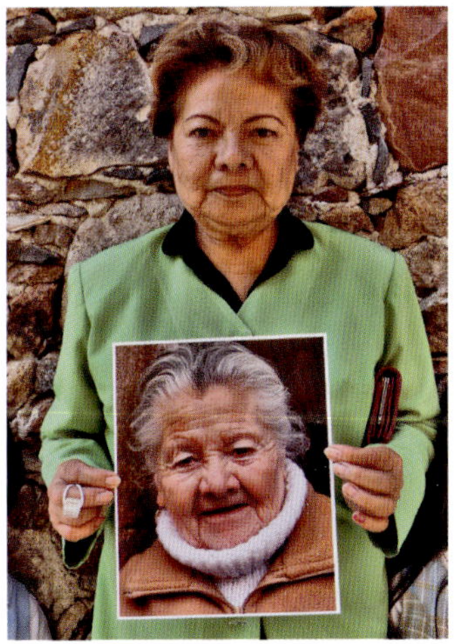

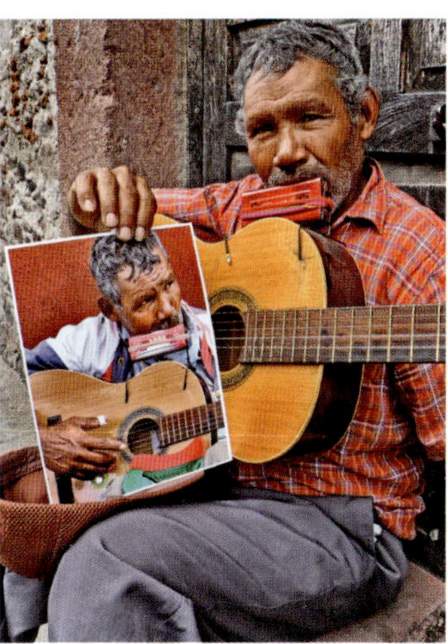

Steven has, over the years, photographed the lives, births, deaths, and celebrations of our many friends and neighbors, shown holding their portraits.

Biography

Cathi and Steven House are partners in the award-winning firm of House + House Architects. For forty years, House + House has crafted intimate, personal architecture and soulful living experiences for a vast array of clients. Deeply sensitive to form, color, natural light, and movement, they create a tangible spirit within each project, molded to the process of living. Their diverse body of work in California, Hawaii, Mexico, Honduras, Africa, and the Caribbean reflects their passion for site-specific, well-choreographed buildings.

House + House has received more than fifty design awards, and their work has been featured in prestigious publications throughout the world, including two monographs: *House + House Architects: Choreographing Space* and *Houses in the Sun: light movement embrace.*

Cathi and Steven have lectured throughout the United States and Mexico and have traveled throughout Europe, Asia, Africa, and Central and South America documenting cultures. Their stunning books, *Mediterranean Villages: an architectural journey* and *Villages of West Africa: an intimate journey across time*, celebrate the people, villages, textiles, and architecture of places that have much to teach us about community and sustainability.

Dedicated to continuing education through travel, they acknowledge the profound influence their intimate study of Indigenous cultures around the world has had on their lives and their work. Having traveled to over sixty-five countries to study living environments and to embrace the importance of travel, they established CASA, the Center for Architecture Sustainability + Art, a study abroad program based in San Miguel. In CASA, they endeavor to instill in international architecture students a way to see past the surface to the soul of a place, to understand and learn in ways that will help their work create a more soulful future.

In 1988, while searching for a stone quarry in Mexico, Cathi and Steven discovered the historic town of San Miguel de Allende. That was the beginning of a love affair with a place that has offered them new opportunities in the refinement of their craft. Cathi designed a home for them in San Miguel in 1992 and has since designed over forty homes in Mexico.

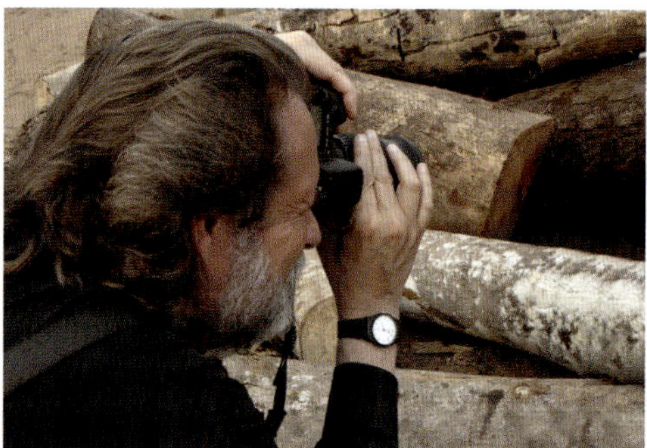

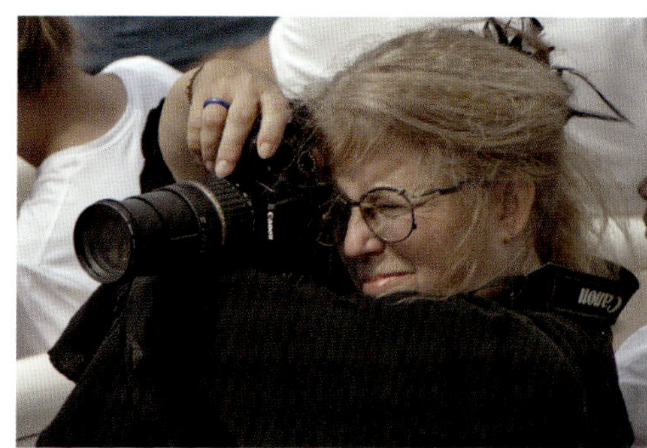

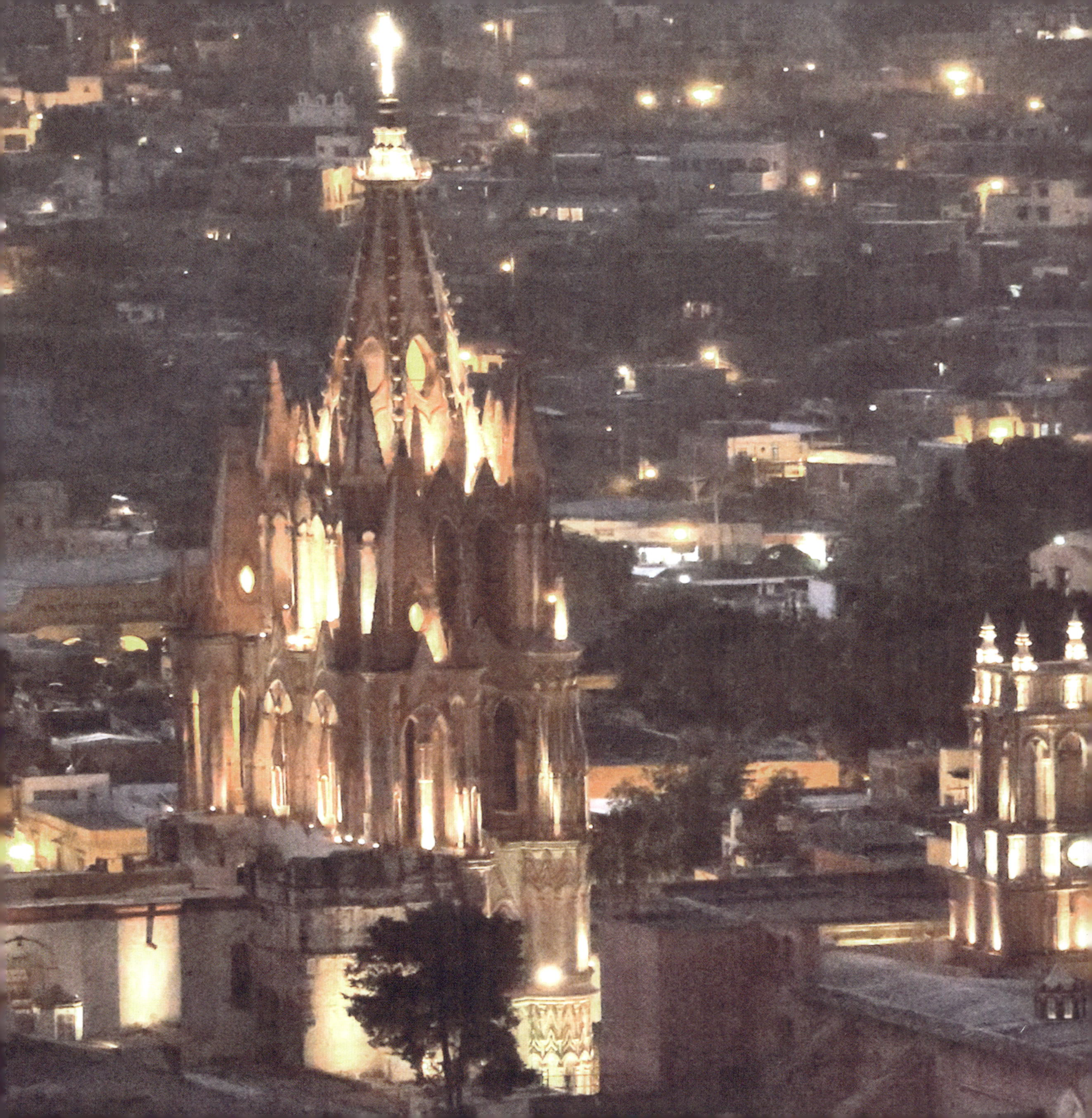